S. H. IRVINE

Psychological Testing

THE MACMILLAN COMPANY
NEW YORK • CHICAGO
DALLAS • ATLANTA • SAN FRANCISCO
LONDON • MANILA
IN CANADA
BRETT-MACMILLAN LTD.
GALT, ONTARIO

Psychological Testing

Second Edition

ANNE ANASTASI

Professor of Psychology,
Graduate School, Fordham University

The Macmillan Company   New York

Second Printing 1962

Library of Congress catalog card number: 61–5389

The Macmillan Company, New York
Brett-Macmillan Ltd., Galt, Ontario

Printed in the United States of America

Previous edition copyright 1954 by
The Macmillan Company

Preface

Although the primary objectives and basic plan of this text have remained the same as in the first edition, the present revision places relatively more emphasis on principles of psychological testing. This has been accomplished both by the expansion of Part 1 and by the frequent discussion of special issues and methodological or interpretive problems throughout the text. Even more than in the earlier edition, the book is designed to teach the student how to evaluate psychological tests and interpret test results. The specific tests discussed in Parts 2, 3, and 4 provide continuing opportunities for illustrating and applying the principles introduced in Part 1.

The pace at which psychological testing is developing can be gauged from the fact that about a third of the tests discussed in this edition have either originated or been revised since the publication of the first edition. For many of the others, there are revised manuals, technical supplements, or major research publications that provide important new information. Little of what was said about specific tests in 1954 has remained unchanged in 1961.

In such a field, one must be ready to judge the merits of new tests as they appear. To enable the reader to do this has been a constant aim of the book. In line with this goal, Chapter 2 provides an expanded discussion of sources of information about tests. Bibliographies at the end of each chapter include many references to publications about specific tests, as well as to more advanced or specialized readings on each topic. In this connection it should be noted that the practice of citing references by number has been retained in the present edition. The citation by author and date, currently recommended by the APA Council of Editors for journal use, appears to be too unwieldy for textbook purposes, especially in an area where many references may have to be cited for a single statement. Under these conditions, the page would become cluttered with names and dates of little intrinsic interest to the college student. Through the unobtrusive bibliography numbers given in parentheses, any desired reference can easily be located at the end of the chapter.

As a further aid to the evaluation of tests and the interpretation of test scores, new sections on elementary statistical concepts have been included in Chapters 4 and 5. The computation of the most common measures is illustrated with simple examples. Special attention has also been given to a clarification and systematization of the various procedures for determining test reliability and validity. The treatment of validity has been expanded to cover two chapters, while the chapter on item analysis from the earlier edition has been condensed and integrated with other topics. More detailed treatment has also been given to the interpretation of aptitude profiles, the identification of traits through factor analysis, and the evaluation of the various multiple aptitude batteries developed within the past decade.

A sample of new topics covered in the present edition includes: research on test anxiety, on coaching, and on the influence of examiner variables on test performance (Ch. 3); clinical versus statistical utilization of test results (Ch. 7); decision theory in the interpretation of test scores (Ch. 7); research on the measurement of creativity (Ch. 15); the changing relation between achievement and aptitude tests (Ch. 16 and 17); procedures for improving teacher-made classroom tests (Ch. 16); the social desirability variable in personality inventories (Ch. 18); the place of interests in personality theory (Ch. 19); a re-evaluation of projective techniques in the light of recent, well-controlled studies (Ch. 20); and an overview of many new approaches to personality assessment (Ch. 21).

In a real sense, this book has evolved in the classroom. Much of the discussion centers around recurrent questions that students ask about tests. Although intended primarily as a college text, such a book should also prove helpful to the practitioner in a number of fields. It provides a comprehensive view of current tests and testing problems for anyone who uses tests, such as the counselor, school psychologist, personnel psychologist in industry or government, and clinical psychologist. Among the parts of special relevance to clinical psychology, for example, may be mentioned the chapters on individual intelligence tests, projective techniques, and other personality measures. The book should likewise aid in the proper understanding and interpretation of test scores on the part of teachers, principals, social workers, psychiatrists, and others who utilize the results of tests in their daily activities. Educators will be particularly interested in the two chapters on achievement tests, as well as in the several chapters on group intelligence and aptitude tests. For the general psychologist, the book furnishes a background for the critical evaluation of the growing body of research data obtained through psychological tests.

It is a pleasant task to acknowledge the cooperation of colleagues in the preparation of this book. I wish to express my sincere appreciation to the many authors and test publishers who provided photographs of test materials, specimen tests, manuals, reprints, and unpublished manuscripts. In each of these cases, specific acknowledgment has been made in the text. I am especially grateful for the promptness, courtesy, and thoroughness with which my innumerable questions were answered by mail and telephone. Thanks are also extended for the thoughtful recommendations submitted by course instructors, several of which were utilized in preparing this revision. I am happy to record the contribution of my husband, Dr. John P. Foley, Jr., who discussed and helped to solve countless problems as they arose throughout the preparation of the manuscript. To my colleague, Dr. Dorothea McCarthy, I am indebted for her helpful suggestions and her ready cooperation in many ways. Grateful acknowledgment is made to Miss Rowena Plant and Miss Margaret Tighe of the Fordham University library staff for their gracious and efficient assistance in bibliographic matters and to Miss Mary Ellen Anderson for her competent help in proofreading and indexing.

A. A.

New York City

Contents

PART 1

Principles of Psychological Testing

CHAPTER 1

Functions and Origins of Psychological Testing

Anyone reading this book today could undoubtedly illustrate what is meant by a psychological test. It would be easy enough to recall a test the reader himself has taken in school, in college, in the armed services, in the counseling center, or in the personnel office. Or perhaps the reader has served as a subject in an experiment in which standardized tests were employed. This would certainly not have been the case fifty years ago. Psychological testing is a relatively young branch of one of the youngest of the sciences.

CURRENT USES OF PSYCHOLOGICAL TESTS

Basically, the function of psychological tests is to measure differences between individuals or between the reactions of the same individual on different occasions. One of the first problems that stimulated the development of psychological tests was the identification of the feebleminded. To this day, the detection of intellectual deficiency remains an important application of certain types of psychological tests. Related clinical uses of tests include the examination of the emotionally maladjusted, the delinquent, and other types of subnormal deviants. A strong impetus to the early development of tests was likewise provided by problems arising in education. At present, schools are among the largest test users. The classification of children with reference to their ability to profit from different types of school instruction, the identification of the intellectually retarded on the one hand and the gifted on the other, the diagnosis of academic failures, the educational and vocational counseling of high school and college students, and the selection of applicants for professional and other special schools are some of the many educational uses to which tests are being put. In a somewhat different setting, the testing

3

of children for adoption placement illustrates another specific way in which tests aid in practical decisions.

The selection and classification of industrial personnel represent relatively recent and rapidly expanding applications of psychological testing. From the assembly-line operator or filing clerk to top management, there is scarcely a type of job for which some kind of psychological test has not proved helpful in such matters as hiring, job assignment, transfer, promotion, or termination. To be sure, the effective employment of tests in many of these situations, especially in connection with high-level jobs, usually requires that the tests be used as an adjunct to skillful interviewing, so that test scores may be properly interpreted in the light of other background information about the individual. Nevertheless, testing constitutes an important part of the total personnel program. A closely related application of psychological testing is to be found in the selection and classification of military personnel. From simple beginnings in World War I, the scope and variety of psychological tests employed in military situations showed a phenomenal increase during World War II. Subsequently, research on test development has been continuing on a large scale in all branches of the armed services.

It is clearly evident that psychological tests are currently being employed in the solution of a wide range of practical problems. One should not, however, lose sight of the fact that such tests are also serving important functions in basic research. Nearly all problems in differential psychology, for example, require testing procedures as a means of gathering data. As illustrations, reference may be made to studies on the nature and extent of individual differences, the identification of psychological traits, the measurement of group differences, and the investigation of biological and cultural factors associated with behavioral differences. For all such areas of research—and for many others—the precise measurement of individual differences made possible by well-constructed tests is an essential prerequisite. Similarly, psychological tests provide standardized tools for investigating such varied problems as age changes within the individual, the effects of education, the outcome of psychotherapy, the impact of propaganda, and the influence of distraction on performance.

From the many different uses of psychological tests, it follows that some knowledge of such tests is needed for an adequate understanding of most fields of contemporary psychology. It is primarily with this end in view that the present book has been prepared. The book is not designed to make the individual either a skilled examiner and test administrator, or an expert on test construction. It is directed, not to the test specialist, but to the general student of psychology. Some acquaintance with the leading current tests is necessary in order to understand references to the use of such tests in the psychological literature. And a proper evaluation and interpretation of test results must ultimately rest upon a knowledge of how the tests were constructed, what they can be expected to accomplish, and what are their peculiar limitations. Today a familiarity with tests is required, not only by those who give or construct tests, but by the general psychologist as well.

A brief overview of the historical antecedents and origins of psychological testing will provide perspective and should aid in the understanding of present-day tests.[1] The direction in which contemporary psychological testing has been progressing can be clarified when considered in the light of the precursors of such tests. The special limitations as well as the advantages that characterize current tests likewise become more intelligible when viewed against the background in which they originated.

EARLY INTEREST IN THE CLASSIFICATION AND TRAINING OF THE FEEBLEMINDED

The nineteenth century witnessed a strong awakening of interest in the humane treatment of the feebleminded and the insane. Prior to that time, neglect, ridicule, and even torture had been the common lot of these unfortunates. With the growing concern for the proper care of mental deviates came a realization that some uniform criteria for identifying and classifying these cases were required. The establishment of many special institutions for the care of the feebleminded in both Europe and America made the need for setting up admission standards and an objective system of classification especially urgent. First it was necessary to differentiate between the insane and the feebleminded. The former manifested emotional disorders which might or might not be accompanied by intellectual deterioration from an initially normal level; the latter were characterized essentially by intellectual defect which had been present from birth or early infancy. What is probably the first explicit statement of this distinction is to be found in a two-volume work published in 1838 by the French physician, Esquirol (9), in which over one hundred pages are devoted to feeblemindedness.

Esquirol also pointed out that there are many degrees of feeblemindedness, varying along a continuum from normality to low-grade idiocy. In the effort to develop some system for classifying the different degrees and varieties of feeblemindedness, Esquirol tried several procedures, but concluded that the individual's use of language provides the most dependable criterion of

---

[1] A detailed account of the early origins of psychological tests can be found in Goodenough (12) and Peterson (26). Cf. also Boring (6) and Murphy (23) for more general background, and Anastasi (1, Ch. 1) for historical antecedents of the study of individual differences.

his intellectual level. On this basis, he distinguished between two grades of imbecility and three grades of idiocy. In the higher degree of imbecility, he maintained, speech is employed readily and easily; in the lower-grade imbecile, speech is more difficult and the vocabulary more limited. The highest grade of idiot uses only a few words or very short phrases; the second level of idiot is able to utter only monosyllables and cries; and in the lowest-level idiot, no language is found at all (9, vol. II, p. 340). It is interesting to note that current criteria of feeblemindedness are also largely linguistic, and that present-day intelligence tests are heavily loaded with verbal content. The important part verbal ability plays in our concept of intelligence will be repeatedly demonstrated in subsequent chapters.

Of special significance are the contributions of another French physician, Seguin, who pioneered in the training of the feebleminded. Having rejected the prevalent notion of the "incurability" of mental deficiency, Seguin experimented for many years with what he designated the "physiological method" of training (cf. 28), and in 1837 he established the first school devoted to the education of mentally defective children. In 1848 he emigrated to America, where his ideas gained wide recognition. Many of the "sense training" and "muscle training" techniques currently in use in institutions for the feebleminded were originated by Seguin. By these methods, low-grade mental defectives are given intensive exercise in sensory discrimination and in the development of motor control. Some of the procedures developed by Seguin for this purpose were eventually incorporated into "performance" or nonverbal tests of intelligence. An example is the Seguin Form Board, in which the individual is required to insert variously shaped blocks into the corresponding recesses as quickly as possible.

THE FIRST EXPERIMENTAL PSYCHOLOGISTS

The early experimental psychologists of the nineteenth century were not, in general, concerned with the measurement of individual differences. The principal aim of psychologists of that period was the formulation of generalized descriptions of human behavior. It was the uniformities rather than the differences in behavior that were the focus of attention. Individual differences were either ignored or were accepted as a necessary evil which limited the applicability of the generalizations. Thus the fact that one individual reacted differently from another when observed under identical conditions was regarded as a form of "error." The presence of such error, or individual variability, rendered the generalizations approximate rather than exact. This was the attitude toward individual differences that prevailed in such laboratories as that founded by Wundt at Leipzig in 1879, where many of the early experimental psychologists received their training.

In their choice of topics, as in many other phases of their work, the founders of experimental psychology reflected the influence of their backgrounds in physiology and physics. The problems studied in their laboratories were concerned largely with sensitivity to visual, auditory, and other sensory stimuli, and with simple reaction time. Such an emphasis upon sensory phenomena was in turn reflected in the nature of the first psychological tests, as will be apparent in subsequent sections.

Still another way in which nineteenth-century experimental psychology influenced the course of the testing movement may be noted. The early psychological experiments brought out the need for rigorous control of the conditions under which observations were made. For example, the wording of directions given to the subject in a reaction-time experiment might appreciably increase or decrease the speed with which the subject responded. Or again, the brightness or color of the surrounding field would markedly alter the appearance of a visual stimulus. The importance of making observations on all subjects under standardized conditions was thus vividly demonstrated. Such standardization of procedure eventually became one of the special earmarks of psychological tests.

THE CONTRIBUTIONS OF FRANCIS GALTON

It was the English biologist, Sir Francis Galton, who was primarily responsible for launching the testing movement on its course. A unifying factor in Galton's numerous and varied research activities was his interest in human heredity. In the course of his investigations on heredity, Galton realized the need for measuring the characteristics of related and unrelated persons. Only in this way could he discover, for example, the exact degree of resemblance between parents and offspring, brothers and sisters, cousins, or twins. With such an end in view, Galton was instrumental in inducing a number of educational institutions to keep systematic anthropometric records on their students. In 1882, he established an anthropometric laboratory in South Kensington Museum, London, where by the payment of a small fee individuals could be measured in certain physical traits and could undergo tests of keenness of vision and hearing, muscular strength, reaction time, and other simple sensorimotor functions. By such methods, the first large, systematic body of data on individual differences in simple psychological processes was gradually accumulated.

Galton himself devised most of the simple tests administered at his anthropometric laboratory, many of which are still familiar either in their original or in modified forms. Examples include the "Galton bar" for visual discrimination of length, the "Galton whistle" for determining the highest audible pitch, and graduated series of weights for measuring kinaesthetic discrimination, as well as tests of strength, speed of reaction, and other traits. It was Galton's belief that tests of sensory discrimination could serve as a means of gauging a person's intellect. In this respect, he was partly influenced by the theories of Locke. Thus Galton wrote: "The only information that reaches us concerning outward events appears to pass through the avenue of our senses; and the more perceptive the senses are of difference, the larger is the field upon which our judgment and intelligence can act" (10, p. 27). Galton had also noted that idiots tend to be defective in the ability to discriminate heat, cold, and pain—an observation that further strengthened his conviction that sensory discriminative capacity "would on the whole be highest among the intellectually ablest" (10, p. 29).

Galton also pioneered in the application of rating scale and questionnaire methods, as well as in the use of the "free association" technique subsequently employed for a wide variety of purposes. A further contribution of Galton is to be found in his development of statistical methods for the analysis of data on individual differences. Galton selected and adapted a number of techniques previously derived by mathematicians. These techniques he put in such form as to permit their use by the mathematically untrained investigator who might wish to treat test results quantitatively. He thereby extended enormously the application of statistical procedures to the analysis of test data. This phase of Galton's work has been carried forward by many of his students, the most eminent of whom was Karl Pearson.

CATTELL AND THE EARLY "MENTAL TESTS"

An especially prominent position in the development of psychological testing is occupied by the American psychologist, James McKeen Cattell. The newly established science of experimental psychology and the still newer testing movement merged in Cattell's work. For his doctorate at Leipzig, he completed a dissertation on individual differences in reaction time, despite Wundt's resistance to this type of investigation. While lecturing at Cambridge in 1888, Cattell's own interest in the measurement of individual differences was reinforced by contact with Galton. Upon his return to America, Cattell was active both in the establishment of laboratories for experimental psychology and in the spread of the testing movement.

In an article written by Cattell in 1890 (7), the term "mental test" was used for the first time in the psychological literature. This article described a series of tests which were being administered annually to college students in the effort to determine their intellectual level. The tests, which had to be administered individually, included measures of muscular strength, speed of movement, sensitivity to pain, keenness of vision and of hearing, weight discrimination, reaction time, memory, and the like. In his choice of tests, Cattell shared Galton's view that a measure of intellectual functions could be obtained through tests of sensory discrimination and reaction time. Cattell's preference for such tests was also bolstered by the fact that simple functions could be measured with precision and accuracy, whereas the development of objective measures for the more complex functions appeared at that time a well-nigh hopeless task.

Cattell's tests were typical of those to be found in a number of test series developed during the last decade of the nineteenth century. Some efforts to tap more complex psychological functions may be seen in the inclusion of tests of reading, verbal association, memory, and simple arithmetic (22, 29). Such test series were administered to school children, college students, and miscellaneous adults. At the Columbian Exposition held in Chicago in 1893, Jastrow set up an exhibit at which visitors were invited to take tests of sensory, motor, and simple perceptual processes and to compare their skill with the norms (cf. 26, 27). A few attempts to evaluate such early tests yielded very discouraging results. The individual's performance showed little correspondence from one test to another (29, 37), and it exhibited little or no relation to independent estimates of intellectual level based on teachers' ratings (5, 11) or academic grades (37).

A number of test series assembled by European psychologists of the period tended to cover somewhat more complex functions. Kraepelin (20), who was interested primarily in the clinical examination of psychiatric patients, prepared a long series of tests to measure what he regarded as basic factors in the characterization of an individual. The tests, employing chiefly simple arithmetic operations, were designed to measure practice effects, memory, and susceptibility to fatigue and to distraction. A few years earlier, Oehrn (24), a pupil of Kraepelin, had employed tests of perception, memory, association, and motor functions in an investigation on the interrelationships of psychological functions. Another German psychologist, Ebbinghaus (8), administered tests of arithmetic computation, memory span, and sentence completion to school children. The most complex of the three tests, sentence completion, was the only one that showed a clear correspondence with the children's scholastic achievement.

Like Kraepelin, the Italian psychologist, Ferrari, and his students were interested primarily in the use of tests with pathological cases (13). The test series they devised ranged from physiological measures and motor tests to apprehension span and the interpretation of pictures. In an article published in France in 1895, Binet and Henri (3) criticized most of the available test series as being too largely sensory and as concentrating unduly on simple, specialized abilities. They argued further that, in the measurement of the more complex functions, great precision is not necessary, since individual differences are larger in these functions. An extensive and varied list of tests was proposed, covering such functions as memory, imagination, attention, comprehension, suggestibility, aesthetic appreciation, and many others. In these tests, we can readily recognize the trends that were eventually to lead to the development of the famous Binet "intelligence scales."

BINET AND THE RISE OF INTELLIGENCE TESTS

Binet and his co-workers devoted many years to active and ingenious research on ways of measuring intelligence. Many approaches were tried, including even the measurement of physical traits, handwriting analysis, and palmistry! The results, however, led to a growing conviction that the direct, even though crude, measurement of complex intellectual functions was the best solution. Then a specific situation arose which brought Binet's efforts to immediate practical fruition. In 1904, the Minister of Public Instruction appointed a commission to study procedures for the education of subnormal children attending the Paris schools. It was to meet this practical demand that Binet, in collaboration with Simon, prepared the first Binet-Simon Scale (4).

This scale, known as the 1905 Scale, consisted of 30 problems or tests arranged in ascending order of difficulty. The difficulty level was determined empirically by administering the tests to 50 normal children aged 3 to 11 years, and to some retarded and feebleminded children. The tests were designed to cover a wide variety of functions, with special emphasis upon judgment, comprehension, and reasoning, which Binet regarded as essential components of intelligence. Although sensory and perceptual tests were included, a much greater proportion of verbal content was found in this scale than in most test series of the time. The 1905 Scale was presented as a preliminary and tentative instrument, and no precise objective method for arriving at a total score was formulated.

In the second, or 1908 Scale, the number of tests was increased, some unsatisfactory tests from the earlier scale were eliminated, and all tests were grouped into age levels. Thus in the 3-year level were placed all tests normal

3-year-olds could pass, in the 4-year level all tests passed by normal 4-year-olds, and so on to age 13. The child's score on the test could then be expressed as a *"mental age,"* i.e., the age of normal children whose performance he equaled. The use of such mental age norms, which achieved considerable popularity in later stages of psychological testing, will be discussed in more detail in Chapter 4. Since "mental age" is such a simple concept to grasp, its introduction undoubtedly did much to popularize intelligence testing.

A third revision appeared in 1911, the year of Binet's untimely death. In this scale, no fundamental changes were introduced. Minor revisions and relocations of specific tests were instituted. More tests were added at several year levels, and the scale was extended to the adult level.

Even prior to the 1908 revision, the Binet-Simon tests attracted wide attention among psychologists throughout the world. Translations and adaptations appeared in many languages. In America, a number of different revisions were prepared, the most famous of which is the one developed under the direction of L. M. Terman at Stanford University, and known as the Stanford-Binet (34). It was in this test that the Intelligence Quotient (IQ), or ratio between mental age and chronological age, was first used. The latest revision of this test is widely employed today and will be more fully considered in Chapter 8. Of special interest, too, is the first Kuhlmann-Binet revision, which extended the scale downward to the age level of 3 months (21). This scale represents one of the earliest efforts to develop preschool and infant tests of intelligence.

GROUP TESTING

The Binet tests, as well as all their revisions, are *individual scales* in the sense that they can be administered to only one person at a time. Many of the tests in these scales require oral responses from the subject or necessitate the manipulation of materials. Some call for individual timing of responses. For these and other reasons, such tests are not adapted to group administration. Another characteristic of the Binet type of test is that it requires a highly trained examiner. Such tests are essentially clinical instruments, suited to the intensive study of individual cases.

Group testing, like the first Binet scale, was developed to meet a pressing practical need. When the United States entered World War I in 1917, a committee was appointed by the American Psychological Association to consider ways in which psychology might aid in the conduct of the war. This committee, under the direction of Robert M. Yerkes, recognized the need for the rapid classification of the million and a half recruits with respect to general intellectual level. Such information was of assistance in many administrative decisions, including rejection or discharge from military service, assignment to different types of service, or admission to officer training camps. It was in this setting that the first group intelligence test was developed. In this task, the Army psychologists drew upon all available test materials, and especially upon an unpublished group intelligence test prepared by Arthur S. Otis, which he turned over to the Army.

The tests finally developed by the Army psychologists have come to be known as the Army Alpha and the Army Beta. The former was designed for general routine testing; the latter was a non-language scale employed with illiterates and with foreign-born recruits who were unable to take a test in English. Both were suitable for administration to large groups.

Shortly after the termination of World War I, the Army tests were released for civilian use. Not only did the Army Alpha and Army Beta themselves pass through many revisions, the latest of which are even now in use, but they also served as models for most group intelligence tests. The testing movement underwent a tremendous spurt of growth. Soon group intelligence tests were being devised for all ages and types of persons, from preschool children to graduate students. Large-scale testing programs, previously impossible, were now being launched with zestful optimism. Since group tests were designed as mass testing instruments, they not only permitted the simultaneous examination of large groups, but they also simplified the instructions and administration procedures so as to demand a minimum of training on the part of the examiner. School teachers began to give tests to their classes. College students were routinely examined prior to admission. Extensive studies of special adult groups, such as prisoners, were undertaken. And soon the general public became "IQ-conscious."

The application of such group intelligence tests far outran their technical improvement. That the tests were still crude instruments was often forgotten in the rush of gathering scores and drawing practical conclusions therefrom. When the tests failed to meet unwarranted expectations, skepticism and hostility toward all testing often resulted. Thus the testing boom of the twenties, based upon the indiscriminate use of tests, may have done as much to retard as to advance the progress of psychological testing.

TESTS OF SPECIAL APTITUDES

Although intelligence tests were originally designed to sample a wide variety of functions in order to estimate the individual's "general intellectual level," it soon became apparent that such tests were quite limited in their coverage. Not all important functions were represented. In fact, most intelligence tests were primarily measures of verbal ability and, to a lesser extent, of the ability to handle numerical and other abstract and symbolic relations. Gradually psychologists came to recognize that the term "intelligence test" was a misnomer, since only certain aspects of intelligence were measured by such tests.

To be sure, the tests covered abilities that are of prime importance in our culture. But it was realized that more precise designations, in terms of the type of information these tests are able to yield, would be preferable. For example, a number of tests that would probably have been known as "intelligence tests" during the twenties were now described as "scholastic aptitude tests." Such a shift in terminology was made in recognition of the fact that many so-called intelligence tests measure that combination of abilities demanded by academic work.

Some intelligence tests have been given the name of "general classification tests" or "screening tests." An example is the Army General Classification Test (AGCT) developed during World War II to serve the same general purposes as the Army Alpha of World War I. Tests for use in industrial personnel selection are also frequently designated as general classification tests. Such a name itself has grown out of the fact that intelligence tests, and especially group intelligence tests, are often used as rough, preliminary screening instruments and are then followed by more detailed measures of special aptitudes. Among the latter are to be found tests of mechanical, clerical, musical, and artistic aptitudes. Standardized tests in all these areas are available and are widely used today for educational and vocational counseling, personnel selection, and other purposes.

The need for special aptitude tests to supplement so-called intelligence tests is now generally recognized. In this connection, it is interesting to note the results of a "poll of experts" conducted in 1944 among a representative group of psychologists in the testing field (18). Of the 79 psychologists replying, 55 believed that "most will be accomplished if psychologists concentrate on measuring separate intellectual factors." At the other extreme, only 5 expressed the opinion that test development should be oriented primarily toward the measurement of general intelligence. It should not be inferred from such replies, of course, that these test experts were dissatisfied with current intelligence tests or that they advocated the abolition of such tests. On the contrary, when asked how well intelligence tests meet the practical needs for classifying people as to general ability in the army, in schools, and in industry, over 75 per cent chose the response, "Rather well, much better than is done without tests." The comments following this question, however, again indicated that intelligence tests were regarded as approximate or preliminary screening instruments which ought to be supplemented by tests of special aptitudes.

Mention may also be made of the contrast between the testing programs in World War I and World War II. Such a comparison vividly illustrates the direction in which psychological testing had progressed during the intervening quarter-century. Although in World War I the Army Alpha and Army Beta represented the major part of the psychological testing in the armed forces, in World War II the AGCT and similar general tests constituted a relatively small portion of the total test construction effort. The chief contribution of test psychologists during World War II was in the development of specialized test "batteries," or combinations of tests. Research on such batteries was conducted on a vast scale and attained heretofore undreamed-of proportions. Special batteries were constructed for pilots, bombardiers, radio operators, range finders, and scores of other military specialists. A report of the batteries prepared in the Air Force alone occupies at least nine of the nineteen volumes devoted to the aviation psychology program during World War II (2). Some available tests of special aptitudes, especially in the mechanical and motor areas, were utilized in the military test batteries; but many of the tests were specially devised for the purpose. Such military tests also illustrate another aspect of current test development which will be considered in the following section.

MULTIPLE APTITUDE BATTERIES

The critical evaluation of intelligence tests which followed their widespread and indiscriminate use during the twenties also revealed another noteworthy fact, namely, that an individual's performance on different parts of such a test often showed marked variation. This was especially apparent on group tests, in which the items are commonly segregated into subtests of relatively homogenous content. For example, a person might score relatively high on a verbal subtest and low on a numerical subtest, or vice versa. To some extent, such internal variability is also discernible on a test like the Stanford-Binet, in which, for example, all items involving words might prove very difficult for a particular individual, while items employing pictures or geometric diagrams may place him at an advantage.

Test users, and especially clinicians, frequently utilized such intercomparisons in order to obtain more insight into the individual's psychological make-up. Thus not only the "IQ," or other total score, but also scores on subtests would be examined in the evaluation of the individual case. Such a practice is not to be generally recommended, however, since intelligence tests were not designed for the purpose of differential aptitude analysis. Often the subtests being compared contain too few items to yield a stable or reliable estimate of a specific ability. As a result, the obtained difference between subtest scores might be reversed if the individual were retested on a different day or with another form of the same test. If such intra-individual comparisons are to be made, tests are needed that are specially designed to reveal differences in performance in various functions.

While the practical application of tests demonstrated the need for differential aptitude tests, a parallel development in the study of trait organization was gradually providing the means for constructing such tests. Statistical studies on the nature of "intelligence" had been exploring the interrelations among scores obtained by many persons on a wide variety of different tests. Such investigations were begun by the English psychologist, Charles Spearman, during the first decade of the present century (31, 32). Subsequent methodological developments, based upon the work of such American psychologists as T. L. Kelley (17) and L. L. Thurstone (35, 36), as well as upon that of other American and English investigators, have come to be known as *factor analysis*.

The contributions that the methods of factor analysis have made to test construction will be more fully examined and illustrated in Chapter 13. For the present, it will suffice to note that the data gathered by such procedures have indicated the presence of a number of relatively independent "factors," or traits. Some of these traits were represented, in varying proportions, in the traditional intelligence tests. Verbal comprehension and numerical reasoning are examples of this type of trait. Others, such as spatial, perceptual, and mechanical aptitudes, had been touched upon only slightly, if at all, in most intelligence tests.

One of the chief practical outcomes of factor analysis was the development of *multiple aptitude batteries*. These batteries are designed to provide a measure of the individual's standing in each of a number of traits. In place of a total score or "IQ," a separate score is obtained for such traits as verbal comprehension, numerical aptitude, spatial visualization, arithmetic reasoning, and perceptual speed. Such batteries thus provide a suitable instrument for making the kind of intra-individual analysis, or differential diagnosis, that clinicians had been trying for many years to obtain from intelligence tests, with crude and often erroneous results. These batteries also incorporate into a comprehensive and systematic testing program much of the information formerly obtained from special aptitude tests, since the multiple aptitude batteries cover some of the traits not ordinarily included in intelligence tests.

Multiple aptitude batteries represent a relatively late development in the testing field. Nearly all have appeared since 1945. In this connection, the work of the military psychologists during World War II should again be cited. Much of the test research conducted in the armed services was based on factor analysis and was directed toward the construction of differential aptitude batteries. This was especially true of the previously mentioned work of the Air Force psychologists. Research along these lines is still in progress under the sponsorship of various branches of the armed services. A number of differential aptitude batteries have likewise been developed for civilian use, and are being widely applied in educational and vocational counseling, personnel selection, and similar areas. The principal examples of such batteries will be discussed in Chapter 13.

MEASUREMENT OF PERSONALITY

A phase of psychological testing that is still in its infancy is represented by the various efforts to measure non-intellectual aspects of behavior. Tests designed for this purpose are commonly known as "personality tests," although some psychologists prefer to use the term "personality" in a broader sense, to refer to the entire individual. Intellectual as well as non-intellectual traits would thus be included under this heading. In the terminology of psychological testing, however, the designation "personality test" most often refers to measures of such characteristics as emotional adjustment, social relations, motivation, interests, and attitudes.

An early precursor of personality testing may be recognized in Kraepelin's use of the *free association test* with abnormal patients. In such a test, the subject is given specially selected stimulus words and is required to respond to each with the very first word that comes to mind. Kraepelin also employed this technique to study the psychological effects of fatigue, hunger, and drugs, and concluded that all these agents increase the relative frequency of superficial associations (19). Sommer (30), also writing during the last decade of the nineteenth century, suggested that the free association test might be used to differentiate between the various forms of mental disorder. The free association technique has subsequently been utilized for a variety of testing purposes and is still currently employed. Mention should also be made of the work of Galton, Pearson, and Cattell in the development of standardized questionnaire and rating-scale techniques. Although originally devised for other purposes, these procedures were eventually employed by others in constructing some of the most common types of current personality tests.

The prototype of the personality questionnaire, or *self-report inventory,* is the Personal Data Sheet developed by Woodworth during World War I (cf. 33, Ch. 5). This test was designed as a rough screening device for identifying seriously neurotic men who would be unfit for military service. The inventory consisted of a number of questions dealing with common neurotic symptoms, which the individual answered about himself. A total score was obtained, in terms of the number of symptoms reported. Immediately after the war, civilian forms of this questionnaire were prepared, including a special form for use with children. The Woodworth Personal Data Sheet, moreover, served as a model for most subsequent emotional adjustment inventories. In some of these questionnaires, an attempt was made to subdivide emotional adjustment into more specific forms, such as home adjustment, school adjustment, and vocational adjustment. Other tests concentrated more intensively upon a narrower area of behavior, or were concerned with more distinctly social responses, such as ascendance-submission in personal contacts. A later development was the construction of tests for quantifying the expression of interests and attitudes. These tests, too, were based essentially upon questionnaire techniques.

Another approach to the measurement of personality is through the application of *performance* or *situational tests*. In such tests, the subject has a task to perform whose purpose is generally disguised. Most of these tests simulate everyday-life situations quite closely. The subject's reactions in these situations are observed without his knowledge. The first extensive application of such techniques is to be found in the tests developed in the late twenties and early thirties by Hartshorne and May (14, 15, 16). This series, standardized on school children, was concerned with such behavior as cheating, lying, stealing, cooperativeness, and persistence. Objective, quantitative scores could be obtained on each of a large number of specific tests. A more recent illustration, for the adult level, is provided by the series of situational tests developed during World War II in the Assessment Program of the Office of Strategic Services (35). These tests were concerned with relatively complex and subtle social and emotional behavior, and required rather elaborate facilities and trained personnel for their administration. The interpretation of the subject's responses, moreover, was relatively subjective.

Projective techniques represent a third approach to the study of personality, and one that has shown phenomenal growth, especially among clinicians. In such tests, the subject is given a relatively "unstructured" task which permits wide latitude in its solution. The assumption underlying such methods is that the individual will "project" his characteristic modes of response into such a task. Like the performance and situational tests, projective techniques are more or less disguised in their purpose, thereby reducing the chances that the subject can deliberately create a desired impression. The previously cited free association test represents one of the earliest types of projective technique. A certain form of sentence-completion test has likewise been used in a similar manner. Other tasks commonly employed in projective techniques include drawing, arranging toys to create a scene, extemporaneous dramatic play, ranking photographs in order of preference, and interpreting a series of pictures or inkblots.

All the available types of personality tests present serious difficulties, both practical and theoretical. Each approach has its own special advantages and weaknesses. The specific problems encountered in personality test construction will be considered in later chapters. For the present, it will suffice to point out that personality testing lags far behind aptitude testing in its positive accomplishments. Nor is such lack of progress to be attributed to insufficient effort. Research on the measurement of personality has reached vast proportions during the past decade, and many ingenious devices and technical improvements are under investigation. It is rather the special difficulties encountered in the measurement of personality that account for the slow advances in this area.

REFERENCES

1. Anastasi, Anne. *Differential psychology.* (3rd ed.) N. Y.: Macmillan, 1958.
2. *Army Air Forces aviation psychology program, research reports.* Rep. Nos. 1-19. Washington: Govt. Printing Office, 1947-1948.
3. Binet, A., and Henri, V. La psychologie individuelle. *Année psychol.*, 1895, 2, 411-463.
4. Binet, A., and Simon, Th. Méthodes nouvelles pour le diagnostic du niveau intellectuel des anormaux. *Année psychol.*, 1905, 11, 191-244.
5. Bolton, T. L. The growth of memory in school children. *Amer. J. Psychol.*, 1891-92, 4, 362-380.
6. Boring, E. G. *A history of experimental psychology.* (Rev. ed.) N. Y.: Appleton-Century-Crofts, 1950.
7. Cattell, J. McK. Mental tests and measurements. *Mind*, 1890, 15, 373-380.
8. Ebbinghaus, H. Über eine neue Methode zur Prüfung geistiger Fähigkeiten und ihre Anwendung bei Schulkindern. *Z. Psychol.*, 1897, 13, 401-459.
9. Esquirol, J. E. D. *Des maladies mentales considérées sous les rapports médical, hygiénique, et médico-légal.* Paris: Baillière, 1838. 2 vols.
10. Galton, F. *Inquiries into human faculty and its development.* London: Macmillan, 1883.
11. Gilbert, J. A. Researches on the mental and physical development of school children. *Stud. Yale Psychol. Lab.*, 1894, 2, 40-100.

12. Goodenough, Florence L. *Mental testing: its history, principles, and applications.* N. Y.: Holt, Rinehart and Winston, 1949.

13. Guicciardi, G., and Ferrari, G. C. I testi mentali per l'esame degli alienati. *Riv. sper. Freniat.,* 1896, 22, 297-314.

14. Hartshorne, H., and May, M. A. *Studies in deceit.* N. Y.: Macmillan, 1930.

15. Hartshorne, H., May, M. A., and Maller, J. B. *Studies in service and self-con-control.* N. Y.: Macmillan, 1929.

16. Hartshorne, H., May, M. A., and Shuttleworth, F. K. *Studies in the organization of character.* N. Y.: Macmillan, 1930.

17. Kelley, T. L. *Crossroads in the mind of man: a study of differentiable mental abilities.* Stanford Univer., Calif.: Stanford Univer. Press, 1928.

18. Kornhauser, A. Replies of psychologists to a short questionnaire on mental test developments, personality inventories, and the Rorschach test. *Educ. psychol. Measmt.,* 1945, 5, 3-15.

19. Kraepelin, E. *Über die Beeinflüssung einfacher psychischer Vorgänge durch einige Arzneimittel.* Jena: Fischer, 1892.

20. Kraepelin, E. Der psychologische Versuch in der Psychiatrie. *Psychol. Arbeit.,* 1895, 1, 1-91.

21. Kuhlmann, F. A revision of the Binet-Simon system for measuring the intelligence of children. *J. Psycho-Asthenics, Monogr. Suppl.,* 1912, 1, 1-41.

22. Münsterberg, H. Zur Individualpsychologie. *Zbl. Nervenheilk. Psychiat.,* 1891, 14, 196-198.

23. Murphy, G. *An historical introduction to modern psychology.* (Rev. ed.) N. Y.: Harcourt, Brace, 1949.

24. Oehrn, A. *Experimentelle Studien zur Individualpsychologie.* Dorpater disser., 1889. (Also in *Psychol. Arbeit.,* 1895, 1, 95-152.)

25. OSS Assessment Staff. *Assessment of men: selection of personnel for the Office of Strategic Services.* N. Y.: Holt, Rinehart and Winston, 1948.

26. Peterson, J. *Early conceptions and tests of intelligence.* Tarrytown-on-Hudson, N. Y.: World Book Co., 1926.

27. Philippe, J. Jastrow—exposition d'anthropologie de Chicago—testes psychologiques, etc. *Année psychol.,* 1894, 1, 522-526.

28. Seguin, E. *Idiocy: its treatment by the physiological method.* (Rep. from original ed. of 1866.) N. Y.: Teach. Coll., Columbia Univer., Bur. Publ., 1907.

29. Sharp, Stella E. Individual psychology: a study in psychological method. *Amer. J. Psychol.,* 1898-99, 10, 329-391.

30. Sommer, R. *Diagnostik der Geisteskrankheiten für praktische Ärzte und Studierende.* Wien und Leipzig: Urban und Schwarzenberg, 1894.

31. Spearman, C. "General intelligence" objectively determined and measured. *Amer. J. Psychol.,* 1904, 15, 201-293.

32. Spearman, C. *The abilities of man.* N. Y.: Macmillan, 1927.

33. Symonds, P. M. *Diagnosing personality and conduct.* N. Y.: Appleton-Century-Crofts, 1931.

34. Terman, L. M. *The measurement of intelligence.* Boston: Houghton Mifflin, 1916.

35. Thurstone, L. L. *Vectors of mind: multiple-factor analysis for the isolation of primary traits.* Chicago: Univer. Chicago Press, 1935.
36. Thurstone, L. L. *Multiple factor analysis.* Chicago: Univer. Chicago Press, 1947.
37. Wissler, C. The correlation of mental and physical traits. *Psychol. Monogr.,* 1901, 3, No. 16.

CHAPTER 2

Principal Characteristics of Psychological Tests

The general public still identifies psychological tests primarily with intelligence tests. The rapid growth and widespread application of group intelligence tests following World War I have left their mark upon the popular concept of what constitutes a psychological test. Moreover, such tests are often loosely described as "IQ tests." Such a designation undoubtedly reflects the popular appeal of age norms and of the intelligence quotient as a technique for reporting the individual's intellectual status. The term "IQ test" is, however, misleading. It is to be hoped that its use will gradually disappear as the public learns more about psychological tests. The IQ refers not to a type of test but to a particular way of interpreting scores on certain psychological tests. Moreover, the IQ is applicable to relatively few psychological tests, as will be seen in Chapter 4. Other, more precise and more widely applicable scoring procedures have been developed and are being employed increasingly in present-day tests.

Intelligence tests themselves represent only one of several types of currently available psychological tests. As can be seen from the historical introduction in Chapter 1, many other kinds of psychological tests have been devised. In terms of both technical excellence and practical value, these other types of tests are often superior to the general intelligence tests. It thus seems appropriate, before proceeding further, to inquire into the exact nature of a psychological test. Psychological tests are more varied and broader in scope than might at first appear. What, then, constitutes a psychological test? What are its essential characteristics?

WHAT IS A PSYCHOLOGICAL TEST?

A psychological test is essentially an objective and standardized measure of a sample of behavior. Psychological tests are like tests in any other sci-

21

ence, in so far as observations are made upon a small but carefully chosen *sample* of an individual's behavior. In this respect, the psychologist proceeds in much the same way as the chemist who tests a shipment of iron ore or a supply of water by analyzing one or more samples of it. If the psychologist wishes to test the extent of a child's vocabulary, or a clerk's ability to perform arithmetic computations, or a pilot's eye-hand coordination, he examines their performance with a representative set of words, or arithmetic problems, or motor tests. Whether or not the test adequately covers the behavior under consideration obviously depends upon the number and nature of items in the sample. For example, an arithmetic test consisting of only five problems, or one including only multiplication items, would be a poor measure of the individual's computational skill. A vocabulary test composed entirely of baseball terms would hardly provide a dependable estimate of a child's total range of vocabulary.

The *diagnostic* or *predictive value* of a psychological test depends upon the degree to which it serves as an indicator of a relatively broad and significant area of behavior. Measurement of the behavior sample directly covered by the test is rarely, if ever, the goal of psychological testing. The child's knowledge of a particular list of 50 words is not, in itself, of great interest. Nor is the job applicant's performance on a specific set of 20 arithmetic problems of much importance. If, however, it can be demonstrated that there is a close correspondence between the child's knowledge of the word list and his total mastery of vocabulary, or between the applicant's score on the arithmetic problems and his computational performance on the job, then the tests are serving their purpose.

It should be noted in this connection that the test items need not resemble closely the behavior the test is to predict. It is only necessary that an empirical correspondence be demonstrated between the two. The degree of similarity between the test sample and the predicted behavior may vary widely. At one extreme, the test may coincide completely with a part of the behavior to be predicted. An example might be a foreign vocabulary test in which the students are examined on 20 of the 50 new words they have studied; another example is provided by the road test taken prior to obtaining a driver's license. A lesser degree of similarity is illustrated by many vocational aptitude tests administered prior to job training, in which there is only a moderate resemblance between the tasks performed on the job and those incorporated in the test. At the other extreme one finds projective personality tests such as the Rorschach inkblot test, in which an attempt is made to predict from the subject's associations to inkblots how he will react to other people, to emotionally toned stimuli, and to other complex, everyday-life situations. Despite their superficial differences, all these tests consist of samples of the individu-al's behavior. And each must prove its worth by an empirically demonstrated correspondence between the subject's performance on the test and in other situations.

Whether the term "diagnosis" or "prediction" is employed in this connec-tion also indicates a minor distinction. Prediction commonly connotes a tem-poral estimate, the individual's future performance on a job, for example, being forecast from his present test performance. In a broader sense, how-ever, even the diagnosis of present condition, such as feeblemindedness or emotional disorder, implies a prediction of what the individual will do in situ-ations other than the present test. It is logically simpler to consider all tests as behavior samples from which predictions regarding other behavior can be made. Different types of tests can then be characterized as variants of this basic pattern.

Another point that should be considered at the outset pertains to the con-cept of *capacity*. It is entirely possible, for example, to devise a test for pre-dicting how well an individual can learn French before he has even begun the study of French. Such a test would involve a sample of the types of behavior required to learn the new language, but would in itself presuppose no knowl-edge of French. It could then be said that this test measures the individual's "capacity" or "potentiality" for learning French. Such terms should, however, be used with caution in reference to psychological tests. Only in the sense that a present behavior sample can be used as an indicator of other, future behavior can we speak of a test measuring "capacity." No psychological test can do more than measure behavior. Whether such behavior can serve as an effective index of other behavior can be determined only by empirical try-out.

Standardization. It will be recalled that in the initial definition a psycho-logical test was described as a standardized measure. Standardization implies *uniformity of procedure* in administering and scoring the test. If the scores obtained by different individuals are to be comparable, testing conditions must obviously be the same for all. Such a requirement is only a special application of the need for controlled conditions in all scientific observations. In a test situation, the single independent variable is usually the individual being tested.

In order to secure uniformity of testing conditions, the test constructor provides detailed directions for administering each newly developed test. The formulation of such directions is a major part of the standardization of a new test. Such standardization extends to the exact materials employed, time limits, oral instructions to subjects, preliminary demonstrations, ways of handling queries from subjects, and every other detail of the testing situation. Many other, more subtle factors may influence the subject's performance on certain tests. Thus in giving instructions or presenting problems orally, consideration must be given to the rate of speaking, tone of voice, inflection, pauses, and facial expression. In a test involving the detection of absurdities, for example, the correct answer may be given away by smiling or pausing when the crucial word is read.

In so far as possible, the surroundings should also be standardized. Certainly adequate lighting, proper ventilation, and freedom from discomfort and distraction should be common requirements in all testing situations. Attention should also be given to motivating the subject, arousing his interest, eliciting his cooperation, and establishing "rapport." The question of rapport will be considered more fully in Chapter 3. In the present connection, however, it should be noted that in this regard, as in other aspects of testing, conditions must be standardized as much as possible for all subjects.

Norms. Another important step in the standardization of a test is the establishment of norms. Without norms, test scores cannot be interpreted. Psychological tests have no predetermined standards of "passing" or "failing." An individual's score can be evaluated only by comparing it with the scores obtained by others. As its name implies, a norm is the "normal" or average performance. Thus if normal 8-year-old children complete 12 out of 50 problems correctly on a particular arithmetic reasoning test, then the 8-year-old norm on this test corresponds to a score of 12. The latter is known as the "raw score" on the test. It may be expressed as number of correct items, time required to complete a task, number of errors, or some other objective measure appropriate to the content of the test. Such a raw score is meaningless until evaluated in terms of a suitable set of norms.

In the process of standardizing a test, it must be administered to a large, representative sample of the type of subjects for whom it is designed. This group, known as the standardization sample, serves to establish the norms. Such norms indicate not only the average performance but also the relative frequency of varying degrees of deviation above and below the average. It is thus possible to evaluate different degrees of superiority and inferiority. The specific ways in which such norms may be expressed will be considered in Chapter 4. All permit the designation of the individual's position with reference to the normative or standardization sample.

It might also be noted that norms are established for personality tests in essentially the same way as for aptitude tests. The norm on a personality test is not necessarily the most desirable or "ideal" performance, any more than a perfect or errorless score is the norm on an aptitude test. On both types of tests, the norm corresponds to the performance of typical or average individuals. On ascendance-submission tests, for example, the norm falls at an intermediate point representing the degree of ascendance or submission manifested by the average individual. Similarly, in an emotional adjustment inventory, the norm does not ordinarily correspond to a complete absence of unfavorable or maladaptive responses, since a few such responses occur in the majority of "normal" individuals in the standardization sample. It is thus apparent that psychological tests, of whatever type, are based upon empirically established norms.

Objective Measurement of Difficulty. Reference to the definition of a psychological test with which this discussion opened will show that such a test was characterized as an objective as well as a standardized measure. In what specific ways are such tests objective? Some aspects of the objectivity of psychological tests have already been touched upon in the discussion of standardization. Thus the administration, scoring, and interpretation of scores are objective in so far as they are independent of the subjective judgment of the individual examiner. Any one individual should theoretically obtain the identical score on a test regardless of who happens to be his examiner. This is not entirely so, of course, since perfect standardization and objectivity have not been attained in practice. But at least such objectivity is the goal of test construction and has been achieved to a reasonably high degree in most tests.

There are other major ways in which psychological tests can be properly described as objective. The determination of the difficulty level of an item or of a whole test, and the measurement of test reliability and validity, are based upon objective, empirical procedures. The concepts of reliability and validity will be considered in subsequent sections. We shall turn our attention first to the concept of difficulty.

When Binet and Simon prepared their original, 1905 Scale for the measurement of intelligence (cf. Ch. 1), they arranged the 30 items of the scale in order of increasing difficulty. Such difficulty, it will be recalled, was determined by trying out the items on 50 normal and a few retarded and feebleminded children. The items correctly solved by the largest proportion of subjects were, *ipso facto,* taken to be the easiest; those passed by relatively few subjects were regarded as more difficult items. By such a procedure, an empirical order of difficulty was established. This early example typifies the objective measurement of difficulty level, which is now common practice in psychological test construction.

Not only the arrangement but also the selection of items for inclusion in a test can be determined by the proportion of subjects in the trial samples who pass each item. Thus if there is a bunching of items at the easy or difficult end of the scale, some items can be discarded. Similarly, if items are sparse in certain portions of the difficulty range, new items can be added to fill in the gaps.

Frequency of correct response is also employed in constructing age scales, such as the later revisions of the Binet scales. In such a case, the proportion of children at each age level who pass each item is determined. The item is then assigned to that age level at which a certain proportion pass it.

The difficulty level of the test as a whole is, of course, directly dependent upon the difficulty of the items that make up the test. A comprehensive check of the difficulty of the total test for the population for which it is designed is provided by the distribution of total scores. If the standardization sample is a representative cross section of such a population, then it is generally expected that the scores will fall roughly into a *normal distribution curve*. In other words, there should be a clustering of individuals near the center of the range, and a gradual tapering off as the extremes are approached. A theoretical normal curve, with all irregularities eliminated, is shown in Figure 1. In

Fig. 1. A Normal Distribution Curve.

plotting such a frequency distribution, scores are indicated on the baseline, and frequencies, or number of persons obtaining each score, on the vertical axis. A smooth curve like the one illustrated above is closely approximated when very large samples are tested.[1]

Let us suppose, however, that the obtained distribution curve is not "normal," but clearly skewed, as illustrated in Figures 2A and 2B. The former distribution, with a piling of scores at the low end, suggests that the test has too high a "floor" for the group under consideration, lacking a sufficient number of easy items to discriminate properly at the lower end of the range. The result is that persons who would normally scatter over a considerable range obtain zero or near-zero scores on this test. A peak at the low end of the scale is therefore obtained. Such an artificial piling of scores is illustrated

[1] For a fuller discussion of the implications of the normal curve, as well as for illustrations of obtained distributions of test scores, cf. Anastasi (3, Ch. 2).

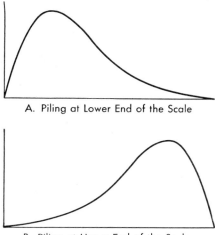

A. Piling at Lower End of the Scale

B. Piling at Upper End of the Scale

Fig. 2.   Skewed Distribution Curves.

schematically in Figure 3, in which a normally distributed group yields a skewed distribution on a particular test. The opposite skewness is illustrated in Figure 2B, with the scores piled up at the upper end, a finding which suggests insufficient test "ceiling." Administering a test designed for the general population to selected samples of college or graduate students will usually yield such a skewed distribution, a number of students obtaining nearly perfect scores. With such a test, it is impossible to measure individual differences among the more able subjects in the group. If more difficult items had been included in the test, some individuals would undoubtedly have scored higher than the present test permits.

When the standardization sample yields a markedly non-normal distribution on a test, the difficulty level of the test is ordinarily modified until a

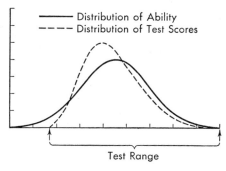

———— Distribution of Ability
‒ ‒ ‒ ‒ Distribution of Test Scores

Test Range

Fig. 3.   Skewness Resulting from Insufficient "Test Floor."

normal curve is approximated. Depending upon the type of deviation from normality that appears, easier or more difficult items may be added, other items eliminated or modified, the position of items in the scale altered, or the scoring "weights" assigned to certain responses revised. Such adjustments are continued until the distribution becomes at least roughly normal. Under these conditions, the most likely score, obtained by the largest number of subjects, usually corresponds to about 50 per cent correct items. To the layman who is unfamiliar with the methods of psychological test construction, a "50 per cent" score may seem shockingly low. It is sometimes objected, on this basis, that the examiner has set too low a "standard of passing" on the test. Or the inference is drawn that the group tested is a particularly poor one. Both conclusions, of course, are totally meaningless when viewed in the light of the procedures followed in developing psychological tests. Such tests are deliberately constructed and specifically modified so as to yield a mean score of approximately 50 per cent correct. Only in such a way can the maximum differentiation between individuals at all ability levels be obtained with the test. With a mean of approximately 50 per cent correct items, there is the maximum opportunity for a normal distribution, with individual scores spreading widely at both extremes.[2]

Reliability. "How good is this test?" "Does it really work?" These questions could—and occasionally do—lead to long hours of futile discussion. Subjective opinions, hunches, and personal biases may lead, on the one hand, to extravagant claims regarding what a particular test can accomplish and, on the other hand, to stubborn rejection. The only way in which questions such as these can be conclusively answered is by empirical trial. The *objective evaluation* of psychological tests involves primarily the determination of the reliability and the validity of the test in specified situations.

As used in psychometrics, the term "reliability" always means stability or consistency. Test reliability is the consistency of scores obtained by the same persons when retested with the identical test or with an equivalent form of the test. If a child receives an IQ of 110 on Monday and an IQ of 80 when retested on Friday, it is obvious that little or no confidence can be put in either score. Similarly, if one set of 50 words enables an individual to identify 40 correctly, while on another, supposedly equivalent set, he can get a score of only 20 right, then neither score can be taken as a dependable index of

---

[2] Actually, the normal curve provides finer discrimination at the ends than at the middle of the scale. Equal discrimination at all points of the scale would require a rectangular distribution. The normal curve, however, has an advantage if subsequent statistical analyses of scores are to be conducted, since many current statistical techniques assume approximate normality of distribution. For this and other reasons, it is likely that most tests designed for general use will continue to follow a normal-curve pattern for some time to come. In the construction of custom-made tests to serve clearly defined purposes, however, the form of the distribution of scores should depend upon the type of discrimination desired (cf. 11, 15).

his verbal comprehension. To be sure, in both illustrations it is possible that only one of the two scores is in error, but this could be demonstrated only by further retests. From the given data, we can conclude only that both scores cannot be right. Whether one or neither is an adequate estimate of the individual's true ability we cannot determine without additional information.

Before a psychological test is released for general use, a thorough, objective check of its reliability must be carried out. The different types of test reliability, as well as methods of measuring each, will be considered in Chapter 5. Reliability can be checked with reference to temporal fluctuations, the particular selection of items or behavior sample constituting the test, the role of different examiners or scorers, and other aspects of the testing situation. It is essential to specify the type of reliability and method employed to determine it, since the same test may vary in these different aspects. The number and nature of individuals on whom reliability was checked should likewise be reported. With such information, the test user can predict whether the test will be about equally reliable for the group with which he expects to use it, or whether it is likely to be more reliable or less reliable.

Validity. Undoubtedly the most important question that needs to be raised regarding any psychological test concerns its validity, i.e., the degree to which the test actually measures what it purports to measure. Validity provides a direct check on how well the test fulfills its function. The determination of validity usually requires independent, external *criteria* of whatever the test is designed to measure. For example, if a medical aptitude test is to be used in selecting promising applicants for medical school, ultimate success in medical school would be a criterion. In the process of validating such a test, it would be administered to a large group of students at the time of their admission to medical school. Some measure of performance in medical school would eventually be obtained for each student, on the basis of grades, ratings by instructors, success or failure in completing training, and the like. Such a composite measure constitutes the criterion with which each student's initial test score is to be correlated. A high correlation, or *validity coefficient,* would signify that those individuals who scored high on the test had been relatively successful in medical school, while those scoring low on the test had done poorly in medical school. A low correlation would indicate little correspondence between test score and criterion measure, and hence poor validity for the test. The validity coefficient enables us to determine how closely the criterion performance could have been predicted from the test scores.

In a similar manner, tests designed for other purposes can be validated against appropriate criteria. A vocational aptitude test, for example, can be validated against on-the-job success of a trial group of new employees. A pilot aptitude battery can be validated against achievement in flight training and eventually against combat performance, if the latter records become available. Tests designed for broader and more varied uses are validated against a number of criteria. Thus intelligence tests have been validated against such criteria as school achievement, ratings by teachers or supervisors, or scores on other, previously validated tests. If, as in the case of intelligence tests, it is reasonable to expect scores to increase with age up to a certain level, then an examination of the mean scores obtained by successive age groups provides another check on validity. Similarly, the test performance of institutionalized mental defectives may be compared with that of normal school children. In tests of emotional instability, the responses of persons known to be neurotic or psychotic may be checked against those of unselected normal adults.

The reader may have noticed an apparent paradox in the concept of test validity. If it is necessary to follow up the subjects or in other ways to obtain an independent measure of what the test is trying to predict, why not dispense with the test? The answer to this riddle is to be found in the distinction between the validation group on the one hand, and the groups on which the test will eventually be employed for predictive purposes on the other. Before the test is ready for use, its validity must be established on a representative sample of subjects. The scores of these persons are not themselves employed for predictive purposes, but serve only in the process of "testing the test." If the test proves valid by this method, then it can be used on other samples, in the absence of criterion measures.

It might still be argued that we would only need to wait for the criterion measure to "mature," or become available, on *any* group, in order to obtain the information that the test is trying to predict. But such a procedure would be so wasteful of time and energy as to be prohibitive in most instances. Thus we could determine which applicants will succeed on a job or which students will satisfactorily complete college by admitting all who apply and waiting for subsequent developments! It is the very wastefulness of such a procedure that tests are designed to reduce. By means of tests, the individual's eventual performance in such situations can be predicted with a determinable margin of error. The more valid the test, of course, the smaller will be this margin of error.

An essential precaution in determining the validity of a test is to make certain that the test scores do not themselves influence any individual's criterion status. For example, if a college instructor or a foreman in an industrial plant knows that a particular individual scored very poorly on an aptitude test, such knowledge might influence the grade given to the student or the rating assigned to the worker. Or a high-scoring individual might be given the benefit of the doubt when academic grades or on-the-job ratings are being prepared. Such influences would obviously raise the correlation between test scores and criterion in a manner that is entirely spurious or artificial. This possible source of error in test validation is known as *criterion contamination,* since the criterion ratings become "contaminated" by the rater's knowledge of the test scores. To prevent the operation of such an error, it is absolutely essential that no person who participates in the assignment of criterion ratings have any knowledge of the subjects' test scores. For this reason, test scores employed in "testing the test" must be kept strictly confidential. It is sometimes difficult to convince teachers, employers, military officers, and other line personnel that such a precaution is essential. In their urgency to utilize all available information for practical decisions, such persons may fail to realize that the test scores must be put aside until the criterion data mature and validity can be checked.

The special problems encountered in determining the validity of different types of tests, as well as the specific criteria and statistical procedures employed, will be discussed in Chapters 6 and 7. One further point, however, should be considered at this time. Validity tells us more than the degree to which the test is fulfilling its function. It actually tells us *what* the test is measuring. By examining the criterion data, together with the validity coefficients of the test, we can objectively determine what the test is measuring.[3] It is for this reason that some psychologists prefer to define validity as the extent to which we know what the test measures. The interpretation of test scores would undoubedly be clearer and less ambiguous if tests were regularly named in terms of the criteria against which they had been validated (cf. 2). A tendency in this direction can be recognized in such test labels as "scholastic aptitude test" (6) and "personnel classification test" (23) in place of the vague title "intelligence test."

VARIETIES OF PSYCHOLOGICAL TESTS

Major Types of Psychological Tests. It is customary to classify psychological tests with reference to the aspects of behavior which they sample. Such a classification is somewhat arbitrary and fluid, as will shortly become apparent. For practical convenience, however, there are certain advantages in grouping tests in this manner. Moreover, the terms designating these various test categories are widely used in the psychological literature. Conse-

[3] Several specific procedures for determining what a test measures will be discussed in Chapter 6. In most of these, however, the basic step is the correlation of test scores with some independently obtained criterion data.

quently, familiarity with such terms is helpful in itself. Outstanding examples
of current tests in each category will be examined in Parts 2, 3, and 4. In
general, the organization of tests in the chapters included under Parts 2, 3,
and 4 will follow the classification given below.

As indicated in Chapter 1, the development of *general intelligence tests,*
to estimate over-all level of intellectual functioning, was one of the earliest
goals of psychological testing. The early efforts to identify and classify mental
defectives, the original Binet-Simon tests, and even the research of Galton
and Cattell with sensorimotor tests were oriented toward the measurement of
general intelligence. This type of test, with its many varieties and levels,
still constitutes one of the largest groups of available psychological tests. The
most widely used tests in this category, ranging from the infant level to
graduate school, will be discussed in Part 2 (Chs. 8 to 12).

Multiple aptitude batteries are rapidly replacing general intelligence tests
for a number of purposes, especially in the counseling of adolescents and
adults. Although they cover a wide sampling of psychological functions, even
broader than that included in the traditional intelligence tests, these batteries
do not ordinarily provide a single over-all score, such as an IQ. Rather, it is
the principal aim of such batteries to permit differentiation among the individual's special assets and liabilities—among the high and low spots in his
"intellectual profile." The construction of multiple aptitude batteries also
utilizes the latest developments in factor analysis, since the tests that make
up such batteries are ordinarily chosen to represent the principal traits identified by factor analysis. A more comprehensive coverage of abilities, with a
minimum of needless overlap of test content, is thereby assured. The major
multiple aptitude batteries in current use, together with the methods employed in their construction, will be considered in Chapter 13.

Tests of *special aptitudes* will be illustrated in Chapters 14 and 15. His-
torically, this type of test antedates the multiple aptitude batteries, having
been first developed to fill in some of the obvious gaps left by the general intelligence tests. Attention was first focused on highly specialized areas that
intelligence tests made no effort to cover, such as musical, artistic, and mechanical aptitudes. Interest in vocational selection also stimulated the development of certain special aptitude tests, such as those for the prediction of
clerical aptitude. To some extent, special aptitude tests overlap the functions
covered by multiple aptitude batteries, although some areas not included in
the latter can be measured by certain special aptitude tests. Today, special
aptitude tests are available for a wide variety of purposes. They range from
very specific and simple measures of sensory acuity or speed of finger movement to complex tests of art appreciation or of aptitude for law or dentistry.

A traditional distinction is that between aptitude tests and *achievement tests.* The latter are designed to assess the effects of a specified course of training. The principal examples of achievement tests are to be found in educational testing. In fact, any standardized examination on a school course represents an achievement test. Such tests are now extremely common, ranging from the elementary school to the graduate and professional schools, and covering practically all subjects of instruction. Trade tests, for use in screening and selecting industrial and business employees, constitute another type of achievement test. As in educational achievement tests, such trade tests assume that the testees have had a specific course of instruction, job apprenticeship, or other relatively uniform experience. Achievement tests for use in both education and industry will be covered in Chapters 16 and 17. Following the more detailed discussion in those chapters, it will be seen that the distinction between achievement and aptitude tests is relative rather than absolute, since each type of test can be used, under certain conditions, to appraise the effects of past experience and to predict future accomplishment.

The last major category of psychological tests, to be considered in Chapters 18 to 21, is a very broad one and concerns the measurement of *personality characteristics.* The types of tests conventionally placed under this heading include measures of emotional adjustment, also known as tests of neuroticism or emotional instability, or simply as "personality inventories." The category also covers measures of social traits, involving primarily relations with other persons, such as ascendance-submission, introversion-extroversion, and self-sufficiency. Social intelligence, covering the knowledge and skills demanded in social situations, is sometimes classified with special aptitudes and sometimes with personality. Tests of character traits, such as honesty, perseverance, and cooperativeness, are traditionally included under personality tests, as are measures of motivation, interests, and attitudes. The questionnaire, projective, and situational tests briefly described in Chapter 1 would all, of course, fall under the heading of personality tests. Each of these three techniques has been applied to the measurement of several of the areas listed above.

Like many of the distinctions made in classifying tests, the dichotomy between ability and personality tests is to some extent artificial and debatable. In taking any test, the individual is undoubtedly influenced both by ability factors and by emotional, motivational, interest, and other non-intellectual characteristics. Some tests, in fact, have been employed to measure either ability or personality factors, when administered or scored in different ways. In the construction of psychological tests, however, emphasis is generally placed upon one or another aspect of behavior. Such emphasis is reflected in the instructions to the subjects, the techniques for establishing rapport, scoring procedures, and other features of the test.

A useful distinction has been proposed in this connection by Cronbach (8, pp. 29-34), who differentiates between tests of *maximum performance* and tests of *habitual performance.* The former correspond to ability tests (intelligence, special aptitudes, etc.), the latter to personality tests. It is certainly true that the object of ability tests is characteristically to discover how well the individual can perform in a certain area, under the most favorable conditions that can be provided. Every effort is made in such tests to control motivation, interest, surrounding conditions, and other contributing factors in such a way as to insure that the individual is "doing his best" on the test. On the other hand, in personality tests it is the usual or habitual reaction of the individual that is sought—not what the individual believes is the best solution or what he would like to do, but what he actually does in the specified situation.

Other Bases for Classifying Psychological Tests. Psychological tests are commonly classified in a number of other ways, some of which may cut across the major divisions outlined in the preceding section. For example, it is useful to distinguish between *individual* and *group* tests. This dichotomy is regularly employed with intelligence tests, as indicated in Chapter 1. But it is equally applicable to any other type of test. For practical purposes, it is of course very important to know whether a test must be administered singly to each subject, like the Stanford-Binet, or whether it can be given simultaneously to large groups. Many individual tests also require a highly trained examiner and are designed primarily as clinical instruments for the intensive study of single cases.

Individual tests enable the examiner to make valuable auxiliary observations regarding the subject's work methods and other qualitative aspects of performance, his social and emotional reactions, and the like. It has been said, for example, that the Stanford-Binet is in effect a standardized interview, the experienced clinician obtaining much more information from it than just the IQ. Individual tests also give the examiner a better opportunity to establish rapport, obtain cooperation, and maintain the interest of the subject in the test. Any special conditions that may handicap the subject in his performance are also more readily noted and remedied in an individual testing situation. Group tests, on the other hand, not only permit the "mass testing" characteristic of many contemporary testing programs, but they also insure more uniformity of procedure, since the role of the examiner is reduced and simplified, and scoring can be made highly automatic.

Another basis for classifying psychological tests is to be found in the *testing medium*. The most familiar differentiation in this connection is that between *paper-and-pencil* and *performance* tests. This distinction, too, has been applied primarily to intelligence tests, although it has more recently proved useful with other types, especially personality tests. The familiar paper-and-pencil type of test provides each subject with a test form on which all items are printed. Responses are written by the subject on either the test form itself or on a separate answer sheet. In some paper-and-pencil tests, the stimuli are presented on phonograph records or tape recordings. Examples include tests of musical aptitude (Ch. 15) and tests designed to measure either aptitude or achievement in foreign languages (Ch. 17).

In performance tests, the individual may be required to manipulate objects, pictures, blocks, or mechanical apparatus, or he may perform more complex activities in a typical everyday-life situation. Performance tests have traditionally been restricted to individual testing. One reason for such a limitation

Fig. 4. The Administration of a Performance Test to a Small Group: Two-Hand Coordination Test Used in Air Force Classification Program. (Courtesy U. S. Air Force; for description of test, cf. Melton, 16.)

is the difficulty of providing duplicate sets of materials, owing to bulkiness, purchase cost, and expense of checking and maintenance in the case of certain types of equipment. Another reason is that in most performance tests each subject could easily see what others are doing. In contemporary, large-scale testing programs, however, performance tests are sometimes administered in small groups. Table screens may be employed to conceal each subject's test materials. In the case of many sensorimotor coordination tests, moreover, such a precaution may be unnecessary, since observation of another's performance would be of no help. Figure 4 illustrates the procedure followed by the Air Force in administering apparatus tests for classification purposes during World War II.

A testing medium that has been extensively explored since 1940 is the *motion-picture film*. This medium received considerable attention, for example, in the Air Force testing program during World War II (12). Further research on the development of motion-picture tests was conducted, as part of an extensive project on the instructional use of films, by Carpenter and his associates under the joint auspices of the Army and Navy (5). In this connec-

Fig. 5. The Motion Picture as a Testing Medium: "Classroom Communicator" with Response Stations Used by Subjects in Recording Responses. (From 5; courtesy C. R. Carpenter.)

tion, special equipment was developed for the recording and immediate scoring of subject responses during motion-picture tests. Figure 5 shows the individual "response stations" to be used by each subject in the group being tested (5). The subject inserts his hand under the cover and registers each response by depressing the appropriate key.

Although presenting certain technical problems in the preparation of the film and in the administration of the test—problems relating to seating arrangements, lighting, and the like—motion-picture tests have many advantages. If combined with a sound track, such tests can achieve a high degree of standardization in instructions and presentation of stimuli. The time allowed for each item can likewise be controlled. Moreover, certain perceptual problems involving motion can be effectively presented through this medium. The realism of the situations portrayed by a motion picture is a further asset in certain types of tests.

Mention should also be made of what is undoubtedly the newest of testing mediums, *television.* Preliminary research suggests that this, too, is a promising medium for highly standardized, large-scale testing programs (cf. 17). One advantage of televised tests is the speed with which they can be revised, as contrasted to films. In a rapidly changing field, television can thus combine timeliness with the high degree of standardization of procedure offered by the film medium. Figure 6 shows a group of subjects taking a televised test and recording their responses on specially devised response units.

A further distinction made in the classification of psychological tests is that between *language* and *non-language* tests. In the non-language test, no language is required, either written or spoken, in either the instructions or the test items. To be sure, language may be and often is employed in administering these tests, but alternative non-language procedures are available for special circumstances. Non-language tests are especially designed for the illiterate, foreign-speaking, deaf, or others who for any reason are unable to take a language test. A non-language test can be either a performance or a paper-and-pencil test. In the latter, the test content generally consists of pictures, diagrams, and non-linguistic symbols, the subject being required to respond by making relatively simple marks. Instructions are given by gesture, pantomime, and demonstrations involving charts and diagrams. The Army Beta, developed during World War I, was the first group non-language test for measuring intelligence.

Tests have also occasionally been classified with reference to their predominant *content,* as verbal, numerical, pictorial, spatial, and the like. Such a superficial characterization is, however, gradually giving way to more precise descriptions in terms of the factorial composition of tests. Pictorial mate-

Fig. 6. Television as a Testing Medium: Television Screens, Sound Equipment, and Individual Response Indicators in Use. (Cf. 17; courtesy R. T. Rock.)

rials, for example, can be employed to measure verbal comprehension. Thus, in a number of tests for preschool and primary grade children, the subject is required to mark the picture that fits the word, phrase, or sentence spoken by the examiner. Another objection to classifying tests in terms of content stems from the fact that individuals may employ different methods to perform the same task. Consequently, a problem involving spatial content, such as geometric forms, may be solved by some subjects through spatial visualization and by others through verbal reasoning.

Finally, mention should be made of the differentiation between *speed* and *power* tests. A pure speed test is one in which individual differences depend entirely upon speed of performance. Such a test is ordinarily constructed from items of uniformly low difficulty level, all of which are well within the ability of the subjects taking the test. The time limit is then made so short that no one can finish all the items. Under such conditions, each person's score reflects only the speed with which he worked. A pure power test, on the other hand, has a time limit long enough to permit everyone to attempt all items. The difficulty of the items is steeply graded, and the test includes some items too difficult for anyone to solve, so that nobody can get a perfect score. It will be noted that both speed and power tests are designed to prevent the achievement of perfect scores. The reason for such a precaution is that perfect scores are indeterminate, since it is impossible to know how much higher the individual's score would have been if more items, or more difficult items, had been included. To enable each individual to show fully what he is able to accomplish, the test must provide adequate ceiling, either in number of items or in difficulty level.

The distinction between power and speed tests is one of degree, rather than being a twofold division. Most tests actually depend upon both power and speed, in varying proportions. It is important to know the extent to which speed and power enter into performance on any particular test. Not only is such information essential for the proper interpretation of scores on any given test, but it is also needed in the technical evaluation of the test. As will be seen in Chapter 5, the estimation of certain forms of test reliability may be seriously in error if the role of speed is ignored.

SOURCES OF INFORMATION ABOUT TESTS

The active test user in any branch of testing needs to keep informed regarding the new tests constantly being developed. The large number available, as well as the rapidity with which revisions and new tests appear, makes the task of locating pertinent material a particularly difficult one. Familiarity with at least the major sources of information is thus a necessity for anyone interested in tests.

One of the most important sources is the series of *Mental Measurements Yearbooks* edited by Buros (4). These yearbooks cover nearly all commercially available psychological, educational, and vocational tests published in English-speaking countries. The coverage is especially complete for paper-and-pencil tests. Each yearbook includes tests published during a specified period, thereby supplementing rather than supplanting the earlier yearbooks. Thus, *The Fifth Mental Measurements Yearbook,* published in 1959, is concerned with tests appearing between 1952 and 1958. The first two publications in the series, appearing in 1935 and 1936, were simply bibliographies of tests. Beginning in 1938, however, the yearbook assumed its current form, which includes critical reviews of most of the tests by one or more test experts. Such data as publisher, price, forms, and age or other characteristics of subjects for whom the test is suitable are regularly given. Another valuable feature of the yearbooks is their listing of books dealing with testing and related fields, together with excerpts from published reviews of each book.

A bibliography on psychological tests, prepared by Hildreth in 1939 (13), covers a 50-year period and includes over four thousand titles. A supplement (14) published in 1945 contains about one thousand additional items. In this bibliography, an effort was made to list all available standardized tests, with the exception of sensory and physical measures. The entries are grouped under such broad headings as intelligence, vocational, psychomotor, and personality tests. Besides tests published in America, some foreign ones are also included, principally from England, France, and Germany. Tests not commercially available are likewise listed, provided they are adequately described in a printed source. Other compilations published at about the same time as the Hildreth bibliography are *An Annotated Bibliography of Mental Tests and Scales* by Wang (22) and *An Index of Periodical Literature on Testing* by South (19).

Information regarding many tests can also be obtained from handbooks that survey tests for special purposes. An early classic is Whipple's *Manual of Mental and Physical Tests,* first published in 1910 (24). Detailed descriptions of many sensory, motor, and simple psychological tests are given in this source. A much more recent publication is the book by Super (21), which surveys psychological tests with special reference to their usefulness in vocational counseling. A handbook by Dorcus and Jones (9) is devoted to tests for which validation data in terms of an industrial criterion are available; this collection would thus be of special interest in connection with personnel selection. Surveys of tests have also been prepared within such specialized areas as mechanical aptitude, clerical aptitude, educational achievement, personality, and projective techniques. References to these sources will be cited in the appropriate chapters dealing with such tests.

Attention should also be called to the listings and reviews of newly published tests provided by a number of psychological and educational journals. *Psychological Abstracts* lists new tests in a special section. Recently published tests are also listed in individual issues of *Educational and Psychological Measurement,* a journal containing many articles on the construction, use, and evaluation of tests. Short reviews of new tests appear from time to time in such publications as the *Journal of Consulting Psychology.* A comprehensive critical survey of all types of psychological and educational tests is published every three years in the February issue of the *Review of Educa-*

tional Research. Initiated in 1932, this triennial cycle includes the years 1953, 1956, 1959, and so on. Since 1954, *Personnel Psychology* has included a section entitled "Validity Information Exchange" which reports in standard summary fashion any new data on the validity of specific tests. Still another section, on "Normative Data Information Exchange," was added in 1956. Current information on tests can also be found in the chapter on "Individual Differences" in each volume of the *Annual Review of Psychology.*

Finally, it should be noted that the most direct source of information regarding specific current tests is provided by the catalogues of test publishers and by the manual that accompanies each test. A comprehensive list of test publishers, with addresses, can be found in the latest *Mental Measurements Yearbook.* For ready reference, the names and addresses of some of the larger American publishers and distributors of psychological tests are given in the Appendix (p. 638). Catalogues of current tests can be obtained from these publishers on request. Manuals and specimen sets of tests can be purchased by qualified users (see Ch. 3).

The test manual should provide the essential information required for administering, scoring, and evaluating a particular test (cf. 1, 7, 10, 18, 20). In it should be found full and detailed instructions, scoring key, norms, and data on reliability and validity. Moreover, the manual should report the number and nature of subjects on whom norms, reliability, and validity were established, the methods employed in computing indices of reliability and validity, and the specific criteria against which validity was checked. In the event that the necessary information is too lengthy to fit conveniently into the manual, references to the printed sources in which such information can be readily located should be given. The manual should, in other words, enable the test user to evaluate the test before choosing it for his specific purpose. It might be added that many test manuals still fall short of this goal. But some of the larger and more professionally oriented test publishers are giving increasing attention to the preparation of manuals that meet adequate scientific standards. An enlightened public of test users provides the firmest assurance that such standards will be maintained and improved in the future.

A succinct but comprehensive guide for the evaluation of psychological tests is to be found in the *Technical Recommendations for Psychological Tests and Diagnostic Techniques* (1), prepared and officially adopted by the American Psychological Association. These recommendations represent a summary of desirable practices in test construction, based upon the current state of knowledge in the field. They are concerned with such questions as reliability, validity, the establishment of norms, and the preparation of a test manual. Relevant portions of these recommendations will be discussed elsewhere in the book, in connection with specific topics.

REFERENCES

1. American Psychological Association. *Technical recommendations for psychological tests and diagnostic techniques.* Washington: Amer. Psychol. Assoc., 1954. (Also in *Psychol. Bull.,* 1954, 51, No. 2, Pt. 2.)
2. Anastasi, Anne. The concept of validity in the interpretation of test scores. *Educ. psychol. Measmt.,* 1950, 10, 67-78.
3. Anastasi, Anne. *Differential psychology.* (3rd ed.) N. Y.: Macmillan, 1958.
4. Buros, O. K. (Ed.) *The fifth mental measurements yearbook.* Highland Park, N. J.: Gryphon Press, 1959.
5. Carpenter, C. R., Eggleton, R. C., John, F. T., and Cannon, J. B., Jr. The Classroom Communicator. *Technical Report SDC 269-7-14, Special Devices Center, Office of Naval Research,* 1950.
6. College Entrance Examination Board, Aptitude Test Committee. *A description of the College Board Scholastic Aptitude Test.* N. Y.: College Entrance Examination Board, 1956.
7. Conrad, H. S., Information which should be provided by test publishers and testing agencies on the validity and use of their tests: aptitude and intelligence tests. *Proc. 1949 invit. Conf. test. Probl., Educ. Test. Serv.,* 1950, 63-68.
8. Cronbach, L. J. *Essentials of psychological testing.* (2nd ed.) N. Y.: Harper, 1960.
9. Dorcus, R. M., and Jones, Margaret H. *Handbook of employee selection.* N. Y.: McGraw-Hill, 1950.
10. Dressel, P. L. Information which should be provided by test publishers and testing agencies on the validity and use of their tests: achievement tests. *Proc. 1949 invit. Conf. test. Probl., Educ. Test. Serv.,* 1950, 69-74.
11. Ferguson, G. A. On the theory of test discrimination. *Psychometrika,* 1949, 14, 61-68.
12. Gibson, J. J. (Ed.) *Motion picture testing and research.* (AAF Aviation Psychology Program, Research Reports. Rep. No. 7.) Washington: Govt. Printing Office, 1947.
13. Hildreth, Gertrude H. *A bibliography of mental tests and rating scales.* (2nd ed.) N. Y.: Psychol. Corp., 1939.
14. Hildreth, Gertrude H. *A bibliography of mental tests and rating scales, 1945 supplement.* N. Y.: Psychol. Corp., 1946.
15. Jackson, R. W. B., and Ferguson, G. A. A functional approach in test construction. *Educ. psychol. Measmt.,* 1943, 3, 23-28.
16. Melton, A. W. (Ed.) *Apparatus tests.* (AAF Aviation Psychology Program, Research Reports. Rep. No. 4.) Washington: Govt. Printing Office, 1947.
17. Rock, R. T., Duva, J. S., and Regan, J. J. Training by television. *Report No:*

NAVEXOS P-850-1, Special Devices Center, Office of Naval Research, 1953.

18. Shaffer, L. F. Information which should be provided by test publishers and testing agencies on the validity and use of their tests: personality tests. *Proc. 1949 invit. Conf. test. Probl., Educ. Test. Serv.,* 1950, 75-78.

19. South, E. B. *An index of periodical literature on testing.* N. Y.: Psychol. Corp., 1937.

20. Stuit, D. B. The preparation of a test manual. *Amer. Psychologist,* 1951, 6, 167-170.

21. Super, D. E. *Appraising vocational fitness by means of psychological tests.* N. Y.: Harper, 1949.

22. Wang, C. K. A. *An annotated bibliography of mental tests and scales.* Peiping, China: Catholic Univer. Press, 1939-1940. 2 vols.

23. Wesman, A. G. *Personnel Classification Test.* N. Y.: Psychol. Corp., 1946-1951.

24. Whipple, G. M. *Manual of mental and physical tests.* Baltimore: Warwick & York, 1914-1915. 2 vols. (Original, single-volume ed. publ. in 1910.)

CHAPTER 3

Use of Psychological Tests

"May I have a Stanford-Binet blank? I'd like to find my little sister's IQ. The family think she's precocious."

"Last night I answered the questions in an intelligence test published in our newspaper, and I got an IQ of 80—I think psychological tests are silly."

"I'd like to borrow the Ishihara color-blindness test to show my brother. He's applying for a Navy commission and would like some practice so he can pass that test."

"My roommate is studying psych. She gave me a personality test and I came out neurotic. I've been too upset to go to class ever since."

"I represent the school paper. We'd like a list of the IQ's of the entering freshmen to publish in our first Fall issue."

The above remarks are not imaginary. Each is based on a real incident, and the list could easily be extended by any psychologist. Such remarks illustrate potential misuses of psychological tests in such ways as to render the tests worthless or to hurt the individual. Like any scientific instrument or precision tool, psychological tests must be properly used to be effective. In the hands of either the unscrupulous or the well-meaning but uninformed user, such tests can cause serious damage.

CODE OF PROFESSIONAL ETHICS PERTAINING TO PSYCHOLOGICAL TESTS

In order to circumvent the misuse of psychological tests, it has become necessary to erect a number of safeguards around both the tests themselves and the test scores. The distribution and use of psychological tests constitutes a major area in *Ethical Standards of Psychologists* (3), the code of professional ethics officially adopted by the American Psychological Associa-

44

tion. It will be helpful at this point to take a quick look at some of the highlights in the relevant portions of this code. Some of these points are also covered in *Technical Recommendations for Psychological Tests and Diagnostic Techniques* (2), cited in the preceding chapter.

The first and most fundamental principle is that the sale and distribution of tests should be restricted to qualified users. The necessary qualifications will, of course, vary with the type of test. Thus, a relatively long period of intensive training and supervised experience is required for the proper use of individual intelligence tests and most personality tests, and a minimum of specialized psychological training is needed in the case of educational achievement or vocational proficiency tests. It should also be noted that students who take tests in class for instructional purposes are not usually equipped to administer the tests to others or to interpret the scores properly.

Test scores should likewise be released only to persons qualified to interpret them. When an individual is given his own score, not only should the score be interpreted by a properly qualified person, but facilities should also be available for counseling any individual who may become emotionally disturbed by a knowledge of his score. For example, a college student might become seriously discouraged when he learns of his poor performance on a scholastic aptitude test. A gifted school child might develop habits of laziness and shiftlessness, or he might become uncooperative and unmanageable, if he discovers that he is much brighter than any of his associates. A severe personality disorder may be precipitated when a maladjusted individual is given his score on a personality test. Such detrimental effects may, of course, occur regardless of the correctness or incorrectness of the score itself. Even when a test has been accurately administered and scored, and properly interpreted, a knowledge of such a score without the opportunity to discuss it further may be detrimental to the individual. The possible harm is further compounded if the score itself is in error.

A question arising particularly in connection with personality tests is that of "invasion of privacy." In so far as some tests of emotional, motivational, or attitudinal traits are necessarily disguised, the subject may reveal characteristics in the course of such a test without realizing that he is so doing. Although there are few available tests whose approach is subtle enough to fall into this category, the possibility of developing such indirect testing procedures imposes a grave responsibility upon the psychologist who uses them. For purposes of testing effectiveness it may be necessary to keep the examinee in ignorance of the specific ways in which his responses on any one test are to be interpreted. Nevertheless, a person should not be subjected to any testing program under false pretenses. Of primary importance in this connection is the obligation to have a clear understanding with the examinee regarding the use that will be made of his test results. Two statements contained in *Ethical Standards of Psychologists* are especially relevant to this problem (3, p. 280):

> The psychologist who asks that an individual reveal personal information in the course of interviewing, testing, or evaluation, or who allows such information to be divulged to him, does so only after making certain that the person is aware of the purpose of the interview, testing, or evaluation and of the ways in which the information may be used.
>
> The psychologist in industry, education, and other situations in which conflicts of interest may arise among varied parties, as between management and labor, defines for himself the nature and direction of his loyalties and responsibilities and keeps these parties informed of these commitments.

Still other professional problems concern the marketing of psychological tests by authors and publishers. Tests should not be released prematurely for general use. Nor should any claims be made regarding the merits of a test in the absence of sufficient objective evidence. When a test is distributed early for research purposes only, this condition should be clearly specified and the distribution of the test restricted accordingly. As already indicated in the preceding chapter, the test manual should provide adequate data to permit an evaluation of the test itself, as well as full information regarding administration, scoring, and norms. The manual should be a factual exposition of what is known about the test, rather than a selling device designed to put the test in a favorable light. It is the responsibility of the test author and publisher to revise tests and norms often enough to prevent obsolescence. The rapidity with which a test becomes outdated will, of course, vary widely with the nature of the test.

Finally, tests or parts of tests should not be published in a newspaper, popular magazine, or book, either for descriptive purposes or for self-evaluation. Under such conditions, self-evaluation would not only be subject to such drastic errors as to be well-nigh worthless, but it might also be detrimental to the individual for the reasons already discussed. Moreover, any publicity given to specific test items will tend to invalidate the future use of the test with other persons. It might also be added that presentation of test materials in this fashion tends to create an erroneous and distorted picture of psychological testing in general. Such publicity may foster either naïve credulity or indiscriminate resistance on the part of the public toward all psychological testing.[1]

---

[1] For teaching or expository purposes, it is permissible to reproduce sample test items constructed so as to resemble those of the test itself, or items which are used for demonstration purposes only in the test. This is the practice followed, for example, in the present text.

PRINCIPAL REASONS FOR CONTROLLING THE
USE OF PSYCHOLOGICAL TESTS

It should be apparent that there are two principal reasons for controlling the use of psychological tests: (*a*) to prevent general familiarity with test content, which would invalidate the test; and (*b*) to insure that the test is used by a qualified examiner. Obviously, if an individual were to memorize the correct responses on a test of color blindness, such a test would no longer be a measure of color vision for him. Under these conditions, the test would be completely invalidated. Test content clearly has to be restricted in order to forestall deliberate efforts to fake scores.

In other cases, however, the effect of familiarity may be less obvious, or the test may be invalidated in good faith by misinformed persons. A school teacher, for example, may give her class special practice in problems closely resembling those on an intelligence test, "so that the pupils will be well prepared to take the test." Such an attitude is simply a carry-over from the usual procedure of preparing for a school examination. When applied to an intelligence test, however, it is likely that such specific training or coaching will raise the scores on the test without appreciably affecting the broader area of behavior the test tries to sample. Under such conditions, the validity of the test as a predictive instrument is reduced.

The need for a qualified examiner is evident in each of the three major aspects of the testing situation—selection of the test, administration and scoring, and interpretation of scores. Tests cannot be chosen like lawn mowers, from a mail-order catalogue. They cannot be evaluated by name, author, or other easy marks of identification. To be sure, it requires no psychological training to consider such factors as cost, bulkiness and ease of transporting test materials, testing time required, ease and rapidity of scoring, and the like. Information on these practical points can usually be obtained from a test catalogue and should be taken into account in planning a testing program. For the test to serve its function, however, an evaluation of its technical merits in terms of such characteristics as validity, reliability, and norms is essential. Only in such a way can the test user determine the appropriateness of any test for his particular purpose and its suitability for the type of persons with whom he plans to use it.

The introductory discussion of test standardization in Chapter 2 has already suggested the importance of a trained examiner. An adequate realization of the need to follow instructions precisely, as well as a thorough familiarity with the standard instructions, is required if the test scores obtained by different examiners are to be comparable, or if any one individual's score is to be evaluated in terms of the published norms. Careful control of testing conditions and effectiveness in establishing rapport are also essential. Similarly, incorrect or inaccurate scoring may render the test score worthless. In the absence of proper checking procedures, scoring errors are far more likely to occur than is generally realized.

The proper interpretation of test scores requires a thorough understanding of the test, the individual, and the testing conditions. What is being measured can be objectively determined only by reference to the specific procedures in terms of which the particular test was validated. Other information, pertaining to reliability, nature of the group on which norms were established, and the like, is likewise relevant. Some background data regarding the individual being tested are essential in interpreting any test score. The same score may be obtained by different persons for very different reasons. The conclusions to be drawn from such scores would therefore be quite dissimilar. Finally, some consideration must also be given to special factors that may have influenced a particular score, such as unusual testing conditions, temporary emotional or physical state of the subject, recent experiences, response sets, and "test sophistication" or extent of the subject's previous experience with tests.

Some of the special problems associated with each of the major aspects of test administration and interpretation cited above will be considered in the sections that follow.

MOTIVATION, TEST ANXIETY, AND RAPPORT

Motivation. Underlying all tests of ability is the assumption that the subject is "doing his best." Consequently, if conditions are to be kept uniform in this regard, every subject should be motivated to put forth his maximum efforts on the test. A fairly large number of studies have been concerned with the possible influence of different incentives upon test performance. Almost any added incentive, however mild, may raise or lower the scores of at least certain groups. In one pair of studies, for example, praise and reproof were both found to improve the performance of school children on group intelligence tests, as well as on arithmetic tests (40, 41). Praise, however, proved to be more effective than reproof, especially when the incentives were administered repeatedly. Similar verbal incentives, including encouragement and discouragement, sarcasm, ridicule, and "razzing," have been used by other investigators in the effort to influence the subject's self-confidence and to arouse feelings of success or failure. Among the other incentives studied may be mentioned individual competition, group rivalry, knowledge of results, presence of observers, presence of co-workers, prizes, and monetary rewards.

With emotionally disruptive conditions, scores are likely to drop even for subjects accustomed to taking tests. In one study (30), for example, eighth-grade pupils were given the Stanford-Binet and retested two weeks later under conditions designed to evoke discouragement. On this retest, the children scored significantly lower than a control group retested under normal conditions. Similar results were obtained when three groups of college students were given tests of verbal analogies, arithmetic, and cancellation under the following conditions: (*a*) normal, control conditions; (*b*) with instructions to work as accurately as possible; (*c*) with instructions to work as rapidly as possible and with a buzzer sounding every 30 seconds, at which time the examiner stated how many items should have been completed (66). The third set of conditions was designed to arouse tension. It also tended to induce feelings of inferiority and failure, since the level of attainment specified at each interval was set just beyond the capacities of the subjects. The results of this study showed that the group working under "tension" conditions made significantly more errors than the other two groups. The instructions to be accurate produced no appreciable effect.

In the administration of such tests as the Stanford-Binet, the standard procedure is to continue with the presentation of increasingly difficult tasks until all tests within a single year level are failed. It has been suggested that with some children such a procedure may produce a mounting awareness of failure, which prevents the child from doing as well as he might on some of the later tasks (42). To test this hypothesis, one investigator altered the procedure in such a way that every failure was followed by an easier item (42). Poorly adjusted children were found to score higher when tested by this method than by the standard procedure, but well-adjusted children did equally well by either method. It should be noted, of course, that standardized test procedure should not be altered in this manner under ordinary circumstances, when it is desired to evaluate an individual's performance in terms of norms. The study is cited merely to illustrate the part motivational factors may play in the test performance of maladjusted subjects.

Another investigation of interest in this connection was conducted on kindergarten children (49). The subjects were given the Stanford-Binet upon entering kindergarten and were retested two months later with a parallel form. A significant rise in mean IQ was found on the retest. This gain was attributed by the investigator largely to the effect of the kindergarten experience in reducing shyness, fear of strangers, and other attitudes inhibiting oral expression. Support for such a hypothesis was found in the fact that the average test-retest improvement in manipulatory tasks was only 4.7 per cent, as contrasted to a gain of 11.2 per cent in the oral items. In certain ethnic minority groups, such as the American Negro, attitudes that inhibit oral speech may be fostered by the culture, rather than gradually eliminated. It has been suggested that overt verbalization increases the possibility of incurring the hostility of the dominant social group. Consequently, habits of inarticulateness might be encouraged by cultural factors in such minority groups (11). Verbalization, of course, plays as important a part in the individual's general intellectual development, as in his test performance. Hence more than just test scores would be adversely affected by such a culturally imposed handicap.

Most middle-class American school children and college students today are not only fairly test-wise, but they are also generally motivated to succeed in academic work and in test situations. In such groups, cooperation can be obtained with little difficulty. Special motivational problems are encountered, however, in testing certain other groups. Emotionally disturbed persons, prisoners, or juvenile delinquents, especially when tested in an institutional setting, are likely to manifest a number of unfavorable attitudes, such as suspicion, insecurity, fear, or cynical indifference. Specific abnormal factors in the past experience of such persons are also likely to influence their test performance adversely. Such individuals may, for example, have developed feelings of hostility and inferiority toward any academic material, as a result of early failures and frustrations in school (cf. 62, Chs. 4 and 6; 64).

There is also ample evidence to suggest that test-taking motivation varies widely in different ethnic and socioeconomic groups (cf. 5, p. 552; 23, pp. 20-21). One illustration is provided by the following statement, appearing in a summary of socioeconomic differences in test performance:

Observation of the performance of lower-class children on speed tests leads one to suspect that such children often work very rapidly through a test, making responses more or less at random. Apparently they are convinced in advance that they cannot do well on the test, and they find that by getting through the test rapidly they can shorten the period of discomfort which it produces (23, p. 21).

It is interesting to note that a reaction almost identical with that described above was observed among Puerto Rican school children tested in New York City (6) and in Hawaii (65).

Test Anxiety. Closely related to test-taking motivation is the question of test anxiety. The nature, correlates, and effects of such anxiety have been studied with both school children and college students, much of this research having been conducted by Sarason and his associates at Yale (50, 62, 63, 77). First, a questionnaire was constructed to assess the individual's test-taking attitudes. The children's form, for example, contains 43 items such as the following:

Do you worry a lot before taking a test?

When the teacher says she is going to find out how much you have learned, does your heart begin to beat faster?

While you are taking a test, do you usually think you are not doing well?

Children were also rated by their teachers for overt expressions of anxiety, including such behavior as fidgeting when called upon to recite, working better alone than in front of a class, and performing poorly under time pressure.

In one investigation on 600 children in grades two to five, anxiety questionnaires and teachers' ratings were significantly correlated in all grades (63). Test anxiety also tended to increase from the second to the fifth grade. Of primary interest is the finding that both school achievement and intelligence test scores yielded significant negative correlations with test anxiety. Such correlations support the hypothesis that children who become over-anxious in a test situation are thereby handicapped in their performance. Such correlations, of course, do not indicate the direction of causal relation. It is possible that children develop test anxiety because they do poorly on tests and have thus experienced failure and frustration in previous test situations.

Sarason and his co-workers, however, point to several lines of evidence suggesting that at least some of the association results from the deleterious effects of anxiety upon test performance. In one investigation (77), high-anxious and low-anxious children equated in intelligence test scores were given repeated trials in a learning task. Although initially equal in the learning test, the low-anxious group improved significantly more than the high-anxious. Supporting evidence is also provided by a series of learning experiments on college students (50). For example, ego-involving instructions, such as telling subjects that everyone is expected to finish in the time allotted, had a beneficial effect on the performance of low-anxious subjects, but a deleterious effect on that of high-anxious subjects.

It thus appears that test anxiety does interfere with effective learning and test performance. More research is needed, however, before a definitive statement can be made. It is likely, for instance, that the relation between anxiety and performance is curvilinear, a slight degree of anxiety being beneficial, a high degree detrimental. The finding that ego-involving instructions exert a positive influence on the performance of initially low-anxious subjects and a negative influence on the performance of initially high-anxious subjects fits in with this hypothesis.

What, specifically, do the experimental findings on motivation and test anxiety imply regarding testing procedure? First, such findings highlight the importance of adhering to the prescribed motivating conditions in administering any test. The addition of any other incentive, however mild, may raise or lower scores appreciably, especially with certain types of subjects. Standing over the subject with a stop watch, peering over his shoulder, uttering some word of exhortation or criticism, or telling the subject how much time remains, all illustrate ways in which motivating conditions might be inadvertently altered. A second implication is that, in the interpretation of scores, any unusual motivating conditions should be taken into consideration. This is especially true for subjects whose experiential background is unlike that of the standardization sample. Finally, it is apparent that the establishment of rapport, prior to the administration of a test, is an important part of the testing procedure. In so far as the situation permits, the examiner must make certain that the subject is ready to do his best before the test is begun.

Rapport. The specific techniques for establishing rapport vary somewhat with the nature of the test and the type of subjects to be tested. Thus, in testing preschool children,[2] special factors to be considered include shyness with strangers, distractability, and negativism. A friendly, cheerful, and relaxed manner on the part of the examiner helps to reassure the child. The shy, timid child needs more preliminary time to become familiar with his surroundings. For this reason it is better for the examiner not to be too demonstrative at the outset, but rather to wait until the child is ready to make the first contact. Test periods should be brief, and the tasks should be varied and intrinsically interesting to the child. The testing should be presented to the child as a game, and his curiosity aroused before each new task is introduced. A certain flexibility of procedure is necessary at this age level, because of possible refusals, loss of interest, and other manifestations of negativism.

Children in the first two or three grades of elementary school present many of the same testing problems as the preschool child. The "game" appeal is still the most effective way of arousing their interest in the test. The

---

[2] A detailed description of recommended procedures for testing young children can be found in 29. This account has been reprinted by Goodenough (28, pp. 298-304).

older school child can usually be motivated through an appeal to his competitive spirit and his desire to do well on a test. It should be borne in mind, however, that every test presents an implied threat to the individual's prestige. Some reassurance should therefore be given at the outset. It is helpful to explain, for example, that no one is expected to finish or to get all the items correct. The individual might otherwise experience a mounting sense of failure as he finds that he is unable to finish any part of the test within the time allowed.

It is also desirable to eliminate the element of surprise from the test situation as far as possible, since the unexpected and unknown are likely to produce anxiety. Many group tests provide a preliminary explanatory statement which is read to the group by the examiner. An even better procedure is to announce the tests a few days in advance and to give each subject a printed statement that explains the purpose and nature of the tests, offers general suggestions on how to take the tests, and possibly contains a few sample items. Such printed statements are used regularly by the College Entrance Examination Board (14), Educational Records Bureau (47, pp. 345-347), and other organizations. A more general booklet entitled *Taking a Test* (51), published by World Book Company, is designed for use with senior high school and college students.

In the absence of any formal printed statement, it can probably be assumed that any announcement is better than none. Care should be taken, of course, not to arouse anxiety by making the coming test sound like a formidable event. If such announcements are made in an objective, straightforward, and matter-of-fact manner, however, they will serve to reduce rather than to heighten tension and worry. In a group of junior high school students, for example, increases of approximately one to two per cent in mean score were found as a result of a two-day advance notice of the test (75).

The testing of college students and adults presents some of the same problems as the testing of school children, including the need for reducing threat and surprise. In addition, adults out of school are generally more resistant to tests. Unlike the school child, the adult is not so likely to work hard at a task merely because it is assigned to him. It therefore becomes more important to "sell" the purpose of the tests to the adult, although high school and college students also respond to such an appeal. Cooperation of the subject can usually be secured by convincing him that it is in his own interests to obtain a valid score, i.e., a score correctly indicating what he can do, rather than overestimating or underestimating his abilities. Most subjects can readily be made to realize that an incorrect decision, which might result from invalid test scores, would mean subsequent failure, loss of time, and frustration for them. This approach is usually effective not only in motivating the subject to try his best, but also in preventing cheating, since the subject realizes that he himself would eventually be the loser. It is certainly not in the best interests of the individual to be admitted to a course of study for which he is not qualified or assigned to a job he cannot perform.

INFLUENCE OF PRACTICE AND COACHING UPON TEST PERFORMANCE

Breadth of Influence. In evaluating the effect of coaching or practice upon test scores, a fundamental question to consider is the breadth of such influence. Is the improvement limited to the specific items included in the test, or does it extend to the broader area of behavior that the test is designed to predict? The answer to this question represents the difference between coaching and education. Obviously any educational experience the individual undergoes, either formal or informal, in or out of school, should be reflected in his performance on tests sampling the relevant aspects of behavior. Such broad influences would in no way invalidate the test, since the test score would in such cases present an accurate picture of the individual's standing in the abilities under consideration. The difference is, of course, one of degree. An influence is not either narrow or broad, but obviously varies widely in scope, from factors affecting only a single administration of a single test, through those affecting performance on all items of a certain type, to those influencing the individual's performance in the large majority of his activities. From the standpoint of effective testing, however, a workable distinction can be made. Thus it can be stated that a test score is invalidated only when a particular experience raises it *without appreciably affecting the behavior domain that the test is designed to predict.*[3] It is the latter, invalidating type of influence that will now be considered with reference to coaching and practice.

Coaching. A number of investigations have dealt with the effects of coaching upon test performance. Early studies with the Stanford-Binet demonstrated that children can be taught intelligence test items they were formerly incapable of executing correctly (12, 33). Large and significant gains in IQ were obtained in one experiment as a result of two hours of coaching on tests the child had failed on a previous administration of the Stanford-Binet (33). Groups coached on similar rather than on identical material showed smaller gains. The effects of coaching declined on successive retests. At the end of three years, no significant differences remained between the

---

[3] For a fuller discussion of this point, cf. 4.

groups coached on identical and on similar material or between these and the control group which had been retested with no intervening coaching. Such a result is to be expected, partly because of forgetting and partly because the nature of the Stanford-Binet items varies at different age levels. The children were therefore being tested on tasks unlike those on which they had been coached.

More recent research on several group as well as individual tests has likewise shown that, in general, coaching produces significant gains in mean scores (20, 24, 37, 43, 76, 83, 84, 85). Many of these studies were conducted by British psychologists, who have been concerned about the effects of practice and coaching upon the tests used in assigning 11-year-old children to different types of secondary schools. As might be expected, the extent of improvement depends upon the ability and earlier educational experiences of the subjects, the nature of the tests, and the amount and type of coaching provided. Subjects with deficient educational backgrounds are more likely to benefit from special coaching than are those who have had superior educational opportunities and are already prepared to do well on the tests. It is obvious, too, that the closer the resemblance between test content and coaching material, the greater will be the improvement in test scores.

In America, the College Entrance Examination Board has felt concern over the prevalence of ill-advised coaching courses for college applicants. To clarify the issue, the College Board conducted several well-controlled experiments to determine the effects of coaching on its Scholastic Aptitude Test (24). In a formal statement subsequently issued by the College Board trustees, it was pointed out that, although intensive drill on the types of material covered by this test may produce a significant mean rise in score in certain groups, the amount of probable gain in individual cases is not such as to affect college admission decisions (15).

The distinction between coaching and education is highlighted by an investigation with kindergarten children (39). Two kindergarten classes totaling 53 children were put through a 14-week program based on the *Learning to Think* series (70, 71). Prepared by the author of the tests of Primary Mental Abilities for Ages 5 to 7 (see Ch. 13), this training material is closely similar to the test content. Before and after the training program, the children were given both the Primary Mental Abilities tests and the Wechsler Intelligence Scale for Children (see Ch. 12). Two control classes of 54 children took the same pretests and posttests, with no intervening training. All groups improved on the second testing. The trained subjects, however, improved no more than the controls on the Wechsler test, although they improved significantly more than the controls on the Primary Mental Abilities tests. Such findings suggest that the training provided by the *Learning to Think* materials operates as specific coaching on the Primary Mental Abilities tests rather than serving a broader educational function.

Practice. The effects of sheer repetition, or practice, upon test performance are similar to the effects of coaching, but usually less pronounced. It should be noted that practice, as well as coaching, may alter the nature of the test, since the subjects may employ entirely different *work methods* in solving the same problems. In general, those tests in which work methods change little with repetition show little improvement in score as a result of practice; those in which performance undergoes marked qualitative changes with repetition show large gains in score. Some evidence for this relationship may be found in a study on college students in which the objective test scores were supplemented with qualitative observations of performance and with introspective reports of the methods employed in solving problems (32). In this study, tests measuring speed of simple movements and tests of auditory discrimination showed little or no practice effect. In taking such tests the subjects performed essentially the same functions on initial and later trials. Tests involving precision of movement and those depending upon prior information, such as vocabulary tests, yielded retest gains ranging from 6 to 25 per cent of the initial scores. Maze and block-design tests, in which a generalized rule could be formulated during the initial test, showed increases of from 76 to 200 per cent. Even greater improvements were found in mechanical aptitude tests in which a mechanical object had to be assembled from its constituent parts. In such tests, the earlier solutions could be recalled and reapplied to the same test materials.

Current intelligence tests frequently contain items whose nature can be expected to change with repetition. Retest scores on such tests, whether derived from a repetition of the identical test or from a parallel form, should therefore be carefully scrutinized. A number of studies have been concerned with the effects of the *identical repetition* of intelligence tests over periods ranging from a few days to several years (1, 13, 16, 19, 35, 36, 45, 79). Both adults and children, and both normal and mentally defective subjects have been employed. Most of the studies have utilized group tests, although some data on individual tests are also available. All agree in showing significant mean gains in score upon retests. Nor is improvement necessarily limited to the initial repetitions. Whether gains persist or level off in successive administrations seems to depend upon the difficulty of the test and the ability level of the subjects (16, 35, 36).

The implications of such findings are illustrated by the results obtained when 3500 school children were retested annually with a variety of intelligence tests (19). When the same test was re-administered in successive years, the median IQ of the group rose from 102 to 113, but it dropped to 104 when another test was substituted. Because of the retest gains, the meaning of an IQ obtained on an initial and later trial proved to be quite different. For example, an IQ of 100 fell approximately at the average of the distribution on the initial trial, but in the lowest quarter on a retest (19, p. 134). Such IQ's, though numerically identical and derived from the same test, might thus signify normal ability in the one instance and inferior ability in the other.

Gains in score are also found upon retesting with *parallel forms* of the same test, although such gains tend in general to be smaller. Significant mean gains have been reported when alternate forms of a test were administered in immediate succession (68), at one-day intervals (68), and one month apart (55, 56). Similar results have been obtained with British children (55, 56), normal and intellectually gifted American school children (68), and American high-school, college, and graduate students (68). Contemporary test constructors recognize such a practice effect and often make allowances for it. In the Minnesota Preschool Scale, for example, it is suggested that 3 IQ points be deducted as a correction for practice effect when alternate forms are administered within a few weeks (29).

The general problem of *test sophistication* should also be considered in this connection. The individual who has had extensive prior experience in taking psychological tests enjoys a certain advantage in test performance over one who is taking his first test (36, 60). Part of this advantage stems from having overcome an initial feeling of strangeness, as well as from having developed more self-confidence and better test-taking attitudes. Part is the result of a certain amount of overlap in the type of content and functions covered by many tests. Probably other factors also operate in more subtle and indirect ways. It is particularly important to take test sophistication into account when comparing results from children in different types of schools, where the extent of psychological testing may vary widely.

MALINGERING AND CHEATING

The problem of malingering and cheating is largely a motivational one. Theoretically, it should be possible to forestall attempts to fake scores on psychological tests by convincing the subject that a valid score is in his own best interests, on the grounds that an incorrect decision based upon invalid scores will only cause him difficulties later on. With certain types of subjects, however, such an appeal may not be very effective. School children, for example, may not be sufficiently farsighted to be influenced by a relatively distant goal. Maladjusted persons will in many cases respond too emotionally to the test to be susceptible to such a rational argument. There are, moreover, a few testing situations, especially in the examination of criminal offenders and in the screening of draftees for military service, in which the objectives of individual subjects may be fundamentally at cross-purposes to those of the examiner, a conflict which no amount of rapport may be able to reconcile. To be sure, proper motivation and rapport should go far toward reducing malingering and cheating. But other precautionary measures are undoubtedly necessary. When strong motivation to achieve a certain result is combined with a feeling of insecurity regarding the outcome of a given test, attempts to fake scores are likely to occur.

The faking of psychological test scores may be conveniently considered under three headings, viz., (*a*) cheating to raise scores on ability tests, (*b*) attempts to appear in a more favorable light on personality tests, and (*c*) simulation of inferiority or abnormality on either personality or ability tests.

Raising Scores on Ability Tests. A common example of the first type of cheating is the utilization of *outside assistance,* such as referring to books and notes, or copying from a neighbor. Several measures may be taken to reduce such practices. As is true of all types of faking, however, no preventive is completely successful. Adequate proctoring, proper seating arrangements, and the simultaneous use of alternate test forms are generally effective. If cheating is suspected during or after the test, certain statistical checks are available to aid in its detection. These checks are based upon an analysis of the number of identical errors among the responses of the subjects suspected of copying from each other (7, 10, 21).

Cheating to improve the score on an ability test may also take the form of an unwarranted *extension of time limit.* This can occur through "jumping the gun," or premature starting, before the signal to begin. Thus the subject may start to work on the first few items of the test proper while the examiner is still giving the directions or discussing the sample items. Similarly, the subject may continue to work after the signal to stop is given. The best safeguards against this type of cheating are provided by more careful test administration and more extensive proctoring. Premature starting can also be greatly minimized by the proper layout of items in the test booklets. All instruction materials and sample items, as well as questions regarding name and other personal data, should be printed on a separate page, containing none of the items of the test proper. Moreover, the items should be so arranged that it is necessary to turn a page when proceeding from the preliminary material to the test proper, or when going from one separately timed part of the test to the next.

Still another spurious procedure for raising scores on ability tests is the acquisition of *prior knowledge* regarding test items. In an institution for defective delinquents, for example, it was discovered that subjects were giving the "right answers" on a common individual intelligence scale (Wechsler-Bellevue) even when an essential part of the question was omitted (8). Thus to the question, "How many oranges can you buy for thirty-six cents?" the subject would reply "Nine," although the examiner had omitted the second part of the problem which normally follows, "if one orange costs four cents." In this case, the items were being circulated in the institution through the help of those who had been tested earlier. It might be added that this large-scale cheating program became organized as a result of a misapprehension regarding dependence of parole on intelligence test scores; proper orientation regarding the purposes of the test would probably have done much to prevent such cheating. More specific procedures for avoiding the dissemination of prior knowledge include the safeguarding of test materials, the use of a test with several alternate forms, and scheduling the testing so as to minimize the possibility of intercommunication. When communication is likely, as in an institutional setting, a group test has certain advantages over an individual test. For the same reason, the administration of such a test in one large group would be preferable to the successive testing of several smaller groups.

"Faking Good" on Personality Tests. The second major type of faking, namely, the faking of personality test responses so as to appear in a more favorable light, is especially likely to occur on self-report inventories. Despite introductory statements to the contrary, most items in such inventories have one answer which is pretty clearly the desirable or socially acceptable response. Consequently there is a strong tendency for the individual to check what he recognizes as the "right" answer, rather than the answer which corresponds to his own habitual behavior. This may occur even when there is no deliberate or recognized attempt to alter the score. If, in addition, the individual is motivated to "put his best foot forward," as in the case of a job applicant, it is quite easy for him to create the desired impression on such a test.

Evidence of the success with which subjects can dissemble on personality inventories is plentiful (cf. 25, 31, 54, 81). A common classroom demonstration consists in asking different groups to fake responses in specified ways. For example, one section of the class is directed to answer each question as it would be answered by a happy and well-adjusted college student; another section is told to respond in the manner of a severely maladjusted subject; and the last section is instructed to answer the items truthfully with reference to their own behavior. Or the same subjects may take the test twice, first with instructions to simulate in a specified way and later under ordinary conditions. The results of such studies clearly demonstrate the facility with which the desired impression can be deliberately created on such inventories. To be sure, subjects of lower educational or intellectual level are probably less successful in disguising their responses than are the college groups on which most of these studies have been conducted. As long as a subject has sufficient education to enable him to answer a personality inventory, however, he probably has the ability to alter his score appreciably in the desired direction.

It is interesting to note that specific faking for a particular vocational objective can also be successfully carried out. Thus in one study (81), the responses of the same group of students were compared on two administrations of a personality inventory (Bernreuter) taken a week apart. On the first testing, the subjects were instructed to pretend they were applying for the position of salesman in a large industrial organization and to answer in a manner designed to increase their chances of employment. On the second testing, the same instructions were given, but the position of librarian was substituted for that of salesman. When the responses were scored for the trait of self-confidence, a conspicuous difference was found in the distributions of scores on the two occasions, the simulated-salesman scores being much higher than the corresponding librarian scores.

That job applicants do in fact fake personality test responses was demonstrated in another study (31), in which the scores obtained by a group of applicants were compared with the scores of a comparable group of job holders who were tested for research purposes only. Under these contrasting motivating conditions, the scores of the two groups differed in the expected direction. Although such faking is relatively easy on the self-report type of personality test, there is some evidence to indicate that it can also occur in certain widely used projective techniques (cf., e.g., 80).

"Faking Bad" on Personality or Ability Tests. The last form of faking to be considered involves the simulation of mental deficiency or emotional disturbance by deliberately obtaining a "poor" score on an intelligence or personality test. Such malingering is of special concern in military testing. A variant of this performance is the differential failure on certain portions of a classification battery in the effort to be assigned to a more desirable specialty. For example, Air Force cadets sometimes tried deliberately to miss items on the bombardier and navigator parts of the classification battery, in the hope that such a performance would increase their chances of being assigned to pilot training.

The problems presented by such malingering on aptitude tests are similar to those arising from either favorable or unfavorable faking on personality tests. The same general approaches are therefore being explored in the effort to cope with all these forms of simulation. One solution is to disguise the purpose of the test, as when a measure of masculinity-femininity is presented as a survey of interests and attitudes. Such a procedure is effective only in a few types of tests. Most personality test items have enough "visibility" for the alert subject to discover the true purpose of the test. A more effective sort of disguise is to be found in the forced-choice technique, in which the subject must choose one of two answers which appear to be equally acceptable or unacceptable. One of the answers, however, has been shown empirically to be a favorable indicator of the criterion under consideration, while the other answer is neutral or unfavorable.[4]

Another common procedure is directed not toward the prevention but toward the detection of faking. Essentially, this technique involves the construction of a special key from which a malingering score can be derived. Such a procedure is applicable to both aptitude and personality tests. The fundamental fact upon which the malingering keys are based is that when an individual tries to fake his responses, he tends to overdo it. For example, in an intelligence test on which the individual may be trying to appear dull, he will probably pass more of the difficult items and fail more of the easy items than a genuine mental defective. In such a situation it is difficult for the individual to gauge accurately the relative difficulty of different items. A malingering key can be empirically derived by comparing the responses of a group of subjects instructed to appear stupid with the responses of bona fide feebleminded cases (cf. 26, 57).

Similar keys have been prepared for use with certain personality tests (e.g., 34). These will be considered in connection with the specific tests to be discussed in Chapter 18. In some instances, the various malingering scores are simply used to determine whether the regular test scores should be accepted or rejected. In other cases a numerical correction can be applied to the regular scores, on the basis of the subject's score on the malingering key.

PROBLEMS OF TEST ADMINISTRATION

A whole volume could easily be devoted to a discussion of desirable procedures of test administration. But such a survey falls outside the scope of

[4] A fuller discussion of this and other techniques employed in specific personality inventories will be found in Chapter 18.

the present book. Moreover, it is more practicable to acquire such techniques within specific settings, since no one individual would normally be
concerned with all forms of testing, from the examination of infants to the
clinical testing of psychotic patients or the administration of a mass testing
program for military personnel. The present discussion will therefore deal
principally with the common rationale of test administration rather than
with specific questions of implementation.[5]

Advance Preparation of Examiners. The most important requirement for
good testing procedure is advance preparation. In testing there can be no
emergencies. Special efforts must therefore be made to foresee and forestall
emergencies. Only in this way can uniformity of procedure be assured.

Advance preparation for the testing session takes many forms. Memorizing
the verbal instructions is essential in most individual testing. Even in a group
test in which the instructions are read to the subjects, some previous familiarity with the statements to be read prevents misreading and hesitation, and
permits a more natural, informal manner during test administration. The
preparation of test materials is another important preliminary step. In individual testing, and especially in the administration of performance tests,
such preparation involves the actual layout of the necessary materials to
facilitate subsequent use with a minimum of search or fumbling. Materials
should generally be placed on a table near the testing table, so that they are
within easy reach of the examiner but do not distract the subject. When apparatus is employed, frequent periodic checking and calibration may be
necessary. In group testing, all test blanks, answer sheets, special pencils, or
other materials needed should be carefully counted, checked, and arranged
in advance of the testing day.

Rehearsal of procedure with one or more trial subjects is another essential
prerequisite in both individual and group testing. In the case of group testing,
and especially in large-scale projects, such preparation may include the advance briefing of examiners and proctors, so that each is thoroughly familiar
with the functions he is to perform. In general, the examiner reads the instructions, takes care of timing, and is in charge of the group in any one
testing room. The proctors hand out and collect test materials, make certain
that subjects are following instructions, answer individual questions of subjects within the limitations specified in the manual, and prevent cheating.

Some attention should also be given to the selection of a suitable testing
room. Such a room should be free from undue noise and distraction, and

---

[5] For detailed suggestions regarding testing procedure, the reader is referred to Goodenough
(28, Ch. 20) and Watson (78, Ch. 12) for the testing of preschool children; Terman and Merrill
(67, pp. 45-59) for individual testing of older children and adults; and Lindquist (47, Ch. 10),
Thorndike (69, Ch. 9), and Ligon (46) for group test ng.

should provide adequate lighting, ventilation, seating facilities, and working space for the subjects. Special steps should also be taken to prevent interruptions during the test. Posting a sign on the door to indicate that testing is in progress is effective, provided all personnel have learned that such a sign means no admittance under any circumstances. In the testing of large groups, locking the doors or posting an assistant outside each door may be necessary to prevent the entrance of late-comers.

Testing Conditions. It is important to realize the extent to which testing conditions may influence scores. Even apparently minor aspects of the testing situation may appreciably alter the subjects' performances. Such a factor as the use of desks or of chairs with desk arms, for example, proved to be significant in a group testing project with high school students, the groups using desks tending to obtain higher scores (44, 73). Similarly, whether the examiner is a stranger or someone familiar to the subjects has been found to make a significant difference in test scores (61, 74). In another study, the general manner and behavior of the examiner, as illustrated by smiling, nodding, and making such comments as "Good" or "Fine," were shown to have a decided effect upon test results (82). In a projective test requiring the subject to write stories to fit given pictures, the presence of the examiner in the room tended to inhibit the inclusion of strongly emotional content in the stories (9).

Previous Activities of Subjects. The subjects' activities immediately preceding the test may affect their performance, especially when such activities produce emotional disturbance, fatigue, or other handicapping conditions. Thus in an investigation with third- and fourth-grade school children, there was some evidence to suggest that IQ on a non-verbal intelligence test was influenced by the children's preceding classroom activity (48). On one occasion, the class had been engaged in writing a composition on "The Best Thing That Ever Happened to Me"; on the second occasion, they had again been writing, but this time on "The Worst Thing That Ever Happened to Me." The IQ's on the second test, following what may have been an emotionally depressing experience, averaged 4 or 5 points lower than on the first test.

These findings were corroborated in a study specifically designed to determine the effect of immediately preceding experience upon test performance (59). The same test was employed as in the earlier study. In the later investigation, children who had had a gratifying experience involving the successful solution of an interesting puzzle, followed by a reward of toys and candy, showed more improvement in their test scores than those who had undergone neutral or less gratifying experiences.

Response Sets. Test performance may also be affected by the response sets with which subjects approach the test (cf. 17). Owing to the nature of the instructions and to the form in which test items are expressed, the subject may be set to respond in a particular way. In such cases, changing the item form or modifying the instructions would alter the subject's responses. The response set thus represents a condition specific to the particular test and may be quite irrelevant to the aptitude being measured. Moreover, when test instructions are ambiguous or fail to specify certain aspects of procedure, response sets may differ from person to person, thereby introducing another source of variation in testing conditions.

One illustration of response sets is to be found in the tendency to guess, or take a chance when not sure of the answer, rather than omit the item. If no instructions regarding guessing are provided, the more "reckless" subjects may guess on every uncertain item, leaving no omissions. Other, more cautious individuals may only mark those answers of which they feel very confident. This difference in response set probably reflects personality characteristics rather than aptitude, and would therefore serve only to reduce the validity of aptitude scores. In general, the subject who guesses will have a certain advantage, since at least some of his guesses will be correct by chance. Except in purely blind guessing, individuals will tend to be more often right than wrong in their guesses, since they usually have some knowledge about the items on which they guess; for this reason common correction formulas for guessing, such as "number right minus number wrong" for true-false tests, tend to undercorrect. On the other hand, item writers usually try to make the incorrect alternatives sound so plausible that every examinee who guesses will choose a wrong answer. In so far as this goal is achieved, the usual correction formulas would overcorrect.

The correction for guessing will, of course, be smaller on multiple-choice than on true-false tests, and the greater the number of alternative responses the smaller will be the correction.[6] Thus the probability of guessing correctly on a true-false item would be one out of two; while on a five-alternative multiple-choice item, it would be one out of five. It should also be noted that if all subjects are instructed to omit no items and to guess when not sure, no correction for guessing is needed. In such a case, each subject's relative position in the group would be identical whether or not any correction is applied. Such a procedure also provides a uniform response set, thus eliminating the effects of individual differences in willingness to take a

---

[6] The general correction formula for guessing is:

Corrected score $= R - \dfrac{W}{n-1}$, in which R is the number of items right, W the number of items wrong, and n is the number of alternative responses per item. In a true-false test, in which there are only two alternative answers per item, the corrected score reduces to $R - W$.

chance. For these reasons, many psychological tests specify that no omissions are to be made.

The question of how to handle guessing on psychological tests is still a controversial one. Should subjects be instructed to guess or not to guess? Should a correction for guessing be applied in scoring? Arguments can be found in support of different practices, the most desirable solution probably varying with the situation. The test manual, however, should recognize these problems and indicate how they ought to be handled.

A similar question pertains to the relative emphasis to be put upon speed and accuracy. On certain clerical aptitude tests, for example, a very careful worker may be handicapped because he proceeds too slowly, in order to avoid errors. The individual who races through the test, on the other hand, may complete twice as many items and make only a few errors. His overall score would therefore be much higher than that of the slow, cautious worker. Before beginning a test, subjects should be given a clear picture of the relative importance of speed and accuracy in determining their scores.

Other, more specific examples of response sets include the tendency to answer "true" rather than "false" when not sure about a true-false item, and the tendency to check many or few responses when the subject is free to check as many responses as he chooses. The latter response set could occur, for example, if the subject is required to check all the statements that follow from a certain premise in a logical reasoning test.

In general, the problem of response sets is the concern of the test constructor. The test user, however, should take response sets into account in choosing tests. Other things being equal, a test that reduces individual differences in response sets is to be preferred. Multiple-choice items requiring a single response are the most satisfactory in this regard. The test instructions, moreover, should be checked for the clarity with which such matters as guessing and the relative importance of speed and accuracy are treated. Finally, in the process of administering a test, the examiner should be on his guard against the introduction of any response sets not covered by the standardized instructions. This caution is especially pertinent to the answering of questions raised by subjects and to preliminary announcements regarding the purpose of the test.

Clinical Interaction. A comprehensive analysis of the operation of examiner and situational variables in test performance has been provided by Sarason (62) under the general concept of "clinical interaction." By reference to published studies, as well as to his own research and case reports, Sarason demonstrates that test scores are susceptible to the interaction of individual subject characteristics with examiner and situational variables. Among the significant examiner variables are included age, sex, race, professional and socioeconomic status, appearance, and such behavioral characteristics as self-confidence, aggressiveness, responsiveness, and social warmth. Situational variables are illustrated by the place where the test is administered (school, clinic, hospital, jail, psychology laboratory, etc.); the expectations and attitudes built up by the way in which the forthcoming test experience was presented to the subject; and the nature of specific instructions. That the effect of all such conditions can be best conceptualized in terms of interaction is exemplified by the finding that such factors as ego-involving instructions and appearance of the examiner have a different influence on subjects with different personality characteristics. A more recent survey of studies on the effects of interpersonal and situational variables on test performance was prepared by Masling (53).

Although most of the studies reported by Sarason and by Masling concern individual clinical examinations with projective techniques, all testing will to some extent be subject to social and situational interaction. There is evidence, for example, that the emotional interaction of examiner and subjects influences the results obtained with individual intelligence tests (52). It is not to be inferred, however, that we should abandon the practice of administering tests under standardized conditions. Rather the examiner should be all the more alert to control those conditions that can be kept uniform, so as to retain the applicability of norms. At the same time, any aspects of the particular test situation that cannot be controlled should be clearly recognized and taken into account in interpreting the subject's responses on the test. Ignoring inevitable sources of variation is no protection against their effects.

PROBLEMS OF SCORING

The principal considerations in the selection and application of scoring procedures are accuracy, speed, and economy. The last two are especially important in large-scale testing programs. Efficient operation of the scoring program, with a minimum of wasted effort, helps to reduce cost. An even more important factor in determining the cost of scoring is the selection of tests that provide appropriate scoring techniques. Speed of scoring is a major consideration in many testing programs in which results must be made available promptly, as in testing military personnel and college or professional-school applicants. Accuracy is of course an essential requirement of all types of scoring, whether in individual or group testing. Research on the development and improvement of scoring techniques is directed toward this triple objective of accuracy, speed, and economy, although the relative emphasis given to the three aspects varies with the nature of the test and with the use to which it is put.

Individual Tests. Whether of the verbal or performance type, individual tests are generally scored by the examiner. While administering the test, the examiner records the subject's responses on a printed record form. Some tests, such as the Stanford-Binet, need to be scored during the process of test administration, since the presentation of further items depends upon the subject's performance on prior items; other individual tests may be scored later. In so far as subjective judgment enters into the evaluation of any response, the results obtained by independent scorers should be checked on a representative sample of record sheets. This check provides a measure of one aspect of the reliability of the test, and will be discussed further in Chapter 5. A different type of checking is the routine repetition of certain steps in the scoring to correct any clerical or computational errors. Even such a simple operation as the computation of an IQ reveals such common errors that checking is imperative. A vivid demonstration of this fact can easily be arranged by having any class compute an IQ from a given mental age and a given date of birth. The range of IQ's reported by different students should prove impressive.

Group Tests. Since speed and economy are major considerations in group testing, such tests do not as a rule need to be scored by a trained examiner, but usually permit either hand scoring by a clerk or machine scoring.[7] The latter always requires a specially printed answer sheet. But manual scoring can also be done more efficiently through the use of a separate answer sheet on which the subjects record their responses. Such an arrangement not only provides greater compactness of records and saves scoring labor, but it also permits the repeated use of the same test booklets by different subjects.

One of the most common hand-scoring procedures utilizes the *fan* or *accordion key*. The correct answers for each page of the test booklet are printed in a separate column. When the key is folded vertically, in accordion fashion, only one column is visible at a time. With such a key, scoring involves the comparison of the subject's answers with the corresponding answers given on the key. This type of scoring requires more time than many other available techniques. It is most often used with tests in which the subject writes in each response, instead of selecting and marking the correct response to each item.

An efficient type of scoring key for hand scoring is the *punched* or *cut-*

---

[7] For a comprehensive and critical survey of a large number of available scoring techniques, cf. Lindquist (47, pp. 365-413).

out scoring stencil. Such a key is applicable to multiple-choice items in which each alternative response occupies a different position on the answer sheet. Holes or windows are cut on the scoring stencil to correspond to the positions of the correct alternatives. Superimposing such a stencil over the answer sheet immediately reveals all items that have been correctly marked by the subject. A few items from a test that utilizes this type of scoring are shown in Figure 7. In this test, the subjects are instructed to mark the word in each line that means the opposite of the first word.

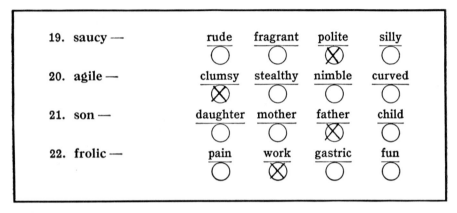

Fig. 7. Sample Items from a Test Booklet Scored with a Punched Scoring Stencil. (From Pintner-Durost Elementary Test; copyright by World Book Company.)

A number of tests utilize *self-scoring answer sheets.* An example is the self-scoring carbon pad provided with the tests of Primary Mental Abilities (see Ch. 13). In these tests, the subject records his responses on the outside of a two-page answer booklet which is folded together and cannot be opened without tearing. Squares corresponding to the position of the correct answer for each item are printed on the inner side of the booklet, where the subject's responses are automatically recorded through the carbon backing of the answer sheet. The subject, of course, cannot see the inside of the booklet without tearing the booklet apart, which would invalidate his test. To score the test, it is only necessary to tear the booklet open and count the number of x's that fall within the printed squares. A section of this answer sheet is reproduced in Figure 8.

Another self-marking device is the *pin-punch answer pad* used, for instance, with the Kuder Preference Record, a measure of vocational interests (see Ch. 19). In this case, the subject is provided with a metal pin, with which he punches holes in the appropriate circles on the answer sheet to indicate his preferences (see Fig. 112, p. 537). On the inside of the answer booklet are printed sets of circles corresponding to the responses to be scored within each interest area. The subject's score in each of these areas is found by counting the number of holes punched within the appropriate set of circles.

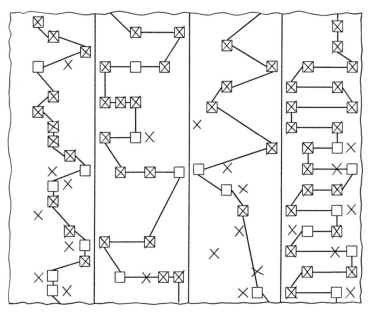

Fig. 8. A Portion of the Self-Scoring Carbon Answer Pad Used with the SRA Tests of Primary Mental Abilities for Ages 11 to 17. The illustration shows the inner or "scorer's eye" view, never seen by the subject. (Reproduced by permission of Science Research Associates.)

Parenthetically, it may be added that another type of so-called self-scorer is designed, not for the convenience of the examiner, but for the instruction of the subject. In such a test, for example, the subject keeps on choosing answers in a multiple-choice item until the correct one is found. The scoring device may be a punchboard, in which a full hole can be punched only through correct answers, since these correspond to apertures in the perforated stencil inserted under the answer sheet. Incorrect answers produce only a small pin prick. Or, the holes for the wrong answers may show red on the backing sheet, while the correct one appears black. The subject's score on such a test can be determined by counting the number of holes punched; the fewer the holes or attempts he requires to reach the correct answers, the better his score. The self-scorer principle underlies many of the so-called *teaching machines* currently being used for research purposes (18, 22, 38, 58). Further reference to these machines will be made in Chapter 16.

For large-scale testing programs, *machine scoring* is the most efficient procedure. The IBM Test-Scoring Machine, developed by the International Business Machines Corporation, is probably the best-known device for this purpose. Use of this machine requires specially prepared, patented answer sheets, on which the subject records his responses by blackening the space between two lines. Part of such an answer sheet is shown in Figure 9. Sub-

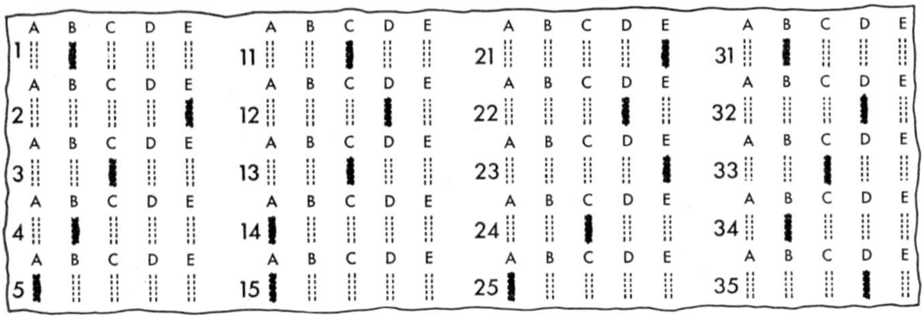

Fig. 9. Part of an Answer Sheet for Use with the IBM Test-Scoring Machine. (Reproduced by permission of International Business Machines Corporation.)

jects are also provided with special soft pencils for marking the answers. The test-scoring machine operates essentially in terms of electrical contacts. The graphite pencil-marks on the answer sheet establish contact across a set of contact brushes in the machine. These electrical contacts are counted by the machine and the total thus obtained represents the subject's score. When a scoring stencil with holes cut over the correct responses is inserted in the machine, contacts are made only with the marks in the correct spaces. Thus the number of correct responses can be read from the machine. Errors and omissions can also be scored by inserting another, appropriately cut scoring stencil.

A special precaution to be observed with machine-scored answer sheets is the inspection of the answer sheets prior to scoring. If subjects have not followed directions carefully, some of their pencil-marks may not be heavy enough to establish proper contact in the machine. Similarly, stray, unintentional pencil-marks may be counted as wrong responses by the machine. Investigation has shown that such carelessly marked answer sheets may significantly lower the mean score of a group; in individual cases, the scores may be lowered by more than 25 per cent (72). Much of this difficulty, of course, can be avoided by proper instructions and demonstration during the administration of the test, as well as by adequate proctoring. Nevertheless, all answer sheets should be inspected before machine scoring.

Systematic procedures for checking the actual scoring represent an essential step in all large-scale testing programs. Such checking is designed to detect both chance and constant errors. The first type of error generally results from incorrect reading or transcribing of scores, or from other routine clerical inaccuracies. Such errors can be checked by the independent repetition of those scoring operations subject to clerical errors, for all papers. Constant errors may result from procedural mistakes, such as the use of the wrong scoring key. They can be caught by spot checking all operations, through the complete and independent rescoring of a sample of papers.

Scorer Bias. A subtle kind of constant error that may affect the scoring of certain types of individual as well as group tests results from the mental set or "unconscious bias" of the scorer. An example will suggest how such errors may operate. In a study of the errors made by a school teacher in grading spelling papers, the number and direction of the scoring errors were found to be significantly related to the ratings for "personal attractiveness" given by the teacher to the same children (cf. 27, p. 376). Although the teacher had tried to score the papers accurately, the errors she made tended to raise the scores of children whom she found personally more attractive, and to lower the scores of children whom she considered less attractive.

Such constant errors resulting from personal bias could also operate in reference to a whole group. For example, in the comparison of ethnic groups, socioeconomic levels, or urban and rural samples, the scorer's own expectation of superiority or inferiority in certain groups could influence his scoring errors. Similarly, in an experimental investigation, the experimenter's hypothesis might lead him to expect a certain group difference and might thus bias his scoring. It should be noted that such constant errors occur despite the scorer's sincere efforts to be accurate and objective. The surest way to prevent such errors is to keep the scorer—and if possible, the examiner— in ignorance of the subject's group membership. This can be accomplished by removing names and other identifying marks and by coding the test papers prior to scoring. Such precautions are especially important in the case of tests whose scoring involves a certain degree of subjectivity, such as projective techniques and many individual intelligence scales.

REFERENCES

1. Adkins, Dorothy C. The effects of practice on intelligence test scores. *J. educ. Psychol.*, 1937, 28, 222-231.

72   *Principles of Psychological Testing*

2. American Psychological Association. *Technical recommendations for psychological tests and diagnostic techniques.* Washington: Amer. Psychol. Assoc., 1954. (Also in *Psychol. Bull.,* 1954, 51, No. 2, Pt. 2.)
3. American Psychological Association. *Ethical standards of psychologists. Amer. Psychologist,* 1959, 14, 279-282.
4. Anastasi, Anne. The concept of validity in the interpretation of test scores. *Educ. psychol. Measmt.,* 1950, 10, 67-78.
5. Anastasi, Anne. *Differential psychology.* (3rd ed.) N. Y.: Macmillan, 1958.
6. Anastasi, Anne, and Cordova, F. A. Some effects of bilingualism upon the intelligence test performance of Puerto Rican children in New York City. *J. educ. Psychol.,* 1953, 44, 1-19.
7. Anikeeff, A. M. Index of collaboration for test administrators. *J. appl. Psychol.,* 1954, 38, 174-177.
8. Berk, R. L. Coaching in an institution for defective delinquents: an evaluation by means of the critical incident technique. *Amer. J. ment. Def.,* 1952, 56, 615-621.
9. Bernstein, L. The examiner as an inhibiting factor in clinical testing. *J. consult. Psychol.,* 1956, 20, 287-290.
10. Bird, C. The detection of cheating in objective examinations. *Sch. and Soc.,* 1927, 25, 261-262.
11. Brown, F. An experimental and critical study of the intelligence of Negro and white kindergarten children. *J. genet. Psychol.,* 1944, 65, 161-175.
12. Casey, Mary L., Davidson, Helen P., and Harter, Doris I. Three studies on the effect of training in similar and identical material upon Stanford-Binet test scores. *27th Yearb., nat. Soc. Stud. Educ.,* 1928, Part I, 431-439.
13. Cattell, Psyche. Constant changes in Stanford-Binet IQ. *J. educ. Psychol.,* 1931, 22, 544-550.
14. College Entrance Examination Board, Aptitude Test Committee. *A description of the College Board Scholastic Aptitude Test.* N. Y.: College Entrance Examination Board, 1956.
15. College Entrance Examination Board, Trustees. A statement by the College Board trustees on test "coaching." *Coll. Bd. News,* 1959, No. 5, 2-3.
16. Crane, V. R., and Heim, Alice W. The effects of repeated retesting: III. Further experiments and general conclusions. *Quart. J. exp. Psychol.,* 1950, 2, 182-197.
17. Cronbach, L. J. Response sets and test validity. *Educ. psychol. Measmt.,* 1946, 6, 475-494.
18. Crowder, N. Intrinsically-programmed teaching devices. *Proc. 1959 invit. Conf. test. Probl., Educ. Test. Serv.,* 1960, 40-52.
19. Dearborn, W. F., and Rothney, J. *Predicting the child's development.* Cambridge, Mass.: Sci-Art Pub., 1941.
20. Dempster, J. J. B. Symposium on the effects of coaching and practice in intelligence tests: III. Southampton investigation and procedure. *Brit. J. educ. Psychol.,* 1954, 24, 1-4.
21. Dickenson, H. F. Identical errors and deception. *J. educ. Res.,* 1945, 38, 534-542.
22. Diederich, P. B. Self-correcting homework in English. *Proc. 1959 invit. Conf. test. Probl., Educ. Test. Serv.,* 1960, 70-86.

23. Eells, K., Davis, A., Havighurst, R. J., Herrick, V. E., and Tyler, R. W. *Intelligence and cultural differences.* Chicago: Univer. Chicago Press, 1951.

24. French, J. W. An answer to test coaching: public school experiment with SAT. *Coll. Bd. Rev.,* 1955, No. 27, 5-7.

25. Gehman, W. S. A study of ability to fake scores on the Strong Vocational Interest Blank for Men. *Educ. psychol. Measmt.,* 1957, 17, 65-70.

26. Goldstein, H. A. A malingering key for mental tests. *Psychol. Bull.,* 1945, 42, 104-118.

27. Goodenough, Florence L. Some special problems of nature-nurture research. *39th Yearb., nat. Soc. Stud. Educ.,* 1940, Part I, 367-384.

28. Goodenough, Florence L. *Mental testing.* N. Y.: Holt, Rinehart and Winston, 1949.

29. Goodenough, Florence L., Maurer, Katherine M., and Van Wagenen, M. J. *Minnesota Preschool Scales: manual of instructions.* Minneapolis: Educ. Test. Bur. 1940.

30. Gordon, L. V., and Durea, M. A. The effect of discouragement on the revised Stanford-Binet scale. *J. genet. Psychol.,* 1948, 73, 201-207.

31. Green, R. F. Does a selection situation induce testees to bias their answers on interest and temperament tests? *Educ. psychol. Measmt.,* 1951, 11, 503-515.

32. Greene, E. B. Practice effects on various types of standard tests. *Amer. J. Psychol.,* 1937, 49, 67-75.

33. Greene, Katherine B. The influence of specialized training on tests of general intelligence. *27th Yearb., nat. Soc. Stud. Educ.,* 1928, Part I, 421-428.

34. Hathaway, S. R., and McKinley, J. C. *Minnesota Multiphasic Personality Inventory.* (Rev. ed.) N. Y.: Psychol. Corp., 1951.

35. Heim, Alice W., and Wallace, Jean G. The effects of repeatedly retesting the same group on the same intelligence test: I. Normal adults. *Quart. J. exp. Psychol.,* 1949, 1, 151-159.

36. Heim, Alice W., and Wallace, Jean G. The effects of repeatedly retesting the same group on the same intelligence test: II. High grade mental defectives. *Quart. J. exp. Psychol.,* 1950, 2, 19-32.

37. Heim, Alice W., and Watts, K. P. Symposium: contributions to intelligence testing and the theory of intelligence: V. An experiment on practice, coaching, and discussion of error in mental testing. *Brit. J. educ. Psychol.,* 1957, 27, 199-210.

38. Holland, J. G. Teaching machines: an application of principles from the laboratory. *Proc. 1959 invit. Conf. test. Probl., Educ. Test. Serv.,* 1960, 53-69.

39. Holloway, H. D. Effects of training on the SRA Primary Mental Abilities (Primary) and WISC. *Child Develpm.,* 1954, 25, 253-263.

40. Hurlock, Elizabeth B. The value of praise and reproof as incentives for children. *Arch. Psychol.,* 1924, No. 71.

41. Hurlock, Elizabeth B. An evaluation of certain incentives used in school work. *J. educ. Psychol.,* 1925, 16, 145-159.

42. Hutt, M. L. "Consecutive" and "adaptive" testing with the revised Stanford-Binet. *J. consult. Psychol.,* 1947, 11, 93-103.

43. James, W. S. Symposium on the effects of coaching and practice in intelli-

gence tests: II. Coaching for all recommended. *Brit. J. Psychol.,* 1953, 23, 155-162.

44. Kelley, T. L. Cumulative significance of a number of independent experiments: reply to A. E. Traxler and R. N. Hilkert. *Sch. and Soc.,* 1943, 57, 482-484.

45. Levine, R. L., and Angoff, W. H. The effect of practice on scores on the Scholastic Aptitude Test of the College Entrance Examination Board. *Amer. Psychologist,* 1956, 11, 423.

46. Ligon, E. M. The administration of group tests. *Educ. psychol. Measmt.,* 1942, 2, 387-399.

47. Lindquist, E. F. (Ed.) *Educational measurement.* Washington: Amer. Council Educ., 1951.

48. McCarthy, Dorothea. A study of the reliability of the Goodenough drawing test of intelligence. *J. Psychol.,* 1944, 18, 201-216.

49. McHugh, G. Changes in IQ at the public school kindergarten level. *Psychol. Monogr.,* 1943, 55, No. 2.

50. Mandler, G., and Sarason, S. B. A study of anxiety and learning. *J. abnorm. soc. Psychol.,* 1952, 47, 166-173.

51. Manuel, H. T. *Taking a test: how to do your best.* Tarrytown-on-Hudson, N. Y.: World Book Co., 1956.

52. Masling, J. The effects of warm and cold interaction on the administration and scoring of an intelligence test. *J. consult. Psychol.,* 1959, 23, 336-341.

53. Masling, J. The influence of situational and interpersonal variables in projective testing. *Psychol. Bull.,* 1960, 57, 65-85.

54. Noll, V. H. Simulation by college students of a prescribed pattern on a personality scale. *Educ. psychol. Measmt.,* 1951, 11, 478-488.

55. Peel, E. A. A note on practice effects in intelligence tests. *Brit. J. educ. Psychol.,* 1951, 21, 122-125.

56. Peel, E. A. Practice effects between three consecutive tests of intelligence. *Brit. J. educ. Psychol.,* 1952, 22, 196-199.

57. Pollaczek, P. P. A study of malingering on the CVS abbreviated individual intelligence scale. *J. clin. Psychol.,* 1952, 8, 75-81.

58. Pressey, S. L. Development and appraisal of devices providing immediate automatic scoring of objective tests and concomitant self-instruction. *J. Psychol.,* 1950, 29, 417-447.

59. Reichenberg-Hackett, Wally. Changes in Goodenough drawings after a gratifying experience. *Amer. J. Orthopsychiat.,* 1953, 23, 501-517.

60. Rodger, A. G. The application of six group intelligence tests to the same children, and the effects of practice. *Brit. J. educ. Psychol.,* 1936, 6, 291-305.

61. Sacks, Elinor L. Intelligence scores as a function of experimentally established social relationships between the child and examiner. *J. abnorm. soc. Psychol.,* 1952, 47, 354-358.

62. Sarason, S. B. *The clinical interaction, with special reference to the Rorschach.* N. Y.: Harper, 1954.

63. Sarason, S. B., Davidson, K., Lighthall, F., and Waite, R. A test anxiety scale for children. *Child Develpm.,* 1958, 29, 105-113.

64. Sears, R. Motivational factors in aptitude testing. *Amer. J. Orthopsychiat.,* 1943, 13, 468-493.

65. Smith, S. Language and non-verbal test performance of racial groups in Honolulu before and after a 14-year interval. *J. gen. Psychol.,* 1942, 26, 51-93.
66. Staudt, Virginia M. The relationship of testing conditions and intellectual level to errors and correct responses in several types of tasks among college women. *J. Psychol.,* 1948, 26, 125-140.
67. Terman, L. M., and Merrill, Maud A. *Stanford-Binet Intelligence Scale: manual for the third revision, Form L-M.* Boston: Houghton Mifflin, 1960.
68. Thorndike, E. L. Practice effects on intelligence tests. *J. exp. Psychol.,* 1922, 5, 101-107.
69. Thorndike, R. L. *Personnel selection: test and measurement techniques.* N. Y.: Wiley, 1949.
70. Thurstone, Thelma G. *Learning to think series. The red book.* Chicago: Sci. Res. Assoc., 1948.
71. Thurstone, Thelma G. *Learning to think series. Teacher's manual for play and learn. The red book.* Chicago: Sci. Res. Assoc., 1948.
72. Traxler, A. E. Accuracy of machine scoring of answer sheets marked with different degrees of excellence. *Proc. Research Forum, Endicott, N. Y., August 26-30, 1946.* N. Y.: International Business Machines Corp., 1947, pp. 89-94.
73. Traxler, A. E., and Hilkert, R. N. Effect of type of desk on results of machine-scored tests. *Sch. and Soc.,* 1942, 56, 277-296.
74. Tsudzuki, A., Hata, Y., and Kuze, T. (A study of rapport between examiner and subject.) *Jap. J. Psychol.,* 1957, 27, 22-28.
75. Tyler, F. T., and Chalmers, T. M. Effect on scores of warning junior high school pupils of coming tests. *J. educ. Res.,* 1943, 37, 290-296.
76. Vernon, P. E. Symposium on the effects of coaching and practice in intelligence tests: V. Conclusions. *Brit. J. educ. Psychol.,* 1954, 24, 57-63.
77. Waite, R. R., Sarason, S. B., Lighthall, F. F., and Davidson, K. S. A study of anxiety and learning in children. *J. abnorm. soc. Psychol.,* 1958, 57, 267-270.
78. Watson, R. I. *The clinical method in psychology.* N. Y.: Harper, 1951.
79. Watts, K. P. Intelligence test performance from 11 to 18: a study of grammar school girls. *Brit. J. educ. Psychol.,* 1958, 28, 112-119.
80. Weisskopf, Edith A., and Dieppa, J. Experimentally induced faking of TAT responses. *J. consult. Psychol.,* 1951, 15, 469-474.
81. Wesman, A. G. Faking personality test scores in a simulated employment situation. *J. appl. Psychol.,* 1952, 36, 112-113.
82. Wickes, T. A., Jr. Examiner influence in a testing situation. *J. consult. Psychol.,* 1956, 20, 23-26.
83. Wiseman, S. Symposium on the effects of coaching and practice in intelligence tests: IV. The Manchester experiment. *Brit. J. educ. Psychol.,* 1954, 24, 5-8.
84. Wiseman, S., and Wrigley, J. The comparative effects of coaching and practice on the results of verbal intelligence tests. *Brit. J. Psychol.,* 1953, 44, 83-94.
85. Yates, A. Symposium on the effects of coaching and practice in intelligence tests: I. An analysis of some recent investigations. *Brit. J. educ. Psychol.,* 1953, 23, 147-154.

CHAPTER 4

Norms: Their Nature and Interpretation

It will be recalled from Chapter 2 that a "raw score" on any psychological test is, in itself, quite meaningless. Obviously, to say that an individual has correctly solved 15 problems on an arithmetic reasoning test, or identified 34 words in a vocabulary test, or successfully completed a mechanical puzzle in 57 seconds conveys little or no information about his standing in any of these functions.

Nor do the familiar "percentage scores" provide a satisfactory solution to the problem of interpreting test scores. A score of 65 per cent correct on one vocabulary test, for example, might be equivalent to 30 per cent correct on another, and to 80 per cent correct on a third. The difficulty level of the items making up each test will, of course, determine the meaning of the score. In a test in which the items are answered correctly, on the average, by 90 per cent of the subjects, the average score of the group will be 90 per cent of a perfect score. Such a test would be very unsatisfactory for differentiating among superior individuals, since the upper half of the group would be bunched between scores of 90 per cent and 100 per cent. On the other hand, a test in which 50 per cent of the subjects, on the average, answer each item correctly would yield an average score of 50 per cent right, and would permit finer discrimination among individuals throughout the range. A score of 50 per cent on the latter test would correspond to a score of 90 per cent on the former. Like all raw scores, such percentage scores can be interpreted only by reference to *norms*.

Essentially, psychological test norms represent the test performance of the standardization sample. The norms are thus empirically established by determining what a representative group of persons actually do on the test. Any individual's raw score is then referred to the distribution of scores obtained by the standardization sample, to discover where he falls in such a distribution. Does his score coincide with the average performance of the standardization group? Is he slightly below average? Or does he fall near the upper end of the distribution?

In order to determine more precisely the individual's exact position with reference to the standardization sample, the raw score is converted into some relative measure. Such converted scores are designed to serve a dual purpose. First, they indicate the individual's relative standing in the normative sample and thus permit an evaluation of his performance in reference to other persons. Secondly, they provide comparable measures which make possible a direct comparison of the individual's performance on different tests. If, for example, we find that a given individual has a raw score of 40 on a vocabulary test and 22 on an arithmetic reasoning test, we obviously know nothing about his relative performance on the two tests. Is he better in vocabulary or in arithmetic, or equally good in both? Since raw scores on different tests are usually expressed in different units, a direct comparison of such scores is impossible. The difficulty level of the particular test would also affect such a comparison between raw scores. Converted scores, on the other hand, can be expressed in the same units and referred to the same or to closely similar normative samples for different tests. The individual's relative performance in many different functions can thus be compared.

There are various ways in which raw scores may be converted to fulfill the two objectives stated above. Fundamentally, however, test scores are of three major types: age scores, percentiles, and standard scores. These types, together with some of their common variants, will be considered in separate sections of this chapter. But first it will be necessary to examine a few elementary statistical concepts that underlie the development and utilization of norms. The following section is included simply to clarify the meaning of certain common statistical measures. Simplified computational examples are given only for this purpose and not to provide training in statistical methods. For computational details and specific procedures to be followed in the practical application of these techniques, the reader is referred to any recent textbook on psychological or educational statistics, such as Blommers and Lindquist (6), Garrett (12), Guilford (14), or Walker and Lev (27). Shorter and more elementary introductions to statistical method have also been published by Garrett (11) and by Walker and Lev (28).

SOME ELEMENTARY STATISTICAL CONCEPTS

A major object of statistical method is to organize and summarize quantitative data in order to facilitate their understanding. A list of 1000 test scores can be an overwhelming sight. In that form, it conveys little meaning.

A first step in bringing order into such a chaos of raw data is to tabulate the scores into a *frequency distribution,* as illustrated in Table 1. Such a distribution is prepared by grouping the scores into convenient class intervals and tallying each score in the appropriate interval. When all scores have been entered, the tallies are counted to find the frequency, or number of cases, in each class interval. The sums of these frequencies will equal *N,* the total number of cases in the group. Table 1 shows the scores of 1000 college students in a code-learning test in which one set of artificial "words," or nonsense syllables, was to be substituted for another. The raw scores, giving number of correct syllables substituted during a two-minute trial, ranged from 8 to 52. They have been grouped into class intervals of 4 points, from 52-55 at the top of the distribution down to 8-11. The frequency column reveals that 2 persons scored between 8 and 11, 3 between 12 and 15, 8 between 16 and 19, and so on.

TABLE 1. **Frequency Distribution of Scores of 1000 College Students on a Code-Learning Test**
(From Anastasi, 1, p. 34)

Class Interval	Frequency
52-55	1
48-51	1
44-47	20
40-43	73
36-39	156
32-35	328
28-31	244
24-27	136
20-23	28
16-19	8
12-15	3
8-11	2
	1000

The information provided by a frequency distribution can also be presented graphically in the form of a distribution curve. Figure 10 shows the data of Table 1 in graphic form. On the baseline, or horizontal axis, are the scores, grouped into class intervals; on the vertical axis are the frequencies, or number of cases falling within each class interval. The graph has been plotted in two ways, both forms being in common use. In the *histogram,* the height of the column erected over each class interval corresponds to the number of persons scoring in that interval. We can think of each individual standing on another's shoulders to form the column. In the *frequency poly-*

gon, the number of persons in each interval is indicated by a point placed in the center of the class interval and across from the appropriate frequency. The successive points are then joined by straight lines.

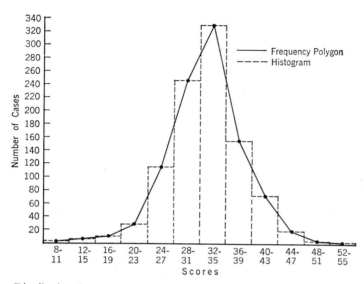

Fig. 10. Distribution Curves: Frequency Polygon and Histogram. (Data from Table 1.)

Except for minor irregularities, the distribution portrayed in Figure 10 resembles the bell-shaped *normal curve.* A mathematically determined, perfect normal curve is reproduced in Figure 12. This type of curve has important mathematical properties and provides the basis for many kinds of statistical analyses. For the present purpose, however, only a few features will be noted. Essentially, the curve indicates that the largest number of cases cluster in the center of the range, and the number drops off gradually in both directions as the extremes are approached. The curve is bilaterally symmetrical, with a single peak in the center. Most distributions of human traits, from height and weight to aptitudes and personality characteristics, approximate the normal curve. In general, the larger the group, the more closely will the distribution resemble the theoretical normal curve.

A group of scores can also be described in terms of some measure of *central tendency.* Such a measure provides a single, most typical or representative score to characterize the performance of the entire group. The most familiar of these measures is the average, more technically known as the *mean (M).* As is well known, this is found by adding all scores and dividing the sum by the number of cases *(N).* Another measure of central tendency is the *mode,* or most frequent score. In a frequency distribution, the mode is the midpoint of the class interval with the highest frequency. Thus in Table 1, the mode falls midway between 32 and 35, being 33.5. It will be noted that this score corresponds to the highest point on the distribution curve in Figure 10. A third measure of central tendency is the *median,* or middlemost score when all scores have been arranged in order of size. The median is the point that bisects the distribution, half the cases falling above it and half below.

Further description of a set of test scores is given by measures of *variability,* or the extent of individual differences around the central tendency. The most obvious and familiar way of reporting variability is in terms of the *range* between the highest and lowest score. The range, however, is extremely crude and unstable, since it is determined by only two scores. A single unusually high or low score would thus markedly affect its size. A more precise method of measuring variability is based on the difference between each individual's score and the mean of the group.

At this point it will be helpful to look at the example in Table 2, in which the various measures under consideration have been computed on 10 cases. Such a small group was chosen in order to simplify the demonstration, although in actual practice we would rarely perform these computations on so few

TABLE 2. Illustration of Central Tendency and Variability

		Score (X)	Diff. (x)	Diff. Squared (x^2)
	50% of cases	48	+ 8 ⎫	64
		47	+ 7 ⎪	49
		43	+ 3 ⎬ + 20	9
		41	+ 1 ⎪	1
		41	+ 1 ⎭	1
Median = 40.5 →	50% of cases	40	0 ⎫	0
		38	− 2 ⎪	4
		36	− 4 ⎬ − 20	16
		34	− 6 ⎪	36
		32	− 8 ⎭	64
		$\Sigma X = 400$	$\Sigma |x| = 40$	$\Sigma x^2 = 244$

$$M = \frac{\Sigma X}{N} = \frac{400}{10} = 40$$

$$AD = \frac{\Sigma |x|}{N} = \frac{40}{10} = 4$$

$$\text{Variance} = \sigma^2 = \frac{\Sigma x^2}{N} = \frac{244}{10} = 24.40$$

$$SD \text{ or } \sigma = \sqrt{\frac{\Sigma x^2}{N}} = \sqrt{24.40} = 4.9$$

cases. Table 2 serves also to introduce certain standard statistical symbols which should be noted for future reference. Original raw scores are conventionally designated by a capital X, and a small x is used to refer to deviations of each score from the group mean. The Greek letter Σ means "sum of." It will be seen that the first column in Table 2 gives the data for the computation of mean and median. The mean is 40; the median is 40.5, falling midway between 40 and 41—five cases (50 per cent) are above the median and five below. There is little point in finding a mode in such a small group, since the cases do not show clear-cut clustering on any one score. Technically, however, 41 would represent the mode, since two persons obtained this score, while all other scores occur only once.

The second column shows how far each score deviates above or below the mean of 40. The sum of these deviations will always equal zero, since the positive and negative deviations around the mean necessarily balance, or cancel each other out ($+20 - 20 = 0$). If we ignore signs, of course, we can average the absolute deviations, thus obtaining a measure known as the *average deviation* (*AD*). The symbol $|x|$ in the *AD* formula indicates that absolute values were summed, without regard to sign. Although of some descriptive value, the *AD* is not suitable for use in further mathematical analyses, because of the arbitrary discarding of signs.

A much more serviceable measure of variability is the *standard deviation* (symbolized by either *SD* or σ), in which the negative signs are legitimately eliminated by squaring each deviation. This procedure has been followed in the last column of Table 2. The sum of this column divided by the number of cases $\left(\dfrac{\Sigma x^2}{N}\right)$ is known as the *variance,* or *mean square deviation,* and is symbolized by σ^2. The variance has proved extremely useful in sorting out the contributions of different factors to individual differences in test performance. For the present purposes, however, our chief concern is with the *SD,* which is the square root of the variance, as shown in Table 2. This measure is commonly employed in comparing the variability of different groups. In Figure 11, for example, are two distributions having the same mean but differing in variability. The distribution with wider individual differences yields a larger *SD* than the one with narrower individual differences.

The *SD* also provides the basis for expressing an individual's scores on different tests in terms of norms, as will be shown in the section on standard scores. The interpretation of the *SD* is especially clear-cut when applied to a normal or approximately normal distribution curve. In such a distribution, there is an exact relationship between the *SD* and the proportion of cases, as shown in Figure 12. On the baseline of this normal curve have been marked

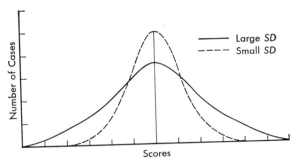

Fig. 11. Frequency Distributions with the Same Mean but Different Variability.

distances representing one, two, and three standard deviations above and below the mean. For instance, in the example given in Table 2, the mean would correspond to a score of 40, $+1\sigma$ to 44.9 (40 + 4.9), $+2\sigma$ to 49.8 (40 + 2 × 4.9), and so on. The percentage of cases that fall between the mean and $+1\sigma$ in a normal curve is 34.13. Since the curve is symmetrical, 34.13 per cent of the cases are likewise found between the mean and -1σ, so that between $+1\sigma$ and -1σ on both sides of the mean there are 68.26 per cent of the cases. Nearly all the cases (99.72 per cent) fall within $\pm3\sigma$ from the mean. These relationships are particularly relevant in the interpretation of standard scores and percentiles to be discussed in later sections.

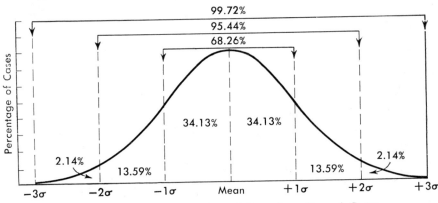

Fig. 12. Percentage Distribution of Cases in a Normal Curve.

AGE SCORES

The concept of mental age, it will be recalled, was introduced in the 1908 revision of the Binet-Simon scales. In age scales such as the Binet and its revisions, individual items are grouped into year levels. For example, those items passed by the majority of 7-year-olds in the standardization sample are placed at the 7-year level, those passed by the majority of 8-year-olds are assigned to the 8-year level, and so forth.[1] A child's score on this test will then correspond to the highest year level that he can successfully complete. If, for example, a 10-year-old child can satisfactorily complete the 12-year items, his mental age (MA) is 12, although his chronological age (CA) is 10. He is thus two years accelerated, since he equals the performance of an average child two years his senior.

In actual practice, the individual's performance on age scales such as the Binet shows a certain amount of *scatter*. In other words, the subject fails some tests below his mental age level and passes some above it. For this reason, it is customary to compute the *basal age,* i.e., the highest age at and below which all tests are passed. Partial credits, in months, are then added to this basal age for all tests passed at higher year levels. The child's mental age on the test is the sum of the basal age and the additional months of credit earned at higher age levels.

Mental age norms may also be employed with tests that are not divided into year levels. In such a case, the subject's raw score is first determined. Such a score may be the total number of correct items on the whole test; or it may be based on time, on number of errors, or on some combination of such measures. The mean raw scores obtained by the children in each year group within the standardization sample constitute the age norms for such a test. The mean raw score of the 8-year-old children, for example, would represent the 8-year norm. If an individual's raw score is equal to the mean 8-year-old raw score, then his mental age on the test is 8 years. All raw scores on such a test would be transformed in a similar manner by reference to the age norms.

It should be noted that the mental age unit does not remain constant with age, but tends to shrink with advancing years. For example, a child who is one year retarded at age 4 will be approximately three years retarded at age 12. One year of mental "growth" from ages 3 to 4 is equivalent to three years of growth from ages 9 to 12. Since intellectual development progresses more rapidly at the earlier ages and gradually decreases as the individual approaches his mature limit, the mental age unit shrinks correspondingly with age. This relationship may be more readily visualized if we think of the individual's height as being expressed in terms of "height age." The difference, in inches, between a "height age" of 3 and 4 years would be greater than that between a "height age" of 10 and 11. Owing to the progressive shrinkage of the MA

1 The exact percentage who must pass an item varies somewhat at different year levels. This percentage must decrease from the lower to the upper year levels, if the IQ is to remain constant. For a fuller explanation of this point, cf. McNemar (20, p. 9).

unit, one year of acceleration or retardation at, let us say, age 5 represents a greater deviation from the norm than a similar amount of acceleration or retardation at age 10.

In order to provide a measure that, unlike mental age, permits a uniform interpretation regardless of the age of the subject, the Intelligence Quotient (IQ) was introduced. Although the need for such a ratio measure had been previously indicated by Stern and by Kuhlmann, the IQ was first employed in the 1916 form of the Stanford-Binet. The IQ is the ratio of mental age to chronological age, the fraction being customarily multiplied by 100 in order to avoid the use of decimals, as shown below:

$$IQ = 100\frac{MA}{CA}$$

If a child's mental age equals his chronological age, his IQ will be exactly 100. An IQ of 100 thus represents normal or average performance. IQ's below 100 indicate retardation, and those above 100, acceleration. The shrinkage in the mental age unit is automatically adjusted by the use of the ratio. For example, if a 4-year-old has a mental age of 3, his IQ will be 75 ($100 \times 3/4 = 75$). The same child at age 12 will probably have a mental age of 9, and his IQ will still be 75 ($100 \times 9/12 = 75$). Such an IQ indicates the same relative standing in the group, whether obtained by a 4-year-old or by a 12-year-old. The IQ is thus comparable at different ages, in the sense that the interpretation of a particular IQ remains the same regardless of the age of the subject.

The IQ, however, will remain constant only when the mental age unit *shrinks in direct proportion with age*. This condition must be met if the IQ is to be meaningfully employed with a particular test. When the mental age unit shrinks, individual differences measured in terms of such a unit will increase proportionately. This follows arithmetically, in the same way that individual differences in height will be 12 times as large when measured in inches as when measured in feet, since the inch is $1/12$ as large as the foot. Accordingly, individual differences in mental age should, for example, be twice as large at age 14 as at age 7. Only when the *SD* of mental ages increases proportionately with age will the *SD* of IQ's remain constant. It is only under such conditions that a given IQ will have the same meaning at all ages.

This condition was met closely enough in the 1937 Stanford-Binet (20, 24) to make the IQ applicable to this test. Figure 13 shows the spread of Stanford-Binet mental ages from ages 6 to 18, as indicated by the range of approximately the middle 68 per cent of the cases at each age. It will be recalled that this is the approximate percentage of cases falling between $+1$ *SD* and -1 *SD* from the mean in a normal curve. The trend toward greater variability in mental age with increasing chronological age is clearly apparent in Figure 13. Even in such a carefully constructed test as the Stanford-Binet, however, some inequalities remained in the *SD*'s of the IQ at different ages (13, 24), a difficulty that was handled by the preparation of a correction table to be used with IQ's at certain age levels (20, pp. 173-174). In the 1960 revision of the Stanford-Binet (25), the problem was circumvented by replacing the ratio IQ with deviation IQ's, to be discussed later in this chapter.

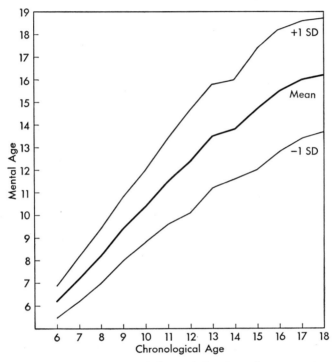

Fig. 13. Means and Standard Deviations of Stanford-Binet Mental Ages. (Data from McNemar, 20, pp. 32-33.)

In several other intelligence tests that provide age norms, however, the conditions for IQ constancy are not met. In such tests, the same IQ may signify different degrees of superiority or inferiority at different ages. In the Merrill-Palmer scale, for example, an IQ of 114 at one age may indicate the same degree of superiority as an IQ of 141 at another age (23). Despite its apparent logical simplicity, the IQ is not directly applicable to most psychological tests. Its use should be preceded by a thorough check of variability at different ages, to insure that the condition of uniform IQ variability, or proportionately increasing MA variability, has been met.

A further limitation in the applicability of the IQ is to be found in adult testing. A consideration of the very concept of age norms will indicate that their usefulness is largely restricted to children. To say that a 10-year-old child has a mental age of 12 conveys a vivid and objectively definable picture. It is one of the chief advantages of the mental age concept that it can be clearly grasped by the layman. Such an advantage is greatly reduced, however, with adult mental ages. On such a test as the Stanford-Binet, for example, the average adult does not improve much beyond the 15-year level. Hence the average adult mental age on this test is under 16 (actually 15 years-9 months). To be sure, superior adult levels have been added to give the test adequate ceiling, and mental ages above 15-9 may thus be obtained. But to say that a particular adult received a mental age of 20 on such a test does not permit the same clear-cut interpretation as would be possible with a mental age of 8 or 10. Certainly a mental age of 20 cannot be defined as what the average 20-year-old can do, since the average 20-year-old obtains a mental age of 15-9. In testing a feebleminded adult whose mental age is below 15-9, of course, the mental age concept is as applicable as with children. With normal and superior adults, however, other types of scores, such as percentiles or standard scores, are now commonly employed.

Still another limitation of age scores arises from the fact that they can be employed only with functions that show a clear and consistent change with age. Traits that exhibit little relation to age obviously do not lend themselves to measurement in terms of age units. Most personality characteristics, for example, would fall into this category.

PERCENTILES

Percentile scores are expressed in terms of the percentage of persons in the standardization sample who fall below a given raw score. For example, if 28 per cent of the subjects obtain fewer than 15 problems correct on an arithmetic reasoning test, then a raw score of 15 corresponds to the 28th percentile (P_{28}). A percentile indicates the individual's relative position in the standardization sample. Percentiles can also be regarded as ranks in a group of 100, except that in ranking it is customary to start counting at the top, the best person in the group receiving a rank of one. With percentiles, on the other hand, we begin counting at the bottom, so that the lower the percentile, the poorer the individual's standing.

The 50th percentile (P_{50}) corresponds to the median, already discussed as a measure of central tendency. Percentiles above 50 represent above-average performance, those below 50 signify inferior performance. The 25th and 75th percentile are known as the first and third quartile points (Q_1 and Q_3), since they cut off the lowest and highest quarters of the distribution. Like the median, they provide convenient landmarks for describing a distribution of scores and comparing it with other distributions.

Percentiles should not be confused with the familiar "percentage scores." The latter are raw scores, expressed in terms of the percentage of correct items; percentiles are converted scores, expressed in terms of percentage of persons. A raw score lower than any obtained in the standardization sample would have a percentile rank of zero (P_0); one higher than any score in the standardization sample would have a percentile rank of 100 (P_{100}). These percentiles, however, do not imply a zero raw score and a perfect raw score.

In test manuals, percentile norms are sometimes reported in the form of a graph, as illustrated in Figure 14. Such a graph, known as an *ogive*, shows the cumulative percentage of cases falling below each score. As in the previously discussed frequency graphs, scores are given on the baseline, frequencies (i.e., cumulative percentages) on the vertical axis. Figure 14 was

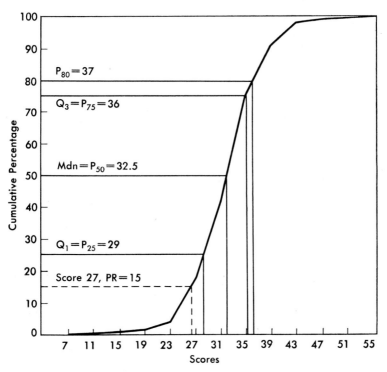

Fig. 14. Cumulative Frequency Graph Used in Finding Percentiles. (Data from Table 3.)

plotted from the data of Table 3, which shows the same 1000 scores given in Table 1. The first two columns of Table 3, giving class intervals and frequencies, are identical with those of Table 1. In the third column are the cumulative frequencies, found by adding frequencies from the bottom up. Thus the number of cases falling at or below a score of 11 is 2; the number at or below 15 is 5 (3 + 2); the number at or below 19 is 13 (8 + 5). In the fourth column, these cumulative frequencies have been changed to percentages by dividing each by 10 (since $N = 1000$).

TABLE 3. Cumulative Frequency Distribution

Class Interval	Frequency	Cumulative Frequency	Cumulative Percentage Frequency
52-55	1	1000	100.0
48-51	1	999	99.9
44-47	20	998	99.8
40-43	73	978	97.8
36-39	156	905	90.5
32-35	328	749	74.9
28-31	244	421	42.1
24-27	136	177	17.7
20-23	28	41	4.1
16-19	8	13	1.3
12-15	3	5	0.5
8-11	2	2	0.2

The ogive in Figure 14 shows the cumulative percentage frequency below the upper limit of each class interval.[2] Such an ogive can be read in either direction. For example, if we wish to find the median, we locate the 50 per cent point on the vertical axis, draw a horizontal line from this point to the graph, and at the point where the line meets the graph drop a perpendicular to the baseline. This has been done in Figure 14, showing that the median is 32.5. Similarly, Q_1 is found to be approximately 29 and Q_3 approximately 36. The raw score corresponding to any other percentile can be found in the same manner; for the 80th percentile, for example, it is 37. Working in the opposite direction, we can start with an individual's raw score and locate the percentile rank corresponding to it. Thus for a raw score of 27, we raise a perpendicular above 27 on the baseline until it meets the curve; a horizontal line drawn from that point to the vertical axis shows the percentile rank to be 15.

2 The observant reader may have noticed that the points on the graph have been plotted slightly to the right of the score values on the baseline. In a continuous scale, the numbers 11, 15, etc., correspond to the *midpoints* of scores. The *upper limits* of the scores, at which cumulative percentage frequencies have been plotted, fall on 11.5, 15.5, etc.

Not only do percentiles show where the individual stands in the normative sample, but they are also useful in comparing the individual's own performance on different tests. For example, if a child obtains a raw score of 30 on an arithmetic test and 58 on a reading test, we cannot compare these two scores directly because they are expressed in different units. Suppose, however, that reference to percentile norms shows that a score of 30 on the arithmetic test corresponds to a percentile rank of 65, and a score of 58 on the reading test to a percentile rank of 40. Now we can conclude that the child did much better in arithmetic than in reading.

Percentile scores have several advantages. They are easy to compute and can be readily understood, even by relatively untrained persons. Moreover, percentiles are universally applicable. They can be used equally well with adults and children, and are suitable for any type of test, whether it measures aptitude or personality variables.

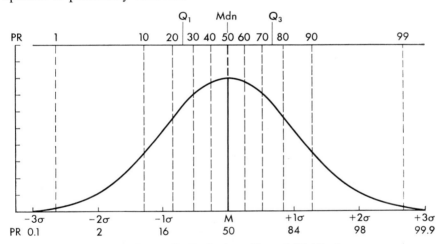

Fig. 15. Percentile Ranks in a Normal Distribution.

The chief drawback of percentile scores arises from the marked inequality of their units, especially at the extremes of the distribution. If the distribution of raw scores approximates the normal curve, as is true of most test scores, then raw score differences near the median or center of the distribution are exaggerated in the percentile transformation, while raw score differences near the ends of the distribution are greatly shrunk. This distortion of distances between scores can be seen in Figure 15. In a normal curve, it will be recalled, cases cluster closely at the center and scatter more widely as the extremes are approached. Consequently, any given percentage of cases near the center covers a shorter distance on the baseline than the same percentage near the ends of the distribution. In Figure 15, this discrepancy in the gaps between percentile ranks (*PR*) can readily be seen if we compare the distance between a *PR* of 40 and a *PR* of 50 with that between a *PR* of 10 and a *PR* of 20. Even more striking is the discrepancy between these distances and that between a *PR* of 10 and a *PR* of 1. (In a mathematically derived normal curve, zero percentile is not reached until infinity and hence cannot be shown on the graph.)

The same relationship can be seen from the opposite direction if we examine the percentile ranks corresponding to equal σ-distances from the mean of a normal curve. These percentile ranks are given under the graph in Figure 15. Thus the percentile difference between the mean and $+1\sigma$ is 34 (84 — 50). That between $+1\sigma$ and $+2\sigma$ is only 14 (98 — 84).

It is apparent that percentiles give a correct picture of each individual's *relative position* in the normative sample, but not of the *amount* of difference between his score and that of another person. For this reason, percentiles are unsuitable for the computation of means, standard deviations, and several other statistical measures. The results of such computations with percentiles would differ from those obtained with raw scores. For example, the mean of two percentiles does not equal the percentile corresponding to the mean of the two raw scores. Percentiles thus provide a crude though simple and widely applicable method of indicating the individual's standing in reference to the test norms.

STANDARD SCORES

Current tests are making increasing use of standard scores, which are the most satisfactory type of transformed score from most points of view. Standard scores express the individual's distance from the mean in terms of the standard deviation of the distribution.

Linear Standard Scores. Standard scores may be obtained by either linear or non-linear transformations of the original raw scores. When found by a linear transformation, they retain the exact numerical relations of the original raw scores, since they are computed by subtracting a constant from each raw score and then dividing the result by another constant. The relative magnitude of differences between standard scores derived by such a linear transformation corresponds exactly to that between the raw scores. All properties of the original distribution of raw scores are duplicated in the distribution of these standard scores. For this reason, any computations that can be carried out with the original raw scores can also be carried out with linear standard scores, without any distortion of results.

Linearly derived standard scores are often designated simply as "standard scores," or "z scores." To compute a z score, we find the difference between the individual's raw score and the mean of the normative group, and then divide this difference by the *SD* of the normative group. Table 4 shows the computation of z scores for two individuals, one of whom falls 1 *SD* above the group mean, the other .40 *SD* below the mean. Any raw score that is exactly equal to the mean is equivalent to a z score of zero. It is apparent that such a procedure will yield derived scores that have a negative sign for all subjects falling below the mean. Moreover, since the total range of most groups extends no farther than about 3 *SD*'s above and below the mean, such standard scores will have to be reported to at least one decimal place in order to provide sufficient differentiation among individuals.

TABLE 4. Computation of Standard Scores

$$z = \frac{X - M}{SD} \qquad M = 60 \qquad SD = 5$$

JOHN'S SCORE	BILL'S SCORE
$X_1 = 65$	$X_2 = 58$
$z_1 = \dfrac{65 - 60}{5}$	$z_2 = \dfrac{58 - 60}{5}$
$= +1.00$	$= -0.40$

Both of the above conditions, viz., the occurrence of negative values and of decimals, tend to produce awkward numbers that are confusing and difficult to use for both computational and reporting purposes. For this reason, some further linear transformation is usually applied, simply to put the scores into a more convenient form. For example, the scores on the AGCT (Army General Classification Test) employed during World War II were standard scores adjusted to a mean of 100 and an *SD* of 20. Thus a standard score of -1 on this test would be expressed as 80 ($100 - 20 = 80$). Similarly, a standard score of $+1.5$ would correspond to 130 ($100 + 1.5 \times 20 = 130$). To convert an original standard score to the new scale, it is simply necessary to multiply the standard score by the desired *SD* (20) and add it to or subtract it from the desired mean (100).

Any other convenient values can be arbitrarily chosen for the new mean and *SD*. The College Entrance Examination Board employs a mean of 500 and an *SD* of 100. Scores on the separate subtests of the Wechsler Intelligence Scales (see Ch. 12) are converted to a distribution with a mean of 10 and an *SD* of 3. All such measures are examples of linearly transformed standard scores.

Normalized Standard Scores. It will be recalled that one of the reasons for transforming raw scores into any derived scale is to render scores on different tests comparable. The linearly derived standard scores discussed in the preceding section will be comparable only when found from distributions that have approximately the same form. Under such conditions, a score corresponding to 1 *SD* above the mean, for example, signifies that the individual occupies the same position in relation to both groups. His score exceeds approximately the same percentage of persons in both distributions, and this percentage can be determined if the form of the distribution is known. If, however, one distribution is markedly skewed and the other normal, a *z* score of $+1.00$ might exceed only 50 per cent of the cases in one group, but would exceed 84 per cent in the other.

In order to achieve comparability of scores from dissimilarly shaped distributions, non-linear transformations may be employed to fit the scores to any specified type of distribution curve. The mental age and percentile scores described in earlier sections represent non-linear transformations, but they are subject to other limitations already discussed. Although under certain circumstances it may be preferable to fit scores to some other type of distribution (cf. 9, pp. 725 ff.; 10), the normal curve is usually employed for this purpose. One of the chief reasons for such a practice is that raw score distributions more often approximate the normal curve than any other type of curve. Moreover, physical measures such as height and weight, which use equal-unit scales derived through physical operations, generally yield normal distributions.[3] Another important advantage of the normal curve is that it has many useful mathematical properties, which facilitate further computations.

Normalized standard scores are standard scores expressed in terms of a distribution that has been transformed to fit a normal curve. Such scores can be computed by reference to tables giving the percentage of cases falling at different σ-distances from the mean of a normal curve. First, the percentage of persons in the standardization sample falling at or above each raw score is found. Such a percentage is then located in the normal curve frequency table, and the corresponding normalized standard score is obtained. Normalized standard scores are expressed in the same form as linearly derived standard scores, viz., with a mean of zero and an *SD* of 1. Thus a normalized score of zero indicates that the individual falls at the mean of a normal curve, excelling 50 per cent of the group. A score of -1.00 means that he surpasses approximately 16 per cent of the group; and a score of $+1.00$, that he surpasses 84 per cent. These percentages correspond to a distance of 1 *SD* below and

---

[3] Partly for this reason and partly as a result of other theoretical considerations, it has frequently been argued that, by normalizing raw scores, an equal-unit scale could be developed for psychological measurement, similar to the equal-unit scales of physical measurement. This, however, is a debatable point which involves certain questionable assumptions. For a good introduction to the logic of scales of measurement, with special reference to problems of psychological measurement, cf. Bergman and Spence (5), Comrey (7), Lorge (18), and Stevens (22).

1 *SD* above the mean of a normal curve, respectively, as can be seen by reference to Figure 15.

Like linearly derived standard scores, normalized standard scores can be put into any convenient form. If the normalized standard score is multiplied by 10 and added to or subtracted from 50, it is converted into a *T score,* a type of score first proposed by McCall (19). On such a scale, a score of 50 corresponds to the mean, a score of 60 to 1 *SD* above the mean, and so forth. Another well-known transformation is represented by the *stanine* scale employed by the United States Air Force during World War II (cf. 9, pp. 727 ff.). This scale provides a single-digit system of scores, with a mean of 5 and an *SD* of approximately 2.[4] The name "stanine" (a contraction of "standard nine") is based on the fact that the scores run from 1 to 9. The restriction of scores to single-digit numbers has certain computational advantages, especially in machine computation.

Raw scores can readily be converted to stanines by arranging the original scores in order of size and then assigning stanines in accordance with the normal curve percentages reproduced in Table 5. For example, if our group

TABLE 5.   **Normal Curve Percentages for Use in Stanine Conversion**

Percentage	4	7	12	17	20	17	12	7	4
Stanine	1	2	3	4	5	6	7	8	9

consists of exactly 100 persons, the four lowest-scoring persons receive a stanine score of 1, the next 7 a score of 2, the next 12 a score of 3, and so on. When the group contains more or fewer than 100 cases, the number corresponding to each designated percentage is first computed; these numbers of cases are then given the appropriate stanines. Thus out of 200 cases, 8 would be assigned a stanine of 1 (4 per cent of 200 = 8). With 150 cases, 6 would receive a stanine of 1 (4 per cent of 150 = 6).

Although normalized standard scores are the most satisfactory type of score for the majority of purposes, there are nevertheless certain technical objections to normalizing all distributions routinely. Such a transformation should be carried out only when the sample is large and representative and when there is reason to believe that the deviation from normality results from defects in the test rather than from characteristics of the sample or from other factors affecting the behavior under consideration. It should also be noted that when the original distribution of raw scores approximates normality, the linearly derived standard scores and the normalized standard scores will be very

---

[4] Kaiser (16) has proposed a slight modification of the stanine scale which yields an *SD* of exactly 2, thus being easier to handle quantitatively.

similar. Although the methods of deriving these two types of scores are quite dissimilar, the resulting scores will be nearly identical under such conditions. Obviously, the process of normalizing a distribution that is already virtually normal will produce little or no change. Whenever feasible, it is generally more desirable to obtain a normal distribution of raw scores by proper adjustment of the difficulty level of test items, rather than by subsequently normalizing a markedly non-normal distribution. With an approximately normal distribution of raw scores, the linearly derived standard scores will serve the same purposes as normalized standard scores.

Normal Percentile Graphs. Increasing use is being made of a graphical technique for reporting test scores that combines some of the advantages of percentiles and normalized standard scores. Reference to Figure 15 will suggest how such a combination can be effected. If successive percentile units are spaced closer together at the center and farther apart as the extremes of the distribution are approached, they can be made to correspond to equal units on the baseline of a normal curve. The plotting of such percentile points is facilitated by the use of arithmetic probability paper, a cross-section paper in which the vertical lines are spaced in the same way as the percentile points in a normal distribution, while the horizontal lines are uniformly spaced.

When percentile scores are indicated on such a graph, the relationships among them can be properly visualized in terms of normally distributed scores. For example, if individuals A, B, C, and D receive percentile scores of 10, 20, 40, and 50, respectively, it will be apparent on such a graph that the difference in performance between individuals A and B is much larger than that between individuals C and D. If standard scores are also indicated along the axis of such a graph, percentiles can be converted to standard scores at a glance.

A relatively early use of such a combination of percentiles and standard scores is to be found in the *Normal Percentile Chart* prepared by Otis (21). This chart is designed for recording the performance of a whole group on one or two tests. It can be used to facilitate the computation of norms in terms of both percentiles and normalized standard scores, as well as for a number of other purposes related to the interpretation of test results.

Normal percentile graphs have also proved helpful in plotting individual *profiles*. Such profiles show the subject's relative standing on different tests, all scores being expressed in comparable units and with reference to a common norm. The profile method of reporting scores has become especially prominent in connection with the growing use of batteries for the differential testing of aptitudes. Among the current batteries that employ normal percentile graphs in plotting profiles are the tests of Primary Mental Abilities published by Science Research Associates and the Differential Aptitude Tests prepared by The Psychological Corporation. Since the percentile points are spaced in accordance with normal curve distances, the individual's relative standing on different tests is not distorted. If, as in the Differential Aptitude Tests, standard score equivalents are also provided on the graph, numerical scores that are likewise free from distortion can be read directly from the graph. Part of a sample report form from the Differential Aptitude Tests is reproduced in Figure 16.

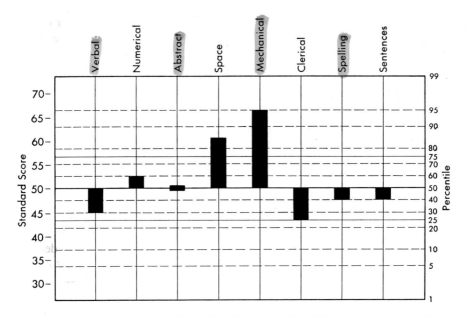

Fig. 16. Individual Report Form for Use with the Differential Aptitude Tests, Illustrating the Application of Normal Percentile Graphs in Plotting Profiles. (From Bennett, Seashore, and Wesman, 4, p. 22; reproduced by permission of The Psychological Corporation.)

The Deviation IQ. Another adaptation of standard scores is to be found in the recently developed concept of a deviation IQ. These so-called IQ's are actually standard scores with a mean of 100 and an *SD* that approximates the *SD* of the familiar Stanford-Binet IQ distribution. Although the *SD* of the 1937 Stanford-Binet IQ was not exactly constant at all ages, it fluctuated around a median value slightly greater than 16 (24, p. 40). Hence if an *SD* close to 16 is chosen in reporting standard scores on a newly developed test, the resulting scores can be interpreted in the same way as Stanford-Binet IQ's. Since Stanford-Binet IQ's have been in use for many years, testers and clinicians have become accustomed to interpreting and classifying test performance in terms of such IQ levels. They have learned what to expect from individuals with IQ's of 40, 70, 90, 130, and so forth. There are therefore certain practical advantages in the use of a derived scale that corresponds to the familiar distribution of Stanford-Binet IQ's. Such a correspondence of score units can be achieved by the selection of numerical values for the mean and *SD* that agree closely with those in the Stanford-Binet distribution.

It should be added that the use of the term "IQ" to designate such standard scores may at first be somewhat misleading. Such IQ's are not derived by the same methods employed in finding traditional ratio IQ's. They are not ratios of mental ages and chronological ages. For this reason, some criticism of the practice of calling such scores "IQ's" has been expressed. The justification lies in the general familiarity of the term "IQ," and in the fact that such scores *can* be interpreted as IQ's provided that their *SD* is approximately equal to that of previously known IQ's. The more precise expression, "deviation IQ," should eventually succeed in eliminating any confusion regarding the derivation of such measures. Among the first tests to express scores in terms of deviation IQ's were the Wechsler Intelligence Scales. In these tests, the mean is 100 and the *SD* 15. Deviation IQ's are also used in a number of current group tests of intelligence and in the 1960 revision of the Stanford-Binet.

At this stage in our discussion of converted scores, the reader may have become aware of a rapprochement among the various types of scores. Percentiles have gradually been taking on at least a graphic resemblance to normalized standard scores. Linear standard scores are indistinguishable from normalized standard scores if the original distribution of raw scores closely approximates the normal curve. Finally, standard scores are becoming IQ's, and vice versa. In connection with the last point, a re-examination of the meaning of a ratio IQ on such a test as the Stanford-Binet will show that these IQ's can themselves be interpreted as standard scores. If we know that the 1937 Stanford-Binet IQ distribution had a mean of 100 and an *SD* of approximately 16, we can conclude that an IQ of 116 falls at a distance of 1 *SD* above the mean and represents a standard score of $+1.00$. Similarly, an IQ of 132 corresponds to a standard score of $+2.00$, an IQ of 76 to a standard score of -1.50, and so forth. Moreover, a Stanford-Binet ratio IQ of 116 corresponds to a percentile rank of approximately 84, since it will be recalled that in a normal curve 84 per cent of the cases fall below $+1.00$ *SD* (Fig. 15).

In Figure 17 are summarized the relationships that exist in a normal distribution among the types of scores discussed in this chapter. These include *z* scores, AGCT scores, College Entrance Examination Board (CEEB) scores, Wechsler deviation IQ's ($SD = 15$), *T* scores, stanines, and percentiles. Ratio IQ's on any test will coincide with the given deviation IQ scale if they are normally distributed and have an *SD* of 15. Any other normally distributed IQ could be added to the chart, provided we knew its *SD*. If the *SD* is 20, for instance, then an IQ of 120 corresponds to $+1\sigma$, an IQ of 80 to -1σ, etc.

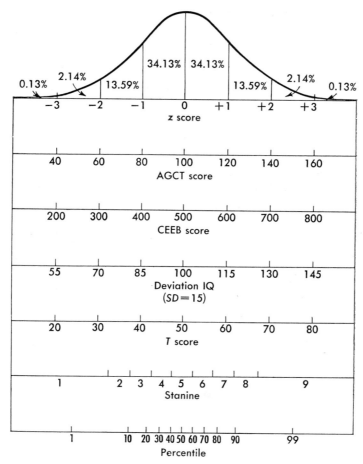

Fig. 17. Relationships among Different Types of Test Scores in a Normal Distribution.

In conclusion, the exact form in which scores are reported is dictated largely by convenience, familiarity, and ease of developing norms. Standard scores in any form (including the deviation IQ) appear to be gradually replacing other types of scores, because of certain advantages they offer with regard to test construction and statistical treatment of data. All types of converted scores, however, are fundamentally similar if carefully derived and properly interpreted. When certain statistical conditions are met, each of these scores can be readily translated into any of the others.

SPECIFICITY OF NORMS

Any norm, however expressed, is restricted to the particular normative population from which it was derived. The test user should never lose sight of the way in which norms are established. Psychological test norms are in no sense absolute, universal, or permanent. They merely represent the test performance of the subjects constituting the standardization sample. In choosing such a sample, an effort is usually made to obtain a representative cross section of the population for which the test is designed.

In statistical terminology, a distinction is made between *sample* and *population*. The former refers to the group of individuals actually tested. The latter designates the larger, but similarly constituted, group from which the sample is drawn. For example, if we wish to establish a norm of test performance for the population of native-born, white, 10-year-old, urban, public school boys, we might test a carefully chosen sample of 500 native-born, white, 10-year-old boys attending public schools in several American cities. The sample would be checked with reference to geographical distribution, socioeconomic level, and other relevant characteristics to insure that it was truly representative of the desired population.

In the development and application of test norms, considerable attention should be given to the standardization sample. It is apparent that the sample on which the norms are based should be large enough to provide stable values. Another, similarly chosen sample of the same population should not yield norms that diverge appreciably from those obtained. Norms with a large "sampling error" would obviously be of little value in the interpretation of test scores.

Equally important is the requirement that the sample be representative of the population under consideration. Subtle selective factors that might make the sample unrepresentative should be carefully investigated. A number of such selective factors are illustrated in institutional samples. Since such samples are usually large and readily available for testing purposes, they offer an alluring field for the accumulation of normative data. The special limitations of these samples, however, should be carefully analyzed. Testing subjects in school, for example, will yield an increasingly superior selection of cases in the successive grades, owing to the progressive dropping out of the less able pupils. Nor does such elimination affect different subgroups equally. For example, the rate of selective elimination from school is greater for boys than for girls (cf. 2, p. 456), and it is greater in lower than in higher socioeconomic classes (15).

Selective factors likewise operate in other institutional samples, such as prisoners, patients in mental hospitals, or institutionalized mental defectives. Because of many special factors that determine institutionalization itself, such groups are not representative of the entire population of criminals, psychotics, or mental defectives. Mental defectives with physical handicaps, for example, are more likely to be institutionalized than are the physically fit. Similarly, the relative proportion of lower-grade defectives will be much greater in institutional samples than in the total population.

Closely related to the question of representativeness of sample is the need for defining the specific population to which the norms apply. Obviously, one way of insuring that a sample is representative is to restrict the population to fit the specifications of the available sample. For example, if the population is defined to include only 14-year-old school children, rather than all 14-year-old children, then a school sample would be representative. Ideally, of course, the desired population should be defined in advance in terms of the objectives of the test. Then a suitable sample should be assembled. Practical obstacles in obtaining subjects, however, often make such a goal unattainable. In such a case, it is far better to redefine the population more narrowly than to report norms on an ideal population which is not adequately represented by the standardization sample. In actual practice, very few tests are standardized on such broad populations as is popularly assumed. No test provides norms for the human species! And it is doubtful whether any tests give truly adequate norms for such broadly defined populations as "adult American men," "American 10-year-old children," and the like.

Because of the differences in the nature of the samples upon which different tests have been standardized, the same individual may appear to be superior when measured by one test and average or inferior when measured by another. To take an extreme example, if one set of norms were based on college freshmen and another on unselected persons of the same age, any one individual would obviously rate higher in terms of the latter norms than in terms of the former. Another possible reason for the apparent discrepancy in an individual's performance on different tests designed for the same purpose is to be found in a lack of comparability of units. As explained in the preceding section, if the IQ's on one test have an *SD* of, let us say, 10, and the IQ's on another have an *SD* of 15, then an individual who received an IQ of 110 on the first test will probably obtain an IQ of 115 on the second.

It should also be noted that performance may vary appreciably from one test to another because the tests differ in content, despite the fact that such tests may be given the same label. So-called intelligence tests provide many illustrations of this situation. Although commonly described by the same blanket term, intelligence tests often vary considerably in the functions they measure. To be sure, lack of comparability of either content or test units can usually be detected by reference to the test itself or to the test manual. Differences in the respective normative samples, however, are more likely to be overlooked. Such differences probably account for many otherwise unexplained discrepancies in test results.

There is considerable evidence to indicate that scores on many tests that are commonly used interchangeably do in fact differ materially. In the Harvard Growth Study (8), the performance of elementary school children on a number of common group intelligence tests revealed consistent differences among the tests. For example, the median IQ of the entire group of 320 children was 94 on one test, 102 on another, and 110 on a third. Similarly, an IQ of 108 on the first-mentioned test corresponded to an IQ of 118 on the second and to an IQ of 124 on the third, all three scores falling at the 80th percentile of the group. In the light of the marked variations found, the authors conclude that "an IQ of 100, which is commonly interpreted as indicating average ability and a position near the center of an unselected group, represents, on tests given for the first time, positions varying from the 19th to the 65th percentile . . . from one in the lower quarter of the group, representing an ability which is supposed to approximate dullness, to one near the upper third of the distribution, indicating brightness of a promising nature" (8, p. 134).

Another, more recent analysis illustrating the same point was based upon data gathered by the World Book Company on high school students (17). Three groups of students were selected so as to be closely matched in age, grade, age-within-grade, and performance on a comprehensive academic achievement battery. The three groups thus assembled totaled nearly 1200 cases. Each of the matched groups had taken one of three widely used group intelligence tests, viz., Terman-McNemar Test of Mental Ability, Otis Quick Scoring Mental Ability Tests, and Pintner General Ability Tests (Verbal Series). From these results, a table of equivalent IQ's on the three tests was prepared by finding the scores that corresponded to given percentile points in the three distributions. This analysis revealed consistent differences between the tests. Thus the Pintner test yielded IQ's 2 to 5 points lower than those on the Terman-McNemar throughout the range. The Otis IQ's were found to have a lower *SD* than either the Pintner or the Terman-McNemar, a finding which corroborated earlier results on other groups. This discrepancy in *SD* has the effect of making IQ's fall closer to the mean on the Otis than they would on the other two tests. An IQ of 66 on the Terman-McNemar, for example, corresponds to an IQ of 76 on the Otis, while an IQ of 141 on the Terman-McNemar corresponds to one of 134 on the Otis.

To be truly comparable, scores on different tests must be expressed not only in the same units, but also with reference to comparable standardization samples. When these conditions are not met, adjustments or corrections should be applied, as illustrated by the table of equivalent IQ's cited above. In any event, an IQ or any other score should always be accompanied by the name of the test on which it was obtained. Test scores cannot be properly interpreted in the abstract; they must be referred to particular tests. If the school records show that Bill Jones received an IQ of 94 and Tom Brown an IQ of 110, such IQ's cannot be accepted at face value without further information. The positions of these two students might have been reversed by exchanging the particular tests that each was given in his respective school.

Similarly, any one individual's relative standing in different functions may be grossly misrepresented through lack of comparability of test norms. Let us suppose that an individual has been given a verbal comprehension and a spatial aptitude test to determine his relative standing in the two fields. If the verbal ability test was standardized on a random sample of high school students, while the spatial test was standardized on a selected group of boys attending elective shop courses, the examiner might erroneously conclude that the individual is much more able along verbal than along spatial lines, when the reverse may actually be the case.

Much of the confusion in the interpretation of scores from different tests could probably be avoided if the *normative populations* were defined in more specific terms. It is very difficult to obtain truly representative samples of broadly defined populations. Consequently, the samples obtained by different test constructors often tend to be unrepresentative and biased in different ways, and the resulting norms are not comparable. As already suggested, a more practicable and effective procedure is to standardize the test on a more narrowly defined population, chosen to suit the specific purposes of the test. The limitations of such a population should then be clearly stated in reporting the norms. For example, a test may be standardized on "American-born children in urban, Midwestern public schools," or upon "employed clerical workers in large business organizations," or upon "first-year engineering students." If the test proves its worth in actual practice, it may be deemed advantageous to expand the boundaries of the normative population by testing additional samples. The description of the norms would then be accordingly generalized.

For many purposes, however, highly specific norms are desirable. Thus, even when representative norms are available for a broadly defined population, it is often helpful to have separately reported *subgroup norms.* This is true whenever recognizable subgroups yield appreciably different scores on a particular test. The subgroups may be formed with respect to age, grade, type of curriculum, sex, geographical region, urban or rural environment, socioeconomic level, and many other factors. The use to be made of the test determines the type of differentiation that is most relevant, as well as whether general or specific norms are more appropriate (3, 26).

That subgroup norms do reveal marked discrepancies in many tests has been repeatedly demonstrated. On the Differential Aptitude Tests, for example, sizable sex differences in favor of boys were found in the Space Relations and Mechanical Reasoning Tests, while the girls clearly excelled in the Clerical, Spelling, and Sentences Tests (29). If a boy obtains a raw score of 40 on the Mechanical Reasoning Test, he would fall at approximately the 75th percentile in the combined distribution for both sexes. He might thus appear to show promise for a curriculum or vocation requiring mechanical understanding. In such a curriculum or occupation, however, he would compete almost entirely with other males. When evaluated in terms of the male distribution only, his raw score of 40 places him only at the 50th percentile. He would therefore be just average in reference to the type of individuals with whom he would have to compete. Similarly, a girl receiving a raw score of 53 on the Clerical Test would fall at the 40th percentile in the combined distribution, but at the 30th percentile in the girls' distribution. The latter percentile is of more practical significance, since the competition encountered in clerical training and in clerical jobs would be predominantly female (29).

Another illustration of the practical implications of subgroup norms is provided by a comparison of public and private school norms employed by the Educational Records Bureau in reporting scores on scholastic aptitude and achievement tests (26). In reading ability and on English achievement tests, for example, private high school students were about two grades ahead of public high school students. On the American Council Psychological Examination for College Freshmen, the median scores obtained by juniors and seniors in private high schools consistently excelled the medians for entering college freshmen. Selective factors probably account in large part for these differences. Because of the discrepancies in such norms, however, the evaluation of any individual's score should take cognizance of which set of norms was employed. Otherwise a college applicant from a private school, for example, would be handicapped by being judged against a higher norm.

Mention should also be made of *local norms,* often developed by the test users themselves within a particular setting. The groups employed in deriving such norms are even more narrowly defined than the subgroups considered above. Thus an employer may accumulate norms on applicants for a given type of job within his company. Or a college admissions office may develop norms on its own student population. Similarly, in selecting pilots or bombardiers, the Air Force utilized norms on applicants for pilot and bombardier training. These norms obviously permit a more accurate prediction of the individual's performance than could be made with norms derived from "men in general."

In summary, normative populations should be clearly defined. The characteristics of such populations should be taken into consideration in interpreting test scores. For many purposes, moreover, specific norms, based on more narrowly defined normative populations, are more useful than general norms.

REFERENCES

1. Anastasi, Anne. Practice and variability. *Psychol. Monogr.*, 1934, 45, No. 5.
2. Anastasi, Anne. *Differential psychology.* (3rd ed.) N. Y.: Macmillan, 1958.
3. Bauernfeind, R. H. Are sex norms necessary? *J. counsel. Psychol.*, 1956, 3, 57-63.
4. Bennett, G. K., Seashore, H. G., and Wesman, A. G. *Differential Aptitude Tests: manual.* (2nd ed.) N. Y.: Psychol. Corp., 1952.
5. Bergman, G., and Spence, K. W. The logic of psychophysical measurement. *Psychol. Rev.*, 1944, 51, 1-24.
6. Blommers, P., and Lindquist, E. F. *Elementary statistical methods in psychology and education.* Boston: Houghton Mifflin, 1960.
7. Comrey, A. L. Mental testing and the logic of measurement. *Educ. psychol. Measmt.*, 1951, 11, 323-334.
8. Dearborn, W. F., and Rothney, J. *Predicting the child's development.* Cambridge, Mass.: Sci-Art Pub., 1941.
9. Flanagan, J. C. Units, scores, and norms. In E. F. Lindquist (Ed.), *Educational measurement.* Washington: Amer. Council Educ., 1951. Pp. 695-763.
10. Gardner, E. F. Value of norms based on a new type of scale unit. *Proc. 1948 invit. Conf. test. Probl., Educ. Test. Serv.*, 1949, 67-74.
11. Garrett, H. E. *Elementary statistics.* N. Y.: Longmans, Green, 1956.
12. Garrett, H. E. *Statistics in psychology and education.* (5th ed.) N. Y.: Longmans, Green, 1958.
13. Goodenough, Florence L. Studies of the 1937 revision of the Stanford-Binet Scale: I. Variability of the IQ at successive age-levels. *J. educ. Psychol.*, 1942, 33, 241-251.
14. Guilford, J. P. *Fundamental statistics in psychology and education.* (3rd ed.) N. Y.: McGraw-Hill, 1956.
15. Havighurst, R. J. Sociological and psychological factors affecting the supply of talent. *Proc. 1951 invit. Conf. test. Probl., Educ. Test. Serv.*, 1952, 24-33.

16. Kaiser, H. F. A modified stanine scale. *J. exp. Educ.*, 1958, 26, 261.
17. Lennon, R. T. A comparison of results of three intelligence tests. *Test Service Notebook, World Book Co.*, 1952, No. 11.
18. Lorge, I. The fundamental nature of measurement. In E. F. Lindquist (Ed.), *Educational measurement.* Washington: Amer. Council. Educ., 1951. Pp. 533-559.
19. McCall, W. A. *How to measure in education.* N. Y.: Macmillan, 1922.
20. McNemar, Q. *The revision of the Stanford-Binet Scale: an analysis of the standardization data.* Boston: Houghton Mifflin, 1942.
21. Otis, A. S. *Normal Percentile Chart: manual of directions.* Tarrytown-on-Hudson, N. Y.: World Book Co., 1938.
22. Stevens, S. S. On the theory of scales of measurement. *Science,* 1946, 103, 677-680.
23. Stutsman, Rachel. *Mental measurement of preschool children with a guide for the administration of the Merrill-Palmer Scale of Mental Tests.* Tarrytown-on-Hudson, N. Y.: World Book Co., 1931.
24. Terman, L. M., and Merrill, Maud A. *Measuring intelligence.* Boston: Houghton Mifflin, 1937.
25. Terman, L. M., and Merrill, Maud A. *Stanford-Binet Intelligence Scale: manual for the third revision, Form L-M.* Boston: Houghton Mifflin, 1960.
26. Traxler, A. E. Norms for scholastic aptitude and achievement tests of independent secondary school pupils. *Proc. 1948 invit. Conf. test. Probl., Educ. Test. Serv.,* 1949, 81-94.
27. Walker, Helen M., and Lev, J. *Statistical inference.* N. Y.: Holt, Rinehart and Winston, 1953.
28. Walker, Helen M., and Lev, J. *Elementary statistical methods.* (Rev. ed.) N. Y.: Holt, Rinehart and Winston, 1958.
29. Wesman, A. G. Separation of sex groups in test reporting. *J. educ. Psychol.,* 1949, 40, 223-229.

CHAPTER 5

Test Reliability

The reliability of a test refers to the consistency of scores obtained by the same individuals on different occasions or with different sets of equivalent items. This concept of reliability underlies the *error of measurement* of a single score, whereby we can predict the range of fluctuation likely to occur in a single individual's score as a result of irrelevant, chance factors.

Test reliability should not be confused with the reliability of statistical measures. When, for example, we speak of the reliability of means, standard deviations, or correlations, or when we inquire whether a difference betwen two means is statistically significant, we refer primarily to *sampling error.* In other words, we wish to know the consistency of these statistical measures when redetermined on a different sample of the same population. Such a question is obviously basic to the interpretation of any experimental results, since the conclusions of scientific investigations are rarely, if ever, restricted to the particular sample studied.

In common with other psychological investigations, analyses of test scores frequently involve questions of sampling error. Such an error, however, should be differentiated from the error of measurement, with which the present chapter is concerned. Sampling error pertains to the consistency of results obtained when observations are repeated on *different individuals;* error of measurement, to the consistency of results obtained when observations are repeated on the *same individuals.*

TYPES OF TEST RELIABILITY

The concept of test reliability itself has been used to cover not one but several aspects of score consistency. During the past quarter-century, attention has been called repeatedly to the ambiguity of the blanket term, "test reliability," and several more specific designations have been proposed from

105

time to time. The *Technical Recommendations for Psychological Tests and Diagnostic Techniques* (1), prepared by the American Psychological Association, have helped to systematize terminology in this area. It should be noted that no one type or measure of test reliability is universally preferable. The choice depends upon the use to which the test scores are to be put.

In its broadest sense, test reliability indicates the extent to which individual differences in test scores are attributable to chance errors of measurement, and the extent to which they are attributable to true differences in the characteristic under consideration. To state it in more technical terms, every measure of test reliability denotes what proportion of the total variance of test scores is "error variance." The crux of the matter, however, lies in the definition of error variance. Factors that might be considered error variance for one purpose would be classified under true variance for another. For example, if we are interested in measuring fluctuations of mood, then the day-by-day changes in scores on a test of cheerfulness-depression would be relevant to the purpose of the test and would hence be part of the true variance of the scores. If, on the other hand, the test is designed to measure more permanent personality characteristics, the same daily fluctuations would fall under the heading of error variance.

Essentially, any condition that is irrelevant to the purpose of the test represents error variance. Thus when the examiner tries to maintain uniform testing conditions by controlling the testing environment, instructions, time limits, rapport, and other similar factors, he is reducing error variance and making the test scores more reliable. Despite optimum testing conditions, however, no test is a perfectly reliable instrument. Hence every test should be accompanied by a statement of its reliability. Such a measure of reliability characterizes the test when administered under standard conditions and given to subjects similar to those constituting the normative sample. The characteristics of such a sample should therefore be specified, together with the type of reliability that was measured.

There could, of course, be as many varieties of test reliability as there are conditions affecting test scores, since any such conditions might be irrelevant for a certain purpose and would thus be classified as error variance. The types of reliability computed in actual practice, however, are relatively few. The principal sources of error variance underlying the common measures of test reliability will be considered below. In a later section of the chapter, the relation between different concepts of reliability and specific techniques currently employed to measure test reliability will be examined.

Temporal Stability. An obvious source of error variance for most testing purposes is to be found in the random fluctuations of performance occurring from one test session to another. These variations may result in part from uncontrolled testing conditions, such as extreme changes in weather, sudden noises and other distractions, or a broken pencil point. To some extent, however, they arise from changes in the condition of the subject himself, as illustrated by illness, fatigue, emotional strain, worry, recent experiences of a pleasant or unpleasant nature, and the like. Temporal stability indicates the degree to which scores on a test are affected by the random daily fluctuations in the condition of the subject or of the testing environment. It is obvious that the temporal stability of a test depends in part upon the length of interval over which stability is measured. Illustrations could readily be cited of tests showing high reliability over periods of a few days or weeks, but whose scores reveal an almost complete lack of correspondence when the interval is extended to as long as ten or fifteen years. Many preschool intelligence tests, for example, yield moderately stable measures within the preschool period, but are virtually useless as predictors of late childhood or adult IQ's.

In actual practice, however, a simple distinction can usually be made. Short-range, random fluctuations that occur during intervals ranging from a few hours to a few months are generally included under the error variance of the test score. Thus in checking this type of test reliability, an effort is made to keep the interval short. In testing young children, the period should be even shorter than for older subjects, since at early ages progressive developmental changes are discernible over a period of a month or even less. For any type of subject, the interval between retests should rarely exceed six months.

Any additional changes in the relative test performance of individuals that occur over longer periods of time are apt to be cumulative and progressive rather than entirely random. Moreover, they are likely to characterize a broader area of behavior than that covered by the test performance itself. Thus an individual's general level of scholastic aptitude, mechanical comprehension, or artistic judgment may have altered appreciably over a ten-year period, owing to unusual intervening experiences. The individual's status may have either risen or dropped appreciably in relation to others of his own age, because of circumstances peculiar to his own home, school, or community environment, or for other reasons such as illness or emotional disturbance.

The extent to which such factors can affect an individual's psychological development provides an important problem for investigation. This question, however, should not be confused with the stability of a particular test. Thus when we measure the reliability of the Stanford-Binet or the Minnesota Preschool Test, we would not ordinarily check the stability of the scores over a period of ten years, or even one year, but over a few weeks. To be sure, long-range retests have been conducted with such tests, but the results are generally discussed in terms of the "constancy of the IQ" or the predictability of adult intelligence from childhood performance, rather than in terms of the reliability of a particular test. The concept of reliability is generally restricted to short-range, random changes that characterize the test performance itself rather than the criterion behavior.

It should be noted that different behavior functions may themselves vary in the extent of daily fluctuation they exhibit. For example, steadiness of delicate finger movements is undoubtedly more susceptible to slight changes in the subject's condition than is verbal comprehension. If we wish to obtain an over-all estimate of the individual's habitual finger steadiness, we would probably require repeated tests on several days, while a single test session would suffice for verbal comprehension. Again we must fall back on an analysis of the purposes of the test and on a thorough understanding of the behavior the test is designed to predict.

Item Sampling. Everyone has probably had the experience of taking a course examination in which he felt he had a "lucky break" because many of the items covered the very topics he happened to have studied most carefully. On another occasion, he may have had the opposite experience, finding an unusually large number of items on areas he had failed to review. This familiar situation illustrates a second source of error variance in test scores. To what extent do scores on this test depend upon factors *specific* to the particular selection of items? If a different investigator, working independently , were to prepare another test in accordance with the same specifications, how much would an individual's score differ on the two tests?

Let us suppose that a 40-item vocabulary test has been constructed as a measure of general word comprehension. Now suppose that a second list of 40 different words is assembled for the same purpose, and that the items are constructed with equal care to cover the same range of difficulty as the first test. The differences in the scores obtained by the same individuals on these two tests illustrate the type of reliability under consideration. Owing to fortuitous factors in the past experience of different subjects, the relative difficulty of the two lists will vary somewhat from person to person. Thus the first list might contain a larger number of words unfamiliar to individual A than does the second list. The second list, on the other hand, might contain a disproportionately large number of words unfamiliar to individual B. If the two individuals are approximately equal in their over-all word knowledge (i.e., in their "true scores"), B will nevertheless excel A on the first list, while A will excel B on the second. The relative standing of these two subjects will therefore be reversed on the two lists, owing to chance differences in the selection of items.

Homogeneity of Items. Test homogeneity refers essentially to *consistency of performance on all items within a test.* For example, if one test includes only multiplication items, while another comprises addition, subtraction, multiplication, and division items, the former test will probably show more interitem consistency than the latter. In the latter, more heterogeneous test, one subject may perform better in subtraction than in any of the other arithmetic operations; another subject may score relatively well on the division items, but more poorly in addition, subtraction, and multiplication; and so on. A more extreme example would be represented by a test consisting of 40 vocabulary items, in contrast to one containing 10 vocabulary, 10 spatial relations, 10 arithmetic reasoning, and 10 perceptual speed items. In the latter test, there might be little or no relationship between a subject's performance on the different types of items.

It is apparent that test scores will be less ambiguous when derived from relatively homogeneous tests. Suppose that in the highly heterogeneous, 40-item test cited above, individuals A and B both obtain a score of 20. Can we conclude that the performances of the two subjects on this test were equal? Not at all. Subject A might have correctly completed 10 vocabulary items, 10 perceptual speed items, and none of the arithmetic reasoning and spatial relations items. In contrast, Subject B could have received a score of 20 by the successful completion of 5 perceptual speed, 5 spatial relations, and 10 arithmetic reasoning items.

Many other combinations could obviously produce the same total score of 20. Such a score would have a very different meaning when obtained through such dissimilar combinations of items. In the relatively homogeneous vocabulary test, on the other hand, a score of 20 would probably mean that the subject had succeeded with approximately the first 20 words, if the items were arranged in ascending order of difficulty. He might have failed two or three easier words and correctly responded to two or three more difficult items beyond the 20th, but such individual variations are slight in comparison with those found in a more heterogeneous test.

A highly relevant question in this connection is whether the criterion that the test is trying to predict is itself relatively homogeneous or heterogeneous. Although homogeneous tests are to be preferred because their scores permit fairly unambiguous interpretation, a single homogeneous test is obviously not an adequate predictor of a highly heterogeneous criterion. Moreover, in the prediction of a heterogeneous criterion, the heterogeneity of test items would not necessarily represent error variance. Traditional intelligence tests provide a good example of heterogeneous tests designed to predict a heterogeneous criterion. In such a case, however, it may be desirable to construct several relatively homogeneous tests, each measuring a different phase of the heterogeneous criterion. Thus unambiguous interpretation of test scores could be combined with adequate criterion coverage.

How does homogeneity differ from adequacy of item sampling, discussed in the preceding section? An extreme example will serve to highlight the difference. Suppose every item in a certain test measures a different and unrelated function. It would be entirely possible to construct another, parallel form of such a test containing the same types and distribution of items as the first form. The scores on the two forms could theoretically agree closely, thus indicating high test reliability in terms of item sampling. The homogeneity of this test, however, would be close to zero, since the consistency of performance from item to item within either form would be no better than chance.

Whether homogeneity should be classified under reliability is a debatable point. Many psychometricians would agree that homogeneity can be more properly regarded as a separate property of tests, distinct from the traditional concepts of either reliability or validity. It is included in the present discussion, however, since it enters into certain measures of reliability to be considered in a later section of the chapter. In any event, the concept of homogeneity should be clearly distinguished from the other forms of reliability already discussed.

Examiner and Scorer Reliability. It should now be apparent that the different concepts of test reliability vary in the factors they subsume under "error variance." In one case, error variance covers temporal fluctuations; in another, it refers to differences between sets of parallel items; and in still another, it includes any interitem inconsistency. On the other hand, the factors excluded from measures of error variance are broadly of two types: (*a*) those factors whose variance should remain in the scores, since they are part of the true differences under consideration; and (*b*) those irrelevant factors that can be experimentally controlled. For example, it is not customary to report the error of measurement resulting when a test is administered under distracting conditions or with a longer or shorter time limit than that specified in the manual. Timing errors and serious distractions can be empirically eliminated from the testing situation. Hence it is not necessary to report special reliability coefficients corresponding to "distraction variance" or "timing variance."

Similarly, most tests provide such highly standardized procedures for administration and scoring that "examiner reliability" and "scorer reliability" can be assumed to be sufficiently high for practical purposes. There is thus no special need for measuring such types of reliability. This is particularly true of group tests designed for mass testing and machine scoring. In such tests we need only to make certain that the prescribed procedures are followed carefully. The problem is thus one of *empirical control of conditions.*

In certain individual tests, however, the role of the examiner is far more complex. As illustrations may be cited the Stanford-Binet and most preschool tests. The testing procedure in such cases is not so rigidly standardized. Much depends upon the examiner's success in establishing rapport and arousing adequate motivation. Often the subject's performance needs to be evaluated by the examiner during the process of test administration, since such performance determines how the examiner is to proceed with the testing. Under such conditions, it is likely that even properly qualified examiners may sometimes obtain different results from the same subjects. These variations in score would constitute error variance attributable to individual differences or idiosyncrasies among examiners.

An illustration of "examiner variance" is provided by an analysis of Stanford-Binet IQ's obtained by different examiners in the Harvard Growth Study (5). Differences as large as 13 points were found between the mean IQ's reported by two examiners for the same group of subjects. For individual subjects, differences of as much as 30 or 40 points were noted. In tests in which examiner idiosyncrasy may play an appreciable part, it appears desirable to obtain some measure of the "examiner reliability" of the test, especially when results by several examiners are to be combined.

Similarly, certain types of tests present a problem of "scorer reliability." In an investigation of the Goodenough Draw-a-Man Test of intelligence, for example, the drawings by 386 children were scored independently by three trained scorers (18). For about 25 per cent of the cases, interscorer discrepancies were found that amounted to a year or more of mental age. Such variations occurred despite the fact that a fairly objective system of credit points has been developed for scoring this test, a system in which the three scorers had been thoroughly trained.

With the widespread use of projective techniques as measures of personality, the question of scorer reliability is receiving increasing attention. Many current projective techniques leave much to the subjective interpretation of the scorer, who is also usually the examiner. With such well-known instruments as the Rorschach inkblot test, for example, the lack of consistency sometimes found between the diagnoses reached from the same records by different experienced scorers is truly astounding (cf., e.g., 11). When specific response categories are compared, the degree of scorer agreement is much higher but still falls far short of perfect reliability (cf. 8, 20, 21). For such tests, there appears to be fully as much need for an index of scorer reliability as for the more usual measures of reliability.

TECHNIQUES FOR MEASURING TEST RELIABILITY

The Correlation Coefficient. Since all types of test reliability are concerned with the degree of consistency or agreement between two independently derived sets of scores, they can all be expressed in terms of a correlation coefficient, whose statistical symbol is r. A discussion of correlation coefficients can be found in any elementary text on statistics (cf., e.g., 4, 9, 10, 12, 24, 25). For the present purpose, it will suffice to note some of the principal characteristics of such coefficients. Essentially, a correlation coefficient expresses the degree of correspondence, or relationship, between two sets of scores. Thus if the top-scoring individual in variable 1 also obtains the top score in variable 2, the second-best individual in variable 1 is second best in variable 2, and so on down to the poorest individual in the group, then there would be a perfect correlation between variables 1 and 2. Such a correlation would have a value of + 1.00.

A hypothetical illustration of a perfect positive correlation is shown in Figure 18. In this figure will be found a scatter diagram, or bivariate distribution. Each tally mark in this diagram indicates the score of one individual

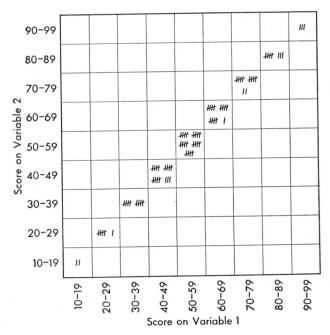

Fig. 18. Bivariate Distribution for a Hypothetical Correlation of +1.00.

in both variable 1 (horizontal axis) and variable 2 (vertical axis). It will be noted that all of the 100 cases in the group are distributed along the diagonal running from the lower left- to the upper right-hand corner of the diagram. Such a distribution indicates a perfect positive correlation (+1.00), since it shows that each individual occupies the same relative position in both variables. The closer the bivariate distribution of scores approaches this diagonal, the higher will be the positive correlation.

Figure 19 illustrates a perfect negative correlation (−1.00). In this case, there is a complete reversal of scores from one variable to the other. The best individual in variable 1 is the poorest in variable 2 and vice versa, this reversal being consistently maintained throughout the distribution. It will be noted that, in this scatter diagram, all individuals fall on the diagonal extending from the upper left- to the lower right-hand corner. This diagonal runs in the reverse direction from that in Figure 18.

A zero correlation indicates complete absence of relationship, such as might occur by chance. If each individual's name were pulled at random out of a hat to determine his position in variable 1, and if the process were repeated for variable 2, a zero or near-zero correlation would result. Under these conditions, it would be impossible to predict an individual's relative standing in variable 2 from a knowledge of his score in variable 1. The top-

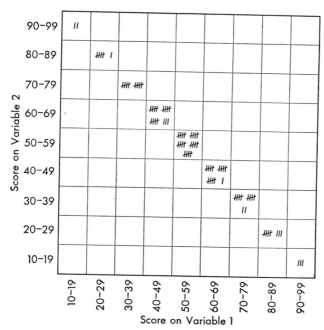

Fig. 19. Bivariate Distribution for a Hypothetical Correlation of −1.00.

scoring subject in variable 1 might score high, low, or average in variable 2. Some individuals might by chance score above average in both variables, or below average in both; others might fall above average in one variable and below in the other; still others might be above the average in one and at the average in the second, and so forth. There would be no regularity in the relationship from one individual to another.

The coefficients found in actual practice generally fall between these extremes, having some value higher than zero but lower than 1.00. Correlations between measures of abilities are nearly always positive, although frequently low. When a negative correlation is obtained between two such variables, it usually results from the way in which the scores are expressed. For example, if time scores are correlated with amount scores, a negative correlation will probably result. Thus if each subject's score on an arithmetic computation test is recorded as the number of seconds required to complete all items, while his score on an arithmetic reasoning test represents the number of problems correctly solved, a negative correlation can be expected. In such a case, the poorest (i.e., slowest) individual will have the numerically highest score on the first test, while the best individual will have the highest score on the second.

Correlation coefficients may be computed in various ways, depending upon the nature of the data. The most common is the *Pearson Product-Moment Correlation Coefficient.* Such a correlation coefficient takes into account not only the individual's position in the group, but also the amount of his deviation above or below the group mean. It will be recalled that when each individual's standing is expressed in terms of standard scores, persons falling above the average receive positive standard scores, while those below the average receive negative scores. Thus an individual who is superior in both variables to be correlated would have two positive standard scores; one inferior in both would have two negative standard scores. If, now, we multiply each individual's standard score in variable 1 by his standard score in variable 2, all of these products will be positive, provided that each individual falls on the same side of the mean on both variables. The Pearson correlation coefficient is simply the mean of these products. It will have a high positive value when corresponding standard scores are of equal sign and of approximately equal amount in the two variables. When subjects above the average in one variable are below the average in the other, the corresponding cross-products will be negative. If the sum of the cross-products is negative, the correlation will be negative. When some products are positive and some negative, the correlation will be close to zero.

In actual practice, it is not necessary to convert each raw score to a standard score before finding the cross-products, since this conversion can be made once for all after the cross-products have been added. There are many short-cuts for computing the Pearson correlation coefficient. One method is demon-strated in Table 6, with hypothetical data for 10 cases. Next to each child's

TABLE 6. Computation of Pearson Product-Moment Correlation Coefficient

Pupil	Arithmetic X	Reading Y	x	y	x^2	y^2	xy
Bill	41	17	+ 1	− 4	1	16	− 4
Carol	38	28	− 2	+ 7	4	49	− 14
Geoffrey	48	22	+ 8	+ 1	64	1	8
Ann	32	16	− 8	− 5	64	25	40
Bob	34	18	− 6	− 3	36	9	18
Jane	36	15	− 4	− 6	16	36	24
Ellen	41	24	+ 1	+ 3	1	9	3
Ruth	43	20	+ 3	− 1	9	1	− 3
Dick	47	23	+ 7	+ 2	49	4	14
Mary	40	27	0	+ 6	0	36	0
Σ	400	210	0	0	244	186	86
M	40	21					

$$\sigma_x = \sqrt{\frac{244}{10}} = \sqrt{24.40} = 4.94 \qquad \sigma_y = \sqrt{\frac{186}{10}} = \sqrt{18.60} = 4.31$$

$$r_{xy} = \frac{\Sigma xy}{N \sigma_x \sigma_y} = \frac{86}{(10)\,(4.94)\,(4.31)} = \frac{86}{212.91} = .40$$

name are his scores in an arithmetic test (X) and a reading test (Y). The sums and means of the 10 scores are given under the respective columns. The third column shows the deviation (x) of each arithmetic score from the arithmetic mean; and the fourth column, the deviation (y) of each reading score from the reading mean. These deviations are squared in the next two columns, and the sums of the squares are used in computing the standard deviations of the arithmetic and reading scores by the method described in Chapter 4. Rather than dividing each x and y by its corresponding σ to find standard scores, we perform this division only once at the end, as shown in the correlation formula in Table 6. The cross-products in the last column (xy) have been found by multiplying the corresponding deviations in the x and y columns. To compute the correlation (r), the sum of these cross-products is divided by the number of cases (N) and by the product of the two standard deviations $(\sigma_x \sigma_y)$.

The correlation of .40 found in Table 6 indicates a moderate degree of positive relationship between the arithmetic and reading scores. There is some tendency for those children doing well in arithmetic also to perform well on the reading test and vice versa, although the relation is not close. If we are concerned only with the performance of these 10 children, we can accept this correlation as an adequate description of the degree of relation existing between the two variables in this group. In psychological research, however, we are usually interested in generalizing beyond the particular *sample* of individuals tested to a larger *population* which they represent. For example, we might want to know whether arithmetic and reading ability are correlated among American school children of the same age as those we tested. Obviously the 10 cases actually examined would constitute a very inadequate sample of such a population. Another comparable sample of the same size might yield a much lower or a much higher correlation.

There are statistical procedures for estimating the probable fluctuation to be expected from sample to sample in the size of correlations, means, standard deviations, and any other group measures. The question usually asked about correlations, however, is simply whether the correlation is significantly greater than zero. In other words, if the correlation in the population is zero, could a correlation as high as that obtained in our sample have resulted from sampling error alone? When we say that a correlation is "significant at the 1 per cent (.01) level," we mean the chances are no greater than one out of 100 that the population correlation is zero. Hence we conclude that the two variables are truly correlated. Significance levels refer to the risk of error we are willing to take in drawing conclusions from our data. If a correlation is said to be significant at the .05 level, the probability of error is 5 out of 100. Most psychological research applies either the .01 or the .05 levels, although other significance levels may be employed for special reasons.

The correlation of .40 found in Table 6 fails to reach significance even at the .05 level. As might have been anticipated, with only 10 cases it is difficult to establish a general relationship conclusively. With this size of sample, the smallest correlation significant at the .05 level is .63. Any correlation below that value simply leaves unanswered the question of whether the two variables are correlated in the population from which the sample was drawn.

The minimum correlations significant at the .01 and .05 levels for groups of different sizes can be found by consulting tables of the significance of correlations in any statistics textbook. For interpretive purposes in this book, however, only an understanding of the general concept is required. Parenthetically, it might be added that significance levels can be interpreted in a similar way when applied to other statistical measures. For example, to say that the difference between two means is significant at the .01 level indicates that we can conclude, with only one chance out of 100 of being wrong, that a difference in the obtained direction would be found if we tested the whole population from which our samples were drawn. For instance, if in the sample tested the boys had obtained a significantly higher mean than the girls on a mechanical comprehension test, we could conclude that the boys would also excel in the total population.

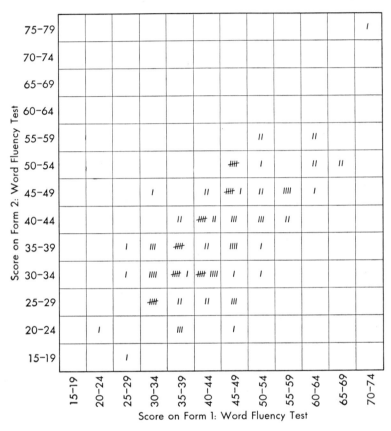

Fig. 20. A Reliability Coefficient of .72. (Data from Anastasi and Drake, 2.)

Correlation coefficients have many uses in the analysis of psychological data. The measurement of test reliability represents one application of such coefficients. An example of a reliability coefficient, computed by the Pearson Product-Moment method, is to be found in Figure 20. In this case, the scores of 104 persons on two equivalent forms of a Word Fluency test[1] were correlated. In one form, the subjects were given five minutes to write as many

---

[1] One of the subtests of the SRA Tests of Primary Mental Abilities for Ages 11 to 17. The data were obtained in an investigation by Anastasi and Drake (2).

words as they could that began with a given letter. The second form was identical, except that a different letter was employed. The two letters were chosen by the test authors as being approximately equal in difficulty for this purpose.

The correlation between the number of words written in the two forms of this test was found to be .72. This correlation is high and significant at the .01 level. With 104 cases, any correlation of .25 or higher is significant at this level. Nevertheless, the obtained correlation is somewhat lower than is desirable for reliability coefficients, which usually fall in the .80's or .90's. An examination of the scatter diagram in Figure 20 shows a typical bivariate distribution of scores corresponding to a high positive correlation. It will be noted that the tallies cluster close to the diagonal extending from the lower left- to the upper right-hand corner; the trend is definitely in this direction, although there is a certain amount of scatter of individual entries. In the following sections, the use of the correlation coefficient in computing different measures of test reliability will be considered.

Retest Reliability. The most obvious method for finding the reliability of a test is by means of a retest, or repetition of the identical test on a second occasion. The reliability coefficient (r_{11}) in this case is simply the correlation between the scores obtained by the same subjects on the two administrations of the test. Such a reliability coefficient is known as the *coefficient of stability* (1) and corresponds to the first concept of reliability discussed in the first part of this chapter.

Although apparently simple and straightforward, this technique presents difficulties when applied to most psychological tests. Practice will probably produce varying amounts of improvement in the retest scores of different individuals. Moreover, if the interval between retests is fairly short, the subjects may recall many of their former responses. In other words, the same pattern of right and wrong responses is likely to recur through sheer memory. Thus the scores on the two administrations of the test are not independently obtained and the correlation between them will be spuriously high. The nature of the test itself may also change with repetition. This is especially true of problems involving reasoning or ingenuity. Once the subject has grasped the principle involved in the problem, or once he has worked out a solution, he can reproduce the correct response in the future without going through the intervening steps. Only tests that are not appreciably affected by repetition lend themselves to the retest technique. A number of sensory discrimination and motor tests would fall into this category. For the large majority of psychological tests, however, the retest technique is not suitable.

It might be added that a coefficient of *scorer reliability* can usually be found by correlating the scores independently obtained by two scorers with the same set of tests. Each subject would thus receive two scores, not from a retest, but from a rescoring of a single test. The limitations of the retest technique would not apply to such a reliability coefficient. In the previously cited study of the Goodenough Draw-a-Man Test, for example, interscorer correlations of .87, .90, and .92 were found among three scorers (18).

Examiner reliability, on the other hand, presents more complications. By its very nature, it involves a retest. Such a retest by different examiners would obviously be subject to the same limitations as retests by the same examiner discussed above. Moreover, the correlation between the two sets of scores thus obtained would reflect both temporal stability and examiner reliability. Through a different type of experimental design, however, it is possible to isolate the error variance attributable to examiners. An application of analysis of variance to this problem can be found in a study on visual acuity tests, conducted by the Pesonnel Research Branch of The Adjutant General's Office (23, pp. 130-131). Three of the 14 tests investigated proved to have significant variance attributable to examiners.

Equivalent-Form Reliability. One way of avoiding the difficulties encountered in retest reliability is through the use of equivalent forms of the test. The subjects can then be tested with one form on the first occasion and with another, comparable form on the second. The correlation between the scores obtained on the two forms represents the reliability coefficient of the test. It will be noted that such a reliability coefficient is a measure of both temporal stability and consistency of response to different item samples. Such a coefficient thus reflects two aspects of test reliability. Since both aspects are important for most testing purposes, however, parallel-form reliability provides a useful index for evaluating many tests. If the two forms are administered in immediate succession or at essentially the same time, the resulting correlation is designated as the *coefficient of equivalence* (1). The error variance measured by such a coefficient reflects variations in performance from one specific set of items to another, but not from one occasion to another.

In the development of parallel forms, care should of course be exercised to insure that they are truly parallel. Fundamentally, parallel forms of a test should be independently constructed tests designed to meet the same specifications. The tests should contain the same number of items, and such items should be expressed in the same form and should cover the same type of content. The range and level of difficulty of the items should likewise be equal. Instructions, time limits, illustrative examples, format, and all other aspects of the test need to be checked for comparability. Only when the two forms are actually equivalent can the differences in score from one form to the other be considered as error variance.

It should be added that the availability of equivalent test forms is desirable for other reasons besides the determination of test reliability. Alternate forms are useful in follow-up studies or in investigations of the effects of some intervening experimental factor upon test performance. The use of several alternate forms also provides a means of reducing the possibility of coaching or cheating.

Although much more widely applicable than retest reliability, equivalent-form reliability also has certain limitations. In the first place, if the behavior functions under consideration are subject to a large practice effect, the use of parallel forms will reduce but not eliminate such an effect. To be sure, if all subjects were to show the same improvement with repetition, the correlation between their scores would remain unaffected, since adding a constant amount to each score does not alter the correlation coefficient. It is much more likely, however, that individuals will differ in amount of improvement, owing to extent of previous practice with similar material, motivation in taking the test, and other factors. Under these conditions the practice effect represents another source of variance that will tend to reduce the correlation between the two test forms. If the practice effect is small, reduction will be negligible.

Another related question to be considered is the degree to which the nature of the test will change with repetition. In certain types of ingenuity problems, for example, any item involving the same principle can be readily solved by most subjects once they have worked out the solution to the first. In such a case, changing the specific content of the items in the second form would not suffice to eliminate this carry-over from the first form. Finally, it should be added that equivalent forms are still unavailable for many tests, because of the practical difficulties of constructing comparable forms. For all of these reasons, some other technique for estimating test reliability is required.

Split-half Reliability. From a single administration of one form of a test it is possible to arrive at a measure of test reliability by various split-half procedures. In such a way, two scores are obtained for each individual by dividing the test into comparable halves. It is apparent that split-half reliability provides a measure of equivalence, or adequacy of item sampling. Temporal stability of the scores does not enter into such a measure, since only one test session is involved.

The first problem is how to split the test in order to obtain the most nearly comparable halves. Any test can be divided in many different ways. In most tests, the first half and the second half would not be comparable, owing to differences in nature and difficulty level of the items, as well as to the cumulative effects of warming up, practice, fatigue, boredom, and any other factors varying progressively from the beginning to the end of the test. A precise and objective way of obtaining two comparable halves is to determine the difficulty level of each item on one group of persons, by finding the percentage who pass each item. Items are then assigned to the two halves on the basis of equivalent difficulty and similarity of content. The reliability is found by correlating the scores obtained on these two halves by a second group of persons.

A procedure that is adequate for most purposes and much less laborious, however, is to find the scores on the odd and even items of the test. If the items were originally arranged in an approximate order of difficulty, such a division yields very nearly equivalent half-scores. One precaution to be observed in making such an odd-even split pertains to groups of items dealing with a single problem, such as questions referring to a particular mechanical diagram or to a given passage in a reading test. In such a case, a whole group of items should be assigned intact to one or the other half. Were the items in such a group to be placed in different halves of the test, the similarity of the half-scores would be spuriously inflated, since any single error in understanding of the problem might affect items in both halves.

Once the two half-scores have been obtained for each subject, they may be correlated by the usual method. It should be noted, however, that such a correlation actually gives the reliability of only a half-test. For example, if the entire test consists of 100 items, the correlation is computed between two sets of scores each of which is based on only 50 items. In both retest and equivalent form reliability, on the other hand, each score is based on the full number of items in the test.

Other things being equal, the longer a test, the more reliable it will be. It is reasonable to expect that, with a larger sample of behavior, we can arrive at a more adequate and stable measure. The effect that lengthening or shortening a test will have upon its reliability coefficient can be estimated by means of the Spearman-Brown formula, given below:

$$r_{11} = \frac{nr'_{11}}{1 + (n-1)r'_{11}}$$

in which r_{11} is the estimated coefficient, r'_{11} the obtained coefficient, and n is the number of times the test is lengthened or shortened. Thus if the number of test items is increased from 25 to 100, n is 4; if it is decreased from 60 to 30, n is $\frac{1}{2}$. The Spearman-Brown formula is widely used in determining test reliability by the split-half method, many test manuals reporting reliability in this form. When applied to split-half reliability, the formula aways involves doubling the length of the test. Under these conditions, it can be simplified as follows:

$$r_{11} = \frac{2r'_{11}}{1 + r'_{11}}$$

A weakness of the Spearman-Brown formula stems from its assumption that the variabilities of the two half-scores are equal. Such an assumption may not always be met, even when the half-scores appear to be comparable. A better procedure, which avoids this assumption, is to use the follwing formula (15):

$$r_{11} = 2 \left(1 - \frac{\sigma^2_a + \sigma^2_b}{\sigma^2_t} \right)$$

in which σ_a and σ_b are the standard deviations of the half-scores and σ_t the standard deviation of total scores on the test. It will be noted that this procedure does not require the computation of a correlation coefficient.

Interitem Consistency. A fourth method employed to determine test reliability is based upon the consistency of the subjects' responses to all items in the test. Such a reliability coefficient provides a measure of both equivalence (as in split-half methods) and homogeneity. Thus two tests that have equally high reliability in terms of equivalent form or split-half coefficients may vary in their coefficients of interitem consistency, if they differ in the degree of homogeneity of their items. In fact, the difference between split-half and interitem consistency coefficients could be used as an index of heterogeneity of the test items.

The most common procedure for finding interitem consistency is that developed by Kuder and Richardson. As in the split-half methods, interitem consistency is found from a single administration of a single test. Rather than requiring two half-scores, however, such a technique is based upon an examination of performance on each item. Of the various formulas developed by Kuder and Richardson, the following is the most widely applicable:

$$r_{11} = \left(\frac{n}{n-1} \right) \frac{\sigma^2_t - \Sigma pq}{\sigma^2_t}$$

in which r_{11} is the reliability coefficient of the whole test, n is the number of items in the test, and σ_t the standard deviation of total scores on the test. The only new term in this formula, Σpq, is found by tabulating the proportion of persons who pass (p) and the proportion who do not pass (q) each item. The product of p and q is computed for each item, and these products are then added for all items, to give Σpq. Since in the process of test construction p is often routinely recorded in order to find the difficulty level of each item, such a method of determining reliability involves little additional computation.

It can be shown that the Kuder-Richardson reliability coefficient given above is actually the mean of all split-half coefficients resulting from different splittings of a test (6). The ordinary split-half coefficient, on the other hand, is based on a planned split designed to yield equivalent sets of items. Hence unless the test items are highly homogeneous, the Kuder-Richardson coefficient will be lower than the split-half reliability. Both split-half and Kuder-Richardson coefficients, as well as any other reliability coefficient derived from a single administration of a single form, are designated as *coefficients of internal consistency* (1). As explained above, however, the information provided by these two kinds of coefficients is not identical. For this reason, it is better to specify the method whereby a particular coefficient of internal consistency was obtained.

Overview. The characteristics of the most common types of reliability coefficients are summarized in Table 7. The first column identifies the procedure followed to obtain the reliability coefficient. In the second column is the conventional designation of each coefficient, as given in the APA *Technical Recommendations for Psychological Tests and Diagnostic Techniques* (1). The third column indicates the factors that are treated as error variance by each technique.

The correlation between retests with the same form administered on different occasions reflects the enduring or lasting characteristics of the individual's

TABLE 7. Types of Reliability Coefficients

Procedure	Conventional Designation	Error Variance
Retest with same form on different occasion	Coefficient of stability	Temporal fluctuation
Retest with parallel form on different occasion	Coefficient of stability and equivalence	Temporal fluctuation and item specificity
Retest with parallel form on same occasion	Coefficient of equivalence	Item specificity
Split-half (odd-even or other parallel splits)	Coefficient of internal consistency	Item specificity
Kuder-Richardson (and other measures of interitem consistency)	Coefficient of internal consistency	Item specificity and heterogeneity

responses. Temporary conditions, which are likely to vary from the first to the second occasion, lower such a correlation and hence constitute error variance in this procedure. If such a correlation is .85, for example, it means that 15 per cent ($100 - 85 = 15$) of the variance of test scores is attributable to temporal fluctuations. The use of parallel forms introduces item specificity as a further source of error variance. The correlation between parallel forms administered on different occasions depends upon those aspects of the subject's performance that are both lasting (over the interval covered) and generalizable beyond the specific items included in any one form. Thus if such a correlation were .72, it would show that 72 per cent of the variance of test scores was attributable to lasting and general response characteristics. Retest correlations with parallel forms administered at the same time treat only item specificity as error variance. If this correlation were .80, for instance, we would conclude that 20 per cent ($100 - 80 = 20$) of the score variance was the result of item specificity.

Split-half techniques provide the same type of information as parallel forms administered on the same occasion. Splits such as that between odd and even items virtually represent equivalent half-tests administered simultaneously. As in the coefficient of equivalence, coefficients of internal consistency based on split-half correlations treat only item specificity as error variance. Such correlations show how generalizable the subject's responses are, but not how stable in time. Finally, the Kuder-Richardson and similar techniques include both item specificity and item heterogeneity under error variance.

RELIABILITY OF SPEEDED TESTS

Internal consistency coefficients based on odd-even, Kuder-Richardson, or similar techniques are inapplicable to speeded tests. To the extent that individual differences in test scores depend upon speed of performance, reliability coefficients found by these methods will be spuriously high. An extreme example will help to clarify this point. Let us suppose that a 50-item test depends entirely on speed, so that individual differences in score are based wholly upon number of items attempted, rather than upon errors. Then if individual A obtains a score of 44, he will obviously have 22 correct odd items and 22 correct even items. Similarly, individual B, with a score of 34, will have odd and even scores of 17 and 17, respectively. Consequently, except for accidental careless errors on a few items, the correlation between odd and even scores would be perfect, or $+1.00$. Such a correlation, however, is entirely spurious and provides no information about the reliability of the test.

An examination of the procedures followed in finding both split-half and Kuder-Richardson reliability will show that both are based upon the consistency in *number of errors* made by the subject. If, now, individual differences in test scores depend, not on errors, but on speed, the measure of reliability must obviously be based on consistency in *speed of work*. To be sure, most psychological tests are neither pure speed nor pure power tests, but represent a combination of both. Under such conditions, the single-trial reliability coefficient will fall below 1.00, but it will still be spuriously high. As long as individual differences in test scores are appreciably affected by speed, single-trial reliability coefficients cannot be properly interpreted.

What alternative procedures are available to determine the reliability of significantly speeded tests? If a simple repetition of the test is applicable, such a procedure would be appropriate. Similarly, equivalent-form reliability may be properly employed with speed tests. Split-half techniques may also be used, provided that the split is made in terms of time rather than in terms of items. In other words, the half-scores must be based on separately timed parts of the test. One way of effecting such a split is to administer two equivalent halves of the test with separate time limits. For example, the odd and even items may be separately printed on different pages, and each set of items given with one-half the time limit of the entire test. Such a procedure is tantamount to administering two equivalent forms of the test in immediate succession. Each form, however, is half as long as the test proper, while the subjects' scores are normally based on the whole test. For this reason, either the Spearman-Brown or some other appropriate formula should be used to find the reliability of the whole test.

If it is not feasible to administer the two half-tests separately, an alternative procedure is to divide the total time into quarters, and to find a score for each of the four quarters. This can easily be done by having the subjects mark the item on which they are working whenever the examiner gives a prearranged signal. The number of items correctly completed within the first and fourth quarters can then be combined to represent one half-score, while those in the second and third quarters can be combined to yield the other half-score. Such a combination of quarters tends to balance out the cumulative effects of practice, fatigue, and other factors. This method is especially satisfactory when the items are not steeply graded in difficulty level.

When is a test appreciably speeded? Under what conditions must the special precautions discussed in this section be observed? Obviously, the mere employment of a time limit does not signify a speed test. If all subjects finish within the given time limit, speed of work plays no part in determining the scores. Percentage of subjects who fail to complete the test might be taken as a crude index of speed versus power. Even when no one finishes the test, however, the role of speed may be negligible. For example, if every subject completes exactly 40 items of a 50-item test, individual differences with regard to speed are entirely absent, although no one had time to attempt all the items.

The essential question, of course, is: "To what extent are individual differences in test scores attributable to speed?" In more technical terms, we want to know what proportion of the total variance of test scores is speed variance. This proportion can be estimated roughly by finding the variance of number of items completed by different persons and dividing it by the variance of total test scores (σ^2_c/σ^2_t). In the example cited above, in which every individual finishes 40 items, the numerator of this fraction would be zero, since there are no individual differences in number of items completed ($\sigma^2_c = 0$). The entire index would thus equal zero in a pure power test. On the other hand, if the total test variance (σ^2_t) is attributable to individual differences in speed, the two variances will be equal and the ratio will be 1.00. Several more refined procedures have been developed for determining this proportion, but their detailed consideration falls beyond the scope of this book (cf. 7, 13, 14, 16, 17).

An example of the effect of speed upon coefficients of internal consistency is provided by data collected in an investigation of the SRA Tests of Primary Mental Abilities for Ages 11 to 17 (2). In this study, the reliability of each test was first determined by the usual odd-even procedure. These coefficients, given in the first row of Table 8, are closely similar to those reported in the test manual. Reliability coefficients were then computed by correlating scores on separately timed halves. These coefficients are shown in the second row of Table 8. Calculation of speed indexes showed that the Verbal Meaning

TABLE 8. Reliability Coefficients of Four of the SRA Tests of Primary Mental Abilities for Ages 11 to 17

(Data from Anastasi and Drake, 2)

Reliability Coefficient Found by:	Verbal Meaning	Reasoning	Space	Number
Single-trial split-half method	.94	.96	.90	.92
Separately timed halves	.90	.87	.75	.83

test is primarily a power test, while the Reasoning test is somewhat more dependent upon speed. The Space and Number tests proved to be highly speeded. It will be noted in Table 8 that, when properly computed, the reliability of the Space test is .75, in contrast to a spuriously high odd-even coefficient of .90. Similarly, the reliability of the Reasoning test drops from .96 to .87, and that of the Number test drops from .92 to .83. The reliability of the relatively unspeeded Verbal Meaning test, on the other hand, shows a negligible difference when computed by the two methods.

DEPENDENCE OF RELIABILITY COEFFICIENTS UPON THE SAMPLE TESTED

An important factor influencing the size of a reliability coefficient is the nature of the group on which reliability is measured. In the first place, any correlation coefficient is affected by the *range of individual differences* in the group. If every member of a group were alike in spelling ability, then the correlation of spelling with any other ability would be zero in that group. It would obviously be impossible, within such a group, to predict an individual's standing in any other ability from a knowledge of his spelling score.

Another, less extreme, example is provided by the correlation between two aptitude tests, such as a verbal comprehension and an arithmetic reasoning test. If these tests were administered to a highly homogeneous sample, such as a group of 300 college sophomores, the correlation between the two would probably be close to zero. There is little relationship, within such a selected sample of college students, between any individual's verbal ability and his numerical reasoning ability. On the other hand, were the tests to be given to a heterogeneous sample of 300 persons, ranging from institutionalized morons to college graduates, a high correlation would undoubtedly be obtained between the two tests. The morons would obtain poorer scores than the college graduates on *both* tests, and similar relationships would hold for other subgroups within this highly heterogeneous sample.

Examination of the hypothetical scatter diagram given in Figure 21 will further illustrate the dependence of correlation coefficients upon the variability, or extent of individual differences, within the group. This scatter diagram shows a high positive correlation in the entire, heterogeneous group, since the entries are closely clustered about the diagonal extending from lower left- to upper right-hand corners. If, now, we consider only the subgroup falling within the small rectangle in the upper right-hand portion of the diagram, it is apparent that the correlation between the two variables is close to zero. Within such a restricted range, small differences in score assume much greater prominence in determining an individual's relative standing in his group.

Like all correlation coefficients, reliability coefficients depend upon the variability of the sampling within which they are found. Thus if the reliability

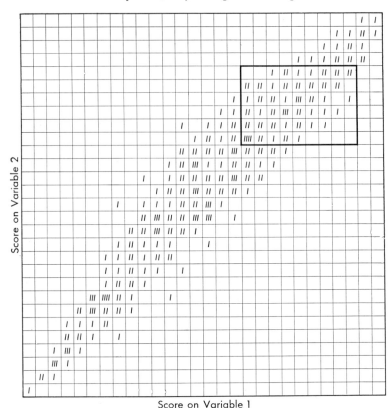

Fig. 21. The Effect of Restricted Range upon a Correlation Coefficient.

coefficient reported in a test manual was determined in a group ranging from fourth-grade children to high school students, it cannot be assumed that the reliability would be equally high within, let us say, an eighth-grade sample. When a test is to be used to discriminate individual differences within a more homogeneous sample than the standardization group, the reliability coefficient should be redetermined on such a sample. Some test manuals make a practice of reporting separate reliability coefficients for relatively homogeneous subsamples within the standardization group (cf., e.g., 3). Formulas for estimating the reliability coefficient to be expected when the standard deviation of the group is increased or decreased are available in any standard statistics textbook. It is preferable, however, to redetermine the reliability coefficient on a group comparable to that on which the test is to be used.

Not only does the reliability coefficient vary with the extent of individual differences in the sample, but it may also vary between groups differing in *average ability level*. These differences, moreover, cannot usually be predicted or estimated by any statistical formula, but can be discovered only by empirical tryout of the test on groups differing in age or ability level. Such differences in the reliability of a single test may arise from the fact that a slightly different combination of abilities is measured at different difficulty levels of the test. Or it may result from the statistical properties of the type of score employed, as in the Stanford-Binet IQ's (cf. 19, Ch. 6). Thus for different ages and for different IQ levels, the reliability coefficient of the Stanford-Binet varies from .83 to .98. In other tests, reliability may be relatively low for the younger and less able groups, since their scores are unduly influenced by guessing. Under such circumstances, the particular test should not be employed at these levels.

It is apparent that every reliability coefficient should be accompanied by a full description of the type of group on which it was determined. Special attention should be given to the variability and the ability level of the sample. The reported reliability coefficient is applicable only to samples similar to that on which it was computed. A desirable and growing practice in test construction is to fractionate the standardization sample into more homogeneous subgroups, with regard to age, sex, grade level, occupation, and the like, and to report separate reliability coefficients for each subgroup. Under these conditions, the reliability coefficients are more likely to be applicable to the samples with which the test is to be used in actual practice.

STANDARD ERROR OF MEASUREMENT

The reliability of a test may be expressed in terms of the standard error of measurement ($\sigma_{meas.}$), also called the standard error of a score. This measure is particularly well suited to the interpretation of individual scores. For many testing purposes, it is therefore more useful than the reliability coefficient. The standard error of measurement can be easily computed from the reliability coefficient of the test, by the following formula:

$$\sigma_{meas.} = \sigma_1 \sqrt{1 - r_{11}}$$

in which σ_1 is the standard deviation of the test scores and r_{11} the reliability coefficient, both computed on the same group. For example, if deviation IQ's on a particular intelligence test have a standard deviation of 15 and a reliability coefficient of .90, the $\sigma_{meas.}$ of an IQ on this test is: $15\sqrt{1 - .90} = 15\sqrt{.10} = 15(.33) = 5$.

To understand what the $\sigma_{meas.}$ tells us about a score, let us assume that we have a series of 100 IQ's obtained with the same test by a single boy, Jim. Because of the types of chance errors discussed in this chapter, these scores will vary, falling into a normal distribution around Jim's "true" score. The true score is the mean of the distribution of the 100 scores and the $\sigma_{meas.}$ is its standard deviation. This standard deviation may be interpreted in terms of the normal curve frequencies that were discussed in Chapter 4 (see Fig. 12). It will be recalled that between the mean and $\pm 1\sigma$ there are approximately 68 per cent of the cases in a normal curve. Thus we can conclude that the chances are roughly 2:1 (or 68:32) that Jim's IQ on this test will fluctuate between $\pm 1\sigma_{meas.}$ or 5 points on either side of his true IQ. If his true IQ is 110, we would expect him to score between 105 and 115 about two-thirds (68 per cent) of the time.

If we want to be more certain of our prediction, we can choose higher odds than 2:1. Reference to Figure 12 in Chapter 4 shows that $\pm 3\sigma$ covers 99.7 per cent of the cases. It can be ascertained from normal curve frequency tables that a distance of 2.58σ on either side of the mean includes exactly 99 per cent of the cases. Hence the chances are 99:1 that Jim's IQ will fall within $2.58\ \sigma_{meas.}$, or $(2.58)(5) = 13$ points, on either side of his true IQ. We can thus state at the .01 level (with only one chance of error out of 100) that Jim's IQ on any single administration of the test will lie between 97 and 123 $(110 - 13$ and $110 + 13)$. If Jim were given 100 equivalent tests, his IQ would fall outside this band of values only once.

In actual practice, of course, we do not know the true IQ, but have only the IQ obtained on a single test. If the reliability coefficient of the test is quite high and the individual's score is not near the upper or lower extremes of the range, the obtained score can be substituted for the true score in computing the band within which the IQ will fall. A more precise method is to estimate the true score first and then compute the band around this estimated score. The true score can be readily estimated from the reliability coefficient by the following formula (cf. 22, p. 611):

$$x_{true} = r_{11}\ x_{obt.}$$

in which $x_{obt.}$ is the deviation of the obtained score from the group mean and x_{true} the deviation of the true score from the same mean. If Jim's obtained IQ was 110, his deviation from the mean of 100 is $+ 10$. With a reliability coefficient of .90, his estimated true score is found as follows:

$$x_{true} = (.90)(+ 10) = + 9 \qquad 100 + 9 = 109$$

Since the estimated true score falls 9 points above the mean IQ of 100, Jim's estimated true score is 109. The band of values within which his IQ is likely to fall at the .01 level is thus: 109 ± 13, or between 96 and 122.

The standard error of measurement and the reliability coefficient are obviously alternative ways of expressing test reliability. Unlike the reliability coefficient, the error of measurement is independent of the variability of the group on which it is computed. Expressed in terms of individual scores, it remains unchanged when found in a homogeneous or a heterogeneous group. On the other hand, being reported in score units, the error of measurement may not be directly comparable from test to test. The usual problems of comparability of units would thus arise when errors of measurement are reported in terms of arithmetic problems, words in a vocabulary test, and the like. Hence if we want to compare the reliability of different tests, the reliability coefficient is the better measure. To interpret individual scores, the standard error of measurement is more appropriate.

INTERPRETATION OF SCORE DIFFERENCES

It is particularly important to consider test reliability and errors of measurement when evaluating the *differences* between two scores. Thinking in terms of the range within which each score may fluctuate serves as a check against overemphasizing small differences between scores. Such caution is desirable both when comparing test scores of different persons and when comparing the scores of the same individual in different abilities. Similarly, changes in scores following instruction or other experimental variables need to be interpreted in the light of errors of measurement.

A frequent question the counselor must answer concerns the individual's relative standing in different areas. Is Jane more able along verbal than along numerical lines? Does Tom have more aptitude for mechanical than for verbal activities? If Jane scored higher on the verbal than on the numerical subtests of an aptitude battery and Tom scored higher on the mechanical than on the verbal, how sure can we be that they would still do so on a retest with another form of the battery? In other words, could the score differences have resulted merely from the chance selection of specific items in the particular verbal, numerical, and mechanical tests employed?

Because of the growing interest in the interpretation of score profiles, test publishers have been developing report forms that permit the evaluation of scores in terms of their errors of measurement. Outstanding examples are provided by the Sequential Tests of Educational Progress (STEP) and the School and College Ability Tests (SCAT), both of which will be discussed in later chapters. Tables of norms and individual profiles for these tests are constructed in terms of "percentile bands" based on the obtained score and its standard error. Each band covers a distance of approximately one standard error of measurement on either side of the obtained score. Illustrations of profiles plotted with such percentile bands are given in Figure 37 (Ch. 9) and Figure 99 (Ch. 16). In interpreting the profiles, the test user is advised to attach no importance to differences between scores whose percentile bands overlap.

Another way of handling the problem of reliability in intra-individual comparisons is illustrated by the Differential Aptitude Tests (DAT), one of whose score profiles was reproduced in the preceding chapter (Fig. 16). In this approach, the standard error of the difference between each pair of scores is computed. It can then be shown that a difference of about 10 standard score points between any two DAT subtests will be significant at the .05 level. The report form was so designed that such a difference corresponded to a distance of 1 inch. Hence the test user can assume that differences of 1 inch or more on the profile are significant at the .05 level or better.

It is well to bear in mind that the standard error of the difference between two scores is larger than the error of measurement of either of the two scores. This follows from the fact that such a difference is affected by the chance errors present in *both* scores. Moreover, when we subtract one score from another any common variance in the two scores cancels out, leaving only specific and error variance. As a result, the error variance constitutes a larger proportion of total variance in the difference score than it does in either of the two original scores. The standard error of the difference between two scores can be found from the standard errors of measurement of the two scores by the following formula:

$$\sigma_{diff.} = \sqrt{\sigma^2_{meas._1} + \sigma^2_{meas._2}}$$

in which $\sigma_{diff.}$ is the standard error of the difference between the two scores, and $\sigma_{meas._1}$ and $\sigma_{meas._2}$ are the standard errors of measurement of the separate scores.[2]

We may illustrate the application of the above procedure to two of the DAT subtests, (1) Verbal Reasoning and (2) Mechanical Reasoning, whose split-half reliabilities are .88 and .85, respectively. DAT scores are reported as standard scores with a mean of 50 and an *SD* of 10. Hence standard errors of the two separate scores and of the differences between them are as follows:

---

[2] By substituting $SD \sqrt{1 - r^2_{11}}$ for $\sigma_{meas._1}$ and $SD \sqrt{1 - r^2_{211}}$ for $\sigma_{meas._2}$, we may rewrite the formula directly in terms of reliability coefficients, as follows:

$$\sigma_{diff.} = SD \sqrt{2 - r_{11} - r_{211}}$$

In this substitution, the same *SD* was used for tests 1 and 2, since their scores would normally be expressed in terms of the same scale before making any comparison between them.

$$\sigma_{meas._1} = 10\sqrt{1 - .88} = 3.46 \qquad \sigma_{meas._2} = 10\sqrt{1 - .85} = 3.87$$

$$\sigma_{diff.} = \sqrt{(3.46)^2 + (3.87)^2} = 5.20$$

It will be noted that the standard error of the difference is considerably larger than the standard errors of the two separate scores. To determine how large a score difference could be obtained by chance at the .05 level, we multiply the standard error of the difference (5.20) by 1.96. The result is approximately 10. Thus the difference between an individual's Verbal and Mechanical scores must be 10 points or greater to be significant at the .05 level.

REFERENCES

1. American Psychological Association. *Technical recommendations for psychological tests and diagnostic techniques.* Washington: Amer. Psychol. Assoc., 1954.
2. Anastasi, Anne, and Drake, J. An empirical comparison of certain techniques for estimating the reliability of speeded tests. *Educ. psychol. Measmt.,* 1954, 14, 529-540.
3. Bennett, G. K., Seashore, H. G., and Wesman, A. G. *Differential Aptitude Tests.* N. Y.: Psychol. Corp., 1947-1959.
4. Blommers, P., and Lindquist, E. F. *Elementary statistical methods in psychology and education.* Boston: Houghton Mifflin, 1960.
5. Cattell, Psyche. Stanford-Binet IQ variations. *Sch. and Soc.,* 1937, 45, 615-618.
6. Cronbach, L. J. Coefficient alpha and the internal structure of tests. *Psychometrika,* 1951, 16, 297-334.
7. Cronbach, L. J., and Warrington, W. G. Time-limit tests: estimating their reliability and degree of speeding. *Psychometrika,* 1951, 16, 167-188.
8. Dana, R. H. Rorschach scorer reliability. *J. clin. Psychol.,* 1955, 11, 401-403.
9. Garrett, H. E. *Elementary statistics.* N. Y.: Longmans, Green, 1956.
10. Garrett, H. E. *Statistics in psychology and education.* (5th ed.) N. Y.: Longmans, Green, 1958.
11. Gilhooly, F. M. The validity and reliability of the Rorschach and the Thematic Apperception Test when these tests are interpreted by the method of blind analysis. Unpublished doctoral dissertation, Fordham Univer., 1952.
12. Guilford, J. P. *Fundamental statistics in psychology and education.* (3rd ed.) N. Y.: McGraw-Hill, 1956.
13. Gulliksen, H. The reliability of speeded tests. *Psychometrika,* 1950, 15, 259-269.
14. Gulliksen, H. *Theory of mental tests.* N. Y.: Wiley, 1950.
15. Guttman, L. A basis for analyzing test-retest reliability. *Psychometrika,* 1945, 10, 255-282.
16. Guttman, L. Reliability formulas for noncompleted or speeded tests. *Psychometrika,* 1955, 20, 113-124.

17. Helmstadter, G. C., and Ortmeyer, D. H. Some techniques for determining the relative magnitude of speed and power components of a test. *Educ. psychol. Measmt.*, 1953, 13, 280-287.
18. McCarthy, Dorothea. A study of the reliability of the Goodenough drawing test of intelligence. *J. Psychol.*, 1944, 18, 201-216.
19. McNemar, Q. *The revision of the Stanford-Binet Scale.* Boston: Houghton Mifflin, 1942.
20. Ramzy, I., and Pickard, P. M. A study in the reliability of scoring the Rorschach Inkblot Test. *J. gen. Psychol.*, 1949, 40, 3-10.
21. Sackman, H. An investigation of certain aspects of the validity of the formal Rorschach scoring system in relation to age, education, and vocabulary score. Unpublished doctoral dissertation, Fordham Univer., 1953.
22. Thorndike, R. L. Reliability. In E. F. Lindquist (Ed.), *Educational measurement.* Washington: Amer. Council Educ., 1951. Pp. 560-620.
23. U.S. Department of the Army, TAGO, Personnel Research Branch. Studies in visual acuity. *PRS Rep.* No. 742, 1948.
24. Walker, Helen M., and Lev, J. *Statistical inference.* N. Y.: Holt, Rinehart and Winston, 1953.
25. Walker, Helen M., and Lev, J. *Elementary statistical methods.* (Rev. ed.) N. Y.: Holt, Rinehart and Winston, 1958.

CHAPTER **6**

Methods for Determining Validity

As indicated in Chapter 2, the question of test validity concerns *what* the test measures and *how well* it does so. In this connection, we should guard against accepting the test name as an index of what the test measures. Test names provide short, convenient labels for identification purposes. Most test names are far too broad and vague to furnish meaningful clues to the behavior area covered, although a trend toward the use of more specific and operationally definable test names is discernible. The trait measured by a given test can be defined only through an examination of the specific criteria or other objective sources of information utilized in establishing its validity (2). Moreover, the validity of a test cannot be reported in general terms. No test can be said to have "high" or "low" validity in the abstract. Its validity must be determined with reference to the particular use for which it is being considered.

Fundamentally, all procedures for determining test validity are concerned with the relationships between performance on the test and other independently observable facts about the behavior characteristic under consideration. The specific techniques employed for investigating these relationships are numerous and have been described by various names. The APA *Technical Recommendations* (1) classified these procedures under four categories, designated as content, predictive, concurrent, and construct validity. Each of these types of validation procedures will be considered in one of the following sections, and the relations among them will be examined in a concluding section. The utilization of validity data in making practical decisions will be discussed in Chapter 7.

CONTENT VALIDITY

Content validity involves essentially the systematic examination of the test content to determine whether it covers a representative sample of the

135

behavior domain to be measured. Such a validation procedure is commonly used in evaluating achievement tests. This type of test, it will be recalled, is designed to measure how well the individual has mastered a specific skill or course of study. It might thus appear that mere inspection of the content of the test should suffice to establish its validity for such a purpose. A test of multiplication, spelling, or American history would seem to be valid by definition if it consists of multiplication, spelling, or American history items, respectively.

The solution, however, is not as simple as it appears to be. One difficulty is presented by the problem of content sampling. The content area to be tested must be systematically analyzed to make certain that all major aspects are adequately covered by the test items, and in the correct proportions. For example, a test can easily become overloaded with those aspects of the field that lend themselves more readily to the preparation of objective items. The content area under consideration needs to be fully described in advance, rather than being defined after the test has been prepared. A well-constructed achievement test should cover the objectives of instruction, not just its subject matter (9, 11). Content thus needs to be broadly defined to include major objectives, such as the application of principles and the interpretation of data, as well as factual knowledge. Moreover, content validity depends upon the relevance of the individual's test responses to the behavior area under consideration, rather than upon the apparent relevance of item content (9, 14). Mere inspection of the test may fail to reveal the processes actually used by subjects in taking the test.

It is also important to guard against any tendency to overgeneralize regarding the content sampled by the test. For instance, a multiple-choice spelling test may measure the ability to recognize correctly and incorrectly spelled words. But it cannot be assumed that such a test also measures ability to spell correctly from dictation, frequency of misspellings in written compositions, and other aspects of "spelling ability" (cf. 7, 13). Still another difficulty arises from the possible inclusion of irrelevant factors in the test scores. For example, a test designed to measure the effects of instruction in such areas as mathematics or mechanics may be unduly influenced by the ability to understand verbal directions or by speed of performing simple, routine tasks.

A number of empirical procedures can be followed to check on the content validity of an achievement test (9, 10, 14). When available, parallel forms of the test can be administered before and after a relevant course of study to see whether there is an appreciable improvement in scores. Other procedures include a study of the types of errors commonly made on the test and an analysis of the work methods employed by subjects, possibly by giving the test individually to subjects with the instructions to "think aloud" in solving each problem. The contribution of speed can be checked by noting how many subjects fail to finish the test or by one of the more refined methods discussed in Chapter 5. To detect the possible irrelevant influence of ability to read instructions upon test performance, scores on the test can be correlated with scores on a reading comprehension test. On the other hand, if the test is designed to measure reading comprehension, giving the questions without the reading passage on which they are based will show how many could be answered simply from the subjects' prior information or other irrelevant cues.

Content validity, especially when bolstered by such empirical checks as those illustrated above, provides an adequate technique for evaluating achievement tests. For aptitude and personality tests, however, content validity is not sufficient and may, in fact, be misleading. Although considerations of appropriateness and effectiveness of content must obviously enter into the initial stages of constructing such tests, eventual validation of the test requires thorough empirical verification by the procedures to be described in the following sections. Aptitude and personality tests bear less intrinsic resemblance to the behavior domain they are trying to sample than do achievement tests. Consequently the content of aptitude and personality tests can do little more than reveal the hypotheses that led the test constructor to choose a certain type of content for measuring a specified trait. Such hypotheses need to be empirically confirmed to establish the validity of the test.

Unlike achievement tests, aptitude and personality tests are not based on a specified course of instruction or uniform set of prior experiences from which test content can be drawn. Hence in the latter tests individuals are likely to vary more in the work methods or psychological processes employed in responding to the same test items. The identical test might thus measure different functions in different persons. Under these conditions, it would be virtually impossible to determine the psychological functions measured by the test from an inspection of its content. For example, college graduates might solve a problem in verbal or mathematical terms, while a mechanic would arrive at the same solution in terms of spatial visualization. Or a test measuring arithmetic reasoning among high school freshmen might measure only individual differences in speed of computation when given to college students. A specific illustration of the dangers of relying upon content analysis of aptitude tests is provided by a study conducted with a digit-symbol substitution test (4). This test, generally regarded as a typical "code-learning" test, was found to measure chiefly motor speed in a group of high school students.

Content validity should not be confused with *face validity*. The latter is not validity in the technical sense; it refers, not to what the test actually measures, but to what it appears superficially to measure. Face validity pertains to whether the test "looks valid" to the subjects who take it, the administrative personnel who decide upon its use, and other technically untrained observers. Fundamentally, the question of face validity concerns rapport and public relations. Although common usage of the term "validity" in this connection may make for confusion, face validity itself is a desirable feature of tests. Certainly if test content appears irrelevant, inappropriate, silly, or childish, the result will be poor cooperation, regardless of the actual validity of the test. When tests originally designed for children and developed within a classroom setting were first extended for adult use, they frequently met with resistance and criticism because of their lack of face validity. Especially in adult testing, it is not sufficient for a test to be objectively valid. It also needs face validity to function effectively in practical situations.

Face validity can often be improved by merely reformulating test items in terms that appear relevant and plausible in the particular setting in which they will be used. For example, if a test of simple arithmetic reasoning is constructed for use with machinists, the items should be worded in terms of machine operations rather than in terms of "how many oranges can be purchased for 36 cents" or other traditional schoolbook problems. Similarly, an arithmetic test for naval personnel can be expressed in naval terminology, without necessarily altering the functions measured. To be sure, face validity should never be regarded as a substitute for objectively determined validity. It cannot be assumed that improving the face validity of a test will improve its objective validity. Nor can it be assumed that when a test is modified so as to increase its face validity, its objective validity remains unaltered. The validity of the test in its final form will always need to be directly checked.

PREDICTIVE VALIDITY

Predictive validity indicates the effectiveness of a test in predicting some future outcome. For this purpose, test scores are checked against a direct measure of the subjects' subsequent performance, technically known as the criterion. This type of validity information is most relevant for tests used in the selection and classification of personnel. Hiring job applicants, selecting students for admission to college or professional schools, and assigning enlisted men to different military specialties represent examples of the sort of decisions requiring a knowledge of the predictive validity of tests. Other examples include the use of tests to screen out men likely to develop emotional disorders under military stress and the use of tests to identify psychiatric patients most likely to benefit from a particular therapy.

In all these instances, the validation procedure is essentially similar. A representative sample of the population under consideration is given the test, but the scores are not used to make any decisions regarding this sample. In fact, scores should not be accessible to anyone in a position to make decisions that influence outcomes for these subjects. As explained in Chapter 2, this precaution is required in order to avoid any possible criterion contamination. Follow-up of the original sample after criterion data have become available will show how closely predictions from the test scores agree with observed outcomes.

Predictive validity against various criteria is commonly reported in test manuals to aid the potential user in understanding what a test measures. Although he may not be directly concerned with the prediction of any of the specific criteria employed, by examining such criteria the test user is able to build up a concept of the behavior domain sampled by the test. The criteria most frequently cited in test manuals include general academic achievement, performance in specialized training, and on-the-job performance.

General Academic Achievement. Probably the most common criterion employed in validating intelligence tests is some index of academic achievement. It is for this reason that such tests have often been more precisely described as measures of scholastic aptitude. The specific indices used as criterion measures include school grades, achievement test scores, promotion and graduation records, special honors and awards, and teachers' or instructors' ratings for "intelligence." In so far as such ratings given within an academic setting are likely to be heavily colored by the individual's scholastic performance, they may be properly classified with the criterion of academic achievement.

The various indices of academic achievement have provided criterion data at all educational levels, from the primary grades to college and graduate school. Although employed principally in the validation of general intelligence tests, they have also served as criteria for certain multiple aptitude and personality tests. In the validation of any of these types of tests for use in the selection of college students, for example, a common criterion is freshman grade-point average. This measure is the average grade in all courses taken during the freshman year, each grade being weighted by the number of course points for which it was received.

Performance in Specialized Training. In the development of special aptitude tests, a frequent type of criterion is based upon performance in a course of specialized training. For example, mechanical aptitude tests may be validated against final achievement in shop courses. Various business school courses, such as stenography, typing, or bookkeeping, provide criteria for aptitude tests in these areas. Similarly, performance in music or art schools has been employed in validating music or art aptitude tests, respectively. Several professional aptitude tests have been validated in terms of achievement in schools of law, medicine, dentistry, engineering, and other areas. In the case of custom-made tests, designed for use within a specific testing program, training records are a frequent source of criterion data. An outstanding illustration is the validation of Air Force pilot selection tests against performance in pilot training.

Among the specific indices of training performance employed for criterion purposes may be mentioned achievement tests administered upon completion of training, formally assigned grades, instructors' ratings, and successful completion of training versus elimination from the program. Multiple aptitude batteries have often been checked against grades in specific high school or college courses, in order to determine their validity as differential predictors. For example, scores on a verbal comprehension test may be compared with grades in English courses, spatial visualization scores with geometry grades, and so forth.

In connection with the use of training records in general as criterion measures, a useful distinction is that between intermediate and ultimate criteria (17). In the development of an Air Force pilot selection test or a medical aptitude test, for example, the ultimate criteria would be combat performance and eventual achievement as a practicing physician, respectively. Obviously it would require a long time for such criterion data to mature. It is doubtful, moreover, whether a truly ultimate criterion is ever obtained in actual practice. Finally, even were such an ultimate criterion available, it would probably be subject to many uncontrolled factors that would render it relatively useless. For example, it would be difficult to evaluate the relative degree of success of physicians practicing different specialties and in different parts of the country. For these reasons, such intermediate criteria as performance records at some stage of training are frequently employed as criterion measures.

On-the-Job Performance. In many ways, the most satisfactory type of criterion measure is that based upon follow-up records of actual job performance. Such a criterion has been used to some extent in the validation of general intelligence as well as personality tests, and to a large extent in the validation of special aptitude tests. It is a common criterion in the validation of custom-made tests for specific jobs. The "jobs" in question may vary widely in both level and kind, including work in business, industry, the professions, the armed forces, and any other field. Most measures of job performance, although probably not representing ultimate criteria, at least provide good intermediate criteria for many testing purposes. In this respect they are to be preferred to training records. On the other hand, the measurement of job performance does not permit as much uniformity of conditions as is possible during training. Moreover, since it usually involves a longer follow-up, the criterion of job performance is likely to entail a loss in the number of available subjects.

A wide variety of indices may be employed to measure degree of job success. Among them may be mentioned quantity and quality of output, accidents and loss through breakage, salary and commissions, job stability and length of service, rate of advancement, and merit ratings by supervisors. The criterion measure may be based on the observation of a limited sample of the individual's job performance, such as a worksample, sales interview, or pilot check flight. Or it may be derived from a cumulative record of output, sales, merit ratings, or job history covering the total available period on the job (cf. 17, pp. 132-159).

CONCURRENT VALIDITY

The relation between test scores and indices of criterion status obtained at approximately the same time is known as concurrent validity. In a number of instances, concurrent validity is found merely as a substitute for predictive validity. It is frequently impracticable to extend validation procedures over the time required for predictive validity or to obtain a suitable preselection sample for testing purposes. As a compromise solution, therefore, tests are administered to a group on whom criterion data are already available. Thus the test scores of college students may be compared with their cumulative grade-point average at the time of testing, or those of employees compared with their current job success.

A variant of the criterion of academic achievement frequently employed with out-of-school adults is the amount of education the individual completed. It is expected that in general the more intelligent individuals continue their education longer, while the less intelligent drop out of school earlier. The assumption underlying this criterion is that the educational ladder serves as a progressively selective influence, eliminating those incapable of continuing beyond each step. Although it is undoubtedly true that college graduates, for example, represent a more highly selected group than elementary school graduates, the relation between amount of education and scholastic aptitude is far from perfect. Especially at the higher educational levels, economic, social, motivational, and other non-intellectual factors may influence the continuation of the individual's education. Moreover, with such concurrent validation, it is difficult to disentangle cause-and-effect relations. To what extent are the obtained differences in intelligence test scores simply the result of the varying amount of education? And to what extent could the test have predicted individual differences in subsequent educational progress? These questions can be answered only when the test is administered before the criterion data have matured, as in predictive validation.

Similarly, when current test scores are compared with the grades earned by college students or the job proficiency of employees, we cannot determine how far the test scores reflect what the students have learned in college or what the workers have learned on the job. Furthermore, when employees or college students are given tests "for research purposes only," their motivation and test-taking attitudes may be quite unlike those of job applicants or students seeking college admission. It is apparent that to generalize from concurrent to predictive validity is a questionable procedure.

For certain uses of psychological tests, on the other hand, concurrent validity is the most appropriate type and can be justified in its own right. The logical distinction between predictive and concurrent validity is based, not on time, but on the objectives of testing. Concurrent validity is relevant to tests employed for *diagnosis* of existing status, rather than prediction of future outcomes. The difference can be illustrated by asking: "Is Smith neurotic?" (concurrent validity) and "Is Smith likely to become neurotic?" (predictive validity).

Since the criterion for concurrent validity is always available at the time of testing, we might ask what function is served by the test in such situations. Basically, such tests provide a simpler, quicker, or less expensive substitute for the criterion data. For example, if the criterion consists of continuous observation of a patient during a two-week hospitalization period, a test that could sort out normals from neurotic and doubtful cases would appreciably reduce the number of persons requiring such extensive observation.

Test manuals frequently contain data on concurrent validity, either as a substitute for predictive validity or as evidence of the diagnostic power of the test. Although especially suitable for personality tests, this type of validity is also reported for many ability tests. Among the most common criteria employed for concurrent validation are contrasted groups, ratings, and other tests.

Contrasted Groups. Validation by the method of contrasted groups generally involves a composite criterion that reflects the cumulative and uncontrolled selective influences of everyday life. This criterion is ultimately based upon survival within a particular group versus elimination therefrom. For example, in the validation of an intelligence test, the scores obtained by institutionalized mental defectives may be compared with those obtained by school children of the same age. In this case, the multiplicity of factors determining commitment to an institution for the feebleminded constitutes the criterion. Similarly, the validity of a musical aptitude or a mechanical aptitude test may be checked by comparing the scores obtained by students enrolled in a music school or an engineering school, respectively, with the scores of unselected high school or college students.

To be sure, contrasted groups can be selected on the basis of any criterion, such as school grades, ratings, or job performance, by simply choosing the extremes of the distribution of criterion measures. The contrasted groups included in the present category, however, are distinct groups that have gradually become differentiated through the operation of the multiple demands of daily living. The criterion under consideration is thus more complex and less clearly definable than those previously discussed.

The method of contrasted groups is used quite commonly in the validation of personality tests. Thus in validating a test of social traits, the test performance of salesmen or executives, on the one hand, may be compared with that of clerks or engineers, on the other. The assumption underlying such a procedure is that, with reference to many social traits, individuals who have entered and remained in such occupations as selling or executive work will as a group excel persons in such fields as clerical work or engineering. Similarly, college students who have engaged in many extracurricular activities may be compared with those who have participated in none during a comparable period of college attendance. Occupational groups have frequently been used in the development and validation of interest tests, such as the Strong Interest Test, as well as in the preparation of attitude scales. Other groups sometimes employed in the validation of attitude scales include political, religious, geographical, or other special groups generally known to represent distinctly different points of view on certain issues.

A number of personality tests concerned with the measurement of emotional or social adjustment are validated on such groups as institutionalized delinquents versus non-delinquents, or on neurotics versus normals. During World War II, for example, comparisons were made between the scores obtained on certain personality tests by the general selectee population and the scores obtained by individuals discharged from service because of neuropsychiatric disability. The criterion in such a case is inability to remain in military service because of personality difficulties.

In the development of certain personality tests, psychiatric diagnosis is used both as a basis for the selection of items and as evidence of test validity. Psychiatric diagnosis may serve as a satisfactory criterion provided that it is based upon prolonged observation and detailed case history, rather than upon a cursory psychiatric interview or examination. In the latter case, there is no reason to expect the psychiatric diagnosis to be superior to the test score itself as an indication of the individual's emotional condition. Such a psychiatric diagnosis could not be regarded as a criterion measure, but rather as an indicator or predictor whose own validity would have to be determined.

Ratings. Mention has already been made, in connection with other criterion categories, of certain types of ratings by school teachers, instructors in specialized courses, and job supervisors. To these can be added ratings by officers in military situations, ratings of students by school counselors, and ratings by co-workers, classmates, fraternity brothers, sorority sisters, and other groups of associates. The ratings discussed in earlier sections represented merely a subsidiary technique for obtaining information regarding such criteria as academic achievement, performance in specialized training, or job success. In this section, however, we are concerned with the use of ratings as the very core of the criterion measure. Under these circumstances, the ratings themselves define the criterion. Moreover, such ratings are not restricted to the evaluation of specific achievement, but involve a personal judgment by an observer regarding any of the variety of traits that psychological tests attempt to measure. Thus the subjects in the validation sample might be rated on such characteristics as dominance, mechanical ingenuity, originality, leadership, or honesty.

Ratings have been employed in the validation of almost every type of test. They are particularly useful in providing criteria for personality tests, since objective criteria are much more difficult to find in this area. Especially is this true of distinctly social traits, in which ratings based upon personal contact may constitute the most logically defensible criterion.

If ratings are obtained from trained raters under carefully controlled conditions, they can provide a valuable source of criterion data. It is generally desirable to secure independent ratings from more than one observer, in order to rule out individual bias and idiosyncrasy of the rater. The accuracy of ratings can be greatly increased by the use of well-constructed rating scales with clearly defined, unambiguous units and with adequate safeguards against common rating errors, such as the "halo effect" (the tendency on the part of raters to be unduly influenced by a single favorable or unfavorable trait, which thus colors their judgment of the individual's other traits). Finally, it is essential that raters have "trait acquaintance" with the individual in the traits they are rating. In other words, it is not enough to have known the individual for a long time. The rater should have had the opportunity to observe the individual in situations in which the particular trait in question was manifested. Raters should not rate an individual on traits for which they lack adequate trait acquaintance.

Ratings are also involved in criterion measures based upon clinical evaluations. In such cases, of course, the clinician's judgment may be aided by other supporting information, such as a detailed case history, test scores, and other objective records. The final evaluation, however, depends upon judgment, as in all ratings. Clinical evaluations are being used increasingly in the validation of personality tests. An example is provided by a project conducted at the USAF School of Aviation Medicine (16). In this project, clinical evaluations by staff psychologists constituted an important part of the criterion employed in investigating the validity of a series of personality screening tests for pilot cadets.

Correlations with Other Tests. Correlations between a new test and previously available tests are frequently cited as evidence of validity. When the new test is an abbreviated or simplified form of a currently available test, the latter can properly be regarded as a criterion measure. Thus a paper-and-pencil test might be validated against a more elaborate and time-consuming performance test whose validity had previously been established. Or a group test might be validated against an individual test. The Stanford-Binet, for example, has repeatedly served as a criterion in validating group tests. In such a case, the new test may be regarded at best as a crude approximation of the earlier one. It should be noted that unless the new test represents a simpler or shorter substitute for the earlier test, the use of the latter as a criterion is indefensible.

CONSTRUCT VALIDITY

The construct validity of a test is the extent to which the test may be said to measure a "theoretical construct" or trait. Examples of such constructs are intelligence, mechanical comprehension, verbal fluency, speed of walking, neuroticism, and anxiety. Focusing on a broader, more enduring, and more abstract kind of behavioral description than the previously discussed types of validity, construct validation requires the gradual accumulation of information from a variety of sources. Any data throwing light on the nature of the trait under consideration and the conditions affecting its development and manifestations are grist for this validity mill. As illustrations of the specific techniques utilized may be mentioned age differentiation, correlations with other tests, factor analysis, internal consistency, and effect of experimental variables on test scores.

Age Differentiation. A major criterion employed in the validation of a number of intelligence tests is age. Such tests as the Stanford-Binet and most preschool tests are checked against chronological age to determine whether the scores show a progressive increase with advancing age. Since abilities are expected to increase with age during childhood, it is argued that the test scores should likewise show such an increase, if the test is valid. The very concept of an age scale of intelligence, as initiated by Binet, is based upon the assumption that "intelligence" increases with age, at least until maturity.

The criterion of age differentiation, of course, is inapplicable to any functions that do not exhibit clear-cut and consistent age changes. In the area of personality measurement, for example, it has found limited use. Moreover, it should be noted that age differentiation is essentially a negative rather than a positive criterion. Thus if the test scores fail to improve with age, such a finding probably indicates that the test is not a valid measure of the abilities it was designed to sample. On the other hand, to prove that a test measures something that increases with age does not define the area covered by the test very precisely. A measure of height or weight would also show regular age increments, although it would obviously not be designated as an intelligence test.

A final point should be emphasized regarding the interpretation of the age criterion. A psychological test validated against such a criterion measures behavior characteristics that increase with age *under the conditions existing in the type of environment in which the test was standardized.* Since different cultures may stimulate and foster the development of dissimilar behavior characteristics, it cannot be assumed that the criterion of age differentiation is a universal one. Like all other criteria, it is circumscribed by the particular cultural setting in which it is derived.

Correlations with Other Tests. Correlations between a new test and similar earlier tests are sometimes cited as evidence that the new test measures approximately the same general area of behavior as other tests designated by the same name, such as "intelligence tests" or "mechanical aptitude tests." Unlike the correlations found in concurrent validity, these correlations should be moderately high, but not too high. If the new test correlates too highly with an already available test, without such added advantages as brevity or ease of administration, then the new test represents needless duplication.

Correlations with other tests are employed in still another way to demonstrate that the new test is relatively free from the influence of certain ir-relevant factors. For example, a special aptitude test or a personality test should have a negligible correlation with tests of general intelligence or scholastic aptitude. Similarly, reading comprehension should not appreciably affect performance on such tests. Thus correlations with tests of general intelligence, reading, or verbal comprehension are sometimes reported as indirect or negative evidence of validity. In these cases, high correlations would make the test suspect. Low correlations, however, would not in themselves insure validity. It will be noted that this use of correlations with other tests is similar to one of the techniques described under content validity.

Factor Analysis. Of particular relevance to construct validity is factor analysis, a statistical procedure for the identification of psychological traits. Essentially, factor analysis is a refined technique for analyzing the interrelationships of behavior data. For example, if 20 tests have been given to 300 persons, the first step is to compute the correlations of each test with every other. An inspection of the resulting table of 190 correlations may itself reveal certain clusters among the tests, suggesting the location of common traits. Thus if such tests as vocabulary, analogies, opposites, and sentence completion have high correlations with each other and low correlations with all other tests, we could tentatively infer the presence of a verbal comprehension factor. Since such an inspectional analysis of a correlation table is difficult and uncertain, however, more precise statistical techniques have been developed to locate the common factors required to account for the obtained correlations. These techniques of factor analysis will be examined further in Chapter 13, together with multiple aptitude tests developed by means of factor analysis. The application of factor analysis to the construction of personality tests will be illustrated in Chapter 18.

In the process of factor analysis, the number of variables or categories in terms of which each individual's performance can be described is reduced from the number of original tests to a relatively small number of factors, or common traits. In the example cited above, five or six factors might suffice to account for the intercorrelations among the 20 tests. Each individual might thus be described in terms of his scores in the five or six factors, rather than in terms of the original 20 scores. A major purpose of factor analysis is to simplify the description of behavior by reducing the number of categories from an initial multiplicity of test variables to a few common factors, or traits.

After the factors have been identified, they can be utilized in describing the factorial composition of a test. Each test can thus be characterized in terms of the major factors determining its scores, together with the weight or

loading of each factor. Such factor loadings also represent the correlations
of the test with each factor, a correlation known as the *factorial validity* of
the test. Thus if the verbal comprehension factor has a weight of .66 in a
vocabulary test, the factorial validity of this vocabulary test as a measure of
the trait of verbal comprehension is .66. It should be noted that factorial
validity is essentially the correlation of the test with whatever is common to
a group of tests or other indices of behavior. The set of variables analyzed
can, of course, include both test and non-test data. Ratings and other criterion
measures can thus be utilized, along with other tests, to explore the factorial
validity of a particular test and to define the common traits it measures.

Internal Consistency. In the published descriptions of certain tests, especially
in the area of personality, the statement is made that the test has been validated by the method of internal consistency. The essential characteristic of
this method is that the criterion is none other than the total score on the test
itself. Sometimes an adaptation of the contrasted group method is used, extreme groups being selected on the basis of the total test score. The performance of the upper criterion group on each test item is then compared with
that of the lower criterion group. Items that fail to show a significantly
greater proportion of "passes" in the upper than in the lower criterion group
are considered invalid, and are either eliminated or revised. Correlational
procedures may also be employed for this purpose. For example, the biserial
correlation between "pass-fail" on each item and total test score can be
computed. Only those items yielding significant item-test correlations would
be retained. A test whose items were selected by this method can be said to
show internal consistency, since each item differentiates in the same direction
as the entire test.

Another application of the criterion of internal consistency involves the
correlation of subtest scores with total score. Many intelligence tests, for
instance, consist of separately administered subtests (such as vocabulary,
arithmetic, picture completion, etc.) whose scores are combined in finding
the total test score. In the construction of such tests, the scores on each
subtest are often correlated with total score and any subtest whose correlation with total score is too low is eliminated. The correlations of the remaining subtests with total score are then reported as evidence of the internal
consistency of the entire instrument.

It is apparent that internal consistency correlations, whether based on
items or subtests, are essentially measures of homogeneity. Since it helps to
characterize the behavior domain or trait sampled by the test, the degree of
homogeneity of a test has some relevance to its construct validity. Nevertheless, the contribution of internal consistency data to test validation is very

limited. In the absence of data external to the test itself, little can be learned about what a test measures.

Effect of Experimental Variables on Test Scores. A further source of data for construct validation is provided by experiments on the effect of selected variables on test scores. Whether pitch discrimination as measured by a particular test is or is not susceptible to practice, for instance, can be checked by administering the test to the same subjects before and after a period of intensive practice. A test designed to measure anxiety-proneness can be administered to subjects who are subsequently put through a situation designed to arouse anxiety, such as taking an examination under distracting and stressful conditions. The initial anxiety test scores can then be correlated with physiological and other indices of anxiety expression during and after the examination.

Except for the artificial introduction of an anxiety-provoking variable, the procedure followed in the above experiment is similar to that used in establishing predictive validity. The direct measures of anxiety expression will be recognized as the criterion against which the predictions made from test scores are validated. A different hypothesis regarding an anxiety test could be evaluated by administering the test before and after an anxiety-arousing experience and seeing whether test scores rise significantly on the retest. Positive findings from such an experiment would indicate that the test scores reflect current anxiety level. In a similar way, experiments can be designed to test any other hypothesis regarding the trait measured by a given test.

A COMPREHENSIVE VIEW

We have considered four major ways of asking, "How valid is this test?" To highlight the distinctive features of these four types of validity, let us apply each in turn to a test consisting of fifty assorted arithmetic problems. This test might be used:

- As an achievement test in elementary school arithmetic (content validity):
  How much has Dick learned in the past?

- As an aptitude test to predict performance in high school mathematics (predictive validity):
  How well will Jim learn in the future?

- As a technique for diagnosing brain damage (concurrent validity):
  Does Bill belong in the brain-damaged or in the normal group?

- As a measure of logical reasoning (construct validity):
  How can we describe Henry's psychological functioning?

Lest the above example should make validity appear clear and simple, let us hasten to inject some disturbing thoughts. The four types of validity are not distinct and logically coordinate. Construct validity is a comprehensive concept, which includes the other three types. All the specific techniques for establishing content, predictive, and concurrent validity, discussed in earlier sections of this chapter, could have been listed again under construct validity. Comparing the test performance of contrasted groups, such as neurotics and normals, is one way of checking the construct validity of a test designed to measure emotional adjustment, anxiety, or other postulated traits. Comparing the test scores of institutionalized mental defectives with those of normal school children is one way to investigate the construct validity of an intelligence test. The correlations of a mechanical aptitude test with performance in shop courses and in a wide variety of jobs contribute to our understanding of the construct measured by the test.

Content validity likewise enters into both the construction and the subsequent evaluation of all tests. In assembling items for any new test, the test constructor is guided by hypotheses regarding the relations between the type of content he chooses and the behavior he wishes to measure. Empirical and concurrent validation, as well as the other techniques discussed under construct validation, represent ways of testing such hypotheses. As for the test user, he too relies in part on content validity in evaluating any test. For example, he may check the vocabulary in an emotional adjustment inventory to determine whether some of the words are too difficult for the subjects he plans to test; he may choose a non-verbal rather than a verbal test of intelligence for examining children with reading disabilities; he may conclude that the scores on a particular test depend too much on speed for his purposes; or he may notice that an intelligence test developed twenty years ago contains many obsolescent items unsuitable for use today. All these observations about content are relevant to the construct validity of a test. In fact, there is no information provided by any validation procedure that is *not* relevant to construct validity.

Following its introduction in the *Technical Recommendations* in 1954, the concept of construct validity was subjected to lively discussion. In a number of provocative articles, construct validity was extensively elaborated (8), favorably reviewed (6), diligently illustrated (12), vigorously attacked (3), partially redefined (15), and incisively sharpened (5). The basic idea of construct validity is not new. The use of theoretical constructs or trait categories is as old as psychological testing. Some of the earliest tests were designed to measure such constructs as attention, memory, and association. Nor should we forget that most notorious of all theoretical constructs, "intelligence."

Similarly, none of the validation techniques specially identified with construct validity is new. Test manuals had been reporting data on age differentiation, correlations with other tests, factorial validity, internal consistency, and the effect of such experimental variables as practice on test scores long before construct validity was given a name and official respectability in the *Technical Recommendations*.

What, then, has the concept of construct validity contributed to psychological testing? First, it has focused attention on the desirability of basing test construction on an explicitly recognized theoretical foundation. Both in devising a new test and in setting up procedures for its validation, the investigator is urged to formulate psychological hypotheses. The proponents of construct validity have tried to integrate psychological testing more closely with psychological theory and experimental methods. A second contribution has been to stimulate the search for novel ways of gathering validation data. Although the major techniques currently employed to estimate construct validity have been familiar for many years, more exploration of different validation techniques can be expected.

A possible danger in the application of construct validity is that it may open the way for subjective, unverified assertions about test validity. Since construct validity is such a broad and loosely defined concept, it has been widely misunderstood. Some textbook writers and test constructors seem to perceive it as content validity expressed in terms of psychological trait names. Hence they present as construct validity purely subjective accounts of what they believe (or hope) their test measures. It is also unfortunate that the chief exponents of construct validity have asserted that this type of validation "is involved whenever a test is to be interpreted as a measure of some attribute or quality which is not 'operationally defined' " (8, p. 282). Such a statement opens the door wider for fuzzy thinking about test scores and the traits they measure.

Actually, the theoretical construct, trait, or behavior domain measured by any test can be defined in terms of the operations performed in establishing the validity of the test. Such a definition would take into account the various criteria with which the test correlated significantly, as well as the conditions found to affect its scores and the groups differing significantly in such scores. These procedures are entirely in accord with the positive contributions made by the concept of construct validity. It would also seem desirable to retain the concept of the criterion in construct validation, not as a specific practical measure to be predicted, but more generally to refer to independently gathered *external data*. The need to base all validation on data, rather than on armchair speculation, would thus be re-emphasized, as would the need for data external to the test scores themselves. Internal analysis of the test, through item-test correlations, factorial analyses of test items, etc., is never an adequate substitute for external validation.

REFERENCES

1. American Psychological Association. *Technical recommendations for psychological tests and diagnostic techniques.* Washington: Amer. Psychol. Assoc., 1954.
2. Anastasi, Anne. The concept of validity in the interpretation of test scores. *Educ. psychol. Measmt.,* 1950, 10, 67-78.
3. Bechtoldt, H. P. Construct validity: a critique. *Amer. Psychologist,* 1959, 14, 619-629.
4. Burik, T. E. Relative roles of the learning and motor factors involved in the digit symbol test. *J. Psychol.,* 1950, 30, 33-42.
5. Campbell, D. T. Recommendations for APA test standards regarding construct, trait, and discriminant validity. *Amer. Psychologist,* 1960, 15, 546-553.
6. Clark, Cherry Ann. Developments and applications in the area of construct validity. *Rev. educ. Res.,* 1959, 29, 84-105.
7. Cook, W. W. The measurement of general spelling ability involving controlled comparisons between techniques. *Univer. Iowa Stud. Educ.,* 1932, 6, No. 6.
8. Cronbach, L. J., and Meehl, P. E. Construct validity in psychological tests. *Psychol. Bull.,* 1955, 52, 281-302.
9. Ebel, R. L. Obtaining and reporting evidence on content validity. *Educ. psychol. Measmt.,* 1956, 16, 269-282.
10. Gulliksen, H. Intrinsic validity. *Amer. Psychologist,* 1950, 5, 511-517.
11. Huddleston, Edith M. Test development on the basis of content validity. *Educ. psychol. Measmt.,* 1956, 16, 283-293.
12. Jessor, R., and Hammond, K. R. Construct validity and the Taylor Anxiety Scale. *Psychol. Bull.,* 1957, 54, 161-170.
13. Knoell, Dorothy M., and Harris, C. W. A factor analysis of spelling ability. *J. educ. Res.,* 1952, 46, 95-111.
14. Lennon, R. T. Assumptions underlying the use of content validity. *Educ. psychol. Measmt.,* 1956, 16, 294-304.
15. Loevinger, Jane. Objective tests as instruments of psychological theory. *Psychol. Rep.,* 1957, 3, 635-694.
16. Sells, S. B. A research program on the psychiatric selection of flying personnel: I. Methodological introduction and experimental design. *Proj. No. 21-37-002. Rep. No. 1, USAF Sch. Aviat. Med.,* 1951.
17. Thorndike, R. L. *Personnel selection: test and measurement techniques.* N. Y.: Wiley, 1949.

CHAPTER 7

Utilization of Validity Data

The test user is concerned with validity at either or both of two stages. First, when considering the suitability of a test for his purposes, he examines available validity reported in the test manual or other published sources. Through such information, he arrives at a tentative concept of what psychological functions the test actually measures and he judges the relevance of such functions to his proposed use of the test. In effect, when a test user relies on published validation data, he is dealing with construct validity, regardless of the specific procedures whereby the data were gathered. Even when predictive or concurrent validity is reported, the criteria employed cannot be assumed to be identical with those the test user wants to predict or diagnose. Jobs bearing the same title in two different companies are rarely, if ever, identical. Two courses in freshman English taught in different colleges may be quite dissimilar. The pronounced variation in apparently similar criteria is borne out by the validity coefficients reported in many test manuals. Thus when scores on a single test are correlated with grades in a particular course, the resulting validity coefficients usually vary widely from one college to another. At least part of this variation results from differences in the specific criterion, although size and heterogeneity of the group tested also affect the correlations.

Because of the specificity of each criterion, test users should check the validity of any chosen test against local criteria whenever possible. Although published data may strongly suggest that a given test should have high validity in a particular situation, direct corroboration is always desirable. The determination of validity against specific local criteria represents the second stage in the test user's evaluation of validity. The techniques to be discussed in this chapter are especially relevant to the analysis of validity data obtained by the test user himself. Most of them are also useful, however, in understanding and evaluating the validity data reported in test manuals.

153

EXPECTANCY TABLES

It will be recalled that in both predictive and concurrent validity, test scores are evaluated against an independent criterion which the test is designed to predict or diagnose, respectively. The relation between subjects' test scores and their criterion status can be analyzed in a number of ways. A simple device for expressing this relation is provided by the expectancy table (1, 2, 35). Such a table shows the likelihood of different criterion outcomes for persons obtaining each test score.

Figures 22 and 23 represent expectancy tables for a dichotomous, or twofold, criterion. Figure 22 shows the relation between scores on the Army

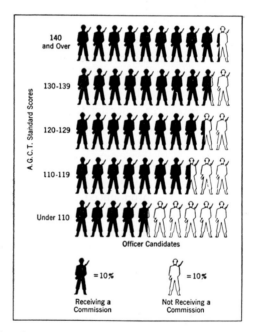

Fig. 22. Validity of Army General Classification Test in Predicting Success in Officer Training Course. (From Boring, 3, p. 242.)

General Classification Test (AGCT) and successful completion of officer training course. The chart gives the percentage of men within each AGCT score interval who actually received a commission in the sample investigated. It will be noted that this percentage increases consistently from the group scoring under 110 to that scoring 140 and over. Figure 23 shows a similar correspondence between percentage of men eliminated in primary flight training and stanine score obtained on a pilot selection battery developed by the Air Force. While 77 per cent of the men receiving a stanine of 1 were eliminated, only 4 per cent of those at stanine 9 failed to complete the course satisfactorily, the percentage decreasing consistently over the intervening stanines.

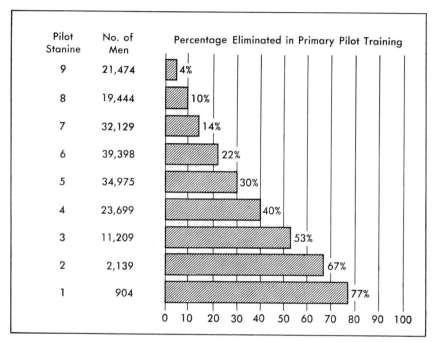

Fig. 23.   Validity of a Pilot Selection Battery in Predicting Success in Primary Flight Training. (From Flanagan, 13, p. 58.)

The percentages given in Figures 22 and 23 provide an estimate of the probabilities that individuals tested in the future will attain the specified criterion status. On the basis of Figure 23, for example, it is predicted that approximately 40 per cent of pilot cadets who obtain a stanine score of 4 will fail, and that approximately 60 per cent will satisfactorily complete primary flight training. Similar statements regarding the expectancy of success or failure can be made about *individuals* who receive each of the stanines. Thus an individual with a stanine of 4 has a 60:40 or 3:2 chance of completing primary flight training.

When the criterion is a continuous rather than a dichotomous variable, the expectancy table can be constructed directly from a scatter diagram. In plotting such a scatter diagram, each individual's standing in both test and criterion is tallied simultaneously, as illustrated in Figure 24. Along the base-line of this diagram are shown the criterion measures, grades in rhetoric, and along the side are given scores on the Sentences Test of the Differential Aptitude Tests (DAT). In this test, the subject is required to locate errors in grammar, punctuation, or word usage in a series of sentences. Each tally mark in Figure 24 shows the test score and rhetoric grade of each of 100 freshman women tested in a state teachers' college. The total frequencies for the different cells, as well as the row totals, have been indicated.

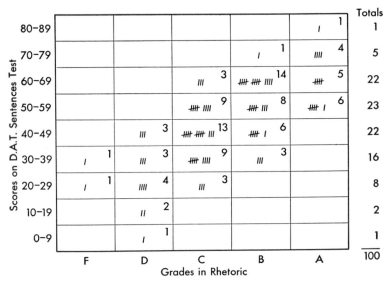

Fig. 24. Bivariate Distribution Showing Relationship between Scores on DAT Sentences Test and Grades in Rhetoric. (From Wesman, 36, p. 2.)

To convert this scatter diagram into an expectancy table, it is only neces-sary to express each cell frequency as a percentage of the corresponding row total. For example, of the 16 subjects who scored between 30 and 39 on the test, 6 per cent (1 case) received a grade of F in the rhetoric course, 19 per cent (3 cases) received D, 56 per cent (9 cases) C, and 19 per cent (3 cases) B. The complete expectancy table will be found in Table 9. Given an individual's test score, it is possible by means of such an expectancy table to predict the chances of his obtaining each grade in the criterion variable. For example, we would expect anyone who scores above 80 to receive a grade of A, and anyone scoring above 70 to receive either A or B. Similarly, we would expect no D or F grades among those scoring above 50 on the test. Other predictions of this sort can readily be made by reference to Table 9.

TABLE 9. **Expectancy Table Showing the Relation between Scores on the DAT Sentences Test and Rhetoric Grades**

(From Wesman, 35, p. 2.)

Test Scores	Percentage Receiving Each Grade				
	F	D	C	B	A
80-89					100
70-79				20	80
60-69			14	63	23
50-59			39	35	26
40-49		14	59	27	
30-39	6	19	56	19	
20-29	13	50	37		
10-19		100			
0- 9		100			

It should be noted, of course, that such predictions are subject to considerable sampling error, especially when the number of cases tested is small. Since the individual percentages are based on the relatively few persons falling within a single cell, the chance fluctuations in such percentages from sample to sample will undoubtedly be large. On the other hand, presentation of validity data by means of expectancy tables is vivid and clear, and it permits an examination of the predictive value of the test in different parts of the range.

VALIDITY COEFFICIENTS

To experienced test users, the most familiar method for reporting test validity is through a validity coefficient, showing the correlation between test and criterion. Not only does such a correlation provide a single, over-all index of the validity of the test, but it is also more stable and less subject to sampling fluctuation than the expectancy table percentages, since it is based on all the cases in the group. A correlation coefficient can be found for any set of data that can be represented by an expectancy table. In the case of two continuous variables, as illustrated in Figure 24 and Table 9, the familiar Pearson Product-Moment Correlation Coefficient can be computed. In the example cited, the correlation between DAT Sentences Test and rhetoric grades is .71.

When the criterion is dichotomized, as in the situations represented by Figures 22 and 23, a *biserial correlation* may be computed. Such a correlation is based upon the difference in mean test scores obtained by the two criterion groups, as well as upon the standard deviation of test scores and the proportion of individuals who fall into the two criterion groups. Other types of correlation coefficients are available for expressing the relationship between test scores and criterion under still different circumstances, as when both variables are dichotomized (tetrachoric correlation), or when the relationship varies at different parts of the range (curvilinear correlation). The specific procedures for computing these different kinds of correlations can be found in any standard statistics text, such as those cited in Chapter 4.

As in test reliability, discussed in Chapter 5, it is essential to specify the nature of the group on which a validity coefficient is determined. The same test may measure different functions when given to individuals who differ in age, sex, educational level, occupation, or any other relevant characteristic. It has already been pointed out in Chapter 6, in connection with content validity, that the work methods employed to arrive at the same solution of a test problem may vary widely from group to group. Consequently, a test could have high validity in predicting a particular criterion in one population, and little or no validity in another. Or it might be a valid measure of different functions in the two populations. Thus, unless the validation sample is representative of the population on which the test is to be used, validity should be redetermined on a more appropriate sample.

The question of *range* of scores is, of course, as relevant to the measurement of validity as it is to the measurement of reliability, since both characteristics are commonly reported in terms of correlation coefficients. It will be recalled that, other things being equal, the wider the range of scores, the higher will be the correlation. This fact should be kept in mind when interpreting the validity coefficients given in test manuals.

A special difficulty encountered in many validation samples arises from *preselection*. For example, a new test that is being validated for job selection may be administered to a group of newly hired employees on whom criterion measures of job performance will eventually be available. It is very likely, however, that such employees represent a superior selection of all those who applied for the job. Hence the range of such a group in both test scores and criterion measures will be curtailed at the lower end of the distribution. The effect of such preselection will therefore be to lower the validity coefficient. In the subsequent use of the test, when it is administered to all applicants for selection purposes, the validity can be expected to be somewhat higher. If adequate information is available regarding the extent of preselection that has occurred in the validation sample, correction formulas can be applied to estimate the effect upon the validity coefficient (cf. 29, pp. 169 ff.).

How high should a validity coefficient be? No general answer to this question is possible, since the interpretation of a validity coefficient must take into account a number of concomitant circumstances. The obtained correlation, of course, should be high enough to be significant at some acceptable level, such as the .01 or .05 levels discussed in Chapter 5. In other words, before drawing any conclusions about the validity of a test, we should be reasonably certain that the obtained validity coefficient could not have arisen through chance fluctuations of sampling from a true correlation of zero.

Having established a significant correlation between test scores and criterion, however, we need to evaluate the size of the correlation in the light of the uses to be made of the test. If we wish to predict an individual's exact criterion score, such as the grade-point average a student will receive in college, the validity coefficient may be interpreted in terms of the *standard error of estimate,* which is analogous to the error of measurement discussed in connection with reliability. It will be recalled that the error of measurement indicates the margin of error to be expected in an individual's score as a result of the unreliability of the test. Similarly, the error of estimate shows the margin of error to be expected in the individual's predicted criterion score, as a result of the imperfect validity of the test.

The error of estimate is found by the following formula:

$$\sigma_{est.} = \sigma_y\sqrt{1 - r^2_{xy}}$$

in which r^2_{xy} is the square of the validity coefficient and σ_y is the standard deviation of the criterion scores. It will be noted that if the validity were perfect ($r_{xy} = 1.00$), the error of estimate would be zero. On the other hand, with a test having zero validity, the error of estimate is as large as the standard deviation of the criterion distribution ($\sigma_{est.} = \sigma_y\sqrt{1 - 0} = \sigma_y$). Under these conditions, the prediction is no better than a guess, and the range of prediction error is as wide as the entire distribution of criterion scores. Between these two extremes are to be found the errors of estimate corresponding to tests of varying validity.

Reference to the formula for $\sigma_{est.}$ will show that the term $\sqrt{1 - r^2_{xy}}$ serves to indicate the size of the error *relative to the error that would result from a mere guess,* i.e., with zero validity. In other words, if $\sqrt{1 - r^2_{xy}}$ is equal to 1.00, the error of estimate is as large as it would be if we were to guess the subject's score. The predictive improvement attributable to the use of the test would thus be nil. If the validity coefficient is .80, the $\sqrt{1 - r^2_{xy}}$ is equal to .60, and the error is 60 per cent as large as it would be by chance. To put it differently, the use of such a test enables us to predict the individual's criterion performance with a margin of error that is 40 per cent smaller than it would be if we were to guess.

It would thus appear that even with a validity of .80, which is unusually high, the error of predicted scores is considerable. If the primary function of psychological tests were to predict each individual's exact position in the criterion distribution, the outlook would be quite pessimistic. When examined in the light of the error of estimate, most tests do not appear very efficient. In most testing situations, however, it is not necessary to predict the specific criterion performance of individual cases, but rather to determine which individuals will exceed a certain minimum standard of performance, or cutoff point, in the criterion. Who will successfully complete medical school, primary flight training, or officer candidate school? Who will prove to be a satisfactory clerk, salesman, or machine operator? Such information is useful not only in group selection but also in individual guidance. For example, it is advantageous to be able to predict that a given person has a good chance of passing all courses in law school, even if we are unable to estimate with certainty whether his grade average will be 74 or 81.

For some purposes, a test may appreciably improve predictive efficiency if it shows *any* significant correlation with the criterion, however low. Under certain circumstances, even validities as low as .20 or .30 may justify inclusion of the test in a selection program. It is gradually being recognized that the traditional evaluation of tests in terms of the error of estimate is unrealistically stringent. Increasing attention is being given to other ways of evaluating the contribution of a test, which take into account the types of decisions to be made from the scores. Some of these procedures will be illustrated in the following section.

TEST VALIDITY AND DECISION THEORY

Let us suppose that 100 applicants have been given an aptitude test and followed up until each could be evaluated for success on a certain job. Figure 25 shows the bivariate distribution of test scores and measures of job success for the 100 subjects. The correlation between these two variables is slightly below .70. The minimum acceptable job performance, or criterion cutoff point, is indicated in the diagram by a heavy horizontal line. The 40 cases falling below this line would represent job failures; the 60 above the line, job successes. If all 100 applicants are hired, therefore, 60 per cent will succeed on the job. Similarly, if a smaller number were hired at random, without reference to test scores, the proportion of successes would probably be close to 60 per cent. Suppose, however, that the test scores are used to select the 45 most promising applicants out of the 100 (selection ratio = .45). In such a case, the 45 individuals falling to the right of the heavy vertical line would be chosen. Within this group of 45, it can be seen that there are 7 job failures, or "misses," falling below the heavy horizontal line, and 38 job successes. Hence the percentage of job successes is now 84 rather than 60 (i.e., $38/45 = .84$). This increase is attributable to the use of the test as a screening instrument. It will be noted that errors in predicted criterion score that do not affect the decision can be ignored. Only those prediction errors that cross the cutoff line and hence place the individual in the wrong category will reduce the selective effectiveness of the test.

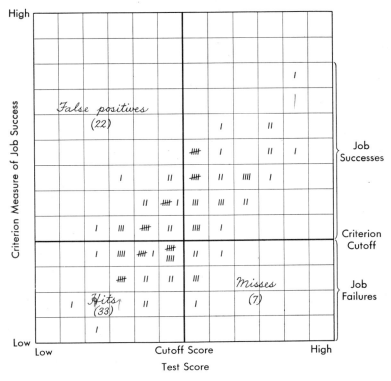

Fig. 25. Increase in the Proportion of "Successes" Resulting from the Use of a Screening Test.

A useful concept in the evaluation of screening effectiveness is that of "false positives." This term has been adopted from the medical field, in which a test for a pathological condition is reported to be positive if the condition is present. A false positive thus refers to a case in which the test erroneously indicates the presence of the pathological condition. In the screening situation, the false positives are the successful workers who are rejected on the basis of the test. Referring again to Figure 25, we find a total of 22 false positives within the upper left-hand quadrant of the graph.

These individuals fall above the criterion cutoff, but below (to the left of) the cutoff score on the test. On the other hand, the 33 "hits" in the lower left-hand quadrant of Figure 25 are job failures who were correctly identified as such by the test.

In setting a cutoff score on a test, attention should be given to the percentage of false positives as well as to the percentages of successes and failures within the selected group. In certain situations, the cutoff point should be set sufficiently high to exclude all but a few possible failures. This would be the case, for example, when the job is of such a nature that a poorly qualified worker could cause serious loss or damage. Under other circumstances, it may be more important to admit as many qualified persons as possible, at the risk of including more failures. In the latter case, the number of false positives can be reduced by the choice of a lower cutoff score. Other factors that normally determine the position of the cutoff score include the available personnel supply, the number of job openings, and the urgency or speed with which the openings must be filled.

In the terminology of decision theory, the example given in Figure 25 illustrates a simple *strategy,* or plan for deciding which applicants to accept and which to reject. In this case, the strategy was to accept the 45 persons with the highest test scores. The increase in percentage of successful employees from 60 to 84 could be used as a basis for estimating the *payoff,* or net benefit to the company resulting from the use of the test.

Statistical decision theory was developed by Wald (33) in the 1940's with special reference to the decisions required in the inspection and quality control of industrial products. Many of its implications for the construction and interpretation of psychological tests have been systematically worked out by Cronbach and Gleser (9). Essentially, decision theory is an attempt to put the decision-making process into mathematical form, so that available information may be used to arrive at the most effective decision under specified circumstances. The mathematical procedures employed in decision theory are often quite complex, and few are in a form permitting their immediate application to practical testing problems. Some of the basic concepts of decision theory, however, are proving helpful in the reformulation and clarification of certain questions about tests. A few of these ideas were introduced into testing before the formal development of statistical decision theory and were later recognized as fitting into that framework (cf. 9).

An example of such a precursor of decision theory in psychological testing is to be found in the Taylor-Russell Tables (28). These tables permit a determination of the net gain in selection accuracy attributable to the use of the test. The information required includes the validity coefficient of the test, the selection ratio or proportion of applicants who must be accepted, and the proportion of successful applicants selected without the use of the test. A change in any of these three factors can alter the predictive efficiency of the test.

For purposes of illustration, one of the Taylor-Russell Tables has been reproduced in Table 10. This table is designed for use when the percentage

TABLE 10. Proportion of "Successes" Expected through the Use of Tests of Given Validity, When Proportion of "Successes" Prior to Use of Test Was .60

(From Taylor and Russell, 28, p. 576)

Validity	Selection Ratio										
	.05	.10	.20	.30	.40	.50	.60	.70	.80	.90	.95
.00	.60	.60	.60	.60	.60	.60	.60	.60	.60	.60	.60
.05	.64	.63	.63	.62	.62	.62	.61	.61	.61	.60	.60
.10	.68	.67	.65	.64	.64	.63	.63	.62	.61	.61	.60
.15	.71	.70	.68	.67	.66	.65	.64	.63	.62	.61	.61
.20	.75	.73	.71	.69	.67	.66	.65	.64	.63	.62	.61
.25	.78	.76	.73	.71	.69	.68	.66	.65	.63	.62	.61
.30	.82	.79	.76	.73	.71	.69	.68	.66	.64	.62	.61
.35	.85	.82	.78	.75	.73	.71	.69	.67	.65	.63	.62
.40	.88	.85	.81	.78	.75	.73	.70	.68	.66	.63	.62
.45	.90	.87	.83	.80	.77	.74	.72	.69	.66	.64	.62
.50	.93	.90	.86	.82	.79	.76	.73	.70	.67	.64	.62
.55	.95	.92	.88	.84	.81	.78	.75	.71	.68	.64	.62
.60	.96	.94	.90	.87	.83	.80	.76	.73	.69	.65	.63
.65	.98	.96	.92	.89	.85	.82	.78	.74	.70	.65	.63
.70	.99	.97	.94	.91	.87	.84	.80	.75	.71	.66	.63
.75	.99	.99	.96	.93	.90	.86	.81	.77	.71	.66	.63
.80	1.00	.99	.98	.95	.92	.88	.83	.78	.72	.66	.63
.85	1.00	1.00	.99	.97	.95	.91	.86	.80	.73	.66	.63
.90	1.00	1.00	1.00	.99	.97	.94	.88	.82	.74	.67	.63
.95	1.00	1.00	1.00	1.00	.99	.97	.92	.84	.75	67	.63
1.00	1.00	1.00	1.00	1.00	1.00	1.00	1.00	.86	.75	.67	.63

of successful applicants selected prior to the use of the test is 60. Across the top are given different values of the selection ratio, and along the side are the test validities. The entries in the body of the table indicate the proportion of successful persons selected after the use of the test. Thus the difference between .60 and any one table entry shows the increase in proportion of successful selections attributable to the test.

Obviously if the selection ratio were 100 per cent, that is, if all applicants had to be accepted, no test, however valid, could improve the selection process. Reference to Table 10 shows that, when as many as 95 per cent of applicants must be admitted, even a test with perfect validity ($r = 1.00$) would raise the proportion of successful persons by only 3 per cent (.60 to .63). On the other hand, when only 5 per cent of applicants need to be chosen, a test with a validity coefficient of only .30 can raise the percentage of successful applicants selected from 60 to 82. The rise from 60 to 82 represents the net effectiveness of the test. It indicates the contribution the test makes to the selection of individuals who will meet the minimum standards in criterion performance. In applying the Taylor-Russell Tables, of course, test validity should be computed on the same sort of group used to estimate percentage of prior successes. In other words, the contribution of the test is not evaluated against chance success unless applicants were previously selected by chance—a most unlikely circumstance. Since applicants are ordinarily selected on the basis of previous job history, letters of recommendation, interviews, and the like, the contribution of the test should be evaluated on the basis of what the test adds to these previous selection procedures.

In many practical situations, what is wanted is an estimate of the effect of the selection test, not on percentage of workers exceeding the minimum performance, but on over-all *output* of the selected workers. How does the actual level of job proficiency or criterion achievement of the workers hired on the basis of the test compare with that of the total applicant sample that would have been hired without the test? Following the work of Taylor and Russell, several investigators addressed themselves to this question (4, 7, 19, 26). Brogden (4) first demonstrated that the expected increase in output is directly proportional to the validity of the test. Thus the improvement resulting from the use of a test of validity .50 is 50 per cent as great as the improvement expected from a test of perfect validity.

The relation between test validity and expected rise in criterion achievement can be readily seen in Table 11. Expressing criterion scores as standard scores with a mean of zero and an *SD* of 1.00, this table gives the expected mean criterion score of workers selected with a test of given validity and with a given selection ratio. It will be noted, for example, that when 20 per cent of the applicants are hired and the validity coefficient is .50, the mean criterion performance is .70 *SD* above the mean of the unselected population of applicants. With the same selection ratio and a perfect test (validity coefficient = 1.00), the mean criterion score of the selected applicants would be 1.40, just twice what it would be with the test of validity .50. Similar direct linear relations will be found if other mean criterion performances are compared within any row of Table 11. For instance, with a selection ratio of 60 per cent, a validity of .25 yields a mean criterion score of .16, while a

TABLE 11. Mean Standard Criterion Score of Selected Cases in Relation to Test Validity and Selection Ratio

(From Brown and Ghiselli, 7, p. 342)

Selection Ratio	Validity Coefficient																				
	.00	.05	.10	.15	.20	.25	.30	.35	.40	.45	.50	.55	.60	.65	.70	.75	.80	.85	.90	.95	1.00
.05	.00	.10	.21	.31	.42	.52	.62	.73	.83	.94	1.04	1.14	1.25	1.35	1.46	1.56	1.66	1.77	1.87	1.98	2.08
.10	.00	.09	.18	.26	.35	.44	.53	.62	.70	.79	.88	.97	1.05	1.14	1.23	1.32	1.41	1.49	1.58	1.67	1.76
.15	.00	.08	.15	.23	.31	.39	.46	.54	.62	.70	.77	.85	.93	1.01	1.08	1.16	1.24	1.32	1.39	1.47	1.55
.20	.00	.07	.14	.21	.28	.35	.42	.49	.56	.63	.70	.77	.84	.91	.98	1.05	1.12	1.19	1.26	1.33	1.40
.25	.00	.06	.13	.19	.25	.32	.38	.44	.51	.57	.63	.70	.76	.82	.89	.95	1.01	1.08	1.14	1.20	1.27
.30	.00	.06	.12	.17	.23	.29	.35	.40	.46	.52	.58	.64	.69	.75	.81	.87	.92	.98	1.04	1.10	1.16
.35	.00	.05	.11	.16	.21	.26	.32	.37	.42	.48	.53	.58	.63	.69	.74	.79	.84	.90	.95	1.00	1.06
.40	.00	.05	.10	.15	.19	.24	.29	.34	.39	.44	.48	.53	.58	.63	.68	.73	.77	.82	.87	.92	.97
.45	.00	.04	.09	.13	.18	.22	.26	.31	.35	.40	.44	.48	.53	.57	.62	.66	.70	.75	.79	.84	.88
.50	.00	.04	.08	.12	.16	.20	.24	.28	.32	.36	.40	.44	.48	.52	.56	.60	.64	.68	.72	.76	.80
.55	.00	.04	.07	.11	.14	.18	.22	.25	.29	.32	.36	.40	.43	.47	.50	.54	.58	.61	.65	.68	.72
.60	.00	.03	.06	.10	.13	.16	.19	.23	.26	.29	.32	.35	.39	.42	.45	.48	.52	.55	.58	.61	.64
.65	.00	.03	.06	.09	.11	.14	.17	.20	.23	.26	.28	.31	.34	.37	.40	.43	.46	.48	.51	.54	.57
.70	.00	.02	.05	.07	.10	.12	.15	.17	.20	.22	.25	.27	.30	.32	.35	.37	.40	.42	.45	.47	.50
.75	.00	.02	.04	.06	.08	.11	.13	.15	.17	.19	.21	.23	.25	.27	.30	.32	.33	.36	.38	.40	.42
.80	.00	.02	.04	.05	.07	.09	.11	.12	.14	.16	.18	.19	.21	.22	.25	.26	.28	.30	.32	.33	.35
.85	.00	.01	.03	.04	.05	.07	.08	.10	.11	.12	.14	.15	.16	.18	.19	.20	.22	.23	.25	.26	.27
.90	.00	.01	.02	.03	.04	.05	.06	.07	.08	.09	.10	.11	.12	.13	.14	.15	.16	.17	.18	.19	.20
.95	.00	.01	.01	.02	.02	.03	.03	.04	.04	.05	.05	.06	.07	.07	.08	.08	.09	.09	.10	.10	.11

validity of .50 yields a mean of .32. Again, doubling the validity doubles the output rise.

Such an evaluation of test validity is obviously much more favorable than that based on the previously discussed error of estimate. The reason for the difference can be seen in the fact that prediction errors that do not affect decisions are irrelevant to the selection situation (36). For example, if Smith and Jones are both superior workers and are both hired on the basis of the test, it does not matter if the test shows Smith to be better than Jones while in job performance Jones excels Smith.

In decision theory, the mathematical payoff function derived for any given strategy incorporates a number of parameters not traditionally considered in evaluating the predictive effectiveness of tests. The selection ratio discussed above is one such parameter. Another is the cost of administering the test. Thus a test of low validity is more likely to be retained if it is short, inexpensive, easily administered by relatively untrained personnel, and suitable for group administration. An individual test requiring a trained examiner or expensive equipment would need a higher validity to justify its use. A further consideration is whether the test assesses an area of criterion-related behavior not otherwise covered by available techniques.

Another major aspect of decision theory is the evaluation of outcomes. The payoff, or expected benefit of a decision strategy, is based on the probability of each outcome (such as job success or failure), together with estimates of the relative value of such outcomes. The lack of adequate systems for assigning values to outcomes is one of the chief obstacles to the wide application of decision theory. In industrial decisions, a dollar and cents value can frequently be employed. Even in such cases, however, certain outcomes pertaining to good will, public relations, and employee morale are difficult to assess in monetary terms. Educational decisions must take into account institutional goals, social values, and other relatively intangible factors. Individual decisions, as in counseling, must consider the individual's preferences and value system. It has been repeatedly pointed out, however, that decision theory did not introduce the problem of values into the decision process, but merely made it explicit. Value systems have always entered into decisions, but they were not heretofore clearly recognized or systematically handled.

Whether a psychological test is to be used in making terminal or sequential decisions also influences its effectiveness. For instance, instead of sorting applicants into accepted and rejected categories only, we might introduce a third category for uncertain cases who are to be examined further with more intensive techniques. Another strategy, suitable for the diagnosis of psychological disorders, would be to use only two categories but to test further *all* cases classified as positives by the preliminary screening test. It should also be noted that many personnel decisions are in effect sequential, although they may not be so perceived. Incompetent employees hired because of prediction errors can usually be discharged after a probationary period; failing students can be dropped from college at several stages. In such situations, it is only adverse selection decisions that are terminal. To be sure, incorrect selection decisions that are later rectified may be costly in terms of several value systems. But they are often less costly than terminal wrong decisions.

Still another condition that may alter the effectiveness of a psychological test is the availability of alternative treatments and the possibility of adapting treatments to individual characteristics (8). An example would be the utilization of different training procedures for workers at different aptitude levels. Such a strategy will further improve the payoff or evaluated outcome of the decisions based on test scores.

To determine what a test contributes to the decision process, we must also consider the *base rate,* or frequency of a given condition in the population to which the test is applied. In a provocative and thorough analysis of this problem, Meehl and Rosen (23) demonstrate that in the case of rare conditions (whose base rate deviates markedly from 50 per cent), the use of tests of low or even moderate validity may actually increase the proportion of wrong decisions. Suppose we have a test that can correctly reveal the presence or absence of a psychiatric disorder in 85 per cent of the cases examined. In other words, the number of abnormals correctly identified as abnormal plus the number of normals correctly identified as normal is 85 out of 100. Let us suppose further that the given disorder occurs in 5 per cent of the intake population of the particular clinic where this test is applied. Under these conditions, if we merely classified everyone as normal, we would be wrong in only 5 per cent of the cases. By applying the test, however, we will be wrong 15 per cent of the time.

In such a situation, increasing the amount of information utilized decreases the probability of correct decisions. This paradoxical consequence results from the large number of false positives, i.e., normal individuals incorrectly diagnosed as abnormal by the test. If everyone is classified as normal, on the other hand, there will be no false positives and the number of misses will be small because of the low frequency of the condition in the population. To identify rare conditions with better than chance success may thus require tests of unattainably high validity. It is obviously more fruitful to design tests for behavior characteristics whose base rates are closer to 50. Another solution is to apply tests within more narrowly defined subgroups, which may have less extreme base rates. For example, only 6 per cent of the intake population of a clinic may have organic brain pathology. But among a subgroup exhibiting certain symtoms, this proportion may be 40 per cent. The use of the test within this subgroup would be more effective.

When the seriousness of a rare condition makes its diagnosis urgent, tests of moderate validity may be employed in an early stage of sequential decisions. For example, all cases might first be screened with an easily administered test of moderate validity. If the cutoff score is set high enough (high scores being favorable), there will be few misses but many false positives. The latter can then be detected through a more intensive individual examination given to all cases diagnosed as positive by the test. This solution would be appropriate, for instance, when available facilities make the intensive individual examination of all cases impracticable.

It might be noted that the base rate we have been considering corresponds to one of the factors utilized in the previously discussed Taylor-Russell Tables, namely, the proportion of applicants who succeed (or fail) prior to the use of the test. Thus if only 5 per cent of present employees fail on a job, it is unlikely that the introduction of a new selection test can improve this outcome appreciably. Nevertheless, such selection decisions differ in certain important respects from the clinical decisions illustrated above. In the employment situation, the selection ratio (proportion of applicants to be hired) is imposed by external requirements, such as number of job openings, rather than being set so as to maximize correct classification. With externally determined selection ratios, the use of a test with any significant degree of validity will increase the total number of correct decisions (23). A further difference is that, in most job-selection decisions, the major emphasis is placed on reducing the number of misses (job failures). In clinical situations, on the other hand, minimizing the number of false positives may be just as important.

The examples cited provide only glimpses into the ways in which decision theory may affect the evaluation of psychological tests. For a more direct acquaintance with this field, the reader should consult the relevant references listed at the end of this chapter (6, 8, 9, 12, 15, 23).

ITEM ANALYSIS AND CROSS-VALIDATION

Both reliability and validity depend ultimately upon the characteristics of the items making up the test. Any test can be improved through the selection, substitution, or revision of items. Item analysis makes it possible to shorten a test, and at the same time increase its validity and reliability. Other things being equal, a longer test is more valid and reliable than a shorter one. The effect of lengthening or shortening a test upon the reliability coefficient was discussed in Chapter 5, where the Spearman-Brown formula for estimating such an effect was also presented. These estimated changes in reliability occur when the discarded items are equivalent to those that remain, or when equivalent new items are added to the test. Similar changes in validity will result from the deletion or addition of items of equivalent validity. All such estimates of change in reliability or validity refer to the lengthening or shortening of tests through a *random* selection of items, without item analysis. When, however, a test is shortened by eliminating the least satisfactory items, the short test may be more valid and reliable than the original, longer instrument.

The validity of any item can be determined by correlating responses to that item with a criterion measure. For example, answers to a personality test question can be correlated with each individual's rating for dominance. Since item responses are often dichotomous (yes-no, right-wrong, etc.), a biserial correlation is often used. If the criterion is also dichotomous (e.g., neurotic vs. normal, successful vs. unsuccessful employees), still other kinds of correlation may be used, such as tetrachoric or phi coefficients. Even when the criterion is continuous, item analysis is sometimes based on a comparison of extreme criterion groups. For example, students falling in the upper and lower thirds of their class in grade-point average may constitute the criterion groups. Whatever the specific procedure for computing item-criterion correlations, those items showing the closest correspondence with the criterion are retained and the other items are discarded in the preparation of the final test.

Item analysis is frequently conducted against total score on the test itself. As was noted in Chapter 6, this procedure yields a measure of *internal consistency*, not external validity. Under certain conditions, the two approaches may lead to opposite results, the items chosen on the basis of external validity being the very ones rejected on the basis of internal consistency. Let us suppose that the preliminary form of a scholastic aptitude test consists of 100 arithmetic items and 50 vocabulary items. In order to select items from this initial pool by the method of internal consistency, the biserial correlation between performance on each item and total score on the 150 items may be computed. It is apparent that such biserial correlations would tend to be higher for the arithmetic than for the vocabulary items, since the total score is based on twice as many arithmetic items. If it is desired to retain the 75 "best" items in the final form of the test, it is likely that most of these items will prove to be arithmetic problems. In terms of the criterion of scholastic achievement, however, the vocabulary items might have been more valid predictors than the arithmetic items. If such is the case, the item analysis will have served to lower rather than raise the validity of the test.

The practice of rejecting items that have low correlations with total score provides a means of purifying or homogenizing the test. By such a procedure, the items with the highest average intercorrelations will be retained. This method of selecting items will increase test validity only when the original pool of items measures a single trait and when this trait is present in the criterion. Most tests developed in actual practice, however, measure a combination of traits required by a complex criterion. Purifying the test in such a case may reduce its criterion coverage and thus lower validity.

Probably the best way to reconcile these objectives is to sort the relatively homogeneous items into separate tests, or subtests, each of which will cover a different aspect of the criterion. Thus breadth of coverage is achieved through a variety of tests, each yielding a relatively unambiguous score, rather than through heterogeneity of items within a single test. By such a procedure, items with low indices of internal consistency would not be discarded, but would be segregated. Within each subtest or item group, fairly high internal consistency could thus be attained. At the same time, internal consistency would not be accepted as a substitute for item validity, and some attention would be given to adequacy of coverage and to the avoidance of excessive concentration of items in certain areas.

After the items have been selected, the validity of the final form of the test must be checked in a new sample. Such an independent determination of test validity is known as *cross-validation* (cf. 25). Any validity coefficient computed on the same sample that was used for item-selection purposes will capitalize on chance errors within that particular sample and will consequently be spuriously high. In fact, a high validity coefficient could result under such circumstances, even when the test has no validity at all in predicting the particular criterion.

Let us suppose that out of a sample of 100 medical students, the 30 with the highest and the 30 with the lowest medical school grades have been chosen to represent contrasted criterion groups. If, now, these two groups are compared in a number of traits actually irrelevant to success in medical school, certain chance differences will undoubtedly be found. Thus there might be an excess of urban-born and of red-haired persons within the upper criterion group. If we were to assign each individual a "score" by crediting him with one point for urban residence and one point for red hair, the mean of such scores would undoubtedly be higher in the upper than in the lower criterion group. This is not evidence for the validity of the predictors, however, since such a validation process is based upon a circular argument. The two predictors were chosen in the first place on the basis of the chance variations that characterized this particular sample. And the *same* chance differences are operating to produce the mean differences in total score. When tested in another sample, however, the chance differences in frequency of urban residence and red hair are likely to disappear or be reversed. Consequently, the validity of the scores will collapse.

A specific illustration of the need for cross-validation is provided by an investigation conducted with the Rorschach inkblot test (21). In an attempt to determine whether the Rorschach could be of any help in selecting sales managers for life insurance agencies, this test was administered to 80 such managers. These managers had been carefully chosen from several hundred employed by eight life insurance companies, so as to represent an upper criterion group of 42 considered very satisfactory by their respective companies, and a lower criterion group of 38 considered unsatisfactory. The 80 test records were studied by a Rorschach expert, who selected a set of 32 signs, or response characteristics, occuring more frequently in one criterion group than in the other. Signs found more often in the upper criterion group were scored $+1$ if present and 0 if absent; those more common in the lower group were scored -1 or 0. Since there were 16 signs of each type, total scores could range theoretically from -16 to $+16$.

When the scoring key based on these 32 signs was reapplied to the original group of 80 persons, 79 of the 80 were correctly classified as being in the upper or lower group. The correlation between test score and criterion would thus have been close to 1.00. However, when the test was cross-validated on a second comparable sample of 41 managers, 21 in the upper and 20 in the lower group, the validity coefficient dropped to a negligible .02. It was thus apparent that the key developed in the first sample had no validity for selecting such personnel.

That such results can be obtained under pure chance conditions was vividly demonstrated by Cureton (10). The criterion to be predicted was the grade-point average of 29 students registered in a particular course. The "items" consisted of 85 tags, numbered from 1 to 85 on one side. To obtain a score for each subject, the 85 tags were thoroughly shaken in a container and dropped on the table. All tags that fell with numbered side up were recorded as indicating the presence of that particular item in the student's test performance. Twenty-nine throws of the 85 tags thus provided complete records for each student, showing the presence or absence of each item or response sign. An item analysis was then conducted, with each student's grade-point average as the criterion. On this basis, 24 "items" were selected out of the 85, 9 of which occurred more frequently among the students with higher grades, and 15 among those with lower grades. The former received a $+1$ weight, the latter -1. The sum of these item weights constituted the total score for each student. Despite the known chance derivation of these "test scores," their correlation with the grade criterion in the original group of 29 students proved to be .82. Such a finding is similar to that obtained with the Rorschach scores in the previously cited study. In both instances, the apparent correspondence between test score and criterion resulted from the utilization of the same chance differences both in selecting items and in determining validity of total test scores.

The amount of "shrinkage" of a validity coefficient in cross-validation depends in part upon the size of the original item pool and the proportion of items retained. When the number of original items is large and the proportion retained is small, there is more opportunity to capitalize on chance differences and thus obtain a spuriously high validity coefficient. Furthermore, if items are chosen on the basis of previously formulated hypotheses, derived from psychological theory or from past experience with the criterion, validity shrinkage in cross-validation will be minimized. For example, if a particular hypothesis required that the answer "Yes" be more frequent among successful students, then the item would *not* be retained if a significantly larger number of "Yes" answers were given by the *unsuccessful* students. The opposite "shotgun" approach would be illustrated by assembling a miscellaneous set of questions with little regard to their relevance to the criterion behavior, and then retaining all items yielding significant positive or negative correlations with the criterion. Under the latter circumstances, we would expect much more shrinkage than under the former.

Still another condition affecting amount of shrinkage in cross-validation is size of sample. Since spuriously high validity in the initial sample results from an accumulation of sampling errors, smaller groups (which yield larger sampling errors) will exhibit greater validity shrinkage. In summary, shrinkage of test validity in cross-validation will be greatest when samples are small, the initial item pool is large, the proportion of items retained is small, and items are assembled without previously formulated rationale.

COMBINING INFORMATION FROM DIFFERENT TESTS

For the prediction of practical criteria, not one but several tests are generally required. Most criteria are complex, the criterion measure depending upon a number of different traits. A single test designed to measure such a criterion would thus have to be highly heterogeneous. It has already been pointed out, however, that a relatively homogeneous and factorially pure test is more satisfactory because it yields less ambiguous scores. Hence it is usually preferable to use a combination of several relatively homogeneous tests, each covering a different aspect of the criterion, rather than a single test consisting of a hodgepodge of many different kinds of items.

When a number of specially selected tests are employed together to predict a single criterion, they are known as a *test battery*. The chief problem arising in the use of such batteries concerns the way in which scores on the different tests are to be combined in arriving at a decision regarding each individual. The procedures followed for this purpose may be subsumed under three major headings: (*a*) multiple regression equation, (*b*) multiple cutoff scores, and (*c*) clinical judgment.

Multiple Regression Equation. The multiple regression equation yields a predicted criterion score for each individual on the basis of his scores on all the tests in the battery. The following regression equation, taken from the manual of the Holzinger-Crowder Uni-Factor Tests (17, p. 22), illustrates the application of this technique to predicting a student's achievement in high school mathematics courses:

$$\text{Mathematics Achievement} = .21\ V + .05\ S + .21\ N + .32\ R + 1.05$$

In using this equation, the student's stanine scores on the verbal (V), spatial (S), numerical (N), and reasoning (R) tests are multiplied by the corresponding weights given in the equation. The sum of these products, plus a constant (1.05), gives the student's predicted stanine position in mathematics courses.

Suppose that Bill Jones receives the following stanine scores:

Verbal	6
Spatial	5
Numerical	4
Reasoning	8

The estimated mathematics achievement of this student is found as follows:

$$\text{Mathematics Achievement} = (.21)(6) + (.05)(5) + (.21)(4)$$
$$+ (.32)(8) + 1.05 = 5.96$$

Bill's predicted stanine is approximately 6. It will be recalled (Ch. 4) that a stanine of 5 represents average performance. Bill would thus be expected to do somewhat better than average in mathematics courses. His very superior performance in the reasoning tests ($R = 8$) and his above-average score on the verbal tests ($V = 6$) compensate for his poor score in speed and accuracy of computation ($N = 4$).

Specific techniques for the computation of regression equations can be found in many texts on psychological statistics (cf., e.g., 16, 34). Essentially, such an equation is based upon the correlation of each test with the criterion, as well as upon the intercorrelations among the tests. Obviously, those tests that correlate higher with the criterion should receive more weight. It is equally important, however, to take into account the correlation of each test with the other tests in the battery. Tests correlating highly with each other represent needless duplication, since they cover to a large extent the same aspects of the criterion. The inclusion of two such tests will not appreciably increase the validity of the entire battery, even though both tests may correlate highly with the criterion. In such a case, one of the tests would serve about as effectively as the pair; only one would therefore be retained in the battery.

Even after the most serious instances of duplication have been eliminated, however, the tests remaining in the battery will correlate with each other to varying degrees. For maximum predictive value, tests that make a more nearly unique contribution to the total battery should receive greater weight than those that partly duplicate the functions of other tests. In the computation of a multiple regression equation, each test is weighted in direct proportion to its correlation with the criterion and in inverse proportion to its correlations with the other tests. Thus the highest weight will be assigned to the test with the highest validity and the least amount of overlap with the rest of the battery.

The validity of the entire battery can be found by computing the multiple correlation (R) between the criterion and the battery. This correlation indicates the highest predictive value that can be obtained from the given battery, when each test is given optimum weight for predicting the criterion in question. The optimum weights are those determined by the regression equation.

It should be noted that these weights are optimum only for the particular sample in which they were found. Because of chance errors in the correlation coefficients used in deriving them, the regression weights may vary from sample to sample. Hence the battery should be cross-validated by correlating the predicted criterion scores with the actual criterion scores in a new sample. Formulas are available for estimating the amount of shrinkage in a multiple correlation to be expected when the regression equation is applied to a second sample, but empirical verification is preferable whenever possible. As in the previously discussed case of item analysis, the shrinkage will be smaller, the larger the sample on which regression weights were derived.

When validity of the battery is redetermined in a different school, factory, or other population from that on which the regression equation was derived, it is likely that the criterion will also differ. Academic success in two colleges, for example, may require a somewhat different constellation of aptitudes. Recomputing the validity of the battery under these circumstances is known as *validity generalization* (25). Through such a process, the test user will be able to detect not only the drop in validity attributable to chance errors, as in cross-validation, but also the drop due to changes in criterion definition.

Multiple Cutoff Scores. An alternative strategy for combining test scores utilizes multiple cutoff points. Briefly, this procedure involves the establishment of a minimum cutoff score on each test. Every individual who falls below such a minimum score on *any one* of the tests is rejected. Only those persons who reach or exceed the cutoff scores in all tests are accepted. An example of this technique is provided by the General Aptitude Test Battery (GATB) developed by the United States Employment Service for use in the occupational counseling program of its State Employment Service offices (31). Of the nine aptitude scores yielded by this battery, those to be considered for each occupation were chosen on the basis of criterion correlations as well as means and standard deviations of workers in that occupation.

The development of GATB occupational standards for machine cutters in the food-canning and preserving industry is illustrated in Table 12. In terms of standard scores with a mean of 100 and an *SD* of 20, the cutoff scores for this occupation were set at 75 in Motor Coordination (*K*), Finger Dexterity (*F*), and Manual Dexterity (*M*). Table 12 gives mean, standard deviation, and correlation with the criterion (supervisory ratings) for each of the nine scores in a group of 57 women workers. On the basis of criterion correlations,

TABLE 12. Illustrative Data Used to Establish Cutoff Scores on GATB

(From 32, p. 10)

	Aptitude	Mean	SD	Criterion Correlation
G	Intelligence	75.1	14.2	− .094
V	Verbal	80.1	11.3	− .085
N	Numerical	73.2	18.4	− .064
S	Spatial	78.9	15.9	.041
P	Form Perception	80.1	23.5	− .012
Q	Clerical Perception	86.3	16.6	.088
K	Motor Coordination	89.3	20.7	.316*
F	Finger Dexterity	92.4	18.1	.155
M	Manual Dexterity	88.2	18.6	.437**

* significant at .05 level.   ** significant at .01 level.

Manual Dexterity and Motor Coordination appeared promising. Finger Dexterity was added because it yielded the highest mean score in the battery, even though individual differences within the group were not significantly correlated with criterion ratings. It would seem that women who enter or remain in this type of job are already selected with regard to Finger Dexterity.[1]

The validity of the composite *KFM* pattern of cutting scores in a group of 194 workers is shown in Table 13. It will be seen that, of 150 good workers,

TABLE 13. Effectiveness of GATB Cutoff Scores on Aptitudes *K*, *F*, and *M* in Identifying Good and Poor Workers

(From 32, p. 14)

Criterion Rating	Aptitude Pattern		Total
	Non-Qualifying	Qualifying	
Good	30	120	150
Poor	30	14	44
Total	60	134	194

120 fell above the cutting scores in the three aptitudes and 30 were false positives, falling below one or more cutoffs. Of the 44 poor workers, 30 were correctly identified (hits) and 14 were not (misses). The over-all efficacy of this cutoff pattern is indicated by a tetrachoric correlation of .70 between predicted status and criterion ratings.

If only scores yielding significant validity coefficients are taken into account, one or more essential abilities in which all workers in the occupation excel might be overlooked. Hence the need for considering also those aptitudes in which workers excel as a group, even when individual differences beyond a certain minimum are unrelated to degree of job success. The multiple cutoff method is preferable to the regression equation in situations such as these, in which test scores are not linearly related to the criterion. For example, up to a point, increasing speed of hand movements may lead to greater output in an assembly-line job. But beyond that point, greater speed may be of no avail because of the mechanical limitations of the operation. In some jobs, moreover, workers may be so homogeneous in a key trait that the range of individual differences is too narrow to yield a significant correlation between test scores and criterion.

The strongest argument for the use of multiple cutoffs rather than a regression equation centers around the question of compensatory qualifications.

---

[1] The data have been somewhat simplified for illustrative purposes. Actually, the final choice of aptitudes and cutting scores was based on separate analyses of three groups of workers on related jobs, on the results obtained in a combined sample of 194 cases, and on qualitative job analyses of the operations involved.

With the regression equation, an individual who rates low in one test may receive an acceptable total score because he rates very high in some other test in the battery. A marked deficiency in one skill may thus be compensated for by outstanding ability along other lines. It is possible, however, that certain types of activity may require essential skills for which there is no substitute. In such cases, individuals falling below the required minimum in the essential skill will fail, regardless of their other abilities. An opera singer, for example, cannot have poor pitch discrimination, regardless of how well he meets the other requirements of such a career. Similarly, operators of sound-detection devices in submarines need good auditory discrimination. Those men incapable of making the necessary discriminations cannot succeed in such an assignment, regardless of superior mechanical aptitude, general intelligence, or other traits in which they may excel. With a multiple cutoff strategy, individuals lacking any essential skill would always be rejected, while with a regression equation they might be accepted.

When the relation between tests and criterion is linear and additive, on the other hand, a higher proportion of correct decisions will be reached with a regression equation than with multiple cutoffs. Another important advantage of the regression equation is that it provides an estimate of each person's criterion score, thereby permitting the relative evaluation of all individuals. With multiple cutoffs, no further differentiation is possible among those accepted or among those rejected. In many situations, the best strategy may involve a combination of both procedures. Thus the multiple cutoff may be applied first, in order to reject those falling below minimum standards on any test, and predicted criterion scores may then be computed for the remaining acceptable cases by the use of a regression equation. If enough is known about the particular job requirements, the preliminary screening may be done in terms of only one or two essential skills, prior to the application of the regression equation.

Clinical Judgment. When tests are employed in the intensive study of individual cases, as in clinical diagnosis, counseling, or the selection of high-level personnel, it is a common practice for scores on separate tests to be utilized by the examiner in arriving at a decision without further statistical manipulation. To be sure, the individual's scores are interpreted with reference to any available general or local norms; but no statistical formula or other automatic procedure is applied in combining scores from different tests or in evaluating the individual's score pattern. Through a relatively subjective process, the examiner interprets the individual's scores in terms of his own past experience with similar cases, his familiarity with particular job requirements, or his knowledge of psychological theory and relevant published research. The result may be presented in the form of a detailed description of personality dynamics, a specific prediction (e.g., Mr. Brown will make a good executive vice-president for this company; Miss Peterson will not respond well to psychotherapy), or both.

In a thought-provoking book entitled *Clinical Versus Statistical Prediction* (22), Meehl discussed the process of clinical judgment and surveyed some 20 investigations comparing the two types of prediction. The criteria predicted in these studies included principally success in some kind of schooling or training (college, Air Force pilot training, etc.), response to therapy on the part of psychotic or neurotic patients, and criminal recidivism as well as institutional adjustment of reformatory inmates. Predictions were made by clinical psychologists, counselors, psychiatrists, and other professional persons with varying amounts of experience in the use of clinical procedures. Focusing only on the process of combining data, rather than on differences in the kind of data obtained, Meehl showed that, with only one questionable exception, the routine application of statistical procedures yielded at least as many correct predictions as clinical analysis, and frequently more. In this connection, Meehl also called attention to the much greater cost of clinical predictions, in terms of both time and level of personnel required. Once a regression equation or other statistical strategy has been developed, it can be applied by a clerk or even a machine.

Although the data are admittedly meager and more research is needed on this question, the consistency of results in Meehl's survey strongly suggests that when statistical formulas of known validity are available for combining test scores, they should be used in preference to subjective clinical judgment. In the light of these findings, it would seem that the clinician's chief contributions to diagnosis and prediction are in areas in which satisfactory tests are unavailable. Systematic interviewing, case histories, and direct observation of behavior are still the principal sources of information on many aspects of personality. Clinical methods also lend themselves better than tests to the evaluation of rare and idiosyncratic events which occur too infrequently to permit the establishment of statistical strategies. Similarly, the clinician can give due consideration to the context in which events occur. For example, the same physical disability may have very different effects on the personality development of two children because of other concomitant traits or circumstances. To be sure, this is a problem of pattern analysis, which theoretically can be handled by appropriate statistical procedures; but when the modifying variables are numerous and each occurs infrequently, the statistical procedures would become too complex to be practicable.

On the other hand, it should be noted that in a few of the studies reported by Meehl, when counselors and clinicians had access to more data than were used in the statistical predictions, the clinical predictions were still no more accurate than the statistical. For example, counselors in a large state university predicted academic success of entering freshmen on the basis of high school percentile rank, an intelligence test, several aptitude and achievement tests, the Strong Vocational Interest Blank, a personality inventory, an individual record form, and interview notes (27). Statistical prediction was carried out by a clerk using a regression equation developed on previous classes in the same university. The only predictor variables in this equation were high school percentile ranks and the intelligence test scores. The validity coefficients of these statistical predictions against actual outcome were .45 and .70 for men and women students, respectively; clinical predictions yielded corresponding validities of .35 and .69.

It is apparent that the validity of clinical predictions against actual outcomes should be systematically investigated whenever feasible. More data are also needed on the consistency of predictions about the same subjects made by different clinicians and by the same clinicians at different times. In so far as possible, the process and cues on which clinical predictions are based should be made explicit in clinical records. Such a practice would not only facilitate research and training, but would also serve to encourage reliance on sound data and defensible interpretations. Finally, the "clinician as instrument" is an important concept in this connection. Undoubtedly the objectivity and skill with which data are gathered and interpreted—and the resulting accuracy of predictions—vary widely with the abilities, personality, professional training, and experience of individual clinicians.

USE OF TESTS FOR CLASSIFICATION DECISIONS

Psychological tests may be used for purposes of selection, placement, or classification. In *selection,* each individual is either accepted or rejected. Deciding whether or not to admit a student to college, to hire a job applicant, or to accept an Army recruit for officer training are examples of selection decisions. When selection is done sequentially, the earlier stages are often called "screening," the term "selection" being reserved for the more intensive final stages. "Screening" may also be used to designate any rapid, rough selection process even when not followed by further selection procedures.

Both placement and classification differ from selection in that no one is rejected, or eliminated from the program. All individuals are assigned to appropriate "treatments" so as to maximize the effectiveness of outcomes. In *placement,* the assignments are based on a single score. This score may be derived from a single test, such as an intelligence test. If a battery of tests has been administered, a composite score computed from a single regression equation would be employed. Examples of placement decisions include the sectioning of college freshmen into different mathematics classes on the basis of their scores on mathematical aptitude tests, assigning applicants to clerical jobs requiring different levels of skill and responsibility, and placing psychiatric patients into "more disturbed" and "less disturbed" wards. It is evident that in each of these decisions only one criterion is employed and that placement is determined by the individual's position along a single predictor scale.

Classification, on the other hand, always involves two or more criteria. In a military situation, for example, classification is a major problem, since each man in an available manpower pool must be assigned to the military specialty where he can serve most effectively. Classification decisions are likewise required in industry, when new employees are assigned to training programs for different kinds of jobs. Other examples include the assignment of students to different curricula in college (science, liberal arts, etc.), as well as the choice of a field of concentration by the student. Counseling is based essentially on classification, since the client is told his chances of succeeding in different kinds of work. Clinical diagnosis is likewise a classification problem, the major purposes of each diagnosis being a decision regarding the most appropriate type of therapy.

Although placement can be done with either one or more predictors, classification requires multiple predictors whose validity is individually determined against each criterion. A classification battery requires a different regression equation for each criterion. Some of the tests may have weights in all the equations, although of different values; others may be included in only one or two equations, having zero or negligible weights in terms of some of the criteria. Thus the combination of tests employed out of the total battery, as well as the specific weights, differs with the particular criterion. An example of such a classification battery is that developed by the Air Force for assignment of personnel to different training programs (11). This battery, consisting of both paper-and-pencil and apparatus tests, provided stanine scores for pilots, navigators, bombardiers, and a few other air-crew specialties. By finding an individual's estimated criterion scores from the different regression equations, it was possible to predict whether, for example, he was better qualified as a pilot than as a navigator.

Such differential prediction of criteria with a battery of tests permits a fuller utilization of available human resources than is possible with a single general test or with a composite score from a single regression equation.

This is illustrated in Figures 26 and 27, which are based on the Aptitude Area scores employed by the Army (30, 37, 38). Each Aptitude Area corresponds to a group of Army jobs requiring common qualifications. Out of a total eleven-test battery, only two tests are used to determine the individual's score in each Aptitude Area. Figure 26 shows the percentages of men in a large sample who obtained standard scores of 100 or higher on the AGCT and in their best Aptitude Area, respectively. As would be expected, a considerably larger proportion of men (75%) reach or exceed a given minimum level of performance in their best Aptitude Area than on a general aptitude test such as the AGCT (53%). More effective utilization of individual talents can thus be achieved by means of a differential aptitude battery than through the use of varying cutoff scores on a "general intelligence" test.

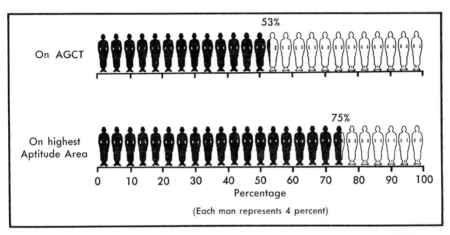

Fig. 26. Percentages of Army Recruits with Standard Scores of 100 or Higher on AGCT and on Aptitude Areas. (From Willemin and Karcher, 37, p. 1.)

The same point is differently illustrated in Figure 27. Both graphs in this figure show the distribution of AGCT scores of the men remaining for non-priority assignments after the top men have been "creamed off" for priority jobs. In the upper graph, AGCT is used to cream off men for priority positions. In other words, men with the highest AGCT scores were assigned to priority jobs. Non-priority openings were then filled from those remaining. In the lower graph, Aptitude Area scores are used, those men being assigned to priority jobs who had the highest scores in the special aptitudes required by each job. For example, if a priority job required chiefly mathematical aptitude, men highest in this aptitude would be assigned to that post, while those high in other aptitudes, such as spatial, motor, or verbal, were left for non-priority assignments that might call for just those aptitudes. It is apparent that a more able group of men is left for non-priority assignments when priority jobs are filled in terms of specific rather than general qualifications. In other words, by utilizing each individual's special talents, it is possible to fill the priority jobs with the men who are best qualified *for those jobs,* and at the same time have men with good qualifications remaining for other, non-priority assignments.

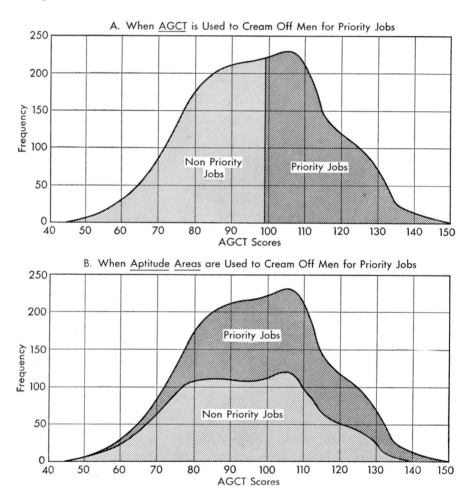

Fig. 27. AGCT Scores of Men Remaining for Non-Priority Jobs When Priority Jobs are Filled by AGCT Scores and by Aptitude Area Scores. (Adapted from Willemin and Karcher, 37, pp. 2 and 3.)

The *differential validity* of a classification test depends upon the difference between its correlations with the separate criteria to be predicted. In a two-criterion classification problem, for example, the ideal test would have a high correlation with one criterion and a zero correlation (or preferably a negative correlation) with the other criterion. General intelligence tests are relatively poor for classification purposes, since they predict success about equally well in most areas. Hence their correlations with the criteria to be differentiated would be too similar. An individual scoring high on such a test would be classified as successful for either assignment, and it would be impossible to predict in which he would do better. In a classification battery, we need some tests that are good predictors of criterion A and poor predictors of criterion B, and other tests that are poor predictors of A and good predictors of B. Statistical procedures have been developed for selecting tests so as to maximize the differential validity of a classification battery (5, 9, 18, 24). When the number of criteria is greater than two, such procedures become quite complex.

An alternative way of handling classification decisions is by means of the *multiple discriminant function* (cf. 14, 20). Essentially, this is a mathematical procedure for determining how closely the individual's scores on a whole set of tests approximate the scores typical of persons in a given occupation, curriculum, psychiatric syndrome, or other category. A person would then be assigned to the particular group he resembles most closely. While the regression equation permits the prediction of degree of success in each field, the multiple discriminant function treats all persons in one category as of equal status. Group membership is the only criterion data utilized by this method. The discriminant function is useful when criterion scores are unavailable and only group membership can be ascertained. Some tests, for instance, are validated by administering them to persons in different occupations, although no measure of degree of vocational success is available for individuals within each field.

The discriminant function is also appropriate when there is a non-linear relation between the criterion and one or more predictors. For example, in certain personality traits there may be an optimum range for a given occupation. Individuals having either more or less of the trait in question would thus be at a disadvantage. It seems reasonable to expect, for instance, that salesmen showing a moderately high amount of social dominance would be most likely to succeed, and that the chances of success would decline as scores move in either direction from this region. With the discriminant function, we would tend to select individuals falling within this optimum range. With the regression equation, on the other hand, the more dominant the score, the more favorable would be the predicted outcome. If the correlation between predictor and criterion were negative, of course, the regression equation would yield more favorable predictions for the low scorers. But there is no way whereby an intermediate score would receive maximum credit. Although in many instances the two techniques would lead to the same choices, there are situations in which persons would be differently classified by regression equations and discriminant functions. For most psychological testing purposes, regression equations provide a more effective technique. Under certain circumstances, however, the discriminant function is better suited to yield the required information.

REFERENCES

1. Bingham, W. V. Great expectations. *Personnel Psychol.*, 1949, 2, 397-404.
2. Bittner, R. H., and Wilder, C. E. Expectancy tables: a method of interpreting correlation coefficients. *J. exp. Educ.*, 1946, 14, 245-252.
3. Boring, E. G. (Ed.) *Psychology for the armed services.* Washington: The Infantry Journal, 1945.
4. Brogden, H. E. On the interpretation of the correlation coefficient as a measure of predictive efficiency. *J. educ. Psychol.*, 1946, 37, 65-76.
5. Brogden, H. E. Increased efficiency of selection resulting from replacement of a single predictor with several differential predictors. *Educ. psychol. Measmt.*, 1951, 11, 173-196.
6. Bross, J. D. J. *Design for decision.* N. Y.: Macmillan, 1953.
7. Brown, C. W., and Ghiselli, E. E. Per cent increase in proficiency resulting from use of selective devices. *J. appl. Psychol.*, 1953, 37, 341-345.
8. Cronbach, L. J. The two disciplines of scientific psychology. *Amer. Psychologist,* 1957, 12, 671-684.
9. Cronbach, L. J., and Gleser, Goldine C. *Psychological tests and personnel decisions.* Urbana, Ill.: Univer. Ill. Press, 1957.
10. Cureton, E. E. Validity, reliability, and baloney. *Educ. psychol. Measmt.*, 1950, 10, 94-96.
11. DuBois, P. H. (Ed.) *The classification program.* (AAF Aviation Psychology Program, Research Reports. Rep. No. 2.) Washington: Govt. Printing Office, 1947.
12. Edwards, W. The theory of decision making. *Psychol. Bull.*, 1954, 51, 380-418.
13. Flanagan, J. C. Scientific development of the use of human resources: progress in the Army Air Forces. *Science,* 1947, 105, 57-60.
14. French, J. W. The logic of and assumptions underlying differential testing. *Proc. 1955 invit. Conf. test. Probl., Educ. Test. Serv.*, 1956, 40-48.
15. Girshick, M. A. An elementary survey of statistical decision theory. *Rev. educ. Res.*, 1954, 24, 448-466.
16. Guilford, J. P. *Fundamental statistics in psychology and education.* (3rd ed.) N. Y.: McGraw-Hill, 1956.
17. Holzinger, K. J., and Crowder, N. A. *Holzinger-Crowder Uni-Factor Tests: manual.* Tarrytown-on-Hudson, N. Y.: World Book Co., 1955.

18. Horst, P. A technique for the development of a differential prediction battery. *Psychol. Monogr.*, 1954, 68, No. 9.

19. Jarrett, R. F. Per cent increase in output of selected personnel as an index of test efficiency. *J. appl. Psychol.*, 1948, 32, 135-146.

20. Johnson, P. O., and Jackson, R. W. B. *Modern statistical methods: descriptive and inductive.* Chicago: Rand McNally, 1959.

21. Kurtz, A. K. A research test of the Rorschach test. *Personnel Psychol.*, 1948, 1, 41-51.

22. Meehl, P. E. *Clinical versus statistical prediction: a theoretical analysis and a review of the evidence.* Minneapolis: Univer. Minn. Press, 1954.

23. Meehl, P. E., and Rosen, A. Antecedent probability and the efficiency of psychometric signs, patterns, or cutting scores. *Psychol. Bull.*, 1955, 52, 194-216.

24 Mollenkopf, W. G. Predicted differences and differences between predictions. *Psychometrika*, 1950, 15, 409-417.

25. Mosier, C. I., Cureton, E. E., Katzell, R. A., and Wherry, R. J. Symposium: the need and means of cross-validation. *Educ. psychol. Measmt.*, 1951, 11, 5-28.

26. Richardson, M. W. The interpretation of a test validity coefficient in terms of increased efficiency of a selected group of personnel. *Psychometrika*, 1944, 9, 245-248.

27. Sarbin, T. R. A contribution to the study of actuarial and individual methods of prediction. *Amer. J. Sociol.*, 1943, 48, 593-602.

28. Taylor, H. C., and Russell, J. T. The relationship of validity coefficients to the practical effectiveness of tests in selection: discussion and tables. *J. appl. Psychol.*, 1939, 23, 565-578.

29. Thorndike, R. L. *Personnel selection: test and measurement techniques.* N. Y.: Wiley, 1949.

30. U.S. Department of the Army, TAGO, Personnel Research Branch. *The Aptitude Area system.* Washington, D.C.: The Adjutant General, Dept. of the Army, October 1958.

31. U.S. Department of Labor, Bureau of Employment Security, USES. *Guide to the use of the General Aptitude Test Battery: Section III. Development.* Washington: Govt. Printing Office, 1952-1956.

32. U.S. Department of Labor, Bureau of Employment Security, USES. Technical report on standardization of General Aptitude Test Battery. *Tech. Rep.* B-381, July 1958.

33. Wald, A. *Statistical decision functions.* N. Y.: Wiley, 1950.

34. Walker, Helen M., and Lev, J. *Statistical inference.* N. Y.: Holt, Rinehart and Winston, 1953.

35. Wesman, A. G. Expectancy tables—a way of interpreting test validity. *Test Serv. Bull., Psychol. Corp.*, 1949, No. 38, 1-5.

36. Wesman, A. G. Better than chance. *Test Serv. Bull., Psychol. Corp.*, 1953, No. 45, 1-5.

37. Willemin, L. P., and Karcher, E. K., Jr. Development of Combat Aptitude Areas. *PRB Tech. Res. Rep.,* No. 1110, January 1958.

38. Zeidner, J., Harper, Bertha P., and Karcher, E. K., Jr. Reconstitution of Aptitude Areas. *PRB Tech. Res. Rep.*, No. 1095, November 1956.

PART 2

General Intelligence Tests

CHAPTER 8

Stanford-Binet Intelligence Scale

In Part 1, we were concerned with the major principles of psychological testing. We are now ready to apply these principles to the evaluation of specific tests. We now know what questions to ask about each test and where to look for the answers. The test manuals, the *Mental Measurements Yearbooks,* special journals and handbooks, and other sources described in Chapter 2 may be consulted to obtain information regarding any of the tests cited.

The purpose of the remaining parts of the book is twofold. One objective is to afford an opportunity to observe the application of testing principles to a wide variety of tests. Another is to acquaint the reader with a few outstanding tests in each of the major areas. No attempt will be made to provide a comprehensive survey of available tests within any area. Such a survey would be outside the scope of this book. Moreover, it would probably be outdated before publication, because of the rapidity with which new tests appear. For these reasons, the discussion will concentrate upon a few representative tests in each category, chosen either because of their widespread use or because they illustrate important developments in testing procedure. Following the categories outlined in Chapter 2, we shall consider general intelligence tests in Part 2, differential testing of abilities in Part 3, and measurement of personality characteristics in Part 4.

It will be recalled that general intelligence tests are designed for use in a wide variety of situations and are validated against relatively broad criteria. They characteristically provide a single score, such as an IQ, indicating the individual's general intellectual level. An effort is made to arrive at such an over-all estimate of intellectual performance by "the sinking of shafts at critical points" (21, p. 4). In other words, a wide variety of tasks is presented to the subject in the expectation that an adequate sampling of all important intellectual functions will thus be covered. In actual practice, the tests are

189

usually overloaded with certain functions, such as verbal ability, and completely omit others.

Since so many intelligence tests are validated against measures of academic achievement, they are often designated as tests of scholastic aptitude. Intelligence tests are frequently employed as preliminary screening instruments, to be followed by tests of special aptitudes. Such a practice is especially prevalent in the testing of normal adolescents or adults for counseling, personnel selection, and similar purposes. Another common use of general intelligence tests is to be found in clinical testing, especially in the identification and classification of mental defectives. For clinical purposes, individual tests such as the Stanford-Binet or Wechsler scales are generally employed.

This chapter will be concerned with the Stanford-Binet Intelligence Scale. Chapter 9 will consider the principal types of group tests available for different ages and educational levels. Non-language and performance scales will be treated in Chapter 10, and tests designed for the preschool and infant levels in Chapter 11. Chapter 12 will be devoted to the Wechsler scales, including both the adult form and the form for children. While they are used for many of the same purposes as the Stanford-Binet, the Wechsler scales include performance as well as verbal tests. Moreover, although administered as individual scales, they share many technical features with group tests. Chronologically, they represent a relatively recent major development in intelligence testing. For all these reasons, the Wechsler scales can be most effectively considered in the last chapter in Part 2, following a discussion of other types of intelligence tests. Chapter 12 will also touch upon the clinical use of tests in detecting intellectual impairment associated with brain damage and psychotic deterioration.

DEVELOPMENT OF STANFORD-BINET SCALES

The original Binet-Simon Scales have already been described briefly in Chapter 1. It will be recalled that the 1905 Scale consisted simply of 30 short tests, arranged in ascending order of difficulty. The 1908 Scale was the first age scale; and the 1911 Scale introduced minor improvements and additions. The age range covered by the 1911 revision extended from 3 years to the adult level. Among the many translations and adaptations of the early Binet tests were a number of American revisions. The earliest were prepared by Goddard (5, 6, 7), who was at that time research director at the Vineland, New Jersey, Training School for mental defectives. The Goddard scales were essentially translations of the various Binet scales, with minor changes necessary to adapt the content to American children. Other early revisions were developed by Kuhlmann (13), who extended the scales downward to the age of 3 months, by Yerkes, Bridges, and Hardwick (24), and by Herring (8). An account of these early American revisions, as well as a detailed description of the original Binet-Simon Scales, can be found in Peterson (17).

The first Stanford revision of the Binet-Simon Scales, prepared by Terman and his associates at Stanford University, was published in 1916 (20). This revision introduced so many changes and additions as to represent virtually a new test. Over one-third of the items were new, and a number of old items were revised, reallocated to different age levels, or discarded. The entire scale was restandardized on an American sample of approximately one thousand children and four hundred adults. Detailed instructions for administering and scoring each test[1] were provided, and the IQ was employed for the first time in any psychological test.

The second Stanford revision, appearing in 1937, consisted of two equivalent forms, L and M (21). In this revision, the scale was greatly expanded and completely restandardized on a new and carefully chosen sample of the American population. A third revision, published in 1960, provided a single form (L-M) in which were incorporated the best items from the two 1937 forms (22). Without introducing any new content, it was thus possible to eliminate obsolescent items and to relocate items whose difficulty level had altered during the intervening years owing to cultural changes.

In preparing the 1960 Stanford-Binet, the authors were faced with a common dilemma of psychological testing. On the one hand, frequent revisions are desirable in order to profit from technical advances and refinements in test construction and from prior experience in the use of the test, as well as to keep the test content up to date. The last-named consideration is especially important for information items and for pictorial material which may be affected by changing fashions in dress, household appliances, cars, and other common articles. The use of obsolete test content may seriously undermine rapport and may alter the difficulty level of items. On the other hand, revision may render much of the accumulated data inapplicable to the new form. Tests that have been widely used for many years have acquired a rich body of interpretive material which should be carefully weighed against the need for revision. It was for these reasons that the authors of the Stanford-Binet chose to condense the two earlier forms into one, thereby steering a course between the twin hazards of obsolescence and discontinuity. The loss of a parallel form was not too great a price to pay for accomplishing

---

[1] The items in the Binet scales are commonly called "tests," since each is separately administered and may contain several parts.

this purpose. As the authors point out, by 1960 there was less need for an alternate form than there had been in 1937 when no other well-constructed individual intelligence scale was available.

Because the 1960 revision is made up entirely of items from the 1937 forms, any evaluation of the 1960 Stanford-Binet requires an examination of the procedures followed in developing the earlier forms (cf. 14; 21, Ch. 2). The construction of the 1937 Stanford-Binet required nearly ten years of research. Much preliminary work went into the assembling of promising new items and their tryout on small groups of children who had taken the earlier form of the test. For every item, curves were plotted showing the percentage of children at each MA level on the 1916 test who passed the new item. Similarly, the mean MA of those passing an item was compared with the mean MA of those failing it. Items not showing a satisfactory degree of correspondence with 1916 MA were discarded at this stage. For preschool children, for whom earlier test scores were unavailable, chronological age was substituted for MA as the criterion in item selection. Except for these younger ages, items were chosen for inclusion in the provisional scales on the basis of their agreement with the earlier Stanford-Binet. Such a procedure insured a certain minimum of similarity in the general area measured by the earlier and later forms.

The major step in the development of the 1937 Stanford-Binet included the administration of the provisional forms to a carefully chosen sample of 3184 subjects, and the final selection and allocation of items. All subjects were given both forms of the test, one-half taking Form L first, the other half Form M first. The interval between the two tests ranged from one day to one week. In this step, the criteria for item analysis were chronological age and composite total score on both provisional forms. The latter is an internal consistency criterion which serves to increase the homogeneity of the test. Three specific measures were employed in the analysis of each item: (*a*) curve of percentages of subjects passing the item in successive chronological ages; (*b*) curve of percentages of subjects passing the item in successive intervals of total score on the two forms; (*c*) correlation of each item with total score on the two forms.

An illustration of the first of these three procedures is to be found in Figure 28, which shows the percentage of subjects at each age who passed two of the items retained in the final forms.[2] It will be noted that for the 3-year test the curve rises more steeply than for the 10-year test. Related to this difference is the fact that the percentage of 3-year-olds who pass the

[2] In the standard citation of Stanford-Binet items, the letter indicates the form (L or M), the Roman numeral designates the year level, and the Arabic numeral specifies the test or item number within that year level. Thus L,III,3 is the third item in the 3-year level of Form L.

3-year test (73 per cent) is greater than the percentage of 10-year-olds who pass the 10-year test (59 per cent). These differences in percentages passing an item are a necessary requirement of an age scale (14, p. 9 and Ch. 8). In the discussion of age scores in Chapter 4, it was seen that the standard deviation of mental ages must increase with age if that of the IQ is to remain constant. Now, if variability of MA is greater in older groups, it means that there must be a greater spread in the performance of older subjects over adjacent year levels. Hence with increasing age, fewer and fewer subjects

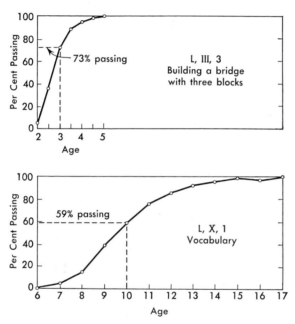

Fig. 28. Distribution of Percentages Passing Two Tests of the 1937 Stanford-Binet. (From Terman and Merrill, 22, p. 15.)

will pass a test that corresponds to their own age level. In the 1937 Stanford-Binet, the percentage of at-age passes dropped from 77 at age 2 to slightly below 50 at the average adult level. Still lower percentages passing were used in selecting items for the superior adult levels, in order to provide adequate ceiling for the test.

In the final selection of items, consideration was given not only to age differentiation and internal consistency, but also to the reduction and balancing of sex differences in percentage passing. An effort was made to exclude items passed by a significantly greater percentage of either sex, on the assumption that such items might reflect purely fortuitous and irrelevant differences in the experiences of the two sexes (14, Ch. 5). Owing to the limited number of items available for each age level, however, it was not possible to eliminate all sex-differentiating items. In order to rule out sex differences in total score, therefore, the remaining sex-differentiating items were balanced, approximately the same number favoring boys and girls. For proper interpretation of test scores, the test user should be aware of such item-selection procedures. A statement that boys and girls do not differ significantly in Stanford-Binet IQ, for example, provides no information whatever regarding sex differences in intelligence. Since sex differences were deliberately eliminated in the process of selecting items for the test, their absence from the final scores merely indicates that this aspect of test construction was successfully executed.

An important feature of the development of the 1937 Stanford-Binet is the care with which the standardization sample was assembled. The 3184 subjects employed for this purpose included approximately one hundred children at each half-year interval from 1½ to 5½ years, two hundred at each age from 6 to 14, and one hundred at each age from 15 to 18. All subjects were within one month of a birthday (or half-year birthday) at the time of testing, and every age group contained an equal number of boys and girls. From age 6 up, most subjects were tested in school, although a few of the older subjects were obtained outside of school in order to round out the sampling. Preschool children were contacted in a variety of ways, many of them being siblings of the school children included in the sample.

In order to obtain an adequate geographical distribution, testing was conducted in 17 communities located in 11 widely separated states. Several indices of socioeconomic level were checked in the effort to include a representative cross section of socioeconomic groups. Despite such precautions, the sampling was somewhat higher in socioeconomic level than the general population. There was also an excess of urban as contrasted to rural subjects, although the testers went to great lengths to sample the relatively inaccessible rural population. Both of these sampling inadequacies would tend to make the intelligence test performance of the standardization group higher than that of the general population. To allow for this condition, adjustments were made in the construction of the test such that the mean IQ of the standardization sample was in fact above 100. It should also be noted that the population sampled was limited to native-born, white subjects. Despite its limitations, however, the normative sampling employed in standardizing the 1937 Stanford-Binet was without doubt more nearly representative of the general population than any that had previously been utilized in the construction of psychological tests. The adequate sampling of such a broadly defined population is a monumental task.

In the preparation of the 1960 Stanford-Binet, items were selected from forms L and M on the basis of the performance of 4498 subjects, aged 2½ to 18 years, who had taken either or both forms of the test between 1950 and 1954. The subjects were examined in six states situated in the Northeast, in the Midwest, and on the West Coast. Although these cases did not constitute a representative sampling of American school children, care was taken to avoid the operation of major selective factors. The group also included two stratified samples of California children, used in special statistical analyses. These samples consisted of 100 6-year-olds stratified with regard to father's occupation and 100 15-year-olds stratified with regard to both father's occupation and grade distribution.

The 1960 Stanford-Binet did not involve a restandardization of the scale. The new samples were utilized only to check changes in item difficulty over the intervening period. Accordingly, the difficulty of each item was redetermined by finding the percentage of children passing it at successive *mental ages* on the 1937 forms. Some items were checked for possible regional and socioeconomic differences through subgroup comparisons within the total sample. No new material was introduced, but in a few items obsolescent drawings of common articles had to be altered. In these instances, the items were pretested on special groups before including them in the scale. Apart from these minor modifications in drawings, the only content changes in the 1960 Stanford-Binet include elimination of items, rescoring of a few items, and relocation of items in different year levels.

DESCRIPTION OF THE 1960 STANFORD-BINET

As in the 1937 forms, the tests in the 1960 Stanford-Binet are grouped into age levels ranging from age II to superior adult. Between the ages of II and V, the test proceeds by half-year intervals. Thus there is a level corresponding to age II, one to age II-6, one to age III, and so forth. Since progress is so rapid during these early ages, it proved feasible and desirable to measure change over six-month intervals. Between V and XIV the age levels correspond to yearly intervals. The remaining levels are designated as Average Adult and Superior Adult levels I, II, and III. Each age level contains six tests, with the exception of the Average Adult level, which contains eight. The tests within any one age level are of approximately uniform difficulty and are arranged without regard to such residual differences in difficulty as may be present. An *alternate* test is also provided at each age level. Being of approximately equivalent difficulty, such alternates may be substituted for any of the tests in the level, if one of these tests should be spoiled during its administration.

The materials needed for administering the Stanford-Binet include a box of standard toy objects for use with younger children, a set of printed cards, a record booklet for recording responses (or an abbreviated record form), and a test manual. Some of the objects employed at the preschool ages can be seen in Figure 29. The tasks to be performed by the subject in the various

Fig. 29. Test Materials Employed in Administering the Stanford-Binet. (Courtesy Houghton Mifflin Company.)

Stanford-Binet tests run the gamut from simple manipulation to abstract reasoning. The following description is intended only to illustrate the wide variety of content covered by these scales and should not be construed as a complete listing of item types. Nor should it be interpreted as a classification of the psychological functions measured by the specific tests. Some information on the latter question is provided by factor analysis data to be discussed in a later section on validity. The present description will be restricted to an objective account of the tasks performed by the subject, with no attempt at interpretation.

A few tests at the earliest age levels involve the manipulation of objects and a certain amount of eye-hand coordination. Among them may be mentioned the simple formboard shown in Figure 29, in which the three pieces must be inserted into the appropriate recesses, as well as tests involving block building and stringing beads. In this category may also be placed the drawing tests which require the child to copy a circle, a square, or a diamond. Certain tests of perceptual discrimination also occur at the lower age levels. Examples include comparing the length of sticks and matching geometric forms.

A relatively large number of tests at the lower levels involve the observation and identification of common objects. Thus at the II-year level, the child is asked to point to parts of the body in a large picture of a doll. Some of the small toy objects reproduced in Figure 29 are employed in identifying objects by name or by use. Pictures of objects are utilized at later age levels for the same purposes. Other tests require the subject to name objects, or pictures of objects. Still others call for the completion of pictures, or the identification of the missing parts. Several tests ask the subject to state the similarities or differences between certain sets of objects named by the examiner. The last-named type of test occurs at different levels of difficulty, extending into the higher ages.

A somewhat related group of tests, also found over a wide age range, may be described under the heading of practical judgment or common sense. In a series of "comprehension" questions, extending from year level III-6 to VIII, the child is asked what he should do in meeting certain everyday-life situations. In other, similar tests at these and higher year levels the subject is required to explain why certain practices are commonly followed or certain objects are employed in daily living. A number of tests calling for the interpretation of pictorially or verbally presented situations, or the detection of absurdities in either pictures or brief stories, also seem to fall into this category. Memory tests are found throughout the scale and utilize a wide variety of materials. The subject is required to recall or recognize objects, pictures, geometric designs, bead patterns, digits, sentences, and the content of passages.

Several tests of spatial orientation occur at widely scattered levels. These include maze-tracing, paper-folding, paper-cutting, rearrangement of geometric figures, and directional orientation. Numerical tests range from rudimentary quantitative concepts and counting, through the simple arithmetic problems encountered in elementary school, to more complex arithmetic reasoning problems involving novel solutions and the inductive formulation of rules.

The most numerous type of test, especially at the upper age levels, is that employing verbal content. In this category are to be found such well-known tests as vocabulary, analogies, sentence completion, disarranged sentences, defining abstract terms, and interpreting proverbs. Some stress verbal fluency, as in naming unrelated words as rapidly as possible, giving rhymes, or building sentences containing three given words. It should also be noted in this connection that many of the tests that are not predominantly verbal in content nevertheless require the understanding of fairly complex verbal instructions. That the scale as a whole is still heavily weighted with verbal ability is indicated by the correlations obtained between the 45-word vocabulary test included in Form L and mental ages on the entire scale. These correlations were found to be .71, .83, .86, and .83 for groups of subjects aged 8, 11, 14, and 18 years, respectively (14, pp. 139-140).[3] These correlations are at least as high as those normally found between tests designed to measure the same functions, and they fall within the range of common reliability coefficients. Such data suggest that the Stanford-Binet scale as a whole measures to a large extent the same functions as the vocabulary test.

In concluding this description of the Stanford-Binet, mention should be made of the *abbreviated scale*. Four tests in each year level were selected on the basis of validity and representativeness to constitute a short scale for use when time does not permit the administration of the entire scale. These tests are marked with an asterisk on the record booklets. Comparisons between full-scale and abbreviated-scale IQ's on a variety of groups (cf. 22, pp. 61-62; 23, p. 262) show a close correspondence between the two, the correlations being approximately as high as the reliability coefficient of the full scale. The mean IQ, however, tends to run slightly lower on the short scale, a discrepancy that is brought out even more vividly when individual cases are considered. Thus over 50 per cent of the subjects received lower IQ's on the short version, while only about 30 per cent scored higher.

ADMINISTRATION AND SCORING

In common with most individual intelligence tests, the Stanford-Binet requires a highly trained examiner. Both administration and scoring are fairly complicated for many of the tests. Considerable familiarity and experience with the scale are therefore required for a smooth performance. Hesitation and fumbling may be ruinous to rapport. Slight inadvertent changes in word-

---

[3] Since these are part-whole correlations, they are spuriously raised by the inclusion of the vocabulary test in the determination of MA. Such effect, however, is slight, since the vocabulary test constitutes less than 5 per cent of the total number of test items (14, p. 140).

ing may alter the difficulty of items. A further complication is presented by the fact that tests must be scored as they are administered, since the subsequent conduct of the examination depends upon the child's performance on previously administered levels.

In taking the Stanford-Binet, no one subject tries all items. Each individual is tested only over a range of age levels suited to his own intellectual level. Testing usually requires no more than thirty to forty minutes for younger children and not more than one hour and a half for older subjects. The standard procedure is to begin testing at a level slightly below the expected mental age of the subject. Thus the first tests given should be easy enough to arouse confidence, but not so easy as to cause boredom and annoyance. If the subject fails any test within the year level first administered, the next lower level is given. Such a procedure continues until a level is reached at which all tests are passed. This level is known as the *basal age*. Testing is then continued upward to a level at which all tests are failed, designated as the *ceiling age*. When this level is reached, the test is discontinued.

Scoring of individual items, or tests, follows an all-or-none system. For each test, the minimal performance that constitutes "passing" is specified in the manual. For example, in identifying objects by use at year level II-6, the child passes if he correctly identifies three out of six designated objects; in repeating five digits from memory at year level VII, correct response on any one of three series is counted as a pass; in answering comprehension questions at year level VIII, any four correct answers out of six represent a passing performance. Certain tests appear in identical form at different year levels, but are scored with a different standard of passing. Such tests are administered only once, the subject's performance determining the year level at which they are credited. The vocabulary test, for example, may be scored anywhere from level VI to Superior Adult III, depending upon the number of words correctly defined.

The items passed and failed by any one individual will show a certain amount of *scatter* among adjacent year levels. We do not find that individuals pass all tests at or below their mental age level and fail all tests above such a level. Instead, the successfully passed tests are spread over several year levels, bounded by the subject's basal age at one extreme and his ceiling age at the other. The subject's mental age on the Stanford-Binet is found by crediting him with his basal age and adding to that age further months of credit for every test passed beyond the basal level. In the half-year levels between II and V, each of the six tests counts as one month; between VI and XIV, each of the six tests corresponds to two months of credit. Each of the adult levels (AA, SA I, SA II, and SA III) covers more than one year of mental age, the months of credit for each test being adjusted accordingly. For example, the Average Adult level includes eight tests, each of which is credited with two months; the Superior Adult I level contains six tests, each receiving four months. The highest mental age theoretically attainable on the Stanford-Binet is 22 years and 10 months. Such a score is not, of course, a true mental age, but a numerical score indicating degree of superiority above the Average Adult performance. It certainly does not correspond to the achievement of the average 22-year-old individual, since the latter would receive a mental age of 15-9. For any adult over 18 years of age, a mental age of 15-9 corresponds to an IQ of 100 on this scale.

A major innovation introduced in the 1960 Stanford-Binet was the substitution of deviation IQ's for the ratio IQ's used in the earlier forms. Such deviation IQ's are standard scores with a mean of 100 and an *SD* of 16. As explained in Chapter 4, the principal advantage of this type of IQ is that it provides comparable scores at all age levels, thus eliminating once for all the vagaries of ratio IQ's. Despite the care with which the 1937 scales were developed in the effort to obtain constant IQ variability at all ages, the *SD's* of ratio IQ's on these scales fluctuated from a low of 13 at age VI to a high of 21 at age II-6. Thus an IQ of 113 at age VI corresponded to an IQ of 121 at age II-6. Special correction tables were developed to adjust for the major IQ variations in the 1937 scales (14, pp. 172-174). All these difficulties were circumvented in the 1960 form through the use of deviation IQ's, which automatically have the same *SD* throughout the age range. To facilitate procedure, Pinneau developed tables in which deviation IQ's can be looked up by entering MA and CA in years and months. These Pinneau tables are reproduced in the Stanford-Binet manual.

A further change introduced in the 1960 form stems from the recognition that improvement on the test continues to age 18, rather than ceasing at age 16 as assumed in the 1937 revision. Several major longitudinal studies conducted by different investigators over the intervening quarter-century strongly suggested that the abilities measured by intelligence tests continue to improve longer than had been supposed. The most direct evidence that improvement on the Stanford-Binet continues beyond age 16 was provided by Bradway, Thompson, and Cravens (4), who retested subjects from the 1937 standardization sample after intervals of 10 and 25 years. When first tested, these subjects had been from 2 to 5½ years old. Mean IQ's remained virtually unchanged from first to second testings, but showed a significant rise of 11.3 points between second and third testings. The latter increase resulted from the fact that the subjects had continued to improve beyond age

16, while the computation of 1937 IQ's assumed termination of growth at that age.

The specific procedure followed in finding MA and IQ on the 1960 Stanford-Binet is illustrated in Table 14. In the upper part of this table is the

TABLE 14. **Computation of Stanford-Binet Mental Ages and Intelligence Quotients**

Year Level	Number of Tests Passed	Months Credit per Test	Total Credit
		6-YEAR-OLD CHILD	
IV	6	Basal age	4 yrs. 0 mos.
IV-6	5	1	5
V	3	1	3
VI	3	2	6
VII	2	2	4
VIII	1	2	2
IX	0	Ceiling age	
			4 yrs. + 20 mos.
	MA = 5-8 CA = 6-4 IQ = 88		
		35-YEAR-OLD ADULT	
XIII	6	Basal age	13 yrs. 0 mos.
XIV	5	2	10
AA	6	2	12
SA I	3	4	12
SA II	2	5	10
SA III	0	Ceiling age	
			13 yrs. + 44 mos.
	MA = 16-8 CA = 18-0 IQ = 106		

record of a child whose chronological age is 6 years and 4 months (CA = 6-4). It will be noted that the basal age is IV and the ceiling age IX. Additional credits total to 20 months, or 1 year and 8 months. The MA is thus 5-8. By reference to the Pinneau tables, this child's IQ is found to be 88. In the lower part of Table 14 will be found the record of a 35-year-old adult. As for anyone whose age is 18 or over, CA is taken as 18 in looking up the IQ. This subject's basal age is XIII, and he earns 44 additional months credit, giving him an MA of 16-8 and an IQ of 106.

RELIABILITY

The reliability of the 1937 Stanford-Binet was determined by correlating IQ's on Forms L and M administered to the standardization group within an interval of one week or less. Such reliability coefficients are thus measures of equivalence and stability over a relatively short period. An exceptionally thorough analysis of the reliability of this test was carried out with reference to age and IQ level of subjects (cf. 14, Ch. 6). In general, the Stanford-Binet tends to be more reliable for the older than for the younger ages, and for the lower than for the higher IQ's. Thus at ages 2½ to 5½, the reliability coefficients range from .83 (for IQ 140-149) to .91 (for IQ 60-69); for ages 6 to 13, they range from .91 to .97, respectively, for the same IQ levels; and for ages 14 to 18, the corresponding range of reliability coefficients extends from .95 to .98.

The fact that high IQ's tend to have lower reliability than low IQ's results from the intrinsic properties of an age scale. The relation between extent of variability and mental age—cited earlier in discussions of the ratio IQ and of the percentage of subjects passing items at different age levels—is also at the root of these reliability differences. For a detailed explanation of how this comes about, the reader is referred to McNemar (14, Ch. 6). The relation between IQ level and reliability within a single age group is illustrated in Figure 30, which shows the bivariate distribution of IQ's obtained by 7-year-old children on Forms L and M. It will be observed that the individual entries fall close to the diagonal at lower IQ levels and spread farther apart at the higher levels. This indicates closer agreement between L and M IQ's at lower levels and wider discrepancies between them at upper levels. With such a "fan-shaped" bivariate distribution, or scatter diagram, a single correlation coefficient is misleading. For this reason, separate reliability coefficients have been reported for different portions of the IQ range.

On the whole, the data indicate that the Stanford-Binet is a highly reliable test, most of the reported reliability coefficients for the various age and IQ levels being over .90. Such high reliability coefficients were obtained despite the fact that they were computed separately within each age group. It will be recalled in this connection that all subjects in the standardization sample were tested within a month of a birthday or half-year birthday. This narrowly restricted age range would tend to produce lower reliability coefficients than found for most tests, which employ more heterogeneous samples. Translated in terms of individual IQ's, a reliability coefficient of .90 and an *SD* of 16 give an error of measurement of approximately 5 IQ points (cf. Ch. 5). In other words, the chances are about 2:1 that a child's true Stanford-Binet IQ differs by 5 points or less from the IQ obtained in a single testing, and the chances are 99:1 that it varies by no more than 13 points. Reflecting the same differences found in the reliability coefficients, these errors of measurement will be somewhat higher for younger than for older children, and somewhat higher for brighter than for duller individuals.

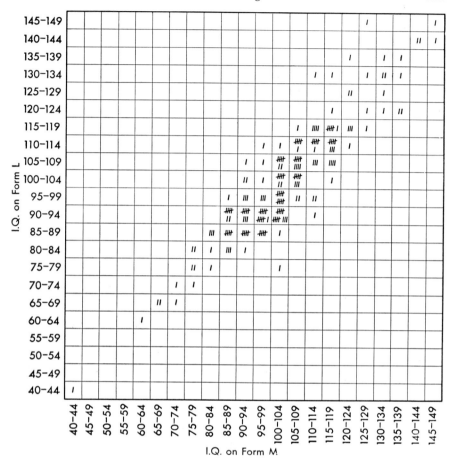

Fig. 30. Parallel-Form Reliability of the Stanford-Binet: Bivariate Distribution of IQ's Obtained by Seven-Year-Old Children on Forms L and M. (From Terman and Merrill, 21, p. 45; reproduced by permission of Houghton Mifflin Company.)

VALIDITY

Some information bearing on the *content validity* of the Stanford-Binet is provided by the description of item types given earlier in this chapter. The tasks were obviously chosen so as to call into play such functions as accuracy of observation, practical judgment, memory for many kinds of material, ability to follow directions, spatial visualization, reasoning, and the handling of abstract concepts. Verbal abilities clearly predominate, especially at the higher mental ages. Skills acquired in school, such as reading and arithmetic, are required for successful performance at the upper year levels. In so far as all of these functions are relevant to what is commonly regarded as "intelligence" the scale may be said to have content validity. The preponderance of verbal content at the upper levels is defended by the test authors on theoretical grounds. Thus they write:

At these levels the major intellectual differences between subjects reduce largely to differences in the ability to do conceptual thinking, and facility in dealing with concepts is most readily sampled by the use of verbal tests. Language, essentially, is the shorthand of the higher thought processes, and the level at which this shorthand functions is one of the most important determinants of the level of the processes themselves (21, p. 5).

Continuity in the functions measured in the 1916, 1937, and 1960 scales was insured by retaining in each revision only those items that correlated satisfactorily with mental age on the preceding form. *Age differentiation* represents the major criterion in the selection of Stanford-Binet items. Hence there is assurance that the Stanford-Binet measures abilities that increase with age during childhood and adolescence in our culture. In each form, *internal consistency* was a further criterion for item selection. That there is a good deal of functional homogeneity in the Stanford-Binet, despite the apparent variety of content, is indicated by a mean item-scale correlation of .66 for the 1960 revision. The predominance of verbal functions in the scale is shown by the higher correlation of verbal than non-verbal items with performance on the total scale (22, p. 34).

Further data pertaining to validity are provided by a series of *factor analyses* of Stanford-Binet items. If IQ's are to be comparable at different ages, the scale should have approximately the same factorial composition at all age levels. For an unambiguous interpretation of IQ's, moreover, the scale should be highly saturated with a single common factor. The latter point has already been discussed in connection with homogeneity (cf. Ch. 5). If the scores were heavily weighted with two group factors, such as verbal and numerical aptitudes, an IQ of, let us say, 115 obtained by different persons might indicate high verbal ability in one case and high numerical ability in the other.

McNemar (14, Ch. 9) conducted separate factorial analyses of Stanford-Binet items at 14 age levels, including half-year groups from 2 to 5 and year groups at ages 6, 7, 9, 11, 13, 15, and 18. The number of subjects employed in each analysis varied from 99 to 200, and the number of items ranged from 19 to 35. In each of these analyses, tetrachoric correlations were computed between the items, and the resulting correlations were factor analyzed. By including items from adjacent year levels in more than one analysis, some evidence was obtained regarding the identity of the common factor at different ages. The examination of tests that recur at several age levels provided further data on this point. In general, the results of these analyses indicated that performance on Stanford-Binet items is largely explicable in terms of a single common factor. Evidence of additional group factors was found at a few age levels, but the contribution of these factors was small. It was likewise demonstrated that the common factor found at adjacent age levels was essentially the same, although such a conclusion may not apply to more widely separated age levels. In fact, there was some evidence to suggest that the common factor becomes increasingly verbal as the higher ages are approached. The common factor loading of the vocabulary test, for example, rose from .59 at age 6 to .91 at age 18.

In a more intensive search for the contribution of group factors, Jones (11, 12) factor analyzed Stanford-Binet items separately in four groups of children aged 7, 9, 11, and 13 years. Each group consisted of 100 boys and 100 girls. At each age level, the results revealed a number of distinct but correlated abilities. Among them were several verbal, memory, reasoning, spatial visualization, and perceptual factors. Moreover, both the factors identified and their relative weights varied somewhat from one age level to another. Further evidence that the Stanford-Binet IQ may depend upon different functions at different ages is provided by Hofstaetter's factor analysis of the performance of a single group of subjects retested over 18 years (9). This investigation suggested that "persistence" is an important determiner of IQ below age 4, but that "manipulation of symbols" is the principal ability measured after that age.

Data on both concurrent and predictive validity of the Stanford-Binet have been reported chiefly in terms of *academic achievement* as a criterion. Since the publication of the original 1916 Scale, many correlations have been computed between Stanford-Binet IQ and school grades, teachers' ratings, and achievement test scores. Most of these correlations fall between .40 and .75. School progress was likewise found to be related to Stanford-Binet IQ, children who were accelerated by one or more grades averaging considerably higher in IQ than those at normal age-grade location, and children who were retarded by one or more grades averaging considerably below (14, Ch. 3).

Like most intelligence tests, the Stanford-Binet correlates highly with performance in nearly all academic courses, but its correlations are highest with the predominantly verbal courses, such as English and history. The following correlations, found between Form L IQ and achievement test scores of high school sophomores are typical (3). The number of cases used in computing these correlations varied from 78 to 200.

Reading comprehension	.73	Spelling	.46
Reading speed	.43	History	.59
English usage	.59	Geometry	.48
Literature acquaintance	.60	Biology	.54

In another study, a correlation of .64 was obtained between Form L IQ and first-year college grades in a group of 67 college freshmen (16). Other studies (2, 18) of college freshmen have yielded correlations in the .50's between Stanford-Binet IQ's and college grades. With college groups, both selective factors and insufficient test ceiling undoubtedly tend to lower the correlations.

The long-range *stability* of Stanford-Binet IQ's may also be regarded as evidence of predictive validity. Longitudinal studies of the same subjects over periods of 10 to 25 years contribute to our understanding of the behavior sampled by such tests as the Stanford-Binet. Such information belongs more properly under the heading of validity than under the heading of reliability, since it concerns broad, enduring behavioral changes rather than temporary fluctuations in specific test performance (cf. Ch. 5).

Several longitudinal studies have provided data on long-range stability of "intelligence" as measured by the Stanford-Binet and other common tests (cf. 1, pp. 231-238; 22, pp. 16-17). As might be expected, retest correlations are higher, the shorter the interval between tests. In one investigation with the Stanford-Binet, for example, the correlation between tests given to the same children at 3 and 4 years of age was .83 (19). Correlations between the 3-year tests and retests at successive ages decreased constantly until at age 12 the correlation had dropped to .46. With constant intervals between tests, retest correlations are generally higher the older the children. This is understandable, since the older the individual, the more of his intellectual development has already occurred. Hence subsequent changes make relatively little difference in his intellectual status. Of special relevance to the Stanford-Binet is the follow-up conducted by Bradway, Thompson, and Cravens (4) on children originally tested between the ages of 2 and 5½ as part of the 1937 Stanford-Binet standardization sample. Initial IQ's correlated .65 with 10-year retests and .59 with 25-year retests. The correlation between the 10-year retest (Mean age = 14 years) and 25-year retest (Mean age = 29 years) was .85.

In terms of group trends, the long-range predictive validity of a Stanford-Binet IQ, especially when obtained with school-age children, is remarkably high. In individual cases, however, large upward or downward shifts in IQ may occur over an interval of a few years. In one extensive longitudinal project (10), individual IQ changes of as much as 50 points were observed. Between the ages of 6 and 18, when retest correlations are generally high,

59 per cent of the cases changed 15 or more IQ points, 37 per cent changed 20 or more points, and 9 per cent changed 30 or more points. Nor were these changes random or erratic in nature. Some children exhibited consistent upward or downward trends over several years. Large shifts in IQ, moreover, were usually associated with the cultural milieu and emotional climate in which the child was reared. Children in underprivileged environments tended to lose and those in superior environments to gain with age, in relation to the norms.

Severe illness, changes in home or familial conditions, therapeutic and remedial programs, and other major environmental variables operating during childhood are likely to be reflected in sharp rises or drops in individual IQ's. The literature on the effects of environmental conditions upon intellectual development is extensive, and it is beyond the scope of this book to survey it (cf. 1). Its findings, however, contribute to our understanding of the construct "intelligence" which such tests as the Stanford-Binet try to measure. It is certainly evident that any one IQ needs to be interpreted in the light of all available background information about the individual.

EVALUATION

One of the chief advantages of the Stanford-Binet derives from the mass of *interpretive data* and extensive clinical experience that have been accumulated regarding this test. For many clinicians, educators, and others concerned with the evaluation of general ability level, the Stanford-Binet IQ has become almost synonymous with intelligence. Much has been learned about what sort of behavior can be expected from a child with an IQ of 50 or 80 or 120 on this test. The distributions of IQ's in the standardization samples for the 1916 Stanford-Binet, and later for the 1937 revision, have provided a common frame of reference for the interpretation of IQ's. In Table 15 will be found the distribution of the composite L and M IQ's of the 1937 standardization sample, showing percentage of cases falling within each 10-point interval of IQ, as well as the descriptive terms commonly applied to these levels. The same data are presented graphically in Figure 31. It will be noted that a close approximation to a normal curve was attained in developing these scales.

The widespread use of such a classification of IQ levels, although of unquestionable help in standardizing the interpretation of test performance, carries certain dangers. Like all classifications of persons, it should not be rigidly applied, nor used to the exclusion of other data about the individual. There are, of course, no sharp dividing lines between the "mentally defective"

TABLE 15. Distribution of Standardization Sample in Composite Stanford-Binet IQ on Forms L and M

(From Merrill, 15, p. 650)

IQ	Percentage of Cases	Classification
160-169	0.03	
150-159	0.2	Very superior
140-149	1.1	
130-139	3.1	
120-129	8.2	Superior
110-119	18.1	High average
100-109	23.5	
90-99	23.0	Normal or average
80-89	14.5	Low average
70-79	5.6	Borderline defective
60-69	2.0	
50-59	0.4	
40-49	0.2	Mentally defective
30-39	0.03	

and the "borderline," or between the "superior" and the "very superior." Individuals with IQ's of 60 have been known to make satisfactory adjustments to the demands of daily living, while some with IQ's close to 100 require institutional care. Persons with IQ's of 160 do occasionally lead undistinguished lives, while some with IQ's much closer to 100 make outstanding contributions. Decisions regarding institutionalization, parole, or discharge of mental defectives must take into account not only IQ but also social maturity, emotional adjustment, physical condition, and other circumstances of the individual case. Nor is high IQ synonymous with genius. High-level achievement may require in addition creativity, originality, special talents, persistence, singleness of purpose, and other propitious emotional and motivational factors.

In interpreting the IQ, it should be borne in mind that the Stanford-Binet is primarily a measure of *scholastic aptitude* and heavily loaded with verbal functions, especially at the upper levels. Individuals with a language handicap, as well as those whose strongest abilities lie along non-verbal lines, will thus score relatively low on such a test. Similarly, there are undoubtedly a number of fields in which scholastic aptitude and verbal comprehension are not of primary importance. Obviously, to apply any test to situations for which it is inappropriate will only reduce its effectiveness. Because of the common identification of Stanford-Binet IQ with the very concept of intelligence, there has been a tendency to expect too much from this one test.

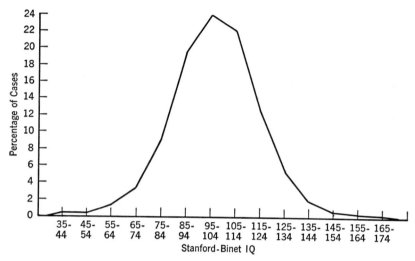

Fig. 31. Distribution of Standardization Sample in Composite IQ on Forms L and M of the Stanford-Binet. (From Terman and Merrill, 21, p. 37; reproduced by permission of Houghton Mifflin Company.)

The Stanford-Binet is likewise unsuited to the measurement of *differential aptitudes*. Although for many years clinicians tried to analyze the individual's performance on different types of items, as a qualitative supplement to the IQ, such a practice is unwarranted and has now been largely abandoned. In the first place, the same types of items do not recur at all age levels. And factorial analyses have corroborated the fact that a somewhat different combination of abilities is measured at different ages. In the second place, the number of items of each type is too small to permit a reliable determination of the individual's performance on separate item groups. The difference between an individual's achievement on, let us say, the spatial orientation and memory items might thus be due entirely to chance. Finally, it is difficult to determine the psychological functions measured by an item through a mere inspection of its content. The previously cited factor analyses of Stanford-Binet items showed that a single general factor accounts for a large part of the variance. Moreover, the scales were deliberately constructed so as to maximize the contribution of such a general factor and to minimize the influence of group factors or separate abilities.

The Stanford-Binet is not suitable for *adult testing,* especially within the normal and superior range. Despite the three Superior Adult levels, there is insufficient ceiling for most superior adults. In such cases, it is often impossible to reach a ceiling age level at which all tests are failed. Moreover, most of the Stanford-Binet tests have more appeal for children than for adults, the content being of relatively little interest to most adults. It will also be recalled that the MA concept is essentially inapplicable to normal and superior adults, mental ages beyond 14 not being interpretable in the same simple and straightforward manner as those below 14.

Many clinicians regard the Stanford-Binet not only as a standardized test, but also as a *clinical interview.* The very characteristics that make this scale so difficult to administer also create opportunities for interaction between examiner and subject, and provide other sources of clues for the experienced clinician. Even more than most other individual tests, the Stanford-Binet makes it possible to observe the subject's work methods, his approach to a problem, and other qualitative aspects of performance. The examiner may also have an opportunity to judge certain personality characteristics, such as willingness, self-confidence, social confidence, and attention. Any qualitative observations made in the course of Stanford-Binet administration should, of course, be clearly recognized as such and ought not to be interpreted in the same manner as objective test scores. The value of such qualitative observations depends to a large extent upon the skill, experience, and psychological sophistication of the examiner, as well as upon his awareness of the pitfalls and limitations inherent in this type of observation.

For the purposes for which it was designed, the Stanford-Binet is undoubtedly a very successful instrument. Its viability over the years attests to the widespread recognition of its merits. No evaluation of the Stanford-Binet would be complete without a reference to the technical quality of the procedures followed in its development. The construction of an age scale requires tremendous expenditure of time and effort. As McNemar wrote in connection with the preparation of the 1937 forms, "Many have pointed out the difficulties in constructing an age scale, but only those who have been through the mill are in a position to appreciate fully the obstacles" (14, pp. 83-84). The procedures followed in determining the reliability of the Stanford-Binet are unusually thorough, and the reliability of the scale is high. A wealth of validation data has accumulated over the years to give meaning to the Stanford-Binet IQ. The elimination of obsolescent item content and the substitution of the deviation IQ for the ratio IQ in the 1960 revision provided the needed rejuvenation for continued use.

REFERENCES

1. Anastasi, Anne. *Differential psychology.* (3rd ed.) N. Y.: Macmillan, 1958.
2. Anderson, E. E., *et al.* Wilson College studies in psychology: I. A comparison of the Wechsler-Bellevue, Revised Stanford-Binet, and American Council on Education tests at the college level. *J. Psychol.,* 1942, 14, 317-326.
3. Bond, E. A. Tenth grade abilities and achievements. *Teach. Coll. Contr. Educ.,* 1940, No. 813.
4. Bradway, Katherine P., Thompson, Clare W., and Cravens, R. B. Preschool IQ's after twenty-five years. *J. educ. Psychol.,* 1958, 49, 278-281.
5. Goddard, H. H. The Binet and Simon tests of intellectual capacity. *Train. Sch.,* 1908, 5, 3-9.
6. Goddard, H. H. A measuring scale for intelligence. *Train. Sch.,* 1910, 6, 146-155.
7. Goddard, H. H. A revision of the Binet Scale. *Train. Sch.,* 1911, 8, 56-62.
8. Herring, J. P. *Herring Revision of the Binet-Simon tests.* Tarrytown-on-Hudson, N. Y.: World Book Co., 1922.
9. Hofstaetter, P. R. The changing composition of "intelligence": a study of T technique. *J. genet. Psychol.,* 1954, 85, 159-164.
10. Honzik, Marjorie P., Macfarlane, Jean W., and Allen, Lucile. The stability of mental test performance between two and eighteen years. *J. exp. Educ.,* 1948, 17, 309-324.
11. Jones, L. V. A factor analysis of the Stanford-Binet at four age levels. *Psychometrika,* 1949, 14, 299-331.
12. Jones, L. V. Primary abilities in the Stanford-Binet, age 13. *J. genet. Psychol.,* 1954, 84, 125-147.
13. Kuhlmann, F. A revision of the Binet-Simon system for measuring the intelligence of children. *J. Psycho-Asthenics, Monogr. Suppl.,* 1912, 1, 1-41.
14. McNemar, Q. *The revision of the Stanford-Binet Scale: an analysis of the standardization data.* Boston: Houghton Mifflin, 1942.
15. Merrill, Maud A. The significance of IQ's on the revised Stanford-Binet Scales. *J. educ. Psychol.,* 1938, 29, 641-651.
16. Mitchell, Mildred B. The Revised Stanford-Binet for university students. *J. educ. Res.,* 1943, 36, 507-511.
17. Peterson, J. *Early conceptions and tests of intelligence.* Tarrytown-on-Hudson, N. Y.: World Book Co., 1926.
18. Sartain, A. Q. A comparison of the New Revised Stanford-Binet, the Bellevue Scale, and certain group tests of intelligence. *J. soc. Psychol.,* 1946, 23, 237-239.
19. Sontag, L. W., Baker, C. T., and Nelson, Virginia L. Mental growth and personality development: a longitudinal study. *Monogr. Soc. Res. Child Develpm.,* 1958, 23, No. 2.
20. Terman, L. M. *The measurement of intelligence.* Boston: Houghton Mifflin, 1916.
21. Terman, L. M., and Merrill, Maud A. *Measuring intelligence.* Boston: Houghton Mifflin, 1937.

22. Terman, L. M., and Merrill, Maud A. *Stanford-Binet Intelligence Scale: manual for the third revision, Form L-M.* Boston: Houghton Mifflin, 1960.
23. Watson, R. I. *The clinical method in psychology.* N. Y.: Harper, 1951.
24. Yerkes, R. M., Bridges, J. W., and Hardwick, R. S. *A point scale for measuring mental ability.* Baltimore: Warwick & York, 1915.

CHAPTER 9

Group Tests

While individual scales such as the Stanford-Binet find their principal application in the clinic, group tests are used primarily in the educational system, in industry, and in the armed services. It will be recalled that mass testing began during World War I with the development of the Army Alpha and the Army Beta for use in the United States Army (cf. Ch. 1). The former was a verbal test designed for general screening and placement purposes. The latter was a non-language test for use with individuals who could not properly be tested with the Alpha owing to foreign-language background or illiteracy. The pattern established by these tests was closely followed in the subsequent development of a large number of group tests for civilian application.

In this chapter, some of the outstanding examples of group tests in current use will be considered. For convenience, these tests have been classified with reference to the age level for which they are designed. Such a classification is only approximate, however, since a number of test series include overlapping forms suitable for widely varying age levels. The same integrated test series may thus yield comparable scores from the primary grades to the high school senior or even the college level. The tests to be discussed in this chapter have been selected to represent the content and scope of available group tests, exclusive of non-language tests, which will be covered in the next chapter. For illustrative purposes only one or two tests will be examined at each level, other widely used tests being cited by name only—for an evaluation of these tests, reference should be made to the test manuals as well as to the *Mental Measurements Yearbooks* and other sources cited in Chapter 2.

TESTS FOR THE PRIMARY LEVEL

The youngest age at which it has proved feasible to employ group tests is the kindergarten and first-grade level. At the preschool ages, individual test-

213

ing is required in order to establish and maintain rapport, as well as to administer the oral and performance type of items suitable for such children. By the age of 5 or 6, however, it is possible to administer printed tests to small groups of no more than 10 or 15 children. In such testing, the examiner must still give considerable individual attention to the subjects to make sure that directions are followed, see that pages are turned properly in the test booklets, and supervise other procedural details. With one or two assistant examiners, somewhat larger groups may be tested if necessary.

Group tests for the primary level generally cover kindergarten and the first two or three grades of elementary school. In such tests, each child is provided with a booklet on which are printed the pictures and diagrams constituting the test items. All instructions are given orally and are usually accompanied by demonstrations. Fore-exercises are frequently included in which subjects try one or two sample items and the examiner or proctor checks the responses to make certain that the instructions were properly understood. The child marks his responses on the test booklet with a crayon or soft pencil. Most of the tests require only marking the correct picture out of a set. A few call for simple motor coordination, as in drawing lines that join two dots.

Obviously tests for the primary level can require no reading or writing on the part of the subject. For this reason, they are sometimes described as "non-verbal tests." This category should not be confused with the non-language tests to be considered in the next chapter. The latter type requires no language at all, either written or spoken, and is suitable for foreign-speaking and deaf as well as for illiterate subjects. Non-language tests for the primary level have also been developed for testing special groups of children, but the usual primary group test involves extensive use of spoken language. The designation "non-verbal" for these tests, although commonly employed, may be somewhat misleading, since it can be properly applied only to the test content and not to the subject's behavior. For example, tests of verbal comprehension can be administered at these age levels through the use of pictorial content. Thus the child's vocabulary or his sentence comprehension can be tested by means of pictures. For this reason, it would seem more accurate to refer to these tests by such a term as "pictorial" or "preliterate," rather than "non-verbal."

One of the best-known group tests for the primary level is the Pintner-Cunningham Primary Test (23), which has been in use in different forms since 1923. This test is part of the Pintner General Ability Tests, Verbal Series (22), which extends through the college freshman level. The Pintner-Cunningham is designed for children in kindergarten, grade 1, and the first

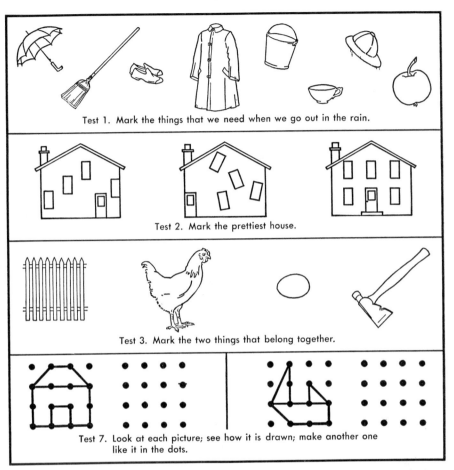

Test 1. Mark the things that we need when we go out in the rain.

Test 2. Mark the prettiest house.

Test 3. Mark the two things that belong together.

Test 7. Look at each picture; see how it is drawn; make another one like it in the dots.

Fig. 32. Illustrative Items from Forms A, B, and C of the Pintner-Cunningham Primary Test. (Copyright by World Book Company.)

half of grade 2. The current revision is available in three equivalent forms, A, B, and C. A few illustrative items taken from each of the three forms are reproduced in Figure 32. Each form consists of the following seven subtests:

1. *Common Observation:* Subject marks all objects in a set that fit a given category, such as all things we need when we go out in the rain (Fig. 32, row 1).

2. *Aesthetic Differences:* Subject marks the prettiest of three drawings of the same object, such as the house shown in Figure 32, row 2.

3. *Associated Objects:* In each row of pictures, subject marks the two things that belong together, such as the chicken and the egg in Figure 32, row 3.

4. *Discrimination of Size:* Subject marks the items of clothing that are the right size for the individual pictured. For each article of clothing, such as shoes, hat, gloves, etc., one is too large, one too small, and one is the correct choice.

5. *Picture Parts:* This test includes a series of pictures of increasing complexity containing children, animals, toys, and other objects. The same objects are reproduced outside the picture, mixed in with other objects. Subject marks all the objects outside the picture that appear in the picture.

6. *Picture Completion:* For each incomplete picture, the subject locates and marks the correct missing part among several parts presented.

7. *Dot Drawing:* Subject copies drawings made by joining dots, as shown in the fourth row of Figure 32.

A total raw score is obtained by adding the point scores on each subtest. By reference to a table of age norms, the mental age corresponding to any given raw score can be found. This can be divided by the CA to find the IQ by the traditional ratio method. Such an IQ, however, is of doubtful significance, since there is no assurance that it will have uniform variability at different age levels. A procedure for converting raw scores into deviation IQ's is also provided in the test manual. Since the *SD* of these deviation IQ's has been set at 16, they are expressed in units that are comparable to those of the Stanford-Binet IQ. It cannot be assumed, of course, that the scores have the same meaning as Stanford-Binet IQ's, since the tests differ in content, mode of administration, and other characteristics. In all cases, IQ's should be accompanied by the name of the test from which they were obtained. An advantage of Pintner-Cunningham IQ's is that they are comparable with the IQ's obtained on other parts of the Pintner General Ability Tests for higher age levels, since the standard score scales developed for different levels are continuous.

Reliability of the Pintner-Cunningham, found by correlating Forms A and B, varied from .83 to .89 within different groups of kindergarten or primary grade children.[1] As in the validation of many group intelligence tests, the Stanford-Binet and certain measures of school achievement served as the criteria. Correlations of .73, .80, and .88 between Pintner-Cunningham and Stanford-Binet were found in three groups of kindergarten and primary grade children. In a group of 260 first-grade pupils, the Pintner-Cunningham correlated .63 with reading test scores.

[1] Unless otherwise indicated, all data reported about a test are taken from the test manual. Complete references for each test cited can be found at the end of each chapter. The dates included in these references are the terminal publication dates of the latest available revision. Frequently, parallel forms of the same edition or supplements to the manual appear in different years. In such cases, more than one year is given in the publication date.

Other tests containing levels suitable for kindergarten and the primary grades are the Otis Quick-Scoring Mental Ability Tests (21), Kuhlmann-Anderson Intelligence Tests (15), California Test of Mental Maturity (25), and The Lorge-Thorndike Intelligence Tests (18). Like the Pintner series, all of these tests provide scores expressed in comparable terms from the primary level through high school or college. All four have been either published or revised since 1952.

TESTS FOR THE ELEMENTARY SCHOOL LEVEL

In general, the tests to be considered in this section are designed for use from grade 4 through grade 8 or 9. Since literacy is presupposed at these levels, such tests are predominantly verbal in content; most also include arithmetic problems or other numerical tests. One of the first group tests constructed for use with school children was the National Intelligence Test (40). This test was prepared shortly after the termination of World War I by a group of psychologists working under the auspices of the National Research Council. It was primarily an adaptation for school children of the group intelligence tests developed for Army recruits during the war. Today this test is of historical interest only, having been replaced by more recently developed instruments. For many years, however, it was one of the most widely used intelligence tests in the elementary school grades and was also employed in many psychological investigations on a wide variety of problems.

The five series of tests cited in the preceding section (Pintner, Otis, Kuhlmann-Anderson, California, and Lorge-Thorndike) contain levels suitable for the elementary school grades. To these may be added the Henmon-Nelson Tests of Mental Ability, revised in 1957 and comprising three batteries designed for grades 3 to 6, 6 to 9, and 9 to 12, respectively (16). Still another example is provided by the Cooperative School and College Ability Tests (SCAT), first developed in 1955 (9). Covering a range from grades 3 to 14, these tests will be more fully discussed in a later section, in connection with their use in testing prospective college students.

As an illustration of tests for elementary school children, we shall examine Level 3 (for grades 4 to 6) of the Lorge-Thorndike tests. The entire series comprises five levels: for kindergarten and first grade, grades 2 to 3, 4 to 6, 7 to 9, and 10 to 12. The two lowest levels are entirely non-verbal. All other levels contain both verbal and non-verbal parts, yielding separate scores. According to the authors, however, all parts of the test were designed to measure abstract intelligence, defined as "the ability to work with ideas and the relationships among ideas." While granting that verbal symbols are the appropriate medium for testing abstract intelligence, the authors have included a parallel set of non-verbal tests to provide a more adequate basis for appraising the abilities of children with inferior educational backgrounds or with special reading disabilities.

Like all other levels, Level 3 is available in two equivalent forms, A and B. The verbal subtests include Sentence Completion, Verbal Classification, Arithmetical Reasoning, and Vocabulary. The non-verbal subtests utilize only pictorial, diagrammatic, or numerical content; they comprise Figure Classification, Number Series, and Figure Analogies. Typical items illustrating each of the seven tests are reproduced in Figures 33A and 33B. The authors recommend that both verbal and non-verbal parts be routinely administered to each child for a more comprehensive picture of his abilities. Total time required is about 45 minutes for the verbal and 40 for the non-verbal parts. Although all subtests have time limits, they are said to be largely power tests.

Within each subtest, items were selected so as to yield an appropriate

---

1. *Sentence Completion:* choose the word that will make the best, the truest, and the most sensible sentence.

There's no book so _____ but something good may be found in it.

A. good   **B.** true   **C.** beautiful   **D.** bad   **E.** excellent

---

2. *Verbal Classification:* think in what way the words in dark type go together. Then find the word on the line below that belongs with them.

cotton   **wool**   **silk**

A. dress   **B.** sew   **C.** fibre   **D.** linen   **E.** cloth

---

3. *Arithmetic Reasoning*

A man has to take a 300-mile trip by car. If he goes 40 miles each hour, how many miles does he still have to travel after driving 5½ hours?

A. 180 mi.   **B.** 100 mi.   **C.** 60 mi.   **D.** 2 mi.   **E.** none of these

---

4. *Vocabulary:* choose the word which has the same meaning, or most nearly the same meaning, as the word in dark type at the beginning of the line.

javelin   **A.** bleach   **B.** coffee   **C.** jacket   **D.** rifle   **E.** spear

---

Fig. 33A. Typical Items from The Lorge-Thorndike Intelligence Tests, Level 3: Verbal Battery. (Reproduced by permission of Irving Lorge and Robert L. Thorndike.)

range of difficulty, as well as high internal consistency. Median item-subtest correlations in Level 3 range from .44 to .70 for the seven subtests. Norms for the complete battery (including all levels) were established by testing about 136,000 children in 44 communities distributed over 22 states. To increase the representativeness of this standardization sample, the communities were selected on the basis of a composite of socioeconomic and educational variables previously found to be related to the intelligence test performance of children within a community. Scores are expressed as deviation IQ's, with a mean of 100 and an *SD* of 16. Age, grade, and percentile norms are also provided. It is interesting to note that on this test the differences between lower and higher socioeconomic levels are about the same in verbal and nonverbal IQ's.

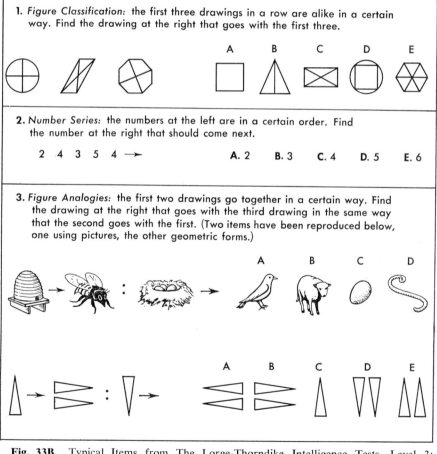

1. *Figure Classification:* the first three drawings in a row are alike in a certain way. Find the drawing at the right that goes with the first three.

2. *Number Series:* the numbers at the left are in a certain order. Find the number at the right that should come next.

2 4 3 5 4 ⟶   A. 2   B. 3   C. 4   D. 5   E. 6

3. *Figure Analogies:* the first two drawings go together in a certain way. Find the drawing at the right that goes with the third drawing in the same way that the second goes with the first. (Two items have been reproduced below, one using pictures, the other geometric forms.)

Fig. 33B. Typical Items from The Lorge-Thorndike Intelligence Tests, Level 3: Nonverbal Battery. (Reproduced by permission of Irving Lorge and Robert L. Thorndike.)

Parallel-form reliability coefficients, found by administering Forms A and B about a week apart, were .896 for the verbal and .814 for the non-verbal parts of Level 3. These coefficients were found on 724 fifth-grade children. Odd-even reliabilities were .940 for both verbal and non-verbal parts. Although varying somewhat in different portions of the score range, the standard error of measurement is about 4 IQ points for the verbal and about 6 for the non-verbal parts. Apart from the a priori choice of test content designed to measure the ability to handle abstract concepts, symbols, and relations, available evidence of validity centers around correlations with other intelligence tests and with tests of educational achievement. For example, in a group of 171 sixth-grade pupils, the correlations of total IQ with Stanford Achievement Tests in Reading and Arithmetic were .87 and .76, respectively. Little information on predictive validity is available, none being reported for Level 3. Empirical data on validity as a whole are meager, but are gradually being accumulated as the test continues in use.

The correlations between verbal and non-verbal parts, separately computed in fourth-, fifth- and sixth-grade groups, ranged from .66 to .68. Although there is considerable overlap, it is apparent that somewhat different functions are measured by verbal and non-verbal IQ's. A factor analysis of the intercorrelations among the seven subtests in Level 3 yielded evidence of a large verbal factor through the verbal tests and a large non-verbal factor through the other three, thus further indicating that these two parts measure distinct functions. In view of these findings, one wonders how well the non-verbal IQ may predict such a highly verbal criterion as school achievement in the case of non-readers and other educationally handicapped children. Empirical data on the predictive validity of the non-verbal IQ against academic criteria are needed to check on the effectiveness of the tests for such purposes.

It is apparent that our knowledge of what these tests measure and how their scores are to be interpreted would benefit from further empirical validation. The chief strengths of the tests stem from the sound theoretical rationale underlying choice of content, the size and representativeness of the standardization sample, the high reliability of the IQ's, and the generally superior quality of test-construction procedures followed in developing the tests.

TESTS FOR HIGH SCHOOL STUDENTS AND UNSELECTED ADULTS

All of the test series mentioned in the preceding section include levels appropriate for testing high school students. However, it should be noted that, as the upper limit of applicability of any test is approached, the test may not be as satisfactory a measure of individual differences as it is nearer the center of its range. Thus the Pintner, Kuhlmann-Anderson, Henmon-Nelson, and Lorge-Thorndike, which extend through grade 12, may not discriminate adequately among high school seniors. The Otis, California, and SCAT, extending into the college level, would be expected to provide a more adequate ceiling for testing the brighter high school seniors. On the other hand, tests designed for the high school level are suitable for unselected adults in the general population. Since the proportion of adults who have attended college is still small, high school tests usually provide sufficient ceiling for unselected adult groups, while tests constructed for college students may be too difficult and would probably fail to differentiate at the lower end of the distribution.

A widely used and carefully constructed test prepared specifically for the high school level is the Terman-McNemar Test of Mental Ability (28), which in 1941 replaced the earlier Terman Group Test. The Terman-Mc-Nemar Test is designed primarily for grades 7 through 12, although the authors report that it may also be used in grade 6 and in the first year of college. It is predominantly a measure of verbal comprehension, consisting of the following seven subtests: Information, Synonyms, Logical Selection, Classification, Analogies, Opposites, and Best Answer. Two numerical tests that had been included in the earlier form were eliminated from the revised form in order to make the test more homogeneous and the scores less ambiguous. The specific instructions and sample items employed with each of the subtests of the Terman-McNemar Test are reproduced in Figure 34. These items are not scored and are considerably easier than those occurring in the test proper.

The Terman-McNemar Test provides two equivalent forms, available in both hand-scored and machine-scored editions. Each form requires approximately fifty minutes to administer and is described in the manual as being essentially a power test, the time limits allowed for each subtest being adequate to enable most subjects to attain their maximum score. Norms were established through a carefully conducted, nationwide testing program, involving 200 communities in 37 states. Scores can be expressed in terms of percentiles, mental ages, and deviation IQ's with an *SD* of 16 points. The last type of score is, of course, the soundest of the three measures and is to be preferred for most purposes.

The reliability coefficient of the total test, adjusted for a single age level, was found to be .96 by both split-half and parallel-form techniques. A correlation of .91 is reported between the present test and the earlier Terman Group Test. Individual scores on the two tests are not, however, directly com-

---

TEST 1. INFORMATION

Mark the answer space which has the same number as the word that makes the sentence TRUE.

SAMPLE. Our first President was
1 Adams   2 Washington   3 Lincoln   4 Jefferson   5 Monroe. ...

1 **2** 3 4 5

TEST 2. SYNONYMS

Mark the answer space which has the same number as the word which has the SAME or most nearly the same meaning as the beginning word of each line.

SAMPLE. correct — 1 neat   2 fair   3 right   4 poor   5 good ....

1 2 **3** 4 5

TEST 3. LOGICAL SELECTION

Mark the answer space which has the same number as the word which tells what the thing ALWAYS has or ALWAYS involves.

SAMPLE. A cat always has
1 kittens   2 spots   3 milk   4 mouse   5 hair...............

1 2 3 4 **5**

TEST 4. CLASSIFICATION

In each line below, four of the words belong together. Pick out the ONE WORD which does not belong with the others, and mark the answer space bearing its number.

SAMPLES.
1 dog   2 cat   3 horse   4 chicken   5 cow..........................

1 2 3 **4** 5

6 hop   7 run   8 stand   9 skip   10 walk...........................

6 7 **8** 9 10

TEST 5. ANALOGIES

Study the samples carefully.

SAMPLES.
Ear is to hear as eye is to
1 cry   2 glasses   3 spy   4 wink   5 see......................

1 2 3 4 **5**

Hat is to head as shoe is to
6 arm   7 leg   8 foot   9 fit   10 glove......................

6 7 **8** 9 10

DO THEM ALL LIKE THE SAMPLES.

TEST 6. OPPOSITES

Mark the answer space which has the same number as the word which is OPPOSITE, or most nearly opposite, in meaning to the beginning word of each line.

SAMPLE. north — 1 hot   2 east   3 west   4 down   5 south.... ....

1 2 3 4 **5**

TEST 7. BEST ANSWER

Read each statement and mark the answer space which has the same number as the answer which you think is BEST.

SAMPLE. We should not put a burning match in the wastebasket because
1 Matches cost money.   2 We might need a match later.
3 It might go out.   4 It might start a fire...................................

1 2 3 **4**

Fig. 34. Sample Items from Terman-McNemar Test of Mental Ability. (Copyright by World Book Company.)

parable, because of differences in test content, standardization sample, and method of computing IQ. The principal evidence for validity derives from the item analysis, which was conducted on a total of 1200 pupils in grades 7, 9, and 11. One criterion for item selection was grade differentiation, or increase in percentage of subjects passing an item from grade 7 to 9, and from grade 9 to 11. The other criterion was the correlation between each item and total score on the entire test. No other statistical data on validity are reported in the manual. It is pointed out, however, that during the many years when the earlier form was widely used in high schools, close correspondence was observed between test scores and indices of academic achievement, such as graduation with honors.

The two principal tests designed for general screening and placement of U.S. military personnel in World Wars I and II also belong in the present category. Both tests have subsequently appeared in civilian editions suitable for high school students and for unselected adults. The original military forms of the Army Alpha (cf. 42, Part II, Ch. 1-4) were validated in terms of such criteria as amount of schooling and ratings of intelligence by officers. In the development of this test, preliminary forms were administered, not only to military personnel, but also to a number of other groups, including college students, school children, and institutionalized mental defectives. Several other criteria were employed in such preliminary testing. For example, the criterion of contrasted groups was applied by comparing the distributions of Alpha scores obtained by college students, officers, enlisted men, and mentally defective adults. For school children, Alpha scores were checked against such criteria as Stanford-Binet MA, chronological age, grade, school marks, and teachers' ratings of pupils' intelligence.

Most of the indices of validity showed the Alpha to correlate fairly well with the criteria employed. For example, a correlation of .82 was found between a preliminary form of Alpha and school grade within a group of unselected 13-year-olds, and a correlation of .86 within a group of unselected 14-year-olds. Correlations with the Stanford-Binet ranged from .58 to .88. Correlations of the final form with ratings of intelligence by officers ranged from .45 to .67, and correlations with amount of schooling were in the .60's and .70's. Correlations of subtests with total scores and intercorrelations among subtests were also employed in the final selection of subtests.

After World War I, the Army Alpha was released for general use. Several revisions were subsequently developed for civilian purposes and were widely administered, especially in testing applicants for industrial jobs (cf. 11). One of the current adaptations of this test is the Modified Alpha Examination, Form 9, developed by Wells (37). Commonly known as "Alpha 9," this test consists of four numerical and four verbal subtests, from which can be obtained separate N and V scores, as well as a combined N + V score. These subtests, together with their corresponding N or V designations, are listed below:

A. Addition (N)
B. Following written directions (V)
C. Arithmetic problems (N)
D. Analogies (V)

E. Number series completion (N)
F. Disarranged sentences (V)
G. Finding largest common divisor (N)
H. Synonym-antonym (V)

Percentile norms are provided for boys and girls in each year of high school, separate norms being given for N, V, and total scores. The manual also includes supplementary norms based on smaller samples of seventh- and eighth-grade pupils, on engineers employed in a single large airplane company, and on men applying for executive positions. Total score reliabilities of about .90 were obtained when Alpha 9 was correlated with comparable earlier forms. No evidence of validity is cited in the manual other than correlations with other group intelligence tests. The mass of data accumulated over the years with earlier forms, however, contributes to the construct validation of the test.

During World War II, the Army General Classification Test (AGCT) was developed to serve many of the functions for which the Army Alpha had been used in the earlier war. The AGCT was administered to over ten million inductees. In 1945, when this test was replaced by a revised edition, the earlier form was released for civilian use (2). The AGCT contains an equal number of vocabulary, arithmetic reasoning, and block-counting items. Some of the easy block-counting items used for demonstration purposes are reproduced in Figure 35. The inclusion of equal proportions of verbal, numerical, and spatial content in this test reflects the influence of the intervening research on factor analysis. The different types of items are arranged in spiral-omnibus form, with blocks of 5 or 10 items of each type following each other in order of increasing difficulty. This layout permits the administration of the entire test with a single time limit. The test proper is preceded by three pages of practice items, including 10 items of each type. The current civilian form is available in both a machine-scoring and a self-scoring edition, the latter employing a pin-punch answer sheet.

AGCT norms were derived from data obtained during the military application of the test. Both percentiles and AGCT standard scores are given. It will be recalled that the latter were adjusted so as to yield a mean of 100 and an *SD* of 20 points (cf. Ch. 4). Retest reliability is .82; split-half and Kuder-Richardson reliabilities cluster about .95 (cf. 35). It is possible that the latter value is spuriously high because of the influence of speed upon test scores, although it is stated in the manual that the time limit allowed is sufficient for most subjects to reach their upper limit of difficulty.

Several measures of validity were found on the basis of the military samples tested. AGCT scores correlated .73 with amount of schooling. Correlations with many other tests are reported, some of which are extremely high. For example, a correlation of .90 was found with Army Alpha, and one of .83 with the Otis Higher Mental Ability Examination. Further data on validity were provided by correlations with performance in military training schools for various occupational specialties, such as that of clerk, radio operator, and mechanic, as well as by correlations with performance in officer candidate schools. The median AGCT scores of men who had been employed in different civilian occupations are likewise given.

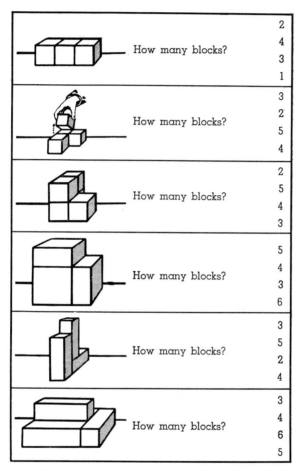

Fig. 35. Sample Block Counting Items from the Army General Classification Test. (Reproduced by permission of Science Research Associates.)

Mention should also be made of the subsequently developed Armed Forces Qualification Test (AFQT). This test was prepared cooperatively by all the armed services for the purpose of screening recruits and providing each service with an equitable distribution of ability among its quota of recruits (5, 6, 14, 36). The AFQT includes vocabulary, arithmetic reasoning, and spatial relations items, the last-named involving the recognition, perception, manipulation, and analysis of relations in two and three dimensions. Items were selected on the basis of difficulty level, as well as on the basis of their correlations with subtests and total test scores. The AFQT has replaced the AGCT as well as other screening tests formerly used by the different services. Following the general preliminary screening by means of the AFQT, each service now administers its own classification batteries, on the basis of which the inductees are assigned to particular specialties within that service.

TESTS FOR COLLEGE STUDENTS AND SUPERIOR ADULTS

A number of tests have been specially developed for use in the admission, placement, and counseling of college students. An outstanding example is the Scholastic Aptitude Test (SAT) of the College Entrance Examination Board (7, 12). Several new forms of this test are prepared each year, a different form being employed in each administration. Separate scores are reported for the Verbal and Mathematics sections of the test. A shorter comparable form, known as the Preliminary SAT, has also been administered since 1959. Generally taken at an earlier stage, this test provides a rough estimate of the high school student's aptitude for college work and has been employed for educational counseling and other special purposes. Both tests are restricted to the testing program of the College Entrance Examination Board.

Another college-level test prepared for restricted use in a special program is the Selective Service College Qualification Test (SSCQT). First administered in 1951, this test was designed to aid in identifying college students with high scholastic aptitude whose military service might profitably be deferred in order to permit them to complete their education (cf. 13). Utilizing a variety of item types, the test gives equal emphasis to verbal ability and quantitative reasoning. In content, it provides a balanced selection of material from the major areas of academic instruction.

A number of tests designed for college-bound high school seniors and for college students are available for distribution to counselors and other qualified persons. Among them may be mentioned the Ohio State University Psychological Test (34), covering only verbal content; the College Placement Test (8), providing verbal and quantitative scores; and the College Qualification Tests (3), yielding scores in verbal and numerical aptitudes as well as in broad areas of academic achievement.

For many years, one of the most widely used instruments for the testing of entering college students was the American Council on Education Psychological Examination for College Freshman, commonly called the ACE. Available also in a high school form, this test yielded a Linguistic (L) and a Quantitative (Q) score. A large number of follow-up studies were conducted to determine the validity of the ACE in predicting college grades. Although the results varied widely with the level and heterogeneity of the sample and with the nature of the courses, correlations with four-year grade-point averages clustered around .45 (4; 26, pp. 120 ff.). In general, the validities were somewhat lower than those reported for other, more recent instruments. Moreover, the L and Q scores seem to be factorially complex and hence difficult to interpret. Speed also plays an unduly prominent part in determining these scores. Following the publication of the 1954 edition, the ACE, which since 1948 had been prepared by the Cooperative Test Division of Educational Testing Service, was discontinued and has been superseded by the Cooperative School and College Ability Tests (SCAT).

As was noted in an earlier section of the chapter, SCAT (9) covers a range from the fourth grade of elementary school through the college sophomore year. At each of the five levels covering this range, the tests are available in two equivalent forms, A and B. Oriented specifically toward the prediction of academic achievement, all levels yield a verbal, a quantitative, and a total score. The verbal score is based on two tests, Sentence Understanding (I) and Word Meanings (III); the numerical score, on Numerical Computation (II) and Numerical Problem Solving (IV). Figure 36 shows a sample item from each of the four parts at Level 1, suitable for college freshmen and sophomores. Administration of any one level requires approximately two class periods.

In line with current trends in testing theory, SCAT undertakes to measure "developed abilities." This is simply an explicit admission of what is more or less true of all intelligence tests, namely that test scores reflect the nature and amount of schooling the individual has received rather than measuring "capacity" independently of relevant prior experiences. Accordingly, SCAT draws freely upon word knowledge and arithmetic processes learned in the appropriate school grades. In this respect, SCAT does not really differ from other intelligence tests, especially those designed for the high school and college levels—it only makes overt a condition sometimes unrecognized in other tests.

Verbal, quantitative, and total scores from all five SCAT levels are expressed on a common scale which permits direct comparison from one level to another. These scores can in turn be converted into percentiles for the appropriate grade, derived from a carefully chosen nationwide standardization sample. A particularly desirable feature of SCAT scores is the provision of a *percentile band* rather than a single percentile for each obtained score. This percentile band, illustrated in Figure 37, covers a distance of approx-

---

Part I. *Sentence Understanding:* select the missing word by deciding which one of the five words *best* fits in with the meaning of the sentence.

A knowledge of history is an antidote for sectionalism and narrow nationalism, leading one instead to realize the eternal (   ) of peoples.

A. differences   **B.** struggle   **C.** self-consciousness   **D.** interdependence

E. evolution

Part II. *Numerical Computation:* choose the correct answer, using scratch paper if necessary.

2) 3 pounds 2 ounces

A. 1 pound 1¼ ounces
B. 1 pound 2 ounces
C. 1 pound 6 ounces
D. 1 pound 9 ounces
E. none of these

Part III. *Word Meanings:* pick the word or phrase whose meaning is closest to the word in large letters.

retaliate

A. buy and sell profitably
B. whisper insults
C. repay evil with evil
D. recheck items in a list
E. return damaged merchandise

Part IV. *Numerical Problem Solving:* choose the correct answer using scratch paper if necessary.

If the average of numbers 1 through 9 is multiplied by 9, the result is

A. 36
B. 40.5
C. 45
D. 54
E. 90

Fig. 36. Typical Items from SCAT, Level 1, for Grades 13 and 14. (Reproduced by permission of Cooperative Test Division, Educational Testing Service.)

imately one standard error of measurement on either side of the corresponding percentile. Such a distance, technically known as a 68 per cent confidence interval, represents the range of percentiles within which the individual's "true" score will fall 68 out of 100 times (roughly a 2:1 chance). As explained in Chapter 4, the error of measurement is a concrete way of taking

SCAT STUDENT PROFILE
School and College Ability Tests

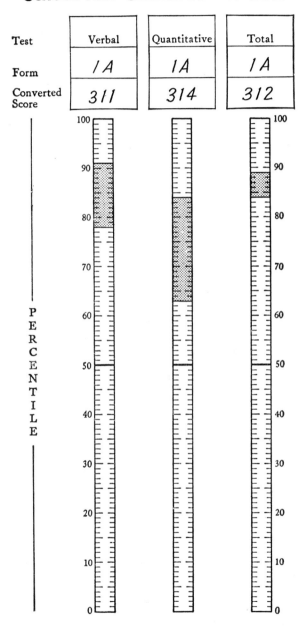

Test	Verbal	Quantitative	Total
Form	*I A*	*I A*	*I A*
Converted Score	*3 I I*	*3 I 4*	*3 I 2*

Fig. 37. SCAT Student Profile, Illustrating Use of Percentile Bands. (Reproduced by permission of Cooperative Test Division, Educational Testing Service.)

the reliability of a test into account when interpreting an individual's score.

Thus if two students were to obtain total SCAT scores that fall in the percentile bands 55-68 and 74-84, we could conclude with fair confidence that the second actually excels the first and would continue to do so on a re-test. Percentile bands likewise help in comparing a single individual's relative standing on verbal and quantitative parts of the test. From Figure 37, for example, we would conclude that the student whose scores are plotted is *not* significantly better in verbal than in quantitative abilities, because his percentile bands for these two scores overlap.

Reliability coefficients for verbal, quantitative, and total scores were separately computed within single grade groups by the Kuder-Richardson technique (cf. Ch. 5). It will be recalled that this is a measure of interitem consistency within a single form administered once. The reported reliabilities are uniformly high. For the separate grade groups investigated, from grade 5 to grade 13, total score reliabilities are all .95 or .96; verbal and quantitative reliabilities vary between .88 and .94. These reliabilities may be spuriously high because the tests are somewhat speeded. It is reported that, in some of the samples tested, the numbers of subjects completing all items were as low as 65 per cent and 80 per cent for the two verbal tests and as low as 48 per cent and 60 per cent for the two quantitative tests. Under these circumstances, equivalent-form reliability would seem more appropriate. When the necessary data have been accumulated, these equivalent-form reliabilities will be reported in supplements to the manual, to be issued from time to time. It is possible that the computed values of the errors of measurement—and hence the percentile bands—may require revision when such equivalent-form reliabilities become available.

A variety of sources provide information about what SCAT measures. Through preliminary experimentation, the four subtests illustrated in Figure 36 were chosen from nine subtests, each representing a different item type designed to sample abilities required for academic success. This selection was based on the correlations of each subtest with total grade averages, English grades, and mathematics grades in groups of ninth- and twelfth-grade students. Intercorrelations among the subtests were also considered, in order to maximize differences between verbal and quantitative measures. Items for the four types of subtests finally chosen were next selected on the basis of item-subtest correlations and appropriateness of difficulty level. This item analysis was conducted on large samples of students representative of the population for which the test was being developed. In the final forms, correlations between verbal and quantitative scores dropped from .71 in the fifth grade to .53 in the thirteenth. Such evidence for increasing differentiation of abilities with increasing age and educational level is consistent with findings on the organization of abilities (cf. 1, Ch. 11).

Special interest attaches to the correlation of SCAT with the ACE, which it was designed to replace. Total scores on the two tests correlated .88 and .87 in high school and college samples, respectively; verbal-linguistic scores correlated .89 and .85; and quantitative scores correlated .75 and .76. Correlations with the College Board SAT are also of interest because of the possibility of predicting SAT scores from earlier SCAT scores, as well as the use of SCAT scores in counseling college-bound high school students. Correlations between these two tests were also found to be in the high .70's and .80's. Charts have been prepared for predicting a student's SAT score from his eleventh- or twelfth-grade SCAT score.

In view of the stated purpose for which SCAT was developed, its predictive validity against academic achievement is of prime relevance. A limited number of studies at elementary, high school, and college levels have so far yielded correlations in the .50's and .60's with grades and correlations in the .80's with achievement test scores. Intervals between test and criterion ranged from a semester to a year. Long-range validation studies at all levels are in progress and will be reported in *Supplements* to the *Technical Report* distributed by the test publishers. The effectiveness of the verbal and quantitative scores as differential predictors of grades in specific courses remains uncertain. English grades tend to correlate higher with verbal than with quantitative scores, and mathematics grades higher with quantitative than with verbal, but the differences are small and not entirely consistent. Moreover, total scores often yield the highest correlations with all types of courses.

On the whole, SCAT is an excellently planned and well-constructed test. Among its chief assets are the carefully chosen standardization samples, the uniform score scale for all levels, the introduction of percentile bands, and the promising evidence of predictive validity. Major gaps to be filled include equivalent-form reliabilities, in place of the questionable single-form reliabilities, and more validity data, especially for long-range predictions.

The practice of testing applicants for admission to college has subsequently been extended to include graduate and professional schools. Most of the tests designed for this purpose, however, represent a combination of general intelligence and achievement tests. A well-known example is the Graduate Record Examination (GRE), administered to applicants or entering students in a large number of graduate schools. Although one portion of this test corresponds closely to the usual scholastic aptitude or intelligence test for superior adults, other parts measure the student's mastery of specific subject-matter areas. Similar tests or batteries of tests have been assembled for the selection of applicants to professional schools, such as schools of medicine, law, dentistry, and the like. This type of test will be covered in Chapter 17, following the discussion of achievement tests.

One test designed for the selection of graduate students that can be properly classified in the present chapter, however, is the Miller Analogies Test (19). Consisting of complex analogies items whose subject matter is drawn from many academic fields, this test has an unusually high ceiling. Although a fifty-minute time limit is imposed, the test is primarily a power test. The Miller Analogies Test was first developed for use at the University of Minnesota, but later forms were made available to other graduate schools. Its administration, however, is restricted to licensed centers, and rigid controls are exercised over the test materials in order to prevent coaching and protect the security of the test. One form is available for testing high-level industrial personnel.

Percentile norms on the Miller Analogies Test are given for several groups of graduate students in different fields and different universities, as well as for a few professional school groups. Marked variations in test performance are found among these different samples. The median of one group, for example, corresponds to the 90th percentile of another. Odd-even reliability coefficients of .92 to .94 were found with different groups of graduate students, and alternate-form reliabilities ranged from .85 to .89. Correlations with graduate course grades and with performance on comprehensive examinations vary widely in different institutions and departments, but more than half fall at or above .40, several being in the .60's and .70's. In general, its validity appears to be as good as that of other longer tests, or better. Correlations in the .70's and .80's have been reported between the Miller Analogies Test and the various parts of the GRE, a test that requires several hours to administer.

Another test that provides sufficient ceiling for the examination of highly superior adults is the Concept Mastery Test (27). Originating as a by-product of Terman's extensive longitudinal study of gifted children, Form A of the Concept Mastery Test was developed for testing the intelligence of the gifted group in early maturity (29). For a still later follow-up, when the gifted subjects were in their mid-forties, Form T was prepared (30). This form, which is somewhat easier than Form A, was subsequently released for more general use. The Concept Mastery Test consists of both analogies and synonym-antonym (same-opposite) items. Like the Miller Analogies Test, it draws on concepts from many fields, including physical and biological sciences, mathematics, history, literature, music, and others. Although predominantly verbal, the test incorporates some numerical content in the analogies items.

Percentile norms are provided for graduate students, college seniors applying for fellowships, and selected adult groups, but the samples are small and such norms must be regarded as tentative. Alternate-form reliabilities range from .86 to .94. Scores show consistent rise with increasing educational level and moderately high correlations with other intelligence tests in superior adult groups. Available evidence of predictive validity, however, is meager.

Mention may also be made of the CAVD, an early test developed by E. L. Thorndike and his associates at the Institute of Educational Research, Teachers College, Columbia University (31, 32). This test derives its name from its four constituent parts, Completion, Arithmetic, Vocabulary, and Directions. The CAVD is highly verbal in content, even the arithmetic problems often demanding a high level of reading comprehension. Although designed to cover a range from a mental age of 3 to superior adult, this test has been used chiefly at its upper levels, which are suitable for college and graduate students. The CAVD is a carefully constructed, pure power test with an unusually high ceiling. It has proved helpful in identifying college and graduate students who are handicapped on speed tests, such as the slow readers or the overcautious. Intercorrelations among its four alternate forms range from .88 to .93.

ABBREVIATED TESTS FOR INDUSTRIAL SCREENING

A number of intelligence tests have been specially developed for the rapid, preliminary screening of industrial personnel. Several of these tests represent abridged versions of earlier tests. Others have been specifically constructed for the purpose, a few introducing interesting innovations in testing procedure. In all these tests, administration and scoring are simplified and streamlined, and an effort is usually made to give the content face validity in an industrial setting.

It should be clearly recognized that general screening tests may have fairly high validity for some jobs and little or no validity for others. The type of behavior sampled by these tests is undoubtedly far more relevant to some types of jobs than to others. Jobs cannot simply be put into a hierarchy in terms of the amount of "intelligence" required, because the type of "intelligence" needed for different jobs varies. For many occupations, especially those requiring mechanical skills, tests of special aptitudes will serve as better predictors of achievement than will the general intelligence tests. This point is not always adequately stressed in the test manuals. In fact, some test manuals tend to create the erroneous impression that the general screening test can be used to predict success in almost every type of industrial work.

An early test that has been widely used in personnel screening is the Otis Self-Administering Test of Mental Ability: Higher Examination (20), which was used as a basis for developing the highest level (Gamma) of the Otis Quick-Scoring Mental Ability Tests. In industry, this test has been used in screening applicants for such varied jobs as those of clerks, calculating-machine operators, assembly-line workers, and foremen and other supervisory personnel. Dorcus and Jones (11) cite 36 validation studies in which the Otis test was checked against an industrial criterion. Not all of these studies yielded significant validity coefficients, of course, but many of them did. In semiskilled jobs, the Otis test correlates moderately well with success in learning the job and ease of initial adaptation, but not with subsequent job achievement (26). This would be expected for jobs that are largely routine, once they are learned. Also, for high-level professional personnel, who represent a select group in terms of academic achievement, correlations between Otis scores and criteria of job success are usually negligible, since this test does not discriminate adequately at the upper levels (cf. 11).

The Wonderlic Personnel Test (41), available in four forms, is an adaptation and abridgment of the Otis Self-Administering Test. Despite its time limit of only twelve minutes, it yields correlations of .81 to .87 with the original, longer Otis test. Parallel-form reliability coefficients between .82 and .94 are reported. The manual provides percentile norms on large industrial samples, totaling approximately 37,000 cases. Correlations with industrial criteria vary widely with the nature of the job, the sample tested, and the type of criterion measure employed (cf. 11). The test appears to have the highest validity in the selection of clerical workers.

Another abbreviated adaptation of an earlier, widely used test is the Thurstone Test of Mental Alertness (33). This test is available in two equivalent forms, each consisting of 126 multiple-choice items of different types arranged in spiral-omnibus order. With a time limit of twenty minutes, the test yields Q and L scores, based on the quantitative and linguistic items, respectively, as well as a total score. Separate percentile norms for these three scores are provided for various educational and occupational samples, although some of the groups employed for this purpose are small. Alternate-form reliability was found to be close to .90. Validity is reported principally in terms of relationships with supervisors' ratings in a number of executive, sales, and clerical groups. Many of these samples are small, and the relations, although significant, provide meager evidence of validity.

A more recently developed test is the Wesman Personnel Classification Test (38). Like most current intelligence tests, it yields Verbal, Numerical, and Total scores. The first is based on an eighteen-minute verbal analogies test, in which each item contains two blanks, as illustrated in Figure 38. The

---

Example 3.   . . . . . is to night as breakfast is to . . . . .   _____

   1. flow   2. gentle   3. supper   4. door
   A. include   B. morning   C. enjoy   D. corner

      Supper is to night as breakfast is to **morning.** So you should have written **3B** on the line at the right.

Fig. 38. Sample Analogies Items from the Wesman Personnel Classification Test. (Reproduced by permission of The Psychological Corporation.)

Numerical score is derived from a ten-minute arithmetic computation test whose items were designed so as to put a premium on ingenuity and ability to perceive numerical relations. Two parallel forms are available. Percentile norms on each of the three scores are reported for groups of students, job applicants, and employees, each group including from 93 to 1476 cases. Parallel-form reliability coefficients for V, N, and T scores fall mostly in the .80's. Correlations of V and N scores vary from .25 to .57, indicating that the overlap of the two parts is small enough to justify retention of separate scores.

Correlations of the Wesman test with the Otis and Wonderlic range from .68 to .84. Mean scores on the test show progressive rise with increasing educational and occupational level in the groups compared. Correlations with criteria of vocational success, usually based on supervisors' ratings, range from .29 to .62. From the nature of the items, as well as from the distribution of scores reported for various groups, it appears that this test may be better suited for higher-level than for lower-level personnel. It also seems likely that the predominantly academic content of the items would not hold the interest of lower-level job applicants and would lack face validity for them.

As a final illustration of rapid screening tests, we may consider the Oral Directions Test (17), in which both directions and test items are presented on either a phonograph or tape recording. This insures more uniformity than would be possible through oral administration by different examiners. Requiring a total time of fifteen minutes, this test has a split-half reliability of approximately .90. Percentile norms are reported for various industrial samples and educational groups. Correlations of an earlier, longer form with the

Alpha 9 and Otis tests clustered around .80. Older persons may be somewhat handicapped on the Oral Directions Test because of its dependence on auditory discrimination and speed. It is rather heavily weighted with perceptual and spatial items, and also depends to a considerable extent upon immediate memory for auditory instructions. Available data suggest that it discriminates somewhat better at the lower intellectual levels and may be particularly useful in screening applicants for such jobs as general laborer, maintenance and service worker, and messenger. In its later, shortened version, the Oral Directions Test is part of a short, low-level intelligence battery, which also includes a five-minute Verbal Test (39) and a twenty-minute Numerical Test (10). A Spanish version of the Oral Directions Test has also been prepared for use with Puerto Ricans and other Latin American groups (cf. 24).

REFERENCES

1. Anastasi, Anne. *Differential psychology.* (3rd ed.) N. Y.: Macmillan, 1958.
2. *Army General Classification Test* (First Civilian Edition). Chicago: Sci. Res. Assoc., 1940-1948.
3. Bennett, G. K., Bennett, Marjorie G., Wallace, W. L., and Wesman, A. G. *College Qualification Tests.* N. Y.: Psychol. Corp., 1955-1958.
4. Berdie, R., Dressel, P., and Kelso, P. Relative validity of the Q and L scores of the ACE Psychological Examination. *Educ. psychol. Measmt.,* 1951, 11, 803-812.
5. Bolanovich, D. J., and Lovelace, N. R. Control of the administration of the Armed Forces Qualification Test to assure applicability of standardized norms. *Amer. Psychologist,* 1952, 7, 388-389. (Abstract)
6. Brandt, H. Development and construction of the Armed Forces Qualification Test: I. Rationale, item content, and construction. *Amer. Psychologist.* 1949, 4, 239. (Abstract)
7. College Entrance Examination Board, Aptitude Test Committee. *A description of the College Board Scholastic Aptitude Test.* N. Y.: College Entrance Examination Board, 1956.
8. *College Placement Test.* Chicago: Sci. Res. Assoc., 1957.
9. *Cooperative School and College Ability Tests.* Princeton, N. J.: Coop. Test Div., Educ. Test. Serv., 1955-1958.
10. Doppelt, J. E. *PTI-Numerical Test.* N. Y.: Psychol. Corp., 1952-1954.
11. Dorcus, R. M., and Jones, Margaret H. *Handbook of employee selection.* N. Y.: McGraw-Hill, 1950.
12. Dyer, H. S., and King, R. G. *College Board scores: their use and interpretation. No. 2.* N. Y.: College Entrance Examination Board, 1955.
13. Findley, W. G. The Selective Service College Qualification Test. *Amer. Psychologist,* 1951, 6, 181-183.
14. Harper, Bertha P., Uhlaner, J. E., and Mosier, C. I. Development and construction of an Armed Services Qualification Test: II. Item analysis and item selection. *Amer. Psychologist,* 1949, 4, 239-240. (Abstract)

15. Kuhlmann, F., and Anderson, Rose G. *Kuhlmann-Anderson Intelligence Tests.* (6th ed.) Princeton, N. J.: Personnel Press, 1952.

16. Lamke, T. A., and Nelson, M. J. *The Henmon-Nelson Tests of Mental Ability, Revised Edition.* Boston: Houghton Mifflin, 1957-1958.

17. Langmuir, C. R. *PTI-Oral Directions Test.* N. Y.: Psychol. Corp., 1954.

18. Lorge, I., and Thorndike, R. L. *The Lorge-Thorndike Intelligence Tests.* Boston: Houghton Mifflin, 1954-1957.

19. Miller, W. S. *Miller Analogies Test.* N. Y.: Psychol. Corp., 1947-1960.

20. Otis, A. S. *Otis Self-Administering Tests of Mental Ability.* Tarrytown-on-Hudson, N. Y.: World Book Co., 1922-1929.

21. Otis, A. S. *Otis Quick-Scoring Mental Ability Tests: New Edition.* Tarrytown-on-Hudson, N. Y.: World Book Co., 1954.

22. Pintner, R., *et al. Pintner General Ability Tests, Verbal Series.* Tarrytown-on-Hudson, N. Y.: World Book Co., 1938-1946.

23. Pintner, R., Cunningham, Bess V., and Durost, W. N. *Pintner-Cunningham Primary Test.* Tarrytown-on-Hudson, N. Y.: World Book Co., 1938-1946.

24. Sanua, V. D. A note on the Spanish language form of the Oral Directions Test of Intelligence. *J. appl. Psychol.,* 1956, 40, 350-352.

25. Sullivan, Elizabeth T., Clark, W. W., and Tiegs, E. W. *California Test of Mental Maturity, 1957 Edition.* Monterey, Calif.: California Test Bur., 1957.

26. Super, D. E. *Appraising vocational fitness by means of psychological tests.* N. Y.: Harper, 1949.

27. Terman, L. M. *Concept Mastery Test.* N. Y.: Psychol. Corp., 1956.

28. Terman, L. M., and McNemar, Q. *Terman-McNemar Test of Mental Ability.* Tarrytown-on-Hudson, N. Y: World Book Co., 1941-1949.

29. Terman, L. M., and Oden, Melita H. *The gifted child grows up: twenty-five years' follow-up of a superior group.* Stanford, Calif.: Stanford Univer. Press, 1947.

30. Terman, L. M., and Oden, Melita H. *The gifted group at mid-life: thirty-five years' follow-up of the superior child.* Stanford, Calif.: Stanford Univer. Press, 1959.

31. Thorndike, E. L., *et al. The measurement of intelligence.* N. Y.: Teach. Coll., Columbia Univer., Bur. Publ., 1927.

32. Thorndike, E. L., Woodyard, Ella, and Lorge, I. Four new forms of the I.E.R. Intelligence Scale for use on the college and higher levels. *Sch. and Soc.,* 1935, 42, 271-272.

33. Thurstone, Thelma G., and Thurstone, L. L. *Thurstone Test of Mental Alertness.* Chicago: Sci. Res. Assoc., 1952-1953.

34. Toops, H. A. *Ohio State University Psychological Test.* Columbus, Ohio: Ohio College Assoc., 1919-1958. (Form 21, 1940, published by Science Research Associates.)

35. U.S. Department of the Army, TAGO, Personnel Research Branch. The Army General Classification Test. *Psychol Bull.,* 1945, 42, 760-768.

36. U.S. Department of the Army, TAGO, Personnel Research Branch. Development of Armed Forces Qualification Test and predecessor screening tests. *PRS Rep.* 976, 1952.

37. Wells, F. L. *Modified Alpha Examination, Form 9.* N. Y.: Psychol Corp., 1942-1951.
38. Wesman, A. G. *Wesman Personnel Classification Test.* N. Y.: Psychol. Corp., 1946-1951.
39. Wesman, A. G. *PTI-Verbal Test.* N. Y.: Psychol. Corp., 1952-1954.
40. Whipple, G. M. The National Intelligence Test. *J. educ. Psychol.,* 1921, 4, 16-31.
41. Wonderlic, E. F. *Wonderlic Personnel Test.* Glencoe, Ill.: Author, 1939-1945.
42. Yerkes, R. M. (Ed.) Psychological examining in the United States Army. *Mem. nat. Acad. Sci.,* 1921, 15.

CHAPTER 10

Performance and Non-Language Tests

The tests brought together in this chapter include both individual and group scales. They have been developed primarily for use with subjects who cannot properly or adequately be measured with such instruments as the Binet scales or the group tests considered in the preceding chapter. Among the special groups for which performance and non-language tests are required may be mentioned the deaf, the speech defective, the illiterate, and the foreign-speaking.

Owing to their general deficiency in linguistic development, the deaf are handicapped on verbal tests, even when the verbal content is visually presented (cf. 5, pp. 145-147; 61). Similarly, the child who has a serious speech defect or whose speech development is retarded for any reason will be unable to take many of the tests on such a scale as the Stanford-Binet, which require oral replies. Such a child, moreover, may be too young or too retarded educationally to take a written test. The illiterate of any age cannot, of course, take the usual individual or group test that calls for a certain amount of reading and writing. Children with special reading disabilities would also fall into this category.

Persons with a foreign-language background may likewise experience special difficulties in taking the common, predominantly verbal intelligence test. Although the bilingual individual may have sufficient mastery of English to communicate on ordinary matters and even to attend an English-speaking school, he may be handicapped when taking a verbal test in English. Such a person may lack the monolingual's vocabulary range, verbal fluency, or facility in handling verbal relations in English. Studies on American-born school children of foreign parentage, for example, often indicate a special deficiency on verbal tests.

The effects of bilingualism are varied and complex. They cannot be adequately summarized in any simple generalization (cf. 5, pp. 558-561; 25). Under certain conditions, intellectual development may be aided by

239

bilingualism; under other conditions, it may be seriously retarded. Emotional as well as intellectual factors probably contribute to the specific effects of bilingualism in particular cases. In testing any bilingual groups, such as immigrants or the children of immigrants, however, the possible influence of language handicap on test performance must be given serious consideration. It cannot be generally assumed that such individuals can be adequately measured with a verbal test, despite their apparent mastery of English.

Performance and non-language tests have also been developed for use in intercultural comparisons. This application would include not only the testing of persons in different nations and in preliterate cultures, but also the comparison of subcultures within a single country. For example, urban and rural groups, as well as individuals reared in different socioeconomic levels, may not have been equally exposed to the sort of educational experiences presupposed by most verbal tests. For these reasons, it has been argued that the performance or non-language type of test may be more suitable for comparisons among these varied groups, since such tests utilize content that is more nearly common to the different groups. The implications of this contention will be examined more fully in a later section of the chapter.

Another purpose for which performance and non-language tests are employed is to supplement the usual type of intelligence test. Certain individuals may score poorly on verbal tests for special reasons. Thus the shy, inarticulate child, or the child who feels discouraged when confronted with verbal tests because of his repeated school failures, may perform more satisfactorily on less academic tasks. On the other hand, the "verbalist" type of individual may obtain a deceptively high score on certain verbal tests, although his understanding of most problems may be very superficial and his practical judgment may be seriously deficient. It is now generally recognized that performance or non-language tests are not simply a substitute for verbal tests. Each type of test taps somewhat different abilities. Together they provide a more complete picture of the individual and serve as mutual correctives in the evaluation of his test performance.

The first section of this chapter will be concerned with *performance tests*. Such tests involve largely the manipulation of objects, rather than oral or written responses. All are designed essentially for individual administration. *Non-language group tests* will be covered in the second section. Although employing paper and pencil, these tests require no knowledge of reading or writing and may be administered without spoken language if necessary. Some of the tests classified in this category do require some oral instructions, but such instructions are sufficiently simple and general that they could presumably be translated into another language without appreciably altering the difficulty of the test. In any event, an attempt is made to reduce and simplify oral directions and to rely upon demonstrations and sample items.

Another type of test, to be considered in the third section, has been designated as "culture-free." Such tests have been developed primarily for *cross-cultural testing*. Like the previously mentioned tests, they are either completely non-language or employ translatable instructions. The test items, besides being non-verbal, are designed so as to be relatively universal in content and to minimize the specific influence of any one culture. Although constructed especially for use in cross-cultural studies, these tests are also applicable in other situations for which non-language tests are desirable. A final section will be devoted to the problem of *testing the physically handicapped*. Consideration will be given to the applicability of previously discussed tests to individuals with sensory or motor handicaps. Reference will also be made to adaptations of existing tests and to specially developed tests available for such purposes.

PERFORMANCE TESTS

One of the earliest performance tests was the formboard developed by Seguin for use with mental defectives. Originally devised in connection with Seguin's program for the sensory and motor training of the mentally deficient, this formboard was subsequently incorporated into a number of performance scales. A photograph of the Seguin Form Board, as used in a current series of performance tests, will be found in Figure 39. In administering this test,

Fig. 39. Seguin Form Board. (From Arthur Point Scale of Performance Tests, Rev. Form II; courtesy The Psychological Corporation.)

the examiner removes the ten pieces and stacks them as shown in the picture, instructing the subject to put them back as fast as he can. Three trials are allowed, the subject's score being the time required for the fastest of the three. The Seguin Form Board is one of the simplest formboards employed in performance scales, being suitable for relatively low mental ages. Many other formboards of increasing complexity have subsequently been developed for higher levels.

A number of other performance tests were developed to meet special testing requirements, following the early application of the Binet scales. In his pioneer psychological work with delinquent children, Healy realized the need for performance tests to supplement the more verbal type of task which predominated in the Binet scales. As a result, the Healy-Fernald test series (41) was assembled in 1911. This series of 23 tests embraced a wide variety of tasks, such as reading, arithmetic, naming opposites of words, code-learning, information questions, memory for a picture, construction puzzles, picture completion, puzzle box, and others. The tests were not combined to yield a single score, as in the Binet, but were analyzed qualitatively in an effort to obtain a picture of the child's strengths and weaknesses.

Several of the performance tests from the Healy-Fernald series have found

Fig. 40. Healy Picture Completion Test I. (From Pintner-Paterson Performance Scale; courtesy C. H. Stoelting Company.)

their way into later scales. An example is the Healy Picture Completion Test I, shown in Figure 40. This picture depicts a rural scene from which ten small squares have been cut out. The square that best completes each part of the picture is to be selected from a large number of pieces and inserted by the subject. In Figure 41 will be seen the Healy Picture Completion Test II, which portrays successive scenes from a typical day in a schoolboy's life. From each scene, a square piece has been cut out, which the subject must select from those in the box and insert in the appropriate place. In each case, the selection of the correct piece depends upon an understanding of the event represented in the scene.

Another early series of performance tests was developed by Knox (50) for testing foreign-speaking immigrants upon arrival in the United States. All tests in this series were of the performance type and were administered without the use of language. Among the tests included in the series was a set of

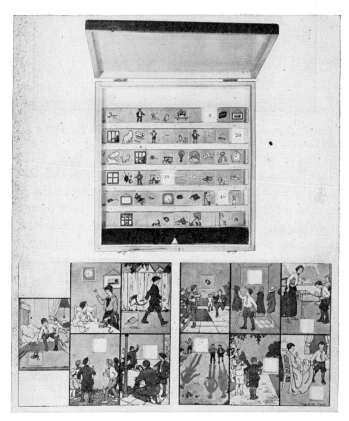

Fig. 41.   Healy Picture Completion Test II. (From Arthur Point Scale of Performance Tests, Rev. Form II; courtesy The Psychological Corporation.)

formboards of increasing difficulty, such as the one illustrated in Figure 42, as well as the Ship Test and the Knox Cube Test. In the Ship Test, ten rectangular pieces are to be arranged within a wooden frame to make a picture of a ship at sea. Undoubtedly this particular picture was chosen because of its appropriateness for testing immigrants who had just disembarked from an ocean liner. The Knox Cube Test is essentially a test of immediate memory for a series of movements. The examiner taps each of four cubes in a predetermined order and then indicates that the subject is to do likewise. The procedure is repeated with successive series of taps, increasing in length and in complexity of sequence.

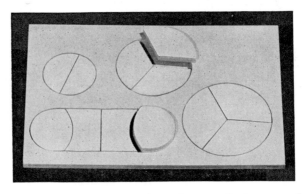

Fig. 42. Casuist Formboard. (From Pintner-Paterson Performance Scale; courtesy C. H. Stoelting Company.)

The Pintner-Paterson Performance Scale (67) represented the first major attempt to develop a standardized series of performance tests with general norms. A number of tests included in this scale were taken from the work of Seguin, Healy, Knox, and others, and have in turn been incorporated into later scales. The entire scale consisted of 15 tests, although for most testing purposes a shorter scale including the 10 most satisfactory tests has been employed. Figures 39, 40, 42, 43, and 44 show 6 tests from this series, all of which have been included in a later scale.

Although the Pintner-Paterson Scale represented a considerable advance over earlier performance tests with regard to scope of tasks, standardization of procedure, and size of normative samples, it still lagged far behind the test-construction standards set by the Stanford-Binet or by some of the group tests described in Chapter 9. Progress in the development of performance tests has been relatively slow. Such tests are still crude, in comparison with most verbal tests. The reliability of the Pintner-Paterson is considerably lower than that of most verbal scales. It should also be noted that correlations between the Pintner-Paterson and such scales as the Stanford-Binet are fairly low, when computed on relatively homogeneous age groups (cf., e.g., 57).

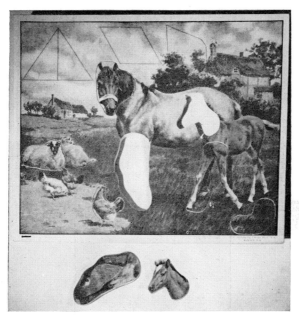

Fig. 43. Mare and Foal Test. (From Pintner-Paterson Performance Scale; courtesy C. H. Stoelting Company.)

The extent to which total scores on the Pintner-Paterson Scale depend upon speed of performance has frequently been recognized as a weakness of the scale. Certain types of individuals may become unduly disturbed by the repeated emphasis upon speed. Moreover, different cultures and sub-cultures vary widely in the degree to which they foster and encourage speed. This fact was vividly brought out, for example, in a comparison of white, Negro, and American Indian boys by means of the Pintner-Paterson (49). Not only did the three groups differ much more in speed than in quality of performance, but marked differences in speed were also found between urban and rural as well as among other subsamples of the three ethnic groups studied. Since speed plays a relatively minor part in the daily life of the reservation Indian or the rural Southern Negro, it is difficult to convey to such subjects the notion that they must hurry through the test as much as possible.

A number of later performance scales have borrowed extensively from the Pintner-Paterson. The Army Performance Scale, developed for individual testing of recruits during World War I, consisted of 10 tests, several of which were taken from the Pintner-Paterson series (84, 85). The Cornell-Coxe Performance Ability Scale (24), developed in 1934, utilized many of the tests from the Army Performance Scale, a few of which had also been part of the Pintner-Paterson. Although familiarity with these various scales is helpful in evaluating published studies that have employed such tests, most of these early scales have been largely replaced by more recently revised and restandardized tests, such as the Arthur Performance Scale, to be considered below. This scale, too, has been constructed primarily from materials taken from earlier series.

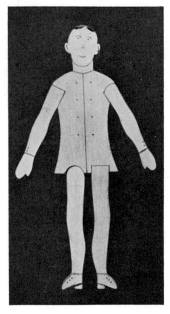

Fig. 44. Manikin Test. (From Pintner-Paterson Performance Scale; courtesy C. H. Stoelting Company.)

Form I of the Arthur Performance Scale (8, 9), first released in 1930, was based on a restandardization of eight of the Pintner-Paterson tests, together with the Porteus Mazes and the Kohs Block Design. All of these tests were restandardized on the same sample of approximately eleven hundred school children between the ages of 5 and 15, about one hundred at each age level. Both the Porteus Mazes and the Kohs Block Design had been widely used as single tests, prior to their incorporation into the Arthur Scale, and are continuing to be so employed. The tests included in the Arthur Scale I are listed below:

1. *Knox Cube:* See earlier description.

2. *Seguin Form Board:* See earlier description and Figure 39.

3. *Two-Figure Form Board:* A more difficult formboard, in which a square and a cross are each divided into four pieces to be fitted together. This test is not scored in the Arthur Scale, being used only to introduce the subject to the "puzzle-test procedure" to be followed in later tests in the series.

4. *Casuist Form Board:* This formboard is rendered more difficult by the close similarity of various pieces, which necessitates finer discriminations. See Figure 42.

5. *Manikin:* A crude wooden figure of a man is to be assembled from arms, legs, head, and trunk. See Figure 44.
   Feature Profile: Given wooden pieces are to be assembled to form a face in profile.

6. *Mare and Foal:* A relatively easy picture-completion test in which each piece, being of a different shape, fits only in its proper recess. No more pieces are provided than are actually needed. See Figure 43.

7. *Healy Picture Completion I:* See earlier description and Figure 40.

8. *Porteus Mazes:* Described below.

9. *Kohs Block Design:* Described below.

The raw score on each test is translated into a point score that weights each test in proportion to its ability to discriminate between successive age levels. Thus tests that show marked progress between successive age levels receive higher weights than those exhibiting smaller age differences in performance. The sum of the point scores is converted into an MA, from which an IQ is computed by the traditional ratio method.

The Porteus Maze Tests (68, 69, 70), first developed by Porteus in 1924, consist of a series of printed line mazes, steeply graded in difficulty. The mazes can be administered with no verbal instructions by using the easier mazes for demonstration purposes. They range from the 3-year to the adult level. The standard procedure is to have the subject trace with a pencil the shortest path from the entrance to the exit of the maze, without ever lifting the pencil from the paper. There is no time limit, and subjects are not hurried in any way. As soon as an "error" is made, by either crossing a line or entering a wrong pathway, the subject is stopped and given a second trial on an identical maze. If an error is made on the second trial, a failure is recorded for that level. At the higher levels, four trials are allowed. Scoring takes into account the trial in which each maze was successfully completed. No spontaneous correction of errors is permitted, the maze being removed as soon as any error is made. In his presentation of this test series, Porteus has repeatedly described it as a measure of foresight and planning capacity. He maintains that it excels verbal tests in measuring those aspects of intelligence most important in practical social sufficiency. The Porteus Mazes have been used in investigations on a wide variety of subjects, including normals, mental defectives, patients with organic brain damage, delinquents, and many different ethnic and cultural groups.

In the Kohs Block Design (51), the subject is presented with a set of identical 1-inch cubes, whose six sides are painted red, blue, yellow, white, yellow-and-blue, and red-and-white, respectively. Colored designs are presented on each of 17 test cards, the subject being required to reproduce each design by assembling the proper blocks. The number of blocks required varies from 4 to 16. Each design has a time limit, extra credit being given for completing it in less time.

In 1947, a Revised Form II of the Arthur Performance Scale was released (10). This form was developed primarily as an alternate for Form I, to be used in retesting. Norms on Form II were derived on 968 pupils from the same "middle-class American district" used in standardizing Form I. Special efforts were made in the development of Revised Form II to prepare directions suitable for deaf children; the use of language is thus reduced to a minimum in its administration. This form consists of five tests, including one newly developed test and revised versions of the Knox Cube, Seguin Form Board (Fig. 39), Porteus Mazes, and Healy Picture Completion Test II (Fig. 41). Most of the revisions concern the instructions or represent minor changes in the specific test materials. The new test is the Arthur Stencil Design Test I, which is pictured in Figure 45. This test is similar to the Kohs Block Design in so far as the subject must reproduce designs of increasing complexity which are presented singly on cards. In the Stencil Design Test, however, the design is reproduced by superimposing cut-out stencils in different colors upon a solid card, several overlapping stencils being required for the more complex designs.

The data on reliability and validity reported by Arthur are meager, although some pertinent information has been obtained by other investigators. A test-retest correlation of .85 was found when Form I was administered over a two-year interval to a small group of mentally defective boys (65). Considerable practice effect was found over this period. Such a result suggests that retests with the same form should be given only when the interval is very long. In reference to validity, the major criterion employed was that of age differentiation, a criterion on the basis of which tests were both selected and weighted.

Fig. 45. Arthur Stencil Design Test I. (Courtesy The Psychological Corporation.)

A number of correlations of the Arthur Scale with the Kuhlmann-Binet and with the Stanford-Binet have been reported, ranging from the .50's to the low .80's (34, 42, 82). Although high, most of these correlations indicate some differences in the information provided by the two types of tests. Some clinicians maintain that an individual's relative performance on the Stanford-Binet and Arthur scales may itself have diagnostic value as an index of emotional and social adjustment. Results on this point, however, are somewhat inconsistent. In interpreting relative performance on these tests, other factors such as the individual's educational and cultural background must be taken into account. No one explanation can be found for all intra-individual differences between verbal and performance test scores. Attempts have also been made to look for diagnostic significance in the relative performance on different tests within the Arthur Scale. An additional point to consider in connection with such a procedure is the relatively low reliability of the separate tests, which makes the obtained differences in test scores of doubtful significance.

Recent studies with both normal and mentally defective children indicate that MA's on the Arthur Form II run significantly lower than on the Stanford-

Binet (31, 36, 60). In particular, it appears that both the Stencil Design Test and the Healy Picture Completion Test II may be standardized at too high a level. Any such differences in test standardization or deficiencies in normative data will, of course, further complicate diagnostic analyses of relative performance.

NON-LANGUAGE GROUP TESTS

The first non-language group test was the Army Examination Beta (84, 85), developed for testing foreign-speaking and illiterate soldiers in the Army during World War I. The Beta was given to all men who fell below a certain score on the Alpha. In this group were included not only those who were handicapped by foreign-language background or illiteracy, but also those who performed poorly on Alpha for any other reason. Since the Beta had a lower test floor than the Alpha, it discriminated better than Alpha at the lower levels.

Instructions for the Army Beta tests were administered by means of gesture, pantomime, and demonstrations on specially prepared blackboard charts. The examiner's task was much more difficult in the Beta than in the Alpha. In addition, the procedure required the services of a trained demonstrator who did before the group what the subjects were later required to do in the test booklets. The subjects responded by drawing lines or making simple marks, except in one test which required the writing of numbers.

In the construction of the Beta, an effort was made to pattern it as closely as possible after the Alpha, since it was designed as a substitute for the Alpha. Subtests for the Beta were selected principally on the basis of their correlations with Alpha and with total Beta scores. The Army Beta placed considerable emphasis on speed. Most of its subtests seem to measure chiefly spatial orientation or perceptual speed and accuracy. The Beta correlated approximately .80 with Alpha and .73 with the Stanford-Binet. It should be noted, however, that these correlations were found on groups of enlisted men representing a wide range of ability. Within more homogeneous samples, the correlations between Beta and verbal tests would undoubtedly be lower.

As in the Army Alpha, several civilian revisions of the Army Beta were developed. A current form is the 1946 restandardization of the Revised Beta Examination (48). This form consists of six subtests, including (*a*) mazes, (*b*) symbol-digit substitution, (*c*) pictorial absurdities, (*d*) paper formboard, (*e*) picture completion, and (*f*) perceptual speed. Both administration and scoring were considerably simplified in this version. Some language is used in giving the instructions, although the explanations rely principally on the practice exercises that precede each subtest. Total scores are expressed as deviation IQ's. One of the chief uses of the Revised Beta is to be found in mass industries employing many persons with foreign background or with little education. It is also sometimes administered in penal institutions as a supplement to verbal group scales.

A well-known non-language scale, designed for elementary school children, is the Pintner Non-Language Test (66). This test was originally constructed for use with deaf children. It was principally for this purpose, too, that the previously described Pintner-Paterson Performance Scale was first developed. In his pioneer studies of deaf children, Pintner found that the linguistic retardation of such children is so great that they cannot be properly tested with any verbal instrument. The performance and non-language scales were thus developed for individual and group testing of deaf children, respectively. Both instruments have subsequently been employed with many other types of subjects.

In its current revision, the Pintner Non-Language Test is available in two equivalent forms, K and L. This test is suitable for grades 4 to 9, and parallels the Intermediate form of the Pintner General Ability Test, Verbal Series discussed in Chapter 9. Since it was standardized on a population of known ability in terms of the Pintner Verbal Test norms, the scores on the two tests are directly comparable. The Pintner Non-Language Test is ordinarily administered with simple oral instructions, but pantomime directions are also available for use with deaf and foreign-speaking children. All items are of the multiple-choice type. Each form consists of six subtests, which are illustrated in Figure 46. All subtests are timed, but the time limits are described as fairly generous. Norms were established on over six thousand school children tested in different parts of the country. Total scores are expressed as deviation IQ's with an *SD* of 16. Mental age and percentile norms are also provided. Split-half reliabilities of the two forms on a single-year group were found to be .86 and .89.

Subtests for the Pintner Non-Language Test were selected on the basis of their parallel-form reliability, correlation with total score, and correlation with the Intermediate Test of the Pintner Verbal series. Within each subtest, items were chosen in terms of grade increment in percentage passing. The criteria employed were thus internal consistency, correlation with a verbal test, and grade differentiation. For homogeneous age groups, correlations in the .60's are reported between the Non-Language and the corresponding Verbal Test of the Pintner series. These correlations are high enough to indicate considerable overlap, but low enough to justify the use of the Non-Language Test as a supplement to the Verbal Test. Such correlations should

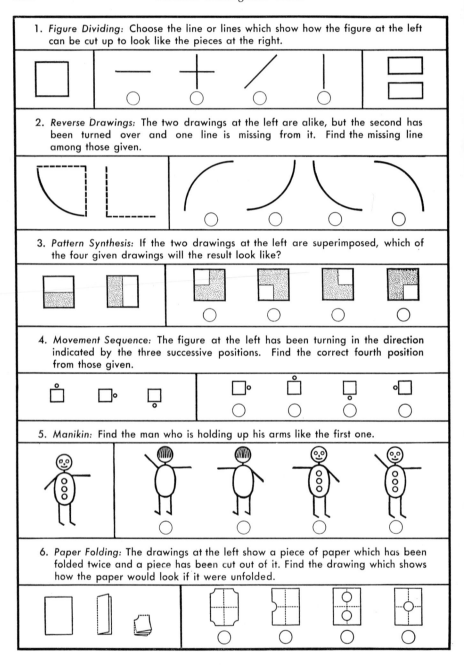

1. *Figure Dividing:* Choose the line or lines which show how the figure at the left can be cut up to look like the pieces at the right.

2. *Reverse Drawings:* The two drawings at the left are alike, but the second has been turned over and one line is missing from it. Find the missing line among those given.

3. *Pattern Synthesis:* If the two drawings at the left are superimposed, which of the four given drawings will the result look like?

4. *Movement Sequence:* The figure at the left has been turning in the direction indicated by the three successive positions. Find the correct fourth position from those given.

5. *Manikin:* Find the man who is holding up his arms like the first one.

6. *Paper Folding:* The drawings at the left show a piece of paper which has been folded twice and a piece has been cut out of it. Find the drawing which shows how the paper would look if it were unfolded.

Fig. 46. Sample Items from the Pintner Non-Language Test. (Copyright by World Book Company.)

also be borne in mind, however, when the test is employed as a substitute for the verbal tests with deaf and other specially handicapped groups. It must be recognized that somewhat different abilities are being tapped by the two types of tests. By their very nature, verbal and non-verbal tests cannot be regarded as completely interchangeable.

An important question to consider regarding non-language tests concerns the extent to which they depend upon spatial and perceptual functions, as contrasted to the symbolic manipulation of abstract relations, concepts, and factual information. The latter functions would seem to resemble more closely those required in the traditional verbal tests of "intelligence." To be sure, the substitution of pictorial for verbal or numerical content may appreciably alter the nature of the test. At the same time, all pictorial or non-language tests cannot be indiscriminately grouped together. Some, like the current form of the Pintner Non-Language Test, stress spatial and perceptual factors almost to the exclusion of other functions. Such tests will be seen to resemble quite closely some of the special aptitude tests to be considered in Part 3. Other non-language tests employ a greater proportion of items calling for ideational or symbolic responses. Examples of the latter type include the Chicago Non-Verbal Examination (17) and the SRA Non-Verbal Form (58). Figure 47 shows sample items from the SRA test. Both tests need

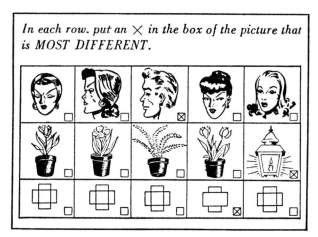

Fig. 47. Sample Items from the SRA Non-Verbal Form. (McMurry and King, 58. Copyright by Science Research Associates.)

further standardization and other technical improvements. In their present form they are of interest chiefly because they illustrate attempts to measure conceptual abilities without the use of verbal or numerical content.

A similar approach is illustrated by the recently developed Tests of General Ability, or TOGA (29). These tests consist of a series of five overlapping batteries, extending from kindergarten to grade 12. In some ways, they resemble the tests for primary grades discussed in Chapter 9, except that they utilize similar pictorial and diagrammatic material at all grade levels. They are not truly non-language, since extensive use of oral language is

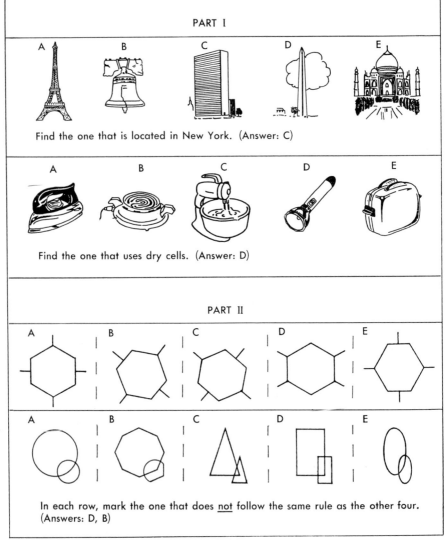

Fig. 48. Practice Items from Tests of General Ability (TOGA), Grades 9 to 12. (Reproduced by permission of John C. Flanagan.)

made throughout. Each battery requires a total of 35 to 45 minutes of testing time and consists of two parts. Part I uses pictures to test general information and the understanding of concepts learned in school, home, or community. Part II is a classification test employing geometric forms. This part is designed to test abstract reasoning with material that is relatively free from specific cultural content. Sample items of both types from the highest level (grades 9 to 12) are illustrated in Figure 48. More information would be desirable on just what is measured by the items in Part I, especially at the upper levels. Some require the application of concrete factual knowledge or of a principle that is described in fairly simple terms. Many of the items, however, depend upon the understanding of a key word, such as "resiliency" or "pachyderm." One wonders, incidentally, why an individual who has mastered such vocabulary needs a non-reading test. Illiteracy and reading disabilities are unlikely to be associated with such knowledge.

Because of the recency of their publication, the TOGA batteries cannot be adequately evaluated. Available data on reliability and concurrent validity, however, appear favorable. In single grade levels, split-half reliabilities of total scores range from .80 to .90, correlations with general achievement tests range from .52 to .81, and correlations with school grades range from .38 to .50. A correlation of .65 is reported with the Stanford-Binet, and correlations from .41 to .80 were found with a number of predominantly verbal group tests. Two types of norms are provided, in terms of grade level and ratio IQ. No information is given to show that the variability of the IQ remains constant with age. Although major emphasis is placed on total scores, some normative data are also included that permit a comparison of an individual's scores on Parts I and II and an evaluation of the significance of the difference between the two part scores. Such comparisons are recommended for children with unusual cultural backgrounds.

"CROSS-CULTURAL" TESTING

One of the purposes for which non-language tests were designed was the testing of individuals reared in different cultures or subcultures. It is apparent, however, that persons from certain cultures would still be handicapped on most non-language tests, primarily because of specific information that the tests presuppose. The picture-completion test of the Army Beta, for example, requires familiarity with such articles as a violin, postage stamp, gun, and pocketknife. Similarly, the Chicago Non-Verbal Examination includes pictures of cooking utensils, tools, a telephone, a radio, a piano player, telegraph poles, a basketball game, and many other culturally linked objects or activities. Some of the pictures employed in such performance scales as the Pintner-Paterson and the Arthur likewise require knowledge that is specific to our culture. In so far as speed influences scores on any of these tests, moreover, individuals from certain cultures or subcultures would have a decided advantage.

To reduce the cultural restrictions characterizing most non-language and performance tests, several attempts have been made to construct "culture-free" tests. In order to evaluate such tests properly, a number of points should be noted at the outset. In the first place, no test can be truly "culture-free." Since every test measures a sample of behavior, it will reflect any factor that influences behavior. Persons do not react in a cultural vacuum. There is a mass of evidence to indicate the basic role that cultural factors play in behavior development (cf. 5, Ch. 18). It is, however, theoretically possible to construct a test that presupposes only experiences that are common to different cultures. Such a test would not be *free* from cultural influences, but would utilize only elements *common* to many cultures. For this reason, the term "cross-cultural" has been employed here to characterize these tests, in preference to the more common but misleading term "culture-free."

It should also be noted, however, that no existing test is universally applicable or entirely unrestricted in its cultural reference. The difference is one of degree, cross-cultural tests being less restricted than others. Any test tends to favor individuals from the culture in which it was developed. The mere use of paper and pencil or the presentation of abstract tasks having no immediate practical significance will favor some cultural groups and handicap others. Emotional and motivational factors likewise influence test performance. Among the many relevant conditions differing from culture to culture may be mentioned the intrinsic interest of the test content, rapport with the examiner, drive to do well on a test, desire to excel others, and past habits of solving problems individually or cooperatively (cf. 5, pp. 561-568).

Each culture encourages and fosters certain abilities and ways of behaving, and discourages or suppresses others. It is therefore to be expected that, on tests developed within the American culture, American subjects will generally excel. If a test were constructed by the same procedures within a culture differing markedly from ours, American subjects would probably appear deficient in terms of test norms. Data bearing on this type of cultural comparison are very meager. What evidence is available, however, suggests that persons from our culture may be just as handicapped on tests prepared within other cultures as members of those cultures are on our tests (cf. 5, pp. 566-568). It is interesting to observe that the same relationship holds in the case of urban and rural subcultures. When two forms of a test, developed on urban and rural groups, respectively, were administered to new samples of urban and rural children, the urban groups excelled on the urban form and the rural groups on the rural form (5, p. 533; 78).

Three distinct approaches to the testing of persons in different cultures should be recognized. Each differs in its fundamental objectives. First, different tests may be developed within each culture and validated against local criteria only. This approach is exemplified by the many revisions of the original Binet scales for use in different European, Asiatic, and African groups, as well as by a few tests whose development was initiated within particular cultural groups (e.g., 59, 62, 83). In such instances, the tests are validated against the specific criteria they are designed to predict, and performance is evaluated in terms of local norms. Each test is applied only within the culture in which it was developed and no cross-cultural comparisons are attempted. It might be added that, in comparison with the mass of tests available in America, the number developed for use in other national or cultural groups is small. Psychological testing is a predominantly American movement. Moreover, even when not constructed by American psychologists, the tests prepared in other countries frequently follow the pattern set by American tests.

A second major approach is to make up a test within one culture and administer it to individuals with different cultural backgrounds. Such a procedure would be followed when the object of testing is prediction of a local criterion within a particular culture. In such a case, if the specific cultural loading of the test is reduced, the test validity may also drop, since the criterion itself is culturally loaded (cf. 4). For example, an individual who scores poorly on a verbal test will probably also be handicapped in school work or in jobs calling for verbal ability within that particular culture. On the other hand, we should avoid the mistake of regarding any test developed within a single cultural framework as a universal yardstick for measuring "intelligence." Nor should we assume that a low score on such a test has the same explanation when obtained by a member of another culture as when obtained by a member of the test culture.

The third approach to the testing of different cultural groups involves the choice of items common to many cultures and the validation of the resulting test against local criteria in many different cultures. This is the basic approach of the cross-cultural tests, although the repeated validation in different cultures has often been either neglected altogether or inadequately executed. Without such a step, however, we cannot be sure that the test is relatively free from culturally restricted elements. Moreover, it is possible that a test constructed entirely from elements that are equally familiar in many cultures might measure trivial functions and possess little validity in terms of practical criteria in any culture. For both reasons, therefore, validity should be rechecked in terms of criteria considered important within each culture.

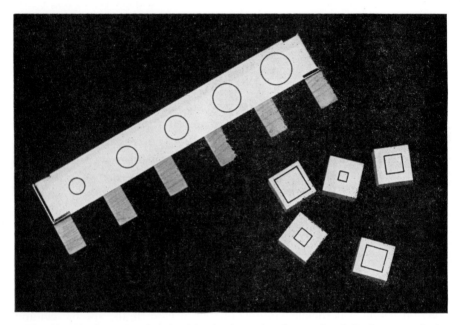

Fig. 49. Typical Materials for Use in the Leiter International Performance Scale. The test illustrated is the Analogies Progression Test from the Six-Year Level. (Courtesy C. H. Stoelting Company.)

An example of a cross-cultural test is provided by the Leiter International Performance Scale (54, 55). This series of tests was developed through several years of use with different ethnic groups in Hawaii, including elementary and high school pupils. It was subsequently applied to several African groups by Porteus and to a few other national groups by other investigators. A later revision, issued in 1948, was based upon further testing of American children, high school students, and Army recruits during World War II. A distinctive feature of the Leiter scale is the almost complete elimination of instructions, either spoken or pantomime. Each test begins with a very easy task of the type to be encountered throughout that test. The comprehension of the task is treated as part of the test. The materials consist of a response frame, shown in Figure 49, with an adjustable card holder. All tests are administered by attaching the appropriate card, containing printed pictures, to the frame. The subject chooses the blocks with the proper response pictures and inserts them into the frame.

The Leiter scale was designed to cover a wide range of functions, similar to those found in verbal scales. Among the tasks included may be mentioned: matching identical colors, shades of gray, forms, or pictures; copying a block design; picture completion; number estimation; analogies; series completion; recognition of age differences; spatial relations; footprint recognition; similarities; memory for a series; and classification of animals according to habitat. These tests are arranged into year levels from 2 to 18.[1] They are administered individually with no time limit. The scale is scored in terms of MA and ratio IQ, although there is no assurance that such an IQ retains the same meaning at different ages. In fact, the published data show considerable fluctuation in the standard deviation of the IQ's at different age levels. Split-half reliabilities of .91 to .94 are reported from several studies, but the samples varied widely in age and probably in other characteristics. Validation data are based principally on age differentiation and internal consistency. Some correlations are also reported with teachers' ratings of intelligence and with scores on other tests, chiefly the Stanford-Binet. The latter correlations range from .64 to .81 but were obtained on rather heterogeneous groups.

The IPAT Culture Free Intelligence Test (22) was developed by Cattell at the Institute for Personality and Ability Testing, University of Illinois. This test is now available in three levels: Scale 1, for ages 4 to 8 and feebleminded adults; Scale 2, for ages 8 to 12 and unselected adults; and Scale 3, covering a range from high school pupils to superior adults. Each scale has been prepared in two parallel forms, A and B. Scale 1 requires individual administration for at least some of the tests; the other scales may be given either as individual or as group tests. Scale 1 comprises eight tests, only four of which are described by the author as "culture-free." The other four involve both verbal comprehension and specific cultural information. It is suggested that the four "culture-free" tests can be used as a sub-battery, separate norms being provided for this abbreviated scale. Scales 2 and 3 are alike, except for difficulty level. Each consists of the following four tests, sample items from which are shown in Figure 50.

---

[1] The tests in year levels 2 to 12 are also available as the Arthur Adaptation of the Leiter International Performance Scale, standardized as a point scale by Dr. Grace Arthur (11). This scale is considered suitable for testing children between the ages of 4 and 8 years.

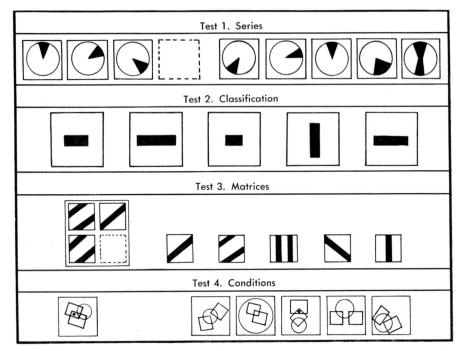

Fig. 50. Sample Items from IPAT Culture Free Test of Intelligence, Scale 2. (Copyright by Institute for Personality and Ability Testing.)

1. *Series:* Select the item that completes the series.

2. *Classification:* Mark the one item in each row that does not belong with the others.

3. *Matrices:* Mark the item that correctly completes the given matrix, or pattern.

4. *Conditions:* Insert a dot in one of the alternative designs so as to meet the same conditions indicated in the sample design. Thus in the example reproduced in Figure 50, the dot must be in the two rectangles, but not in the circle. This condition can be met only in the third response alternative, which has been marked.

For Scale 1, only ratio IQ's are provided. In Scales 2 and 3, scores can be converted into deviation IQ's with SD's of either 24 or 16 points. The latter conversion was added later in order to insure more comparability with IQ's obtained on other familiar tests. In interpreting IQ's from the IPAT test, it is thus important to note which conversion was used. Scale 2 has been standardized on larger samples than either of the other two scales, but the representativeness of the samples and the number of cases at some age levels still fall short of desirable test-construction standards (21). Although the tests are highly speeded, some norms are provided for an untimed version. Fairly extensive verbal instructions are required, but the author asserts that giving these instructions in a foreign language or in pantomime will not affect the difficulty of the test.

Reliability and validity data appear to have been gathered largely on Scale 2, some having been obtained with an earlier, longer form of the test (20, 23). Split-half reliabilities between .70 and .92 are reported for Forms A and B combined. Results changed little when the test was given under unspeeded conditions. However, no information is given on the nature of the groups on which these coefficients were found. Immediate retests yielded reliabilities in the .80's, but retests over a longer interval in one sample correlated as low as .53. Validity is discussed chiefly in terms of saturation with Spearman's general ability factor (g). Factorial validity of the IPAT test was accordingly determined from its correlations with a pool of intelligence tests, including both verbal and performance types. Data on concurrent and predictive validity in terms of non-test criteria are virtually non-existent. The IPAT tests have been administered in several European countries, in America, and in certain African and Asiatic cultures. Norms tended to remain unchanged in cultures moderately similar to that in which the tests were developed; in other cultures, however, performance fell considerably below the original norms.

The Progressive Matrices (71, 72, 73), developed in Great Britain by Raven, were also designed as a measure of Spearman's g factor. Requiring chiefly the eduction of relations among abstract items, this test is regarded by most British psychologists as the best available measure of g. It consists of 60 matrices, or designs, from each of which a part has been removed. The subject chooses the missing insert from six or eight given alternatives. The items are grouped into five series, each containing 12 matrices of increasing difficulty but similar in principle. The earlier series require accuracy of discrimination; the later, more difficult series involve analogies, permutation and alteration of pattern, and other logical relations. Two sample items are reproduced in Figure 51. The test is administered with no time limit, and can be given individually or in groups. Very simple oral instructions are required.

Percentile norms are provided for each half-year interval between 8 and 14 years, and for each five-year interval between 20 and 65 years. These norms are based on British samples, including 1407 children, 3665 men in military service tested during World War II, and 2192 civilian adults. Closely similar norms were obtained by Rimoldi (75) on 1680 children in Argentina.

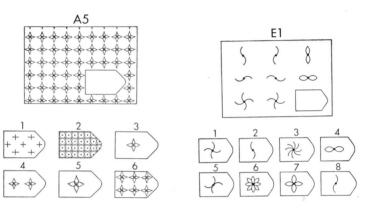

Fig. 51. Sample Items from the Progressive Matrices. (Reproduced by permission of J. C. Raven.)

Use of the test in several European countries likewise indicated the applicability of available norms. Studies in a number of non-European cultures, however, have raised doubts about the suitability of this test for groups with very dissimilar backgrounds (13, 19, 45, 52, 53, 63, 64). In such groups, moreover, the test was found to reflect amount of education and to be susceptible to considerable practice effect.

The manual for the Progressive Matrices (72) is quite inadequate, giving little information on reliability and none on validity. Many investigations have been published, however, that provide relevant data on this test. In a review of publications appearing prior to 1957, Burke (19) lists over 50 studies appearing in England, 14 in America, and 10 elsewhere. Since that time, research has continued at a rapid pace, especially in America where this test has received growing recognition.

Retest reliability in groups of older children and adults that were moderately homogeneous in age varies approximately between .70 and .90. At the lower score ranges, however, reliability falls considerably below these values. Correlations with both verbal and performance tests of intelligence range between .40 and .75, tending to be higher with performance than with verbal tests. Studies with mental defectives and with different occupational and educational groups indicate fair concurrent validity. Predictive validity coefficients against academic criteria run somewhat lower than those of the usual verbal intelligence tests. Several factorial analyses suggest that the Progressive Matrices are heavily loaded with a factor common to most intelligence tests (identified with Spearman's *g* by British psychologists), but that spatial aptitude, inductive reasoning, perceptual accuracy, and other group factors also influence performance (19).

An easier, colored form of the Progressive Matrices has been prepared for use with children between the ages of 5 and 11 and with feebleminded adults (73). At this level, the test is available in both book form and board form, the latter requiring the subject to insert the right piece rather than choose the correct completion. The book form, however, is more readily obtainable and is described as adequate for most testing purposes. Another form, with a higher ceiling, has been specially developed for testing superior groups (30, 71), but its distribution is restricted to approved and registered users.

On the whole, the Progressive Matrices show considerable promise for a variety of testing purposes, but more systematic data are needed on norms, reliability at different levels, and validity. It should be noted that this test, as well as other so-called culture-free tests, are applicable to most situations for which non-language tests were devised. In comparison with non-language tests, the culture-free tests have the advantage of requiring less culturally restricted information. A further advantage is that current culture-free tests depend more heavily upon abstract reasoning and less on spatial aptitudes than is true of available well-standardized non-language tests.

Another example of a completely non-language cross-cultural test is the Semantic Test of Intelligence (STI) constructed at Harvard University under contract with the Army (76, 77). Designed primarily as a power test and utilizing only pantomime and demonstration in the instructions, STI was developed to identify illiterates in military service who can profit from literacy training. This test requires the learning of a new set of semantic symbols, which are then combined into short "sentences." Figure 52 shows two sample items employed at the two-symbol stage. By reference to the key at the top of the page, it will be seen that the first symbol stands for "cow," the second for "jumping," the third for "woman," and the fourth for "lying down." The first sample item contains the symbols for "cow" and "jumping." Hence the correct picture is that of the jumping cow, and this picture has been encircled. The second item has the symbols for "woman" and "lying down." Accordingly, the woman lying down has been encircled.

The highest semantic level reached by the STI test is the four-symbol sentence, such as "woman kicks lying-down dog." In the more difficult items, the subject must abstract the common feature associated with the particular symbol and apply it to objects unlike any of those in the key. A parallel-form reliability coefficient of .855 was found in a group with narrowly restricted ability range. In follow-up studies of 314 Marine Corps recruits in slow-learning classes, STI predicted subsequent performance on subject-matter examinations and reading instructors' grades better than these could be predicted from either General Classification Test or Army Beta scores.

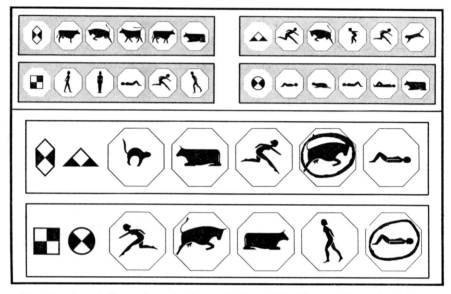

Fig. 52. Sample Items from the Semantic Test of Intelligence. (Reproduced by permission of P. J. Rulon.)

A somewhat different approach is illustrated by the Goodenough Draw-a-Man Test (32), in which the subject is simply instructed to "make a picture of a man; make the very best picture that you can." This test was in use without change from its original standardization in 1926 until 1961. An extension and revision was published in 1961 under the title of Harris-Goodenough Test of Psychological Maturity (37, 38). In the revision, as in the original test, emphasis is placed upon the child's accuracy of observation and upon the development of conceptual thinking, rather than upon artistic skill. Credit is given for the inclusion of individual body parts, clothing details, proportion, perspective, and similar features. A total of 73 scorable items were selected on the basis of age differentiation, relation to total score on the test, and relation to group intelligence test score. Data for this purpose were obtained by testing samples of 50 boys and 50 girls at each grade level from kindergarten to the ninth grade in urban and rural areas of Minnesota and Wisconsin, stratified according to father's occupation.

In the revised scale, subjects are also asked to draw a picture of a woman and of themselves. The Woman Scale is scored in terms of 71 items similar to those in the Man Scale. The Self Scale has been developed as a projective test of personality, although available findings from this application are not promising. Norms on both Man and Woman Scales were established on new samples of 300 children at each year of age from 5 to 15, selected so as to be representative of the U.S. population with regard to father's occupation and geographical region. Point scores on each scale are transmuted into deviation IQ's with a mean of 100 and an *SD* of 15. In Figure 53 will be found three illustrative drawings produced by children aged 5-8, 8-8, and 12-11, together with the corresponding raw point scores and deviation IQ's.

Man: Raw Score 7   Woman: Raw Score 31   Man: Raw Score 66
CA 5-8   IQ 73   CA 8-8   IQ 103   CA 12-11   IQ 134

Fig. 53. Specimen Drawings Obtained in Harris-Goodenough Test of Psychological Maturity. (Courtesy Dale B. Harris.)

The reliability of the Draw-a-Man Test has been repeatedly investigated by a variety of procedures. In one carefully controlled study of the earlier form administered to 386 third- and fourth-grade school children, the retest correlation after a one-week interval was .68, and split-half reliability was .89 (56). Rescoring of the identical drawings by a different scorer yielded a scorer reliability of .90, and rescorings by the same scorer correlated .94. Studies with the new form (38) have yielded similar results. Readministration of the test to groups of kindergarten children on consecutive days revealed no significant difference in performance on different days. Examiner effect was also found to be negligible, as was the effect of art training in school (38). The old and new scales are apparently quite similar, their scores correlating between .91 and .98 in homogeneous age groups. The correlation of the Man and Woman Scales is about as high as the split-half reliability of the Man Scale found in comparable samples. On this basis, Harris recommends that the two scales be regarded as alternate forms and that the mean of their deviation IQ's be used for greater reliability.

Apart from the item-analysis data gathered in the development of the scales, information regarding the construct validity of the test is provided by correlations with other tests. For the earlier form, correlations between .41 and .80 have been reported with other intelligence tests, principally the Stanford-Binet (cf. 6). In a study with 100 fourth-grade children, correlations were found between Draw-a-Man IQ and scores on a number of tests of known factorial composition (6). Such correlations indicated that, within the ages covered, the Draw-a-Man Test correlates highest with tests of reasoning, spatial aptitude, and perceptual accuracy. Motor coordination plays a negligible role in the tests at these ages. For kindergarten children, the Draw-a-Man IQ correlated higher with numerical aptitude and lower with perceptual speed and accuracy than it did for fourth-grade children (38). Such findings suggest that the test may measure somewhat different functions at different ages.

The original Draw-a-Man Test has been administered widely in clinics as a supplement to the Stanford-Binet and other verbal scales. It has also been employed in a large number of studies on different cultural and ethnic groups, including several American Indian samples. Such investigations have indicated that performance on this test is more dependent upon differences in cultural background than was originally assumed by its author (cf. 33). In a review of studies pertaining to this test, Goodenough and Harris expressed the opinion that "the search for a culture-free test, whether of intelligence, artistic ability, personal-social characteristics, or any other measurable trait is illusory (33, p. 399). This view was reaffirmed by Harris in the 1961 book (38, Ch. 3). Certainly any test requiring the use of paper and pencil and involving representational drawing may be expected to show significant cultural differences.

Attempts to develop tests based upon common cultural content have been extended to social classes within the American culture. A group of investigators at the University of Chicago, under the general direction of Davis and Havighurst, compared the performance of children from different socioeconomic classes upon individual items taken from current intelligence tests (28). Such studies showed wide variation in "cultural differentials" from item to item. The role of such factors as practice, motivation, testing conditions, and form of items has also been investigated in relation to socioeconomic level of subjects (35).

As a result of these studies, a test designed to be relatively free from "social-class bias" was developed. Known as the Davis-Eells Games (26), this test is applicable from the first to the sixth school grade. The test requires no reading, all instructions being given orally by the examiner. The content is entirely pictorial and consists of problems chosen from the everyday-life experiences of children in the urban American culture. All parts of the test are presented as games, the administration being designed to induce a comfortable and relaxed atmosphere. Praise and encouragement are also freely given to increase motivation. Several of the items represent humorous situations, introduced as a further appeal to the interests of children. The role of speed is reduced to a minimum. The subtests include Verbal Problems, Money Problems, Best Ways Problems, and Analogies. These subtests appear to have been designed to measure primarily verbal comprehension, number ability, spatial visualization and mechanical comprehension, and reasoning, respectively. Two sample items will be found in Figure 54.

The Davis-Eells Games were standardized on a sample of 19,756 school children in 17 cities and 2 counties, situated in 15 states. The subjects were selected so as to constitute a representative sample of the urban American population with respect to geographical distribution, size of community, racial background, and parental occupation. Scores are expressed as deviation IQ's with a mean of 100 and an *SD* of 16. The authors recommend, however, that the score on this test be described, not as an IQ, but as an Index of Problem-Solving Ability (IPSA), the latter being a more specific designation of what the test undertakes to measure. Split-half reliability coefficients were found to be in the .80's from grade 2 to grade 6. In grade 1, however, in which a shorter form of the test is employed, the reliability coefficient was only .68. Retests within a two-week interval yielded coefficients of .72 and .90 in grades 2 and 4, respectively. But these coefficients may have been somewhat inflated by the subjects' recall of their previous responses.

Although reporting a number of moderately high correlations with other group intelligence tests and with educational achievement tests, the authors justify the test primarily in terms of its content validity. They point out, in fact, that this test is not intended to be a measure of scholastic aptitude, and hence should not correlate too highly with either educational achievement tests or with other currently available intelligence tests. In some thirty studies which have appeared since its publication in 1953, this test has not fared well. Predictive and concurrent validity coefficients against achievement tests

Verbal Problems: Examiner reads three statements about each picture, instructing the subject to mark the one which is true.

Problem A
1. They are waving at a *boy.*
2. They are waving at a *girl.*
3. We *cannot tell* from this picture *whom* they are waving to.

Problem B
1. The man fell down and hit his head.
2. A ball came through the window and hit the man's head.
3. The picture *does not show how* the man got the bump on his head. Nobody can tell because the picture doesn't show how the man got the bump.

"Best Ways" Problems: Which boy is *starting* to load the packages *the best way* so he can take all three home?

Fig. 54. Sample Items from the Davis-Eells Games: A Test of General Intelligence. (Copyright by World Book Company.)

and teachers' ratings have almost always been lower for the Davis-Eells than for conventional intelligence tests. To be sure, the test authors would not regard this as a serious drawback. A more telling criticism, however, stems from the common finding that lower-class children perform as poorly on this test as on other intelligence tests. Thus the test seems to have sacrificed predictive validity without eliminating "cultural bias."

TESTING THE PHYSICALLY HANDICAPPED

The growing emphasis upon rehabilitation and training of the physically handicapped has created an increasing demand for appropriate testing instruments. The testing of *deaf* children has already been noted as the primary object in the development of the original Pintner-Paterson Performance Scale, as well as the Pintner Non-Language Test. Similarly, deaf children represent one of the special groups for which the Arthur Performance Scale was prepared. In the Revised Form II of this scale, the verbal instructions required in Form I were further reduced in order to increase the applicability of the test to deaf children (10). Many other tests that have been discussed in this chapter can be used with the deaf.

Although adapted to the testing of the deaf, all of these tests have been standardized primarily on hearing subjects. For many purposes it is of course desirable to compare the performance of the deaf with general norms established on hearing persons. At the same time, norms obtained on deaf children are also useful in a number of situations pertaining to the educational development of such children.

To meet this need, the Nebraska Test of Learning Aptitude, developed by Hiskey (43), was standardized on deaf and hard-of-hearing children. This is an individual test suitable for ages 4 to 10. Speed was eliminated, since it is difficult to convey the idea of speed to young deaf children. An attempt was also made to sample a wider variety of intellectual functions than those covered by most performance tests. Pantomime and practice exercises to put across the instructions, as well as intrinsically interesting items to establish rapport, were considered important requirements for such a test. All items were chosen with special reference to the limitations of deaf children, the final item selection being based chiefly upon the criterion of age differentiation.

The Nebraska Test consists of eleven subtests, as follows:

1. Memory for Colored Objects
2. Bead Stringing
3. Pictorial Associations
4. Block Building
5. Memory for Digits
6. Completion of Drawings
7. Pictorial Identification
8. Paper Folding
9. Visual Attention Span
10. Puzzle Blocks
11. Pictorial Analogies

Norms are based on 466 children, aged 4 to 10 years, who were attending residential state schools for the deaf in six states. Norms for hearing children were added later. A split-half reliability of .96 is reported. Correlations of subtests with total score range from .63 to .84. A correlation of .829 was found between Nebraska and Stanford-Binet tests on 380 hearing children. The manual contains a general discussion of desirable practices in testing deaf children.

Testing the *blind* presents a very different set of problems from those encountered with deaf subjects. Oral tests can be most readily adapted for blind subjects, while performance tests are least likely to be applicable. A good introduction to procedures for testing the blind—together with a summary of the principal intelligence, special aptitude, achievement, and personality tests prepared for this purpose—may be found in a manual prepared by Bauman and Hayes (12) and in a survey by Rawls (74).

In addition to the usual oral presentation by the examiner, other suitable testing techniques have been utilized, such as phonograph records and tape or wire recordings. Some tests are also available in braille. The latter technique is somewhat limited in its applicability, however, by the greater bulkiness of materials printed in braille as compared with inkprint, by the slower reading rate for braille, and by the number of blind persons who are not facile braille readers. The subject's responses may likewise be recorded in braille or on a typewriter. Specially prepared embossed answer sheets or cards are also available, especially for use with true-false, multiple-choice, and other objective-type items. In many individually administered tests, of course, oral responses can be obtained.

Among the principal examples of general intelligence tests that have been adapted for blind subjects are the Binet and the Wechsler. The first Hayes-Binet revision for testing the blind was based on the 1916 Stanford-Binet. In 1942, the Interim Hayes-Binet [2] was prepared from the 1937 Stanford-Binet (39, 40). All items that could be administered without the use of vision were selected from both Form L and Form M. This procedure yielded six tests for each year level from VII to XIV, and eight tests at the Average Adult level. In order to assemble enough tests for year levels III to VI, it was necessary to draw upon some of the special tests devised for use in the earlier Hayes-Binet. Most of the tests in the final scale are oral, a few requiring braille materials. A retest reliability of .90 and a split-half reliability of .91 are reported by Hayes. A correlation of .83 was found between this test and the earlier Hayes-Binet. Correlations with braille editions of standard achievement tests ranged from .82 to .93. The validity of this test was also checked against school progress.

---

[2] Originally designated as an interim edition because of the tentative nature of its standardization, th s revision has now come to be known by this name in the literature.

The Wechsler scales, to be discussed in Chapter 12, have also been adapted for blind subjects (cf. 12). These adaptations consist essentially in using the verbal tests and omitting the performance tests. A few items inappropriate for blind subjects have also been replaced by alternates. When tested under these conditions, blind subjects as a group have been found to equal or excel the general seeing norms (12). A number of the group intelligence tests discussed in Chapter 9 have likewise been adapted for use with the blind. Among them may be mentioned the Kuhlmann-Anderson, Otis, Pintner Verbal Series, and the Scholastic Aptitude Test of the College Entrance Examination Board.

A type of subject that has only recently begun to receive special attention in psychological testing is the *orthopedically handicapped* (1, 14, 15, 27, 44, 46, 47, 79, 80). Although usually able to receive auditory and visual stimulation, these individuals may have such severe motor handicaps as to make either oral or written responses impracticable. The manipulation of formboards or other performance materials would likewise meet with difficulties. Working against a time limit or in strange surroundings often increases the motor disturbance in the orthopedically handicapped. Their greater susceptibility to fatigue makes short testing sessions necessary.

Some of the severest motor handicaps are found among the cerebral palsied. Yet surveys of these cases have frequently employed common intelligence tests such as the Stanford-Binet or the Arthur Performance Scale. In such studies, the most severely handicapped were usually excluded as untestable. Frequently, informal adjustments in testing procedure are made in order to adapt the test to the child's response capacities (cf. 16). Both of these procedures, of course, are makeshifts.

A more satisfactory approach lies in the development of testing instruments suitable for even the most severely handicapped individuals. Considerable research is now in progress on the development of special tests and the adaptation of existing tests for use with the physically handicapped. A number of relevant techniques are still in an experimental stage and have not yet been fully described in the literature. Adaptations of the Leiter International Performance Scale and the Porteus Mazes, suitable for administration to cerebral-palsied children, have been prepared (1, 7). In both adapted tests, the examiner manipulates the test materials, while the subject responds only by appropriate head movements. A similar adaptation of the Stanford-Binet has been worked out (47).

The previously cited Progressive Matrices provide a promising tool for this purpose. Since it is given with no time limit and since the response may be indicated orally, in writing, or by pointing or nodding, it appears to be especially appropriate for the orthopedically handicapped. Despite the flexibility and simplicity of its response indicator, this test covers a wide range of difficulty and provides a fairly high test ceiling. Successful use of this test has been reported in studies of cerebral-palsied children and adults (1, 44, 81).

Another test that permits the utilization of a simple pointing response is the Full-Range Picture Vocabulary Test (2, 3). This test was designed as a rapid measure of "use" vocabulary, especially for persons unable to vocalize well, such as the cerebral palsied. The test consists of 16 plates, each containing four cartoon-like drawings. As the examiner speaks each word, the subject indicates by pointing or other signal which of the drawings best fits the given word. Two forms are available, each including 85 words of increasing difficulty. Norms are provided from a mental age of 2 to the superior adult level. These norms are based on a total of 589 cases, including 15 boys and 15 girls at each year of age from 2 to 17, and some additional adult subjects. Although the individual normative samples are small, they were chosen so as to be representative of the general population in occupational level and in age-grade placement. Preliminary data suggest that the test has satisfactory reliability and that it correlates highly with Stanford-Binet vocabulary scores.

A test that was originally developed for estimating the intellectual level of cerebral-palsied children is the Columbia Mental Maturity Scale (18). This scale comprises 100 items, each consisting of a set of three, four, or five drawings printed on a 6-by-19-inch card. The subject is required to identify the drawing that does not belong with the others, indicating his choice by pointing or nodding. To heighten interest and appeal, the cards and drawings are varicolored. Scores are expressed as mental ages and ratio IQ's. In studies with non-handicapped subjects, these IQ's yielded a median correlation of .77 with Stanford-Binet IQ's for single-age groups. Split-half reliability of the tests is estimated at .94. This scale appears promising for testing children with severe motor handicaps, although more data are needed to evaluate its effectiveness.

REFERENCES

1. Allen, R. M., and Collins, Marjorie G. Suggestions for the adaptive administration of intelligence tests for those with cerebral palsy. *Cerebral Palsy Rev.*, 1955, 16, 11-14.
2. Ammons, R. B., and Ammons, Helen S. *Full-Range Picture Vocabulary Test.* Missoula, Montana: Psychol. Test Specialists, 1948.
3. Ammons, R. B., Arnold, P. R., and Herrmann, R. S. The Full-Range Picture

Vocabulary Test: IV. Results for a white school population. *J. clin. Psychol.,* 1950, 6, 164-169.

4. Anastasi, Anne. Some implications of cultural factors for test construction. *Proc. 1949 Invit. Conf. Test. Probl., Educ. Test. Serv.,* 1950, 13-17.
5. Anastasi, Anne. *Differential psychology.* (3rd ed.) N. Y.: Macmillan, 1958.
6. Ansbacher, H. L. The Goodenough Draw-a-Man Test and primary mental abilities. *J. consult. Psychol.,* 1952, 16, 176-180.
7. Arnold, Gwen F. A technique for measuring the mental ability of the cerebra! palsied. *Psychol. Serv. Cent. J.,* 1951, 3, 171-180.
8. Arthur, Grace. *A Point Scale of Performance Tests.* Vol. II. *The process of standardization.* N. Y.: Commonwealth Fund, 1933.
9. Arthur, Grace. *A Point Scale of Performance Tests.* Vol. I. *Clinical manual.* (2nd ed.) Chicago: Stoelting, 1943.
10. Arthur, Grace. *A Point Scale of Performance Tests. Revised Form II. Manual for administering and scoring the tests.* N. Y.: Psychol. Corp., 1947.
11. Arthur, Grace. *The Arthur Adaptation of the Leiter International Performance Scale.* Washington: Psychol. Serv. Center Press, 1952.
12. Bauman, Mary K., and Hayes, S. P. *A manual for the psychological examination of the adult blind.* N. Y.: Psychol. Corp., 1951.
13. Berlioz, L. Étude des "progressive matrices" faites sur les Africains de Douala. *Bull. Cent. Étud. Rech. psychotech.,* 1955, 4, 33-44.
14. Blank, L., and Rawn, M. L. An experimental method to measure intellectual functioning with verbal and motor factors minimal. *J. Psychol.,* 1956, 41, 119-126.
15. Blum, Lucille H., Burgemeister, Bessie, and Lorge, I. Trends in estimating the mental maturity of the cerebral palsied child. *J. except. Child.,* 1951, 17, 174-177.
16. Braen, B. B., and Masling, J. M. Intelligence tests used with special groups of children. *J. except. Child.,* 1959, 26, 42-45.
17. Brown, A. W., Stein, S. P., and Rohrer, P. L. *The Chicago Non-Verbal Examination.* N. Y.: Psychol. Corp., 1936-1947.
18. Burgemeister, Bessie, Blum, Lucille H., and Lorge, I. *Columbia Mental Maturity Scale—Revised.* Tarrytown-on-Hudson, N. Y.: World Book Co., 1959.
19. Burke, H. R. Raven's Progressive Matrices: a review and critical evaluation. *J. genet. Psychol.,* 1958, 93, 199-228.
20. Cattell, R. B. A culture-free test of intelligence. I. *J. educ. Phychol.,* 1940, 3, 161-179.
21. Cattell, R. B. Classical and standard score IQ standardization of the I.P.A.T. Culture-Free Intelligence Scale 2. *J. consult. Psychol.,* 1951, 15, 154-159.
22. Cattell, R. B., and Cattell, A. K. S. *IPAT Culture Free Intelligence Test.* Champaign, Ill.: Inst. Pers. Abil. Test., 1950-1959.
23. Cattell, R. B., Feingold, S. N., and Sarason, S. B. A culture-free test of intelligence: II. Evaluation of cultural influence on test performance. *J. educ. Psychol.,* 1941, 2, 81-100.
24. Cornell, Ethel L., and Coxe, W. W. *A Performance Ability Scale: examination manual.* Tarrytown-on-Hudson, N. Y.: World Book Co., 1934.

25. Darcy, Natalie T. A review of the literature on the effects of bilingualism upon the measurement of intelligence. *J. genet. Psychol.*, 1953, 82, 21-57.
26. Davis, A., and Eells, K. *Davis-Eells Games: Davis-Eells Test of General Intelligence or Problem-Solving Ability.* Tarrytown-on-Hudson, N. Y.: World Book Co., 1953.
27. Doll, E. A. Mental evaluation of children with expressive handicaps. *Amer. J. Orthopsychiat.*, 1951, 21, 148-154.
28. Eells, K., Davis, A., Havighurst, R. J., Herrick, V. E., and Tyler, R. W. *Intelligence and cultural differences.* Chicago: Univer. Chicago Press, 1951.
29. Flanagan, J. C. *Tests of General Ability* (TOGA). Chicago: Sci. Res. Assoc., 1959-1960.
30. Foulds, G. A., and Raven, J. C. An experimental survey with Progressive Matrices (1947). *Brit. J. educ. Psychol.*, 1950, 20, 104-110.
31. Gellerman, S. W. Forms I and II of the Arthur Performance Scales with mental defectives. *J. consult. Psychol.*, 1952, 16, 127-131.
32. Goodenough, Florence L. *Measurement of intelligence by drawings.* Tarrytown-on-Hudson, N. Y.: World Book Co., 1926.
33. Goodenough, Florence L., and Harris, D. B. Studies in the psychology of children's drawings: II. 1928-1949. *Psychol. Bull.*, 1950, 47, 369-433.
34. Goodenough, Florence L., and Maurer, Katherine M. *The mental growth of children from two to fourteen years.* Minneapolis: Univer. Minn. Press, 1942.
35. Haggard, E. A. Social-status and intelligence: an experimental study of certain cultural determinants of measured intelligence. *Genet. Psychol. Monogr.*, 1954, 49, 141-186.
36. Hamilton, Mildred E. A comparison of the revised Arthur Performance Tests (Form II) and the 1937 Binet. *J. consult. Psychol.*, 1949, 13, 44-49.
37. Harris, D. B., and Goodenough, Florence L. *Harris-Goodenough Measure of Intellectual Maturity.* Tarrytown, N. Y.: Harcourt, Brace and World, (in press).
38. Harris, D. B., and Goodenough, Florence L. *Children's drawings as measures of intellectual maturity: a revision and extension of the Goodenough Draw-a-Man Test.* Tarrytown, N. Y.: Harcourt, Brace and World, (in press).
39. Hayes, S. P. Alternative scales for the mental measurement of the visually handicapped. *Outlook for the Blind,* 1942, 36, 225-230.
40. Hayes, S. P. A second test scale for the mental measurement of the visually handicapped. *Outlook for the Blind,* 1943, 37, 37-41.
41. Healy, W., and Fernald, Grace M. Tests for practical mental classification. *Psychol. Monogr.*, 1911, 13, No. 2.
42. Hilden, A. H., and Skeels, H. M. A comparison of the Stanford-Binet Scale, the Kuhlmann-Anderson Group Test, the Arthur Point Scale of Performance Tests, and the Unit Scales of Attainment. *J. exp. Educ.*, 1935, 4, 214-230.
43. Hiskey, M. S. *Nebraska Test of Learning Aptitude.* Lincoln, Neb.: Author, 1941-1955.
44. Holden, R. H. Improved methods in testing cerebral palsied children. *Amer. J. ment. Defic.*, 1951, 56, 349-353.

45. Jahoda, G. Assessment of abstract behavior in a non-Western culture. *J. abnorm. soc. Psychol.*, 1956, 53, 237-243.
46. Jewell, B. T., and Wursten, H. Observations on the psychological testing of cerebral palsied children. *Amer. J. ment. Defic.*, 1952, 56, 630-637.
47. Katz, E. The "Pointing Modification" of the Revised Stanford-Binet Intelligence Scales, Forms L and M, Years II through VI: a report of research in progress. *Amer. J. ment. Defic.*, 1958, 62, 698-707.
48. Kellogg, C. E., Morton, N. W., Lindner, R. M., and Gurvitz, M. *Revised Beta Examination.* N. Y.: Psychol. Corp., 1946-1957.
49. Klineberg, O. An experimental study of speed and other factors in "racial" differences. *Arch. Psychol.*, 1928, No. 93.
50. Knox, H. A. A scale based on the work at Ellis Island for estimating mental defect. *J. Amer. med. Assoc.*, 1914, 62, 741-747.
51. Kohs, S. C. *Intelligence measurement: a psychological and statistical study based upon the Block-Design Tests.* N. Y.: Macmillan, 1923.
52. Laroche, J. L. L'analyse des erreurs sur le matrix 38. *Bull. Cent. Étud. Rech. psychotech.*, 1956, 6, 161-174.
53. Laroche, J. L. Effets de répétition du matrix 38 sur les résultats d'enfants katangais. *Bull. Cent. Étud. Rech. psychotech.*, 1959, 8, 85-99.
54. Leiter, R. G. Part II of the manual for the 1948 revision of the Leiter International Performance Scale. *Psychol. Serv. Cent. J.*, 1950, 2, 259-343. (Test distributed by C. H. Stoelting Co.)
55. Leiter, R. G. Part I of the manual for the 1948 revision of the Leiter International Performance Scale. Psychol. Serv Cent. J., 1959, 11, 1-72.
56. McCarthy, Dorothea. A study of the reliability of the Goodenough Test of intelligence. *J. Psychol.*, 1944, 18, 201-216.
57. MacMurray, D. A comparison of gifted children and of dull-normal children measured by the Pintner-Paterson Scale, as against the Stanford-Binet Scale. *J. Psychol.*, 1937, 4, 273-280.
58. McMurry, R. N., and King, J. E. *SRA Non-Verbal Form.* Chicago: Sci. Res. Assoc., 1947.
59. Mann, C. W. A test of general ability in Fiji. *J. genet. Psychol.*, 1939, 54, 435-454.
60. Manolakes, G., and Sheldon, W. D. A comparison of the Grace Arthur, Revised Form II, and the Stanford-Binet, Revised Form L. *Educ. psychol. Measmt.*, 1952, 12, 105-108.
61. Myerson, L. A psychology of impaired hearing. In W. M. Cruickshank (Ed.), *Psychology of exceptional children and youth.* Englewood Cliffs, N. J.: Prentice-Hall, 1955. Pp. 120-183.
62. Ojha, J. M. An intelligence test in the Gujarati language. *Educ. and Psychol., Delhi,* 1954, 1 (1), 39-50.
63. Ombredane, A. Étude du comportement intellectuel des noirs congolais. *Psychol. franç.*, 1957, 1 (2), 19.
64. Ombredane, A., Robaye, Francine, and Plumail, H. Résultats d'une application répétée du matrix-couleur à une population de noirs congolais. *Bull. Cent. Étud. Rech. psychotech.*, 1956, 6, 129-157.
65. Patterson, R. M. The significance of practice effect upon readministration of

the Grace Arthur Performance Scale to high grade mentally deficient children. *Amer. J. ment. Defic.,* 1946, 50, 393-401.

66. Pintner, R. *Pintner General Ability Tests, Non-Language Series: Intermediate Test.* Tarrytown-on-Hudson, N. Y.: World Book Co., 1945.

67. Pintner, R., and Paterson, D. G. *A Scale of Performance Tests.* N. Y.: Appleton-Century-Crofts, 1917.

68. Porteus, S. D. *Guide to Porteus Maze Test.* Vineland, N. J.: The Training School, 1924.

69. Porteus, S. D. *The Porteus Maze Test.* N. Y.: Psychol. Corp., 1933-1959.

70. Porteus, S. D. *The Maze Test and clinical psychology.* Palo Alto, Calif.: Pacific Books, 1959.

71. Raven, J. C. *Progressive Matrices (1947) Sets I and II.* Dumfries: The Crichton Royal, (n.d.).

72. Raven, J. C. *Guide to using Progressive Matrices (1938).* London: Lewis, 1956. (U. S. distributor: Psychol. Corp.)

73. Raven, J. C. *Guide to using the Coloured Progressive Matrices (1947), Sets A, Ab, B.* London: Lewis, 1958. (U. S. distributor: Psychol. Corp.)

74. Rawls, R. F. Objective tests and testing of blind children. *New Outlook for the Blind,* 1954, 48, 39-45.

75. Rimoldi, H. J. A. A note on Raven's Progressive Matrices Test. *Educ. psychol. Measmt.,* 1948, 8, 347-352.

76. Rulon, P. J. A Semantic Test of Intelligence. *Proc. 1952 Invit. Conf. Test. Probl., Educ. Test. Serv.,* 1953, 84-92.

77. Rulon, P. J., and Schweiker, R. F. *Validation of a non-verbal test of military trainability (STI—Semantic Test of Intelligence).* Final Report, Department of the Army, Research Contract #DA-49-083 OSA-363, 1953.

78. Shimberg, Myra E. An investigation into the validity of norms with special reference to urban and rural groups. *Arch. Psychol.,* 1929, No. 104.

79. Sievers, Dorothy J., and Norman, R. D. Some suggestive results in psychometric testing of the cerebral palsied with Gesell, Binet, and Wechsler scales. *J. genet. Psychol.,* 1953, 82, 69-90.

80. Strother, C. R. The psychological appraisal of children with cerebral palsy. In *Psychological problems of cerebral palsy: a symposium.* Chicago: Nat. Soc. Crippled Children and Adults, 1952.

81. Tracht, V. S. Preliminary findings on testing the cerebral palsied with Raven's "Progressive Matrices." *J. except. Child.,* 1948, 15, 77-79.

82. Wallin, J. E. W. A comparison of the Stanford 1916 and 1937 (Form L) test results with those from the Arthur Performance Scale (Form I) based on the same subjects. *J. genet. Psychol.,* 1946, 69, 45-55.

83. Warburton, F. W. The ability of the Gurkha recruit. *Brit. J. Psychol., gen. Sect.,* 1951, 42, 114-133.

84. Yerkes, R. M. (Ed.) Psychological examining in the United States Army. *Mem. nat. Acad. Sci.,* 1921, 15.

85. Yoakum, C. S., and Yerkes, R. M. *Army mental tests.* N. Y.: Holt, Rinehart and Winston, 1920.

CHAPTER 11

Infant and Preschool Tests

All tests designed for infants and preschool children require individual administration. Some kindergarten children can be tested in small groups with the types of tests constructed for the primary grades. In general, however, group tests are not applicable until the child has reached school age. Most tests for children below the age of 6 are either performance or oral tests. A few involve rudimentary manipulation of paper and pencil.

It is customary to subdivide the first five years of life into the infant period and the preschool period. The first extends from birth to the age of approximately 18 months; the second, from 18 to 60 months. From the viewpoint of test administration, it should be noted that the infant must be tested while he is either lying down or supported on a person's lap. Little or no speech is possible during this period. Most of the tests deal with sensory and motor development. The preschool child, on the other hand, can walk, sit at a table, use his hands in manipulating test objects, and communicate by language. At the preschool level, the child is also much more responsive to the examiner as a person, while for the infant the examiner serves primarily as a means of providing specific objects. Preschool testing is a more highly interpersonal process—a feature that augments both the opportunities and the difficulties presented by the test situation.

In the following sections, infant and preschool tests will be considered separately. The distinction cannot be rigidly applied, however, since a number of current scales overlap both periods. Moreover, it should be borne in mind that all such stages are arbitrary, since behavior development is actually gradual and continuous. Dividing lines are introduced only to facilitate description.

INFANT TESTS

One of the most extensive series of investigations of infant behavior is that conducted at the Yale Clinic of Child Development under the direction of

Gesell (19, 21, 22). In 1927, Gesell and his co-workers began a longitudinal study of the normal course of behavior development in the human infant (22). The principal data were obtained by repeated observations of 107 infants constituting a relatively "normal" and homogeneous sample. Only healthy children free from any known defects were included in the survey. The children were carefully selected so that the parents were of middle socio-economic status and close to the general average in amount of education and in occupational level. All parents were American born and of north-European extraction.

The infants in this group were examined at the ages of 4, 6, and 8 weeks, and at every 4-week interval thereafter until the age of 56 weeks. Later follow-ups were made at 18 months, and at 2, 3, 4, 5, and 6 years. Re-examinations were continued over a 10-year period with as many cases as were available. Only a portion of the entire group was examined at any one age level, the numbers varying from 28 to 60 through age 5; at age 6, only 18 cases were included. Approximately the same number of boys and girls were observed at each age. The study of the normative sample was supplemented by extensive observations on large numbers of clinical cases.

From the results obtained in the normative sample, as well as supplementary data on other cases, the Gesell Developmental Schedules were prepared (20). These schedules are employed in determining the level of behavior development the child has attained in four major areas (21, pp. 5-6):

1. *Motor behavior:* covers both gross bodily control and finer motor coordination. This category includes postural reactions, head balance, sitting, standing, creeping, walking, reaching for and grasping objects, and manipulation of objects.

2. *Adaptive behavior:* covers eye-hand coordination in reaching for and handling objects, solution of practical problems, and exploration and manipulation of objects. Examples include reactions to such stimuli as toy cubes, a ringing bell, and a dangling ring, as well as drawing and the solution of simple formboards.

3. *Language behavior:* covers all means of communication, such as facial expression, gesture, postural movements, prelinguistic vocalizations, and speech. Comprehension of communication by others is also included.

4. *Personal-social behavior:* covers "the child's personal reactions to the social culture in which he lives." Among the types of behavior in this category are feeding, toilet-training and response to training in other socially imposed situations, play, development of a "sense of property," smiling and other responses to persons, and responses to mirror.

In general, the Gesell Developmental Schedules represent a standardized procedure for observing and evaluating the course of behavior development in the child's daily life. Although a few may be properly described as tests, most of the items in these schedules are purely observational. A set of standard toys and other test objects, reproduced in Figure 55, is employed in making these observations. Specifications regarding clinical crib, infant-supporting chair, test table, observation play pen, and other equipment required in the course of the behavior examinations are also provided (cf. 21, pp. 448-455). The direct examination of the infant is supplemented by interview data obtained from the mother.

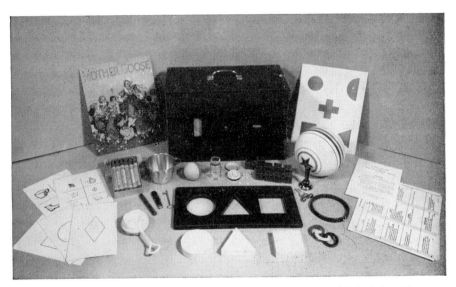

Fig. 55. Test Objects Employed with the Gesell Developmental Schedules. (Courtesy The Psychological Corporation.)

No single score is computed for the entire behavior schedule, the authors arguing against such a composite measure. Instead, the record indicates the approximate developmental level, in months, that the child has attained in each of the four major areas covered. This is found by comparing the child's behavior with that given as typical of eight "key ages," viz., 4, 18, 28, and 40 weeks; and 12, 18, 24, and 36 months (cf. 21, Ch. 3). In the preparation of these developmental scales, behavior items were classified into "increasing," "decreasing," and "focal" items. The first category includes behavior whose frequency of occurrence increases with age; the second covers behavior that decreases with age; and the third, behavior that increases up to a certain age and then decreases. Increasing and decreasing behavior items were allocated to those age levels at which the frequency of occurrence was closest to 50 per cent; focal items were assigned to the age levels at which they occurred with the highest frequency.

Below is a "condensed narrative picture" used with the Developmental Schedules to indicate steps in the examination and to describe typical behavior at the 28-week level. In Figure 56 will be found four of the draw-

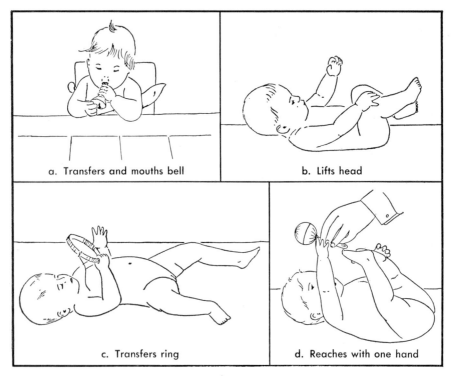

a. Transfers and mouths bell b. Lifts head

c. Transfers ring d. Reaches with one hand

Fig. 56. Drawings Employed with the Gesell Developmental Schedules to Illustrate Typical Behavior at 28 Weeks of Age. (From *Developmental Diagnosis,* by Arnold Gesell and Catherine S. Amatruda. Copyright 1941, 1947, by Arnold Gesell. By permission of Paul B. Hoeber, Inc., publisher.)

ings that accompany this description (21, pp. 44-46). Italics in the text indicate behavior that characteristically appears for the first time at this key age.

The 28-week-old infant sits with support, his trunk erect and head steady. After a brief period with an introductory toy, it is removed and the examiner presents the FIRST of three CUBES. The baby seizes it *immediately* with a *radial palmar* grasp and carries it to his mouth. He *retains* it as the SECOND CUBE is presented. He does not grasp the second cube but he holds *2 cubes more than momentarily* when they are placed in his hands. As the THIRD CUBE is presented, he drops a cube. He does not grasp the third cube, but mouths, *transfers,* drops and resecures the cube in hand.

He follows the screen as it is removed from the MASSED CUBES, then approaches the mass with both hands, grasping one cube and scattering the others. *Holding one cube he grasps another;* he may pick up 3 in all.

He follows the examiner's hand away as the PELLET is presented; gives delayed, intent regard to the pellet, and *rakes* at it with his fingers, *contacting it.*

He makes an *immediate one-handed* approach on the BELL, taking it by the bowl or junction. He *bangs,* mouths, and *transfers* the bell, *retaining* it without dropping [Fig. 56a].

The RING AND STRING are presented, the string obliquely aligned to the right, but within reach. He *reaches toward the ring,* slaps and scratches the table, and finally sees the string; he either *abandons the effort or fusses.*

The test table is removed. He is placed on his back on the platform. His SUPINE posturings are symmetrical, with the legs lifted high in extension or semi-extension. He *lifts the head* as though striving to sit up [Fig. 56b]. He is none too tolerant of the supine position and this and the following three situations may have to be curtailed or omitted.

He grasps, *transfers* and mouths the DANGLING RING, regarding it in hand [Fig. 56c].

He makes an *immediate one-handed approach* upon the RATTLE [Fig. 56d], *shakes* it vigorously, regards it and fingers it with the free hand. If it is placed on the platform at his side, he reaches for it unsuccessfully.

When auditory responses are tested by RINGING A BELL opposite first one ear, then the other, he turns his head correctly and promptly.

The examiner now takes his hands and he lifts his head and assists in the PULL-TO-SITTING. In the SITTING position he *sits for a moment, leaning forward, propped* on his hands. He also shows some *active balance, sitting erect for a fleeting, unsteady moment.*

Held in the STANDING position, he sustains a *large fraction of weight* on his extended legs as he *bounces* actively.

Placed PRONE, he holds the head well lifted, his weight on his abdomen and hands. He *lifts one arm* toward a lure and he *tries, unsuccessfully, to pivot.*

Seated before a MIRROR, he regards his image, smiles, vocalizes, and *pats the glass.*

His LANGUAGE includes cooing, squealing, and *combined vowel sounds.* He says *m-m-mum* when he cries.

His mother REPORTS that he discriminates strangers, "talks" to his toys, *takes solids well,* and even *brings his feet to his mouth.* He rolls from supine to prone and sits propped about half an hour.

Both observation and scoring procedures are less highly standardized in the Gesell Schedules than in the usual psychological test. A certain amount of subjectivity enters into the examination at several points. The restriction in both size and nature of the normative sample should also be kept in mind. No statistical analysis of reliability or validity is reported. In general, these schedules may be regarded as a refinement and elaboration of the qualitative observations routinely made by pediatricians and other specialists concerned with infant development. The investigations from which the schedules were derived represent an important contribution to child psychology. As testing instruments, however, the Gesell Developmental Schedules are relatively crude.

Another type of measuring instrument suitable for the infant level is provided by several special revisions and downward extensions of the Binet scales. Kuhlmann's 1922 revision of the Binet extended the scales down to a 3-month level (30). This represents one of the earliest attempts to develop a standardized test for infants. The 1939 revision of the Kuhlmann-Binet likewise covers most of the infant period, the easiest tests being designed for the age of 4 months (31).

A scale that many psychologists consider one of the most satisfactory instruments for infant testing is the Cattell Infant Intelligence Scale (12). This scale was developed as a downward extension of the 1937 Stanford-Binet, Form L. In addition to Stanford-Binet items, the Cattell scale utilizes material from the Gesell Developmental Schedules and from other available infant tests, together with some original items. The items are grouped into age levels, and the MA and ratio IQ are computed by the same procedures followed in the 1937 Stanford-Binet. The Cattell scale extends from 2 to 30 months. During the first year, age levels are spaced at intervals of one month; during the second year, at two-month intervals; and during the first half of the third year, at three-month intervals.

If the child passes any test at the 30-month level, testing is continued with the Stanford-Binet, beginning at Year Level III. Between 22 and 30 months, Stanford-Binet items are intermingled with other items in the Cattell scale. Each age level contains five items, with one or two alternates. The small intervals between age levels, as well as the relatively large number of tests at each level, permit more precise measurement with this scale than is possible with most other available infant tests. Continuity and comparability with the Stanford-Binet are further advantages. In order to insure close comparability of scores on the two scales, certain groups within the standardization samples were retested at the age of 3 years with Form L of the Stanford-Binet. The placement of items in the Cattell scale was then adjusted so as to yield approximately the same median IQ as that obtained by each group on the Stanford-Binet.

The Cattell scale was standardized on a total group of 274 children, varying numbers within this sample being retested at the ages of 3, 6, 9, 12, 18, 24, 30, and 36 months. As is nearly always true in longitudinal studies, the entire group was not available for all retests. Nor did it prove possible to administer all preliminary items suitable for a particular age to all children of that age. The children came from lower-middle-class families, as judged by income level and father's occupation, and were of north-European extraction. Like other groups employed in longitudinal studies, this sample was somewhat selected in terms of stability of residence and willingness of parents to cooperate in the study.

The principal statistical criterion employed for item selection was increase in percentage of children passing an item from one age to the next. Several other practical criteria, however, were applied in retaining or discarding items. Thus items were eliminated if they were difficult to administer or score, involved an undue amount of subjectivity on the part of the examiner, required cumbersome apparatus, or failed to hold the attention of young children. An effort was also made to minimize the number of items testing primarily muscular coordination or depending unduly upon specific home training.

All items in the Cattell scale are administered without a time limit. The author points out that timed tests are undesirable in testing infants or preschool children. Not only do younger children often fail to understand the need for hurrying, but a timed test may penalize the bright child who is talkative and imaginative in his use of test materials, as well as the slow, deliberate child who plans carefully before he acts. For most children, the Cattell scale requires no more than twenty to thirty minutes. The order of administration of the tests is not prescribed, but is modified to suit the interests of the child and other specific circumstances. For example, tests that the child takes in a prone position should usually precede those in which he is held on the lap, since he is more likely to object to the prone position after he has been sitting up.

The standardized materials required to administer these tests are very similar to those employed with the Gesell Developmental Schedules and at the lower levels of the Stanford-Binet. At the youngest ages, the tests are largely perceptual, comprising such activities as attending to a voice or bell, following a dangling ring or a moving person with the eyes, looking at a spoon or a cube, and inspecting own fingers. A few motor items, such as lifting head, manipulating fingers, or transferring objects from hand to hand, are also included. With increasing age, more complex manipulatory tasks are introduced and increasing use is made of verbal functions. Blocks, pegboards, formboards, cups, spoons, dolls, and other toy objects are employed at these levels. At the higher ages, the child follows oral instructions in using these materials. Naming objects or pictures of objects and identifying or pointing to objects named by the examiner are among the more highly verbal tasks utilized.

Other examples of infant scales include the California First-Year Mental Scale developed by Bayley (4, 5) for use in the Berkeley Growth Study, the Northwestern Intelligence Tests prepared by Gilliland (23), and The Griffiths Mental Development Scale more recently standardized in England (26, 27). Like most infant scales, these tests have borrowed items extensively from each other and from the Gesell and Binet scales. In content, they thus have much in common. They differ considerably, however, in adequacy of standardization and in amount of information available on reliability and validity. In their present form, some are crude and serve only to suggest promising testing techniques. Others are sufficiently well developed for immediate practical application. For specific information and evaluation, the reader is urged to consult the *Mental Measurements Yearbooks* and other relevant publications cited for each test.

EVALUATION OF INFANT TESTS

The testing of infants presents many difficulties in *administration and scoring,* and hence requires special procedures (cf., e.g., 12, Ch. 3). Oral directions cannot be used for most tests. The examiner must rather set the stage so that the desired response is elicited. Similarly, the infant is not motivated to "do his best on the test." Intrinsic interest of the test stimuli and rapport with the examiner must be relied upon to provide motivation. Moreover, some infants may have been adversely conditioned to the environment of a clinic, doctor's office, or hospital because of previous uncomfortable or painful experiences during medical examinations or treatment. The easy fatigability of the infant, which makes long testing sessions impracticable, must likewise be taken into account. Distractability presents another problem. The infant is readily distracted by any competing stimuli, and it is consequently difficult to hold or direct his attention.

For many items, scoring is rendered more difficult and subjective by the lack of any objective record of the child's response. Did the child lift his head? Did his eyes actually follow a moving object? The test record in such cases depends upon relatively fleeting observations by the examiner. Few infant test responses leave a permanent record that may be studied at leisure or rescored.

The *normative samples* employed in standardizing infant scales are smaller and often less representative than those used in developing tests for older children. On the other hand, a longitudinal approach has generally been followed in the construction of infant scales, in contrast to the cross-sectional approach characteristic of tests standardized on older children. An advantage of the longitudinal method stems from the greater uniformity of sampling it provides, since the same subjects are tested at successive ages. The cross-sectional method is subject to selective factors that may operate differentially at different ages. For example, if school children are tested, those in the upper grades represent a relatively superior sampling, since the less able tend to drop out.

The *reliability* of infant tests has generally proved to be lower than that of tests for older children. Such a finding is not surprising, in the light of some of the previously mentioned difficulties of infant testing. Some of the more recently developed infant scales, however, have yielded more promising results with reference to reliability. The reliability coefficients of the Cattell scale, found at different age levels within the standardization sample, are given in Table 16. With the exception of the 3-month level, at which the reli-

TABLE 16. **Split-Half Reliability of the Cattell Infant Intelligence Scale**
(Adapted from Cattell, 12, p. 49)

Age in Months	Number of Cases	Reliability Coefficient
3	87	.56
6	100	.88
9	85	.86
12	101	.89
18	100	.90
24	80	.85
30	56	.71

ability coefficient is only .56, all other reliabilities fall between .71 and .90. For comparative purposes, it may be noted that in a group of 62 3-year-old children drawn from the same sample, Cattell found a reliability of .87 for the Stanford-Binet, Form L. The Infant Intelligence Scale thus compares favorably in this respect with the Stanford-Binet.

Closely similar results were obtained by Bayley with the California First-Year Mental Scale (5). For the ages of 1, 2, and 3 months, the reliabilities were only .63, .51, and .74, respectively. Beyond 4 months, however, the coefficients ranged from .75 to .95, with a median value of .86. It should be noted that items for infant scales are usually selected so as to sample a wide variety of functions. Such heterogeneous content is unlikely to yield comparable halves for the computation of split-half reliability. If closely comparable forms had been available, the obtained reliability coefficients would probably have been still higher.

The determination of *validity* for infant tests is hampered by a dearth of suitable criteria. Independent estimates of the intelligence of infants are not readily available. We do not have school grades, records of job achievement, or officers' ratings on infants! To be sure, for extreme deviants, independent evidence of ability level can sometimes be obtained. This is especially true of feebleminded children falling into clinical types that have clearly recognizable physical symptoms, such as mongolism. Such a criterion, for example, was applied by Gilliland to a small sample employed in the validation of the Northwestern Intelligence Tests. For less extreme deviants, however, and especially for the superior deviant, few criterion data can be found.

As a result, the validation of infant tests has been based largely upon two criteria, viz., age differentiation and prediction of subsequent status. The first of these criteria is generally employed in the original selection of items, although it is also used to check both item performance and total scores on the final forms. In terms of this criterion, infant tests in general show good validity. Clear-cut and progressive age changes in performance are found, even over as short a time as a month.

With regard to the second criterion, evidence for validity is much less satisfactory. This criterion has aroused considerable interest, since one of the practical uses of infant tests is the prediction of later intellectual level in children considered for adoption. It might be argued that the correlation of infant test scores with subsequent test scores should be regarded as a measure of reliability rather than validity. Two points may be noted in this connection. First, the subsequent intelligence test scores are often derived from a different test, such as the Stanford-Binet. In this respect, then, the correlation would represent a validity coefficient against another, well-established test as a criterion. Such a procedure is similar to the validation of group tests or of abridged screening tests against individually administered and longer tests.

The second point concerns the time interval. In this connection, reference may be made to the discussion of the coefficient of stability in Chapter 5. It will be recalled that, for most tests, retest reliability is determined over fairly short intervals, ranging from a few days to a few months. Even tests with high stability over such short intervals yield much lower retest correlations after a lapse of several years. Such is the case, for example, with the Stanford-Binet. Long-range prediction of behavior is always a difficult matter, since so many fortuitous circumstances may influence the individual's development in the interim. To be sure, the older the individual, the easier in general will the prediction be, since a larger proportion of his development will have already occurred (cf. 1, pp. 231-238; 2).

Any long-term prediction involves more factors than are operative in the usual retest reliability coefficient. Certainly a two-year retest coefficient obtained with an infant scale should not be compared with a two-month retest coefficient on an adult test. It should be further noted, in this connection, that intellectual development progresses much more rapidly in infancy than it does among older children. Consequently, the nature of the items in infant tests may show considerable variation over relatively short intervals. Items suitable for the 3-month level may be quite unlike those suitable for the 6-month level. This condition further complicates the interpretation of retest correlations at the infant level, even when the interval is only three or four months.

In the light of the two points discussed, it would seem that the retest coefficients generally reported for infant tests are not truly comparable with retest reliability as usually measured in other tests. Whether such coefficients are classed under "validity" or placed in a separate category is of little consequence. They may properly be considered measures of validity, provided that subsequent performance is specified as the criterion and the length of the interval is indicated.

We may now examine some typical retest correlations. In Bayley's longitudinal study with the California First-Year Mental Scale, correlations between tests administered under the age of 1 year and retests at 18 months were close to zero (5, 6). With subsequent retests, negative correlations as high as —.21 were obtained. From such findings, Bayley concluded that intelligence test scores at age 3 or later can be predicted better on the basis of parental education than from tests administered to the child during his first year.

The results for the first year are only slightly better with the Cattell Infant Intelligence Scale. Table 17 shows the correlations between Cattell IQ's obtained at the ages of 3, 6, 9, 12, 18, 24, and 30 months, respectively, with the Stanford-Binet (Form L) IQ subsequently obtained by the same children at the age of 3 years. It will be noted that below the age of 12 months the predictive correlations are only .10, .34, and .18. These correlations are little better than chance and indicate that such tests had virtually no predictive value in terms of the 3-year Stanford-Binet IQ. This lack of predictive validity of Cattell IQ's obtained prior to the age of 1 year has been confirmed by other investigators (13). Beginning with the age of 12 months, however, the correlations are considerably higher, rising steadily from .56 to .83. It might be noted for comparative purposes that the Stanford-Binet Form L IQ's obtained by the same children at ages 3 and 3½ correlated .75.

TABLE 17.   Validity Coefficients of the Cattell Infant Intelligence Scale

(Adapted from Cattell, 12, p. 49)

Age in Months	Number of Cases	Correlation with Stanford-Binet IQ at Age of 3 Years
3	42	.10
6	49	.34
9	44	.18
12	57	.56
18	52	.67
24	52	.71
30	42	.83

In the California First-Year Mental Scale, a relatively large proportion of the tests administered below the age of 1 year are sensorimotor in nature. The Cattell scale contains fewer tests of this type, a special effort having been made to exclude them. It should be noted that, when sensorimotor tests are given to older children and adults, they show little or no correlation with intellectual functions. Nor do such tests correlate highly with each other. A fairly high degree of specificity has generally been found among sensorimotor functions. It is therefore to be expected that those infant scales that contain a large proportion of sensorimotor items will show little or no correlation with subsequently administered intelligence tests. In so far as it is possible to construct infant tests with items more closely resembling those occurring in traditional intelligence tests, better prediction of future intellectual status seems likely.

A promising approach to the testing of infant intelligence involves greater utilization of the verbal factor, which is so closely identified with later intelligence (3, 32). Items based on the use of language and the understanding of words tend to have better predictive validity than the more usual sensorimotor items. In very young infants, prelinguistic vocalization appears to bear a significant relation to subsequent IQ. Systematic analyses of infant speech have revealed consistent developmental trends in such characteristics as number of different consonants uttered and ratio of consonants to vowels (10). Even within the first six months of life, such speech indices exhibit differences among socioeconomic levels which parallel group differences in intelligence observed at later ages (10). Infants reared in their own homes, moreover, excel institutional infants in such speech characteristics (18, 29), a finding that is likewise in line with intelligence test results on older children. An exploratory follow-up study of 23 cases yielded significant correlations as high as .45 between certain speech indices at the ages of 6 to 18 months and Stanford-Binet IQ's at the ages of 3 to 4½ years (11). Prelinguistic vocalization thus appears to be one area worth further investigation in constructing infant tests of the future.

PRESCHOOL TESTS

Among tests specially designed for the preschool level, the best known are the Merrill-Palmer Scale and the Minnesota Preschool Scale. The former was developed by Stutsman (36) at the Merrill-Palmer School in Detroit, Michigan. The tests for this scale were originally assembled from many sources, including performance scales, children's games, verbal tests such as the Woodworth-Wells Association Tests, and others. From a total of 78 tests tried out on groups of nursery school children at the Merrill-Palmer School, 38 were finally retained. The bases of test selection were popularity with children, practicality in administration, relation with age, and differentiation of children judged by nursery school staff to be bright or dull.

The normative sample to which the final 38 tests were administered consisted of 631 children, 300 boys and 331 girls, between the ages of 18 and 77 months. The subjects, all of whom were in Detroit, Michigan, were obtained from 20 different sources, including public and private schools, Merrill-Palmer waiting list, orphanages, day nurseries, child-care agencies, and health clinics. These children were classified into 6-month age groups, each group containing from 49 to 81 cases.

The 38 tests in the scale yield a total of 93 scorable test elements, since several tests are scored at different levels, depending upon the child's performance. For each of these test elements, the "age at par" was computed, that is, the age at which 50 per cent of the normative sample passed it. The test elements were then arranged in ascending order of difficulty, according to their age at par. The test elements, or items, were also grouped into 6-month age levels, on the same basis. For example, items whose age at par ranged from 21.0 to 23.4 were placed into the 18-to-23-months level. The scale is suitable for testing children between the ages of 24 and 63 months.

The Merrill-Palmer Scale is administered as an age scale but scored as a point scale. Testing is usually begun at a level within which the child's chronological age falls. It is continued downward to a level at which all tests are passed and upward to a level at which one-half or more of the tests are failed.

Although the tests are arranged in order of difficulty within each level, the order of administration is flexible. It is customary to begin with a particularly appealing test and to let the child's interests influence the course of the testing. The tests are presented in individual, brightly colored, and differently shaped boxes, a practice which stimulates curiosity and greatly enhances the appeal of these tests for young children.

The score is determined by crediting one point for each test element passed, including all tests below the basal age. In view of the difficulties frequently encountered in testing preschool children, an adjustment is made for refusals and omissions. Any test element that could not be administered is credited as passed if it falls below the raw score finally attained, and as failed if it falls above that score. Normative data are provided for translating raw point scores into mental ages, percentiles, and standard scores. The computation of IQ's with the mental ages found from this scale is not advocated, since the *SD* of the mental ages does not increase proportionately with age. In fact, it increases up to a certain age, and then decreases.

The Merrill-Palmer Scale includes relatively few language tests, most of the tests being of the performance type. The language tests consist of memory span for words and for meaningful word groups; answering simple questions (e.g., "What does a doggie say?" "What is this?"—pencil. "What is it for?"); and action-agent association (e.g., "What runs?" "What cries?"). A number of tests measure predominantly sensorimotor coordination, as illustrated by throwing a ball, pulling a string, crossing feet, standing on one foot, closing fist and moving thumb, cutting with scissors, buttoning, folding paper, building with blocks, and fitting cubes into a box. Some involve matching colors or pictures, reconstruction of cut-out picture puzzles, or copying a drawing of a circle, cross, or star. A few familiar performance tests are also included, such as the Seguin Form Board, Mare and Foal, and Manikin. Speed plays an important part in many of these tests, the level at which the test is passed often depending upon the time required to complete it. The materials used in administering the Merrill-Palmer tests are pictured in Figure 57.

The validity of the Merrill-Palmer Scale was determined in part by the method of selecting tests in terms of age differentiation and relation to ability as judged by nursery school staff. Within the standardization sample of 631 cases, a correlation of .92 was found between chronological age and total score on the Merrill-Palmer. This step may be regarded as a cross-validation of the initial item selection in terms of the criterion of age differentiation. The degree of overlap of scores between adjacent age groups was also found to be slight in the standardization sample. Validity was further checked by comparing the performance of 29 mentally defective children, aged 4½ to 12½, with the norms. Finally, correlations in the high .70's are reported between Merrill-Palmer and Stanford-Binet mental ages in one mentally defective and two normal samples. These correlations are misleading, however, since chronological age varied widely within these groups. Subsequent studies with more homogeneous samples have yielded lower correlations with the Stanford-Binet and the Kuhlmann-Binet (cf. 41).

Fig. 57. Materials for Use in Administering the Merrill-Palmer Scale. Each test is presented in an individual, gaily colored box. (Courtesy C. H. Stoelting Company.)

No information regarding reliability is given in the test manual, but later studies (cf. 41) report retest reliabilities ranging from .72 to .96 with intervals of two months or less. These coefficients were obtained on small groups of children aged approximately 2 to 5 years and varying widely in ability. Such reliabilities, too, would undoubtedly be lower in more homogeneous samples.

The major weaknesses of the Merrill-Palmer Scale center about its emphasis upon motor skills and upon speed. For the preschool child, speed has not yet become an important goal. The procedures for evaluating scores are also crude, when judged in terms of current standards of test construction. The principal asset of this scale is its undoubted appeal to young children, both because of the intrinsic interest of the tasks and because of the manner of presenting tests in attractive, gaily colored boxes. Another advantage, from the standpoint of preschool testing, stems from the scoring adjustments available for handling refusals and omissions.

It should also be noted that a revision of the Merrill-Palmer Scale is in progress. It is anticipated that this revision will extend the scale upwards to about the 12-year level and downwards to include a new infant scale prepared by Nancy Bayley. An attempt will be made to measure the same abilities, as identified through factor analysis, at all age levels.[1]

The Minnesota Preschool Scale (24, 25) is available in two equivalent forms, A and B, each consisting of 26 tests. These tests were derived largely from the Kuhlmann-Binet; some were taken from other scales and some are original tests. The standardization sample consisted of a carefully selected group of 900 children, including 100 at each half-year from 1½ to 6 years of age. They were obtained from nursery schools, public and private schools, clinics, and settlement houses, and were selected in terms of father's occupation so as to constitute a representative sampling of the population of Minneapolis.

The Minnesota scale contains relatively few motor items. None of the tests is timed. The tests are classified as verbal and non-verbal, each type yielding a separate score. Among the verbal tests are to be found: pointing to parts of the body on a large doll; pointing to objects in pictures; naming objects; telling what a picture is about; following directions; comprehension, or answering practical questions such as "What should you do when you are hungry?"; naming objects from memory; naming colors; identifying incomplete pictures; digit span; detecting absurdities; vocabulary; opposites; and number of words in longest sentence used spontaneously by the child during the examination. The similarity of many of these tests to Stanford-Binet items is apparent.

The non-verbal tests include: copying drawings of circle, triangle, and diamond; imitative drawing of horizontal stroke and vertical cross; block-building; Knox cube; form discrimination; form recognition; tracing forms; rearrangement of cut-out picture puzzles; paper-folding; indicating missing parts in pictures; and imitating position of hands of clock. The materials employed in administering the tests are shown in Figure 58. Many of the pictorial materials are bound into an examination booklet, which may be seen in the illustration.

Norms are provided for each month of age between 1½ and 6 years. Scores on verbal, non-verbal, and total scale can be expressed as IQ equiv-

[1] Personal communication from Dr. Rachel Stutsman Ball, Arizona State University, Tempe, Arizona.

alents or in terms of specially developed equal-unit scales indicating the difficulty level of tasks the child can pass as well as his position in a normal distribution. Parallel-form reliability, with intervals of one to seven days, ranged from .68 to .94 for the verbal scales, from .67 to .92 for the non-verbal, and from .80 to .94 for the total scale. These coefficients were found in the standardization sample by correlating Forms A and B within single half-year age groups.

Fig. 58.   Materials Employed in the Minnesota Preschool Scale. (Reproduced by permission of Educational Test Bureau, Minneapolis.)

Validity of the Minnesota Preschool Scale was initially determined through the criteria of age differentiation and internal consistency, both of which were employed in the selection and placement of tests. Relationship of test scores to father's occupational level was taken as further corroborative evidence of validity. In two extensive follow-up studies (24, 33), the predictive validity of the Minnesota Preschool Scale was checked against intelligence test performance in later childhood and adulthood. The principal criteria used in these follow-ups were scores on the Stanford-Binet and the Army Alpha. The correlations varied widely, but in general indicated some predictive value.

For example, 1937 Stanford-Binet IQ's obtained between the ages of 4½ and 13½ years showed a median correlation of .68 with Minnesota Preschool IQ's obtained at 4 years of age and over. With Minnesota IQ's obtained between 3 and 4 years, the median correlation was .61; and with Minnesota IQ's obtained before the age of 3 years, it was .21.

In the adult follow-up (33), 226 subjects who had been tested with the Minnesota Preschool Scale before the age of 6 years were located and given the Army Alpha at ages ranging from 16½ to 22 years. The principal objective of this follow-up was the selection of the most discriminative items in terms of the criterion of adult Alpha score. Within a subsample of 46 cases, however, correlations were computed between adult Alpha score and initial scores on the Minnesota Preschool Scales A and B (33, p. 74). These correlations were found to be .31 and .33, respectively. It is interesting to note that approximately the same correlations were obtained in this subsample between Alpha scores and Minnesota Preschool scores based only on the items selected in terms of the follow-up criterion. Such a finding suggests that, if more items of the same degree of predictive efficiency were added, higher correlations might be obtained.

All in all, the outstanding features of the Minnesota Preschool Scale appear to be the careful procedures followed in standardization and in development of norms, the availability of parallel forms, the high parallel-form reliability, the elimination of speed, the reduction in number of motor items, and the extensive follow-up data. On the negative side, the tests in this scale have not proved to be as appealing to young children, especially under the age of 3, as other preschool tests. This scale is probably most useful in testing normal children between the ages of 3 and 5 years. The lack of any provision for handling refusals and omissions is also a handicap in testing preschool children. Similarly, the practice of beginning with the easiest items in the scale, regardless of the child's age, makes the scale unduly long and boring for the older and brighter subjects.

Mention may also be made of an intelligence test developed in England by Valentine (38), suitable for children between the ages of 1½ and 15. Although crudely standardized, this scale combines a relatively large number of tests from earlier sources (Binet, Gesell, Merrill-Palmer, etc.) and includes a few ingenious new tests. No data on reliability or validity are reported by the test author. In an investigation by Wakelam (39) on kindergarten and primary grade children, however, promising results were obtained regarding retest reliability, as well as concurrent and predictive validity against several academic criteria.

Attention should likewise be called to a number of well-standardized and widely used tests suitable for the preschool ages but extending either downward into the infant level or upward into the school period. These tests have already been discussed in connection with other age levels. Among them are the Kuhlmann-Binet and the Cattell Infant Intelligence Scale, which bridge the gap completely from infancy to school age. When the Cattell scale is considered together with the Stanford-Binet, for which it was designed as a downward extension, the entire preschool period is adequately covered. Because of the wide use and careful standardization of the Stanford-Binet and its continuity to the adult level, there is much to recommend the combination of Cattell and Stanford-Binet as a means of testing preschool children.

Among the performance scales discussed in Chapter 10, the Leiter International Performance Scale extends down to Year Level 2 and is considered suitable for testing normal children at age 4 and over. The point scale adaptation of the lower levels of this scale was prepared by Arthur as a downward extension of the Arthur Performance Scale.

The Gesell Developmental Schedules include a Preschool as well as an Infant Schedule. The Preschool Schedule (19) extends from the age of 15 months to 6 years. The general approach is similar to that followed in the Infant Schedule. The items are largely observational and are classified under the same four types of development, viz., motor, adaptive, language, and personal-social. Descriptive norms are provided for every three-month interval between 15 months and 6 years. The normative data were obtained from further follow-ups of the infants observed in the standardization of the Infant Schedule, as well as from data on several hundred children subsequently examined in the Yale Clinic of Child Development.

Two other types of developmental scales may be considered in this connection, namely, the Oseretsky Tests of Motor Proficiency and the Vineland Social Maturity Scale. Both of these scales extend well beyond the preschool level, through later childhood and adolescence. They are of special relevance to the present discussion, however, because of certain similarities to the Gesell scales in content and in general approach. They are also more suitable for use at the lower age or intellectual levels than at higher levels.

The Oseretsky Tests of Motor Proficiency were originally published in Russia in 1923. They were subsequently translated into several languages and used in a number of European countries. In 1946, Doll (14), then Director of Research for the Vineland Training School, sponsored and edited an English translation of the Portuguese adaptation of these tests. A scale of motor development is especially useful in testing mental defectives, who are also frequently retarded in motor functions. Other applications of the Oseretsky tests are found in the testing of children with motor disorders, in connection with the administration of therapeutic and training programs. The age range covered by the original Oseretsky tests extended from 4 to 16 years, the tests being arranged into year levels as in the Stanford-Binet. A "motor age" was likewise computed by a procedure similar to that followed in the Stanford-Binet. The Oseretsky scale was designed to cover all major types of motor behavior, from postural reactions and gross bodily movements to finger coordination and control of facial muscles. Administration of these tests requires only simple and easily obtainable materials, such as matchsticks, wooden spools, thread, paper, rope, boxes, rubber ball, and the like. Directions are given orally and by demonstration.

In their original form, some of the Oseretsky tests involved the comprehension and recall of fairly complex instructions. Such "intellectual loading" of the tests would tend to produce spuriously high correlations with intelligence tests and to make interpretation of scores ambiguous. Instructions and scoring procedures for some of the tests were unclear and inadequately standardized. In 1955, the Lincoln-Oseretsky Motor Development Scale (35) was issued as a revision and restandardization of the Oseretsky tests. Covering only ages 6 to 14, this revision includes 36 of the original 85 items. Further standardization to cover younger ages is anticipated. The tests, which in this revision are arranged in order of difficulty, were chosen on the basis of age correlation, reliability, and certain practical considerations. Tentative percentile norms were found on a standardization sample of 380 boys and 369 girls attending public schools in central Illinois. Split-half reliabilities computed for single age and sex groups fell mostly in the .80's and .90's. A one-year retest yielded a correlation of .70. A factor analysis of a slightly longer, earlier version indicated a single common factor identified as motor development.

The Vineland Social Maturity Scale (15, 16) is a developmental schedule concerned with the individual's ability to look after his practical needs and to take responsibility. Although covering a range from birth to over 25 years, this scale has been found most useful at the younger ages, as well as with mental defectives. The entire scale consists of 117 items grouped into year levels. The information required for each item is obtained, not through test situations, but through an interview with an informant or with the subject himself. The scale is based on what the subject has actually done in his daily living. The items fall into eight categories: general self-help, self-help in eating, self-help in dressing, self-direction, occupation, communication, locomotion, and socialization. A social age (SA) and a social quotient (SQ) can be computed from the subject's record on the entire scale.

The Vineland Scale was tentatively standardized on 620 subjects, including 10 males and 10 females at each year from birth to 30 years. Validity of this scale was determined chiefly on the basis of age differentiation, comparison of normals and mental defectives, and correlation of scores with judgments of observers who knew the subjects well. A retest reliability of .92 has been reported for 123 cases, the retest intervals varying from one day to 9 months. The use of different examiners or informants did not appreciably affect results in this group, as long as all informants had had an adequate opportunity to observe the subjects. An adaptation for blind preschool children has been developed and standardized by Maxfield and Buchholz (34).

Correlations between the Vineland Scale and the Stanford-Binet vary widely but are sufficiently low, in general, to indicate that different facets of behavior are being tapped by the two scales. The Vineland Social Maturity Scale has proved helpful to clinicians in diagnosing feeblemindedness and in reaching decisions regarding institutionalization. For example, an individual who is intellectually deficient in terms of the Stanford-Binet may be able to adjust satisfactorily outside of an institution if his social age on the Vineland Scale is adequate. Discrepancies between MA and SA may likewise contribute to an understanding of certain cases manifesting behavior problems or delinquency.

On the other hand, the available norms must be regarded as tentative. The standardization sample obviously included too few cases at each age to insure desirable stability and representativeness of norms. Moreover, the subjects came chiefly from middle-class American homes. It is apparent that many items, such as those relating to going out alone, use of spending money, and the like, would have a different significance for children in different socioeconomic levels or in certain minority groups. Cultural differences in child-rearing customs, rather than the child's ability level, might in such cases account for deviations from the norms. Similarly, a considerable number of items are unsuitable for institutional children.

EVALUATION OF PRESCHOOL TESTS

Many of the problems encountered in the *administration* of infant tests are also met at the preschool level. Although oral directions can now be relied upon to a much greater extent, the problems of motivation and interest, short attention span, and susceptibility to fatigue remain. In scoring at least some preschool tests, moreover, subjectivity is likely to enter, since many test responses at this level leave no permanent record. Apart from these difficulties, which are shared with infant tests, preschool testing presents certain problems peculiar to its own level (cf. 19, Ch. 11; 25, pp. 11-18; 40, pp. 340-

344). As the child's sphere of activity widens, and as he reacts increasingly to the interpersonal aspects of the test situation, new problems emerge.

The principal characteristics that may interfere with satisfactory test performance at the preschool age are shyness, distractability, and negativism (cf. 25). A shy child may be frightened by strange surroundings or a strange examiner. He may cry, cling to his mother, refuse to try the tests, and object to remaining in the examination room. Especially with younger preschool children, permitting the mother to remain in the examination room or even to hold the child on her lap may reassure a shy child. A further problem arises from the fact that some preschool children are highly distractable and hyperactive. They cannot remain seated and are constantly running about the room, handling materials, performing acrobatics, and inquiring about a variety of unrelated and irrelevant matters. The very talkative child of this age may try to take over the examination himself.

The negativism often exhibited by children of this age level has been extensively discussed in the literature of child psychology. In the test situation, this behavior may take the form of flat refusals to perform, complete silence and general unresponsiveness, failure to follow directions in the use of test materials, or screaming and temper tantrums. In all but the most resistant cases, the examiner may elicit the cooperation of such a negativistic child by a number of subterfuges and indirect appeals to his interests, or by a brief delay (17, 37). Sometimes the testing session must be postponed because of extreme manifestations of any of the three types of behavior described.

With regard to *standardization procedures,* preschool tests have more in common with school-age tests than with infant tests. Norms have usually been obtained by a cross-sectional rather than a longitudinal approach. Two important exceptions, however, are the Gesell and the Cattell scales, which obtained longitudinal norms for the preschool as well as for the infant levels. Normative samples are, in general, larger than those used in the infant tests, and are more often chosen so as to be representative of a well-defined population. Parallel forms appear for the first time. Contemporary criteria are more often employed for validation purposes, although the interest in prediction of subsequent status persists.

Some of the *follow-up studies* conducted with reference to preschool tests have fairly broad implications, which extend beyond the specific tests employed. In the investigation by Bradway (7) cited in Chapter 8, 138 subjects who had been tested between the ages of 2 and 5½ years during the standardization of the Stanford-Binet Scale were retested with Form L 10 years later, when they were from 12 to 15½ years old. The data were analyzed separately for those children whose age at initial test was between 2 and

3½ ($N = 52$) and those whose age was between 4 and 5½ years ($N = 86$). In the younger group, correlations between initial IQ and 10-year retest were .58 and .67 for initial Forms L and M, respectively. In the older group, the corresponding correlations were .67 and .63. An analysis of individual Stanford-Binet items showed that verbal and memory items had higher predictive validity against the 10-year criterion than did non-verbal items (8). The correlation of preschool IQ's with a 25-year retest, at a mean age of 29 years, was .59 (9).

Although these correlations are too low to permit accurate predictions in individual cases, they show a substantial stability of test performance over periods of 10 and even 25 years. When the same, well-constructed instrument is employed in initial test and retest, the predictive value of IQ's obtained by 2- or 3-year-old children appears to be much higher than was previously supposed. It should also be borne in mind that these correlations are based on a single initial test for each individual. Gesell and others have repeatedly pointed out that better prediction of subsequent status can be made on the basis of repeated preschool tests. Such retests provide a more reliable estimate and also permit the observation of developmental trends.

The previously cited follow-up study by Maurer (33) with the Minnesota Preschool Scale represents an effort to increase the predictive value of preschool tests by item selection. Biserial correlations were found between each item on the Minnesota Preschool Scale and Alpha scores obtained by the same subjects as adults. Despite the crudeness of the criterion measure and the small number of cases available for the computation of individual item-criterion correlations, certain suggestive findings emerged from this study.

A comparison of the items retained with those discarded on the basis of predictive value reveals differences that also appear reasonable on other grounds. Thus the least-predictive items included several that were unduly influenced by motor coordination. It will be recalled that in infant tests, too, such items were found to be least satisfactory for measuring intellectual development. Similarly, tests lacking sufficient interest for young children, as well as those employing confusing or complicated directions, often fell into the non-predictive category. Items of this sort would usually be judged faulty for any testing purpose. Another group of items with low predictive value depended largely upon rote memory for information that the child might or might not have acquired during his prior experience. Examples of these items include naming objects or parts of pictures, and pointing to body parts or to objects named by the examiner. In such tasks, too many fortuitous circumstances may have influenced the child's knowledge of the names.

Among the most predictive tests in Maurer's investigation were those emphasizing perception of spatial relations, controlled attention, memory, and logical relations. Specific examples include incomplete pictures, mutilated pictures, block-building, discrimination of colors and forms, cut-out picture puzzles, Knox cube, definitions, word opposites, detection of verbal absurdities, and vocabulary. Once more, verbal tests and those involving abstract concepts and relations proved to be effective predictors of later intelligence.

That the functions measured by available intelligence tests change systematically from infancy to school age was demonstrated in a factorial analysis of the IQ's obtained in the Berkeley Growth Study (28). The basic data for this analysis were the intercorrelations among IQ's obtained by the same children on successive retests between the ages of 1 month and 18 years. During the first year, the children were examined monthly with the California First-Year Mental Scale; later retests at increasingly longer intervals employed other appropriate tests, such as the Stanford-Binet and the Terman-McNemar Group Test. Factorial analysis of the intercorrelations revealed three factors. The first, identified as sensorimotor alertness, was prominent during the first two years of life. The second factor reached its peak between the ages of 2 and 4, its weight being negative in early IQ's and dropping gradually to zero in later childhood. This factor was tentatively described as persistence, or a tendency to act in accordance with an established set, as opposed to responsiveness to momentary stimulation. It was suggested that this factor may also underlie the stubbornness and negativism often exhibited by children at these ages. The third factor, characterized as abstraction and the manipulation of symbols, begins to emerge at about 2 years of age and becomes the principal factor in the IQ from age 4 on.

A final word may be added regarding the construction of both preschool and infant tests. In one respect, such tests present the same problem as that encountered in cross-cultural testing. Unlike the school child, the infant and preschool child have not been exposed to the standardized series of experiences represented by the school curriculum. In developing tests for school-age children or for adults who have completed a prescribed amount of schooling, the test constructor has a large fund of common experiential material from which he can draw test items. Prior to school entrance, on the other hand, the individual's experiences are far less standardized, despite certain broad cultural uniformities in child-rearing practices. Under these conditions, the development of satisfactory tests is much more difficult.

REFERENCES

1. Anastasi, Anne. *Differential psychology.* (3rd ed.) N. Y.: Macmillan, 1958.
2. Anderson, J. E. The prediction of terminal intelligence from infant and pre-school tests. *39th Yearb., nat. Soc. Stud. Educ.,* 1940, Part I, 385-403.
3. Anderson, L. D. The predictive value of infancy tests in relation to intelligence at five years. *Child Develpm.,* 1939, 10, 203-212.
4. Bayley, Nancy. The California First-Year Mental Scale. *Univer. Calif. Syllabus Series,* 1933, No. 243.
5. Bayley, Nancy. Mental growth during the first three years. *Genet. Psychol. Monogr.,* 1933, 14, 1-93.
6. Bayley, Nancy. On the growth of intelligence. *Amer. Psychologist,* 1955, 10, 805-818.
7. Bradway, Katherine P. IQ constancy on the Revised Stanford-Binet from the preschool to the junior high school level. *J. genet. Psychol.,* 1944, 65, 197-217.
8. Bradway, Katherine P. Predictive value of Stanford-Binet preschool items. *J. educ. Psychol.,* 1945, 36, 1-16.
9. Bradway, Katherine P., Thompson, Clare W., and Cravens, R. B. Preschool IQ's after twenty-five years. *J. educ. Psychol.,* 1958, 49, 278-281.
10. Brodbeck, A., and Irwin, O. C. The speech behavior of infants without families. *Child Develpm.,* 1946, 17, 145-156.
11. Catalano, F. L., and McCarthy, Dorothea. Infant speech as a possible predictor of later intelligence. *J. Psychol.,* 1954, 38, 203-209.
12. Cattell, Psyche. *The measurement of intelligence of infants and young children.* N. Y.: Psychol. Corp., 1947.
13. Cavanaugh, Maxine C., Cohen, I., Dunphy, D., Ringwell, E. A., and Goldberg, I. D. Prediction from Cattell Infant Intelligence Scale. *J. consult. Psychol.,* 1957, 21, 33-37.
14. Doll, E. A. (Ed.) *The Oseretsky Tests of Motor Proficiency.* Minneapolis: Educ. Test Bur., 1946.
15. Doll, E. A. *Vineland Social Maturity Scale: manual of directions.* Minneapolis: Educ. Test Bur., 1947.
16. Doll, E. A. *The measurement of social competence.* Minneapolis: Educ. Test Bur., 1953.
17. Dwyer, R. M. A note on resistance and rapport in psychological tests for young children. *J. genet. Psychol.,* 1937, 51, 451-454.
18. Fisichelli, Regina M. A study of the pre-linguistic speech development of institutionalized infants. Unpublished doctoral dissertation, Fordham University, 1950.
19. Gesell, A., *et al. The first five years of life.* N. Y.: Harper, 1940.
20. Gesell, A., *et al. Gesell Developmental Schedules.* N. Y.: Psychol. Corp., 1949.
21. Gesell, A., and Amatruda, Catherine S. *Developmental diagnosis.* (2nd ed.) N. Y.: Hoeber, 1947.
22. Gesell, A., Thompson, Helen, and Amatruda, Catherine S. *The psychology of early growth.* N. Y.: Macmillan, 1938.

23. Gilliland, A. R. The measurement of the mentality of infants. *Child Developm.*, 1948, 19, 155-158.
24. Goodenough, Florence L., and Maurer, Katharine M. *The mental growth of children from two to fourteen years: a study of the predictive value of the Minnesota Preschool Scales.* Minneapolis: Univer. Minn. Press, 1942.
25. Goodenough, Florence L., Maurer, Katharine M., and Van Wagenen, M. J. *Minnesota Preschool Scales.* Minneapolis: Educ. Test Bur., 1932-1940.
26. Griffiths, Ruth. *The Griffiths Mental Development Scale for Testing Babies from Birth to Two Years.* London: Author, 1951-1955.
27. Griffiths, Ruth. *The abilities of babies: a study in mental measurement.* N. Y.: McGraw-Hill, 1954.
28. Hofstaetter, P. R. The changing composition of "intelligence": a study in *T* technique. *J. genet. Psychol.*, 1954, 85, 159-164.
29. Irwin, O. C., and Chen, H. Speech sound elements during the first year of life; a review of the literature. *J. Speech Disord.*, 1943, 8, 109-121.
30. Kuhlmann, F. *A handbook of mental tests.* Baltimore: Warwick & York, 1922.
31. Kuhlmann, F. *Tests of mental development.* Minneapolis: Educ. Test Bur., 1939.
32. McCarthy, Dorothea A. Measurement of cognitive abilities at the preschool and early childhood level. *Proc. 1958 invit. Conf., Educ. Test. Serv.*, 1959, 10-25.
33. Maurer, Katharine M. *Intellectual status at maturity as a criterion for selecting items in preschool tests.* Minneapolis: Univer. Minn. Press, 1946.
34. Maxfield, Kathryn B., and Buchholz, Sandra. *A social maturity scale for blind preschool children: a guide to its use.* N. Y.: Amer. Found. Blind, 1957.
35. Sloan, W. The Lincoln-Oseretsky Motor Development Scale. *Genet. Psychol. Monogr.*, 1955, 51, 183-252. (Test distributed by C. H. Stoelting Co.)
36. Stutsman, Rachel. *Mental measurement of preschool children.* Tarrytown-on-Hudson, N. Y.: World Book Co., 1931. (Test distributed by C. H. Stoelting Co.)
37. Symmes, E. F. Some techniques in securing rapport with preschool children. *Amer. J. Orthopsychiat.*, 1933, 3, 181-190.
38. Valentine, C. W. *Intelligence Tests for Children.* London: Methuen, 1945-1958.
39. Wakelam, B. B. The application of a new intelligence test in an infant school and the prediction of backwardness. *Brit. J. educ. Psychol.*, 1944, 14, 142-150.
40. Watson, R. I. *The clinical method in psychology.* N. Y.: Harper, 1951.
41. Wellman, Beth L. The intelligence of preschool children as measured by the Merrill-Palmer Scale of Performance Tests. *Univer. Iowa Stud. Child Welf.*, 1938, 15, No. 3.

CHAPTER 12

The Wechsler Scales and
Other Clinical Instruments

This chapter is concerned with two intelligence scales prepared by David Wechsler, one for adults and one for children. Although administered as individual tests and designed for many of the same uses as the Stanford-Binet, these scales differ in several important ways from the earlier test. Both are point scales rather than age scales. All items of a given type are grouped into subtests and arranged in increasing order of difficulty within each subtest. In this respect the Wechsler scales follow the pattern established for group tests. Another characteristic feature of these scales is the inclusion of verbal and performance subtests, from which separate verbal and performance IQ's are computed.

Besides their use as measures of general intelligence, the Wechsler scales have been investigated as a possible aid in psychiatric diagnosis. Beginning with the observation that brain damage, psychotic deterioration, and emotional difficulties may affect some intellectual functions more than others, Wechsler and other clinical psychologists argued that an analysis of the individual's relative performance on different subtests should reveal specific psychiatric disorders. The problems and results pertaining to such a profile or scatter analysis of the Wechsler scales will be considered in a separate section. In the final section of this chapter, other types of tests designed to detect intellectual impairment will be briefly examined.

MEASUREMENT OF ADULT INTELLIGENCE

The first form of the Wechsler scales, known as the Wechsler-Bellevue Intelligence Scale, was published in 1939. One of the primary objectives in its preparation was to provide an intelligence test suitable for adults. In first presenting this scale, Wechsler (70) pointed out that previously available intelligence tests had been designed primarily for school children and had been adapted for adult use by adding more difficult items of the same kinds. The content of such tests was often of little interest to adults. Unless the test items have a certain minimum of face validity, rapport cannot be properly established with adult subjects. Many intelligence test items, written with special reference to the daily activities of the school child, clearly lack face validity for most adults. As Wechsler expressed it, "Asking the ordinary housewife to furnish you with a rhyme to the words, 'day,' 'cat,' and 'mill,' or an ex-army sergeant to give you a sentence with the words, 'boy,' 'river,' 'ball,' is not particularly apt to evoke either interest or respect" (70, p. 17).

The overemphasis on speed in most tests also tends to handicap the older person. Similarly, Wechsler believed that relatively routine manipulation of words receives undue weight in such tests. He likewise called attention to the inapplicability of mental age norms to adults, and pointed out that few adults had previously been included in the standardization samples for individual intelligence tests. It was to meet these various objections that the original Wechsler-Bellevue was developed.

In form and content, this scale was closely similar to the more recent Wechsler Adult Intelligence Scale (WAIS) which has now supplanted it. A description of the latter, to be given in the next section, thus serves also to characterize the Wechsler-Bellevue. The earlier scale, however, had a number of technical deficiencies which have been largely corrected in the current form. A proper evaluation of the many published studies that used the Wechsler-Bellevue requires some familiarity with its special limitations.

The chief weakness of the Wechsler-Bellevue stemmed from the unrepresentativeness of its normative sample, which was drawn largely from New York City and its environs. The total number of adults of both sexes included in this sample was only 1081. The reliability of some of the subtests was quite low, especially for the proposed profile analysis of subtest scores. Obsolescent items, meager validity data, and inadequacies of the manual were among the other deficiencies of this scale. The Wechsler-Bellevue provided norms down to the age of 10 years, its total standardization sample including 670 children between the ages of 7 and 16. The scale was not well suited for testing children, however, and was soon replaced at these levels by the Wechsler Intelligence Scale for Children (WISC), also to be considered in this chapter.

The amount of interest aroused by the publication of the Wechsler-Bellevue, as well as the extent of its use in clinical testing and in research, can be seen in the bibliography of 625 references listed in the *Fifth Mental Measurements Yearbook* for this test alone, exclusive of publications on the WISC and WAIS. Two special surveys appearing in the *Psychological Bulletin* covered research with the Wechsler-Bellevue published during the years 1945-1950 (55) and 1950-1955 (30).

WECHSLER ADULT INTELLIGENCE SCALE

Description. Published in 1955, the WAIS (73) comprises eleven subtests. Six subtests are grouped into a Verbal Scale and five into a Performance Scale. These subtests are listed and briefly described below, in the order of their administration.

VERBAL SCALE

1. *Information:* 29 questions covering a wide variety of information that adults have presumably had an opportunity to acquire in our culture. An effort was made to avoid specialized or academic knowledge. It might be added that questions of general information have been used for a long time in informal psychiatric examinations to establish the individual's intellectual level and his practical orientation.

2. *Comprehension:* 14 items, in each of which the subject explains what should be done under certain circumstances, why certain practices are followed, the meaning of proverbs, etc. Designed to measure practical judgment and common sense, this test is similar to the Stanford-Binet Comprehension items, but its specific content was chosen so as to be more consonant with the interests and activities of adults.

3. *Arithmetic:* 14 problems similar to those encountered in elementary school arithmetic. Each problem is orally presented and is to be solved without the use of paper and pencil.

4. *Similarities:* 13 items requiring the subject to say in what way two things are alike.

5. *Digit Span:* Orally presented lists of three to nine digits are to be orally reproduced. In the second part, the subject must reproduce lists of two to eight digits backwards.

6. *Vocabulary:* 40 words of increasing difficulty are presented both orally and visually. The subject is asked what each word means.

PERFORMANCE SCALE

7. *Digit Symbol:* This is a version of the familiar code-substitution test which dates back to the early Woodworth-Wells Association Tests and has often

been included in non-language intelligence scales. The key contains 9 symbols paired with the 9 digits. The subject's score is the number of symbols correctly written within 1½ minutes.

8. *Picture Completion:* 21 cards, each containing a picture from which some part is missing. Subject must tell what is missing from each picture.

9. *Block Design:* This test is similar to the previously described Kohs Block Design Test (cf. Ch. 10). In the Wechsler adaptation, however, the blocks have only red, white, and red-and-white sides. Subject reproduces designs of increasing complexity requiring from four to nine cubes.

10. *Picture Arrangement:* Each item consists of a set of cards containing pictures to be rearranged in the proper sequence so as to tell a story. Figure 59

Fig. 59. Demonstration Item from the WAIS Picture Arrangement Test. (Reproduced by permission of The Psychological Corporation.)

shows one set of cards in the order in which they are presented to the subject. This set shows the easiest of 8 items making up the test.

11. *Object Assembly:* Modeled after the Pintner-Paterson Manikin and Feature Profile, this test includes improved versions of both of these objects, together with two additional objects to be assembled.

Both speed and accuracy of performance are taken into account in scoring Arithmetic, Digit Symbol, Block Design, Picture Arrangement, and Object Assembly.

Norms and Scoring Procedures. The WAIS standardization sample was chosen with exceptional care to insure its representativeness. The principal normative sample consisted of 1700 cases, including an equal number of men and women distributed over seven age levels between 16 and 64 years. Subjects were selected so as to match as closely as possible the proportions in the 1950 U.S. census with regard to part of the country, urban-rural residence, race (white versus non-white), occupational level, and education. At each age level, one man and one woman from an institution for mental defectives were also included. Supplementary norms for older persons were established by testing an "old-age sample" of 475 persons, aged 60 years and over, in a typical Midwestern city (18).

Raw scores on each WAIS subtest are transmuted into standard scores with a mean of 10 and an *SD* of 3. These scaled scores were derived from a reference group of 500 cases which included all persons between the ages of 20 and 34 in the standardization sample. All subtest scores are thus expressed in comparable units. Verbal, Performance, and Full Scale scores are found by adding the scaled scores on the six Verbal subtests, the five Performance subtests, and all eleven subtests, respectively. By reference to appropriate tables provided in the manual, these three scores can be expressed as deviation IQ's with a mean of 100 and an *SD* of 15. Such IQ's, however, are found with reference to the individual's own age group. They therefore show the individual's standing in comparison with persons of his own age level.

As can be seen in Figure 60, in the WAIS standardization sample Full Scale scores rise until the late twenties and then decline slowly until 60. A sharper rate of decline was found beyond age 60 in the old-age sample.

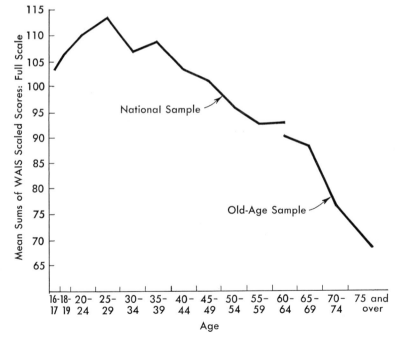

Fig. 60. Decline in WAIS Scaled Scores with Age. (Data from Wechsler, 74, p. 95.)

By deriving IQ's separately for each age level, individuals are thus compared with a declining norm beyond the peak age. The age decrement is greater in Performance than in Verbal scores and also varies from one subtest to another (18). Thus Digit Symbol, with its heavy dependence on speed and visual perception, shows the maximum age decline. In the other Performance subtests, however, speed may not be an important factor in the observed decline. In a special study of this point, subjects in the old-age sample were given these tests under both timed and untimed conditions. Not only were the differences in scores under these two conditions slight, but the decrements from the 60-64 to the 70-74 age group were virtually the same under timed and untimed conditions (74, p. 137).

In this connection it should be noted that in the WAIS standardization sample both the peak scores and the onset of decline occur at older ages than in the Wechsler-Bellevue standardization sample examined some 15 years earlier. These differences could result from a number of factors (74, pp. 140-141). One possible explanation of both the difference between the two standardization samples and the age decrement itself is provided by amount of education received by subjects in different age groups. Because of the rising educational level of the general population, older groups at any one time have received less education on the average than younger groups. Such a difference, of course, is reflected in WAIS and Wechsler-Bellevue standardization samples, and should be if these samples are to be representative of the general U.S. population (1). Moreover, members of the WAIS standardization sample will have received more education on the average than persons of corresponding age in the Wechsler-Bellevue sample, since the latter were educated some 15 years earlier. Examination of educational data on the two samples corroborates all of the above differences.

Also relevant are the findings of a number of longitudinal investigations using other intelligence tests (cf. 2, pp. 242-243). These studies showed that intellectually superior groups that continue their education through college or beyond or engage in relatively intellectual occupations tend to improve in intelligence test performance throughout life, rather than showing a decline. It is likely that with increasing education and other cultural changes the WAIS norms, with their built-in age decrements, may need frequent revision.

Reliability. For each of the eleven subtests, as well as for Verbal, Performance, and Full Scale IQ's, reliability coefficients were computed within the 18-19, 24-34, and 45-54 year samples. These three groups were chosen as being representative of the age range covered by the standardization sample. Odd-even reliability coefficients (corrected for full test length by the Spearman-Brown formula) were employed for every subtest except Digit Span and Digit Symbol. The reliability of Digit Span was estimated from the correlation between Digits Forward and Digits Backward scores. No split-half technique could be utilized with Digit Symbol, which is a highly speeded test. The reliability of this test was therefore determined by parallel-form procedures in a group specially tested with WAIS and Wechsler-Bellevue Digit Symbol subtests.

Full Scale IQ's yielded reliability coefficients of .97 in all three age samples. Verbal IQ's had identical reliabilities of .96 in the three groups, and Performance IQ's had reliabilities of .93 and .94. All three IQ's are thus highly reliable in terms of coefficients of equivalence. As might be expected, the individual subtests yield lower reliabilities, ranging from a few coefficients in the .60's found with Digit Span, Picture Arrangement, and Object Assembly, to coefficients as high as .96 for Vocabulary. It is particularly important to consider these subtest reliabilities when evaluating the significance of differences between subtest scores obtained by the same individual, as in profile analysis. In general, the WAIS subtest reliabilities are higher than those of the Wechsler-Bellevue, since several tests were lengthened and more ceiling was added by the insertion of new items.

The WAIS manual also reports standard errors of measurement for the three IQ's and for subtest scores. For Verbal IQ, such errors were 3 points in each group, for Performance IQ, just under 4 points, and for Full Scale IQ, 2.60. We could thus conclude, for example, that the chances are roughly 2:1 that an individual's true Verbal IQ falls within 3 points of his obtained Verbal IQ. The above values compare favorably with the 5-point error of measurement found for the Stanford-Binet (Ch. 8). It should be remembered, however, that the Stanford-Binet reliabilities were based on parallel forms administered over intervals of one week or less; under such conditions we would anticipate somewhat lower reliability coefficients and greater fluctuation of scores.

Validity. Any discussion of validity of the WAIS must draw upon research done with the earlier Wechsler-Bellevue as well. Because it has been available much longer, the Wechsler-Bellevue has been used in many more investigations than the WAIS. Since all changes introduced in the WAIS represent improvements over the Wechsler-Bellevue (in reliability, ceiling, normative sample, etc.) and since the nature of the test has remained substantially the same, it is reasonable to suppose that validity data obtained on the Wechsler-Bellevue will underestimate rather than overestimate the validity of the WAIS.

The WAIS manual itself contains no validity data, but several aspects of validity are covered in a subsequent book by Wechsler (74). Chapter 5 of that book is devoted to a discussion of the content validity of the Wechsler scales. Wechsler argues that the psychological functions tapped by each of the eleven chosen subtests fit the definition of intelligence, that similar tests have been successfully employed in previously developed intelligence scales, and that such tests have proved their worth in clinical experience. The test author himself places the major emphasis on this approach to validity.

Some empirical data on concurrent validity are summarized by Wechsler in a chapter on the use of the scales in counseling and guidance (74, Ch. 14). These data include mean IQ differences among various educational and occupational groups, as well as a few correlations with job performance ratings and academic grades. Most group differences, though small, are in the expected directions. Persons in white-collar jobs of different kinds and levels averaged higher in Verbal than in Performance IQ, but skilled workers averaged higher in Performance than in Verbal. Verbal IQ correlated in the .30's with over-all performance ratings in studies of industrial executives and psychiatric residents. Both groups, of course, were already selected in terms of the abilities measured by these tests. Correlations in the .40's and .50's were found between Verbal IQ and college or engineering school grades (3; 58; 74, p. 229). In all these groups, the Verbal Scale yielded somewhat higher correlations than the Full Scale; correlations with the Performance Scale were much lower. Even the correlations with the Verbal Scale, however, were not appreciably higher than those obtained with the Stanford-Binet and with well-known group tests.

Of some relevance to the construct validity of the Wechsler scales are the intercorrelations of subtests and of Verbal and Performance IQ's, as well as factorial analyses of the scales. In the process of standardizing the WAIS, intercorrelations of Verbal and Performance Scales and of the eleven subtests were computed on the same three age groups on which reliability coefficients had been found, namely, 18-19, 25-34, and 45-54 (73). Verbal and Performance Scale scores correlated .77, .77, and .81, respectively, in these three groups. Intercorrelations of separate subtests were also very similar in the three age groups, running higher among Verbal than among Performance subtests. Correlations between Verbal and Performance subtests, although still lower on the whole, were substantial. For example, in the 25-34 year group, correlations among Verbal subtests ranged from .40 to .81, among Performance subtests from .44 to .62, and between Performance and Verbal subtests from .30 to .67. Both individual subtest correlations and correlations between total Verbal and Performance Scale scores suggest that the two scales have much in common and that the allocation of tests to one or the other scale may be somewhat arbitrary.

Factorial analyses of the Wechsler scales have been conducted with a variety of subjects ranging from eighth-grade pupils to the old-age standardization sample (aged 60-75 +) and including both normal and abnormal groups. They have also employed different statistical procedures and have approached the analysis from different points of view. Some have been directly concerned with age changes in the factorial organization of the Wechsler subtests, but the findings of different investigators are inconsistent in this regard (6, 14). Surveys of the specific results of this research and references to the original sources may be found in Wechsler (74, Ch. 8), Cohen (14), and Saunders (59). As an example, we may examine the factorial analyses of the WAIS conducted by Cohen (14, 15) with the intercorrelations of subtests obtained on four age groups in the standardization sample (18-19, 25-34, 45-54, and 60-75 +). The major results of this study are in line with those of other investigations using comparable procedures.

That all eleven subtests have much in common was demonstrated in Cohen's study by the presence of a single general factor that accounted for about 50 per cent of the total variance of the battery. In addition, three major group factors were identified. One was a *verbal comprehension* factor, with large weights in the Vocabulary, Information, Comprehension, and Similarities subtests. A *perceptual organization* factor was found chiefly in Block Design and Object Assembly. This factor may actually represent a combination of the perceptual speed and spatial visualization factors repeatedly found in factorial analyses of aptitude tests. The results of an earlier investigation by Davis (16), in which "reference tests" measuring various factors were included with the Wechsler subtests, support this composite interpretation of the perceptual organization factor.

The third major group factor identified by Cohen was described as a *memory* factor. Found principally in Arithmetic and Digit Span, it apparently includes both immediate rote memory for new material and recall of previously learned material. It is suggested that ability to concentrate and to resist distraction may be involved in this factor. Of special interest is the finding that the memory factor increased sharply in prominence in the old-age sample. At that age level it had significant loadings, not only in Arithmetic and Digit Span, but also in Vocabulary, Information, Comprehension, and Digit Symbol. Cohen points out that during senescence memory begins to deteriorate at different ages and rates in different persons. Individual differences in memory thus come to play a more prominent part in intellectual functioning than had been true at earlier ages. Many of the WAIS subtests require memory at all ages. Until differential deterioration sets in, however, individual differences in the retentive ability required in most of the subtests are insignificant.

It should be noted that the results of Cohen's study fail to support the standard practice of grouping tests into Verbal and Performance Scales, each yielding a separate IQ (15). Although the use of a Full Scale IQ is justified by the large general factor content of all subtests, the verbal comprehension factor occurs in only four of the six Verbal Scale subtests. The memory factor is found in the two remaining Verbal subtests, as well as in other subtests from both Scales in the case of older subjects. And the perceptual organization factor has significant loadings in only two of the five Performance Scale subtests. The remaining Performance subtests seem to have largely specific variance, not shared with other subtests in this battery.

Working with normal samples and using item intercorrelations and other procedural variations, Saunders (59, 61, 62, 63) found evidence of at least 10 identifiable factors in WAIS performance. There was not, however, a one-to-one correspondence between these factors and the WAIS subtests. Several subtests proved to be factorially complex, and certain factors cut across more than one subtest. Of particular interest is some suggestive evidence for a deterioration factor common to Wechsler's proposed "Don't Hold" tests, to be discussed later in this chapter (63).

Comparison with Other Tests. The Wechsler scales have been repeatedly correlated with the Stanford-Binet as well as with other well-known tests of intelligence. Several summaries of such correlations have been published (cf. 30; 55; 74, Ch. 7). Correlations with the Stanford-Binet in unselected adolescent or adult groups generally fall in the .80's and .90's. Within more homogeneous samples, such as college students (3, 58), the correlations tend to be considerably lower. Group tests yield somewhat lower correlations with the Wechsler scales, such correlations ranging from about .40 to about .80. For both Stanford-Binet and group scales, correlations are nearly always higher with the Wechsler Verbal Scale than with the Full Scale, while correlations with the Performance Scale are much lower than either.

On the other hand, Performance IQ's correlate more highly than Verbal IQ's with tests of spatial abilities. For example, a correlation of .72 was found between Performance IQ and the Minnesota Paper Form Board Test in a group of 16-year-old boys and girls (36). In other studies, Performance IQ's correlated .70 with Raven's Progressive Matrices (31) and .35 with the Bennett Mechanical Comprehension Test (74, p. 228).

The relative size of IQ's obtained on the Wechsler scales and on other intelligence tests should also be taken into account in interpreting such IQ's.

It has been repeatedly found that brighter subjects tend to score higher on the Stanford-Binet than on the Wechsler scales, while duller subjects score higher on the Wechsler than on the Stanford-Binet. For example, college freshmen obtained significantly higher mean IQ's on the Stanford-Binet than on the Wechsler Full Scale (3, 58). The same relationship holds if comparisons are made between Stanford-Binet and either Verbal or Performance IQ's. Mental defectives, on the other hand, receive higher IQ's on the Wechsler. Within any group, as the IQ's diverge from 100 in either direction, the differences between the two scales become more pronounced (11, 41, 50). As the extremes of the range are approached, IQ's on the two scales may differ by as much as 20 points (11). Although these discrepancies are smaller on the WAIS than on the earlier Wechsler-Bellevue, significant IQ differences still remain (47).

To some extent, the difference in standard deviation of Wechsler and Stanford-Binet IQ's may account for the differences between the IQ's obtained with the two scales. It will be recalled that the *SD* of the Stanford-Binet IQ is 16 (actually fluctuating around this value in the 1937 form), while that of the Wechsler IQ is 15. The discrepancies in individual IQ's, however, are larger than would be expected on the basis of such a difference. Another difference between the two scales is that the Wechsler has less floor and ceiling than the Stanford-Binet and hence does not discriminate as well at the extremes of the IQ range.

The relationship between Stanford-Binet and Wechsler IQ's depends not only upon IQ level, but also upon age. Other things being equal, older subjects tend to obtain higher IQ's on the Wechsler than on the Stanford-Binet, while the reverse is true of younger subjects. One explanation for such a trend is obviously provided by the use of a declining standard in the computation of the Wechsler IQ's of older persons. On the Stanford-Binet, on the other hand, all adults are evaluated in terms of the average peak age on that scale, viz., 18 years (16 years on the earlier form). It is also possible that, since the Stanford-Binet was standardized primarily on children and the Wechsler on adults, the content of the former tends to favor children while that of the latter favors older persons. It will be recalled that in the construction of the original Wechsler-Bellevue a special effort was made to choose material appropriate for adults.

Abbreviated Scales. Since the publication of the original Wechsler-Bellevue scale, a large number of abbreviated scales have been proposed. These scales are formed simply by omitting some of the subtests and prorating scores to obtain a Full Scale IQ comparable to the published norms. The fact that several subtest combinations, while effecting considerable saving in time, correlate over .90 with Full Scale IQ's has encouraged the development and use of abbreviated scales for rapid screening purposes. It is possible that the most effective combination of subtests varies for different intellectual levels or other special populations (55).

Applying a formula developed by McNemar (45) to the intercorrelations of subtests found for the 25-34 year group of the WAIS standardization sample, Maxwell (49) computed the correlations of every possible combination of two, three, four, and five subtests with Full Scale IQ. On this basis, she chose the ten best combinations for each of these battery sizes. It is noteworthy that the variations in the correlations with Full Scale IQ among the reported combinations are slight, all given combinations yielding correlations of .90 or higher. The best two-test combination consists of Vocabulary and Block Design. For three tests, the best combination includes Information, Vocabulary, and Block Design; for four tests, Information, Vocabulary, Block Design, and Picture Arrangement; and for five tests, Information, Similarities, Vocabulary, Block Design, and Picture Arrangement. Other combinations were as good or nearly as good as these. In a comparative analysis of a single four-test combination (one of Maxwell's best ten for this size of battery), Doppelt (17) found correlations of .95 to .97 with Full Scale IQ's at different age levels from 18-19 to 75 and over.

Although an excessive amount of energy seems to have been expended in assembling and checking short forms of the Wechsler scales, it is probably inadvisable to use such abbreviated versions except as rough screening devices. Many of the qualitative observations made possible by the administration of an individual scale are lost in the abbreviated scales. Moreover, the assumption that the original Full Scale norms are applicable to prorated total scores on short scales may not always be justified.

General Evaluation. The WAIS is unquestionably an improvement over its predecessor, the Wechsler-Bellevue. The care with which a representative nationwide normative sample was assembled is a particularly noteworthy feature of the WAIS standardization. The increase in length and difficulty range of subtests has raised reliabilities, although some subtest reliabilities are still too low for the type of intertest analyses often attempted with this scale. The availability of well-established norms for adults of different ages represents a special contribution of the WAIS. In view of the rapidly improving educational and cultural level of the population, however, such norms need frequent rechecking, especially with reference to the expected age decrement. WAIS IQ's vary systematically from Stanford-Binet IQ's, such differences being associated with both intellectual level and age of subjects. These differences need to be considered in interpreting IQ's on the two tests.

More empirical data on WAIS validity would be desirable. It might be noted that nearly all validity data have so far been gathered somewhat incidentally by investigators not directly concerned with the development or distribution of this scale. More systematic investigation of validity would strengthen the interpretation of test scores. Factorial analyses support the use of Full Scale IQ's, because of the large general factor in the test scores. But the standard subdivision into Verbal and Performance IQ's is not well substantiated by the results of such research. Abbreviated scales, though plentiful and correlating highly with Full Scale IQ's, should be used sparingly because they sacrifice much of the qualitative information that an individual clinical instrument should provide.

WECHSLER INTELLIGENCE SCALE FOR CHILDREN

Description. The Wechsler Intelligence Scale for Children (WISC) was prepared as a downward extension of the Wechsler-Bellevue (65, 71). Many items were taken from the Wechsler-Bellevue, easier items of the same types being added to each test. The WISC consists of twelve subtests, of which two are to be used either as alternates or as supplementary tests if time permits. As in the other Wechsler scales, the subtests are grouped into a Verbal and a Performance Scale, as follows:

VERBAL SCALE	PERFORMANCE SCALE
1. General Information	6. Picture Completion
2. General Comprehension	7. Picture Arrangement
3. Arithmetic	8. Block Design
4. Similarities	9. Object Assembly
5. Vocabulary	10. Coding (or Mazes)
(Digit Span)	

The tests listed as alternates were those giving the lowest correlations with the rest of the scale. In the Verbal Scale, Digit Span proved to be the least satisfactory test and was therefore designated as alternate. In the Performance Scale, either Coding or Mazes may be omitted, the decision being left to the examiner. Coding requires less time than Mazes, however, and may be generally preferred for this reason. The Coding Test corresponds to the Digit Symbol Test of the adult scale, with an easier part added. The only subtest that does not appear in the adult scale is the Mazes. This test consists of eight paper-and-pencil mazes of increasing difficulty, performance being scored in terms of both time and errors. If all twelve tests are administered, the total scores must be prorated before the IQ is computed. Figure 61 shows a child working on one of the easier items of the Object Assembly Test.

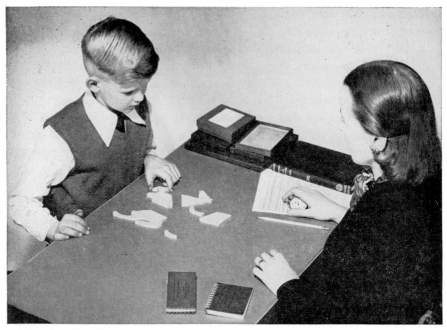

Fig. 61. The Object Assembly Test of the Wechsler Intelligence Scale for Children. (Courtesy The Psychological Corporation.)

Norms and Scoring Procedures. The treatment of scores on the WISC follows the procedures used in the adult scale, with minor differences. Raw scores on each subtest are first transmuted into normalized standard scores within the subject's own age group. Tables of such scaled scores are provided for every 4-month interval between the ages of 5 and 15 years. As in the adult scales, the subtest scaled scores are expressed in terms of a distribution with a mean of 10 and an *SD* of 3 points. The scaled subtest scores are added and converted into a deviation IQ with a mean of 100 and an *SD* of 15. Verbal, Performance, and Full Scale IQ's can be found by the same method. Wechsler (72) subsequently described methods for finding mental age equivalents of WISC scores. Although not required for the computation of IQ's, such MA's were provided to meet legal and other practical needs.

The standardization sample for the WISC included 100 boys and 100 girls at each age from 5 through 15 years, giving a total of 2200 cases. Each child was tested within 1½ months of his midyear. For example, the 5-year-olds ranged in age from 5-years-4-months-15-days to 5-years-7-months-15-days. Only white children were included. All subjects were obtained in schools, with the exception of 55 mental defectives, who were tested in institutions for the feebleminded. Testing was carried out in 85 communities located in 11 states, as well as in 3 institutions for mental defectives. The distribution of subjects conformed closely to the 1940 U.S. census for the country at large, in terms of geographical area, urban-rural proportion, and parental occupation. In many respects, the WISC standardization sample is more representative of the country at large than any other sample employed in standardizing individual tests.

Reliability. Split-half reliability coefficients are reported for each subtest of the WISC, as well as for Verbal, Performance, and Full Scale scores. These reliabilities were computed separately within the 7½-, 10½-, and 13½-year samples, each age group consisting of 200 cases. Since the odd-even technique was inapplicable to Coding and Digit Span, scores on two parts of these tests were correlated. Owing to the lack of complete comparability of the two parts, however, the coefficients obtained for these two tests probably underestimate their reliabilities. The Full Scale reliability coefficients for the three age levels were .92, .95, and .94, respectively. The corresponding reliabilities for the Verbal Scale were .88, .96, and .96; for the Performance Scale, they were .86, .89, and .90. Thus both the Full Scale and the Verbal and Performance IQ's appear to be sufficiently reliable for most testing purposes.

A different picture is presented by the subtest reliabilities. A few of these coefficients are in the .50's. Most are evenly distributed in the .60's, .70's, and .80's. Only one test, Vocabulary, yielded any coefficients in the .90's; and even this test had a reliability of only .77 in the 7½-year group. It might be added that most of the subtests had lower reliability coefficients in the youngest age group than in the other two groups. The test manual rightly cautions the users of this scale against interpreting differences between subtest scores without due reference to the reliability coefficients of the particular subtests.

A four-year follow-up indicated that WISC IQ's are about as stable as Stanford-Binet IQ's over such an interval (25). When 60 fifth-grade pupils were retested in the ninth grade, their Stanford-Binet IQ's correlated .78. On the WISC, the Full Scale, Verbal, and Performance IQ's correlated .77, .77, and .74, respectively.

Validity. No discussion of validity is included in the WISC manual. To be sure, the normative tables of standard score equivalents for each subtest provide evidence of age differentiation, but no evaluation of the data in terms of this criterion is given. It is also relevant to observe that, of the 55 institutionalized mental defectives tested in the standardization sample, only 4 obtained Full Scale IQ's above 70, the mean IQ of this group being 57 (65, p. 109). A few independent investigators have found fairly high concurrent validity coefficients between WISC scores and achievement tests or other academic criteria of intelligence (cf. 43). As would be expected, the Verbal Scale tended to correlate higher than the Performance Scale with such criteria.

The WISC manual reports intercorrelations among the individual subtests, as well as the correlation of each subtest with Verbal, Performance, and Full Scale scores, and of these three composite scores with each other. All correlations are given separately for the 200 cases at each of three age levels in the standardization sample, viz., 7½, 10½, and 13½ years. The correlations between total Verbal and Performance scores were .60, .68, and .56, respectively, in these three age groups. Thus the two parts of the scale have much in common, although the correlations between them are low enough to justify the retention of both parts.

An analysis of occupational differences in Verbal, Performance, and Full Scale IQ is also of interest in this connection (64, 65). When the children in the standardization sample were classified into eight categories in terms of father's occupation, the usual hierarchy of mean IQ's was obtained. In Table

TABLE 18. Mean IQ's on the Wechsler Intelligence Scale for Children in Relation to Paternal Occupation
(Adapted from Seashore, Wesman, and Doppelt, 65, pp. 107-109)

Occupational Category	Mean IQ		
	Verbal	Performance	Full Scale
Professional and semiprofessional workers	110.9	107.8	110.3
Proprietors, managers, and officials	105.9	105.3	106.2
Clerical, sales, and kindred workers	105.2	104.3	105.2
Craftsmen, foremen, and kindred workers	100.8	101.6	101.3
Operatives and kindred workers	98.9	99.5	99.1
Domestic, protective, and other service workers	97.6	96.9	97.0
Farmers and farm managers	96.8	98.6	97.4
Farm laborers and foremen, laborers	94.6	94.9	94.2

18 will be found the mean IQ of each occupational group on the Verbal, Performance, and Full Scales. It will be noted that a difference of 16 points was found between the means of the extreme groups in both Verbal and Full Scale IQ's, and a difference of 13 points between mean Performance IQ's. As in all such comparisons, however, the overlapping of distributions for different occupational categories was very large. Individual cases in the lowest category who excel individual cases in the highest category can easily be found. There is also some evidence indicating that these class differences decline with age, possibly because of exposure to relatively uniform schooling (19, 20).

Attention is also called to the relatively poor performance of the predominantly rural groups. This finding was supported by a separate analysis of scores with reference to urban and rural residence, and reflects the almost universal result obtained with intelligence tests standardized on a predominantly urban sampling.[1] It should likewise be noted that both urban-rural and occupational differences tend to be somewhat smaller on the Performance than on the Verbal Scale. This, too, is a typical finding.

An analysis of the discrepancies between Verbal and Performance scores for each individual throws further light upon these group comparisons (64). For the entire standardization sample, the mean difference between Verbal and Performance IQ was, of course, zero. This follows from the procedure employed in computing deviation IQ's on the WISC. Each age group likewise yielded mean Verbal-Performance differences of practically zero. About half of the individual cases showed Verbal-Performance discrepancies of 8 points or more. In a breakdown with reference to occupational categories, all group differences were small and statistically insignificant, with one exception. The professional and semiprofessional category contains a significantly greater proportion of children with higher Verbal than Performance IQ's. In this group, 62 per cent had a positive V-P difference, 35 per cent a negative difference, and 3 per cent had identical IQ's on both scales. In all other categories, the proportions of positive and negative discrepancies were approximately equal. The differences that did occur, however, were in the expected direction, viz., a greater tendency for rural children and children from lower socioeconomic levels to obtain higher scores on the Performance than on the Verbal Scale.

Comparison with Other Tests. Comparisons of WISC and Stanford-Binet IQ's have yielded results very similar to those obtained with the adult scales. Such comparisons have utilized a variety of groups, including both preschool and school-age children and ranging from mental defectives to gifted children (24, 33, 40, 43, 51, 54, 68). Correlations between WISC and Stanford-Binet range from the .60's to the .90's, varying with the age, intellectual level, and heterogeneity of the samples. The Verbal Scale again correlates more highly with the Stanford-Binet than does the Performance Scale. With such a test as the Arthur Performance Scale, on the other hand, the reverse is true, the WISC Performance IQ yielding a higher correlation than the WISC Verbal IQ (54). As in the adult scales, normal and superior children tend to score higher on Stanford-Binet than on WISC. The discrepancy in favor of the Binet is greater for brighter and younger subjects.

---

[1] For a further discussion of typical findings and of their implications for test construction, cf. Anastasi (2, pp. 525-533).

For the mentally retarded, the WISC yields a significantly higher mean IQ than the Binet.

General Evaluation. On the whole, the WISC compares favorably with the more recently developed WAIS in the quality of its test-construction procedures. The size and representativeness of its normative sample and the careful procedures followed in determining reliability set a particularly high standard in test development. The dearth of validity data remains its principal weakness. More attention should also be given to the consistent discrepancies between WISC and Stanford-Binet IQ's at different ages and intellectual levels. Finally, there seems to be something of a paradox in the underlying rationale of the WISC. It will be recalled that a major reason for the development of the original Wechsler-Bellevue was the need for an adult intelligence test that would not be a mere upward extension of available children's scales. Having presumably achieved this objective, the author then proceeded to prepare a children's scale that was simply a downward extension of the adult scale. Is this a case of "Heads I win and Tails you lose"?

PROFILE ANALYSIS WITH THE WECHSLER SCALES

In addition to their use as general intelligence tests, the Wechsler scales have been widely investigated as instruments for diagnosing intellectual impairment or deterioration resulting from brain damage, psychotic disorders, or other pathological conditions. In this connection, a distinction must be made between mental deficiency, on the one hand, and mental deterioration, on the other. In the former condition, the subject never attains a normal level of intellectual functioning; while in the latter, he declines from a formerly higher level.

Ideally, deterioration or intellectual impairment should be determined by longitudinal techniques that permit a direct comparison of the subject's test performance before and after the onset of his psychological disorder. Since prior tests are not usually available on clinic patients, however, other approaches have been explored. Most current procedures are based upon the expectation that intellectual deterioration occurs in varying amounts in different intellectual functions. Thus some functions are believed to remain relatively unaffected by psychotic and other disturbances. Others are considered to be much more "sensitive" to such pathological conditions. Similarly, it is expected that neurotic anxiety and other emotional disturbances will interfere with performance on certain types of tests, which require careful observation and concentration, while leaving performance on other tests unimpaired.

Techniques of Profile Analysis. Wechsler first discussed the diagnostic use of his scales in the second edition of the Wechsler-Bellevue manual, published in 1941. The 1958 edition of this book, dealing with the WAIS (74), contains a revised and expanded treatment of such a diagnostic use of the scales. Another similar system for clinical interpretation of Wechsler scores was proposed by Rapaport (56). Still other clinicians have recommended other techniques and modifications (cf. 30, 55). All these techniques are based essentially on the individual's relative performance on different subtests. The fact that raw scores on all Wechsler subtests are transmuted into standard scores permits direct comparisons among them and has undoubtedly encouraged the development of an overabundance of diagnostic indices. Specifically, these indices utilize any one of three procedures: measuring amount of scatter, analyzing score patterns, and computing a deterioration index.

Scatter is simply the extent of variation among the individual's scores on the eleven subtests. Wechsler (74, p. 162) proposes that it be measured by finding the average deviation (AD) of the eleven scores around the subject's own mean. The underlying rationale of scatter indices implies that the AD should be larger in pathological than in normal cases. Wechsler illustrates this hypothesis with data on small matched groups of schizophrenics and normals, the former showing significantly greater AD's.

Both Wechsler (74, Ch. 11) and Rapaport (56) have described what they consider characteristic *score patterns* for various clinical syndromes. Wechsler provides such patterns for organic brain disorders, schizophrenia, anxiety states, juvenile delinquency, and mental deficiency. Each pattern is expressed in terms of the position of each subtest with reference to the individual's mean on all eleven subtests. These patterns are supplemented with a number of special diagnostic signs associated with each syndrome. For example, some of the characteristic signs of schizophrenia (74, p. 171) listed by Wechsler are:

Sum of Picture Arrangement plus Comprehension less than Information and Block Design

Object Assembly much below Block Design

Very low Similarities with high Vocabulary and Information

Obviously, a question that must be answered prior to the application of such a system of score patterns and diagnostic signs pertains to the minimum score difference required for statistical significance. With the reliability coefficients obtained in the standardization sample, it is possible to compute for every pair of WAIS subtests the smallest difference that would be significant at any desired probability level. A table giving these differences at the 15 per cent level is reproduced by Wechsler (74, p. 164). The minimum values found in this table for different test pairs vary from 2 to 4 scaled score points, most comparisons requiring 3 points for a significant difference. It should be noted, however, that this level of significance permits a much greater probability of error (15 per cent) than the customary 5 per cent or 1 per cent levels.

Another type of intertest comparison proposed by Wechsler requires the computation of a *deterioration index* (74, Ch. 12). This index was suggested by the observation that in the standardization sample the amount of age decrement varied with the subtest. Tests requiring the utilization of past learning showed less decline than those involving speed, new learning, and the perception of new relations in verbal or spatial content. On the basis of such findings, Wechsler selected a set of "Hold" tests exhibiting little or no age decline and a set of "Don't Hold" tests manifesting relatively steep decline. These tests are listed below:

"HOLD" TESTS	"DON'T HOLD" TESTS
Vocabulary	Digit Span
Information	Similarities
Object Assembly	Digit Symbol
Picture Completion	Block Design

The deterioration index is found by subtracting the sum of the scaled scores on the four Don't Hold tests from the sum of the scaled scores on the four Hold tests, and dividing this difference by the sum of the Hold tests, as shown below:

$$DI = \frac{\text{Hold} - \text{Don't Hold}}{\text{Hold}}$$

Wechsler maintains that at any age individuals with mental disorders show the same differential loss on WAIS subtests found in the general population with advancing age. To allow for normal age decline, the scaled scores used in computing the deterioration index are found by reference to special normative tables for each age level. Hence the individual's relative performance on each subtest is compared with that of his age peers.

Critical Evaluation of Profile Analysis. The diagnostic interpretation of Wechsler profiles by any of the above procedures has been widely criticized from a number of angles (30, 44, 46, 55). The reliabilities of subtests, although higher in the WAIS than in the earlier Wechsler-Bellevue, are still not high enough to permit confident interpretation of any but the largest differences. For instance, to be significant at the .01 level, the difference between Arithmetic and Comprehension must be at least 5 points (46). A related question concerns the frequency with which intertest differences of this magnitude occur in the normal population. Such frequencies can readily be determined for the standardization sample on the basis of the intercorrelations of subtests. Thus McNemar (46) has shown that in the above Arithmetic-Comprehension comparison, 10 per cent of the standardization sample yielded differences of 5 points or more. If we substitute the .15 level of significance proposed by Wechsler for the .01 level, the percentage of differences above the minimum value in the normal population would be far greater.

If the Wechsler scales were to be used as a differential aptitude battery with normal subjects—to compare the individual's relative standing in different abilities—the subtests should have high reliabilities and very low intercorrelations. On the other hand, the rationale underlying the proposed diagnostic interpretations of profile irregularities requires high reliabilities and *high* subtest intercorrelations *in the normal population*. In an abnormal sample, of course, the subtests should have high reliabilities and lower intertest correlations because of the hypothesized increase in scatter of scores.

That the differences regarded as diagnostic by Wechsler do in fact occur frequently in the normal population has been further noted by Jones (37), in reference to a statement in the WAIS manual (73, p. 18). There the number of intertest differences exceeding 3 points and those exceeding 5 points in the normal population is estimated from the results obtained in the standardization sample. As Jones points out, however, the eleven subtests in any one individual's record yield 55 possible intertest comparisons. Hence a difference expected in, let us say, 10 per cent of the cases in any one intertest comparison will actually occur about 5 times in a single individual's record (10 per cent of $55 = 5.5$). Rather than occurring in only 10 per cent of normal persons, therefore, differences of such magnitude would be found, on the average, 5 times in *every* normal person's record.

In individual cases, scatter greater than that found in the normative sample may result, not from pathological conditions, but from differences in educational, occupational, cultural, or other background factors. Language handicap may account for lower Verbal than Performance scores. It will be recalled that skilled laborers tend to score higher on Performance than on Verbal Scales, unlike white-collar groups. Socioeconomic and urban-rural differences in subtest profile have likewise been noted. On the other hand, administration of WISC and WAIS to Jewish subjects from the preschool to the college level revealed a significant tendency for Verbal to exceed Performance IQ (42). This difference, which increased with age, was attributed to the cumulative effect of Jewish cultural values emphasizing verbal abilities. To be sure, Wechsler calls attention to the need for considering background factors in scatter analysis (74, p. 160). But in the zeal to apply diagnostic signs and indices, such precautions are easily forgotten.

The assumption that those subtests showing most normal age decrement are most sensitive to pathological deterioration, which underlies the computation of a deterioration index, is also questionable. The fact that the older subjects in the standardization sample had received less education than the younger makes the interpretation of the observed decrement even more suspect. Furthermore, some of the Hold tests may simply have more flexible scoring standards and may for this reason be less sensitive to change. Some evidence is available to suggest that the apparent resistance of vocabulary tests to decline may be attributable to the substitution of poorer but equally acceptable definitions on the part of deteriorated subjects (13, 21).

Apart from theoretical considerations, extensive data gathered by other investigators have failed to corroborate the various hypotheses regarding diagnostic interpretations of score profiles. That the evidence is predominantly negative is apparent from a survey of the published literature (cf. 30, 55, 69). The original hypotheses were derived either from uncontrolled clinical observations or from comparisons of pathological and control groups that were not equated in age, education, or other factors. Failure to cross-validate likewise accounts for a number of spurious differences. Subsequent studies offer little empirical support to the hypotheses regarding scatter and score patterns. Similarly, mental defectives could not be differentiated from psychotics on the basis of the deterioration index. Schizophrenics obtained no higher deterioration index than neurotics, and patients with brain damage no higher index than those with functional disorders. Even more telling refutation was provided by longitudinal analyses of retest records, which failed to reveal a significant relation between actual decline in test scores and the deterioration index (48, 66). Also relevant are the observations that "normal" deterioration is not found among older institutionalized mental defectives (9), and that vocabulary scores decline in patients hospitalized for long periods (78).

On the other hand, there is some evidence in recent factorial analyses that supports the presence of a common "deterioration factor" through some of the Wechsler subtests (63). The same research indicated a possible relation between performance on certain WAIS subtests and indices of brain functioning derived from electroencephalography. It was also found that relatively low Digit Span scores occurred more often among brain damaged than among normal subjects (60). It is possible that further research will justify the utilization of at least some score patterns on the Wechsler scales for diagnostic purposes.

Like any individual intelligence test, the Wechsler scales can theoretically provide information at various levels. At the most objective level, these scales yield an IQ with high reliability and fair evidence of validity. At a purely qualitative level, any irregularity of performance should alert the clinician to look for peculiarities of past experience, emotional associations, and other individual factors. Bizarreness, overelaboration, or excessive self-reference in responses are often indicative of personality disorders. Even when correct, specific responses may provide promising leads. As Wechsler points out (74, p. 181), if in the Vocabulary test one individual defines "sentence" as a group of words and another as a penalty imposed by a judge, this difference may furnish a clue to important dissimilarities in background or personality.

Such qualitative interpretations, however, are tentative and require further verification. The same response—or score pattern—may have different meanings for different subjects. It may have deep significance for some and only trivial connotations for others. Because of their idiosyncratic meanings, such cues cannot be validated by quantitative methods adapted to group trends. Between these two extremes—from the quantitative, objective IQ to purely qualitative observations—fall the various attempts at semiquantitative profile analysis. It is at this intermediate level that both theoretical analyses and empirical results have so far lent little or no support to the proposed interpretations.

OTHER TESTS OF INTELLECTUAL IMPAIRMENT

A number of tests have been specially designed as clinical instruments for assessing intellectual impairment. Several have been described as indices of "organicity" or brain damage. Most available tests in this category, however, are broader in function, and are employed to detect intellectual deterioration or impairment arising from a variety of possible causes. The many testing techniques proposed for this purpose have been surveyed in a number of books and articles (35, 39, 52, 57, 67, 69, 75, 76, 77). Several are in an experimental stage. Some are designed only to afford the clinician an opportunity for qualitative observations. Others have relatively standardized procedure and objective norms, although the normative samples are often inadequate. Some are subject to one or more of the theoretical objections raised against profile analysis of Wechsler scores. A few have yielded promising empirical data.

All available tests of intellectual impairment are based on the premise of a differential deficit in different functions. Chief among the functions considered to be most sensitive to pathological processes are memory, spatial perception, and abstraction or concept formation. Typical examples of tests in these three areas will be illustrated in this section.

Memory Tests. As early as 1930, Babcock (4) proposed an index of deterioration based on the principle of "Hold" and "Don't Hold" tests. In the subsequently developed Babcock-Levy Test (5), Stanford-Binet vocabulary score furnishes the estimate of previous ability, and deterioration is measured with tests of memory, simple learning, and motor speed. The Hunt-Minnesota Test (34) likewise employs Stanford-Binet vocabulary as a point of reference for evaluating performance on six memory tests. Certain tests require the reproduction of designs, thus detecting disturbances in both memory and spatial perception.

An example of the latter type of test is the Benton Visual Retention Test (10). In this test, 10 designs of increasing complexity are individually presented on cards, the subject being instructed to reproduce each design immediately upon its removal. Performance is scored in terms of number of correct reproductions and number of errors. Other equivalent series of drawings are available for administration with shorter exposure, with a fifteen-second delay, and as a copying test. Scores are interpreted in terms of the subject's IQ as determined by any standard verbal-type intelligence test. If this is unavailable, educational or vocational data are utilized as a rough estimate of the subject's previous intellectual level.

Perceptual Tests. Tasks involving the perception of spatial relations have been used for a long time as qualitative, informal tests of brain damage. They were included, for example, in early test series for the examination of aphasics, and are still employed for this purpose. Frequently, such tests require the subject to copy simple designs. Some investigators have suggested that tests of this type might reveal not only perceptual disorders, but also disturbances in the subject's attitude toward the task (cf., e.g., 53). If that is the case, then these tests might have a broader applicability in the detection of a variety of psychological disorders.

An example of a clinical test in this category is the Bender Visual Motor Gestalt Test, commonly known as the Bender-Gestalt Test (8). In this test, the nine simple designs shown in Figure 62 are presented individually on cards. The subject is instructed to copy each design, with the sample before him. The designs were selected by Bender from a longer series originally employed by Wertheimer, one of the founders of the Gestalt school, in his studies of visual perception. The particular designs were constructed so as to illustrate certain principles of Gestalt psychology, and Bender's own analyses of the test results are formulated in terms of Gestalt concepts. Although for many years the test was administered by Bender and others to children and adults showing a variety of psychological disorders, the data were not reported in objective and systematic form and were therefore difficult to evaluate.

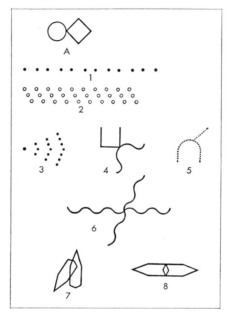

Fig. 62. The Bender-Gestalt Test. (From 8, p. 4; reproduced by permission of Lauretta Bender.)

More recently, Pascal and Suttell (53) undertook a standardization and quantification of the Bender-Gestalt Test on an adult population. On the basis of the drawing errors that significantly differentiated between matched samples of normals and abnormals, a relatively objective scoring key was developed. Cross-validation of this key on new samples of 474 "non-patients" (or normal controls), 187 neurotics, and 136 psychotics yielded the distributions shown in Figure 63. It can be seen that as a group the psychotics and neurotics are clearly differentiated from the controls, the mean scores of the three groups being 81.8, 68.2, and 50, respectively. These scores are standard scores with a mean of 50 and an *SD* of 10, the higher scores indicating more diagnostic errors. The biserial correlation of test scores against the criterion of patient versus non-patient status was .74. This correlation may be regarded as a measure of concurrent validity. In a later study with small groups of children, the test significantly distinguished normals from schizophrenics and mental defectives (26).

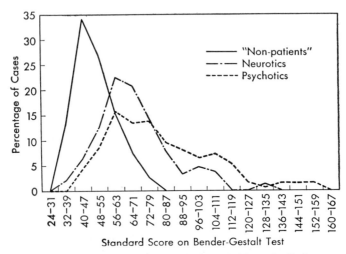

Fig. 63. Percentage Distribution of Psychotic and Neurotic Patients and Control "Non-Patient" Group on Pascal-Suttell Standardization of Bender-Gestalt Test. (Data from Pascal and Suttell, 53, p. 30.)

Retest reliabilities of about .70 were found in normal samples over a twenty-four-hour interval. Scorer reliabilities of approximately .90 are reported for trained scorers. Performance on the test is apparently independent of drawing ability, but is significantly related to amount of education (53) and to mental age (7, 22). In this adaptation, the Bender-Gestalt Test appears to have promise as a rapid screening device, especially for detecting the more serious forms of disturbance. The normative sample, however, is rather restricted geographically, educationally, and in other ways. Extension and revision of the norms on the basis of a larger and more representative sample would be desirable. Further checking of validity in different samples and against other criteria would likewise be of interest.

Another example of a perceptual test is provided by the Grassi Block Substitution Test (29) which represents a special adaptation and extension of the Kohs Block Design. While still in a research stage, this test shows promise, especially as an indicator of brain damage. Mention should also be made of the investigations that have tried to establish "signs of organicity" for the Rorschach inkblot test. Cross-validation has generally failed to substantiate the diagnostic value of the proposed signs. The Rorschach test which may be regarded as a highly unstructured sort of perceptual test, will be discussed in Chapter 20, which deals with projective tests of personality.

Concept Formation Tests. Clinical tests of conceptual thinking are more concerned with the methods employed by the subject than with the end result achieved. Largely for this reason, such tests lean heavily upon qualitative observations and have so far made little use of objective scoring and standardized norms. It is recognized, of course, that normative data would be helpful even in the interpretation of qualitative observations, but such data are difficult to obtain.

A well-known series of concept formation tests was developed by Goldstein and Scheerer (27). This series includes an adaptation and extension of the Kohs Block Design, another design test in which the subject copies simple geometric patterns with sticks and later reproduces them from memory, and several sorting tests. An example is the color-form sorting test, in which pieces differing in both shape and color are to be sorted twice in different ways. In this test, interest centers on the subject's ability to shift spontaneously from one basis of classification to the other.

Fig. 64. Hanfmann-Kasanin Concept Formation Test. (Courtesy C. H. Stoelting Company.)

A somewhat more standardized object-sorting test is the Hanfmann-Kasanin Concept Formation Test (32). In this test, the subject is given the blocks pictured in Figure 64. These 22 blocks vary in color, shape, height, and surface size. A category name (nonsense syllables such as *mur*) is printed on the underside of each block, not visible to the subject in the initial presentation. The subject's task is to discover how the blocks should be classified into four groups, each corresponding to one of the four category names. At the outset, the examiner picks up a sample block, shows the subject the name on the underside, and asks him to select all blocks belonging in that class. When the subject has made an error in grouping blocks, the error is shown to him by reversing the block and exhibiting the class name. With the aid of these clues, the subject works until he arrives at the correct solution. He is then asked to state the principle of classification and to re-sort the blocks. The Hanfmann-Kasanin test is more difficult than the sorting tests in the Goldstein-Scheerer series and is not so satisfactory with persons of low intellectual level. Scoring is quite complex and requires qualitative judgments.

Other sorting tests on which research is being conducted include the Kahn Test of Symbol Arrangement (38) and the Wisconsin Card-Sorting Test (12, 23, 28). The latter is unusual in the objectivity of its administration and scoring and in the number of well-controlled experiments performed with it. In studies with schizophrenic, brain-injured, and mentally defective subjects, it has shown considerable promise as a diagnostic tool.

It should be noted that many of the tests cited in this chapter show a close kinship with personality tests, to be discussed in Part 4. Clinical tests provide a particularly clear illustration of the arbitrary distinction between personality and ability tests. At least some of the techniques considered in this chapter could have been included in one of the chapters of Part 4. They have been treated at this point because, in either their construction or their application, they resemble ability tests somewhat more closely than they do personality tests. But the differentiation is minor and is made solely for ease of discussion.

REFERENCES

1. Anastasi, Anne. Age changes in adult test performance. *Psychol. Rep.*, 1956, 2, 509.
2. Anastasi, Anne. *Differential psychology.* (3rd ed.) N. Y.: Macmillan, 1958.
3. Anderson, E. E., *et al.* Wilson College studies in psychology: I. A comparison of the Wechsler-Bellevue, Revised Stanford-Binet, and American Council on Education tests at the college level. *J. Psychol.*, 1942, 14, 317-326.
4. Babcock, Harriet. An experiment in the measurement of mental deterioration. *Arch. Psychol.*, 1930, No. 117.
5. Babcock, Harriet, and Levy, Lydia. *The Revised Examination for the Measurement of Efficiency of Mental Functioning.* Chicago: Stoelting, 1940.
6. Balinsky, B. An analysis of the mental factors of various age groups from nine to sixty. *Genet. Psychol. Monogr.*, 1941, 23, 191-234.
7. Baroff, G. S. Bender-Gestalt visuo-motor function in mental deficiency. *Amer. J. ment. Defic.*, 1957, 61, 753-760.

8. Bender, Lauretta. A visual motor Gestalt test and its clinical use. *Amer. Orthopsychiat. Assoc., Res. Monogr.,* 1938, No. 3.
9. Bensberg, G. J., and Sloan, W. A study of Wechsler's concept of "normal deterioration" in older mental defectives. *J. clin. Psychol.,* 1950, 6, 359-362.
10. Benton, A. L. *Benton Visual Retention Test, Revised Edition.* N. Y.: Psychol. Corp., 1955.
11. Benton, A. L., Weider, A., and Blauvelt, J. Performance of adult patients on the Bellevue Intelligence Scales and the Revised Stanford-Binet. *Psychiat. Quart.,* 1941, 15, 802-806.
12. Berg, Esta A. A simple objective technique for measuring flexibility in thinking. *J. gen. Psychol.,* 1948, 39, 15-22.
13. Chodorkoff, B., and Mussen, P. Qualitative aspects of the vocabulary responses of normals and schizophrenics. *J. consult. Psychol.,* 1952, 16, 43-48.
14. Cohen, J. The factorial structure of the WAIS between early adulthood and old age. *J. consult. Psychol.,* 1957, 21, 283-390.
15. Cohen, J. A factor-analytically based rationale for the Wechsler Adult Intelligence Scale. *J. consult. Psychol.,* 1957, 21, 451-457.
16. Davis, P. C. A factor analysis of the Wechsler-Bellevue Scale. *Educ. psychol. Measmt.,* 1956, 16, 127-146.
17. Doppelt, J. E. Estimating the Full Scale score of the Wechsler Adult Intelligence Scale from scores on four subtests. *J. consult. Psychol.,* 1956, 20, 63-66.
18. Doppelt, J. E., and Wallace, W. L. Standardization of the Wechsler Adult Intelligence Scale for older persons. *J. abnorm. soc. Psychol.,* 1955, 51, 312-330.
19. Estes, Betsy W. Influence of socioeconomic status on Wechsler Intelligence Scale for Children: an exploratory study. *J. consult. Psychol.,* 1953, 17, 58-62.
20. Estes, Betsy W. Influence of socioeconomic status on Wechsler Intelligence Scale for Children: addendum. *J. consult. Psychol.,* 1955, 19, 225-226.
21. Feifel, H. Qualitative differences in the vocabulary responses of normals and abnormals. *Genet. Psychol. Monogr.,* 1949, 39, 151-204.
22. Feldman, I. Psychological differences among moron and borderline mental defectives as a function of etiology: I. visual-motor functioning. *Amer. J. ment. Defic.,* 1953, 57, 484-494.
23. Fey, Elizabeth T. The performance of young schizophrenics on the Wisconsin Card-Sorting Test. *J. consult. Psychol.,* 1951, 15, 311-319.
24. Frandsen, A. N., and Higginson, J. B. The Stanford-Binet and the Wechsler Intelligence Scale for Children. *J. consult. Psychol.,* 1951, 15, 236-238.
25. Gehman, Ila H., and Matyas, R. P. Stability of the WISC and Binet tests. *J. consult. Psychol.,* 1956, 20, 150-152.
26. Goldberg, F. H. The performance of schizophrenic, retarded, and normal children on the Bender-Gestalt test. *Amer. J. ment. Defic.,* 1957, 61, 548-555.
27. Goldstein, K., and Scheerer, M. Abstract and concrete behavior; an experimental study with special tests. *Psychol. Monogr.,* 1941, 53, No. 2. (Test materials distributed by Psychol. Corp.)

28. Grant, D. A. Perceptual versus analytical responses to the number concept of a Weigl-type card sorting test. *J. exp. Psychol.*, 1951, 41, 23-29.
29. Grassi, J. R. *The Grassi Block Substitution Test: For Measuring Organic Brain Pathology.* Los Angeles: Western Psychol. Services, 1947-1953.
30. Guertin, W. H., Frank, G. H., and Rabin, A. I. Research with the Wechsler-Bellevue Intelligence Scale: 1950-1955. *Psychol. Bull.*, 1956, 53, 235-257.
31. Hall, J. A correlation of a modified form of Raven's Progressive Matrices (1938) with Wechsler Adult Intelligence Scale. *J. consult. Psychol.*, 1957, 21, 23-26.
32. Hanfmann, Eugenia, and Kasanin, J. Conceptual thinking in schizophrenia. *Nerv. ment. Dis. Monogr.*, 1942, No. 67. (Test distributed by C. H. Stoelting Co.)
33. Harlow, J. E., Jr., Price, A. C., Tatham, L. J., and Davidson, J. F. Preliminary study of comparison between Wechsler Intelligence Scale for Children and Form L of revised Stanford-Binet Scale at three age levels. *J. clin. Psychol.*, 1957, 13, 72-73.
34. Hunt, H. F. *The Hunt-Minnesota Test for Organic Brain Damage.* Minneapolis: Univer. Minn. Press, 1943.
35. Hunt, J. McV., and Cofer, C. N. Psychological deficit. In J. McV. Hunt (Ed.), *Personality and the behavior disorders.* Vol. II. N. Y.: Ronald, 1944. Pp. 971-1032.
36. Janke, L. L., and Havighurst, R. J. Relations between ability and social status in a midwestern community: II. Sixteen-year-old boys and girls. *J. educ. Psychol.*, 1945, 36, 499-509.
37. Jones, H. G. The evaluation of the significance of differences between scaled scores on the WAIS: perpetuation of a fallacy. *J. consult. Psychol.*, 1956, 20, 319-320.
38. Kahn, T. C. *Kahn Test of Symbol Arrangement.* Missoula, Montana: Psychol. Test Specialists, 1949-1957.
39. Klebanoff, S. G., Singer, J. L., and Wilensky, H. Psychological consequences of brain lesions and ablations. *Psychol. Bull.*, 1954, 51, 1-41.
40. Krugman, Judith I., Justman, J., Wrightstone, J. W., and Krugman, M. Pupil functioning on the Stanford-Binet and the Wechsler Intelligence Scale for Children. *J. consult. Psychol.*, 1951, 15, 475-483.
41. Kutash, S. B. A comparison of the Wechsler-Bellevue and the Revised Stanford-Binet, Form L. *Psychiat. Quart.*, 1945, 19, 677-685.
42. Levinson, B. M. Traditional Jewish cultural values and performance on the Wechsler tests. *J. educ. Psychol.*, 1959, 50, 177-181.
43. Littell, W. M. The Wechsler Intelligence Scale for Children: review of a decade of research. *Psychol. Bull.*, 1960, 57, 132-156.
44. McNemar, Q. Review of Wechsler, D. The measurement of adult intelligence (3rd ed.). *Amer. J. Psychol.*, 1945, 58, 420-422.
45. McNemar, Q. On abbreviated Wechsler-Bellevue Scales. *J. consult. Psychol.*, 1950, 14, 79-81.
46. McNemar, Q. On WAIS difference scores. *J. consult. Psychol.*, 1957, 21, 239-240.
47. Madow, A. A., Daniel, J. P., and Throne, J. M. A comparison of WAIS and

Revised Stanford-Binet IQ's in adult mental defectives. Paper read at North Central Region, Amer. Assoc. ment. Defic., Des Moines, October, 1955.

48. Magaret, Ann, and Simpson, Mary. A comparison of two measures of deterioration in psychotics. *J. consult. Psychol.,* 1948, 12, 265-270.

49. Maxwell, Eileen. Validities of abbreviated WAIS scales. *J. consult. Psychol.,* 1957, 21, 121-126.

50. Mitchell, Mildred B. Performance of mental hospital patients on the Wechsler-Bellevue and the Revised Stanford-Binet, Form L. *J. educ. Psychol.,* 1942, 33, 538-544.

51. Nale, S. The Children's Wechsler and the Binet on 104 mental defectives at the Polk State School. *Amer. J. ment. Defic.,* 1951, 56, 419-423.

52. Parker, J. W. The validity of some current tests for organicity. *J. consult. Psychol.,* 1957, 21, 425-528.

53. Pascal, G. R., and Suttell, Barbara J. *The Bender-Gestalt Test: quantification and validity for adults.* N. Y.: Grune & Stratton, 1951.

54. Pastovic, J. J., and Guthrie, G. M. Some evidence on the validity of the WISC. *J. consult. Psychol.,* 1951, 15, 385-386.

55. Rabin, A. I., and Guertin, W. H. Research with the Wechsler-Bellevue Test: 1945-1950. *Psychol. Bull.,* 1951, 48, 211-248.

56. Rapaport, D., *et al. Diagnostic psychological testing.* Vol. I. Chicago: Year Book Publ., 1945.

57. Rosenzweig, S., and Kogan, Kate L. *Psychodiagnostics.* N. Y.: Grune & Stratton, 1949.

58. Sartain, A. Q. A comparison of the new Revised Stanford-Binet, the Bellevue Scale, and certain group tests of intelligence. *J. soc. Psychol.,* 1946, 23, 237-239.

59. Saunders, D. R. On the dimensionality of the WAIS battery for two groups of normal males. *Psychol. Rep.,* 1959, 5, 529-541.

60. Saunders, D. R. Digit span and alpha frequency: a cross-validation. *Res. Bull., Educ. Test. Serv.,* RB-60-3, 1960.

61. Saunders, D. R. A factor analysis of the Information and Arithmetic items of the WAIS. *Psychol. Rep.,* 1960, 6, 367-383.

62. Saunders, D. R. A factor analysis of the Picture Completion items of the WAIS. *J. clin. Psychol.,* 1960, 16, 146-149.

63. Saunders, D. R. Further implications of Mundy-Castle's correlations between EEG and Wechsler-Bellevue variables. *J. nat. Inst. Personnel Res., Johannesburg,* in press.

64. Seashore, H. G. Differences between verbal and performance IQ's on the Wechsler Intelligence Scale for Children. *J. consult. Psychol.,* 1951, 15, 62-67.

65. Seashore, H., Wesman, A., and Doppelt, J. The standardization of the Wechsler Intelligence Scale for Children. *J. consult. Psychol.,* 1950, 14, 99-110.

66. Sloan, W. Validity of Wechsler's deterioration quotient in high grade mental defectives. *J. clin. Psychol.,* 1947, 3, 187-188.

67. Strauss, A. A., and Kephart, N. C. *Psychopathology and education of the brain-injured child.* N. Y.: Grune & Stratton, 1955.

68. Triggs, Frances O., and Cartee, J. K. Preschool pupil performance on the Stanford-Binet and the Wechsler Intelligence Scale for Children. *J. clin. Psychol.,* 1953, 9, 27-29.
69. Watson, R. I. *The clinical method in psychology.* N. Y.: Harper, 1951.
70. Wechsler, D. *The measurement of adult intelligence.* Baltimore: Williams & Wilkins, 1939.
71. Wechsler, D. *Wechsler Intelligence Scale for Children.* N. Y.: Psychol. Corp., 1949.
72. Wechsler, D. Equivalent test and mental ages for the WISC. *J. consult. Psychol.,* 1951, 15, 381-384.
73. Wechsler, D. *Wechsler Adult Intelligence Scale.* N. Y.: Psychol. Corp., 1955.
74. Wechsler, D. *The measurement and appraisal of adult intelligence.* (4th ed.) Baltimore: Williams & Wilkins, 1958.
75. Weider, A. (Ed.) *Contributions toward medical psychology.* Vol. II. N. Y.: Ronald, 1953.
76. Wells, F. L., and Ruesch, J. *Mental examiner's handbook.* N. Y.: Psychol. Corp., 1945.
77. Yates, A. J. The validity of some psychological tests of brain damage. *Psychol. Bull.,* 1954, 51, 359-379.
78. Yates, A. J. The use of vocabulary in the measurement of intellectual deterioration—a review. *J. ment. Sci.,* 1956, 102, 409-440.

PART 3

Differential Testing of Abilities

CHAPTER 13

Multiple Aptitude Batteries

One of the chief distinguishing features of contemporary psychological testing is its *differential approach* to the measurement of ability. To be sure, the general intelligence tests discussed in Part 2 are still widely used in preliminary screening and in the clinical examination of extreme deviates. The period since World War II, however, has witnessed a rapid increase in the development and application of instruments that permit an analysis of performance with regard to different aspects of intelligence. Such instruments yield, not a single, global measure such as an IQ, but a set of scores in different aptitudes. They thus provide an intellectual *profile* showing the individual's characteristic strengths and weaknesses.

A number of events have contributed to the growing interest in differential aptitude testing. First, there has been an increasing recognition of intra-individual variation in performance on intelligence tests. Crude attempts to compare the individual's relative standing on different subtests or item groups antedated the development of multiple aptitude batteries by many years. As has been repeatedly pointed out, however, intelligence tests were not designed for such a purpose. The subtests or item groups are often too unreliable to justify intra-individual comparisons. In the construction of intelligence tests, moreover, items or subtests are generally chosen to provide a unitary and internally consistent measure. In such a selection, an effort is therefore made to minimize, rather than maximize, intra-individual variation. Subtests or items that correlate very low with the rest of the scale would, in general, be excluded. Yet these are the very parts that would probably have been retained if the emphasis had been on the differentiation of abilities. Another illustration of the same trend is to be found in the more defensible practice of reporting two scores on intelligence tests, such as verbal and numerical, linguistic and quantitative, verbal and non-verbal, etc.

The development of multiple aptitude batteries has been further stimulated by the gradual realization that so-called general intelligence tests are in fact less general than was originally supposed. It soon became apparent that many such tests were primarily measures of verbal comprehension. Certain areas, such as that of mechanical abilities, were usually untouched, except in some of the performance and non-language scales. As these limitations of intelligence tests became evident, psychologists began to qualify the term "intelligence." Distinctions between "academic" and "practical" intelligence were suggested by some. Others spoke of "abstract," "mechanical," and "social" intelligence. Tests of "special aptitudes" were likewise designed to supplement the intelligence tests. But closer analysis showed that the intelligence tests themselves could be said to measure a certain combination of special aptitudes, such as verbal and numerical aptitudes, although the area covered by such tests was loosely and inconsistently defined.

A strong impetus to differential aptitude testing was also provided by the growing activities of psychologists in vocational counseling, as well as in the selection and classification of industrial and military personnel. The early development of specialized tests in clerical, mechanical, and other vocational areas is a reflection of such interests. The assembling of test batteries for the selection of applicants for admission to schools of medicine, law, engineering, dentistry, and other professional fields represents a similar development which has been in progress for many years. Moreover, a number of differential aptitude batteries, such as those prepared by the Air Force and by the United States Employment Service, were the direct result of vocational selection or classification work.

Finally, the application of factor analysis to the study of trait organization provided the theoretical basis for the construction of multiple aptitude batteries. Through such factorial techniques, the different abilities loosely grouped under "intelligence" could be more systematically identified, sorted, and defined. Tests could then be selected so that each represented the best available measure of one of the traits or factors identified by factor analysis.

FACTOR ANALYSIS

The principal object of factor analysis is to simplify the description of data by reducing the number of necessary variables or "dimensions." Such reduction was illustrated in the brief introduction to factor analysis given in Chapter 6. Thus if we find that five factors are sufficient to account for all the common variance in a battery of 20 tests, we can for most purposes substitute 5 scores for the original 20 without sacrificing any essential information. The usual practice is to retain from among the original tests those providing the best measures of each of the factors.

All techniques of factor analysis begin with a complete table of intercorrelations among a set of tests. Such a table is known as a correlation matrix. Every factor analysis ends with a *factor matrix,* i.e., a table showing the weight or loading of each of the factors in each test. A hypothetical factor matrix involving only two factors is shown in Table 19. The factors are listed across the top and their weights in each of the 10 tests are given in the appropriate rows.

TABLE 19.   A Hypothetical Factor Matrix

Test	Factor I	Factor II
1. Vocabulary	.74	.54
2. Analogies	.64	.39
3. Sentence Completion	.68	.43
4. Disarranged Sentences	.32	.23
5. Reading Comprehension	.70	.50
6. Addition	.22	−.51
7. Multiplication	.40	−.50
8. Arithmetic Problems	.52	−.48
9. Equation Relations	.43	−.37
10. Number Series Completion	.32	−.25

Several different methods for analyzing a set of variables into common factors have been derived. As early as 1901, Pearson (32) pointed the way for this type of analysis. T. L. Kelley (29) and Thurstone (42) in America and Burt (7) in England did much to advance the method. Alternative procedures, modifications, and refinements have been developed by many others.[1] The availability of electronic computers is rapidly leading to the adoption of more refined and laborious techniques. Although differing in their initial postulates, most of these methods yield similar results. Currently the most widely used technique, especially in America, is the *centroid method* formulated by Thurstone (42). The factor matrix given in Table 19 is typical of those found by this method. For brief and simple introductions to factorial procedures, the student is referred to Guilford (23, Ch. 16) and Adcock (1). A more detailed treatment of the methodology of factor analysis can be found in Fruchter (19).

It is clearly beyond the scope of this book to cover the mathematical basis or the computational procedures of factor analysis. But an understanding of the results of factor analysis need not be limited to those who have mastered its specialized methodology. Even without knowing how the factor loadings were computed, the student will be able to see how a factor matrix is utilized

[1] For specific references and for a fuller discussion of the methods, problems, and results of factor analysis, see Anastasi (3, Chs. 10 and 11).

in the identification and interpretation of factors. For an intelligent reading of reports of factorial research, however, familiarity with a few other concepts and terms is helpful.

It is customary to represent factors geometrically as *reference axes* in terms of which each test can be plotted. Figure 65 illustrates this procedure.

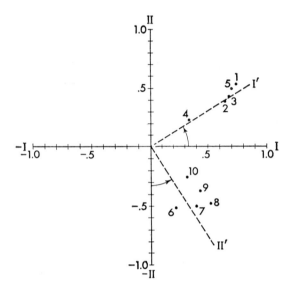

Fig. 65. A Hypothetical Factor Pattern, Showing Weights of Two Group Factors in Each of Ten Tests.

In this graph, each of the 10 tests from Table 19 has been plotted against the two factors, which correspond to axes I and II. Thus the point representing Test 1 is located by moving .74 of the distance along axis I and .54 of the distance along axis II. The points corresponding to the remaining 9 tests are plotted in the same way, using the weights given in Table 19. Although all the weights on Factor I are positive, it will be noted that on Factor II some of the weights are positive and some negative. This can also be seen in Figure 65, where Tests 1 to 5 cluster in one part of the graph and Tests 6 to 10 in another.

In this connection it should be noted that the position of the reference axes is not fixed by the data. The original correlation table determines only the position of the tests (points in Figure 65) in relation to each other. The same points can be plotted with the reference axes in any position. For this reason, factor analysts usually rotate axes until they obtain the most satisfactory and easily interpretable pattern. This is a legitimate procedure, somewhat analogous to measuring longitude from, let us say, Chicago rather than Greenwich.

The reference axes in Figure 65 were rotated to positions I′ and II′, shown by the broken lines. This rotation was carried out in accordance with Thurstone's criteria of *positive manifold* and *simple structure*. The former requires the rotation of axes to such a position as to eliminate all significant negative weights. Most psychologists regard negative factor loadings as inapplicable to aptitude tests, since such a loading implies that the higher the individual rates in the particular factor, the poorer will be his performance on the test. The criterion of simple structure means that each test shall have loadings on as few factors as possible. Both of these criteria are designed to yield factors that can be most readily and unambiguously interpreted.

It will be seen that on the rotated axes in Figure 65 all the verbal tests (Tests 1 to 5) fall along or very close to axis I′. Similarly, the numerical tests (Tests 6 to 10) cluster closely around axis II′. Parenthetically, the reader may feel that rotated axis II′ should have been labeled —II′, to correspond to the unrotated axis —II. Which pole of the axis is labeled plus and which minus, however, is an arbitrary matter. In the present example, the rotated axis II′ has been "reflected" in order to eliminate negative weights.

The new factor loadings, measured along the rotated axes, are given in Table 20. The reader may easily verify these factor loadings by preparing a

TABLE 20. Rotated Factor Matrix
(Data from Figure 65)

Test	Factor I′	Factor II′
1. Vocabulary	.91	—.06
2. Analogies	.75	.02
3. Sentence Completion	.80	.00
4. Disarranged Sentences	.39	—.02
5. Reading Comprehension	.86	—.04
6. Addition	—.09	.55
7. Multiplication	.07	.64
8. Arithmetic Problems	.18	.68
9. Equation Relations	.16	.54
10. Number Series Completion	.13	.38

paper "ruler" with a scale of units corresponding to that in Figure 65. With this "ruler," distances can be measured along the rotated axes. The factor loadings in Table 20 include no negative values except for very low, negligible amounts attributable to sampling errors. All of the verbal tests have high loadings on Factor I′ and practically zero loadings on Factor II′. The numerical tests, on the other hand, have high loadings on Factor II′ and low, negligible loadings on Factor I'. The identification and naming of the two factors and the description of the factorial composition of each test have thus been simplified by the rotation of reference axes. In actual practice, the number of factors is often greater than two—a condition that complicates the geometrical representation as well as the statistical analysis, but does not alter the basic procedure. The fact that factor patterns are rarely as clear-cut as the one illustrated in Figure 65 adds further to the difficulty of rotating axes and of identifying factors.

Once the rotated factor matrix has been computed, we can proceed with the interpretation and naming of factors. This step calls for psychological insight rather than statistical training. To learn the nature of a particular factor, we simply examine the tests having high loadings on that factor and we try to discover what psychological processes they have in common. The more tests there are with high loadings on a given factor, the more clearly we can define the nature of the factor. In Table 20, for example, it is apparent that Factor I' is verbal and Factor II' is numerical.

Factor loadings also represent the correlation of each test with the factor. It will be recalled that this correlation is the factorial validity of the test (Ch. 6). From Table 20 we can say, for instance, that the factorial validity of the Vocabulary test as a measure of the verbal factor is .91. The factorial validity of the Addition test, in terms of the numerical factor, is .55. Obviously the first five tests have negligible validity as measures of the numerical factor, and the last five have practically no validity as measures of the verbal factor. The concept of factorial validity is especially relevant to the type of tests to be discussed in this chapter.

Another type of information that can be obtained from a factor matrix is the proportional contribution of each factor to the total variance of a test. This contribution is simply the square of the factor loading. For example, if we examine the loadings of Test 8, Arithmetic Problems, in Table 20, we can see that 3 per cent of its variance ($.18^2 = .03$) is attributable to the verbal factor and 46 per cent ($.68^2 = .46$) to the numerical factor. The total variance of this test attributable to common factors is thus 49 per cent ($.46 + .03 = .49$). This is known as its communality. Let us now suppose that the reliability of this test had been found to be .85. We can then conclude that 15 per cent of the test variance is error variance. So far we have accounted for 64 per cent of the test variance ($.49 + .15 = .64$). The remaining 36 per cent is the specificity of the test, covering any specific factors occurring only in this test. The variance of any test can be broken down in a similar fashion, if we know its common factor loadings and its reliability coefficient.

The axes employed in Figure 65 are known as *orthogonal axes,* since they are at right angles to each other. Occasionally, the test clusters are so situated that a better fit can be obtained with *oblique axes.* In such a case, the factors would themselves be correlated. Some investigators have maintained that orthogonal, or uncorrelated, factors should always be employed, since they provide a simpler and clearer picture of trait relationships. Others insist that oblique axes should be used when they fit the data better, since the most meaningful categories need not be uncorrelated. An example cited by Thurstone is that of height and weight. Although it is well known that height and weight are highly correlated, they have proved to be useful categories in the measurement of physique.

When the factors are themselves correlated, it is possible to subject the intercorrelations among the factors to the same statistical analyses we employ with intercorrelations among tests. In other words, we can "factorize the factors" and derive *second-order factors.* This process has been followed in a number of studies with both aptitude and personality variables. Certain investigations with aptitude tests have yielded a single second-order general factor. As a rule, American factor analysts have proceeded by accounting for as much of the common variance as possible through group factors and then identifying a general factor as a second-order factor if the data justified it. British psychologists, on the other hand, usually begin with a general factor, to which they attribute the major portion of the common variance, and then resort to group factors to account for any remaining correlation. These procedural differences reflect differences in theoretical orientation to be discussed in the following section.

THEORIES OF TRAIT ORGANIZATION

The Two-Factor Theory. The first theory of trait organization based upon a statistical analysis of test scores was the Two-Factor theory developed by the British psychologist, Charles Spearman (34, 35). In its original formulation, this theory maintained that all intellectual activities share a single common factor, called the "general factor," or *g.* In addition, the theory postulated numerous specific or *s* factors, each being strictly specific to a single activity. Positive correlation between any two functions was thus attributed to the *g* factor. The more highly the two functions were "saturated" with *g,* the higher would be the correlation between them. The presence of specifics, on the other hand, tended to lower the correlation between functions.

It follows from the Two-Factor theory that the aim of psychological testing should be to measure the amount of each individual's *g.* If this factor runs through all abilities, it furnishes the only basis for prediction of the subject's performance from one situation to another. It would be futile to measure specific factors since each by definition operates in only a single activity. Accordingly, Spearman proposed that a single test, highly saturated with g, be substituted for the heterogeneous collection of items found in intelligence tests. He suggested that tests dealing with abstract relations are probably the best measures of g and could be used for this purpose. Examples of tests constructed as measures of g include Raven's Progressive Matrices and the IPAT Culture Free Intelligence Test, both discussed in Chapter 10.

From the outset, Spearman realized that the Two-Factor theory must be qualified. When the activities compared are very similar, a certain degree of correlation may result over and above that attributable to the g factor. Thus in addition to general and specific factors, there might be another, intermediate class of factors, not so universal as g nor so strictly specific as the s factors. Such a factor, common to a group of activities but not to all, has been designated as a *group factor*. In the early formulation of his theory Spearman admitted the possibility of very narrow and negligibly small group factors. Following later investigations by several of his students, he included much broader group factors such as arithmetic, mechanical, and linguistic abilities.

Multiple-Factor Theories. The prevalent contemporary American view of trait organization recognizes a number of moderately broad group factors, each of which may enter with different weights into different tests. For example, a verbal factor may have a large weight in a vocabulary test, a smaller weight in an analogies test, and a very small weight in an arithmetic reasoning test. The publication in 1928 of Kelley's *Crossroads in the Mind of Man* (28) paved the way for a large number of studies in quest of particular group factors. Chief among the factors proposed by Kelley were manipulation of spatial relationships, facility with numbers, facility with verbal material, memory, and speed. This list has been modified and extended by subsequent investigators employing the more modern methods of factor analysis discussed in the preceding section.

One of the leading exponents of Multiple-Factor theory was Thurstone. On the basis of extensive research by himself and his students, Thurstone proposed about a dozen group factors which he designated as "primary mental abilities." Those most frequently corroborated in the work of Thurstone and of other independent investigators (16, 24, 39, 43) include the following:

> *V. Verbal Comprehension:* The principal factor in such tests as reading comprehension, verbal analogies, disarranged sentences, verbal reasoning, and proverb matching. It is most adequately measured by vocabulary tests.

W. *Word Fluency:* Found in such tests as anagrams, rhyming, or naming words in a given category (e.g., boys' names or words beginning with the same letter).

N. *Number:* Most closely identified with speed and accuracy of simple arithmetic computation.

S. *Space:* It is possible that this factor may represent two distinct factors, one covering perception of fixed spatial or geometric relations, the other manipulatory visualization, in which changed positions or transformations must be visualized. There is also evidence of a third factor of "kinaesthetic imagery" (31).

M. *Associative Memory:* Found principally in tests demanding rote memory for paired associates. There is some evidence to suggest that this factor may reflect the extent to which memory crutches are utilized (12). The evidence is against the presence of a broader factor through all memory tests. Other restricted memory factors, such as memory for temporal sequences and for spatial position, have been suggested by some investigations.

P. *Perceptual Speed:* Quick and accurate grasping of visual details, similarities, and differences. This factor may be the same as the speed factor identified by earlier investigators. This is one of several factors subsequently identified in perceptual tasks (41).

I (or *R*). *Induction* (or *General Reasoning*): The identification of this factor was least clear. Thurstone originally proposed an inductive and a deductive factor. The latter was best measured by tests of syllogistic reasoning and the former by tests requiring the subject to find a rule, as in a number series completion test. Evidence for the deductive factor, however, was much weaker than for the inductive. Moreover, other investigators suggest a general reasoning factor, best measured by arithmetic reasoning tests (30).

It should be noted that the distinction between general, group, and specific factors is not so basic as may at first appear. If the number or variety of tests in a battery is small, a single general factor may account for all the correlations among them. But when the same tests are included in a larger battery with a more heterogeneous collection of tests, the original general factor may emerge as a group factor, common to some but not all tests. Similarly, a certain factor may be represented by only one test in the original battery, but may be shared by several tests in the larger battery. Such a factor would have been identified as a specific in the original battery, but would become a group factor in the more comprehensive battery. In the light of these considerations, it is not surprising to find that intensive factorial investigations of special areas have yielded many factors in place of the one or two primary mental abilities originally identified in each area. Such has been the case in studies of verbal (11), perceptual (41), memory (12), and reasoning (21) tests.

Factorial research seems to have produced a bewildering multiplication of factors. On the basis of his own and other published studies, Guilford (24, 25) listed some fifty factors and pointed to gaps in his schema where other factors may eventually be identified. He proposed a threefold model for the "structure of intellect." In this model, intellectual activities are classified with regard to operations (cognition, memory, divergent thinking, convergent thinking, evaluation), products (units, classes, relations, systems, transformations, implications), and contents (figural, symbolic, semantic, behavioral). Such a classification yields 120 cells, each corresponding to a potential factor. A certain amount of order has been achieved by cross-identification of factors reported by different investigators and often given different names (2, 16). Such cross-identification can be accomplished when there are several tests common to the investigations being compared. To facilitate this process, a group of factor analysts assembled a kit of "reference tests" measuring the principal aptitude factors so far identified. This kit, which is distributed by Educational Testing Service (17, 18), makes it easier for different investigators planning factorial research to include some common tests in their batteries.

It is apparent that even after these efforts at simplification and coordination, the number of factors remains large. Human behavior is varied and complex, and perhaps it is unrealistic to expect a dozen or so factors to provide an adequate description of it. For specific purposes, of course, we can choose appropriate factors with regard to both nature and breadth. For example, if we are selecting applicants for a difficult and highly specialized mechanical job, we would probably want to measure fairly narrow perceptual and spatial factors that closely match the job requirements. In selecting college students, on the other hand, a few broad factors such as verbal comprehension, numerical facility, and general reasoning would be most relevant. Illustrations of the different ways in which factorial results have been utilized in test development will be given later in this chapter.

Hierarchical Theories. An alternative schema for the organization of factors has been proposed by a number of British psychologists, including Burt (9) and Vernon (49). A diagram illustrating Vernon's application of this system is reproduced in Figure 66. At the top of the hierarchy, Vernon places Spearman's g factor. At the next level are two broad group factors, corresponding to verbal-educational ($v{:}ed$) and to practical-mechanical ($k{:}m$) aptitudes, respectively. These major factors may be further subdivided. The verbal-educational factor, for example, yields verbal and numerical sub-factors. Similarly, the practical-mechanical factor splits into mechanical-information, spatial, and manual subfactors. Still narrower subfactors can be identified by further analysis, let us say, of the verbal tasks. At the lowest level of the hierarchy are the specific factors. Such a hierarchical structure thus resembles a genealogical tree, with *g* at the top, *s* factors at the bottom, and progressively narrower group factors in between.

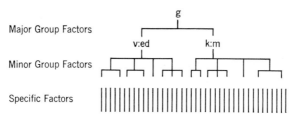

Fig. 66.   Diagram Illustrating Hierarchical Theory of Human Abilities. From Vernon, 49, p. 22. Copyright, 1960, Methuen & Co., Ltd.)

Factors as Operational Unities. That different investigators may arrive at dissimilar schemas of trait organization becomes less perplexing when we recognize that the traits identified through factor analysis are simply an expression of correlation among behavior measures. They are not underlying entities or causal factors, but descriptive categories. Hence it is conceivable that different principles of classification may be applicable to the same data.

The concept of factors as descriptive categories is explicit in the writings of Thomson (37, 38), Burt (7, 8), and Vernon (49) in England, and those of Tryon (46) in America. All of these writers have called attention to the vast multiplicity of behavioral elements, which may become organized into clusters through either hereditary or experiential linkages. For example, a broad verbal-educational factor is likely to develop through all activities learned in school. A narrower factor of numerical aptitude may result from the fact that all arithmetic processes are taught together by the same teacher in the same classroom. Hence the child who is discouraged, antagonized, or bored during the arithmetic period will tend to fall behind in his learning of *all* these processes; the one who is stimulated and gratified in his arithmetic class will tend to learn well all that is taught in that class period and to develop attitudes that will advance his subsequent numerical learning.

It might be added that other factor analysts have from time to time expressed essential agreement with these interpretations of factors. Thurstone (40), for instance, suggested that factors are not to be regarded as ultimate psychological entities but rather as "functional unities" or aggregates of more elementary components. Nevertheless, Thurstone's discussion of factors in other publications and his continued use of the term "primary mental abilities" have tended to foster the impression of factors as underlying entities.

MULTIPLE APTITUDE BATTERIES FOR GENERAL USE

The most direct effect of factor analysis upon test construction can be seen in the development of multiple aptitude batteries. Among the best-known examples of such batteries designed for general use are the SRA Primary Mental Abilities (PMA), Differential Aptitude Tests (DAT), Flanagan Aptitude Classification Tests (FACT), Guilford-Zimmerman Aptitude Survey, Holzinger-Crowder Uni-Factor Tests, and Multiple Aptitude Tests (MAT). All of these batteries have been thoroughly reviewed in the fourth and fifth volumes of the *Mental Measurements Yearbooks,* as well as in a special survey edited by Super (36). The reader is urged to consult these sources for several independent evaluations of each instrument. This discussion will touch upon a few highlights only.

The publication of the original Chicago PMA tests in 1941 (44) was a direct outcome of Thurstone's pioneer research on the identification of the primary mental abilities discussed in the preceding section (39). For each factor, those tests with the highest factorial validities were assembled into a battery requiring six testing sessions. By reducing the number of tests for each factor, this series was later shortened to a single-booklet, two-hour edition. Subsequent development included further condensation, yielding the SRA Primary Mental Abilities for Ages 11-17, as well as downward extensions to include similar short batteries for ages 7-11 and 5-7 (45). Illustrative items from the 11-17 battery are reproduced in Figure 67.

Not all the primary mental abilities listed in the preceding section are represented in all these batteries. The factor scores provided in each battery are summarized below:

Chicago PMA: { separate-booklet ed. } (Ages 11-17) { single-booklet ed. }	M	V	W	N	S	R	
SRA: PMA Ages 11-17		V	W	N	S	R	
SRA: PMA Ages 7-11		V		N	S	R	P
SRA: PMA Ages 5-7		V	(Q)	S	(Q)	P	Mo

In the 5-7 year battery, a rudimentary Quantitative (Q) factor replaces the Numerical (N) and Reasoning (R) factors found at later ages. A Motor (Mo) test, involving speed and accuracy in the use of a pencil, was also added at the 5-7 year level. With regard to content, the PMA tests at this level are very similar to most group intelligence tests for the primary level (cf. Ch. 9). Subsequent research has shown, in fact, that multiple aptitude batteries contribute little at these ages, since the abilities of young children are very highly intercorrelated (3, pp. 357-360; 10; 20). In fact, it is not until the high school level that differentiation of abilities has progressed far enough to justify the practical use of multiple aptitude batteries.

VERBAL-MEANING is measured by a multiple-choice vocabulary test made up of the following type of item:

ANCIENT: A. Dry   B. Long   C. Happy   D. Old

The word which means the same as the first word is to be marked.

SPACE is measured by items similar to the one below:

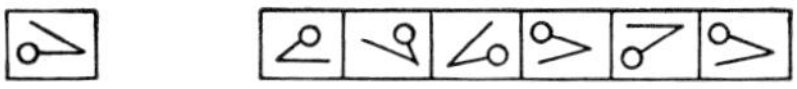

Every figure in the row that is the same as the first figure, even though it is rotated, is to be marked. Figures that are mirror-images of the first figure are not to be marked.

REASONING is measured by items like the following:

a b x c d x e f x g h x

The letters in the row form a series based on a rule. The problem is to mark the letter that should come next in the series.

NUMBER is measured by a series of addition items, such as the following:

$$\begin{array}{r} 17 \\ 84 \\ 29 \\ \hline 140 \end{array}$$

R W

The sum of each column of figures is given, but some of the solutions are right and others wrong. The answer given is to be marked right or wrong.

WORD-FLUENCY is measured by a test requiring the writing of as many words as possible beginning with a certain letter.

Fig. 67. Description and Illustration of Items from the SRA Tests of Primary Mental Abilities for Ages 11 to 17. (Reproduced by permission of Science Research Associates.)

The current PMA batteries have been widely criticized because of technical faults. The early forms were based on extensive research and represented an important breakthrough in test construction. Rather than providing the needed refinement and empirical validation, however, the subsequent evolution of these tests has proceeded chiefly in the direction of abridgment and simplification. Inadequacies of normative data, questionable types of scores (such as ratio IQ's), unsupported interpretations of scores, meager validity data, improper procedures for computing reliability of speeded tests, excessive dependence of scores on speed, and low reliabilities of factor scores are among the chief weaknesses of these tests. In their present form, they are of interest primarily to illustrate the nature of the factors identified in the original research.

The DAT (5) was developed principally for use in educational and vocational counseling of high school students. Designed for grades 8 through 12, it is also suitable for unselected adults. Although not utilizing factor analysis in its construction, the authors of the DAT were guided in their choice of tests by the accumulated results of factorial research, as well as by practical counseling needs. Rather than striving for factorial purity, they included tests that might be factorially complex if they represented well-recognized vocational or educational areas. The DAT yields the following eight scores: Verbal Reasoning, Numerical Ability, Abstract Reasoning, Space Relations, Mechanical Reasoning, Clerical Speed and Accuracy, Language Usage I— Spelling, and Language Usage II—Sentences. A sample item from each test is reproduced in Figures 68A and 68B.

The DAT manual provides an unusually clear and thorough account of the test-construction procedures followed in developing the battery. Norms were derived from a large, representative national sample. With the exception of Clerical Speed and Accuracy, all tests are essentially power tests. Reliability coefficients are high and permit interpretation of intertest differences with considerable confidence. By combining information on test reliabilities and intercorrelations found in the standardization sample, the test authors determined the proportion of differences in excess of chance between each pair of tests. This can be done by reference to the chart reproduced in Figure 69. For boys, the percentages of such differences ranged from 29 to 52; for girls, they ranged from 20 to 48.

The amount of validity data available on the DAT is overwhelming, including several thousand validity coefficients. Most of these data are concerned with predictive validity in terms of high school and college achievement. Many of the coefficients are high, even with intervals as long as three years between test and criterion data. The results are somewhat less encouraging with regard to differential prediction. Although, in general, verbal tests correlate more highly with English courses and numerical tests with mathematics courses, there is evidence of a large general factor underlying performance in all academic work. Verbal Reasoning, for example, gives high correlations with most courses.

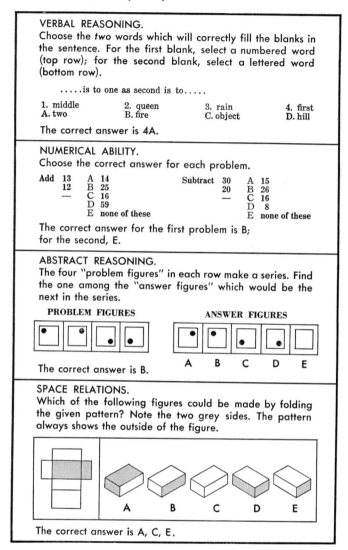

VERBAL REASONING.
Choose the *two* words which will correctly fill the blanks in the sentence. For the first blank, select a numbered word (top row); for the second blank, select a lettered word (bottom row).

.....is to one as second is to.....

1. middle   2. queen   3. rain   4. first
A. two   B. fire   C. object   D. hill

The correct answer is 4A.

NUMERICAL ABILITY.
Choose the correct answer for each problem.

Add 13   A 14   Subtract 30   A 15
     12   B 25   20   B 26
     —   C 16   —   C 16
           D 59   D 8
           E none of these   E none of these

The correct answer for the first problem is B; for the second, E.

ABSTRACT REASONING.
The four "problem figures" in each row make a series. Find the one among the "answer figures" which would be the next in the series.

PROBLEM FIGURES   **ANSWER FIGURES**

The correct answer is B.   A   B   C   D   E

SPACE RELATIONS.
Which of the following figures could be made by folding the given pattern? Note the two grey sides. The pattern always shows the outside of the figure.

A   B   C   D   E

The correct answer is A, C, E.

Fig. 68A. Sample Items from the Differential Aptitude Tests. (Reproduced by permission of The Psychological Corporation.)

Scores on the DAT are reported on normalized percentile charts. Thus the individual's relative standing on different tests is not distorted by the inequalities of percentile units. Corresponding standard scores with a mean of 50 and an *SD* of 10 can also be read from the profile charts (cf. Fig. 16, Ch. 4). In order to facilitate the interpretation of intra-individual differences in test scores, the profile charts were designed so that a distance of 1 inch cor-

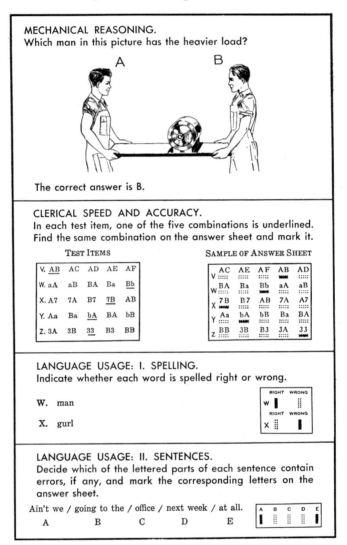

MECHANICAL REASONING.
Which man in this picture has the heavier load?

A   B

The correct answer is B.

CLERICAL SPEED AND ACCURACY.
In each test item, one of the five combinations is underlined.
Find the same combination on the answer sheet and mark it.

TEST ITEMS

V. AB	AC	AD	AE	AF
W. aA	aB	BA	Ba	Bb
X. A7	7A	B7	7B	AB
Y. Aa	Ba	bA	BA	bB
Z. 3A	3B	33	B3	BB

SAMPLE OF ANSWER SHEET

	AC	AE	AF	AB	AD
V	::::	::::	::::	▓▓▓	::::
W	BA	Ba	Bb	aA	aB
	::::	::::	▓▓▓	::::	::::
X	7B	B7	AB	7A	A7
	▓▓▓	::::	::::	::::	::::
Y	Aa	bA	bB	Ba	BA
	::::	▓▓▓	::::	::::	::::
Z	BB	3B	B3	3A	33
	::::	::::	::::	::::	▓▓▓

LANGUAGE USAGE: I. SPELLING.
Indicate whether each word is spelled right or wrong.

W. man

X. gurl

	RIGHT	WRONG
W	▮	⫴
X	⫴	▮

LANGUAGE USAGE: II. SENTENCES.
Decide which of the lettered parts of each sentence contain
errors, if any, and mark the corresponding letters on the
answer sheet.

Ain't we / going to the / office / next week / at all.
   A   B   C   D   E

A	B	C	D	E
▮	⫴	⫴	⫴	▮

Fig. 68B. Sample Items from the Differential Aptitude Tests. (Reproduced by permission of The Psychological Corporation.)

responds to 10 standard score points.[2] By computing the standard errors of intra-individual differences between each pair of tests (cf. Ch. 5), it can be shown that a difference of approximately 10 standard score points between any two tests is significant at the .05 level or better. On this basis it is recommended that if the vertical distance between any two tests on a profile is 1 inch or more, it may be assumed that a true difference exists. Differences be-

2 This is true in the actual profile charts, not in the reduced reproduction given in Figure 16.

tween ½ inch and 1 inch are considered doubtful; and those less than ½ inch, negligible.

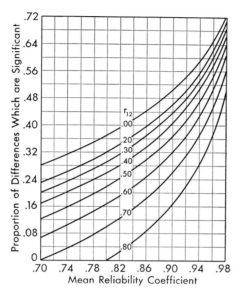

Fig. 69. Chart for Determining the Proportion of Differences in Excess of Chance between Pairs of Tests. (From Bennett and Doppelt, 4, p. 322; reproduced by permission of *Educational and Psychological Measurement.*)

No regression equations or other statistical procedures for predicting specific criteria with DAT scores are provided, except for an index of over-all scholastic ability. In the third edition of the Manual, published in 1958, data are presented to show that the sum of the Verbal Reasoning and Numerical Ability scores yields coefficients of .70 to .86 with subsequent academic criteria. The combination of these two scores thus functions as an especially valid "intelligence" test in this context. Test users may, of course, work out other score combinations and regression equations in terms of other specific criteria. The test authors themselves recommend a clinical rather than a statistical interpretation of scores (cf. Ch. 7), once the profiles have been plotted. In a casebook entitled *Counseling from Profiles* (6), they report 30 cases actually submitted by high school counselors, together with the DAT profiles, to illustrate the ways in which such profiles can be used in making individual recommendations.

A still different approach to the construction of multiple aptitude batteries is illustrated by the Flanagan Aptitude Classification Tests, or FACT (15). Beginning as an outgrowth of Flanagan's research on the development of Air Force classification tests during World War II, this battery is oriented principally toward vocational counseling and employee selection. Job analyses of many occupations led to the identification of 21 "critical job elements," or abilities differentiating successful from unsuccessful workers on each job. Any one job element is common to many types of jobs. Three examples of such job elements are given below (from p. 10, FACT Technical Report, 1959):

Assembly: Ability to visualize the appearance of an object assembled from a number of separate parts (see Fig. 70).

Planning: Ability to plan, organize, and schedule; ability to foresee problems that may arise, and to anticipate the best order for carrying out the various steps.

Ingenuity: Creative or inventive skill; ability to devise ingenious procedures, equipment, or presentations (see Fig. 70).

Assembly: In each figure, parts are to be assembled so that places having the same letter are put together. Which of the five assemblies below shows the parts put together correctly?

Ingenuity: Think of a word or words that will complete a clever and ingenious solution to the stated problem. Then choose the alternative having the same first and last letters and the same number of letter spaces as your answer.

> S1. A hostess for a children's party wanted to serve ice cream in an interesting manner, and she decided to make a clown for each child. She placed a ball of ice cream to represent the clown's head on a round cookie which served for a collar, and on top of this she inverted a
>
> A. t __ __ e.
> B. u __ __ i.
> C. r __ __ s.
> D. c __ __ e.
> E. t __ __ r.

Answers: *Assembly, C*   *Ingenuity, D (cone)*

Fig. 70. Sample Items from Flanagan Aptitude Classification Tests. (Reproduced by permission of John C. Flanagan.)

A battery of paper-and-pencil tests was prepared to test 19 of the 21 job elements. The remaining two, *Carving* and *Tapping,* require performance tests. Norms were established on a national sample of approximately 11,000 students in grades 9 to 12. On the basis of the initial, qualitative job analyses, test scores were combined into 38 Occupational Aptitude Scores, including one score for predicting general college aptitude and scores for specific occupations ranging from humanities teacher to plumber. The individual tests have rather low reliabilities and some of the score distributions suggest inadequate differentiations among individuals. Reliabilities of the composite Occupational Aptitude Scores are higher. These composite scores, however, show much more overlap than the individual test scores. Intercorrelations among the tests indicate that fairly distinct aptitudes are measured; but apparently many occupations require similar combinations of aptitudes. A correlation of .90 between the occupational scores for telephone operator and office clerk is not surprising; but a correlation of .95 between the aptitude scores of airplane pilot and draftsman suggests inadequate differential validity!

The Occupational Aptitude Scores are being validated longitudinally, by following up the subsequent educational and vocational careers of high school students tested in the standardization sample. This represents an ambitious and commendable plan. Available data from a one-year follow-up of the present form of the battery and follow-ups of earlier forms of as much as five-years' duration have so far provided moderately promising evidence of validity. The battery has shown good predictive validity against professional training criteria. But validity data in terms of job entry and advancement are meager and sometimes difficult to evaluate because of criterion inadequacies and the influence of fortuitous factors in occupational careers. The continuing research program carried on with the FACT battery will eventually permit a more definitive evaluation of its contribution.

Another battery resulting from wartime Air Force research is the Guilford-Zimmerman Aptitude Survey (26). This battery, which is still in the process of development and standardization, provides tests for seven factors: (1) Verbal Comprehension, (2) General Reasoning, (3) Numerical Operations, (4) Perceptual Speed, (5) Spatial Orientation, (6) Spatial Visualization, and (7) Mechanical Knowledge. It is suggested that Tests 1 and 2 may be combined to yield an estimate of "abstract intelligence," Tests 3 and 4 an estimate of "clerical aptitude," and Tests 5, 6, and 7 an estimate of "mechanical aptitude." For counseling or personnel classification, however, the use of the entire battery is recommended.

A distinctive feature of the Guilford-Zimmerman battery is its inclusion of two separate spatial scores. Spatial Orientation refers to the perception of spatial relations of objects with reference to the observer's own position. This ability proved important in learning to pilot a plane and may be involved in many jobs requiring the operation of machines. Spatial Visualization is the ability to manipulate or to transform an object into another visual arrangement. These two factors are illustrated by the items reproduced in Figure 71. Validity data for each of the seven parts of the battery include factor loadings as well as a few concurrent and predictive correlations with college grades and industrial criteria. The Verbal Comprehension and General Reasoning tests yield significant and moderately high correlations with grades in most courses. The Numerical and the two Spatial tests show some

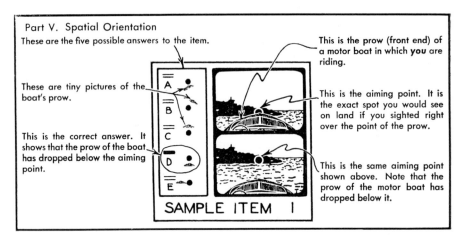

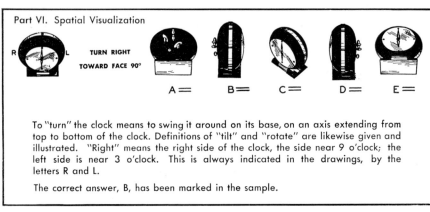

Fig. 71. Sample Items from Guilford-Zimmerman Aptitude Survey. (Reproduced by permission of Sheridan Supply Company.)

significant correlations with grades in certain courses and with industrial criteria, but evidence for differential validity is very meager.

The Holzinger-Crowder Uni-Factor Tests (27) have aimed more deliberately than most other batteries toward factorial purity and independence of factor scores. Partly as a consequence of these aims, these tests measure rather simple and narrowly limited functions. The battery provides four scores: Verbal, Spatial, Numerical, and Reasoning. Each of the first three scores is derived from two tests; the fourth from three tests. The battery is technically sound and the manual is unusually thorough and objective in its presentation of data. Norms are based on a large, nationwide sample of junior and senior high school students. Regression equations are provided for combining the factor scores so as to predict general scholastic aptitude, as well as achievement in science, social studies, English, and mathematics (cf. Ch. 7, p. 173). Validity has been checked principally against concurrent criteria of achievement tests and school grades. Some promising evidence of differential validity is available.

A relatively recent addition to differential testing is the MAT (33). Employing nine tests, this battery yields scores in Verbal Comprehension, Perceptual Speed, Numerical Reasoning, and Spatial Visualization. Similar in purpose and approach to the DAT, this battery has not been in use long enough to permit an adequate judgment of its effectiveness. The tests have been well constructed and carefully evaluated. Good techniques for score reporting have been worked out, including provision for evaluating the significance of differences between factor scores obtained by the same individual. Evidence of differential validity against grades in specific courses is inconclusive.

In commenting upon multiple aptitude batteries as a group, we may note first that available instruments differ considerably in approach, technical quality, and amount of available evaluative data. A common feature, however, is their disappointing performance with regard to *differential validity*. In this connection, the student is urged to reread the section on the use of tests for classification decisions, given in Chapter 7. It will be noted that counseling—for which most if not all the batteries discussed in the present section were developed—is essentially a classification decision. And it will be recalled that differential validity is the major requirement for classification batteries.

Perhaps academic criteria, against which most multiple aptitude batteries have so far been validated, are not clearly differentiable on the basis of aptitudes. It is possible that differences in performance in specific courses depend principally on interests, motivation, and emotional factors. Unpredictable contingency factors, such as interpersonal relations between an individual student and a particular instructor, may also play a part. With regard to aptitudes, the large common contribution of verbal comprehension to achievement in all academic areas has been repeatedly demonstrated. If dependable criteria of occupational success (rather than performance in vocational *training*) can be developed, it is likely that better differential predictions can be made with batteries designed for this purpose. In terms of available data, however, multi-factor batteries have fallen short of their initial promise.

MULTIPLE APTITUDE BATTERIES FOR SPECIAL PROGRAMS

Factor analysis underlies the development of classification batteries widely employed in the armed services and in certain civilian agencies. The General Aptitude Test Battery (GATB) was developed by the United States Employment Service for use by employment counselors in the State Employment Service offices (14, 22). Prior to the preparation of this battery, factorial analyses were conducted on preliminary batteries of 15 to 29 tests, which had been administered to nine groups of men. These groups included a total of 2156 men between the ages of 17 and 39, most of whom were trainees in vocational courses. A total of 59 tests was covered by the nine overlapping batteries. On the basis of these investigations, 10 factors were identified and 15 tests chosen to measure them. In a later revision of the GATB, the number of tests was reduced to 12 and the number of factors to 9.

The factors covered by the GATB are as follows:

G. *Intelligence:* Found by adding the scores on three tests also used to measure other factors (Vocabulary, Arithmetic Reason, Three-Dimensional Space).

V. *Verbal Aptitude:* Measured by a Vocabulary test requiring examinee to indicate which two words in each set have either the same or opposite meaning.

N. *Numerical Aptitude:* Includes both Computation and Arithmetic Reason tests.

S. *Spatial Aptitude:* Measured by Three-Dimensional Space test, involving the ability to comprehend two-dimensional representation of three-dimensional objects and to visualize effects of movement in three dimensions.

P. *Form Perception:* Measured by two tests requiring the subject to match identical drawings of tools in one test and of geometric forms in the other.

Q. *Clerical Perception:* Similar to P, but requiring the matching of names rather than pictures or forms.

K. *Motor Coordination:* Measured by a simple paper-and-pencil test requiring the subject to make specified pencil marks in a series of squares.

F. *Finger Dexterity:* Two tests requiring the assembling and disassembling, respectively, of rivets and washers.

M. *Manual Dexterity:* Two tests requiring the subject to transfer and reverse pegs in a board.

The last four tests (for measuring factors F and M) require simple apparatus; the other eight are paper-and-pencil tests. Alternative forms are available for the first seven tests. The entire battery requires approximately two and one-quarter hours.

The nine factor scores on the GATB are converted into standard scores with a mean of 100 and an SD of 20. These standard score norms were derived from a sample of 4000 cases representative of the 1940 working population of the United States in terms of age, sex, educational, occupational, and geographical distribution. By testing many groups of employees, applicants, and trainees in different kinds of jobs, Occupational Ability Patterns (OAP) have subsequently been established, showing the critical aptitudes and minimum standard scores required for each occupation. For example, accounting was found to require a minimum score of 105 in Intelligence (G) and 115 in Numerical Aptitude (N). Plumbing called for a minimum score of 85 in intelligence (G) and of 80 in Numerical Aptitude (N), Spatial Aptitude (S), and Manual Dexterity (M). An individual's standard score profile is matched with all those OAP's whose cutoff scores he reaches or exceeds. The occupations classified under these OAP's are then considered in counseling him.

The development of an OAP was illustrated in Chapter 7 (pp. 175-176). The procedure followed with each group includes job analysis, selection of suitable criterion data (output records, supervisors' ratings, training performance, etc.), and administration of the 12-test battery. The significant factors are chosen on the basis of their criterion correlations, as well as the means and SD's of scores on each factor and the qualitative job-analysis information. For example, if workers on the job under consideration average considerably above the normative sample in a particular factor and also show relatively low variability in their scores, that factor would probably be included in the OAP even if it fails to show a significant criterion correlation. Such a situation could occur if employees on a certain job were a highly selected group with regard to that aptitude. Specific occupations are grouped together on the basis of similar OAP's. Thus 22 OAP's have so far been developed, covering over 500 occupations. Slightly less than half of these occupations have been directly studied by the procedure outlined above. The others were added on the basis of similarity in job duties.

The GATB is used in State Employment Service offices in the counseling and job referral of nearly half a million applicants a year. In addition, the battery may be obtained by non-profit organizations such as colleges, universities, Veterans' Administration hospitals, and prisons, under arrangements with the appropriate State Employment Service. Permission has also been granted to individuals and organizations in many foreign countries to translate the GATB and use it for research purposes. Foreign editions are available or in preparation in over twenty countries distributed over every continent (13).

Through the facilities of the United States Employment Service and the various State offices, a vast body of data has been gathered on the GATB, and a continuing research program is in progress. The normative sample is unusually large and representative. A large amount of information on predictive and concurrent validity of individual OAP's is reported in the manual (22) and in the Validity Information Exchange published in *Personnel Psychology* since 1954. Although cross-validation has not been systematically carried out and rather crude statistical procedures have been employed, available cross-validation data are promising. Despite the shortness of the tests, reliabilities of the factor scores are generally satisfactory. Both equivalent-form and retest correlations cluster in the .80's and low .90's, although the reliabilities of the motor tests tend to be somewhat lower.

Certain limitations of the battery should be noted. All tests are highly speeded. Coverage of aptitudes is somewhat limited. No mechanical comprehension test is included, nor are tests of reasoning and inventiveness well represented. The factorial structure of the battery rests on a series of early exploratory studies. A more comprehensive investigation with a large sample and a wider variety of tests would provide a more solid foundation. In terms of the over-all empirical evidence, however, the GATB has proved to be one of the most successful multiple aptitude batteries in current use.

The armed services also make extensive use of multiple aptitude batteries. These batteries are given for classification purposes after preliminary screening with such instruments as the Army General Classification Test (AGCT) and the Armed Forces Qualification Test (AFQT) (cf. Ch. 9). Although the Air Force pioneered in the development of classification batteries, all branches of the armed services eventually prepared multifactor batteries for assigning personnel to specialized military jobs.

In the Air Force, the Aircrew Classification Battery was developed and employed during World War II for selecting pilots, navigators, bombardiers, and other flight personnel (47). Later, an Airman Classification Test Battery (48) was prepared for use with other Air Force personnel. Both batteries were constructed by means of factor analysis. In applying these batteries, the scores on each test are substituted in the appropriate regression equation for the particular specialty. The individual's predicted score, or Aptitude Index, for that specialty serves as a basis for job assignments. For example, in computing the Aptitude Index for clerical specialties, significant weights are given to tests of arithmetic reasoning, background for current affairs, dial- and table-reading, numerical operations, and word knowledge. The index for radio operator is based upon tests of arithmetic reasoning, dial- and table-reading, electrical information, memory for landmarks, and numerical operations. A score on a biographical inventory, derived with a different key for each specialty, is also employed in the determination of each Aptitude Index.

On the whole, both the GATB and the various multi-factor batteries developed for military use have proved relatively successful as classification instruments. Both differ from the general counseling batteries discussed in the preceding section in that they have been validated chiefly against occupational rather than academic criteria. To be sure, training criteria have sometimes been substituted for actual job performance, but the training programs were job-oriented and quite unlike school work. Both training and job activities of airplane pilots, bakers, beauticians, and the many other kinds of workers included in these testing programs are far removed from traditional academic tasks. With criteria differing more widely from each other and from the verbally loaded academic criterion, there is more room for differential validity.

Another advantage enjoyed by the military batteries is that the number of occupational fields to be covered is smaller than in a general counseling battery. This was especially true of the Aircrew Classification Battery, whose task was limited to the assignment of personnel to four or five jobs. As a result, it was possible to work with relatively narrow group factors, which specifically matched the criterion requirements. In the Air Force research, for example, a large number of different sensorimotor, perceptual, and spatial factors were identified and utilized in test construction. A general counseling battery, on the other hand, must concentrate on a few broad group factors, each of which is common to many jobs. To do otherwise would require the administration of a prohibitive number of tests to each person. But with such an instrument distinctions are blurred and differential validity drops.

REFERENCES

1. Adcock, C. J. *Factorial analysis for non-mathematicians.* Carlton, N. 3, Victoria: Melbourne Univer. Press; N. Y.: Cambridge Univer. Press, 1954.
2. Ahmavaara, Y. *On the unified factor theory of mind.* Helsinki: Suomalaisen Kirjallisuuden Kirjapaino Oy, 1957.
3. Anastasi, Anne. *Differential psychology.* (3rd ed.) N. Y.: Macmillan, 1958.
4. Bennett, G. K., and Doppelt, J. E. The evaluation of pairs of tests for guidance use. *Educ. psychol. Measmt.,* 1948, 8, 319-325.
5. Bennett, G. K., Seashore, H. G., and Wesman, A. G. *Differential Aptitude Tests.* N. Y.: Psychol. Corp., 1947-1959.
6. Bennett, G. K., Seashore, H. G., and Wesman, A. G. *Counseling from profiles: a casebook for the Differential Aptitude Tests.* N. Y.: Psychol. Corp., 1951.
7. Burt, C. *The factors of the mind: an introduction to factor-analysis in psychology.* N. Y.: Macmillan, 1941.
8. Burt, C. Mental abilities and mental factors. *Brit. J. educ. Psychol.,* 1944, 14, 85-89.
9. Burt, C. The structure of the mind; a review of the results of factor analysis. *Brit. J. Psychol.,* 1949, 19, 176-199.
10. Burt, C. The differentiation of intellectual ability. *Brit. J. educ. Psychol.,* 1954, 24, 76-90.
11. Carroll, J. B. A factor analysis of verbal abilities. *Psychometrika,* 1941, 6, 279-308.
12. Christal, R. E. Factor analytic study of visual memory. *Psychol. Monogr.,* 1958, 72, No. 13.
13. Dvorak, Beatrice J. GATB in foreign countries. *J. appl. Psychol.,* 1954, 38, 373-374.
14. Dvorak, Beatrice J. The General Aptitude Test Battery. *Personnel Guid. J.,* 1956, 35, 145-154.
15. Flanagan, J. C. *Flanagan Aptitude Classification Tests.* Chicago: Sci. Res. Assoc., 1953-1959.
16. French, J. W. The description of aptitude and achievement tests in terms of rotated factors. *Psychometr. Monogr.,* 1951, No. 5.
17. French, J. W. *Manual for kit of selected reference aptitude and achievement factors.* Princeton, N. J.: Educ. Test. Serv., 1954.
18. French, J. W. Kit of factor reference tests. *Amer. Psychologist,* 1959, 14, 416.
19. Fruchter, B. *Introduction to factor analysis.* Princeton, N. J.: Van Nostrand, 1954.
20. Garrett, H. E. A developmental theory of intelligence. *Amer. Psychologist,* 1946, 1, 372-378.
21. Green, R. F., Guilford, J. P., Christensen, P. R., and Comrey, A. L. A factor-analytic study of reasoning abilities. *Psychometrika,* 1953, 18, 135-160.
22. *Guide to the use of the General Aptitude Test Battery. Section III: Development.* Washington: Govt. Printing Office, 1952-1958.

23. Guilford, J. P. *Psychometric methods.* (Rev. ed.) N. Y.: McGraw-Hill, 1954.
24. Guilford, J. P. The structure of intellect. *Psychol. Bull.,* 1956, 53, 267-293.
25. Guilford, J. P. Three faces of intellect. *Amer. Psychologist,* 1959, 14, 469-479.
26. Guilford, J. P., and Zimmerman, W. S. *The Guilford-Zimmerman Aptitude Survey.* Beverly Hills, Calif.: Sheridan Supply Co., 1947-1956.
27. Holzinger, K. J., and Crowder, N. A. *Holzinger-Crowder Uni-Factor Tests.* Tarrytown-on-Hudson, N. Y.: World Book Co., 1952-1955.
28. Kelley, T. L. *Crossroads in the mind of man: a study of differentiable mental abilities.* Stanford Univer., Calif.: Stanford Univer. Press, 1928.
29. Kelley, T. L. *Essential traits of mental life.* Cambridge, Mass.: Harvard Univer. Press, 1935.
30. Kettner, N., Guilford, J. P., and Christensen, P. R. A factor-analytic investigation of the factor called general reasoning. *Educ. psychol. Measmt.,* 1956, 16, 438-453.
31. Michael, W. B., Guilford, J. P., Fruchter, B., and Zimmerman, W. S. The description of spatial-visualization abilities. *Educ. psychol. Measmt.,* 1957, 17, 185-199.
32. Pearson, K. On lines and planes of closest fit to systems of points in space. *Phil. Mag.,* Series 6, 1901, 2, 559-572.
33. Segel, D., and Raskin, Evelyn. *Multiple Aptitude Tests.* Monterey, Calif.: Calif. Test Bur., 1955.
34. Spearman, C. "General intelligence" objectively determined and measured. *Amer. J. Psychol.,* 1904, 15, 201-293.
35. Spearman, C. *The abilities of man.* N. Y.: Macmillan, 1927.
36. Super, D. E. (Ed.) *The use of multifactor tests in guidance.* Washington: Amer. Personnel Guid. Assoc., 1958. (Reprinted from *Personnel Guid. J.,* 1956-1957.)
37. Thomson, G. H. A hierarchy without a general factor. *Brit. J. Psychol.,* 1916, 8, 271-281.
38. Thomson, G. H. *The factorial analysis of human ability.* (3rd ed.) Boston: Houghton Mifflin, 1948.
39. Thurstone, L. L. Primary mental abilities. *Psychometr. Monogr.,* 1938, No. 1.
40. Thurstone, L. L. Current issues in factor analysis. *Psychol. Bull.,* 1940, 37, 189-236.
41. Thurstone, L. L. A factorial study of perception. *Psychometr. Monogr.,* 1944, No. 4.
42. Thurstone, L. L. *Multiple factor analysis.* Chicago: Univer. Chicago Press, 1947.
43. Thurstone, L. L., and Thurstone, Thelma G. Factorial studies of intelligence. *Psychometr. Monogr.,* 1941, No. 2.
44. Thurstone, L. L., and Thurstone, Thelma G. *The Chicago Tests of Primary Mental Abilities.* Chicago: Sci. Res. Assoc. Six-Booklet Edition, 1941; Single-Booklet Edition, 1943.
45. Thurstone, L. L., and Thurstone, Thelma G. *SRA Primary Mental Abilities—Ages 5 to 7; Ages 7 to 11; Ages 11 to 17.* Chicago: Sci. Res. Assoc., 1946-1958.

46. Tryon, R. C. A theory of *psychological components*—an alternative to "mathematical factors." *Psychol. Rev.,* 1935, 42, 425-454.

47. U.S. Air Force. *Aviation psychology research reports.* Washington: Govt. Printing Office, 1947. Reports No. 1, 5, 11.

48. U.S. Air Force. Development of the Airman Classification Test Battery. *Air Train. Com. Res. Develpm. Progr., Res. Bull.,* 48-4, Nov. 1948.

49. Vernon, P. E. *The structure of human abilities.* (Rev. ed.) London: Methuen, 1960.

CHAPTER 14

Special Aptitude Tests: I

Even prior to the development of multiple aptitude batteries, it was generally recognized that intelligence tests were limited in their coverage of abilities. Efforts were soon made to fill the major gaps by means of special aptitude tests. Among the earliest were those designed to measure mechanical aptitude. Since intelligence tests concentrate chiefly upon "abstract" functions involving the use of verbal or numerical symbols, a particular need was felt for tests covering the more "concrete" or "practical" abilities. Mechanical aptitude tests were developed partly to meet this need.

The demands of vocational selection and counseling likewise stimulated the development of tests to measure mechanical, clerical, musical, and artistic aptitudes. Tests of vision, hearing, and motor dexterity have also found their principal applications in the selection and classification of personnel for industrial and military purposes. It is thus apparent that a strong impetus to the construction of all special aptitude tests has been provided by the urgent problems of matching job requirements with the specific pattern of abilities characterizing each individual.

A word should be added about the concept of special aptitudes. The term originated at a time when the major emphasis in testing was placed upon general intelligence. Mechanical, musical, and other special aptitudes were thus regarded as supplementary to the "IQ" in the description of the individual. With the advent of factor analysis, however, it was gradually recognized that intelligence itself comprises a number of relatively independent aptitudes, such as verbal comprehension, numerical reasoning, numerical computation, spatial visualization, associative memory, and the like. Moreover, several of the traditional special aptitudes, such as mechanical and clerical, are now incorporated in some of the multiple aptitude batteries.

What, then, is the justification for a separate chapter on special aptitude tests? First, there are certain areas, such as vision, hearing, motor dexterity, and artistic talents, that are rarely included in multiple aptitude batteries.

365

From the practical viewpoint of test administration, it is probably more convenient to employ independent tests in these fields. Such a practice permits more flexibility, not only in the choice of relevant functions, but also in the fullness with which each function is to be measured for specific purposes. The second reason for a separate discussion of special aptitude tests pertains to those tests that do overlap the content of multiple aptitude batteries. The various clerical and mechanical aptitude tests fall into this category. In certain types of testing programs, it is still current practice to employ tests of general intelligence as screening instruments and to supplement them with more detailed special aptitude tests in relevant areas. In part, the continuation of this procedure may reflect inertia. But to some extent it undoubtedly results from the availability of vocational norms and validation data for the special aptitude tests. Such data are not yet generally available for the subtests of the various differential batteries, which have been more recently developed.

This chapter covers sensory, motor, mechanical, and clerical tests. In the following chapter will be considered tests for measuring aptitudes in the artistic, musical, and literary fields, as well as tests of reasoning and creativity. Some of the tests designed to predict professional aptitudes, to be considered in Chapter 17, could likewise be included under the measurement of special aptitudes. It is apparent that the designation "special aptitude tests" has become somewhat of a catch-all. In it are included a miscellaneous collection of tests, each measuring a more narrowly defined area than either intelligence tests or multiple aptitude batteries.

SENSORY CAPACITIES

Use of Sensory Tests in Psychology. Among the earliest topics investigated in laboratories of experimental psychology were sensory acuity, sensory discrimination, and the influence of various factors upon sensitivity. Today, research on sensory capacities is an important phase of applied experimental psychology, or human engineering. It is one of the principal aims of this field of research to adapt equipment design for effective use by the human operator (cf. 10, 40). Such laboratory studies on sensitivity, however, are concerned primarily with principles or with general characteristics, rather than with the measurement of individual differences. This approach does not, therefore, fall within the scope of psychological testing, although it has occasionally contributed to methodology and to the accumulation of normative data.

Even if we limit the present discussion to standardized tests, we shall find that the measurement of sensory capacities has served a variety of functions in the field of psychological testing. The reader will recall the early attempts by Galton and others to measure intelligence by means of sensory tests (Ch. 1). Although these efforts proved futile, a number of later studies on school children have suggested the detrimental effects that visual or auditory handicaps may have upon intellectual development, educational progress, and social adjustment (cf. 1, pp. 142-147). The examination of school children for the detection of minor visual or auditory deficiencies is now routine practice in many school systems. These examinations serve a screening function. The children whose test performance shows evidence of defect are then referred for individual examination and clinical diagnosis by a specialist. The results of such clinical examinations may serve as a basis for corrective treatment, assignment to special classes, transfer to special schools, or other appropriate action. Screening tests for visual or auditory defects may also be utilized as a check prior to the administration of any group tests that require reading or oral instructions. A child who falls below the minimum standard on a sensory test can then be excluded from the regular testing session and examined by more suitable procedures.

Another application of sensory tests is to be found in the psychological clinic. It is frequently desirable to check for unsuspected sensory deficiencies as a possible source of the patient's difficulties. This is especially important in cases of reading disabilities and speech defects. But many other conditions, such as behavior disorders or school retardation in children, and depression or abnormal suspiciousness in adults, may have been induced or aggravated by an uncorrected sensory deficiency (cf., e.g., 4, 12).

One of the chief current uses of sensory tests is in the selection of industrial or military personnel. A large amount of research is available that indicates the effects of sensory handicaps upon quantity and quality of output, spoilage and waste of materials, job turnover, and accidents (cf., e.g., 59, Chs. 5 and 14). Many types of military specialties likewise make heavy demands upon visual or auditory capacities (cf. 10, 60). Special attention has been given to the role of both auditory and visual defects in the causation of accidents. Relevant data have been obtained, not only among industrial employees and transportation workers, but also among automobile drivers. The psychology of traffic thus represents a related field in which increasing use of sensory tests is being made (cf. 15).

Although psychological research on sensory capacities has extended to all sense modalities, standardized tests for the measurement of individual differences have been limited primarily to vision and hearing. These, of course, are the most important modalities for modern man. It is also interesting to note that most available sensory tests are designed chiefly to detect deficiencies. The identification of superior capacities has received relatively little attention. Perhaps the medical point of view, which is concerned with pathological deviations rather than with the whole range of human variation, has influenced the orientation of sensory tests in this direction.

In the present section, we shall consider some of the most widely used standardized testing techniques in the fields of vision and hearing. Only screening instruments designed for general testing will be discussed. No mention will be made of the more elaborate and refined techniques that have been developed for special purposes. The latter category includes clinical instruments for the use of such medical specialists as oculists and otologists, as well as laboratory apparatus for research in experimental psychology or in other sciences concerned with vision and hearing.

Vision. Visual sensitivity includes not one but many functions. It is common knowledge, for example, that color perception may be impaired or even totally lacking in an individual whose vision is otherwise normal. That a number of other aspects of vision must be differentiated is not, however, so generally recognized. Among the visual characteristics found to be of greatest practical importance may be mentioned: near acuity at "reading distance" (13-16 inches), far acuity (usually measured at 20 feet), perception of distance or depth, muscular balance of the eyes (phoria), and color discrimination.

The principal characteristic tested by the usual type of wall chart is far acuity. The Snellen Chart, containing rows of letters of gradually decreasing size, is undoubtedly the most familiar of these charts. In the administration of this test, the subject is seated at a distance of 20 feet from the chart. If he can correctly read the row of letters that the average person can perceive at 20 feet, he is said to have normal, or 20/20 vision. If he can read the letters normally identified at 15 feet, he has superior far acuity, as represented by 20/15 vision. A ratio of 20/100, on the other hand, signifies that at 20 feet he can perceive only letters that the average person can identify at 100 feet. His far acuity is therefore quite poor. Charts employing pictures, dots, or diagrams have been prepared on the same principle, for testing preschool children, older children with reading disabilities, or illiterate adults.

Sometimes such an acuity test is administered by employing letters (or other objects) of constant size, recognizable at 20 feet by the normal eye, and varying the distance until the subject can correctly read the letters. Although identical in principle, this procedure yields a score that appears somewhat different. Thus 20/40 visual acuity on the Snellen Chart now becomes 10/20. In both cases, the numerator indicates the distance at which the subject correctly identifies the letters; the denominator, the distance at which the average person identifies them. If expressed as decimals or percentages, the two types of ratios are identical. In the example cited, both are equal to .50.

In certain measures of acuity, especially those obtained under more precise laboratory conditions, acuity is reported in terms of the visual angle subtended by the smallest object the person can see. As an object of constant size moves farther away, it will, of course, subtend a smaller visual angle and will become increasingly difficult to see. A large, distant object may subtend the same visual angle as a small object close at hand. The most common test object employed in determining the visual angle of the smallest discriminable detail is known as the "Landolt C" or "Landolt ring." This is a small circle with a break at one point. Both the size and position of the gap are varied in the course of the examination. In each case, the subject is required to state the position of the break. The object of the test is to find the smallest gap that the subject can correctly locate. If the subject is seated at a standard distance from the test object, the visual angle subtended by this gap can be readily determined.

In general, it has been found that the average person can just barely see an object (or detail, such as the above-mentioned break) that subtends a visual angle of one minute (i.e., 1/60th of a degree). This angle corresponds to a visual acuity of 20/20 as determined by the Snellen Chart or similar tests. Because of the relationship between the two types of tests, visual acuity can be readily converted into a visual angle, or vice versa. The visual angle, in minutes, is simply the reciprocal of the visual acuity ratio. For example, 20/40 acuity corresponds to a visual angle of 2 minutes; 20/100, to an angle of 5 minutes; and 20/10, to an angle of ½ minute.

The above discussion has dealt only with far acuity tests. What of the other important aspects of vision? Measures of a number of different visual characteristics have been incorporated in certain visual screening instruments specially designed for large-scale testing in industry or in schools. The three best-known instruments for this purpose are the Ortho-Rater (Bausch and Lomb), the Sight-Screener (American Optical Company), and the Telebinocular (Keystone View Company). A picture of the Ortho-Rater in use is reproduced in Figure 72. The three instruments are essentially similar in principle, each providing measures of near and far acuity, depth perception, lateral and vertical phorias, and color discrimination.

These instruments have been used extensively in industry, where efforts have been made to set up visual qualifications for specific jobs. Some of the results obtained in a survey of 3025 workers in 51 industrial jobs can be

Differential Testing of Abilities

Fig. 72. The Bausch and Lomb Ortho-Rater for Testing Visual Functions. (Courtesy Bausch & Lomb Optical Company.)

seen in Figure 73. This graph shows the relation between performance on Ortho-Rater far acuity test and measures of job success. Among the employees obtaining each far acuity score, the graph indicates the proportion who fell into the high criterion group in terms of job performance. These re-

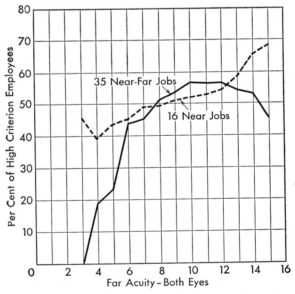

Fig. 73. Relation between Criteria of Job Success and Ortho-Rater Far Acuity Scores in a Group of 3025 Industrial Employees. (From McCormick, 39, p. 56; reproduced by permission of American Psychological Association.)

sults are reported separately for 16 jobs requiring predominantly "near" vision, and for 35 jobs requiring varying combinations of "near" and "far" vision.

A thorough investigation of 14 types of wall charts, together with the three machine tests described above, was conducted by the Personnel Research Branch of The Adjutant General's Office, United States Army (63). In introducing the study, the authors pointed out that great inconsistency in the application of visual standards for military service had resulted from the use of different instruments, as well as from inadequate standardization of testing and scoring procedures. One part of the study was concerned with the reliability of wall charts. For this purpose, 261 men were retested with each chart after a 24-hour interval. On the whole, the reliabilities were found to be satisfactory. The Snellen Chart, for example, yielded a reliability of .88. Most of the others had reliabilities close to .80. In another part of the study, similar reliability coefficients were found for most of the measures obtained with the three machine tests.

A major portion of the investigation consisted of factor analyses of the intercorrelations among the various tests. The most prominent factor revealed by these analyses was a *retinal resolution* factor. Retinal resolution, or the ability to "resolve" or distinguish points in the visual field, is essentially what is meant by visual acuity. All tests had significant loadings in this factor, but its loadings were highest in the far acuity tests. The purest measures of this factor were those employing, not letters, but a checkerboard pattern, such as that illustrated in Figure 74. This type of pattern is also used in the Ortho-Rater far acuity test. Letter charts, such as the Snellen Chart, had additional significant loadings in a form perception factor. A further complication in the development of letter tests arises from the inequalities in ease of recognizing different letters. Such a problem is avoided in the checkerboard tests.

All near tests had significant loadings in a factor of *accommodation.* This appears to be the principal distinguishing characteristic of near vision. It is this factor that shows impairment with advancing age. Among the other factors identified were *depth perception, lateral phoria, vertical phoria,* and *convergence efficiency* (at the normal reading distance). It should be noted that all tests measuring these factors also had appreciable loadings in other factors. These non-pertinent factors included the previously mentioned retinal resolution factor, which occurred in all the tests, as well as minor group and specific factors. Moreover, the factorial composition of similarly named tests from the different machines varied considerably. It may be added that the factorial analyses likewise suggested the presence of certain *brightness dis-*

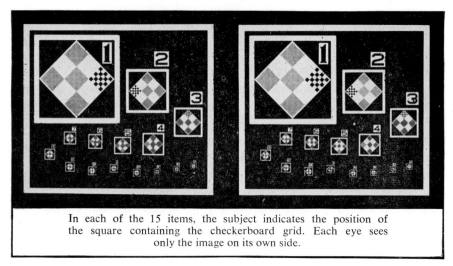

In each of the 15 items, the subject indicates the position of the square containing the checkerboard grid. Each eye sees only the image on its own side.

Fig. 74. "Checkerboard" Slide for Measuring Far Acuity with the Ortho-Rater. (Courtesy Bausch & Lomb Optical Company.)

crimination and *form perception* factors. Although these factors do not seem to be adequately measured by any existing instruments, they provide fruitful leads for further research. Such factors could have considerable practical significance in certain situations. On the whole, this investigation indicates that much remains to be done in the development of satisfactory and unambiguous measures for the different visual characteristics.

Because of the special interest that attaches to color vision, separate tests of color discrimination have been available for a long time. The importance of color signals in many forms of transportation is well known. Industry is likewise making increasing use of color coding in many kinds of operations. The correct and rapid identification of colors is also required in the performance of numerous military functions. It is apparent that a dependable and easily administered test for the detection of deficient color vision is needed for a variety of purposes.

One of the earliest and crudest techniques for the detection of color blindness was that employing the Holmgren woolens. This is a sorting test, in which the subject is given a large skein of green wool and told to select all the small skeins that approximately match it in color. The procedure may be repeated with a large rose skein and a large red skein as samples.

A more refined technique is based upon the use of pseudo-isochromatic plates. The Ishihara[1] and its many revisions and adaptations are familiar

[1] Obtainable from C. H. Stoelting Company and other companies dealing in psychological or optical equipment.

examples of this approach. Pseudo-isochromatic plates employ colors so chosen as to appear alike in certain types of color blindness, while appearing distinctly different to the normal eye. The background consists of dots in one of these colors, while a number or pattern is traced in dots of the other color. The color-blind subject will be unable to see any numbers or patterns on some of the plates; on others, he will see a different number from that seen by the normal person. The responses to each plate expected from red-blind, green-blind, and totally color-blind persons are indicated in the manual. Another test constructed on the same principle is the Dvorine Pseudo-Isochromatic Plates (17). Some normative data are available that permit an evaluation of degree of handicap in terms of number of errors on this test (51).

A different approach is illustrated by two color vision tests developed by Farnsworth. The Farnsworth Dichotomous Test for Color Blindness (18) is a screening device designed to distinguish the color blind, on the one hand, from the moderately color defective and the normal, on the other. By setting the standard of "passing" somewhat lower than in the Ishihara type of test, it avoids classifying those who are merely color deficient with the color blind. The author points out that the color deficient person is employable in a number of occupations requiring only gross color discriminations. In the Farnsworth test, the subject is required to arrange 15 colored caps, or "buttons," in order according to color, beginning with a given cap. Each cap is numbered on the reverse side. To score the test, the examiner reverses the rack and records the order in which the caps were arranged by the subject. When errors are present, the resulting pattern on the scoring sheet reveals the presence and type of color blindness.

A similar procedure is followed in the Farnsworth-Munsell 100 Hue Test (19), except that 85 caps are used and the subject sorts the caps in four series.[2] The score on this test provides a quantitative measure of the subject's ability to discriminate colors. In addition to identifying the different varieties of color blindness, as in the dichotomous test, this instrument can differentiate among individuals with weak, normal, or superior color discrimination. The number and extent of incorrect placements, as well as the location of errors on the color chart, are taken into consideration in evaluating performance.

Two difficulties encountered in the administration of most commercially available color vision tests arise from the effect of varying illumination and from the fading and soiling of colors. All tests specify the use of a standard illuminant, but owing to inadequate facilities the illuminant often deviates

---

[2] Although this test is based on the Munsell 100-hue equal-chromaticity series, only 85 colors are used since preliminary research indicated that 15 of the pairs were too often confused by normal subjects to be discriminative.

widely from the prescribed standard. Either varying illumination or the fading or soiling of test materials may affect different hues unequally and hence alter the relationship between colored stimuli. Thus despite careful selection of original colors in the construction and printing of the test, a color-blind person might pass such a test because of poorly controlled conditions.

The Illuminant-Stable (I-S) Color Vision Test (28, 29), was designed especially to meet these difficulties. The author states that the particular colors chosen are such as to yield approximately the same results under widely varying conditions of illumination. Some empirical evidence of such stability of scores is reported from a study of 100 normal and 100 color-blind subjects (29). To reduce soiling and fading, a transparent plastic coating is employed. The principle on which this test is constructed is that of pseudo-isochromatic plates, as in the Ishihara and Dvorine tests. A definitive evaluation of the I-S test is not possible until more data have been accumulated.

Hearing. Like vision, hearing is not a unitary capacity. An individual may be normal or superior in one aspect of hearing and seriously deficient in another. The aspect of most general interest is auditory acuity. Also known as the absolute threshold of hearing, this measure refers to the faintest sound that the individual can just barely hear. A number of other questions can, however, be asked regarding a person's hearing. Some assume major importance if we wish to predict how effectively the individual will function in certain situations. Thus we may want to test his tolerance for very loud sounds. At what intensity does sound become painful or uncomfortable for him? Or it may be necessary to measure his ability to recognize words against a background of loud and confusing noise, as in an airplane intercommunication system. The answers to these questions can usually be obtained by adaptations of the basic techniques employed in measuring auditory acuity.

In other situations, the individual may have to make fine auditory discriminations, as in distinguishing the pitch or loudness of different tones. In the submarine service, for example, the control of a number of instruments, such as sonar, depends upon such auditory discriminations. Since the ability to make fine differentiations between sounds is also of primary importance to musicians, the Seashore Measures of Musical Talents include a series of auditory discrimination tests for pitch, intensity, time, and timbre. These tests have been in use for a long time in connection with the selection and counseling of prospective music students. More recently, however, they have demonstrated a wider applicability, having proved helpful in the selection of personnel for certain military and civilian jobs. Because of their predominant orientation toward the prediction of musical performance, a discussion of the Seashore Tests will be deferred to the next chapter, which covers the measurement of musical aptitudes. At least some of these tests, however, could have been included in this section. This is especially true of the pitch discrimination test, which has been widely applied outside the field of music.

The remainder of the section will provide a rapid overview of typical techniques for the measurement of auditory acuity. For a fuller discussion of these techniques, the reader is referred to such books as Davis (13), Hirsh (35), and Watson and Tolan (64). Among the simplest procedures employed for testing auditory acuity are the *whispered speech* and *watch tick* tests. In both of these tests, the examiner gradually increases or decreases his distance from the subject in order to determine at what distance the subject can just barely hear the spoken words or the watch. While the whispered speech test checks acuity over the pitch range usually necessary to understand speech, the watch test samples higher frequencies. The latter thus provides a useful supplement, since loss of hearing often begins with decreased sensitivity for higher frequencies.

The chief weakness of these tests, of course, is the lack of standardization of both stimuli and surroundings. The amount of distracting noise, echoes, and other acoustic properties of the room influence the results. Similarly, the voices and speech of different examiners and the ticking of different watches are far from uniform. It is probably for these reasons that when using such crude tests, each examiner generally applies his own norms. Some degree of uniformity is at least possible within each examiner's application of the technique.

A more precise determination of auditory acuity can be obtained with one of the many types of electronic *audiometers* that are now available. For *individual testing,* pure tone audiometers are generally employed. In administering such a test, it is customary to test one ear at a time, the subject receiving the sound through a headphone or receiver held against the ear. Beginning with a sound too faint for the subject to hear, the examiner gradually increases the intensity of the tone until the subject indicates that he hears it. The threshold is determined in both an ascending and descending direction. In other words, the intensity is increased until the subject can just barely hear the sound, and it is decreased until he can no longer hear it. This will be recognized as the psychophysical method of limits commonly employed in experimental psychology laboratories. The entire procedure is repeated at several frequency levels in order to check for differential hearing loss.

At each frequency level, the subject's hearing loss in decibels can be read directly from the audiometer dial. The zero point on this dial represents

Differential Testing of Abilities

the intensity of sound that the "normal" ear can just barely hear on that audiometer. This point was empirically determined in the process of calibrating each instrument, by testing a large normative sampling of persons. The subject's hearing loss, as indicated on the audiometer, represents the number of decibels by which sound intensity must be increased above the normal threshold in order to be audible to him. The audiometer dial readings are used to plot the subject's *audiogram,* a graph showing his hearing loss at different frequency levels. An audiogram of a school child is reproduced in Figure 75. It illustrates differential hearing loss at the higher frequencies in a subject whose hearing is virtually normal at lower frequencies.

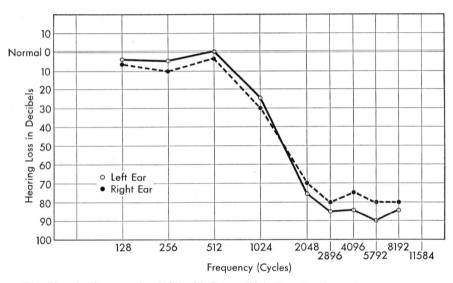

Fig. 75.   Audiogram of a Child with Severe High Tone Deafness. (From Watson and Tolan, 64, p. 247; copyright by L. A. Watson.)

In employing the audiometer, it is of course essential to observe the rules of all good test administration. Such problems as uniformity of testing conditions, adequate comprehension of instructions by the subject, rapport, and the detection of malingering deserve particular attention. If, for example, the subject fails to concentrate upon the stimulus, he is less likely to hear faint sounds. As in any auditory test, the avoidance of distracting noise is especially important. Frequent checking of the instrument, and particularly of the headphones, is essential. It is obvious that without such precautions misleading results might be obtained even with the most carefully constructed precision instrument. When properly administered, audiometers have been found to yield retest reliabilities ranging from .70 to .87 (cf. 60). As would be expected, the reliability of informal, unstandardized techniques such as the whispered speech and watch tick tests is much lower. Moreover, the latter tests do not correlate very highly with audiometer tests. The median correlations found in one survey were .34 and .35 for the whispered speech and watch tick tests, respectively (cf. 60).

Since one of the most important functions of hearing is the understanding of speech, a more direct measure of this ability may be desirable. Speech audiometers are sometimes employed for this purpose. In this case, the sound stimulus the subject receives through the earphone is the human voice pronouncing numbers, words, or sentences. As in the pure tone audiometer, the intensity is varied to determine the point at which the subject can correctly understand speech. This intensity is usually higher than that at which the subject can just barely *hear* speech. Such a procedure provides a more functional measure of the social adequacy of the subject's hearing.

Other types of audiometers are available for *group screening tests*. These audiometers are often used in surveys of school children, as many as 40 children being tested simultaneously by this method. For many years, group audiometer tests have been conducted with phonographic-type audiometers in which speech provides the test stimuli. The most common procedure is that involving the so-called fading numbers test. In this test, two-place numbers are presented at decreasing intensities, the subjects being required to write the numbers as they hear them. No attempt is made to explore differential hearing loss at different frequency levels. That such a procedure may provide misleading results is illustrated by the case whose audiogram was reproduced in Figure 75. Despite the severe hearing loss at higher frequencies, this child had been classified as normal in a group audiometer fading numbers test (64, p. 247). The hearing loss indicated by that test was only 3 decibels, in contrast to the losses of from 80 to 90 decibels revealed by the more thorough examination.

More recently, pure tone audiometers have been adapted for group use (cf. 36). Equipment is now available that permits the utilization of the same set of earphones with either a speech phonographic audiometer or a pure tone audiometer. Pure tone group tests are scored as either passed or failed; they are not designed to yield measures of auditory thresholds. The stimulus is a signal tone presented at each of three frequency levels, six trials being given at each level. The subject merely underlines *yes* or *no* next to the appropriate trial number to indicate whether or not he hears the signal. In some of the trials, no signal is actually given, the position of these trials being specified on the examiner's master sheets. An illustration of a pure tone group audiometer in use is given in Figure 76. This type of test shows a

Fig. 76. A Pure Tone Group Audiometer in Use. (Courtesy The Maico Company.)

significantly closer agreement with the results of individual audiometric tests than is obtained with speech audiometer tests (36). Although the pure tone group test described above has been used principally with children in grades 3 to 12, there is evidence that it can also be successfully applied in the first two grades (36).

MOTOR FUNCTIONS

Types of Available Tests. Many tests have been devised to measure speed, coordination, and other characteristics of movement responses. Most are concerned with manual dexterity, but a few involve leg or foot movements that may be required in performing specific jobs. Some measure a combination of motor and perceptual, spatial, or mechanical aptitudes, thus overlapping the tests to be discussed in the next sections. Others have been incorporated into mechanical aptitude batteries and will be considered in connection with such batteries in the following section. Mention should also be made of the previously discussed Lincoln-Oseretsky tests (Ch. 11). Since they are concerned chiefly with motor development in children, these tests could be most conveniently considered with other types of developmental scales.

Motor tests are characteristically apparatus tests, although several paper-and-pencil adaptations have been designed for group administration. Both the GATB and the FACT discussed in Chapter 13 include examples of such paper-and-pencil motor tests. Some of these printed motor tests may prove valid in their own right as predictors of practical criteria. Available evidence indicates, however, that there is little or no correlation between printed tests and apparatus tests designed to measure the same motor functions (25, 44).

The principal application of motor tests has been in the selection of industrial and military personnel. Frequently, they have been custom-made to meet the requirements of specific jobs. Many are constructed on the principle of the "job miniature." This means that the test closely reproduces all or part of the movements required in the performance of the job itself. These tests are not miniatures in the sense of involving smaller movements. On the contrary, to insure validity, the test and the job should call for the use of the same muscle groups.

Many examples of motor coordination tests, ranging from simple to very complex, are provided by the classification testing program conducted by the Air Force during World War II (44). One of the tests developed for this purpose, the Two-Hand Coordination Test, was illustrated in Chapter 2 (Fig. 4). In this test, the subject must keep a pointer in contact with a small, irregularly moving, metal target. With the right hand, he turns a handle which moves the pointer forward or backward; with the left hand, he simultaneously operates another handle which controls lateral movements of the pointer. The time during which each subject succeeds in keeping the pointer in contact with the target is automatically recorded on an electric clock in front of the examiner. Each man's score can thus be read directly from his own clock. This is one of many kinds of "pursuit" or "tracking" tests that have been developed to predict performance in different military or civilian tasks.

Another example of a test constructed for use in the same Air Force program is the Complex Coordination Test illustrated in Figure 77. This is a typical job miniature type of test, in which the subject is required to manipulate three controls similar to the rudder and stick controls used in piloting a plane. The test stimuli consist of different patterns of signal lights on a vertical panel.

Since they are not designed for use beyond their immediate situation, such custom-made tests fall outside the scope of this book and will not be discussed further. Similarly, we shall not be concerned with a vast array of laboratory techniques for the measurement of muscular strength, reaction time, speed of tapping with a stylus or a telegraph key, simple and complex hand coordinations, hand or arm steadiness, bodily sway, and many others well known to the experimental and industrial psychologist. Although such techniques have been put to a variety of uses and have frequently been incorporated into industrial and military batteries, they are not generally available as standardized tests with broadly applicable norms. They represent a rich resource of raw test material for the research worker, but they are not a ready-made tool for the test user.

Fig. 77. Complex Coordination Test Used in Air Force Classification Program. (Courtesy U. S. Air Force; for description of test, cf. Melton, 44.)

A comprehensive survey of commercially available, standardized tests for motor and mechanical aptitudes appearing prior to 1942 is provided by Bennett and Cruikshank (7). Data on the industrial validity of the tests cited in this and later sections of this chapter can be found in Dorcus and Jones (16), as well as in the *Mental Measurements Yearbooks* and the test manuals. Also relevant is Patterson's (50) survey of all published results on the validity of tests in predicting success in trade and vocational schools.

Two tests measuring simple hand and finger movements required by certain routine assembly jobs are the O'Connor Finger Dexterity and Tweezer Dexterity Tests (45). These tests measure the speed with which the subject can insert pins into small holes by hand or with a tweezer, respectively. In the former, three pins are placed into each hole; in the latter, the holes are smaller, and a single pin is inserted in each. Although the reliability of these tests seems to be satisfactory, their validity needs to be carefully checked in terms of specific criteria. The tests are probably fairly valid for selecting individuals for jobs requiring the manipulation of small objects with fingers or tweezers. But they may show little or no relationship to other types of manipulative ability.

The Crawford Small Parts Dexterity Test (11), shown in Figure 78, covers a wider variety of manipulative skills. In Part I of this test, the subject

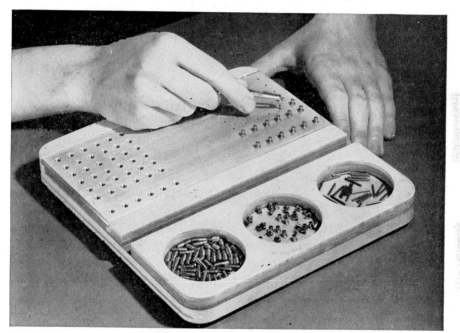

Fig. 78. Crawford Small Parts Dexterity Test. (Courtesy The Psychological Corporation.)

uses tweezers to insert pins in close-fitting holes, and then places a small collar over each pin. In Part II, small screws are placed in threaded holes and screwed down with a screwdriver. The score is the time required to complete each part. Split-half reliability coefficients between .80 and .95 are reported for the two parts of this test. Despite the apparent similarity of the functions required by Parts I and II, the correlations between the two parts ranged from .10 to .50 in several industrial and high school samples, with a median correlation of .42.

Another manual dexterity test which, however, utilizes no tools is the

Purdue Pegboard (57, 58). This test is said to provide a measure of two types of activity, one requiring gross movements of hands, fingers, and arms, and the other involving "tip of the finger" dexterity needed in small assembly work. First, pins are inserted individually in small holes with the right hand, left hand, and both hands together, in successive trials. In another part of the test, pins, collars, and washers are assembled in each hole. The prescribed procedure for this activity involves the simultaneous use of both hands.

Two tests requiring a similar type of gross manual dexterity are the Minnesota Rate of Manipulation Test (65) and the Stromberg Dexterity Test (56). The former consists of a board containing 60 circular holes into which 60 cylindrical blocks are to be placed. In the second part of this test, each block is removed from the board, turned over with the other hand, and returned to its hole. It is interesting to note that a correlation of only .57 was found between the "placing" and "turning" parts of this test.

The Stromberg Dexterity Test is illustrated in Figure 79. Red, yellow, and blue blocks are to be inserted in a prescribed sequence in the correspondingly colored sections of the board. Before each trial, the blocks are arranged in standard order, with only one color to a row in one trial, and only one color to a column in another. The subject is required to pick up the blocks in a specified pattern that prevents the placement of two blocks of the same color in immediate succession.

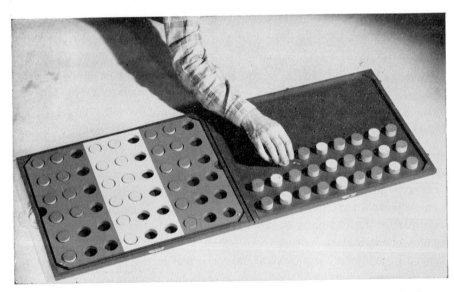

Fig. 79. Stromberg Dexterity Test. (Courtesy The Psychological Corporation.)

As a final example, we may consider the Bennett Hand-Tool Dexterity Test (cf. Fig. 80). This test was designed "to provide a measure of proficiency in using ordinary mechanics' tools" (6). Although performance is undoubtedly influenced by the subject's past experience in handling tools, the test was constructed so as to maximize the role of manipulative skill rather than mechanical information. The task is simply to remove all the nuts and bolts (of different sizes) from the left upright and mount them on the right upright in a prescribed sequence. The score is the total time required to complete this task.

Fig. 80. Bennett Hand-Tool Dexterity Test. (Courtesy The Psychological Corporation.)

Evaluation of Motor Tests. What can be said about the effectiveness of motor tests as a whole? The most important point to note in evaluating such tests is the high degree of *specificity* of motor functions. Intercorrelations and factor analyses of large numbers of motor tests have failed to reveal broad group factors such as those found for intellectual functions. The most extensive factorial research on motor functions has been conducted with Air Force data, principally by Fleishman (21, 22, 25, 26, 27, 44). Among the major factors identified by Fleishman in a series of factorial analyses are the following:

Control Precision: Ability to make fine, highly controlled but not overcontrolled muscular adjustments—important in the rapid and accurate operation of controls by hand, arm, and foot movements (as in Complex Coordination and Rotary Pursuit Air Force tests).

Multi-Limb Coordination: Ability to coordinate gross movements requiring the simultaneous use of more than one limb in any combination.

Response Orientation: Ability to select the appropriate response under highly speeded conditions—identified in complex coordination tests in which each pattern of signals requires a different choice of controls and direction of movement.

Reaction Time: Speed with which an individual is able to respond to a stimulus when it appears—found to be independent of specific response required and of whether the stimulus is auditory or visual.

Speed of Arm Movement: Speed with which gross arm movements can be made, regardless of precision.

Rate Control: Ability to make continuous anticipatory motor adjustments relative to changes in speed and direction of a moving target—the common factor in pursuit and tracking tests.

Manual Dexterity: Ability to make skillful, well-controlled arm-hand movements in manipulating fairly large objects under speed conditions.

Finger Dexterity: Ability to make skillful, controlled manipulations of small objects, involving primarily finger movements.

Arm-Hand Steadiness: Ability to make precise arm-hand positioning movements where strength and speed are minimized.

Wrist-Finger Speed: Traditionally called "tapping," this ability is best measured by paper-and-pencil tests requiring rapid tapping of the pencil in relatively large areas.

Aiming: A narrowly defined ability measured chiefly by paper-and-pencil "dotting" tests which require subject to place a dot accurately and rapidly in each of a series of small circles.

Still other factors have been identified in the area of gross bodily movements, as manifested in athletic skills (34). These include limb strength, trunk strength, limb flexibility, trunk flexibility, energy mobilization (ability to exert maximum energy at a given moment), static balance, dynamic balance, and gross body coordination (involving trunk and limbs). As new data are gathered, this list of motor factors is constantly undergoing revision and redefinition, but most of the factors named have been verified in several independent investigations.

It has also been shown that the abilities called into play by motor tests may change with *practice* (23, 26). In a study involving continued practice on the Complex Coordination Test illustrated in Figure 77, both the number and nature of factors identified at different stages of practice varied (26). At the early stages, non-motor factors such as spatial orientation, visualization, mechanical experience, and perceptual speed entered into performance together with motor factors. With increasing practice, the importance of the intellectual factors declined and that of the motor factors increased. In the last stages of practice, the only common factors having significant weights were speed of arm movement and control precision. A factor specific to the Complex Coordination Test also increased in weight with practice. Similar results were obtained in later analyses of other complex motor tests (23, 26).

The factorial composition of a motor test may also be affected by its *difficulty level* (24). This relation was investigated with a specially designed motor test requiring the subject to press a button on the response panel that corresponded to the position of a light appearing on the display panel. By varying the reference point on the display panel, the relation between stimulus lights and response buttons could be made more complicated and the difficulty of the task increased. Under the simplest conditions, individual differences in performance proved to be largely a function of perceptual speed. As the task was made more difficult, performance depended increasingly on the spatial orientation and response orientation factors. The finding that both practice and difficulty affect the factors determining performance on a motor task suggests that the validity of the same test for a given criterion may vary accordingly. Moreoever, subjects of different ability levels may solve the same task through the use of different processes.

The change in nature of many motor tests with practice complicates the determination of *reliability*. Increasing the length of a motor test does not usually result in as great a rise in reliability as found with intellectual tests, since the different portions of the motor test may not measure quite the same functions. In general, the reliabilities of motor tests are not as high as those of other types of tests, many falling in the .70's and .80's. Some of the simple motor tests described in this section, however, have higher reliabilities. In such simple tasks, there is less likelihood that practice will alter the nature of the test.

In considering the *validity* of motor tests, we need to differentiate between complex motor tests that closely resemble the particular criterion performance they are trying to predict and tests of simple motor functions designed for more general use. The former are well illustrated by some of the Air Force tests. Such complex, custom-made tests that reproduce the combination of motor aptitudes required by the criterion have shown fair validity. The Complex Coordination Test of the Air Force, for example, considerably improved the prediction of performance in pilot training. For most purposes, however, the use of such tests is not practicable, since a very large number of tests would have to be devised to match different criteria. Moreover, there is a question as to whether the same result might not be achieved through a combination of intellectual tests and simple motor tests. For counseling purposes, of course, such highly specific tests would be of little use.

With regard to commercially available motor tests, the functions they measure are very simple and their validities against most criteria are not high. For this reason, such tests can serve best as part of a selection battery, rather than as single predictors. In general, motor tests have been most successful in predicting performance on routine assembling and machine-operating jobs (21, 31). As the jobs become less repetitive, perceptual and intellectual factors come to play a more important part. Because of the specificity of motor functions, validity should be reported in terms of specific criteria and should be rechecked whenever the test is applied in a different situation.

In this connection it should also be noted that different results may be obtained through the use of quality or quantity criteria, when the latter are applied to the same job. In one study on power sewing-machine operators (46), certain tests proved to be valid predictors of quality, while other tests gave high correlations with speed of work. In general, the motor tests included in this study correlated higher with speed than with quality of output, as might be expected. For example, the O'Connor Tweezer Dexterity Test yielded correlations of .46 and .07 with speed and quality criteria, respectively. The corresponding correlations obtained with the Minnesota Rate of Manipulation Test were .31 and .08. Thus in a factory that specializes in high-quality merchandise, the motor dexterity tests might be poorer predictors than in one concerned with rapid production for a mass market.

MECHANICAL APTITUDE

Mechanical aptitude tests cover a variety of functions. Motor factors enter into some of the tests in this category, either because the rapid manipulation of materials is required in the performance of the test, or because special subtests designed to measure motor dexterity are included. In terms of the factors discussed in the preceding chapter, perceptual and spatial aptitudes play an important part in many of these tests. Finally, mechanical reasoning and sheer mechanical information predominate in a number of mechanical aptitude tests.

It is important to recognize the diversity of functions subsumed under the heading of mechanical aptitude, since each function may be differently related to other variables. For example, mechanical information tests are much more dependent upon past experience with mechanical objects than are abstract spatial or perceptual tests. Similarly, sex differences may be reversed from one of these functions to another. Thus in manual dexterity and in perceptual discrimination tests, women generally excel; in abstract spatial tests, a small but significant average difference in favor of males is usually found; while in mechanical reasoning or information tests, men are markedly superior, the difference increasing with age (cf. 1, Ch. 14).

In an attempt to clarify the nature of mechanical aptitude, Harrell (33) conducted a factor analysis of 31 tests that had been administered to a group of 91 machine-fixers in a cotton mill. Apart from three verbal tests, all were designed to measure some aspect of mechanical aptitude. In addition, the factor analysis included scores on an interest test, ratings, age, amount of schooling, and mechanical experience. Three principal factors were found to have significant loadings in the mechanical aptitude tests. These were described as perceptual, spatial, and agility or manual dexterity. It might be noted that no mechanical information tests were administered in this study. Had such tests been included, one or more additional factors would probably have been identified.

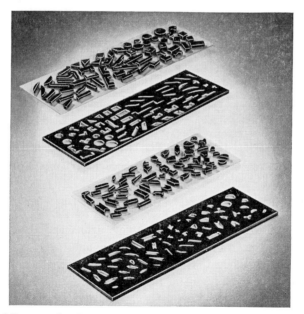

Fig. 81. Minnesota Spatial Relations Test. (Courtesy C. H. Stoelting Company.)

We may now consider some examples of different types of tests designed to measure "mechanical aptitude." Among the tests emphasizing *abstract spatial and perceptual abilities* are to be found formboards, construction puzzles, and diagrammatic paper-and-pencil tests. The Minnesota Spatial Relations Test (49), illustrated in Figure 81, falls into this category. This is one of the tests standardized in an extensive investigation of mechanical aptitude conducted at the University of Minnesota (47). It consists of four form-boards, each containing 58 variously shaped cutouts. One set of blocks is used with Boards A and B, another with Boards C and D. Both time and errors are scored. It might be noted that in the Harrell study (33) this test had its highest loading in the perceptual factor.

Another test developed in the same Minnesota study is the Minnesota Paper Form Board. A later revision employing multiple-choice items was prepared by Likert and Quasha (38). This test is now available in two equivalent forms, obtainable in either hand-scored or machine-scored editions. Two sample items are reproduced in Figure 82. Each item in the test

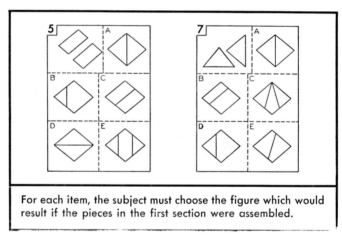

For each item, the subject must choose the figure which would result if the pieces in the first section were assembled.

Fig. 82. Sample Items from the Revised Minnesota Paper Form Board. (Reproduced by permission of The Psychological Corporation.)

consists of a figure cut into two or more parts. The subject determines how the pieces would fit together into the complete figure, and chooses the drawing that correctly shows this arrangement. An unusually large number of studies have been conducted with the Minnesota Paper Form Board Test. The results indicate that it is one of the most valid available instruments for measuring the ability to visualize and manipulate objects in space (38). Among the criteria employed in this research were performance in shop courses, grades in engineering and in other technical and mechanical courses, supervisors' ratings, and objective production records. The test has also shown some validity in predicting the achievement of dentistry and art students.

Reference should likewise be made to the Spatial Relations Test of the DAT battery, discussed in Chapter 13. It will be recalled that each of the tests in this battery is printed in a separately obtainable booklet and has its own norms. Such a test can therefore be used when only a measure of spatial aptitude is desired. Since it requires a somewhat more complex type of three-dimensional visualization, it may tap a different aspect of spatial ability than that covered by the Minnesota Paper Form Board.

A test that undertakes to measure several aspects of mechanical aptitude is the MacQuarrie Test for Mechanical Ability (41). This test comprises the following seven subtests: Tracing, Tapping, Dotting, Copying, Location, Blocks, and Pursuit. The first three subtests were included as measures of speed and accuracy of eye-hand coordination. In the Harrell study, however, dotting was the only subtest of the three having a high loading in the agility factor (.501). A sample item from this test is shown in Figure 83. The remaining four subtests were designed to measure spatial ability. According to Harrell's findings, all four have their highest loading in the spatial factor. Sample items from the three tests most heavily saturated with this factor are reproduced in Figure 83.

It might be added that most of Harrell's findings regarding the MacQuarrie test were corroborated in a subsequent factorial analysis of the subtest scores of 329 radio assembly operators (31). In this study, a spatial factor was the most prominent in the entire battery, although its highest loadings were in the Location, Copying, Blocks, and Pursuit tests. A controlled movement factor, probably corresponding to Harrell's agility factor, showed significant weights in Tapping, Dotting, and Tracing. Slight evidence of a third factor, described as visual inspection, was found in the Tracing, Dotting, and Pursuit tests, all of which require careful observation of visual details.

Norms are provided for total scores on the MacQuarrie test, as well as for each subtest. The use of specific subtest score patterns for different jobs is recommended in the manual. In this connection it might be noted that an early study of retest reliability yielded a coefficient of .90 for total scores and coefficients ranging from .72 to .86 for subtests (42). No data on reliability are cited in the manual, nor is any information provided regarding subtest intercorrelations. A number of validity studies employing various industrial criteria have been conducted with this test (41). A few of the reported validity coefficients for either individual subtests or combinations of subtests fall between .40 and .50; others are lower.

Like spatial aptitude tests, measures of *mechanical reasoning and information* can also be divided into performance and paper-and-pencil types. The former are "assembly tests," requiring the subject to put together common

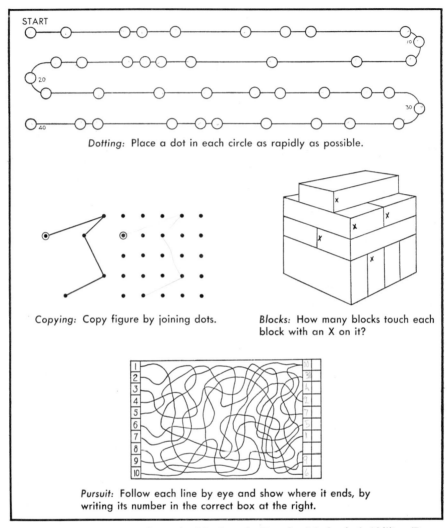

Dotting: Place a dot in each circle as rapidly as possible.

Copying: Copy figure by joining dots.   Blocks: How many blocks touch each block with an X on it?

Pursuit: Follow each line by eye and show where it ends, by writing its number in the correct box at the right.

Fig. 83. Sample Items from the MacQuarrie Test for Mechanical Ability. (Reproduced by permission of California Test Bureau.)

mechanical objects from the given parts. One of the earliest tests of this type is the Stenquist Assembly Test (55), developed during World War I. A revision and extension of this test was standardized in the previously cited Minnesota study (47) and is now available as the Minnesota Mechanical Assembly Test (48). The three boxes containing the mechanical objects to be assembled are shown in Figure 84. A shorter form involving fewer objects is also available. Time limits are long enough to render the contribution of agility minimal. Although norms for other groups are available, these tests are especially suitable for high school boys. On such a group, the long form yielded an odd-even reliability of .94 and a correlation of .53 with a carefully measured, comprehensive criterion of success in shop work (47). The practical usefulness of such assembly tests is limited by difficulties of administration, scoring, and maintenance, as well as by the impossibility of testing more than a few subjects simultaneously.

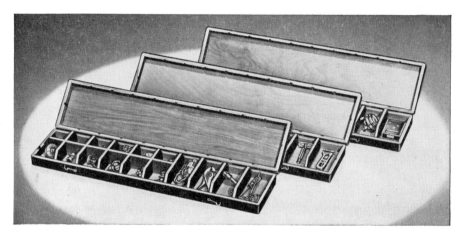

Fig. 84. Minnesota Mechanical Assembly Test. (Courtesy C. H. Stoelting Company.)

To meet these practical problems, pictorial tests of mechanical comprehension have been developed. Such tests were also initiated by Stenquist with an early test requiring the subject to match pictures of mechanical objects or of parts of objects that belong together. A more recent application of the same approach is found in the Mellenbruch Mechanical Motivation Test (43). The rationale underlying this test is that individuals who are mechanically adept and interested in tools and machinery are more likely to have acquired the information required on the test. To what extent scores on this test reflect interest or motivation, mechanical aptitude, or sheer amount of mechanical experience cannot be determined from the available data. In view of the paucity of information on this test, it must be regarded as being still in an experimental stage.

A combination of pictures and questions, which permits wider coverage of content and more emphasis on the understanding of mechanical principles, is found in the Bennett Test of Mechanical Comprehension (5). This test has been widely used for both military and civilian purposes. The currently available civilian forms include: Form AA, suitable for boys in high school or trade school, for unselected adult men, and for certain industrial groups;

Form BB, a more difficult form designed for engineering school applicants and other similarly selected groups; Form CC (Owens-Bennett), a still more difficult form permitting finer discrimination at high ability levels; and Form W1 (Bennett-Fry) for women. To these should be added the Mechanical Reasoning Test of the DAT, discussed in Chapter 13, which is essentially another form of the same test. Two sample items from Form AA are illustrated in Figure 85.

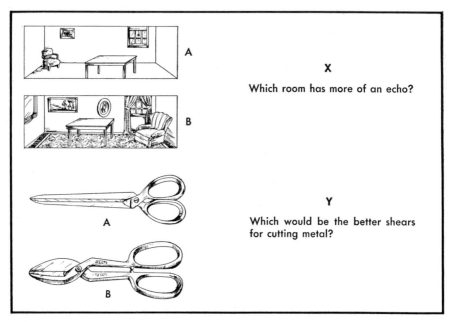

Fig. 85.   Sample Items from the Bennett Mechanical Comprehension Test, Form AA. (Reproduced by permission of The Psychological Corporation.)

Despite its widespread use, little information regarding the validity of the Bennett Test of Mechanical Comprehension is reported in the manual. Other published studies either with this test or with one of its military forms, however, provide good evidence of both concurrent and predictive validity for mechanical trades and engineering. Correlations between .30 and .60 have been found with either training or job-proficiency criteria for many kinds of mechanical jobs (30, 50). During World War II, this test proved to be one of the best predictors of pilot success (32, p. 843). Its validity for this purpose seems to have resulted chiefly from the contribution of a mechanical information factor and a spatial visualization factor, which together accounted for about 60 per cent of the variance of its scores (32, pp. 336-339).

Another paper-and-pencil test, the SRA Mechanical Aptitudes test (54), includes three subtests designed to measure mechanical knowledge, space relations, and shop arithmetic, respectively. In the first test, the subject identifies tools by checking the correct name or use of each. The second test is constructed on the principle of fitting pieces together, as in the Minnesota Paper Form Board. In the third, the subject solves arithmetic problems involving tables or diagrams such as might be encountered in shop work. These skills were chosen because they were thought to be important in many mechanical jobs. In this connection it is interesting to note that, in the extensive surveys by Ghiselli (30) and Patterson (50), shop arithmetic tests proved to be good predictors of industrial-training criteria as well as success in trade and vocational schools.

The three scores on the SRA Mechanical Aptitudes test may be evaluated separately, combined with equal weights into a total score, or combined with different weights in terms of local criterion data obtained by the test user. Norms are provided for the first two uses. It should be noted, however, that the reported reliability coefficients of the three subtests are too low to justify a differential use of the scores. Although the authors state that the item types included in these tests closely parallel those used in successful Army tests, no validity data are given in the manual.

CLERICAL APTITUDE

Tests designed to measure clerical aptitude are characterized by a common emphasis upon perceptual speed. A well-known example is the Minnesota Clerical Test (2), which consists of two separately timed subtests, Number Comparison and Name Comparison. In the first, the examinee is given 200 pairs of numbers, each containing from 3 to 12 digits. If the two numbers in the pair are identical, he places a check mark between them. The task is similar in the second subtest, proper names being substituted for numbers. Sample items from both subtests are reproduced in Figure 86. Although a deduction is made for errors, the scores depend predominantly upon speed. Performance on this test is influenced by the subject's response set. Occasionally a very careful worker will obtain a poor score because he proceeds slowly in order to avoid errors. By contrast, the examinee who emphasizes speed at the expense of accuracy will complete many more items and will be penalized only a few points as a result of errors. The possible effect of response set should therefore be taken into account when interpreting a low score, especially when such a score is obtained by an otherwise able or promising person.

When the two numbers or names in a pair are <u>exactly the same,</u> make a check mark on the line between them.

66273894_____66273984

527384578_____527384578

New York World_____New York World

Cargill Grain Co._____Cargil Grain Co.

Fig. 86. Sample Items from the Minnesota Clerical Test. (Reproduced by permission of The Psychological Corporation.)

Data on both concurrent and predictive validity of the Minnesota Clerical Test are provided by a number of scattered studies (cf. 2, 16). Moderately high correlations have been found between scores on this test and ratings by office supervisors or by commercial teachers, as well as performance records in courses and in various kinds of clerical jobs. Several studies employed the method of contrasted groups. Thus comparisons are reported between different levels of clerks, between clerical workers and persons engaged in other occupations, and between employed and unemployed clerks. All these comparisons yielded significant differences in mean scores in the expected direction. A marked and consistent sex difference in favor of women has been found on this test, beginning in childhood and continuing into adulthood.

It is apparent, of course, that such a relatively homogeneous test as the Minnesota Clerical Test measures only one aspect of clerical work. Clerical jobs cover a multiplicity of functions. Moreover, the number and particular combination of duties vary tremendously with the type and level of job. Even specific jobs designated by the same name, such as typist, filing clerk, or shipping clerk, may differ considerably from one company to another, owing to the size of the company, degree of possible specialization of jobs, nature of the work, and other local conditions. Despite such a diversity of activities, however, job analyses of general clerical work indicate that a relatively large proportion of time is spent in such tasks as classifying, sorting, checking, collating and stapling, stuffing and sealing envelopes, and the like (cf. 8). Speed and accuracy in perceiving details, together with a certain minimum of manual dexterity, would thus seem to be of primary importance for the clerical worker.

To be sure, many other types of jobs require perceptual speed and accuracy. Inspectors, checkers, packers, and a host of other factory workers obviously need this ability. It is interesting to note in this connection that the Minnesota Clerical Test has also been found to have some validity in predicting the performance of such workers (cf. 16). However, it is likely that higher validity may be obtained in such cases by designing a similar test with pictorial rather than with verbal or numerical material. It will be recalled that, in the GATB prepared by the United States Employment Service, separate tests are included for the *Q* and *P* factors. The *Q* factor appeared in number- and word-checking tests similar to those that make up the Minnesota Clerical Test. The *P* factor, on the other hand, occurred in tests requiring the perception of similarities and differences in spatial items, and is probably more closely related to the inspection of materials.

Several tests of clerical aptitude combine perceptual speed and accuracy with other functions required for clerical work. Among the measures used for the latter functions are "job sample" types of tests for such activities as alphabetizing, classifying, coding, and the like. In addition, some measure of

Instructions: After each name, write the number of the drawer in which that record should be filed. Work quickly and accurately. The first two are marked correctly.

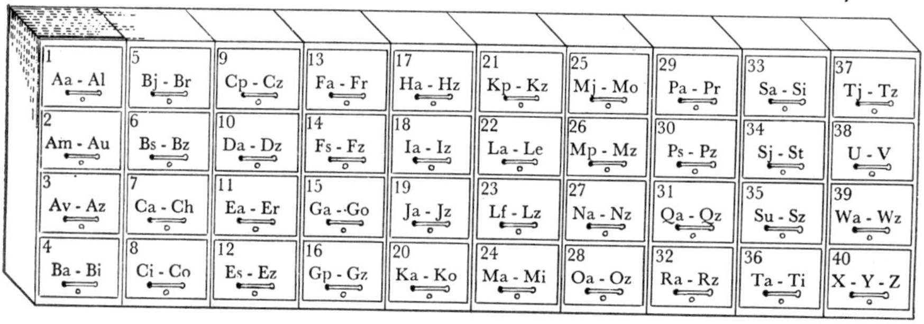

| Kuczma, H. G. | *21* |
| Davidson, C. H. | *10* |

Fig. 87. Alphabetizing Subtest from the General Clerical Test, Showing Two Practice Items. (Reproduced by permission of The Psychological Corporation.)

verbal and numerical ability may be included, to serve in lieu of a "general intelligence" test. An example of such a composite test of clerical aptitude is the Psychological Corporation General Clerical Test (52). This test consists of nine subtests, grouped so as to yield clerical, numerical, and verbal scores, as well as a total score. The first two tests, Checking and Alphabetizing, are designed to measure speed and accuracy in routine clerical tasks. The Alphabetizing test, which has considerable face validity for clerical workers, is illustrated in Figure 87. The numerical score is derived from tests of Arithmetic Computation, Error Location, and Arithmetic Reasoning. Four tests are combined to yield the verbal score, namely, Spelling, Reading Comprehension, Vocabulary, and Grammar. The entire battery requires approximately fifty minutes.

Other clerical tests covering a combination of aptitudes include the Turse Clerical Aptitudes Test (62), SRA Clerical Aptitudes test (53), Short Employment Tests (9), and Purdue Clerical Adaptability Test (37). Mention should also be made of the Clerical Speed and Accuracy test of the DAT (Ch. 13). In selecting clerical workers, this test could be used singly or in combination with the two Language Usage tests and possibly some of the other parts of the battery.

A survey of clerical aptitude tests appearing prior to 1949 can be found in Bennett and Cruikshank (8). Data on the validity of various tests in predicting the training performance and job proficiency of clerical workers are provided by Dorcus and Jones (16) and Ghiselli (30). The Ghiselli survey indicates that tests of general intelligence and those requiring perception of details have good validity in this situation, but motor tests do not. A factor analysis (3) of 17 subtests taken from commonly used clerical aptitude tests yielded three factors, identified as perceptual analysis, speed in making simple discriminations, and comprehension of relations (primarily verbal, but also appearing in some numerical tests). It is interesting to note that the Minnesota Clerical Test had substantial loadings in all three of these factors.

A few aptitude tests for typing and shorthand have also been developed, to predict a student's performance in learning these skills. Such tests are designed for use prior to training and are thus to be distinguished from proficiency tests in typing or shorthand, to be discussed under achievement tests (Ch. 17). Examples of aptitude tests in this area include the Turse Shorthand Aptitude Test (61), E. R. C. Stenographic Aptitude Test (14), and Flanagan's Tapping Test (20) for predicting performance in typing courses. The last-named test utilizes an ingenious procedure in which the subject wears felt dots on her fingertips, with which she makes differently colored marks in a set of circles on the answer sheet. Since each finger is assigned to a different letter, words and other letter combinations can be transcribed from a key. Flanagan points out that this task involves two job elements found to be important in typing, namely (a) rapid and accurate tapping with each finger separately and (b) responding to each symbol with the appropriate finger. Preliminary data on both the concurrent and predictive validity of this test appear promising.

REFERENCES

1. Anastasi, Anne. *Differential psychology.* (3rd ed.) N. Y.: Macmillan, 1958.
2. Andrew, Dorothy M. and Paterson, D. G. *Minnesota Clerical Test.* N. Y.: Psychol. Corp., 1933-1959.
3. Bair, J. T. Factor analysis of clerical aptitude tests. *J. appl. Psychol.,* 1951, 35, 245-249.
4. Barker, R. G., *et al. Adjustment to physical handicap and illness: a survey of the social psychology of physique and disability.* (Rev. ed.) N. Y.: Soc. Sci. Res. Coun., 1953.
5. Bennett, G. K. *Test of Mechanical Comprehension: Forms AA, BB, CC* (with W. A. Owens), and *WI* (with Dinah E. Fry). N. Y.: Psychol. Corp., 1940-1954.
6. Bennett, G. K. *Hand-Tool Dexterity Test.* N. Y.: Psychol. Corp., 1946.
7. Bennett, G. K., and Cruikshank, Ruth M. *A summary of manual and mechanical ability tests.* N. Y.: Psychol. Corp., 1942.
8. Bennett, G. K., and Cruikshank, Ruth M. *A summary of clerical tests.* N. Y.: Psychol. Corp., 1949.
9. Bennett, G. K., and Gelink, Marjorie. *The Short Employment Tests.* N. Y.: Psychol. Corp., 1951-1956.
10. Chapanis, A., Garner, W. R., and Morgan, C. T. *Applied experimental psychology.* N. Y.: Wiley, 1949.
11. Crawford, J. E., and Crawford, Dorothea M. *Small Parts Dexterity Test.* N. Y.: Psychol. Corp., 1946-1956.
12. Cruickshank, W. M. (Ed.) *Psychology of exceptional children and youth.* Englewood Cliffs, N. J.: Prentice-Hall, 1955.
13. Davis, H. (Ed.) *Hearing and deafness.* N. Y.: Murray Hill Books, 1947.
14. Deemer, W. L., Jr. *E. R. C. Stenographic Aptitude Test.* Chicago: Sci. Res. Assoc., 1944.
15. de Silva, H. R. *Why we have automobile accidents.* N. Y.: Wiley, 1942.
16. Dorcus, R. M., and Jones, Margaret H. *Handbook of employee selection.* N. Y.: McGraw-Hill, 1950.
17. Dvorine, I. *Dvorine Pseudo-Isochromatic Plates, Second Edition.* Los Angeles: Western Psychol. Serv., 1953-1955.
18. Farnsworth, D. *The Farnsworth Dichotomous Test for Color Blindness.* N. Y.: Psychol. Corp., 1947.
19. Farnsworth, D. *The Farnsworth-Munsell 100 Hue Test for the Examination of Color Discrimination.* Baltimore: Munsell Color Co., 1942-1957.
20. Flanagan, J. C. *The Tapping Test.* Pittsburgh: Psychometric Techniques Assoc., 1959.
21. Fleishman, E. A. Testing for psychomotor abilities by means of apparatus tests. *Psychol. Bull.,* 1953, 50, 241-262.
22. Fleishman, E. A. Dimensional analysis of psychomotor abilities. *J. exp. Psychol.,* 1954, 48, 437-454.
23. Fleishman, E. A. A comparative study of aptitude patterns in unskilled and skilled psychomotor performances. *J. appl. Psychol.,* 1957, 41, 263-272.

24. Fleishman, E. A. Factor structure in relation to task difficulty in psychomotor performance. *Educ. psychol. Measmt.*, 1957, 17, 522-532.
25. Fleishman, E. A. Dimensional analysis of movement reactions. *J. exp. Psychol.*, 1958, 55, 438-453.
26. Fleishman, E. A. The description and prediction of perceptual-motor skill learning. Paper read at Symposium on "Training research and its implications for education," sponsored by Univer. of Pittsburgh and Office of Naval Research, Pittsburgh, February, 1960.
27. Fleishman, E. A., and Hempel, W. E. Factorial analyses of complex psychomotor performance and related skills. *J. appl. Psychol.*, 1956, 40, 96-104.
28. Freeman, E. An illuminant-stable color vision test: I. *J. opt. Soc. Amer.*, 1948, 38, 532-538.
29. Freeman, E. *The Illuminant-Stable Color Vision Test, Second Edition.* Sarasota, Fla.: Freeman Tech. Assoc., 1954.
30. Ghiselli, E. E. The measurement of occupational aptitude. *Univer. Calif. Publ. Psychol.*, 1955, 8 (2), 101-216.
31. Goodman, C. H. The MacQuarrie Test for Mechanical Ability: II. Factor analysis. *J. appl. Psychol.*, 1947, 31, 150-154.
32. Guilford, J. P., and Lacey, J. I. (Eds.) *Printed classification tests.* (AAF Aviation Psychology Program, Research Reports. Rep. No. 5.) Washington: Govt. Printing Office, 1947.
33. Harrell, T. W. A factor analysis of mechanical ability tests. *Psychometrika*, 1940, 5, 17-33.
34. Hempel, W. E., and Fleishman, E. A. A factor analysis of physical proficiency and manipulative skill. *J. appl. Psychol.*, 1955, 39, 12-16.
35. Hirsh, I. J. *The measurement of hearing.* N. Y.: McGraw-Hill, 1952.
36. Johnson, P. W. The Massachusetts Hearing Test. *J. acoust. Soc. Amer.*, 1948, 20, 697-703.
37. Lawshe, C. H., Tiffin, J., and Moore, H. *Purdue Clerical Adaptability Test, Revised Edition.* West Lafayette, Ind.: University Book Store, 1956.
38. Likert, R., and Quasha, W. H. *Revised Minnesota Paper Form Board Test.* N. Y.: Psychol. Corp., 1941-1948.
39. McCormick, E. J. An analysis of visual requirements in industry. *J. appl. Psychol.*, 1950, 34, 54-61.
40. McCormick, E. J. *Human engineering.* N. Y.: McGraw-Hill, 1957.
41. MacQuarrie, T. W. *MacQuarrie Tests for Mechanical Ability.* Monterey, Calif.: California Test Bur., 1925-1943.
42. MacQuarrie, T. W. A mechanical ability test. *J. Personnel Res.*, 1927, 5, 329-337.
43. Mellenbruch, P. L. *Mellenbruch Mechanical Motivation Test.* Chicago: Psychometric Affiliates, 1956-1957.
44. Melton, A. W. (Ed.) *Apparatus tests.* (AAF Aviation Psychology Program, Research Reports. Rep. No. 4.) Washington: Govt. Printing Office, 1947.
45. O'Connor, J. Administration and norms for the Finger Dexterity Test, Worksample No. 16, and Tweezer Dexterity Test, Worksample No. 17. *Tech. Rep. Hum. Engineer. Lab.*, 1938, No. 16. (Also test manuals distributed by Stoelting.)

46. Otis, J. L. The prediction of success in power sewing machine operating. *J. appl. Psychol.,* 1938, 22, 350-366.

47. Paterson, D. G., *et al. Minnesota mechanical ability tests.* Minneapolis: Univer. Minn. Press, 1930.

48. Paterson, D. G., *et al. Minnesota Mechanical Assembly Test.* Chicago: Stoelting, 1930.

49. Paterson, D. G., *et al. Minnesota Spatial Relations Tests.* Minneapolis: Educ. Test Bur., 1930.

50. Patterson, C. H. Predicting success in trade and vocational courses: review of the literature. *Educ. psychol. Measmt.,* 1956, 16, 352-400.

51. Peters, G. A. A color-blindness test for use in vocational guidance. *Personnel Guid. J.,* 1956, 34, 572-575.

52. Psychological Corporation Staff. *General Clerical Test.* N. Y.: Psychol. Corp., 1944-1950.

53. Richardson, Bellows, Henry & Co., Inc. *SRA Clerical Aptitudes.* Chicago: Sci. Res. Assoc., 1947-1950.

54. Richardson, Bellows, Henry & Co., Inc. *SRA Mechanical Aptitudes.* Chicago: Sci. Res. Assoc., 1947-1950.

55. Stenquist, J. L. Measurement of mechanical ability. *Teach. Coll. Contr. Educ.,* 1923, No. 130.

56. Stromberg, E. L. *Stromberg Dexterity Test.* N. Y.: Psychol. Corp., 1947-1951.

57. Tiffin, J. *Purdue Pegboard.* Chicago: Sci. Res. Assoc., 1941-1948.

58. Tiffin, J., and Asher, E. J. The Purdue Pegboard: norms and studies of reliability and validity. *J. appl. Psychol.,* 1948, 32, 234-247.

59. Tiffin, J., and McCormick, E. J. *Industrial psychology.* (4th ed.) Englewood Cliffs, N. J.: Prentice-Hall, 1958.

60. Tufts College Institute of Applied Experimental Psychology. *Handbook of human engineering data.* (2nd ed.) NAVEXOS P-643. Tech. Rep.—SDC 199-1-2. Spec. Devices Cent., ONR, 1951.

61. Turse, P. L. *Turse Shorthand Aptitude Test.* Tarrytown-on-Hudson, N. Y.: World Book Co., 1940.

62. Turse, P. L. *Turse Clerical Aptitudes Test.* Tarrytown-on-Hudson, N. Y.: World Book Co., 1955.

63. U.S. Department of the Army, TAGO, Personnel Research Branch. Studies in visual acuity. *PRS Rep.* No. 742, 1948.

64. Watson, L. A., and Tolan, T. *Hearing tests and hearing instruments.* Baltimore: Williams & Wilkins, 1949.

65. Ziegler, W. A. *Minnesota Rate of Manipulation Tests.* Minneapolis: Educ. Test Bur., 1946.

CHAPTER 15

Special Aptitude Tests: II

Continuing the survey of special aptitude tests begun in Chapter 14, this chapter is concerned with tests in the areas of art, music, literary appreciation, and creativity. Tests in the general field of reasoning, inventiveness, originality, and creativeness have constituted an important and growing focus of research interest since the end of World War II. Much of this activity stems from a concern with the identification and training of high-level scientists. Although oriented principally toward scientific productivity, such research also sheds some light on artistic creativity.

The development of tests specifically designed for measuring aesthetic abilities, on the other hand, has been slow and sporadic. Little progress in the testing of artistic, musical, or literary aptitudes has been made since the early 1940's. In number, scope, and technical refinements, tests in this area have lagged far behind other aptitude tests. In part, this condition may result from the resistance artistically trained persons have exhibited toward objective measurement, quantification, and the "scientific" approach to artistic talent. Traditionally, art and science have been regarded as fundamentally dissimilar and mutually incompatible in their points of view. Even today, many artists and art teachers look upon psychological testing with suspicion or skepticism.

Another reason for the scarcity of well-constructed tests of artistic aptitudes may be found in the value systems of our contemporary culture. The greatest effort will, in general, be exerted in constructing those tests that meet the most urgent social needs. To a large extent, the development of tests reflects the demand for such instruments. In our culture, the demand for testing office clerks, engineers, or Air Force pilots has proved more widespread and more insistent than the demand for testing poets, musicians, or painters.

Aesthetic aptitudes represent a broad and varied category of traits. It is apparent, of course, that a different constellation of talents is required in music, the graphic arts, and literature. Further specialization within each of these fields is also undoubtedly associated with a diversity of personal quali-

400

fications. The poet and the biographer, the traditional portraitist and the surrealist painter, the coloratura soprano in grand opera and the saxophonist in a dance orchestra—all must obviously meet a very different set of requirements.

Within the same form of art, moreover, the individual may play any one of a variety of roles, each with its own characteristic set of qualifications. Thus the creative artist, art teacher, critic, collector, dealer, and museum worker approach art with a different pattern of skills, knowledge, interests, attitudes, feelings, and motives. In music, similar differences can be recognized between the composer, performer, critic, teacher, and appreciative public, not to mention the obvious differences associated with type of instrument, or with popular versus classical music. The field of literature can likewise be subdivided in a corresponding fashion. It is evident that a thorough coverage of artistic aptitudes would require many different "job specifications," some of which might have little in common.

Turning now to available tests for the measurement of aesthetic aptitudes, we find that such tests fall principally into three major classes, namely, art (in the narrow sense of graphic arts), music, and literature. Each will be considered in a separate section. Within each of these categories, a further distinction can usually be made between tests of appreciation and tests of production.

It is obvious, of course, that appreciation does not require productive skills. A person may be a highly discriminating and sophisticated connoisseur of paintings without himself being able to paint. But artistic production, except at a routine and mechanical level, undoubtedly presupposes superiority in both appreciative and productive skills. Thus tests of art appreciation have a broader applicability than tests of production. Moreover, productive skills are more closely dependent upon specific training. The measurement of such skills is therefore more likely to fall under the heading of achievement tests. As we consider specific tests it will become apparent, however, that in the measurement of artistic talents the distinction between aptitude and achievement tests is especially tenuous.

ARTISTIC APTITUDES

Tests of *artistic appreciation* have generally followed a common pattern. In each item, the subject is requested to express his preference regarding two or more variants of the same object. One variant is either an original by an eminent artist or a version preferred by the majority of a group of art experts. The other versions represent deliberate distortions designed to violate some accepted principle of art. Any controversial items, on which a clear consensus of experts cannot be obtained, are normally eliminated from such a test.

In the development of art appreciation tests, both original item selection and subsequent validation procedures depend heavily upon the opinions of contemporary art experts within our culture. It is well to bear this fact in mind when interpreting scores. Essentially, such tests indicate the degree to which the individual's aesthetic "taste" agrees with that of contemporary art experts. The representativeness of the particular group of experts employed in developing the test is obviously an important consideration. In so far as aesthetic standards or "taste" may change with time, the periodic rechecking of scoring key and item validities is likewise desirable.

The McAdory Art Test (41, 54) represents one of the earliest attempts to measure artistic appreciation. First published in 1929, this test is now of historical interest only, because many of its items are outdated. The test employed contemporary materials taken from art and trade magazines, as well as art objects chosen from museums and art books. The items cover such varied categories as furniture and household utensils, textiles and clothing, automobiles, and painting and other graphic arts. Each item consists of four variations, to be ranked in order of preference by the subject. The alternative versions differ in shape and line arrangement, massing of dark and light, or color.

The Meier Art Judgment Test (45), a revision of the earlier Meier-Seashore Test (47), is undoubtedly the most widely used test of artistic appreciation. This test, whose first edition also appeared in 1929, was revised in 1940. The revision consisted essentially in the elimination of the 25 items having the lowest correlations with total score and, within the remaining 100 items, the allotment of double credit to the 25 having the highest correlations with total score.

The Meier Art Judgment Test differs in a number of ways from the McAdory. The materials from which the Meier test was constructed consist of relatively timeless art works, which will not readily go out of date. Most are paintings or drawings by acknowledged masters, while a few represent vases or designs suitable for pottery. All reproductions are in black and white. Each item contains only two versions, an original and a variation in which the symmetry, balance, unity, or rhythm has been altered. This test thus concentrates upon the judgment of *aesthetic organization,* which Meier considers to be the key factor in artistic talent. In order to rule out the contribution of perceptual accuracy, the subject is told in what detail the two versions of each picture differ. An illustrative item is reproduced in Figure 88.

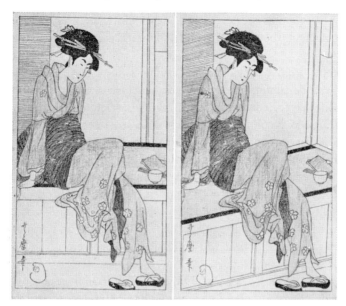

Fig. 88. Item Similar to Those Employed in the Meier Art Judgment Test. This item does not appear in the current revised form. The difference between the two versions is in the angle at which the window seat crosses the picture. (Courtesy Norman C. Meier.)

For more than two decades, Meier and his associates at the University of Iowa conducted research on the nature of artistic talent. Although most of their subjects were children, data on adult groups, including professional artists, were also obtained. This research led Meier to the conclusion that artistic aptitude comprises six interlinked traits, viz., manual skill, volitional perseveration, aesthetic intelligence, perceptual facility, creative imagination, and aesthetic judgment. The Meier Art Judgment Test is designed to measure only the last of these six traits. The original plans called for the preparation of creative imagination and aesthetic perception tests, but little progress was made on the development of these tests. It might be added that the six traits listed were not identified by factor analysis, but are based upon the author's interpretation of a mass of relevant observations. Corroboration by means of factor analysis would be desirable. More objective evidence on the relation between aesthetic judgment and the quality of artistic production should likewise be provided.

Percentile norms are given for three groups: 1445 junior high school students; 892 senior high school students; and 982 adults, including college and art school students. All norms were derived largely from students in art courses, whether in high school, college, or special art schools. Data were gathered in 25 schools scattered throughout the United States. Split-half reliability coefficients between .70 and .84 are reported for relatively homogeneous samples.

Most of the available evidence regarding validity of the Meier Art Judgment Test can be summarized under the headings of item selection and contrasted group performance, although a few correlations with independent criteria of artistic accomplishment have also been reported. First, it should be noted that the original items were chosen from reputable art works and that the distortions were such as to violate accepted art principles. A large number of items thus assembled were then submitted to 25 art experts, and only those items showing clear-cut agreement among the experts were retained. Finally, items were selected on which from 60 to 90 per cent of a group of 1081 miscellaneous subjects chose the original as the preferred version. In the revised edition, it will be recalled, items were further selected on the basis of internal consistency.

Total scores on the Meier Art Judgment Test exhibit a sharp differentiation in terms of age, grade, and art training. Thus art faculty score higher than non-art faculty, art students higher than comparable non-art students. The extent to which these group differences result from selection or from previous art training cannot be determined from available data. Although no validity coefficients are given in the manual, a few are reported in other published sources. Correlations ranging from .40 to .69 have been found between scores on this test and art grades or ratings of creative artistic ability (8, 34, 48).

As in most artistic aptitude tests, the Meier Art Judgment Test has regularly shown negligible correlation with traditional intelligence tests, such as the Stanford-Binet or group verbal tests. This does not mean, however, that abstract intelligence or scholastic aptitude is unrelated to ultimate success in an art career. In fact, there is some evidence to indicate that, for higher levels of artistic accomplishment, superior scholastic aptitude is a decided asset. In one of the investigations conducted at Iowa, for example, the mean IQ of successful artists was found to be 119 (57). Similarly, a group of artistically gifted children studied at the University of Iowa had IQ's ranging from 111 to 166 (46).

While the McAdory Test employed many contemporary dated items, and the Meier Test was constructed from relatively timeless art products, the more recently developed Graves Design Judgment Test (22, 23) consists exclusively of abstract designs. Non-representational figures were chosen in order to evoke a purely aesthetic response, unencumbered by associations with specific objects. In the development of this test, about 150 items were prepared, each consisting of two or three comparable designs. In each item, one design was organized in accordance with certain aesthetic principles, including "unity, dominance, variety, balance, continuity, symmetry, proportion, and rhythm." The other design or designs violated one or more of these principles. The preliminary form of the test was administered to art teachers, art students, and non-art students, with instructions to indicate the preferred design in each set. Items were retained on the basis of: (*a*) agreement among art teachers regarding the preferred design; (*b*) more frequent selection of the "better" design by art students than by non-art students; and (*c*) internal consistency, i.e., "better" design chosen more often by those obtaining high scores than by those obtaining low scores on the entire test.

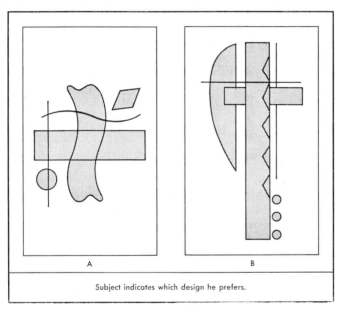

A   B

Subject indicates which design he prefers.

Fig. 89. Item from the Graves Design Judgment Test. (Reproduced by permission of The Psychological Corporation.)

The final test consists of 90 items, 8 containing three designs each, the rest containing only two. The designs are executed in black, white, and gray. Some are line drawings; others are composed of squares, circles, triangles, and similar two-dimensional figures; still others look like reproductions of three-dimensional abstract sculptures. A sample item is reproduced in Figure 89. Percentile norms are given for several art and non-art student groups at the high school and college level, all tested in New York State. Split-half reliability coefficients in fairly homogeneous groups ranged from .81 to .93, with a median of .86. Validity data are meager, being based chiefly on significant differences in mean scores between contrasted criterion groups. Most tests of *creative artistic ability* are actually worksamples. As such, they are undoubtedly influenced to a large extent by formal art training and could be regarded as achievement tests. A number of such tests, however, have been designed specially for use in predicting performance in subsequent training and may therefore be included in the present category. Among the best known are the Lewerenz Tests in Fundamental Abilities of Visual Art (38), the Knauber Art Ability Test (35, 36), and the Horn Art Aptitude Inventory (31). The Lewerenz was designed for grades 3 to 12, the Knauber for grades 7 to 16, and the Horn for grades 12 to 16 and adults. The first two include a variety of subtests, covering art appreciation and information, as well as drawing skills and originality. Both are early tests that have not been revised. Insufficient data are reported to permit an adequate evaluation of their effectiveness. In general, however, they appear to be crude when judged in terms of present test construction standards.

The Horn Art Aptitude Inventory was more recently developed and has undergone a certain amount of revision. Concentrating on the measurement of creative artistic abilities, this test has a fairly high ceiling and shows adequate discrimination among applicants for admission to art schools. The test includes the following three parts:

1. *Scribble Exercise:* The subject is directed to make outline drawings of 20 simple objects, such as book or fork, within time limits of two to six seconds for each drawing. This test is designed partly to give the subject confidence and partly to determine quality of line, appreciation of proportion, and skill in composition or arrangement of object on the page.

2. *Doodle Exercise:* The subject is required to draw simple abstract compositions with given figures, such as six triangles, a rectangle divided by two lines, and the like. This test bears a certain resemblance to the Graves Design Judgment Test, although the subject now produces his own designs instead of judging given designs.

3. *Imagery:* This test provides 12 rectangles, in each of which a few lines have been printed to act as "springboards" for artistic compositions. The subject sketches a picture in each rectangle, building upon the given lines. In Figure 90 will be found one of the given rectangles, together with two different drawings made from the same initial lines.

The Horn Art Aptitude Inventory is scored by means of the product scale technique. Samples of excellent, average, and poor work are furnished as a basis for rating the subject's drawings. As an additional scoring guide, the manual lists certain factors to be considered, such as order, clarity of

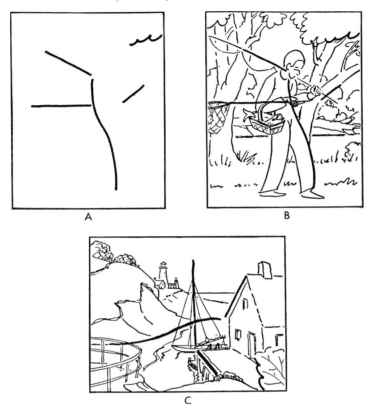

Fig. 90. Sample Item from the "Imagery" Test of the Horn Art Aptitude Inventory. The first rectangle shows the stimulus lines; the other two contain drawings made with these stimulus lines. In the second drawing, the card has been turned to a horizontal position. (From Horn and Smith, 32, p. 351; reproduced by permission of American Psychological Association.)

thought and presentation, quality of line, use of shading, fertility of imagination, and scope of interests. Although the scoring still leaves much to subjective judgment, correlations of .79 to .86 are reported between the results obtained by different scorers.

Some indication of validity is provided by two preliminary studies conducted with the Horn test. Within a group of 52 art school graduates, a correlation of .53 was found between test scores and mean instructors' ratings of performance in a three-year art course. The second study was conducted with 36 high school seniors enrolled in a special art course. In this group, the test scores obtained at the beginning of the year correlated .66 with mean instructors' ratings at the end of the course. A negligible correlation between performance on the Horn test and intelligence test scores was found in the previously mentioned group of 52 art school graduates.

As a measure of the more complex and creative aspects of artistic aptitude at a relatively high level, this test appears to have promise. It has, however, been criticized on the grounds that the scoring puts a premium on conformity to tradition in technique and composition, while great artists often deviate from the norm in these respects. Such a criticism could probably be directed against all current art aptitude tests. Whether a test can be devised to measure the degree of originality characteristic of truly great art remains to be seen. In the meantime, many aspects of artistic aptitude can be measured. The skills involved may represent necessary though not sufficient conditions for artistic production.

A more specific limitation of the Horn Art Aptitude Inventory is that it calls for a certain minimum of artistic training or experience. It could obviously be used as either an achievement or aptitude test. As a further illustration of the tenuousness of such distinctions, it might be noted that this test has even been employed by one investigator as a projective technique in the diagnosis of personality characteristics (28).

What can be concluded regarding the present status of art aptitude tests as a whole? First, much more information is needed regarding the validity of all of these tests in terms of clearly defined training and vocational criteria. There is special need for correlations between test scores obtained prior to specific art courses and measures of subsequent achievement. Some available evidence suggests that terminal grades in art courses correlate higher with worksample tests, such as the Lewerenz and the Knauber, than with art appreciation tests, such as the McAdory and the Meier (3). These correlations, however, may simply reflect the influence of earlier art training in other courses.

Another fruitful approach to the further development of art tests is through the factorial analysis of artistic aptitudes. Most, if not all, existing art aptitude tests are based upon certain assumptions regarding the essential factors in artistic aptitude. An objective verification of these assumptions would be desirable.

It would also be of interest to investigate further the effect of cultural differences upon performance on the various art tests. Some scattered data suggest that these tests are restricted in their applicability to specific cultures. Certainly what is known about cultural differences in artistic expression and artistic standards would support such a view. An investigation of approximately 300 Navajo Indian children with the McAdory test found the Indians to fall far below the norms of New York City whites, despite the high degree of artistic development that characterizes the Navajo Indian culture (55). In view of the nature of the McAdory Test this finding is hardly surprising. The application of the Meier Art Judgment Test to artists, art students, college students, and other adult groups in Brazil likewise indicated the need for certain revisions if the test were to be used in that culture (14).

MUSICAL APTITUDES

During the first four decades of the present century extensive research on the psychology of music was conducted at the University of Iowa under the direction of Carl E. Seashore (51). One of the outcomes of these investigations was the preparation of the Seashore Measures of Musical Talents (50, 52). In its current form, this series consists of six tests covering pitch, loudness, rhythm, time, timbre, and tonal memory. Like most musical aptitude tests, the Seashore tests are reproduced on phonograph records for group administration and uniformity of presentation.

Each item in the Seashore tests consists of a pair of tones or tonal sequences. In the pitch test, the subject indicates whether the second tone is higher or lower than the first. The items are made progressively more difficult by decreasing the difference in pitch between the two tones in each pair. In the loudness test, the subject determines whether the second tone is stronger or weaker than the first. The rhythm test requires the comparison of rhythmic patterns that are either the same or different within each pair. In the time test, the subject records whether the second tone in each pair is longer or shorter than the first. The timbre test calls for the discrimination of tone quality, the two tones in each pair being either the same or different in this respect. In the tonal memory test, short series of three to five tones are played twice in immediate succession. During the second playing, one note is changed, and the subject must write the number of the altered note, i.e., first, second, etc.

The Seashore tests are applicable from the fourth grade to the adult level. The testing of younger children by this procedure has not proved feasible because of the difficulty of sustaining interest and attention. Even above the age of 10 the scores on these tests may be lowered by inattention. Consequently, the tests are not as reliable at these ages as they are for older subjects. The scores are not combined into a single total, but are evaluated separately in terms of percentile norms. These norms are reported for grades 4 to 5, 6 to 8, and 9 to 16, the normative samples for each test and grade level containing from 377 to 4319 cases. Age changes are slight and sex differences are negligible. The tests are probably somewhat susceptible to practice and training, although studies of these effects have yielded conflicting results (18, 51).

Kuder-Richardson reliability coefficients of the six Seashore tests range from .55 to .85 within the three normative grade-level groups. Only content validity is discussed in the manual, Seashore having argued over the years that this is the most appropriate type of validity for such tests. It is undoubtedly true that ability to discriminate pitch, loudness, timbre, and other properties of tones is essential to both appreciation and production of music. To predict musical achievement, however, we need to know much more. What is the minimum cutoff point for different kinds of musical activities? Is there any correlation between test scores and musical performance beyond the cutoff point? What is the relative importance of each of the functions measured by the tests, both in relation to each other and in relation to the entire array of requisite traits? A few scattered studies provide meager evidence of predictive validity against various criteria of performance in music training (5, 40, 52). Many of these validity coefficients are low, few reaching .30 or .40. Apart from the unreliability of criterion measures and the complexity of factors affecting musical achievement, it should be noted that these investigations were conducted on selected samples of music students. Presumably most of the individuals falling below a certain minimum in relevant auditory capacities had already been eliminated from such groups.

Correlations with intelligence tests are negligible, as would be expected for special aptitude tests. Intercorrelations among the six tests are higher than had been anticipated (18). The functions measured by the different tests are thus less independent than had originally been supposed, a fact that has also been confirmed by factor analysis (42). It should also be noted that the Seashore tests or adaptations of them have proved helpful in predicting achievement in certain civilian and military specialties requiring auditory discrimination, such as those of sonar operator and radiotelegrapher (21, 58).

Another test battery that has been used widely by music teachers in elementary and high school classes is the Kwalwasser-Dykema Music Tests (37). This series consist of 10 short tests, requiring a total time of about one hour. The tests were designed to measure the six functions covered by the Seashore tests, together with facility in reading musical notation and certain aspects of musical appreciation. Percentile norms are given for each of the 10 tests and for total scores. Separate norms are provided for each three-grade interval from grades 4 through 12. As a means of evaluating the tests, the Kwalwasser-Dykema manual is of little or no help. No mention is made of reliability or validity. Other investigators, however, have found that the reliabilities of some of these tests are so low as to render their scores practically worthless (5, 18). Most of the tests are too short and contain too few discriminative items, especially in the middle of the difficulty range. The popularity of this battery probably stems from the fact that it seems to yield so much information in so little time. But the information may be incorrect.

An attempt to improve the discriminative value and reliability of the Kwalwasser-Dykema battery without changing the content is reported by Holmes (30). The range of scores on each test was greatly increased by requiring more differentiation in the responses and assigning partial credits in scoring. For example, instead of merely indicating whether two notes are the same or different in pitch, the subject reports whether the second note is equal to the first, different, different and higher, or different and lower. By these procedures, the reliability of the entire battery was raised to .91. Subtest reliabilities, although consistently higher than in the old version, ranged from .43 to .88.

A more recently developed battery that concentrates on only two fundamental components of musical aptitude is the Drake Musical Aptitude Tests (15). These tests are designed for use at ages 8 and over. One part measures musical memory by presenting a two-bar melody which the subject must compare from memory with other versions. If the version is unchanged, the subject indicates so. If it is altered, he must state whether the change was in the key, the time, or the notes. Preliminary illustrations are used to familiarize the subjects with the meaning of these musical terms. The other part is a rhythm test designed to measure the subject's ability to keep time. This test does not appear to measure the same ability as the rhythm test in the Seashore series and correlates low with that test. The memory and rhythm tests of the Drake battery also have low correlations with each other. Both are reported to have high reliabilities, in the .80's and .90's, and unusually high predictive validities against a general criterion of subsequent achievement in music training. These tests are promising and merit further validation studies by other investigators.

A somewhat more comprehensive battery is the Wing Standardized Tests of Musical Intelligence (62), developed in England. These tests too may be used from age 8 on. Like the Drake tests, the Wing tests depart from the "atomistic" sensory approach of the Seashore tests and make use of musically meaningful content. Piano music is utilized in each of the seven tests, which cover chord analysis, pitch change, memory, rhythmic accent, harmony, intensity, and phrasing. The first three tests require sensory discriminations, but at a somewhat more complex level than in the Seashore tests. In the other four, the subject compares the aesthetic merit of two versions. Thus the battery places considerable emphasis on music appreciation.

Norms are provided for total scores on the entire Wing battery. Such a use of total scores is supported by the identification of a general factor of musical ability in factorial analyses of music tests (42, 61). This factor, described as the cognitive aspect of musical ability, accounted for 30 to 40 per cent of the total test variances. For older children and adults, both retest and split-half reliabilities of total scores on the Wing battery are in the .90's. Preliminary studies of validity in small groups yielded correlations of .60 or higher with teachers' ratings of musical ability. The tests have high ceilings and may find their greatest usefulness in the selection of musically talented individuals for further training.

Mention may also be made of various attempts to measure musical attitudes and interests by means of questionnaires or self-ratings. An example is the Seashore-Hevner Tests for Attitude toward Music (53), patterned after the Thurstone scales to be discussed in Chapter 19. More recently, Farnsworth (19) developed a similar series of scales for rating interest in different types of music. In so far as emotional reactions play a significant part in both the appreciation and production of music, the measurement of musical interests would seem to be as important as the measurement of aptitudes in this area.

LITERARY APPRECIATION

Literary aptitude, like aptitude in music or in the graphic arts, represents a multiplicity of skills. Among the measuring instruments employed in this area are to be found tests of literary information; tests concerned with grammar, spelling, word knowledge, and other mechanics of writing; product scales; and tests of literary appreciation. The first two types are predominantly achievement tests which are used to measure the effects of specific courses of study. When more general and more elementary items are employed, such information tests may be incorporated in intelligence or verbal aptitude tests.

In *product scales,* the subject writes an original composition on a more or less narrowly prescribed topic. The products of such an assignment are then graded by "matching" each with a sample product in a previously prepared scale. The raters are usually given a list of specific points to check, such as grammar, spelling, word choice, organization, clarity, and originality.

In so far as creative qualities and other aesthetic characteristics of the writing are judged, such product scales would fall within the scope of the present chapter. In most of these tests, however, the major emphasis is placed upon the individual's ability to use language as a means of factual communication, rather than as an aesthetic medium. Moreover, such tests are employed principally to appraise the educational progress of school children or college students, rather than to select individuals with special literary talents. Thus this type of test, as well as the literary and grammatical information tests, fits more properly into the content of Chapters 16 and 17, which are concerned with achievement tests.

Tests designed to measure *literary appreciation,* on the other hand, have much in common with the tests of music and art appreciation discussed in the preceding sections of this chapter. To be sure, some of the tests labeled as measures of literary appreciation are in effect tests of comprehension or information. With these instruments we shall not be concerned at present. A number of attempts have been made, however, to apply to the literary field the same basic technique used by Meier, Graves, Wing, and others in the development of art and music appreciation tests.

An early test developed in 1921 by Abbott and Trabue (1) established the pattern for this approach to the measurement of literary appreciation. Each item in this test consisted of a short poem or part of a poem, presented in the original and three distorted versions. The three distortions included a sentimental version, in which emotion was falsified by introducing silly, gushy, affected, or otherwise insincere feelings; a prosaic version, in which imagery was reduced to a more pedestrian and commonplace level; and a metrical version, in which movement was rendered awkward or less fine than in the original. In taking the test, subjects were instructed merely to mark the selection they liked best in each set.

The Rigg Poetry Judgment Test (49), published more than twenty years later, utilized essentially the same approach as the Abbott-Trabue. In the Rigg test, only two versions are given in each item, and the number of items has been increased. An example is shown in Figure 91. This test, which is available in two parallel forms, provides norms for high school, college, and adult "expert" groups, although it appears to be too difficult for the high school level. Parallel-form reliabilities in the .70's are reported for high school and college groups. When scores from both forms are combined, the reliabilities rise to the .80's. Validity was "built in" to the test by item selection procedures similar to those followed in the construction of the Meier Art Judgment Test, but no other evidence of validity is presented. The Rigg test has been criticized by teachers of English because the excerpts used are so short that judgments tend to be based on minor details and mechanical aspects of the poetry.

Out of the hills of Habersham, Down the valleys of Hall, I hurry amain to reach the plain, Run the rapid and leap the fall.	My source is in the Habersham Hills, Thence down the valleys of Hall, I flow so fast o'er rocks and rills To reach at last the waterfall.

The subject indicates which selection he regards as the better poetry.

Fig. 91. Sample Item from Rigg Poetry Judgment Test. (Reproduced by permission of Melvin C. Rigg.)

A similar technique has been applied by Carroll (7) to the appreciation of prose. Each item in the Carroll Prose Appreciation Test contains four short passages, approximately equated in length and subject matter, but taken from four sharply differentiated sources. Unlike the Abbott-Trabue test, however, only one version was specially prepared for testing purposes. The four sources of test materials include top-ranking classic literature, books generally regarded as being of mediocre or poor quality, stories from pulp magazines, and a deliberate mutilation written specially for the test. An illustrative item will be found in Figure 92. In this test, the subject is required to rank the four passages for literary merit, giving a rank of 1 to the best and a rank of 4 to the poorest in each set. The score is based on a system of partial credits.

Three levels of the Carroll test were prepared, for use with junior high school, senior high school, and college students. Percentile norms are given separately for each grade. Reliability coefficients of the order of .70 were obtained by both split-half and retest techniques. As in many tests of artistic appreciation, validity was considered in terms of source of material, expert opinion, and performance of contrasted groups. Large and statistically significant differences in mean scores were found between high school and college groups, as well as between college and adult "expert" groups. In addition, the scores increased regularly and significantly with grade, within each school group.

It has been objected that in this test, as in the Rigg test, the individual passages are too brief to permit the proper measurement of literary appreciation. As a result of such brevity, the passages are likely to be judged primarily in terms of their stylistic characteristics. Broader questions of literary

AN INTERIOR

A

I went with the little maid into a gorgeously decorated bedroom, all of cream color and light blue that blended prettily. The bed was a great, wide affair of beautifully carved and ornamented wood, painted creamy white with blue and gold trimmings. There was a wonderful bureau and a dressing table to match, and in one corner of the room a mirror that went from floor to ceiling. I had to hold my breath.

B

Lollie had never seen such a pretty room, and it made her gasp to see how pretty the furniture was, as well as how pretty the rugs were, and the curtains at the windows and the pictures on the wall, but what she really liked best was that furniture, for it looked comfortable as well as pretty, and she knew it must have cost hundreds and hundreds of dollars. She wished she could live and die in that one room, it was so pretty.

C

An air of Sabbath had descended on the room. The sun shone brightly through the window, spreading a golden lustre over the white walls; only along the north wall, where the bed stood, a half shadow lingered . . . The table had been spread with a white cover; upon it lay the open hymn book, with the page turned down. Beside the hymn book stood a bowl of water; beside that lay a piece of white cloth . . . Kjersti was tending the stove, piling the wood in diligently . . . Sorine sat in the corner, crooning over a tiny bundle; out of the bundle at intervals came faint, wheezy chirrups, like the sounds that rise from a nest of young birds.

D

Major Prime had the west sitting-room. It was lined with low bookcases, full of old, old books. There was a fire-place, a winged chair, a broad couch, a big desk of dark seasoned mahogany, and over the mantel a steel engraving of Robert E. Lee. The low windows at the back looked out upon the wooded green of the ascending hill; at the front was a porch which gave a view of the valley.

The subject ranks the four selections in order of literary merit. In this item, the correct order is as follows: 1- C, 2- D, 3- A, 4- B

Fig. 92. Sample Item from Carroll Prose Appreciation Test. (Reproduced by permission of Educational Test Bureau, Minneapolis.)

criticism, such as portrayal of characters, or principles of organization employed in developing a plot, are obviously excluded. The passages are probably long enough, however, to permit judgment of many important aspects of writing.

A test for the appreciation of poetry, developed in England, illustrates still another variation of the same basic procedure (17). In this test, excerpts from representative poems of high literary quality are presented with some portion omitted. Three alternative completions are provided, including the original and two weakened variants. In each item, the subject must choose the best completion. Analysis of the performance of 600 subjects, including secondary school pupils as well as students, research workers, and staff members of two large universities, indicated good differentiation with regard to age and educational level.

From this brief review of the different types of aptitude tests in literature, music, and graphic art, it is apparent that much remains to be done in this field. The available tests are few in number and technically crude. At the same time, several ingenious devices and promising approaches have been developed that warrant further exploration.

CREATIVITY AND REASONING

Of considerable relevance to the understanding of artistic talent is the relatively new area of research on creativity. The large majority of investigators in this field have been concerned primarily with creative talent in science and engineering, but some attention has also been given to creative achievement in the arts. Many studies dealing with reasoning—in the broad sense of problem-solving at a complex level—overlap the area of creativity. In the research literature, the two terms are often used to refer to very similar activities.

In a general discussion of the problem, Thurstone (56) emphasized the fact that creative talent is not synonymous with academic intelligence. He pointed to the possible relation of creativity to ideational fluency, inductive reasoning, and certain perceptual tendencies. Special attention was also given to the contribution of non-intellectual, temperamental factors. For example, creativity may be encouraged by a receptive as contrasted to a critical attitude toward novel ideas, as well as by relaxed, dispersed attention rather than active concentration on a problem. Several studies have approached the problem of creativity through factorial analyses of batteries of tests designed to measure various aspects of creative talent. Some correspondences can be discerned between the factors isolated through these different analyses, although the agreement is far from complete (2, 6, 13, 27, 43, 44).

The most extensive factorial investigation of creativity is that conducted by Guilford and his associates under the auspices of the Office of Naval Research (24, 25, 26, 27, 33, 60). This project set out to explore four areas of thinking, designated as reasoning, creativity, planning, and evaluation. Many new types of tests were developed in the course of the study and were administered, together with tests of previously established factors, to groups of students and military personnel. In the factorial analyses, several familiar factors reappeared, such as Verbal Comprehension, Numerical Facility, Spatial Orientation, Spatial Visualization, Perceptual Speed, General Reasoning (with heavy loading on arithmetic reasoning tests), and several memory factors. But many new factors were identified in the course of the study.

The broader implications of Guilford's research for the nature of intelligence and for the number and organization of intellectual factors were considered in Chapter 13. For the present purpose, interest centers especially on the various fluency, flexibility, and originality factors found to be most closely associated with creativity. These factors come under the heading of "divergent thinking," which Guilford describes as "the kind that goes off in different directions" (26, p. 381). Such thinking permits changes of direction in problem-solving and leads to a diversity of answers. In contrast, "convergent thinking" leads to a single right answer determined by the given facts (26, p. 376). The various divergent-thinking factors identified in Guilford's studies can be illustrated by examining some of the tests found to be heavily loaded with each factor (26, pp. 381-390). A few of these tests have been published and are available for distribution. Others will appear in the near future. Until more data are gathered about these tests, however, all should be regarded as research instruments only.

A test of *word fluency* (10) requires the subject to write words containing a given letter. In this as in all fluency tests, the score is simply the total number of acceptable responses written in the time allowed. Other measures of this factor call for words beginning with a specified prefix or rhymes for a given word. There is some evidence that performance on word fluency tests is correlated with creative achievement of college students in science and art courses (16). In one *ideational fluency* test (10), the subject must name things that belong in a certain class, such as fluids that will burn. In another, he lists different uses for a common object, such as a brick or pencil. *Associational fluency* is illustrated by a test calling for all words similar in meaning to a given word, such as "hard" (10). Words for this test were chosen because each has a variety of meanings. Another test requires the in-

sertion of an adjective to complete each simile (e.g., "As———as a fish").
Expressional fluency can be measured by a test of four-word combinations,
in which the subject writes four connected words, the first letters of which
are given (10). For example, if given Y——— c——— t———
d———, the subject could write, "You can throw dice." The subject continues to write different sentences for each given set until time is called.

Among the tests having high loadings in the various *flexibility* factors identified in Guilford's research may be mentioned Hidden Pictures, Hidden
Figures, and Match Problems (26, p. 386). In the first of these tests, the
problem is to find concealed faces whose lines form parts of larger objects in a picture. In the second, illustrated in Figure 93, the subject must

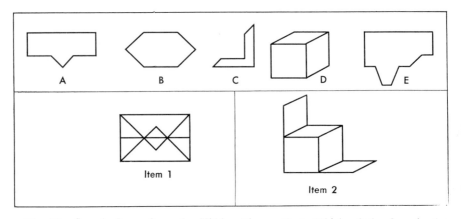

Fig. 93. Sample Items from the Hidden Figures Test. Which of the five simpler
figures at the top is concealed in each of the item figures? Answers: 1, A; 2, D. (From
Guilford, 26, p. 386. Copyright, 1959, McGraw-Hill Book Company, Inc.)

identify a simple geometric figure embedded in a more complex figure. The
Match Problems test requires the removal of a specified number of matchsticks to leave a given number of squares or triangles. One example from
this test is reproduced in Figure 94. In all of these tests, a good performance
requires freedom from persistence of approaches, permitting a restructuring of
the given stimuli.

Originality can be measured by an adaptation of the familiar free association test, in which the subject must respond rapidly to each stimulus word
by giving the first word that occurs to him. In scoring this test, each response
is weighted in inverse proportion to its commonness in the general population. There is some evidence that such groups as scientists, engineers, artists,
musicians, and writers tend to given less common associations than execu-

tives, salesmen, teachers, and politicians (39). Another example is the Consequences test (12), which provides separate scores in ideational fluency and originality. In this test, the subject is told to list as many different consequences of some hypothetical event as he can. For example, "What would be the results if people no longer needed or wanted sleep?" Responses are classified as obvious or remote according to rules given in the manual. The number of obvious responses provides the ideational fluency score; the number of remote responses, the originality score.

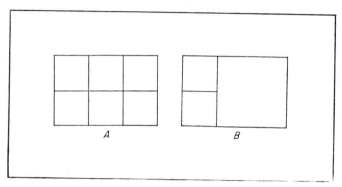

Fig. 94. Sample Item from the Match Problems Test. If each line is a match, can you take away four matches in A, leaving three squares and nothing more? If the subject works under the assumption that all squares must be of the same size, he would be unable to reach the correct solution, shown in B. (From Guilford, 26, p. 387. Copyright, 1959, McGraw-Hill Book Company, Inc.)

Tests of originality similar to those mentioned above have yielded promising criterion correlations in some exploratory investigations. Correlations between .30 and .55 have been reported between such tests and teachers' ratings for creativity of science and art students (16), as well as ratings for originality of military officers (4). Reference should also be made to the Ingenuity test in the FACT battery, discussed in Chapter 13. In a series of preliminary validation studies, scores on this test yielded concurrent validity coefficients of .35 to .50 with criteria of originality in high school art classes, and coefficients of .28 to .46 with similar criteria in high school English classes (20, pp. 49-51).

One investigation was concerned with the effects of varying time limits on performance in the open-end, free-response type of test used to measure creativity (11). Although simple recall tasks show a decreasing production rate with time, the more inventive or creative tasks show a relatively constant rate of production within the time limits investigated. Qualitatively, both uncommonness and remoteness of response increase with time. Thus with longer time limits, subjects gave a larger proportion of responses rated high in these aspects of originality.

Although tests of fluency, flexibility, and originality such as those cited above probably come closest to measuring the essential aspects of creativity, other abilities are undoubtedly needed for effective creative achievement, especially in the sciences. A number of cognitive and evaluative aptitudes usually classified under reasoning are clearly relevant. Two available tests in this area that have emerged from the Guilford project are Logical Reasoning (29), composed of items in syllogistic form, and the Ship Destination Test (9), which is heavily loaded with the general reasoning factor and utilizes problems similar to those found in arithmetic reasoning tests. An earlier test designed to tap several aspects of effective reasoning is the Watson-Glaser Critical Thinking Appraisal (59). Designed for high school and college levels, this test contains five parts, dealing with inference, recognition of assumptions, deduction, interpretation, and evaluation of arguments.

In discussing creative productivity in the arts, Guilford (25) suggests that several of the fluency, flexibility, and originality factors so far identified may play an important part. Those in the verbal area, with which many of the available tests are concerned, are probably related to creative writing. Corresponding factors pertaining to visual, auditory, or even kinaesthetic "figural" content—many of which have not yet been identified—may play an equally important part in the graphic arts, music, and choreography. In addition, creative productivity in the arts, as in the sciences, undoubtedly requires also a certain minimum proficiency in relevant comprehension and memory factors, such as verbal comprehension, spatial orientation, visual or auditory memory, and the like.

It is too early to know what will be the final outcome of current research on the nature of creativity. One point appears to be fairly clear at this time, however. Investigations of scientific talent are becoming increasingly concerned with creative abilities. Interest has shifted from the individual who is merely a cautious, accurate, and critical thinker to the one who also displays ingenuity, originality, and inventiveness. Thus creativity, long regarded as the prime quality in artistic production, is coming more and more to be recognized as a basis for scientific achievement as well. It is also likely that in the years ahead we shall see many new kinds of tests. The traditional emphasis on understanding and recall that has characterized intelligence and aptitude tests will probably give way to a more comprehensive approach with greater concentration on productive thinking.

REFERENCES

1. Abbott, A., and Trabue, M. R. A measure of ability to judge poetry. *Teach. Coll. Rec.,* 1921, 22, 3-19.
2. Adkins, Dorothy C., and Lyerly, S. B. *Factor analysis of reasoning tests.* Chapel Hill, N. C.: Univer. N. Carolina Press, 1952.
3. Barrett, H. D. An examination of certain standardized art tests to determine their relation to classroom achievement and to intelligence. *J. educ. Res.,* 1949, 42, 398-400.
4. Barron, F. The disposition toward originality. *J. abnorm. soc. Psychol.,* 1955, 51, 478-485.
5. Bienstock, Sylvia F. A review of recent studies on musical aptitude. *J. educ. Psychol.,* 1942, 33, 427-442.
6. Botzum, W. A. A factorial study of the reasoning and closure factors. *Psychometrika,* 1951, 16, 361-386.
7. Carroll, H. A. *Prose Appreciation Test.* Minneapolis: Educ. Test Bur., 1932-1935.
8. Carroll, H. A. What do the Meier-Seashore and the McAdory Art Tests measure? *J. educ. Res.,* 1933, 26, 661-665.
9. Christensen, P. R., and Guilford, J. P. *Ship Destination Test.* Beverly Hills, Calif.: Sheridan Supply Co., 1955-1956.
10. Christensen, P. R., and Guilford, J. P. *Fluency Tests: Word Fluency, Expressional Fluency, Ideational Fluency I, Associational Fluency I.* Beverly Hills, Calif.: Sheridan Supply Co., 1957-1958.
11. Christensen, P. R., Guilford, J. P., and Wilson, R. C. Relations of creative responses to working time and instructions. *J. exp. Psychol.,* 1957, 53, 82-88.
12. Christensen, P. R., Merrifield, P. R., and Guilford, J. P. *Consequences.* Beverly Hills, Calif.: Sheridan Supply Co., 1958.
13. Corter, H. M. Factor analysis of some reasoning tests. *Psychol. Monogr.,* 1952, 66, No. 8.
14. D'Annibale Braga, Leonilda. Estudo preliminar da adaptação do teste de Meier ao meio brasileiro. (Preliminary study of the adaptation of the Meier test to the Brazilian environment.) *Arch. brasil. Psicotéc.,* 1951, 3, 7-23.
15. Drake, R. M. *Drake Musical Aptitude Tests.* Chicago: Sci. Res. Assoc., 1954-1957.
16. Drevdahl, J. E. Factors of importance for creativity. *J. clin. Psychol.,* 1956, 12, 21-26.
17. Eppel, E. M. A new test of poetry discrimination. *Brit. J. educ. Psychol.,* 1950, 20, 111-116.
18. Farnsworth, P. R. An historical, critical, and experimental study of the Seashore-Kwalwasser test battery. *Genet. Psychol. Monogr.,* 1931, 9, 291-393.
19. Farnsworth, P. R. Rating scales for musical interests. *J. Psychol.,* 1949, 28, 245-253.

20. Flanagan, J. C. *Flanagan Aptitude Classification Tests: Technical report.* Chicago: Sci. Res. Assoc., 1959.
21. Fleishman, E. A. Predicting code proficiency of radiotelegraphers by means of aural tests. *J. appl. Psychol.,* 1955, 39, 150-155.
22. Graves, M. *The art of color and design.* (2nd ed.) N. Y.: McGraw-Hill, 1951.
23. Graves, M. *Graves Design Judgment Test.* N. Y.: Psychol. Corp., 1948.
24. Green, R. F., Guilford, J. P., Christensen, P. R., and Comrey, A. L. A factor-analytic study of reasoning abilities. *Psychometrika,* 1953, 18, 135-160.
25. Guilford, J. P. Creative abilities in the arts. *Psychol. Rev.,* 1957, 64, 110-118.
26. Guilford, J. P. *Personality.* N. Y.: McGraw-Hill, 1959.
27. Guilford, J. P., *et al.* A factor-analytic study of Navy reasoning tests with the Air Force Aircrew Classification Battery. *Educ. psychol. Measmt.,* 1954, 14, 301-325.
28. Hellersberg, Elizabeth F. The Horn-Hellersberg test and adjustment to reality. *Amer. J. Orthopsychiat.,* 1945, 15, 690-710.
29. Hertzka, A. F., and Guilford, J. P. *Logical Reasoning.* Beverly Hills, Calif.: Sheridan Supply Co., 1955.
30. Holmes, J. A. Increased reliabilities, new keys, and norms for a modified Kwalwasser-Dykema Test of musical aptitude. *J. genet. Psychol.,* 1954, 85, 65-73.
31. Horn, C. C. *Horn Art Aptitude Inventory.* Chicago: Stoelting, 1951-1953.
32. Horn, C. C., and Smith, L. F. The Horn Art Aptitude Inventory. *J. appl. Psychol.,* 1945, 29, 350-355.
33. Kettner, N., Guilford, J. P., and Christensen, P. R. A factor-analytic investigation of the factor called general reasoning. *Educ. psychol. Measmt.,* 1956, 16, 438-453.
34. Kinter, Madeline. *The measurement of artistic abilities.* N. Y.: Psychol. Corp., 1933.
35. Knauber, Alma J. *Knauber Art Ability Test.* Cincinnati: Author, 1932-1935. (Distributed by C. H. Stoelting Co.)
36. Knauber, Alma J. Construction and standardization of the Knauber Art Tests. *Education,* 1935, 56, 165-170.
37. Kwalwasser, J., and Dykema, P. W. *Kwalwasser-Dykema Music Tests.* N. Y.: Fischer, 1930.
38. Lewerenz, A. S. *Tests in Fundamental Abilities of Visual Art.* Monterey, Calif.: Calif. Test Bur., 1927.
39. Licht, M. The measurement of one aspect of personality. *J. Psychol.,* 1947, 24, 83-87.
40. Lundin, R. W. *An objective psychology of music.* N. Y.: Ronald, 1953.
41. McAdory, Margaret. *The McAdory Art Test.* N. Y.: Teach. Coll. Bur. Publ., 1929-1933.
42. McLeish, J. The validation of Seashore's measures of musical talent by factorial methods. *Brit. J. Psychol., Stat. Sect.,* 1950, 3, 129-140.
43. Marron, J. E. The search for basic reasoning abilities: a review of factor analytic studies. *USAF Hum. Resour. Res. Cent. Res. Bull,* 1953, No. 53-28.
44. Matin, L., and Adkins, Dorothy C. A second-order factor analysis of reasoning abilities. *Psychometrika,* 1954, 19, 71-78.

45. Meier, N. C. *The Meier Art Tests: I. Art Judgment.* Iowa City: Bur. Educ. Res. Serv., Univer. Iowa, 1940-1942.

46. Meier, N. C. *Art in human affairs.* N. Y.: McGraw-Hill, 1942.

47. Meier, N. C., and Seashore, C. E. *The Meier-Seashore Art Judgment Test.* Iowa City: Bur. Educ. Res. Serv., Univer. Iowa, 1929.

48. Morrow, R. S. An analysis of the relations among tests of musical, artistic, and mechanical abilities. *J. Psychol.,* 1938, 5, 253-263.

49. Rigg, M. G. *The Rigg Poetry Judgment Test.* Iowa City: Bur. Educ. Res. Serv., Univer. Iowa, 1942.

50. Saetveit, J. G., Lewis, D., and Seashore, C. E. Revision of the Seashore Measures of Musical Talents. *Univer. Iowa Stud., Aims Progr. Res.,* 1940, No. 65.

51. Seashore, C. E. *Psychology of music.* N. Y.: McGraw-Hill, 1938.

52. Seashore, C. E., Lewis, D., and Saetveit, J. G. *Seashore Measures of Musical Talents.* N. Y.: Psychol. Corp., 1939-1956.

53. Seashore, R. H., and Hevner, Kate. A time-saving device for the construction of attitude scales. *J. soc. Psychol.,* 1933, 4, 366-372.

54. Siceloff, Margaret McAdory, *et al. Validation and standardization of the McAdory Art Test.* N. Y.: Teach. Coll. Bur. Publ., 1933.

55. Steggerda, M. The McAdory Art Test applied to Navajo Indian children. *J. comp. Psychol.,* 1936, 22, 283-285.

56. Thurstone, L. L. Creative talent. *Proc. 1950 invit. Conf. test. Probl., Educ. Test. Serv.,* 1951, 55-69.

57. Tiebout, C., and Meier, N. C. Artistic ability and general intelligence. *Psychol. Monogr.,* 1936, 48, 95-125.

58. Tufts College Institute of Applied Experimental Psychology. *Handbook of human engineering data.* (2nd ed.) NAVEXOS P-643. Tech. Rep.—SDC 199-1-2. Special Devices Cent., ONR, 1951.

59. Watson, G., and Glaser, E. M. *Watson-Glaser Critical Thinking Appraisal.* Tarrytown-on-Hudson, N. Y.: World Book Co., 1952-1956.

60. Wilson, R. C., Guilford, J. P., *et al.* A factor-analytic study of creative-thinking abilities. *Psychometrika,* 1954, 19, 297-311.

61. Wing, H. D. A factorial study of musical tests. *Brit. J. Psychol.,* 1941, 31, 341-355.

62. Wing, H. D. *Wing Standardized Tests of Musical Intelligence (Revised Edition).* London: Nat. Found. Educ. Res., 1957-1958.

CHAPTER 16

Achievement Tests: General

In sheer numbers, achievement tests surpass all other types of standardized tests. The principal object of achievement tests is to appraise the effects of a course of instruction or training. Although such tests find their most extensive application in education, they are not restricted to school work. Achievement tests have also been developed for measuring the results of specialized vocational training and experience in many types of jobs.

It is customary to contrast achievement tests with aptitude tests, the latter including general intelligence tests, multiple aptitude batteries, and special aptitude tests. From one point of view, the difference between achievement and aptitude testing is a difference in the degree of uniformity of relevant antecedent experience. Thus achievement tests measure the effects of relatively standardized sets of experiences, such as a course in elementary French, solid geometry, or Gregg shorthand. In contrast, aptitude test performance reflects the cumulative influence of a multiplicity of experiences in daily living. We might say that aptitude tests measure the effects of learning under relatively uncontrolled and unknown conditions, while achievement tests measure the effects of learning that occurred under partially known and controlled conditions.

A second distinction between aptitude and achievement tests pertains to their respective uses. Aptitude tests serve to predict subsequent performance. They are employed to estimate the extent to which the individual will profit from training, or to forecast the quality of his achievement in a new situation. Achievement tests, on the other hand, generally represent a terminal evaluation of the individual's status upon the completion of training. The emphasis in such tests is upon what the individual can do at the time. This difference is perhaps most clearly illustrated by the procedures for estimating the validity of achievement tests, as contrasted to those followed in validating aptitude tests.

It should be recognized, however, that no distinction between aptitude and achievement tests can be rigidly applied. Some aptitude tests may depend upon fairly specific and uniform prior learning, while some achievement tests cover relatively broad and unstandardized educational experiences. Similarly, any achievement test may be used as a predictor of future learning. As such it serves the same purpose as an aptitude test. For example, the progress a pupil has made in arithmetic, as determined by his present achievement test score, may be employed to predict his subsequent success in algebra. Achievement tests on premedical courses can serve as predictors of performance in medical school. Whenever different individuals have had the same or closely similar courses of study, achievement tests based on such courses may provide efficient indices of future performance.

In differentiating between aptitude and achievement tests, we should especially guard against the naïve assumption that achievement tests measure the effects of learning, while aptitude tests measure "innate capacity" independent of learning. This misconception was fairly prevalent in the early days of psychological testing, but has been largely corrected in the subsequent clarification of psychometric concepts. It should be obvious that all psychological tests measure the individual's current behavior, which inevitably reflects the influence of prior learning. The fact that every test score has a "past" does not, however, preclude its having a "future." While revealing the effects of past learning, test scores may, under certain conditions, serve as predictors of future learning.

USES AND MISUSES OF ACHIEVEMENT TESTS

Achievement tests are currently employed in education, business and industry, civil service, and the armed forces. They also constitute a part of the armamentarium of the counselor and the clinical psychologist. In all these fields, they may serve a variety of functions.

Uses. Achievement tests are frequently employed to check the *attainment of minimum performance standards.* Is the industrial or military trainee ready for a specific job assignment? Is the applicant qualified for a license to drive a car, pilot a plane, or practice medicine? This application of achievement tests represents an all-or-none appraisal of current status.

Selection is another function for which achievement tests are often employed. Such tests play a major role in the hiring of applicants for a wide variety of specialized industrial jobs. In civil service employment procedures, the development and application of many kinds of achievement tests represent a gigantic undertaking. The periodic administration of many thousands of educational achievement tests in connection with the admission of students to colleges, graduate schools, and professional schools is well known. Certain scholarship programs likewise include competitive achievement examinations as one instrument for the selection of the most promising candidates.

Placement and *classification* represent other types of decisions utilizing achievement tests. In this connection, the uses of achievement tests range from the classification of military personnel in terms of previous job training and experience, to the "sectioning" or ability grouping of elementary school children. The practice of subdividing school classes into relatively homogeneous ability sections has been followed for several decades. Sectioning on the basis of over-all educational achievement or aptitude, however, has been criticized on the grounds that it ignores trait differences within the individual. For this reason, the use of achievement tests in different areas, as a means of adapting instruction to individual ability patterns, has been strongly advocated (cf., e.g., 35, Ch. 1).

Achievement tests are an important tool in *counseling*. An appraisal of the individual's current skills and knowledge is an obvious first step in the educational and vocational planning that constitute important objectives of the counseling situation. Similarly, achievement tests have a place in *clinical practice*. In the diagnosis of individuals with reading disabilities or other special educational weaknesses, the need for achievement tests is self-evident. A number of available diagnostic tests were specially designed for such intensive individual analyses of academic deficiencies. Many other types of clinical cases may also require the administration of achievement tests. In cases of truancy, behavior problems, and delinquency, for example, educational failures and maladjustment to the school situation may be contributing factors. Similarly, emotional maladjustments among intellectually gifted children are sometimes found to be associated with improper educational placement.

The many roles that achievement tests can play within the specific setting of the school itself have long been recognized. As an aid in the *assignment of grades,* such tests have the advantages of objectivity and uniformity. If properly constructed, they have other merits, such as adequacy of content coverage and reduction of the operation of irrelevant and chance factors in marking procedures. Achievement tests also constitute an important feature of *remedial teaching programs*. In this connection, they are useful both in the identification of pupils with special educational disabilities and in the measurement of progress in the course of remedial work.

For all types of learners, the periodic administration of well-constructed and properly chosen achievement tests serves to *facilitate learning*. Such tests reveal weaknesses in past learning, give direction to subsequent learning, and motivate the learner. The incentive value of "knowledge of results" has been repeatedly demonstrated by psychological experiments in many types of learning situations, with subjects of widely varying age and education. The effectiveness of such self-checking is generally heightened by immediacy. Thus when achievement examinations are employed primarily as a learning aid, it is desirable for the students to become aware of their errors as soon after taking the test as possible.

The use of achievement tests as learning devices is highlighted by the development of "teaching machines," cited in Chapter 3. Such machines may use apparatus for exposing items and recording responses, or a punchboard in which the subject punches holes on an answer sheet to indicate his choice of response, or even simpler paper-and-pencil materials. A feature common to all teaching machines is the provision for immediate self-scoring or "feedback." A number of investigations, principally with college students, have demonstrated a significant superiority in learning by groups using these self-scoring training devices, in comparison to control groups devoting the same amount of time to more traditional learning procedures (cf. 19, 29, 41, 43, 44, 45).

Finally, achievement tests may be employed as aids in the *evaluation of teaching,* the *improvement of instructional techniques,* and the *revision of curriculum content.* Achievement tests can provide information on the adequacy with which essential content is being covered. In situations demanding uniformity of training, as in the military services, such uniformity can be assured by the administration of a common test. Achievement tests can likewise indicate how much of the course content is actually retained and for how long. Are certain types of material retained longer than others? What are the most common errors and misunderstandings encountered? How well can the learners apply their knowledge to new situations? By focusing attention upon such questions and by providing concrete facts, achievement tests stimulate an analysis of training objectives and encourage a critical examination of the content and methods of instruction. The growth of Fall testing programs points up the increasing use of test results as a basis for planning what is to be taught to a class as a whole and what modifications and adjustments need to be made in individual cases. By giving tests at the beginning of the school year, constructive steps can be taken to fill the major gaps in knowledge revealed by the test results.

Misuses. The possible dangers inherent in the unwise application of achievement tests have been as vigorously expounded by educators as have the merits of such tests. One of the strongest objections to the use of achievement tests pertains to the excessive *standardization of instruction* that may thereby be encouraged. In the learning of elementary skills, as well as in a number of vocational and military training situations, such standardization may be a desirable goal. In many other types of learning, however, enforced uniformity is objectionable because it tends to stifle spontaneity, creativity, and original thinking. Moreover, excessive standardization ignores individual differences in both learners and instructors. The adaptation of instruction to local needs and conditions is also incompatible with such a high degree of standardization.

Another objection raised against the indiscriminate use of achievement tests centers about the dangers of *test-oriented instruction.* If achievement tests were so designed as to cover all important goals of education, each weighted in proportion to its importance, this criticism would lose much of its force. Achievement tests, however, tend to overemphasize certain types of learning and neglect others. Not all educational objectives are equally amenable to standardized testing. Despite these limitations of tests, instructors and students are frequently motivated to concentrate upon those aspects of a course that will lead to a better achievement test score. The fact that administrators sometimes place undue emphasis upon test performance also encourages such an attitude.

Like any other type of test, achievement tests should be regarded as tools, not goals. Moreover, it must be remembered that they provide only partial information and need to be supplemented by other observations. In this respect, too, they resemble other tests. When properly used, with due regard to their limitations, they provide an effective instrument for many purposes. It should also be added that achievement tests are constantly being improved in a number of ways. Thus techniques are being developed for testing the more complex and more creative aspects of learning. Although it is relatively difficult to design achievement test items to measure creativity, critical ability, the application of knowledge to new situations, and similar functions, it is not impossible. In fact, one of the most conspicuous changes in educational achievement tests since the 1940's has been the development of tests for measuring the attainment of broader educational goals formerly regarded as inaccessible to objective evaluation. The instruments to be discussed in the last section of this chapter fully illustrate this trend.

CONSTRUCTION OF TEACHER-MADE TESTS

Anyone who has ever prepared a quiz or an examination has constructed an achievement test. Although many of the elaborations and refinements of large-scale test construction would be out of place in the classroom, most examinations could be improved by the judicious application of sound test-construction procedures. Many treatises have been written on the question of how to construct achievement tests. Most of the techniques described in these publications are common to the construction of any type of test. Several of the discussions, however, have been specially oriented toward the preparation of achievement tests for use in education, civil service, or the armed forces. Some are specifically concerned with techniques for improving informal, teacher-made examinations. The major steps in constructing an effective classroom test may be summarized under three headings: (*a*) planning the test, (*b*) item writing, and (*c*) item analysis.

Planning the Test. The test constructor who plunges directly into item writing is likely to produce a lopsided test. Without an advance plan, some areas will be overrepresented while others may remain untouched. It is generally easier to prepare objective items on some topics than on others. And it is easier to prepare items that require the recall of simple facts than to devise items calling for critical evaluation, integration of different facts, or application of principles to new situations. Yet follow-up studies have shown that the factual details learned in a course are most likely to be forgotten, while the understanding of principles and their application to new situations show either no retention loss or an actual gain with time after completion of a course (54, 57). Thus the test constructed without a blueprint is likely to be overloaded with relatively impermanent and less important material. Many of the criticisms of objective tests stem from the common overemphasis of rote memory and trivial details in poorly constructed tests.

To guard against these fortuitous imbalances and disproportions of item coverage, *test specifications* should be drawn up before any items are prepared. For classroom examinations, such specifications should begin with an outline of the objectives of the course as well as of the subject matter to be covered. In listing objectives, the test constructor should ask himself what changes in behavior the course was designed to produce. Such changes may pertain to attitudes, interests, interpersonal relations, and other emotional or motivational characteristics, as well as to the acquisition of knowledge and the development of intellectual skills.

An unusually thorough analysis of educational objectives in the cognitive domain can be found in the *Taxonomy of Educational Objectives* (4). Prepared by a group of specialists in educational measurement, this handbook also provides examples of many types of items to illustrate the testing of each objective. The major categories in this taxonomy include knowledge (in the sense of remembered facts, terms, methods, principles, etc.), comprehension, application, analysis, synthesis, and evaluation. Each broad objective is broken down into finer and finer subdivisions and illustrated from a variety of fields. Some interesting similarities can be noted between this taxonomy of educational objectives and the schema developed by Guilford for classifying the abilities identified through factor analysis (cf. Ch. 13). But the parallel is by no means complete.

The specifications drawn up in planning a classroom test should show the topics to be covered, the kinds of learning to be tested (in terms of objectives), and the relative importance of individual topics and objectives. On this basis, the number of items of each kind to be prepared on each topic can be established. The most systematic way of setting up such specifications is in terms of a two-way table, with objectives across the top and topics in the left-hand column. Not all cells in such a table, of course, need to have items, since certain kinds of learning may be unsuitable or irrelevant for certain topics.

Item Writing. The test constructor must first decide upon the most appropriate item form for his material. The advantages traditionally cited in favor of essay questions are that they test the individual's ability to select, relate, and organize material, as well as his ability to express ideas clearly and accurately. Unfortunately the time available to the examinee in answering essay questions is usually too short to measure these particular skills. It has been suggested, in fact, that essay examinations may be partly responsible for the habits of unclear and careless writing developed by many students (16). Apart from lack of time for effective organization and good writing, the student answering essay questions writes for an instructor who knows more about the subject than he does. Confident in the expectation that even obscure answers will be understood and duly credited, the student rarely takes the trouble to communicate clearly.

With small groups, it may not be worthwhile to prepare objective items, especially in an area that is rapidly changing and would require frequent item revision. Under such circumstances, essay questions that are carefully formulated and scored may provide the most practicable solution. Or a combination of essay and objective items may be chosen. Essay items can be improved by full and explicit formulation of the question and by systematic scoring procedures. A common weakness of essay examinations arises from subjectivity of scoring. It has been repeatedly demonstrated that the same answer may receive very different grades from different examiners or even from the same examiner at different times. To minimize these sources of error variance, it is advisable to list in advance the points to be covered by the answer and the credit to be assigned to each. Preparing sample answers also helps, especially when several persons are to do the scoring.

As the art of item writing develops, more and more of the abilities for merly believed to be amenable only to essay questions are proving to be testable by objective items. Among the chief advantages of objective items are ease, rapidity, and objectivity of scoring. Since each objective item requires much less of the examinee's time than does a typical essay question, objective items also permit a fuller coverage of content and hence reduce an important source of chance errors in total scores.

Among objective items, there is a choice of several specific forms, such as true-false, multiple-choice, completion, matching, and arrangement (in order of magnitude, chronological order, etc.). The content and type of learning to be tested would largely determine the most appropriate item form. Multiple-choice items have proved to be the most widely applicable. They are also easier to score than certain other forms, and reduce the chances of correct guessing by presenting several alternative responses.

Many practical rules for effective item writing have been formulated on the basis of years of experience in preparing items and empirical evaluation of responses. Anyone planning to prepare objective items would do well to consult one of the books summarizing these suggestions, such as Bean (3), Furst (18), Travers (51), or Wood (58). In addition, several books on the general subject of achievement tests or on the use of tests in education contain one or more chapters on item writing for classroom examinations (cf., e.g., 22, 25, 26, 30, 35, 39, 42, 48, 52, 53). Of considerable help, too, are published collections of items. Gerberich (23) provides a detailed classification of items designed for different purposes and illustrates his discussion with over 200 items. A collection of over 13,000 items on various sciences, suitable for college and high school levels, was assembled by Dressel and Nelson (13). References to published item collections in special fields, ranging from accounting and art appreciation to world history and zoology, can be found in Furst (18) and Gerberich (23).

To add one more summary of item-writing "rules" to the many already available would be redundant. However, a few examples will be given to illustrate the kind of pitfalls that await the unwary item writer. Ambiguous or unclear items are a familiar difficulty. Misunderstandings are likely to occur because of the necessary brevity. It is very difficult to write a single sentence that can stand alone with clarity and precision. In ordinary writing, any obscurity in one sentence can be cleared away by the sentences that follow. But it requires unusual skill to compose isolated sentences that can carry the whole burden unaided. The best test of clarity under these circumstances is to have the statement read by someone else. The writer, who knows the context within which he framed the item, may find it difficult to perceive other meanings in it. If read at a later time, however, the writer himself may be able to spot ambiguities.

While students who feel they may have been cheated out of one or two score points by ambiguous items are quick to call it to the instructor's attention, the opposite type of error is less likely to be publicized. Yet many poorly constructed items give an advantage to the observant guesser. For example, one item may give away the answer to another occurring in a different part of the examination. Thus one item may require the student to identify the name of the psychologist who developed the tests of primary mental abilities, while another begins with the words, "In Thurstone's tests of primary mental abilities. . . ." Grammatical cues, such as differences in number or tense of verbs or the use of the indefinite article "a" instead of "an," may reveal the correct alternative in a multiple-choice item or may at least permit the student to eliminate at once one of the wrong alternatives.

In the effort to be clear, the inexperienced item writer frequently makes the correct alternative longer or qualifies it more fully than the other alternatives. Examinees soon learn that the odds are in their favor if they choose such an alternative when they do not know the correct answer. A final example is provided by clang, or alliterative associations, as in the following vocabulary item:

(poor)   illicit: secret   *illegal*   sexual   ignorant   daring
(good)   illicit: secret   *unlawful*   sexual   illiterate   daring

In the first example, the individual who does not know the meaning of "illicit" could get the item right by choosing the word that sounds most nearly like it. Substituting "unlawful" for "illegal" in the second version has eliminated this cue. In addition, the alliterative cue in this version would mislead the guesser, since on this basis he would choose a wrong alternative, "illiterate."

Item Analysis. The application of statistical item-analysis techniques constitutes an important step in the development of standardized tests (cf. Ch. 7). In simplified form, such techniques can serve several purposes in the classroom. In an achievement test, performance on each item is usually checked against total score on the test as a criterion. In general, we would expect each item to be answered correctly by more high-scoring than low-scoring students. When this does not occur, it alerts us to the possibility that something may be wrong either with the item or with the way the point was taught in the course.

To check the relation of item response to total score, we can compare the performance of a group of good students with that of a group of poor students, chosen on the basis of total test score. In a normally distributed sample, it has been shown that the optimum groups for this purpose consist of the upper and lower 27 per cent of the cases (31). Obviously, the more extreme the groups the sharper will be the differentiation. But the use of more extreme groups, such as upper and lower 10 per cent, would reduce the reliability of the results because of the small number of cases utilized. The optimum point at which these two conditions balance is reached in the comparison of upper and lower 27 per cent. When the distribution is flatter than the normal curve, however, the optimum percentage is slightly greater than 27 and approaches 33 (9). With the size of group available in the ordinary class, moreover, the sampling errror of item statistics is so large that only rough results can be obtained. Under these conditions, we need not be too concerned about the exact percentage of cases in the two contrasted groups. Any convenient number between 25 per cent and 33 per cent will serve satisfactorily.

Let us suppose that in a class of 60 students we have chosen the 20 students (33 per cent) with the highest and the 20 with the lowest scores. We now have three groups of papers which we may call the High, Middle, and Low groups. First we need to tally the correct responses to each item given by students in the three groups. This can be done most readily if we list the item numbers in one column and prepare three other columns headed High, Middle, and Low. As we come to each student's paper, we simply place a tally next to each item he answered correctly. This is done for each of the 20 papers in the High group, then for each of the 20 in the Middle group, and finally for each of the 20 in the Low group. We are now ready to count up the tallies and record totals for each group as shown in Table 21. For illustrative purposes, the first seven items have been entered.

The difficulty of an item is indicated by the total number of persons who answered it correctly, the larger this number the easier the item. In large-scale test construction, this number is expressed as a percentage in order to obtain a comparable index regardless of size of group. In a single class, such a conversion is unnecessary. If desired, however, such percentages can be found most readily by dividing 100 by the total number of cases and using this figure as a constant multiplier. In the present example, $100 \div 60 = 1.7$. We could then multiply each of the numbers in the Difficulty column by 1.7 to change them to percentages. Thus item 1 has a difficulty value of 52.7, item 2 of 95.2, and so on.

The discrimination value of each item can be found by subtracting the number of persons answering it correctly in the Low group from the number answering it correctly in the High group. There are many procedures for expressing such discriminative values as correlations with total scores or in the form of specially developed indices (cf. 10; 35, Ch. 9). For the present purposes, however, the simple difference suffices. If an absolute number is desired, which is independent of the number of cases being compared, each obtained difference can be divided by the maximum possible difference (17). In our group, if an item were passed by all students in the High and none in the Low group, the difference would be 20 — 0, or 20. Each obtained difference may thus be divided by 20. The resulting index may fall anywhere between —1.00 and +1.00.

TABLE 21.   Simple Item-Analysis Procedure

Item	H (20)	M (20)	L (20)	Difficulty (H + M + L)	Discrimination (H — L)
1	15	9	7	31	8
2	20	20	16	56*	4
3	19	18	9	46	10
4	10	11	16	37	— 6*
5	11	13	11	35	0*
6	16	14	9	39	7
7	5	0	0	5*	5
•					
•					
•					
•					
75					

* Items chosen for discussion.

To identify questionable items in a class examination, however, we need not go beyond the raw data reported in Table 21. It will be seen that two items, 2 and 7, have been singled out for further discussion because one seems to be too easy, having been passed by 56 out of 60 students, and the other too difficult, having been passed by only 5. Items 4 and 5, while satisfactory with regard to difficulty level, show a negative and zero discriminative value, respectively. We would also consider in this category any items with a very small positive H — L difference, of roughly three or less when groups of approximately this size are being compared. With larger groups, we would expect larger differences to occur by chance in a nondiscriminating item.

The purpose of item analysis in a teacher-made test is to identify deficiencies either in the test or in the teaching. Discussing questionable items with the class is often sufficient to diagnose the problem. If the wording of the item was at fault, it can be revised or discarded in subsequent testing. Discussion may show, however, that the item was satisfactory, but the point being tested had not been properly understood. In that case, the topic may be reviewed and clarified. In narrowing down the source of the difficulty, it is often helpful to carry out a supplementary analysis, as shown in Table 22, with at least some of the items chosen for discussion. This tabulation gives the number of students in the High and Low groups who chose each option in answering the particular items.

TABLE 22. Response Analysis of Individual Items

Item		Response Options *				
		1	2	3	4	5
2	High	0	0	0	*20*	0
	Low	2	0	1	*16*	1
4	High	0	*10*	9	0	1
	Low	2	*16*	2	0	0
5	High	2	3	2	*11*	2
	Low	1	3	3	*11*	2
7	High	*5*	3	5	4	3
	Low	*0*	5	8	3	4
•						
•						
•						

* Correct options have been italicized.

Although item 2 has been included in Table 22, there is little more we can learn about it by tabulating the frequency of each wrong option, since only 4 persons in the Low group and none in the High group chose wrong answers. Discussion of the item with the students, however, may help to determine whether the item as a whole was too easy and therefore of little intrinsic value, whether some defect in its construction served to give away the right answer, or whether it is a good item dealing with a point that happened to have been very effectively taught and well remembered. In the first case, the item would probably be discarded, in the second it would be revised, and in the third it would be retained unchanged.

The data on item 4 suggest that the third option had some unsuspected implications that led 9 of the better students to prefer it to the correct alternative. The point could easily be settled by asking those students to explain why they chose it. In item 5, the fault seems to lie in the wording either of the stem or of the correct alternative, since the students who missed the item were uniformly distributed over the four wrong options. Item 7 is an unusually difficult one, which was answered incorrectly by 15 of the High and all of the Low group. The slight clustering of responses on incorrect option 3 suggests a superficial attractiveness of this option, especially for the more easily misled Low group. Similarly, the lack of choices of the correct response (option 1) by any of the Low group suggests that this alternative was worded so that superficially or to the uninformed it seemed wrong. Both of these features, of course, are desiderata of good test items. Class discussion might show that item 7 is a good item dealing with a point that few class members had actually learned.

These four items have been selected to illustrate the types of information that may be revealed by an item analysis, as well as the decisions to which they may lead. It should be emphasized that items ought not to be discarded merely on the basis of the statistical evidence. Not only may the cause of the unusual statistical findings lie in the teaching rather than in the test, but an item may also show negligible or negative correlation with total score because of heterogeneity of test content. Dropping such items would "overpurify" the test and reduce content coverage. For example, if a test contains 10 items requiring computational skills and 60 requiring numerical reasoning, the first 10 may show zero or negligible correlation with the total score. Eliminating these items, however, would result in a less adequate measure of all the skills the course is trying to develop.

As a final practical suggestion, it might be added that the entire item analysis described above could profitably be carried out by the students themselves during a single class period. In this case, it may be better to divide the class simply into an upper and a lower half on the basis of test scores. While facilitating procedure and permitting everyone to participate, this grouping still provides enough differentiation to identify the items most seriously in need of discussion. Students in the High and Low halves can be seated on opposite sides of the room, and as each item number is called out those who answered it correctly raise their hands. A similar procedure can be followed for the breakdown of response options.

EVALUATION OF STANDARDIZED ACHIEVEMENT TESTS

In the evaluation of achievement tests, the same basic questions need to be asked as in evaluating any psychological test. As seen in Part 1 of this book, these questions pertain chiefly to reliability, validity, and norms. No new problems are encountered regarding the reliability of achievement tests, the same techniques being employed as in all other tests. In connection with validity and norms, however, certain special points may be noted (cf. 11, 47).

Validity. It will be recalled that *content validity* (Ch. 6) finds its principal application in the evaluation of achievement tests. When applied to educational achievement tests, such validity is often called curricular validity. Essentially, this type of validation is based upon the original selection of items to be included in the test. In this respect it is similar to some of the validation procedures followed in the development of artistic appreciation tests (Ch. 15). The preparation of test items is preceded by a thorough and systematic examination of relevant course syllabi and textbooks, as well as by consultation with subject-matter experts. On the basis of the information thus gathered, test specifications are drawn up for the item writers. The resulting blueprint is similar to that described in the preceding section on teacher-made tests, but more elaborate.

In judging the content validity of an achievement test, the first question is whether the test covers a *representative sample* of the curricular content. Does it measure the extent to which the objectives of the curriculum have been achieved? Is the relative weight given to different objectives and topics satisfactory? An equally important question pertains to the *exclusion of irrelevant variables*. Thus a valid mathematics test should not measure reading ability. Nor should a test of creative writing measure speed. Several empirical procedures for checking the possible contribution of such extraneous factors were cited in Chapter 6 (cf. also 27).

A number of supplementary statistical analyses are sometimes reported in test manuals to provide additional information on the *construct validity* of an achievement test. Scores on the test may be correlated with other achievement tests, aptitude tests, grades, and ratings within a given curricular area. Factorial analyses of such measures will help to define the field covered by the test in terms of the factorial composition of its scores. Both quantitative and qualitative analyses of errors made on the test are another source of relevant information. Grade progress in test scores is frequently investigated as a further approach to validation. This is similar to the age progress criterion used in the development of certain intelligence tests. In achievement tests, an item is retained if the percentage of children passing it increases from the lower to the higher grades. Items showing the largest grade increments in percentage passing are preferred. Those showing no change or irregular variations are discarded. Although probably satisfactory for skill subjects such as reading, arithmetic, and language usage, the grade progress criterion may be inappropriate for some of the content areas. For example, if American history is taught in one grade but not in the next, the percentage of pupils who pass a particular item in American history may fail to increase, or may even drop, in the higher of the two grades. The same objection applies to the evaluation of total scores on such tests in terms of the grade progress criterion.

Finally, we must bear in mind that achievement tests are often employed as predictors of subsequent performance. When used for this purpose, the tests should be checked for *predictive validity* in terms of a follow-up criterion. The validation procedures in this situation are no different from those followed in the development of aptitude tests. In any test administered for predictive purposes, there is no substitute for an empirical follow-up.

Norms. It is customary to interpret scores on educational achievement tests in terms of *grade norms*. This practice is understandable, since the tests are employed within an academic setting. To describe a pupil's achievement as equivalent to seventh-grade performance in spelling, eighth-grade in reading, and fifth-grade in arithmetic has the same popular appeal as the use of mental age in the traditional intelligence tests. Frequently such grade equivalents are also employed to plot an achievement profile for the child.

Traditional grade norms are found by computing the median score obtained by children in each grade. Intermediate values, corresponding to fractions of a grade, may be found by interpolation or by testing different groups at different times within the school year. Values beyond the grade range tested are often found by extrapolation.

A refinement of grade norms is represented by *modal-age grade norms,* first proposed by T. L. Kelley (32). In finding such grade norms, only the children who are at the modal, or most frequent, age for their grade are included. This procedure eliminates pupils who are retarded or accelerated, retaining only those whose ages fall within the one-year range typical for that grade. Since the extent of retardation and acceleration varies in different schools and from grade to grade within the same school, traditional norms based on total grade groups will not be comparable from grade to grade. The use of modal-age grade groups tends to make norms more nearly comparable.

Despite their widespread acceptance, grade norms have many defects. In the first place, the content of instruction differs from grade to grade. If a child has not been taught the topics covered in, let us say, seventh-grade history, he cannot be expected to pass many items covering that content. Parenthetically, it might be argued that such information could be acquired by independent outside reading. But in that case, the test would no longer measure how well the individual has learned the content of a uniform course of instruction. Moreover, outside reading is influenced by a number of fortuitous factors, such as the individual's interests, the availability of reading matter, the extent of his participation in other extracurricular activities, his home duties, and the like.

Within a specific course of study, the individual may show superior mastery of the material taught in his own grade and yet be unable to score at a higher grade level. On the other hand, if the test is so constructed that the child who has an excellent grasp of the course content in his own grade obtains a higher "grade equivalent" score, then such a score is misleading. Under these conditions, for example, the child who excels in fifth-grade history may obtain a "seventh-grade equivalent" score. This score seems to indicate that he has mastered seventh-grade history, but it does not really mean that. In other words, the seventh-grade norms on such a test could be reached either by average mastery of seventh-grade content or by superior mastery of fifth-grade content. Scores obtained in this fashion are therefore ambiguous.

Moreover, the amount of improvement in a particular subject of instruction may be much greater, for example, between grades 4 and 5 than between grades 6 and 7. The fourth-grade child who is one grade accelerated on an achievement test in this field would thus excel the average more than the sixth-grade child who is accelerated by one grade. This difficulty is similar to that presented by MA units. But the use of a ratio corresponding to an IQ would be no solution, since the variations in grade units are more irregular, depending upon the peculiarities of the curriculum at different grade levels.

The picture is further complicated by the fact that, during any one grade, progress may be relatively slow in some fields of instruction and relatively rapid in others. The child whose achievement test scores indicate an acceleration of two grades in reading and in arithmetic may actually excel his classmates much more in arithmetic than in reading. This would be true if a larger proportion of individuals in that grade were accelerated by two grades in reading than in arithmetic. In that case, a two-grade acceleration in reading would not represent as much superiority as a two-grade acceleration in arithmetic. It is apparent that an achievement profile plotted in such grade units would be very misleading.

It should also be noted that grade norms tend to be incorrectly regarded as performance standards. A sixth-grade teacher, for example, may assume that all pupils in her class should fall at or close to the sixth-grade norm in achievement tests. Such a misconception is certainly not surprising when grade norms are used. Yet individual differences within any one grade are such that the range of achievement test scores will inevitably extend over several grades.

To express achievement test scores in terms of *educational age norms* offers no solution to these difficulties. Educational ages are to be interpreted in the same manner as mental ages, except that the former are based upon educational achievement test scores, rather than upon intelligence test scores. Educational age norms are usually found by taking the median score of all pupils of a given age, regardless of grade placement. Since most children advance one grade each year, age and grade norms will correspond fairly closely. Discrepancies between them will be partly a reflection of promotion policies and will virtually disappear if modal-age grade groups are used. Regardless of how they are computed, however, educational age norms are subject to the same drawbacks as grade norms.

The computation of an "educational quotient" (EQ) by dividing educational age (EA) by CA meets with the additional type of difficulty described in connection with the IQ. Thus it is likely that the relationship between changes in EA and CA is such as to produce unequal variability of the EQ at different ages. No uniform interpretation could therefore be attached to a given EQ when obtained by children of different ages.

For the majority of testing purposes, the most satisfactory norms for the evaluation of achievement test performance are those showing the individual's position within his own grade level. *Percentile-within-grade norms* are being employed increasingly for this purpose. By means of such norms, the individual's percentile rank is determined in reference to a normative sample of his own grade. Age and grade norms are still widely used, however, because of their familiarity and their apparent ease of interpretation.

A current practice followed in some of the more carefully constructed achievement tests involves the use of a single, composite distribution of standard scores for all grades. One grade level is selected as a reference group, the average and *SD* of this group being used to define the point of origin of the scale and the size of its unit, respectively. The range is extended by supplementary scaling in other grades above and below this primary reference group. The single over-all distribution of standard scores thus obtained is then used in converting raw scores to standard-score equivalents for all individuals, regardless of age or grade. In plotting profiles and in recording the individual's progress from year to year, such a uniform system of standard scores is certainly preferable to age or grade norms.

A further refinement of such uniform score scales is represented by the K-score proposed by Gardner (20, 21) and introduced in the 1953 edition of the Stanford Achievement Test (33). Although similar in principle to normalized standard scores, K-scores are expressed in terms of a more generalized type of curve that may exhibit varying degrees of skewness. It is believed that such curves permit a more accurate representation of the distribution of academic talent within a particular school grade.

For purposes of interpretation, however, it is customary to provide age, grade, or percentile-within-grade norms, which are expressed in terms of the over-all standard scores. These age, grade, or percentile norms are, of course, subject to all the usual limitations of such norms, regardless of the fact that they are found from standard scores rather than from raw scores. All the previously discussed objections to grade norms would still apply. When crude types of norms are superimposed upon the carefully developed scale of standard scores, many of the advantages of the scale are lost.

Despite the availability of supplementary, within-grade norms, the major emphasis in the interpretation of achievement test scores is placed upon the individual's progress along a single, composite scale. It is interesting to note that the traditional procedures for scaling scores are such that in "aptitude" tests the individual is usually compared with a peer group of his own age, while in "achievement" tests he is commonly referred to a single broad distribution within which he is expected to progress as he continues his schooling. The result of these dissimilar approaches to scaling is to yield achievement test scores that rise from year to year, while aptitude test scores tend to remain constant. The deviation IQ on an "intelligence" test, for example, will remain approximately the same when a given individual is retested annually. It will be recalled that such a deviation IQ is none other than a standard score. When the same individual is retested annually with achievement tests, however, his standard scores will show progressive "improvement," in contrast to the "constancy" of his IQ.

Such a traditional difference in the application of standard scores tends to perpetuate the myth that intelligence tests measure the individual's "innate, unchanging capacity," while achievement tests measure the cumulative and ever-changing effects of learning. The distinction is, of course, purely illusory. It would be quite feasible to reverse the relation. Intelligence tests could be so scaled that their deviation IQ's rose each year, and achievement tests could be so scaled that their standard scores remained constant throughout all ages and grades. It is simply a question of what reference group is chosen.

CONCEPT OF DEVELOPED ABILITIES

In the decades since 1940 achievement tests have undergone some major changes. Conspicuous among them is the shift away from the testing of specific subjects, such as geography, English literature, economics, or biology, toward broader content areas. More and more achievement batteries at all levels have been introducing comprehensive sections dealing with the humanities, social studies, or natural science. Concurrently, achievement tests have been moving toward the measurement of improvable intellectual skills or developed abilities. Early achievement tests dealt largely with the mastery of factual content. In the more recent batteries, factual items have been supplemented—and in some instances completely replaced—by items designed to assess critical thinking, the application of principles to the solution of new problems, or the development of habits and attitudes conducive to the appreciation of art and literature.

A characteristic feature of current achievement batteries is their emphasis on work-study skills. These include such basic intellectual skills as reading comprehension, ability to express one's ideas, and arithmetic computation, as well as more specific skills needed in locating and interpreting information. The last are illustrated by tests on the use of indexes, dictionaries, and other reference materials, on map reading, and on the interpretation of tables and graphs.

Several circumstances have led to these changes in the nature of achievement tests. In part, of course, what has been happening to achievement tests reflects underlying changes in curriculum and teaching methods over the intervening period. Courses, units, or projects that cut across traditional subject-matter areas have become a well-known feature of the educational scene. Equally familiar is the decline in drill and memorization in favor of procedures in which the learner plays a more active role.

A second contributing factor was a growing dissatisfaction with the achievement tests themselves. Traditional achievement tests, especially when used in major selection or admission programs, were criticized on the grounds that they tended to impose rigid controls on teaching and encouraged cramming for facts. The College Entrance Examination Board (CEEB), for example, has felt some concern about the prevalence not only of coaching schools but also of coaching courses and sessions in the regular high schools. Although the intensive reviews and drill sessions in preparation for such examinations probably have some educational value, it is generally conceded that the students' time could be more profitably spent. If teachers or schools are judged in part on the basis of how many students pass such tests and are admitted to college, the motivation for organized cramming sessions is understandable.

Partly to minimize these potential misuses of tests and partly in recognition of curricular changes, the CEEB in 1952 initiated a long-range project on what came to be known as the Tests of Developed Abilities, or TDA

(15). What finally emerged from several years of joint effort by subject-matter specialists and test technicians was a six-hour battery covering the humanities, social studies, and science. The tests called for both knowledge and intellectual skills, with major emphasis on the latter.

From an operational standpoint, it was eventually decided not to incorporate these particular tests in the CEEB testing program, chiefly because the predictive validity of the Scholastic Aptitude Test (SAT) in combination with existing Board achievement tests in specific fields proved to be as good as that of the TDA for some purposes and somewhat better for others (40). The flexibility provided by different combinations of achievement tests is an advantage in predicting performance in different curricula or subjects. Moreover, the TDA are more time-consuming to prepare, administer, and score than Board tests already in use. It should also be borne in mind that the failure of TDA to surpass other available instruments as predictors of college performance does not preclude the possibility that TDA-type tests may serve better in other functions for which achievement tests are designed.

The experience gained in constructing the TDA will undoubtedly influence the subsequent development of achievement tests for use in the CEEB program. It is anticipated that some of the most promising features of the TDA may be incorporated either in Board achievement tests or in the SAT. At a broader level, experimentation with the TDA tended to highlight and to define the concept of developed abilities, which underlies many current achievement batteries. Cutting across traditional achievement and intelligence tests, the TDA point up the basic similarity in the behavior measured by the two types of tests. By the same token, they demonstrate that the abilities subsumed under "intelligence" are largely those that education undertakes to develop. It has long been known that intelligence tests correlate about as high with achievemet tests as any two intelligence tests correlate with each other (5). Perhaps the coining of a convenient term like "developed abilities" will succeed in breaking down the dichotomy.

A third influence that has helped shape current achievement tests is to be found in certain major evaluation programs conducted in the schools. Outstanding among these are the Eight-Year Study of the Progressive Education Association, completed in 1942 (1, 46), and the Cooperative Study of Evaluation in General Education, completed in 1954 (12). The many ingenious and novel tests developed for use in these surveys include instruments designed to measure critical thinking, application of scientific principles to everyday-life situations, interpretation of literature, and other broad educational objectives. Further impetus to the development of the new-type achievement tests was provided by the publication in 1946 of the forty-fifth

Yearbook of the National Society for the Study of Education, entitled *The Measurement of Understanding* (38). Covering the appraisal of understanding in a variety of subject-matter areas at both elementary and high school levels, this Yearbook is an excellent source of sample items designed to test different educational objectives.

From a different angle, further momentum was furnished by the testing program conducted under the auspices of the United States Armed Forces Institute to aid in evaluating the educational status of veterans. For this purpose, the Tests of General Educational Development (GED) were developed at both high school and college levels (2, 55, 56). These tests were originally designed to help schools and colleges determine the amount of academic credit that should be granted students for their educational experiences while in military service. As a result of his performance on such tests, an adult who has been out of school for some time may be admitted to college without formal completion of a high school course, or he may be certified as having the equivalent of a high school diploma. At the high school level, the GED battery comprises tests of correctness and effectiveness of expression, general mathematical ability, and interpretation of reading materials in social studies, natural sciences, and literature. In these three major content areas, no factual knowledge is directly required, the student being tested only for his reading comprehension of passages chosen from textbooks and other appropriate sources.

Another probable influence affecting achievement test development stems from recent interest in the identification of high-level talent in science and engineering. Such interest has focused attention on the desirability of measuring creativity, reasoning, and critical thinking in achievement tests as well as in aptitude tests. In fact, several of the aptitude tests discussed in Chapter 15, such as the Watson-Glaser Critical Thinking Appraisal and some of the Guilford tests, could be classified in the present chapter as well. With the recognition that creativity, critical thinking, and similar talents can be stimulated, cultivated, and developed, rather than merely identified, their measurement becomes a goal of achievement testing as well as a goal of aptitude testing.

Finally, a still broader and more pervasive influence can be recognized in the changing viewpoints regarding the contribution of hereditary and environmental factors to intellectual development. With the accumulation of research data and the growing theoretical sophistication about hereditary and environmental mechanisms, psychologists are coming to realize that many behavioral characteristics once believed to be fixed by heredity are in fact susceptible to educational development. As a result, achievement tests are appearing in many areas once reserved for aptitude tests.

GENERAL ACHIEVEMENT BATTERIES

A number of batteries have been developed for measuring the individual's general educational achievement in the areas most commonly covered by academic curricula. This type of test can be used from the primary grades to the adult level, although its major application has been in the elementary school. Most batteries provide individual profiles of subtest scores, in addition to a total score on the entire battery. An advantage of such batteries as against independently constructed achievement tests is that they may permit horizontal or vertical comparisons, or both. Thus an individual's relative standing in different subject-matter areas or educational skills can be compared in terms of a uniform normative sample. Or the child's progress from grade to grade can be reported in terms of a single score scale. The test user should check whether a particular battery was so standardized as to yield either or both kinds of comparability.

Among the most widely used series of achievement tests for the elementary school level are the Metropolitan Achievement Tests (14). In their 1959 revision, these tests include five batteries, ranging from grades 1 to 9. Each battery is available in either three or four equivalent forms. Designed primarily as measures of power rather than speed, each battery requires from about two to four-and-a-half hours distributed over four or five testing sessions. All tests within any one battery are printed in a single booklet. At the upper levels, however, partial batteries are also available.

The composition of the Metropolitan Achievement Tests is summarized in Table 23, which lists the tests included in each battery. It will be noted that the number of tests yielding separate scores ranges from four in the Primary I Battery to thirteen in the Advanced Battery. The content of most of these tests is recognizable from the titles given in Table 23. Word Knowledge is a multiple-choice vocabulary test, which even at the lowest level calls for ability to read words. Word Discrimination, found only at the three lowest levels, requires the discrimination of small differences in the appearance of words, an ability considered important in learning to read. Sample items from the Reading and the Arithmetic Concepts and Skills tests of the Primary I Battery are reproduced in Figure 95. The Language Study Skills tests are concerned with the use of the dictionary and other reference sources. In the tests of Social Studies Study Skills, the pupil reads various kinds of maps, tables, and graphs and draws conclusions from the data therein presented. Although containing a number of items that involve understanding and application of knowledge, the Metropolitan tests as a whole make fairly heavy demands upon specific factual information. This is especially true of the Science tests.

TABLE 23.   Metropolitan Achievement Tests

Test	Battery				
	Prim. I (2nd half of Grade 1)	Prim. II (Grade 2)	Elem. (Grades 3-4)	Intermed. (Grades 5-6)	Adv. (Grades 7-9)
Word Knowledge	•	•	•	•	•
Word Discrimination	•	•	•		
Reading	•	•	•	•	•
Arithmetic:					
Concepts and Skills	•	•			
Problem Solving and Concepts			•	•	•
Computation			•	•	•
Spelling		•	•	•	•
Language:					
Usage			•	•	•
Punctuation and Capitalization			•	•	•
Parts of Speech and Grammar				•	•
Kinds of Sentences					•
Language Study Skills				•	•
Social Studies Information				•	•
Social Studies Study Skills				•	•
Science				•	•

Raw scores on each test are first converted into normalized standard scores with a mean of 50 and an *SD* of 10, which provide horizontal comparability of all tests and all forms of a given battery, but not vertical comparability between different batteries or grade levels. For most practical purposes, these standard scores represent only an intermediate step in looking up the stanines, percentile ranks, or grade equivalents for each test. The stanines are probably the most satisfactory type of score, since they represent equal units (see Ch. 4). It is in terms of stanines that individual score profiles are plotted. Stanines and percentile ranks are found within the appropriate half-year grade group. Grade equivalents are reported to $\frac{1}{10}$ of a grade. For example, if a child's score has a grade equivalent of 6.3, it corresponds to the average score obtained by pupils in the third month of the sixth grade. The normative samples from which all these scores are derived were modal-age grade groups chosen so as to be as nearly as possible a representative sample of the country's public school population.

Split-half reliability coefficients of the Metropolitan tests, computed within single-grade groups, are in the .80's and .90's, except for the separate parts of the Language tests. These part scores, however, are combined in most of the normative evaluations. Content validity is based chiefly on "curricular re-search" involving systematic analysis of syllabi, textbooks, and published statements of educational goals, from which the test specifications were prepared. Further validation utilized item analyses conducted in large-scale tryouts of the experimental forms. In the development of the final forms, items were selected in terms of difficulty, discriminative value against sub-test scores, and grade differentiation.

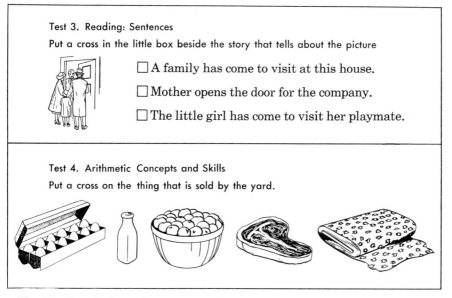

Fig. 95. Sample Items from Metropolitan Achievement Tests, Primary I Battery. (Reproduced by permission of World Book Company.)

An achievement test series that is outstanding in several respects is the Sequential Tests of Educational Progress (STEP), developed by the Co-operative Test Division of the Educational Testing Service (8). These tests are available in four levels, suitable for grades 4 to 6, 7 to 9, 10 to 12, and 13 to 14. At each level, there are seven tests, including multiple-choice tests in Reading, Writing, Mathematics, Science, Social Studies, and Listening, as well as an Essay test. Two parallel forms of each objective test and four parallel forms of the Essay test are available for each level. For maximum flexibility of use, all seven tests at each level are published in separate book-lets and may be obtained individually. The Essay test requires thirty-five minutes. Each of the six objective tests requires seventy minutes and can be administered either in a single session or in two thirty-five minute sessions.

Although the need for specific knowledge in particular fields was recognized in constructing STEP items, major emphasis was placed upon the application of learned skills to the solution of new problems. The tests are concerned more with the outcomes of school learning than with its content. Since teachers are likely to agree more closely on the objectives of instruction than on materials and methods, tests such as these, which concentrate on objectives, are more widely applicable. They also encourage more flexibility with regard to the specific content taught. The STEP item writers have displayed unusual ingenuity and skill in composing items that do in fact measure many of the intellectual skills outlined in the previously discussed *Taxonomy of Educational Objectives.*

Two examples typical of items found in the tests for Science (grades 4-6) and for Social Studies (grades 10-12) are reproduced in Figures 96 and 97. In the Science and Mathematics tests, a problem situation is presented and is followed by a set of related multiple-choice questions. The situations are chosen so as to be as realistic as possible, dealing with events in the home, at camp, on the farm, etc. A possible drawback of this type of item, especially in the Mathematics test, is its heavy loading with verbal comprehension. This is especially true at the lower levels, where a good deal of irrelevant verbal content is introduced to make each "story" appealing to children. It is not surprising, therefore, to find that at the fourth-grade level the STEP Mathematics score correlates more highly with the verbal than with the quantitative scores on SCAT. Even at higher levels, the correlations with SCAT verbal scores are high enough to denote considerable overlap.

A major portion of the STEP batteries is devoted to the testing of communication skills. This is accomplished through an essay test, an objective test of writing ability, a reading comprehension test, and a listening comprehension test. In each of the four forms of the Essay test, the students are assigned a different topic, these topics having been chosen through preliminary experimentation as the most effective. The essays are scored by the classroom teacher, by means of a *product scale* technique. For each topic at each level, five sample essays are provided, together with the ratings assigned to each by a group of experienced teachers. With these samples as a guide, the scorer rates each essay on a 7-point scale, giving prescribed weights to thought quality, style, and mechanics of expression. It might be noted that product scales were among the earliest standardized instruments introduced in educational measurement. They are also used in certain art tests, such as the Horn Art Aptitude Inventory described in Chapter 15.

Situation: Tom wanted to learn which of three types of soil—clay, sand, or loam—would be best for growing lima beans. He found three flowerpots, put a different type of soil in each pot, and planted lima beans in each. He placed them side by side on the window sill and gave each pot the same amount of water.

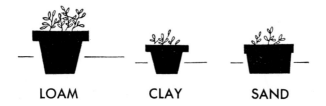

LOAM   CLAY   SAND

The lima beans grew best in the loam. Why did Mr. Jackson say Tom's experiment was NOT a good experiment and did NOT prove that loam was the best soil for plant growth?

23 **A** The plants in one pot got more sunlight than the plants in the other pots.
    B The amount of soil in each pot was not the same.
    C One pot should have been placed in the dark.
    D Tom should have used three kinds of seeds.

Fig. 96. Sample Item from STEP Science Test for Grades 4 to 6. (Reproduced by permission of Cooperative Test Division, Educational Testing Service.)

Scorer unreliability is a common problem in such product scales and has proved to be a persistent weakness of essay tests in general. Preliminary evaluation of scorer reliability for the STEP Essay tests yielded correlations of .50 to .77 between the ratings assigned by different readers to the same papers. The ratings given to each STEP Essay can be further evaluated in terms of percentile norms established on a national sample of 5000 students in grades 4 to 14.

In the objective Writing tests, the students are given a wide variety of written materials ranging from letters and questionnaire replies to editorials and stories. Most of these materials are actual specimens of student writing. Each passage is followed by multiple-choice items covering specific ways in

The students are provided with monthly temperature and rainfall charts for four places, as shown below.

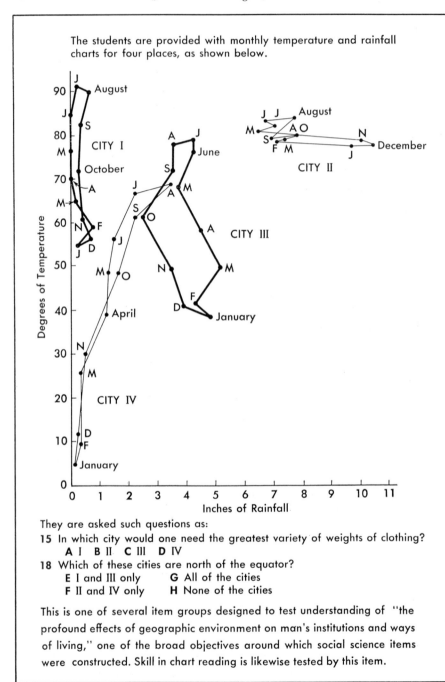

They are asked such questions as:

15 In which city would one need the greatest variety of weights of clothing?
   A I   **B** II   **C** III   **D** IV

18 Which of these cities are north of the equator?
   E I and III only   **G** All of the cities
   F II and IV only   **H** None of the cities

This is one of several item groups designed to test understanding of "the profound effects of geographic environment on man's institutions and ways of living," one of the broad objectives around which social science items were constructed. Skill in chart reading is likewise tested by this item.

Fig. 97. Sample Items from STEP Social Studies Test for Grades 10 to 12. (Reproduced by permission of Cooperative Test Division, Educational Testing Service.)

which the writing could be improved with regard to mechanics of expression as well as organization and effectiveness. It is interesting to note that scores on the objective Writing tests correlate from .61 to .70 with ratings on the Essay tests, while different forms of the Essay test correlate from .64 to .73 with each other. In other words, a student's performance on one essay can be predicted about as well from his score on the objective writing test as from another essay.

In the Reading Comprehension tests, short passages from a variety of content areas are followed by questions designed to test such skills as simple comprehension, interpretation, insight into the writer's motives, and critical evaluation. The measurement of Listening Comprehension, or "auding," is a relatively new development in achievement testing. The ability to understand, interpret, and critically evaluate what one hears is coming to be recognized as an important educational goal. In the STEP Listening tests, the given passages are read by the classroom teacher. The questions and response options are also read by the teacher, although the students have a copy of the response options before them. A typical passage for grades 7-9, together with three sample items, can be seen in Figure 98. The passages sample many types of listening, including directions and simple explanations, exposition, narration, argument and persuasion, and aesthetic material. Presentation by classroom teachers, chosen in favor of recordings for practical reasons, nevertheless introduces an uncontrolled factor. At the upper levels, a further limitation arises from the brevity of the passages. The high school senior and college student—as well as the adult outside of school—must often listen to lectures considerably longer than the one- to four-minute passages of this test.

Raw scores on each STEP test are first converted into a three-digit score scale which, unlike the Metropolitan standard score scale, was designed for vertical rather than horizontal comparability. Thus performance on any one test, such as Mathematics, is expressed in terms of a single scale for all grades, but these scores are not directly comparable from one test to another. By reference to appropriate tables for each grade level, STEP scores can be further transmuted into percentiles. Rather than yielding a single percentile rank, however, the scores are expressed in the form of a *percentile band* for each individual. As in the case of SCAT (see Ch. 9), these percentile bands cover a distance of approximately one standard error of measurement on either side of the corresponding percentile. The chance are thus roughly 2:1 that the student's true position falls within the given band. The STEP Student Profile for the six objective tests is similar to the SCAT profile illustrated in Figure 37 (Ch. 9). For both STEP and SCAT, there is also a simplified Student Report form, used in interpreting scores to the students

---

The examiner reads:

Here is the fourth selection. It is a speech by a student running for school office.

A students, B students, C students, D students, and my friends! As you know, I am running for the office of President of the Student Council. I'd like to tell you what I'll do if I'm elected. In the first place, I think several students ought to sit in on teachers' meetings. They settle too many things for us. I don't think that the teachers always know what's best for us.

In the second place, I'd like to see our Student Council do something. Take the business of the candy machine, for instance. Just because a couple of doctors and dentists don't like it doesn't mean we shouldn't have one. I think they are wrong. I think we should have one. Candy is good for us. It gives us energy, and I, for one, don't think it hurts either your teeth or your appetite. And if it does, so what? You save the lunch money and can go out on a date.

Last, you know that my opponents—and you'll hear from them in a minute—are two girls. Now, everybody says girls are smarter than boys. That might be true—but just because they're smarter doesn't mean they'll make better officers. In fact, I think girls are too smart and can't always get along with people because of that. Maybe we need somebody not so smart, but that can get along. That's me, fellow student—vote for me!

19 The speaker's principal objection to girls as school officers evidently is that they
A talk too much
B support the teacher's point-of-view
C are too smart to get along with people
D don't want a candy machine

22 When the speaker used the word "opponents," he meant
E students from other schools
F students running against him
G the teachers
H doctors and dentists

23 Judging from his comments, how does the speaker feel about the opinions of experts?
A He pretends that the experts agree with him.
B He does not respect the experts if he disagrees with them.
C He pretends to treat the experts with respect.
D He follows expert advice unless he can prove it is wrong.

Fig. 98. Sample Items from STEP Listening Comprehension Test for Grades 7 to 9. (Reproduced by permission of Cooperative Test Division, Educational Testing Service.)

themselves. Figure 99 shows the illustration given on the Student Report to explain how the student's relative standing on different tests may be compared by means of percentile bands.

Although timed, the STEP tests are essentially power tests. Each test is long enough to insure satisfactory reliability. Although only Kuder-Richardson reliabilities were reported at the time of publication, data on correlation of parallel forms and stability will undoubtedly be available later. The de-

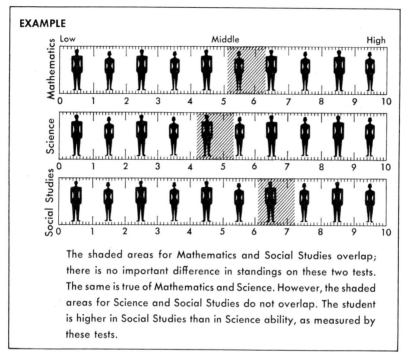

EXAMPLE

The shaded areas for Mathematics and Social Studies overlap;
there is no important difference in standings on these two tests.
The same is true of Mathematics and Science. However, the shaded
areas for Science and Social Studies do not overlap. The student
is higher in Social Studies than in Science ability, as measured by
these tests.

Fig. 99.   Explanatory Example from STEP Student Report. (Reproduced by permission of Cooperative Test Division, Educational Testing Service.)

velopment of STEP represents content validation at its best. Committees of outstanding educators, representing all levels from the elementary school to college and chosen in consultation with national professional organizations, participated with ETS test-construction specialists both in drawing up test specifications and in preparing and reviewing items. Statistical analyses of preliminary forms included the usual determination of difficulty, discriminative power, and grade progress for individual items. The extent to which it proved feasible to construct objective items measuring understanding rather than mere recall of information represents the major contribution of these tests.

The Metropolitan Achievement Tests and STEP have been chosen to illustrate the scope, nature, similarities, and differences of some of the best current achievement batteries. More could be said about both the strengths and weaknesses of either test series. To round out the picture, the student is urged to consult the test manuals and the *Mental Measurements Yearbooks*.

Several other well-known general achievement batteries may be mentioned. One of the earliest standardized educational achievement tests is the

Stanford Achievement Test (33), covering grades 2 to 9. First published in 1923, this battery was revised in 1929, 1940, and 1953. Another revision is in progress and will probably be completed in 1963. Other batteries designed for the elementary and junior high school levels include the Iowa Tests of Basic Skills (37) and the SRA Achievement Series (49). The California Achievement Tests (50) extend from the first grade through the college sophomore year. Batteries designed specifically for the high school level include the Iowa Tests of Educational Development (36) and the Essential High School Content Battery (28).

The Cooperative General Achievement Tests (6) were developed for use with high school seniors and college freshmen, while the Cooperative General Culture Test (7) is intended exclusively for college use, especially at the sophomore level. Mention should also be made of the Area Tests (24) of the Graduate Record Examinations (GRE). Constructed for use from the sophomore year of college to graduate school, the Area Tests are restricted to administration in the GRE Institutional Testing Program. Covering the broad areas of social science, humanities, and natural science as taught at the college level, these tests have succeeded exceptionally well in providing items that assess understanding and the attainment of other complex educational objectives. Longitudinal studies of college students taking alternate forms of the Area Tests in their freshman, sophomore, and senior years revealed significant gains in mean scores (34).

REFERENCES

1. Aikin, W. M. *The story of the Eight-Year Study, with conclusions and recommendations.* N. Y.: Harper, 1942.
2. American Council on Education. *Conclusions and recommendations on a study of the general educational development testing program.* Washington: Amer. Coun. Educ., 1956.
3. Bean, K. L. *Construction of educational and personnel tests.* N. Y.: McGraw-Hill, 1953.
4. Bloom, B. S., et al. *Taxonomy of educational objectives, handbook I: cognitive domain.* N. Y.: Longmans, Green, 1956.
5. Coleman, W., and Cureton, E. E. Intelligence and achievement: the "jangle fallacy" again. *Educ. psychol. Measmt.*, 1954, 14, 347-351.
6. Cooperative Test Division. *Cooperative General Achievement Tests.* Princeton, N. J.: Educ. Test. Serv., 1951-1956.
7. Cooperative Test Division. *Cooperative General Culture Test.* Princeton, N. J.: Educ. Test. Serv., 1954-1956.

8. Cooperative Test Division. *Sequential Tests of Educational Progress.* Princeton, N. J.: Educ. Test. Serv., 1956-1958.
9. Cureton, E. E. The upper and lower twenty-seven per cent rule. *Psychometrika,* 1957, 22, 293-296.
10. Davis, F. B. Item analysis in relation to educational and psychological testing. *Psychol. Bull.,* 1952, 49, 97-121.
11. Davis, F. B., Schwab, J. J., Carroll, J. B., and Gulliksen, H. Criteria for the evaluation of achievement tests. *Proc. 1950 invit. Conf. test. Probl., Educ. Test. Serv.,* 1951, 73-112.
12. Dressel, P. L., and Mayhew, L. B. *General education: explorations in evaluation.* Washington: Amer. Coun. Educ., 1954.
13. Dressel, P. L., and Nelson, C. H. *Questions and problems in science: test item folio no. 1.* Princeton, N. J.: Educ. Test. Serv., 1956.
14. Durost, W. N. (Ed.), Bixler, H. H., Hildreth, Gertrude H., Lund, K. W., and Wrightstone, J. W. *Metropolitan Achievement Tests.* Tarrytown-on-Hudson, N. Y.: World Book Co., 1959-1961.
15. Dyer, H. S., and Coffman, W. S. The Tests of Developed Abilities. *Coll. Bd. Rev.,* 1957, No. 31, 5-10.
16. Findley, W. G. Studying the individual through the school's testing program. In *Modern educational problems: report of the seventeenth educational conference, 1952.* Washington: Amer. Coun. Educ., 1952. Pp. 38-47.
17. Findley, W. G. A rationale for evaluation of item discrimination statistics. *Educ. psychol. Measmt.,* 1956, 16, 175-180.
18. Furst, E. J. *Constructing evaluation instruments.* N. Y.: Longmans, Green, 1958.
19. Galanter, E. (Ed.) *Automatic teaching: the state of the art.* N. Y.: Wiley, 1959.
20. Gardner, E. F. Value of norms based on a new type of scale unit. *Proc. 1948 invit. Conf. test. Probl., Educ. Test. Serv.,* 1949, 67-74.
21. Gardner, E. F. The importance of reference groups in scaling procedure. *Proc. 1952 invit. Conf. test. Probl., Educ. Test. Serv.,* 1953, 13-21.
22. Garrett, H. E. *Testing for teachers.* N. Y.: Amer. Book Co., 1959.
23. Gerberich, J. R. *Specimen objective test items: a guide to achievement test construction.* N. Y.: Longmans, Green, 1956.
24. *The Graduate Record Examinations: The Area Tests.* Princeton, N. J.: Educ. Test. Serv., 1954.
25. Greene, H. A., Jorgensen, A. N., and Gerberich, J. R. *Measurement and evaluation in the elementary school.* (2nd ed.) N. Y.: Longmans, Green, 1953.
26. Greene, H. A., Jorgensen, A. N., and Gerberich, J. R. *Measurement and evaluation in the secondary school.* (2nd ed.) N. Y.: Longmans, Green, 1954.
27. Gulliksen, H. Intrinsic validity. *Amer. Psychologist,* 1950, 5, 511-517.
28. Harry, D. P., Jr., and Durost, W. N. *Essential High School Content Battery.* Tarrytown-on-Hudson, N. Y.: World Book Co., 1951-1952.
29. Jones, R. S. Integration of instructional with self-scoring measuring procedures. *Ohio State Univer., Dissert. Abstr.,* 1954, No. 65, 157-165.
30. Jordan, A. M. *Measurement in education: an introduction.* N. Y.: McGraw-Hill, 1953.

31. Kelley, T. L. The selection of upper and lower groups for the validation of test items. *J. educ. Psychol.,* 1939, 30, 17-24.

32. Kelley, T. L. Ridge-route norms. *Harv. educ. Rev.,* 1940, 10, 309-314.

33. Kelley, T. L., Madden, R., Gardner, E. F., Terman, L. M., and Ruch, G. M. *Stanford Achievement Test.* Tarrytown-on-Hudson, N. Y.: World Book Co., 1953-1956.

34. Lannholm, G. V., and Pitcher, Barbara. *Mean score changes on the Graduate Record Examinations Area Tests for college students tested three times in a four-year period.* Princeton, N. J.: Educ. Test. Serv., 1959.

35. Lindquist, E. F. (Ed.) *Educational measurement.* Washington: Amer. Coun. Educ., 1951.

36. Lindquist, E. F. *Iowa Tests of Educational Development.* Chicago: Sci. Res. Assoc., 1952-1958.

37. Lindquist, E. F., and Hieronymous, A. N. *Iowa Tests of Basic Skills.* Boston: Houghton Mifflin, 1955-1956.

38. *The measurement of understanding.* (45th Yearb., Nat. Soc. Stud. Educ.) Chicago: Univer. Chicago Press, 1946.

39. Noll, V. H. *Introduction to educational measurement.* Boston: Houghton Mifflin, 1957.

40. Olsen, Marjorie. Summary of main findings on the validity of the CEEB Tests of Developed Abilities as predictors of college grades. *Educ. Test. Serv., Stat. Rep.,* SR-57-41, 1957.

41. Pressey, S. L. Development and appraisal of devices providing immediate automatic scoring of objective tests and concomitant self instruction. *J. Psychol.,* 1950, 29, 417-447.

42. Ross, C. C., and Stanley, J. C. *Measurement in today's schools.* (3rd ed.) Englewood Cliffs, N. J.: Prentice-Hall, 1954.

43. Severin, D. G. Appraisal of special tests and procedures used with self-scoring instructional testing devices. *Ohio State Univer., Dissert. Abstr.,* 1955, No. 66, 323-330.

44. Silverman, R. E. Automated teaching: a review of theory and research. *Tech. Rep.: NAVTRADEVCEN 507-2, U.S. Naval Training Device Center,* 1960.

45. Skinner, B. F. Teaching machines. *Science,* 1958, 128, 969-977.

46. Smith, E. R., Tyler, R. W., *et al. Appraising and recording student progress.* N. Y.: Harper, 1942.

47. *Technical recommendations for achievement tests.* Washington: Nat. Educ. Assoc., 1955.

48. Thorndike, R. L., and Hagen, Elizabeth. *Measurement and evaluation in psychology and education.* N. Y.: Wiley, 1955.

49. Thorpe, L. P., Lefever, D. W., and Naslund, R. A. *SRA Achievement Series.* Chicago: Sci. Res. Assoc., 1955-1959.

50. Tiegs, E. W., and Clark, W. W. *California Achievement Tests, 1957 Edition.* Monterey, Calif.: Calif. Test Bur., 1957.

51. Travers, R. M. W. *How to make achievement tests.* N. Y.: Odyssey, 1950.

52. Travers, R. M. W. *Educational measurement.* N. Y.: Macmillan, 1955.

53. Traxler, A. E., *et al. Introduction to testing and the use of test results in public schools.* N. Y.: Harper, 1953.

54. Tyler, R. W. Permanency of learning. *J. higher. Educ.*, 1933, 4, 203-204.

55. Tyler, R. W. *The fact-finding study of the testing program of the United States Armed Forces Institute.* Washington: Off. Armed Forces Inform. Educ., Dept. Defense, 1954.

56. United States Armed Forces Institute. *Tests of General Education Development.* Chicago: Vet. Test. Serv., Amer. Coun. Educ., 1944-1957.

57. Wert, J. E. Twin examination assumptions. *J. higher. Educ.*, 1937, 8, 136-140.

58. Wood, Dorothy A. *Test construction: development and interpretation of achievement tests.* Columbus, Ohio: Merrill, 1960.

CHAPTER 17

Achievement Tests: Special Areas

The preceding chapter dealt with the construction and uses of achievement tests as a whole, as well as with currently available general achievement batteries. In this chapter, we shall consider typical examples of achievement tests designed for more specific purposes. Principal among these are readiness and diagnostic tests in the areas of reading and mathematical skills, which will be discussed in the first two sections. Educational achievement tests in separate content areas will be considered in the third section. The next two sections will be concerned with vocational achievement tests and with the use of achievement tests in admitting students to professional schools and in selecting professional personnel. In the final section, the relation of achievement tests to aptitude tests will be re-examined and the place of achievement tests in the continuum of ability testing will be reviewed.

READINESS TESTS

Readiness or prognostic tests are essentially aptitude tests, since their object is to predict how well the individual will profit from a subsequent course of training. Since they are generally employed in an educational setting, however, they can be more conveniently discussed together with achievement tests. Moreover, many achievement tests can themselves be used as readiness tests, to assess the pupil's readiness for the next more advanced level of instruction. Certain tests, however, have been specifically designed as readiness tests, especially in the areas of reading and mathematical skills. Obviously one stage at which readiness tests can make a significant contribution is that of entrance into the first grade. Readiness tests for this level have much in common with general intelligence tests for the primary grades, discussed in Chapter 9. In the readiness tests, however, special emphasis is placed on those abilities found to be most important in learning to read, some attention also being given to the prerequisites of numerical thinking and to

458

the sensorimotor control required in learning to write. Among the specific functions covered are visual and auditory discrimination, motor control, verbal comprehension, vocabulary, quantitative concepts, and general information.

As an example of readiness tests for the first grade, we may examine the Metropolitan Readiness Tests (25). This battery, a revision of which is in progress, currently includes the following six subtests:

1. *Word Meaning:* In each row of four pictures, the subject selects the one that illustrates the word the examiner names (cf. Fig. 100).

2. *Sentences:* This test is similar to Test 1, except that phrases and sentences are used instead of single words.

3. *Information:* The subject again marks the one picture in each row of four that corresponds to the examiner's oral description, but the objects are now described in terms of use or function. E.g., "mark the one you take pictures with."

4. *Matching:* This test requires the recognition of similarities and differences in visual material, including pictures of objects, geometric forms, numbers, letters, and words (cf. Fig. 100).

5. *Numbers:* Covering a wide variety of quantitative concepts and simple numerical operations, this test resembles closely the quantitative subtests included in intelligence tests for the primary grades.

6. *Copying:* The subject copies simple geometric forms as well as numbers or letters. This test is related to both physical development and intellectual maturity in young children. It also reveals the tendency toward reversals in drawing and writing shown by some children.

The Metropolitan Readiness Tests are available in two equivalent forms. Percentile norms are provided for reading readiness (tests 1-4), number readiness (test 5), and total readiness for first grade school work (tests 1-6). These norms were established on a nationwide sample of more than 15,000 white public school children tested during the first month of the first grade. As a supplementary measure, the test manual recommends the use of a Draw-a-Man Test similar to that standardized by Goodenough and discussed in Chapter 10. The scoring, however, involves the classification of each drawing as a whole into one of five broad categories, rather than the assignment of specific points. Median reliability coefficients, based on retests with parallel forms over intervals of a few days, are given as .83 for reading readiness, .84 for number readiness, and .89 for total readiness scores. The re-

Test 1. *Word Meaning.* In the first row, the subject marks the baby; in the second row, the house.

Test 4. *Matching.* In each row, the subject marks the picture which is identical to the one in the circular frame.

Fig. 100. Sample Items from the Metropolitan Readiness Tests. (Copyright by World Book Company.)

ported data on predictive validity, against achievement tests administered at the end of the first grade as a criterion, look encouraging.

A test designed to assess both arithmetic achievement in the primary grades and readiness for further instruction in arithmetic is the New York Test of Arithmetical Meanings (65). Applicable from the middle of the first grade to the beginning of the third, this test covers such quantitative concepts as size, weight, time, and distance, as well as the use of quantitative symbols and terms, the notion of fractional parts, and simple arithmetic computation. Two sample items from this test are reproduced in Figure 101. Per-

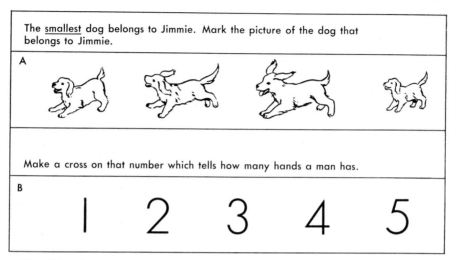

The smallest dog belongs to Jimmie. Mark the picture of the dog that belongs to Jimmie.

A

Make a cross on that number which tells how many hands a man has.

B

1 2 3 4 5

Fig. 101. Sample items from New York Test of Arithmetical Meanings, Level One. (Reproduced by permission of World Book Company.)

centile norms are given for the beginning of the second and the beginning of the third grades, based on approximately 17,000 children tested at each of these two levels in a nationwide sample. Median split-half reliabilities are in the .80's. Content validity was established through curricular analysis of the arithmetic taught in the first two grades.

Prognostic mathematics tests at a more advanced level are illustrated by the Orleans Algebra Prognosis Test (41) and the Orleans Geometry Prognosis Test (42). In both of these tests, the student is provided with simple material to learn from algebra or geometry, and is immediately tested on what he has learned. These tests are thus worksamples, in which the student's subsequent course learning is predicted from his performance in the sample learning tasks. Other prognostic tests in mathematics cover a combination of prerequisite arithmetic skills and new learning. Some contain material similar to that found in the numerical subtests of intelligence tests, such as number series completions. All such prognostic tests are normally validated against subsequent course grades and terminal achievement test scores.

Still another type of readiness test is illustrated by the Modern Language Aptitude Test (12). Designed to assess the capacity of an English-speaking student for learning any foreign language, this test utilizes both paper-and-pencil and tape-recorded materials. It is suitable for high school, college, and adult groups. Two of its subtests require the learning of orally presented numbers and visually presented words in an artificial language. The other three parts test the subject's sensitivity to English grammatical structure, as well as certain word recognition skills with visual and auditory materials. The test may also be administered in a shorter form not requiring a tape recorder. Data on predictive validity in college and high school groups appear promising. In an earlier experimental version, this test proved especially effective in predicting success in intensive language training courses conducted by the Foreign Service Institute of the Department of State, the Air Force, and the Army Language School.

DIAGNOSTIC TESTS

In the measurement of both reading and mathematical skills, a further distinction is made between survey and diagnostic tests. Survey tests indicate the general level of the individual's achievement in reading or arithmetic. For this purpose, they usually provide a single composite score. Among the best examples of such survey tests are the reading and arithmetic subtests of the general achievement batteries discussed in Chapter 16. Diagnostic tests, on the other hand, are designed to analyze the individual's performance and provide information on the causes of difficulty. Such tests typically yield several scores.

Diagnostic tests in *reading* vary widely in the thoroughness of analysis they permit and in the specific procedures followed. They range from group tests yielding two or three subtest scores, which serve little more than a survey function, to intensive clinical programs for individual case studies. Some provide detailed checklists of specific types of errors. The individual batteries frequently employ apparatus, such as tachistoscopes for controlling rate of exposure of printed material, and ophthalmographs for photographing the subject's eye movements while he reads. A few examples will be considered below. More detailed discussions of available reading tests can be found in books on educational measurement (e.g., 21, 22, 29, 40, 45), as well as in books dealing specifically with remedial reading programs and the teaching of reading (e.g., 53, 64).

An example of a relatively short and widely used group test is the Iowa Silent Reading Tests (23). These tests include an elementary battery for grades 4 to 8 and an advanced battery for use in high school and college. Among the common functions covered by both batteries are rate of reading, vocabulary, sentence comprehension, paragraph comprehension, and the use of a simple index. A test of "directed reading" requires the subject to identify the parts of a passage that answer given questions. The elementary battery also includes a test of alphabetizing. The advanced battery contains a test requiring the subject to select the word under which information about a given question might be found in an index. It likewise includes a poetry comprehension test that uses a technique similar to that of the "directed reading" test.

Another example in the same category is the Nelson-Denny Reading Test (39), which was revised in 1960. This test is designed for use with high school, college, and adult groups. Requiring a total working time of 30 minutes, it yields separate scores in vocabulary, reading comprehension, and reading rate. Equivalent-form reliabilities of the three part-scores range from .81 to .93. Norms are based on large, representative, nationwide samples of high school and college populations.

A more intensive approach is illustrated by the series of tests developed by the Committee on Diagnostic Reading Tests (58, 59). Applicable from grades 7 to 13, these tests include a Survey Section for screening purposes and a Diagnostic Battery. All tests are designed for group administration, with the exception of the oral reading test of the Diagnostic Battery. The Survey Section, which can be given within a single class period, yields scores in rate of reading story-type material with satisfactory comprehension, general vocabulary, and comprehension of textbook-type material.

The Diagnostic Battery was likewise designed for classroom administration, although requiring more time than the Survey Section. However, the entire battery need not be given to each individual. Those areas are chosen in which the individual shows greatest difficulty, as determined by the results of the Survey tests. The Diagnostic tests are available in the same three areas covered by the Survey Section, and in one additional area, that of word recognition skills. Specifically, the tests in the Diagnostic Battery comprise: vocabulary, which covers technical vocabulary in grammar, literature, science, social studies, and mathematics; comprehension of textbook material, both when the individual reads it himself and when it is read to him; rates of reading, including rate of reading different types of material, as well as flexibility of rate when reading for different objectives; and word attack, both oral and silent. The last-named test utilizes a variety of procedures to analyze the individual's responses both to the meanings and to the sounds of words. It also provides a checklist for qualitative observations. A bulletin designed for teachers contains many suggestions regarding the use of test results in planning remedial instruction.

A typical battery for intensive individual testing is the Durrell Analysis of Reading Difficulty (17), designed for grades 1 to 6. The Durrell tests utilize series of paragraphs graded in difficulty, a set of cards, and a simple tachistoscope. Scores are provided for rate and comprehension of oral and silent reading, listening comprehension, rapid word recognition, and word analysis.

Supplementary tests of written spelling and speed of handwriting are included. For non-readers, there are measures of visual memory for word
forms, auditory analysis of word elements, letter recognition, rate of learning words, and listening comprehension. All of the comprehension tests actually require simple recall of details read or heard and do not call for much
understanding. One of the chief contributions of this battery is a checklist
based on reading errors identified in a survey of 4000 children. The battery
is better suited for qualitative than for quantitative analysis of performance.
Suggestions for remedial teaching are also provided in the manual.

Among the most common weaknesses of diagnostic reading tests are inadequate reliabilities coupled with high intercorrelations of the subtests from
which separate scores are derived. Especially in some of the shorter group
tests, these two conditions reduce the diagnostic or differential effectiveness of
the tests. Several tests have also been criticized because of the superficiality
of understanding required by the reading comprehension subtests. The
measurement of rate of reading likewise presents special problems. Rate of
reading depends upon such factors as the difficulty of the material and the
purpose for which it is being read. Any individual may thus have, not one,
but many reading rates. This is more likely to be true of the experienced
reader, who adjusts his rate to the nature of the task. Furthermore, in any
one reading test, the response set established by the directions may differ
widely from one person to another. For example, when told to read a passage carefully so as to be able to answer questions about it later, some subjects may skim the material rapidly, while others will try to understand and
memorize specific details. In the previously mentioned Diagnostic Reading
Tests, special efforts were made to tackle this problem by providing several
different measures of reading rate. The effectiveness of this solution, however, has not been objectively demonstrated.

In the area of *mathematical skills,* two of the most comprehensive diagnostic batteries are the Compass Diagnostic Tests in Arithmetic (46) and the
Diagnostic Test for Fundamental Processes in Arithmetic (10, 11). The
former are a series of group tests suitable for use in grades 2 to 8. They comprise 20 tests, each requiring from 18 to 60 minutes and covering different
types of arithmetic operations or problems. The groups of items within each
test permit a further detailed analysis of achievement.

The Diagnostic Test for Fundamental Processes in Arithmetic, prepared
by Buswell and John (10, 11), requires individual administration, since each
problem is solved orally by the subject. It is thus possible to observe the
work methods employed by the child in carrying out the different operations.
Errors as well as undesirable work habits are recorded on a checklist, which

includes the most common difficulties encountered in arithmetic. The problems were specially chosen so as to elicit such difficulties when present. This test is also applicable in grades 2 to 8. There are no time limits, no norms, and no total score, the problems and checklist being designed for qualitative rather than quantitative analysis of arithmetic performance.

In connection with the use of diagnostic tests, one point deserves emphasis. The diagnosis of reading and arithmetic difficulties and the subsequent program of remedial teaching are the proper functions of a trained specialist. No battery of diagnostic tests could suffice for this purpose. The diagnosis and treatment of severe reading disabilities require a thorough clinical case study, including supplementary information on sensory capacities and motor development, medical and health history, complete educational history, data on home and family background, and a thorough investigation of possible emotional difficulties. In some cases, serious reading retardation proves to be only one symptom of a more basic personality maladjustment. Although survey and group diagnostic tests may serve to identify individuals in need of further attention, the diagnosis and therapy of reading disabilities often represent a problem for the clinician. This may also be true in cases of severe arithmetic disabilities.

EDUCATIONAL ACHIEVEMENT TESTS IN SEPARATE CONTENT AREAS

Standardized achievement tests are available for nearly every field of instruction. In the elementary school, with its relatively uniform curriculum, general achievement batteries serve the majority of testing purposes. For more intensive analyses of educational disabilities, these batteries may be supplemented with the diagnostic tests discussed in the preceding section. At the high school and college levels, specialized tests covering particular courses of study are more common. Descriptions and evaluations of available tests in each field can be found in the *Mental Measurements Yearbooks,* as well as in texts dealing specifically with educational measurement (e.g., 22, 29, 40, 45). Books are also available that provide lists of achievement tests in certain special areas, such as business education (24), home economics (5), and physical education (13).

Of particular interest are the *coordinated series of achievement tests* for different courses of study. Three well-known examples of such series are the tests administered in the annual testing program of the College Entrance Examination Board, the achievement tests prepared by the Cooperative Test Division of the Educational Testing Service, and the Evaluation and Adjustment Series published by the World Book Company. A noteworthy feature of these coordinated series is their provision of a single system of comparable norms for all tests. It is thus possible to make direct comparisons among scores obtained in different subject-matter areas.

Unlike the achievement batteries discussed in Chapter 16, however, these coordinated test series cannot be standardized on a single normative population. Moreover, it is likely that the normative samples available for the various academic subjects differ appreciably in general scholastic aptitude. For example, students who have completed two years of Latin are probably a more highly selected group than those who have completed two years of Spanish. And those taking an examination in advanced mathematics are probably more highly selected than those taking an examination in American history. If scores on all these tests were to be evaluated with reference to the means of their respective normative samples, an individual might, for instance, appear to be more proficient in Spanish than in Latin simply because he was compared with a poorer normative sample in the former case.

The three series cited above employ standard score scales which are adjusted for the differences among the normative samples utilized for each test. In the College Board tests, the scores on the Scholastic Aptitude Test (SAT) provide the basis for making such adjustments (18). All raw scores on achievement tests are converted into a standard score scale having a mean of 500 and an *SD* of 100 in the fixed reference group. This group consists of the 10,651 subjects who took the SAT in 1941. The scores obtained by the candidates taking any achievement test during subsequent years are expressed with reference to this group. The adjustment takes into account any differences between the present group and the fixed reference group in the distribution of SAT scores.

The College Board tests are restricted to institutional use on the part of member colleges. The Cooperative achievement tests, on the other hand, are available for general distribution. New forms of these tests are issued periodically. Tests have been developed for the most commonly taught high school courses in English, foreign languages, natural sciences, mathematics, history, and other social studies. The Scaled Scores used in Cooperative achievement tests are normalized standard scores, so adjusted that a score of 50 represents the average score that would be expected if an unselected group of students took the particular course. In the original derivation of these Scaled Scores, students of "average ability" were chosen on the basis of grade placement for age, as well as scores on an intelligence test and on a general achievement battery. It should be noted, however, that beginning in

1960 new tests added to this series are no longer scored in terms of a uniform normative scale.

The Evaluation and Adjustment Series (16), published by the World Book Company, covers a wide variety of high school courses. Some of the tests included in this series pertain to areas not ordinarily measured by traditional achievement tests, such as listening comprehension and study skills. Others deal with the traditional fields of study, such as algebra, geometry, biology, physics, American history, world history, and literature. As in the other test series considered above, the raw scores on all these tests are converted into a single scale of standard scores. The normative samples for each test were compared on the basis of their deviation IQ's on the Terman-McNemar Test of Mental Ability. The standard scores on each test are expressed in the same units as the Terman-McNemar IQ's. Thus in this scale, a score of 100 indicates "average performance." The reference group in terms of which such average performance is defined is the standardization sample of the Terman-McNemar test.

The availability of comparable achievement test scores for different fields is desirable for many purposes. It is also clear that some adjustment must be made to allow for the differences among the examinee populations in different fields. A word of caution is in order, however, regarding the interpretation of the various systems of scaled scores described above. It cannot be assumed that the relative status of different groups on a highly verbal scholastic aptitude or general intelligence test is necessarily the same as their relative status on other tests. For example, if the candidates taking a solid geometry test and those taking a Latin test were to obtain the same distribution of intelligence test scores, they might still differ significantly in their aptitudes for Latin and for geometry. In other words, we cannot assume that the "Latin sample" would have obtained the same scores in solid geometry as the present "solid geometry sample," if both had pursued the same courses.

To be sure, such an assumption is not implied by the use of the above systems of scaled scores. These systems merely express all scores in terms of a fixed standard that can be precisely and operationally defined. But the test user with only a superficial knowledge of how the scores were derived could easily be misled into unwarranted interpretations. It must be borne in mind that the procedures followed in developing these scoring systems provide comparability of a sort. But they do not necessarily yield the identical norms that would be obtained if all students had been enrolled in the same courses of study and had been given all the tests in each series.

We may inquire where the type of achievement test discussed in this section fits into the total testing picture. Such tests are obviously well suited for use as end-of-course examinations. But it is likely that they may continue to serve other functions also. In comparison with the broader tests of educational development discussed in Chapter 16, traditional achievement tests which are more closely linked to specific courses measure more nearly distinct skills and knowledge. For this reason, they are likely to yield lower correlations with intelligence tests than have been found for broad achievement tests. If combined with intelligence tests, therefore, the specialized achievement tests will contribute more unique, non-overlapping variance and may permit better prediction of subsequent outcomes. It will be recalled that it was largely for this reason that the College Board decided to retain the combination of SAT and special achievement tests in preference to the newer experimental Tests of Developed Abilities.

VOCATIONAL ACHIEVEMENT TESTS

So far we have been considering only the uses of achievement tests in education. But we must not lose sight of the fact that a large number of achievement tests are utilized for selection and classification purposes in industry, government, and the armed services. When designed for industrial use, they are commonly designated as *trade tests.* Many vocational achievement tests are custom-made for specific purposes and are not available for general distribution; civil service examinations constitute a major example, and other illustrations can readily be found in industry and in the different branches of the armed forces.

Vocational achievement tests utilize a variety of testing media. The test content may be entirely verbal, or it may involve the use of diagrammatic or pictorial material. Questions may be presented orally or in writing. For many testing purposes, paper-and-pencil content may be replaced by manual or other performance tasks to be executed by the subject.

Many vocational achievement tests represent *standardized worksamples.* In such tests, the task set for the subject is similar to the work he is to perform on the job. The representativeness of the behavior sample and the closeness with which the task duplicates actual job conditions are essential considerations. For practical expediency, worksamples are sometimes presented in the form of "miniature," "analogy," or "simulated" tests. An illustration of a miniature punch press test will be found in Figure 102.

Miniature tests may offer a number of advantages, such as the use of less cumbersome and more easily duplicated equipment, greater condensation of important work processes within a short testing period, and elimination of risk. On the other hand, the reactions called for in miniature tests may be quite unlike those required on the job, despite superficial resemblance of the operations. For example, a different set of movements may be involved, as when hand movements are substituted for arm movements. The miniature task may also represent a highly artificial situation and may arouse different attitudes and emotional reactions than the job itself. When miniature work-samples are employed, it is especially important to check their empirical validity by careful comparison of test scores with on-the-job performance.

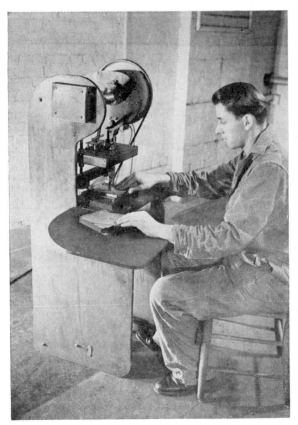

Fig. 102. Miniature Punch Press Test. (From Tiffin and Greenly, 57, p. 451; reproduced by permission of American Psychological Association.)

The scoring of worksamples may be based on either the process, the product, or both. The nature of the task may determine which aspect is scored. For example, piloting a plane, driving a car, or singing an aria in a vocal audition must be appraised in terms of the process. On the other hand, the ability to prepare effective advertising copy would usually be evaluated in terms of the end product, the process being of relatively little interest. In many tasks, both process and product are amenable to observation, but the product lends itself more readily to objective scoring.

Process, or performance, scoring may be facilitated and standardized by the use of checklists indicating the points to observe and the relative importance of each. Such checklists are commonly employed in administering road tests for the driver's license, in rating the performance of student pilots, and in many similar types of activities. Motion-picture records may be helpful in some situations. For example, in evaluating the performance of flexible gunners in bomber planes, a gun camera was used by the Air Force (56, pp. 40-41). This camera was attached to combat-like equipment employed in training flights. A permanent record was thus obtained of the points at which the gun was aimed.

Products of worksample tests can often be scored in terms of objective records. In a typewriting test, for example, the total number of errors in the typewritten copy may be readily counted. Patterns and gauges can be applied to determine whether a mechanical product falls within specified tolerance limits, or how far it deviates from a perfect specimen. Certain types of products, however, require qualitative evaluation by an expert. Rating scales and checklists may be used as aids in such judgments. In other cases, product scales similar to those described for rating drawings or essays are employed, and the product is matched with the scale specimen it resembles most closely and is rated accordingly.

Among the best-known vocational achievement tests available for general use are those designed for clerical jobs, especially typewriting, stenography, and bookkeeping (cf. 7). Some of these tests include parts dealing with English usage and general business information, together with measures of the primary skills under consideration. Stenographic tests usually employ phonographic recording to assure uniformity in speed and clarity of dictation. A typical illustration is the Seashore-Bennett Stenographic Proficiency Test (48). This test requires the subject to take stenographic notes for five letters of increasing length and complexity, and dictated at increasing rates of speed. The notes are then transcribed in the form of typewritten letters. A somewhat different combination of skills is required in the SRA Typing Adaptability Test (60). In this test, the examinee types a corrected copy of a letter containing longhand corrections, copies material involving dates and costs on a printed form, and rearranges names and addresses and types them in alphabetical order.

Another technique for appraising vocational training and experience involves the use of *oral trade tests*. These tests consist of short series of questions about specialized trade knowledge. The items of information are so chosen as to be fairly easy for anyone who has actually worked in a particular type of job, but rarely familiar to other persons. Such questions are often used as interview aids by placement counselors in employment offices. They were also extensively utilized for the rapid classification of military personnel in both World Wars.

Drawing upon oral trade tests previously developed for both military and civilian purposes, the United States Employment Service carried out a thorough restandardization and extension of this technique (cf. 51, Ch. 3 and pp. 156-162). In this program, oral trade questions were formulated for a total of 126 jobs. Each set consists of 15 questions, parallel forms also being available for many of the jobs. Parallel-form reliability for such jobs ranged from .79 to .93. A sample item from the bricklayer's test is given below (51, p. 45):

Question: What do you mean by building up a lead (*leed*)?
Answer : Building up a section (corner) of wall.

In the development of these oral trade tests, questions were first formulated from information gathered through direct observation of jobs and consultation with foremen and highly skilled workers in each field. Preliminary tryouts with foremen and skilled workers in each type of job led to the elimination, revision, or addition of questions. Some questions were discarded because of regional differences in job practices or materials.

The final validation was conducted on workers classified into three categories:

A. Experts, rated as superior workers by their supervisors and usually having a minimum of four years of experience in the given job.

B. Beginners, including apprentices, helpers, and other workers not considered to be thoroughly skilled in their occupation.

C. Persons in related occupations who work in close proximity to the experts in each field. For example, related groups tested with the oral trade tests for painters included carpenters, paper hangers, glaziers, plasterers, and sheet metal workers.

The questions for each occupation were validated on 50 to 100 persons in group A and on 25 to 50 persons in groups B and C, respectively. Questions were chosen on the basis of the size and significance of the difference between percentages of persons answering the question correctly in each group.

The distributions of scores obtained by groups A, B, and C within the brick-layer sample are shown in Figure 103. It will be noted that the groups are sharply differentiated and that overlap is minimal, especially when group A is compared with the other two.

Score	Expert Bricklayers (65 Subjects)	Apprentices and Helpers (25 Subjects)	Related Workers (35 Subjects)
15	OO		
14	OOOOOOO		
13	OOOOOOOOOOOOOOOOO		
12	OOOOOOOOOOOOOOOOOOOOOO		
11	OOOOOOOO	O	
10	OOOOO	OO	
9	OO		O
8	OO	O	
7		OO	
6		O	O
5		OOOOOO	
4		OOOOO	O
3		OO	OOO
2		OO	OO
1		OOO	OOOOOOOOOOO
0			OOOOOOOOOOOOOOO

Fig. 103. Distribution of Scores of Contrasted Validation Samples on Oral Trade Questions for Bricklayers. (Data from Stead, Shartle, *et al.*, 51, p. 41.)

Because of changes in occupational processes and materials, oral trade tests require frequent revision. It should also be emphasized that they are in no sense a substitute for performance or worksample tests. They are intended only as a rapid means of checking on the vocational experience claimed by the job seeker.

TESTING IN THE PROFESSIONS

A rapidly growing application of standardized tests is to be found in large-scale programs for the selection of professional personnel. Many of these programs are directed toward the selection of students for admission to professional training. Tests are currently being administered to candidates for schools of medicine, dentistry, nursing, law, accounting, engineering, theology, and many other professional fields. Although such testing programs emphasize aptitudes and the prediction of subsequent performance in specialized training, achievement tests on preprofessional courses constitute an important part of most batteries.

It should also be noted that in the selection of students for professional schools what is involved is not so much new types of tests as specially administered testing programs. There is no evidence that the various professional fields require any special aptitudes not already covered by available tests. The typical professional school testing program includes a test of scholastic aptitude or general intelligence, one or more achievement tests on preprofessional training, and possibly tests of interests or other personality traits. Test results are often supplemented with biographical data, letters of recommendation, previous academic record, and interview ratings.

The intelligence test employed in such a program may be a previously available instrument such as the ACE (Ch. 9). More often it is specially designed so that the content can be slanted toward the particular professional field under consideration. Such a choice of content increases face validity, in addition to permitting better security control of test materials. There is also some evidence to suggest that the predictive validity of these special tests is a little higher than that of the intelligence or scholastic aptitude tests available for general use. The specialized scholastic aptitude tests often contain measures of reading comprehension for material similar to that which the student will encounter in professional school. Some of the tests yield separate verbal and quantitative scores. Spatial, mechanical, and motor aptitudes may also be separately tested when relevant to the field.

Another level at which standardized testing programs are making major inroads is that of specialty certification and the selection of job applicants following completion of training. Understandably these terminal testing programs draw much more heavily upon achievement tests in specialized content areas; but more general types of tests are not excluded. Examples of testing programs at this level include medical specialty board examinations in surgery, anaesthesiology, and obstetrics and gynecology administered by ETS; the certification of clinical, counseling, and industrial psychologists by the American Board of Examiners in Professional Psychology (ABEPP); the National Teacher Examinations; the NLN Graduate Nurse Qualifying Examination administered by the National League for Nursing; the Officer Selection and Evaluation Program of the U.S. Public Health Service; and the Department of State Foreign Service Examinations. For illustrative purposes, a few typical testing programs at both pretraining and posttraining levels will be examined in the following sections. Examples will be drawn from the fields of medicine, dentistry, law, engineering, teaching, and graduate school studies.

Medicine. Beginning in 1930, the Association of American Medical Colleges sponsored a testing program for selecting medical students. For many years, the test administered for this purpose was one devised by Moss (36), which measured principally knowledge acquired in premedical college courses and ability to understand and retain new material similar to that taught in medical school. Since 1948, this program has employed the Medical College Admission Test (MCAT), originally developed by ETS (50). Requiring slightly over 4½ hours, MCAT consists of four separately scored parts: verbal, quantitative, understanding modern society, and science. The verbal section includes both vocabulary and reading comprehension tests in the fields of science, social studies, and the humanities. Quantitative ability is measured by a variety of mathematical problems involving numbers as well as symbols and requiring reasoning and the utilization of given facts. The applicant's understanding of modern society is tested by multiple-choice items on current economic, social, and political developments. The section on science contains questions on premedical courses in physics, chemistry, and biology. Both information and interpretation are required in this part of the test.

Reliabilities of the four parts, determined by the Kuder-Richardson technique, are in the .80's and low .90's. Since the tests are appreciably speeded, these coefficients probably represent overestimates. Intercorrelations of the four scores average about .60. These high intercorrelations undoubtedly reflect the large verbal saturation of three of the four parts. In reported follow-up studies, validity coefficients of the separate parts against freshman rank were under .40. When senior rank was used as the criterion, nearly all correlations fell below .30. Slightly higher correlations were found with Medical Board examinations.

It should be noted, of course, that such correlations are necessarily based on students admitted to medical schools. Hence a certain amount of preselection has occurred in all groups. This circumstance tends to make the correlations lower than if all applicants could be admitted and followed through medical school. The obtained test correlations, however, are not consistently higher than those found between premedical college grades and medical school grades. In fact, in a number of instances the premedical grades appear to be slightly better predictors than the test scores.

To be sure, the above findings with regard to grades are not peculiar to the MCAT or to the prediction of medical school performance. In all fields, preprofessional grades generally prove to be at least as effective as specially designed tests in the prediction of professional school achievement. But when test scores are combined with grades, a more valid predictor usually results. Admission tests are useful as a supplement rather than as a substitute for preprofessional grades. An intrinsic difficulty presented by grades arises from the lack of comparability of grades in different colleges and different courses. An applicant from a college whose students are not highly selected and whose grading standards are relatively low would have an advantage in terms of grade average. Similarly, students who had elected the minimum of required preprofessional courses and had filled their programs with "snap" courses would probably have a higher over-all grade average than those whose preparation was more thorough and more appropriate for their chosen profession. It is in such situations that a uniform admission test proves helpful.

To evaluate the MCAT solely in terms of its predictive validity, however, would ignore the testing philosophy underlying its development. The MCAT was not specifically designed to sample the kind of learning the student would encounter in medical school. Its object was not so much to predict performance in medical school courses as to assess knowledge, attitudes, and intellectual skills considered to be desirable in a prospective physician. It is on this basis that the test on understanding modern society was included. In 1950, Stalnaker, then director of the medical school testing project, remarked:

> While I should be unwilling to discourage anyone from correlating any two variables, I am neither impressed nor concerned when a low correlation is found between scores on a test in understanding modern society and grades in laboratory work in gross anatomy. I continue to favor selecting the men for the study of medicine who have some awareness of social sciences (50, p. 50).

Such a statement is a clear expression of the viewpoint of content validation. And it is in terms of content validity that the test was originally devised and its use justified.

In a sense, the aim of MCAT appears to be the prediction of a more remote criterion than medical school grades. Thus the inclusion of tests pertaining to general cultural background and current affairs implies an expectation that performance on these tests is related to the ultimate criterion of effective functioning as a physician in our culture. Theoretically, such a criterion could be defined and utilized in determining the predictive validity of these tests. The practical difficulties presented by such a procedure, however, are well-nigh insurmountable. Hence the tests are included on the basis of their content validity and of the undemonstrated but generally accepted assertion that certain characteristics are desirable in a physician. At the same time, it would seem that at least some parts of the MCAT should be designed to predict medical school performance. It is certainly an understatement to say that medical school training is relevant to ultimate achievement in medicine. To be sure, if one desires to go beyond the prediction of medical school achievement, then those parts of the MCAT that are incorporated for this purpose should not be validated against medical school performance as a criterion. But other parts of the MCAT should be evaluated—and improved—as predictors of this training criterion.

Dentistry. Unlike the MCAT, most tests developed for selecting applicants to schools of dentistry have concentrated closely on the aptitudes required in the training program. Possibly for this reason, they have usually proved to be fairly successful predictors of course grades (6, 14, 43, 49, 54, 55). Batteries assembled for this purpose usually include measures of mechanical aptitude and manual dexterity, as well as tests designed to predict achievement in academic or theoretical courses. The former abilities play an important part in the technical and clinical training given in dental schools. According to one survey of dental school curricula, 57 per cent of the dental student's time is devoted to manipulative activities (47).

Early experimentation with such tests conducted at the Universities of Iowa (49) and Minnesota (14) yielded promising results. More recently, a Dental Aptitude Testing Program was developed under the sponsorship of the Council on Dental Education of the American Dental Association, in cooperation with the American Association of Dental Schools (43). Following a five-year experimental period, the battery was adopted in 1951 by all recognized dental schools. For the prediction of performance in technical courses, this battery utilizes a spatial visualization test (similar to the Minnesota Paper Form Board described in Chapter 14) and a worksample requiring the subject to carve relatively simple geometric patterns in chalk. The other tests include a reading comprehension test in the natural sciences; an achievement test measuring factual knowledge and the application of principles in biology and chemistry; and the ACE Psychological Examination. The ACE was chosen because it yields separate linguistic and quantitative scores, and because it provides national norms based on non-dental students. By means of this test, dental school applicants could be compared with current university and college populations.

All of the tests in this battery can be machine scored except the chalk-carving test, which is graded by a committee in terms of specified characteristics. Subtest scores are reported in the form of a standard score profile for each applicant, rather than being combined into a single total. Several combinations of these tests have yielded multiple correlations ranging from .57 to .79 with course grades in a number of dental schools (43). When combined with predental grades, selected tests from this battery raised the multiple correlations by about .10 in two groups of students investigated in one dental school (61). On the other hand, Layton (33) sounds a note of caution regarding the use of national test batteries such as this without local validation. Follow-ups of several classes at the University of Minnesota School of Dentistry yielded lower validities than those found in other published studies, as well as a different pattern of correlations between separate tests and the criterion of dental school grades. Because of differences in student populations, grading standards, curricular emphases, and other local conditions, any such batteries need to be validated within individual schools.

Law. Prior to 1940, tests for the selection of law students were developed at a number of universities for use in their own law schools. The pioneer effort in this direction appears to have been made at Columbia University. However, the first test designed for common use in different law schools was the Ferson-Stoddard Law Aptitude Examination. The preparation of this test was begun in 1925 at the Universities of Iowa and North Carolina, although standardization data were also obtained at several other universities (2, 52).

In 1943 Adams and his co-workers at the University of Iowa developed a new legal aptitude test which was made available for general distribution rather than being restricted to law schools (1, 2, 3). Known as the Iowa Legal Aptitude Test, it originally included the following seven verbal subtests: analogies, mixed relations, opposites, memory for the factual content of a judicial opinion read two hours earlier, judging relevancy of legal arguments, reasoning, and legal information. The last-named test was included on the assumption that students interested in law would have learned certain common facts of law prior to formal study of the subject. Subsequent research with the Iowa Legal Aptitude Test revealed that three of the subtests—reasoning, relevancy, and legal information—yielded a slightly higher multiple correlation with law school grades than did the entire original battery (4). Separate norms were therefore made available for the total score on these three tests, so that they might be used as a short form.

Since 1948, the Law School Admission Test (LSAT) constructed by ETS has been administered to law school candidates on a national basis (27, 28, 32). In about four hours of testing time, the LSAT yields a single score based on six subtests: Principles and Cases, in which the relevance of given principles to described cases is to be judged; Data Interpretation, designed to measure the comprehension of quantitative data in tabular or graphic form (see Fig. 104); Reading Comprehension for passages of general content; Reading Memory, similar to Reading Comprehension but requiring that questions be answered without referring back to passages; Error Recognition, covering proficiency in the mechanics of writing; and Figure Classification, a nonverbal reasoning test. Although the content of some of these subtests is

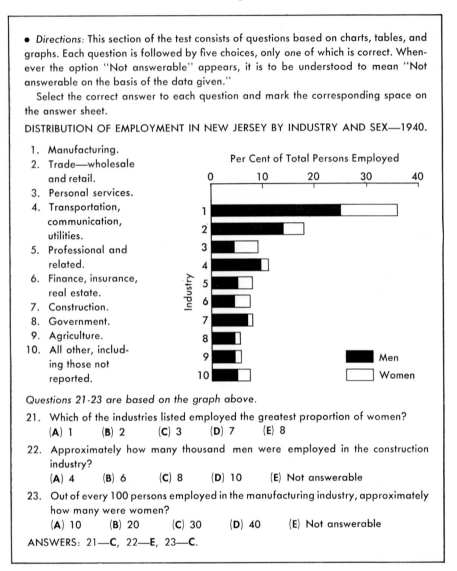

● *Directions:* This section of the test consists of questions based on charts, tables, and graphs. Each question is followed by five choices, only *one* of which is correct. Whenever the option "Not answerable" appears, it is to be understood to mean "Not answerable on the basis of the data given."

Select the correct answer to each question and mark the corresponding space on the answer sheet.

DISTRIBUTION OF EMPLOYMENT IN NEW JERSEY BY INDUSTRY AND SEX—1940.

1. Manufacturing.
2. Trade—wholesale and retail.
3. Personal services.
4. Transportation, communication, utilities.
5. Professional and related.
6. Finance, insurance, real estate.
7. Construction.
8. Government.
9. Agriculture.
10. All other, including those not reported.

Per Cent of Total Persons Employed

Questions 21-23 are based on the graph above.

21. Which of the industries listed employed the greatest proportion of women?
    (A) 1   (B) 2   (C) 3   (D) 7   (E) 8

22. Approximately how many thousand men were employed in the construction industry?
    (A) 4   (B) 6   (C) 8   (D) 10   (E) Not answerable

23. Out of every 100 persons employed in the manufacturing industry, approximately how many were women?
    (A) 10   (B) 20   (C) 30   (D) 40   (E) Not answerable

ANSWERS: 21—C, 22—E, 23—C.

Fig. 104. Sample Items from Data Interpretation Subtest of Law School Admission Test. (From 32, p. 11; reproduced by permission of Educational Testing Service.)

slanted toward the field of law, a deliberate effort was made to exclude items that would favor applicants having prior familiarity with legal terminology. This policy is in sharp contrast with that followed in the previously described Iowa test. Either policy could be defended on theoretical grounds. Specific information tests can be justified if they can be shown empirically to have predictive value.

Follow-up validity studies have been in progress since the initiation of the LSAT program. Available data indicate that, when combined with pre-law grades, this test yields correlations of about .50 to .70 with the criterion of law school grades (44). In a combined survey of 4138 students in 25 law schools, first-year law school grades correlated .36 with undergraduate grades, .45 with LSAT scores, and .54 with the best weighted combination of LSAT scores and undergraduate grades.[1]

Despite the increasing homogeneity of student populations from the first to the third year of law school, LSAT scores tend to correlate as highly with three-year grades as with first-year grades. In one university, the test yielded exactly the same correlation (.56) with first-year law grades and with three-year law grades (8). A study of 601 Yale Law School students graduating between 1953 and 1957 yielded a multiple correlation of .53 between a combination of prelaw grades and LSAT scores and the criterion of three-year law grades (9). This correlation is high in view of the restriction of range resulting from the use of LSAT in admitting candidates and in view of the low reliability of criterion grades. It should nevertheless be borne in mind that validity coefficients vary widely from one law school to another, a finding that highlights the need for local validation.

Engineering. Several batteries for the selection of engineering students have been assembled from time to time (30, 35, 54). These batteries generally utilize previously available standard tests, including mechanical comprehension and assembly tests, spatial visualization tests, a measure of general scholastic aptitude such as the ACE, and achievement tests in mathematics, science, and English. Mathematics achievement tests have usually proved to be the best single predictor of engineering school performance. Pre-engineering high school or college grades have high predictive validity and are likewise employed in conjunction with test scores. English usage, vocabulary, and reading comprehension are relevant to the understanding of lecture and reading material encountered in engineering school, as well as to the preparation of descriptive reports.

A test at a higher level, designed for selection of candidates for graduate engineering training as well as for industrial jobs is the Minnesota Engineering Analogies Test, familiarly known as the MEAT (15). Modeled after the Miller Analogies Test (Ch. 9), the MEAT consists of analogies items with a heavy mathematical and scientific content. The analogies may be expressed wholly in verbal terms, wholly in mathematical terms, or in a mixture of the two. The content of the items is drawn chiefly from the core courses taken by all engineering students during their first two years.

Like the Miller Analogies, the MEAT is a restricted test, administered

[1] Unpublished data, Educational Testing Service, 11/25/59.

only at approved centers. Tentative percentile and stanine norms on engineering students and on employed engineers are provided, but the development of local norms is urged. Internal consistency reliability coefficients of each of the two available forms range from .75 to .85. Because of these rather low reliabilities, use of both forms together is recommended. When administered with an interval of two days or less, the two forms correlated from .71 to .88. Content validity was sought in terms of current curricular coverage. Some data are available on concurrent validity, including correlations with engineering school grades and faculty ratings of students, as well as correlations with supervisory ratings of employed engineers. Although varying widely in specific groups, the former correlations cluster between .40 and .60, the latter between .25 and .35.

It should be noted that an Advanced Test in Engineering is a regular part of the testing program of the Graduate Record Examinations, to be discussed in a later section. The selection of engineers is also closely related to the general problem of identifying high-level talent in science, a problem that has received increasing attention since World War II. Such interest is reflected in studies on the characteristics of successful research workers (19, 34, 62, 63), as well as in the development of tests for measuring reasoning and creativity that were discussed in Chapter 15. Much current research on creativity is directed toward the identification and development of inventive talent in engineering.

Teaching. Considerable research has been done on the use of tests in the selection of prospective teachers at the elementary and high school levels. For the prediction of performance in teacher training courses, the most valid indicators have proved to be previous academic grades, general intelligence tests, and academic achievement tests. In a survey of available published data (54), a median correlation of .51 was found between high school grades and achievement in the first year of teacher training courses. Intelligence tests yield correlations of about the same order of magnitude. Among achievement tests, English tests are generally the most valid predictors. Other measures of achievement frequently employed for this purpose are reading comprehension, general culture, and contemporary affairs tests. Several combinations of high school grades, intelligence tests, and achievement tests have yielded correlations in the .60's with performance in teacher training courses. Practice teaching, on the other hand, shows little or no correlation with these predictors. To some extent, such lack of correlation may result from the inadequacy of the criterion measures themselves. Another factor is undoubtedly to be found in the part that personality characteristics play in the actual teaching situation.

The National Teacher Examinations (38), administered annually at designated centers throughout the country, represent a terminal achievement test given upon completion of teacher training. Developed and conducted by ETS, this testing program is used by school systems as an aid in selecting teachers, as well as by teacher-training institutions as a means of evaluating both the achievement of their students and the effectiveness of their training programs. The National Teacher Examinations are designed to measure the professional background, general cultural knowledge, English usage, and intellectual level of candidates for teaching positions, as well as their preparation in one or two chosen fields. They include a series of Common Examinations, covering the individual's general competence for teaching, and a series of Optional Examinations, covering mastery of subject matter in specialized areas.

The Common Examinations consist of five tests: Professional Information, Social Studies-Literature-Fine Arts, Science and Mathematics, English Expression, and Nonverbal Reasoning. Sample items from each of these tests are reproduced in Figures 105A and 105B. It will be noted that the Nonverbal Reasoning Test is similar in principle to the Progressive Matrices discussed in Chapter 10. Optional Examinations are available in many fields, including elementary school education, early childhood education, English language and literature, social studies, biological sciences, physical sciences, mathematics, art education, industrial arts, physical education, business education, home economics, and music education. All items in both Common and Optional Examinations emphasize understanding and application of knowledge rather than memory for factual details.

Scores on separate tests, as well as weighted totals on each battery, are reported in the form of "Scaled Scores." These are standard scores with a mean of 60, which permit direct comparisons among tests. For normative interpretation, percentile norms are also provided on the basis of the nationwide sample tested each year. Internal-consistency reliability coefficients of separate tests and of weighted composites are all close to or over .90. In the construction of the tests, validity was considered largely in terms of content analysis and internal consistency. Item-test correlations were computed within each separately timed subtest. Some data on concurrent validity are also available. These include significant mean rises in scores among different educational levels, as well as correlations in the .50's between test scores and various ratings of teaching effectiveness in a small group of employed teachers. These data are obviously meager, the major emphasis being placed on content validity.

When first introduced, the National Teacher Examinations aroused con-

---

Professional Information

5. The chief disadvantage of constructing the school curriculum wholly on the basis of an analysis of adult activities is that the

   1—resulting curriculum would be too difficult for pupils

   2—schools would be restricted to vocational training

   3—resulting curriculum would be very different from the typical curriculum at the present time

   4—resulting curriculum would include only the tool subjects of reading, writing, and simple arithmetic

   5—present needs of the pupils would not be taken into consideration

History, Literature, and Fine Arts

10. A rose window would be likely to be found in a

    1—Greek temple

    2—baroque church

    3—Gothic cathedral

    4—Tudor palace

    5—house by Frank Lloyd Wright

Science and Mathematics

11. The most important reason why apple growers frequently place beehives in their orchards is that bees

    A—eat insects which are injurious to apples

    B—produce honey of superior quality when living in apple orchards

    C—are conveniently raised in orchards

    D—help in cross-pollinating apple blossoms

    E—make honey from apple blossoms

English Expression

Which of the underlined parts of the sentence is incorrect? If the sentence contains no error, record 0.

17. The sophomore who transferred from Tulane was the heaviest of all the other
    $\qquad$ 1 $\qquad$ 2 $\quad$ 3 $\qquad$ 4

    candidates for the team.

Fig. 105A. Sample Items from Common Examinations of the National Teacher Examinations. (Reproduced by permission of Educational Testing Service.)

siderable controversy. With continued use, they have gained wider acceptance. It is recognized, of course, that the tests were designed to assess only knowledge. Teacher effectiveness depends also upon attitudes, motivation, emotional adjustment, specific experience in teaching, and other factors that the tests do not undertake to measure. It should be noted that another instrument available at the same level is the Advanced Test in Education of the Graduate Record Examinations. This test is more restricted in its coverage, yielding only a single score on professional knowledge in the field of education.

Nonverbal Reasoning

Directions: Each problem in this test consists of an incomplete pattern. The complete pattern would be made up of nine figures arranged in order. You are to discover how the figures are related and determine the correct figure for space IX. Try the following problems and indicate your answer to each by blackening the corresponding space on the answer sheet.

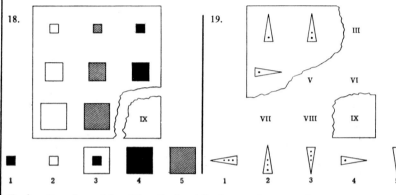

Explanation: In problem 18 notice how the figures change as they go across each row of the pattern. They become darker. As they go down, the figures become larger. Therefore, the correct figure for space IX is large and black. Answer choice 4 is the correct answer.

In problem 19 the figures acquire more dots as they go across the top row. As they go down, the point of the figure is rotated a quarter of a turn to the right. Therefore, the correct figure for space IX has three dots and its point is directed toward the bottom of the page. Answer choice 3 is the correct answer.

Fig. 105B. Sample Items from Common Examinations of the National Teacher Examinations. (Reproduced by permission of Educational Testing Service.)

Graduate School Studies. Standardized tests are widely used in the selection of students for graduate study toward the master's or doctoral degrees in various academic fields. The Miller Analogies Test, discussed in Chapter 9, was designed specially for this purpose. Since it yields a single, over-all score and is in other ways similar to general intelligence tests, it was considered in the section devoted to that type of test, rather than in this chapter. As a group, however, graduate students have much in common with the professional school students discussed in earlier parts of this chapter. Like many professional school students, they are college graduates pursuing specialized, advanced training which is often professionally oriented. A large proportion will eventually engage in research or in teaching at the college level or higher. It is therefore to be expected that some of the general findings regarding professional school students will also apply to graduate school students.

For a number of years, many graduate schools have been making use of the Graduate Record Examinations (20, 26, 31, 37). Known as the GRE, this series of tests originated in 1936 in a joint project of the Carnegie Foundation for the Advancement of Teaching and the graduate schools of four eastern universities. In 1948, the GRE project was transferred to ETS. Currently, the GRE are administered in two types of testing programs. The National Program for Graduate Student Selection is concerned with the testing of students at designated centers prior to their admission to graduate school. The test records are used by the universities for admission purposes, as well as for selecting recipients of scholarships, fellowships, and special appointments. The GRE are also employed in an Institutional Testing Program, in which colleges and universities administer the tests to their own students. In this case, the test records may be utilized as aids in such functions as student guidance, admission of students to candidacy for a degree, and evaluation of the effectiveness of instruction. In both programs, the tests are scored and retained by ETS.

The GRE consist of an Aptitude Test, Area Tests, and Advanced Tests. The Aptitude Test is essentially a general intelligence or scholastic aptitude test suitable for advanced undergraduates or graduate students. Like many such tests, it yields separate verbal and quantitative scores. The Area Tests, providing scores in Social Science, Humanities, and Natural Science, were discussed in Chapter 16 as an example of a general achievement battery for the college level. Advanced Tests are available in many fields of specialization, including Biology, Chemistry, Economics, Education, Engineering, French, Geology, Government, History, Literature, Mathematics, Music, Philosophy, Physics, Psychology, Scholastic Philosophy, Sociology, Spanish, and Speech.

Scores on all GRE tests are reported in terms of a single standard score scale with a mean of 500 and an *SD* of 100. These scores are directly comparable for all tests, having been "anchored" to the Aptitude Test scores of a reference group of 2095 seniors examined in 1952 at 11 colleges. A score of 500 on an Advanced Physics Test, for example, is the score expected from Physics majors whose Aptitude Test score equals the mean Aptitude Test score of the reference group. Since graduate school applicants are a selected sample with reference to academic aptitude, the means of most groups actually taking each Advanced Test in the Graduate Student Selection Program will be considerably above 500. Moreover, there are consistent differences in the intellectual caliber of students majoring in different subjects. For normative interpretation, therefore, the percentiles given for individual groups are more relevant and local norms are still better.

The reliability and validity of the GRE have been investigated in a number of different student samples (20, 31). Kuder-Richardson and odd-even reliability coefficients of the separate tests range from .84 to .95. Retests after an interval of one year yielded reliabilities of .87 to .97; after two years, the reliability coefficients ranged from .71 to .93. Predictive validity has been checked in terms of such criteria as graduate school grades, success versus failure in graduate school, instructors' ratings, and performance on Ph.D. qualifying examinations. Studies conducted in a number of universities indicate that the GRE are not appreciably superior to undergraduate grades as predictors of graduate school performance. But when combined with grades, they permit more effective prediction than can be obtained when grades alone are used. The multiple correlations found with such a combination of predictors were usually in the middle .60's.

It should be noted, however, that these tests are designed to serve other functions besides the prediction of graduate school performance. As in some of the previously described professional aptitude tests, the GRE are employed partly as a measure of the candidate's breadth of cultural background, verbal comprehension, quantitative reasoning, and other qualifications considered important in the selection of graduate students. To the extent that the tests are used for these purposes, their effectiveness is more a matter of content validity than of predictive validity.

THE CONTINUUM OF ABILITY TESTING

It has been repeatedly noted that the distinction between aptitude and achievement tests is not so basic as was once supposed. The new-type, broad achievement batteries considered in Chapter 16 were seen to bridge the gap between traditional course-oriented achievement tests and tests of general intelligence or scholastic aptitudes. It should now be apparent that all ability tests fall along a continuum with regard to their dependence upon specified prior experience. In this respect, traditional achievement tests, broad achievement tests, and intelligence tests differ only in degree. Within the same continuum may be placed special aptitude tests and multiple aptitude batteries. In the general category of intelligence tests, moreover, specific tests may occupy widely separated positions along the continuum, from the highly verbal type of test closely dependent upon schooling, through non-language and performance tests, to the so-called culture-free tests.

As we look over the many kinds of ability tests that have been considered in Parts 2 and 3, we can see that they may all be regarded essentially as tests of "developed abilities." The relations among them can be seen in Figure 106, showing the continuum along which ability tests may be ordered. At

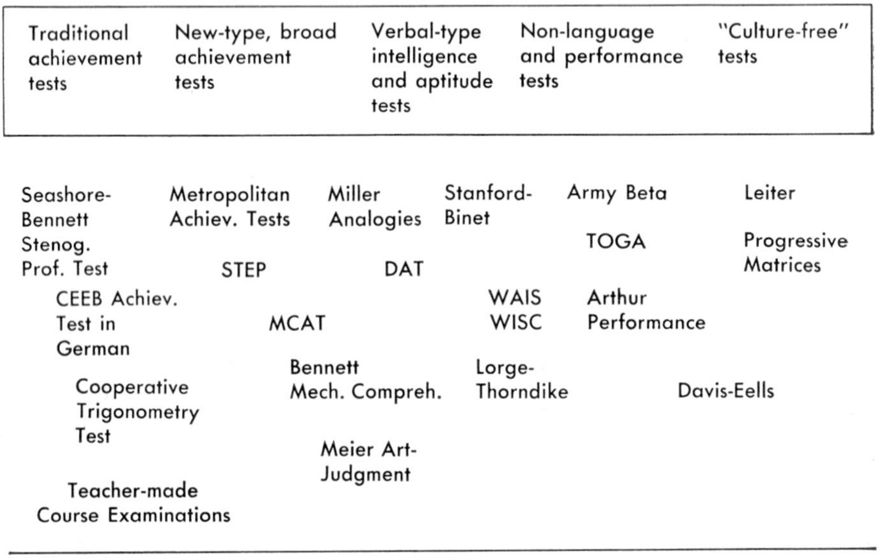

Traditional achievement tests	New-type, broad achievement tests	Verbal-type intelligence and aptitude tests	Non-language and performance tests	"Culture-free" tests

Seashore-Bennett Stenog.	Metropolitan Achiev. Tests	Miller Analogies	Stanford-Binet	Army Beta	Leiter
Prof. Test	STEP	DAT		TOGA	Progressive Matrices
CEEB Achiev. Test in German	MCAT		WAIS WISC	Arthur Performance	
Cooperative Trigonometry Test		Bennett Mech. Compreh.	Lorge-Thorndike		Davis-Eells
Teacher-made Course Examinations		Meier Art-Judgment			

Fig. 106. The Continuum of Ability Tests.

one extreme are the traditional, factual, course-oriented achievement tests. These tests are closely dependent upon a fully specified, uniform course of training. As we move past the new-type achievement tests, which stress intellectual skills rather than course-linked factual content, we come to the predominantly verbal intelligence tests. Situated approximately in the center of the continuum, such intelligence tests characteristically draw upon experiences shared by most persons in a defined cultural group, such as middle-class American urban public school children. Moving on farther, we pass non-language (including non-reading) and performance tests and finally reach the "culture-free" tests which are based upon experiences common to many cultural groups.

For illustrative purposes, a few tests have been placed at various points along this continuum. It will be noted that the tests do not fall into sharply differentiated categories. A test like the Medical College Admission Test

(MCAT), for instance, partakes of the features of both a broad achievement test and a verbal intelligence test. Tests like the WAIS, WISC, and Lorge-Thorndike cut across verbal and non-language or performance types because they have separate parts falling into each of these categories. Teacher-made examinations cover a broad area since they may vary from the most factual, traditional, course-oriented test to much broader types stressing comprehension and application of knowledge.

As a review, the student may try inserting into this continuum other tests that have been discussed in the preceding chapters. The exact position of some tests may prove to be a matter of controversy. A case in point is the relative position of SCAT (Ch. 9) and STEP (Ch. 16). Superficially, SCAT is an intelligence or scholastic aptitude test, STEP an achievement battery. Hence SCAT should be placed to the right of STEP on the continuum. But upon closer inspection, it appears that SCAT draws freely upon specific word knowledge and arithmetic processes learned in school, while STEP has succeeded in measuring reasoning and other intellectual skills fairly independently of specific factual recall. It could be argued that STEP is farther from traditional achievement tests than is SCAT. Nowhere is the increasing rapprochement between traditional intelligence tests and traditional achievement tests more clearly illustrated than in these two concurrently developed test series.

Another example of this relationship is provided by the Aptitude and Area Tests of the GRE. There is evidence that corresponding parts of the Aptitude and Area Tests correlate more highly than the different parts of either test correlate with each other. In one survey, the correlations between the Verbal and Quantitative scores of the Aptitude Test ranged from .41 to .48, but the Verbal score of the Aptitude Test correlated from .71 to .76 with the Social Science and Humanities Area Tests, and the Quantitative score of the Aptitude Test correlated from .61 to .64 with the Natural Science Area Test (20). If the misleading traditional labels are discarded and we recognize that all these tests measure developed abilities, the function served by each test can then be identified more realistically.

REFERENCES

1. Adams, W. M. Prediction of scholastic success in colleges of law: I. The experimental edition of the Iowa Legal Aptitude Test. *Educ. psychol. Measmt.*, 1943, 3, 291-305.
2. Adams, W. M. Prediction of scholastic success in colleges of law: II. An investigation of pre-law grades and other indices of law school aptitude. *Educ. psychol. Measmt.*, 1944, 4, 13-19.

3. Adams, W. M., Funks, L. K., and Stuit, D. B. *Iowa Legal Aptitude Test*. Iowa City: Bur. Educ. Res. Serv., Univer. Iowa, 1948.

4. Adams, W. M., and Stuit, D. B. The predictive efficiency of the 1946 revision of the Iowa Legal Aptitude Test. *Educ. psychol. Measmt.*, 1949, 9, 23-29.

5. Arny, Clara B. *Evaluation in home economics*. N. Y.: Appleton-Century-Crofts, 1953.

6. Bellows, R. M. Status of selection and counseling techniques for dental students. *J. consult. Psychol.*, 1940, 4, 10-15.

7. Bennett, G. K., and Cruikshank, Ruth M. *A summary of clerical tests*. N. Y.: Psychol. Corp., 1949.

8. Breslow, E. The predictive efficiency of the Law School Admission Test at the New York University School of Law. *Psychol. Newsltr., N.Y.U.*, 1957, 9, 13-22.

9. Burnham, P. S., and Crawford, A. B. Law school prediction at mid-century. *J. legal Educ.*, 1957, 10, 201-207.

10. Buswell, G. T., and John, Lenore. *Diagnostic Test for Fundamental Processes in Arithmetic*. Bloomington, Ill.: Public School Publ. Co., 1925.

11. Buswell, G. T., and John, Lenore. Diagnostic studies in arithmetic. *Suppl. educ. Monogr.*, 1926, No. 30.

12. Carroll, J. B., and Sapon, S. M. *Modern Language Aptitude Test*. N. Y.: Psychol. Corp., 1959.

13. Clarke, H. H. *Application of measurement to health and physical education*. Englewood Cliffs, N. J.: Prentice-Hall, 1950.

14. Douglass, H. R., and McCullough, C. M. Prediction of success in the school of dentistry. *Univer. Minn. Stud. Pred. schol. Achiev.*, 1942, 2, 61-74.

15. Dunnette, M. D. *Minnesota Engineering Analogies Test*. N. Y.: Psychol. Corp., 1954-1955.

16. Durost, W. N. (Ed.) *Evaluation and Adjustment Series*. Tarrytown-on-Hudson, N. Y.: World Book Co., 1951-1958.

17. Durrell, D. D. *Durrell Analysis of Reading Difficulty*. Tarrytown-on-Hudson, N. Y.: World Book Co., 1955.

18. Dyer, H. S., and King, R. G. *College Board scores: their use and interpretation. No. 2*. N. Y.: College Entrance Examination Board, 1955.

19. Flanagan, J. C., *et al. Critical requirements for research personnel*. Pittsburgh: Amer. Inst. Res., 1949.

20. *Graduate Record Examinations scores for basic reference groups*. Princeton, N. J.: Educ. Test. Serv., 1960.

21. Greene, H. A., Jorgensen, A. N., and Gerberich, J. R. *Measurement and evaluation in the elementary school*. (2nd ed.) N. Y.: Longmans, Green, 1953.

22. Greene, H. A., Jorgensen, A. N., and Gerberich, J. R. *Measurement and evaluation in the secondary school*. (2nd ed.) N. Y.: Longmans, Green, 1954.

23. Greene, H. A., Jorgensen, A. N., and Kelley, V. H. *Iowa Silent Reading Tests: New Edition, Revised* (Elementary and Advanced Tests). Tarrytown-on-Hudson, N. Y.: World Book Co., 1943.

24. Hardaway, Mathilde, and Maier, T. *Tests and measurements in business education*. (2nd ed.) Cincinnati: South-Western Publ. Co., 1952.

25. Hildreth, Gertrude H., and Griffiths, N. L. *Metropolitan Readiness Tests.* Tarrytown-on-Hudson, N. Y.: World Book Co., 1949-1950.

26. *Institutional Testing Program for Colleges and Universities: handbook for deans and examiners, 1959-1960, The Graduate Record Examinations.* Princeton, N. J.: Educ. Test. Serv., 1960.

27. Johnson, A. P. Tests for law. *Proc. 1950 invit. Conf. test. Probl., Educ. Test. Serv.,* 1951, 30-34.

28. Johnson, A. P., Olsen, Marjorie A., and Winterbottom, J. A. *The Law School Admission Test and suggestions for its use: a handbook for law school deans and admissions officers.* Princeton, N. J.: Educ. Test. Serv., 1955.

29. Jordan, A. M. *Measurement in education: an introduction.* N. Y.: McGraw-Hill, 1953.

30. Kandell, I. L. *Professional aptitude tests in medicine, law, and engineering.* N. Y.: Teach. Coll., Columbia Univer., Bur. Publ., 1940.

31. Lannholm, G. V., and Schrader, W. B. *Predicting graduate school success: an evaluation of the effectiveness of the Graduate Record Examinations.* Princeton, N. J.: Educ. Test. Serv., 1951.

32. *Law School Admission Test: bulletin of information for candidates, 1959-1960.* Princeton, N. J.: Educ. Test. Serv., 1959.

33. Layton, W. L. Predicting success in dental school. *J. appl. Psychol.,* 1953, 37, 251-255.

34. Mandell, M. M., and Adams, S. Selection of physical scientists. *Educ. psychol. Measmt.,* 1948, 8, 575-581.

35. Moore, B. V., Lapp, C. J., and Griffin, C. H. *Engineering and Physical Science Aptitude Test.* N. Y.: Psychol. Corp., 1951.

36. Moss, F. A. Report of the Committee on Aptitude Tests for Medical Schools. *J. Assoc. Amer. med. Coll.,* 1942, 17, 312-315.

37. *National Program for Graduate School Selection: bulletin of information for candidates, 1959-1960, The Graduate Record Examinations.* Princeton, N. J.: Educ. Test. Serv., 1960.

38. *National Teacher Examinations: handbook for school and college officials.* Princeton, N. J.: Educ. Test. Serv., 1959.

39. Nelson, M. J., Denny, E. C., and Brown, J. I. *The Nelson-Denny Reading Test.* (Rev. ed.) Boston: Houghton Mifflin, 1960.

40. Noll, V. H. *Introduction to educational measurement.* Boston: Houghton Mifflin, 1957.

41. Orleans, J. B., and Orleans, J. S. *Orleans Algebra Prognosis Test, Revised Edition.* Tarrytown-on-Hudson, N. Y.: World Book Co., 1950-1951.

42. Orleans, J. B., and Orleans, J. S. *Orleans Geometry Prognosis Test, Revised Edition.* Tarrytown-on-Hudson, N. Y.: World Book Co., 1950-1951.

43. Peterson, S. Tests for dentistry. *Proc. 1950 invit. Conf. test. Probl., Educ. Test. Serv.,* 1951, 35-45.

44. Pitcher, Barbara, and Olsen, Marjorie. The Law School Admission Test as a predictor of first-year law school grades. *Educ. Test. Serv. Stat. Rep.,* SR-59-16, April, 1959.

45. Ross, C. C., and Stanley, J. C. *Measurement in today's schools.* (3rd ed.) Englewood Cliffs, N. J.: Prentice-Hall, 1954.

46. Ruch, G. M., Knight, F. B., Greene, H. A., and Studebaker, J. W. *Compass Diagnostic Tests in Arithmetic.* Chicago: Scott, Foresman, 1925.
47. Schultz, R. S. The relation of general intelligence, motor adaptability, and motor learning to success in dental technical courses. *Psychol. Clinic,* 1932, 21, 226-234.
48. Seashore, H., and Bennett, G. K. *The Seashore-Bennett Stenographic Proficiency Test: A Standard Recorded Stenographic Worksample.* N. Y.: Psychol. Corp., 1946-1956.
49. Smith, R. V. Aptitudes and aptitude testing in dentistry. *J. dent. Educ.,* 1943, 8, 55-70.
50. Stalnaker, J. M. Tests for medicine. *Proc. 1950 invit. Conf. test. Probl., Educ. Test. Serv.,* 1951, 46-51.
51. Stead, W. H., Shartle, C. L., *et al. Occupational counseling techniques.* N. Y.: American Book Co., 1940.
52. Stoddard, G. D. Ferson and Stoddard Law Aptitude Examination. Preliminary report. *Amer. Law Sch. Rev.,* 1927, 6, 78-81.
53. Strang, Ruth, McCullough, Constance M., and Traxler, A. E. *Problems in the improvement of reading.* (2nd ed.) N. Y.: McGraw-Hill, 1955.
54. Stuit, D. B., *et al. Predicting success in professional schools.* Washington: Amer. Coun. Educ., 1949.
55. Thompson, C. E. Motor and mechanical abilities in professional schools. *J. appl. Psychol.,* 1942, 26, 24-37.
56. Thorndike, R. L. (Ed.) *Research problems and techniques.* (AAF Aviation Psychology Program, Research Reports. Rep. No. 3.) Washington: Govt. Printing Office, 1947.
57. Tiffin, J., and Greenly, R. J. Experiments in the operation of a punch press. *J. appl. Psychol.,* 1939, 23, 450-460.
58. Triggs, Frances O., *et al. Diagnostic Reading Tests: a history of their construction and validation.* N. Y.: Comm. on Diagnostic Reading Tests, Inc., 1952.
59. Triggs, Frances O., *et al. Diagnostic Reading Tests: their interpretation and use in the teaching of reading.* N. Y.: Comm. on Diagnostic Reading Tests, Inc., 1952.
60. Tydlaska, Mary, and White, C. *SRA Typing Adaptability Test.* Chicago: Sci. Res. Assoc., 1956.
61. Webb, S. C. The prediction of achievement for first year dental students. *Educ. psychol. Measmt.,* 1956, 16, 543-548.
62. Weislogel, Mary H. *The development of a test for selecting research personnel.* Pittsburgh: Amer. Inst. Res., 1950.
63. Weislogel, Mary H. *The development of tests for evaluating research proficiency in physics and chemistry.* Pittsburgh: Amer. Inst. Res., 1951.
64. Woolf, M. D., and Woolf, Jeanne A. *Remedial reading: teaching and treatment.* N. Y: McGraw-Hill, 1957.
65. Wrightstone, J. W., Justman, J., Pincus, M., and Lowe, Ruth M. *New York Test of Arithmetical Meanings.* Tarrytown-on-Hudson, N. Y.: World Book Co., 1956.

PART 4

Measurement of Personality Traits

CHAPTER 18

Self-Report Inventories

In the classification of psychological tests outlined in Chapter 2, it was noted that tests designed for the measurement of personality characteristics are concerned primarily with the emotional, social, and motivational aspects of behavior. In the next four chapters, the major types of tests currently employed for these purposes will be surveyed. This chapter will deal with personality inventories. Chapter 19 will consider available techniques for the measurement of interests and attitudes. The instruments to be covered in both of these chapters are essentially paper-and-pencil, self-report questionnaires suitable for group administration. The use of projective techniques for the assessment of personality characteristics will be discussed in Chapter 20. In the last chapter, we shall examine a number of miscellaneous approaches to the measurement of personality, many of which are still in an experimental stage.

The number of available personality tests runs into several hundred. Especially numerous are the personality inventories and the projective techniques. In this book, we shall be concerned primarily with the types of approaches that have been explored. A few of the most widely known tests of each type will be briefly described for illustrative purposes. For a more comprehensive survey of existing instruments, the reader should consult such sources as *The Mental Measurements Yearbooks,* as well as books devoted entirely to the measurement of personality (e.g., 1, 46).

In the development of personality inventories, several approaches have been followed in formulating, assembling, selecting, and grouping items. Among the major procedures in current use are the formulation of items in terms of content validity, empirical criterion keying of an item pool, factor analysis of items or subtest scores, forced-choice arrangement of items on the basis of social desirability, and the application of personality theory in choosing variables and constructing items. Each of these approaches will be discussed and illustrated in the following sections. It should be noted, however, that they are not alternative or mutually exclusive techniques. Theoretically, all could be combined in the development of a single personality inventory. In actual practice, several inventories have utilized two or more of these procedures.

CONTENT VALIDATION

The prototype of self-report personality inventories was the Woodworth Personal Data Sheet (cf. 39), developed for use during World War I. This inventory was essentially an attempt to standardize a psychiatric interview and to adapt the procedure for mass testing. Accordingly, Woodworth gathered information regarding common neurotic and preneurotic symptoms from the psychiatric literature as well as through conferences with psychiatrists. It was in reference to these symptoms that the inventory questions were originally formulated. The questions dealt with such behavior deviations as abnormal fears or phobias, obsessions and compulsions, nightmares and other sleep disturbances, excessive fatigue and other psychosomatic symptoms, feelings of unreality, and motor disturbances such as tics and tremors. In the final selection of items, Woodworth applied certain empirical statistical checks, to be discussed in the next section. Nevertheless, it is apparent that the primary emphasis in the construction of this inventory was placed upon content validation, as indicated in the sources from which items were drawn as well as in the common recognition of certain kinds of behavior as maladaptive.

One of the clearest examples of content validation in a current personality inventory is provided by the Mooney Problem Check List (63). Designed chiefly to identify problems for group discussion or for individual counseling, this checklist drew its items from written statements of problems submitted by about 4000 high school students, as well as from case records, counseling interviews, and similar sources. The checklist is available in junior high school, high school, college, and adult forms. The problem areas covered vary somewhat from level to level. In the high school and college forms, they include health and physical development; finances, living conditions, and employment; social and recreational activities; social-psychological relations; personal-psychological relations; courtship, sex, and marriage; home and family; morals and religion; adjustment to school work; the future—vocational and educational; and curriculum and teaching procedure. Although the number of items checked in each area can be recorded, the test does not yield trait scores or measures of degree of adjustment. Emphasis is on individual items as self-perceived and self-reported problems or sources of difficulty.

Another checklist of needs and problems, suitable for grades 4 to 8, is the SRA Junior Inventory (68). The areas sampled by this inventory are designated as: About Me and My School, About Me and My Home, About Myself, Getting along with Other People, and Things in General. A novel feature introduced in this inventory is the use of response boxes of different sizes to enable the child to suggest the magnitude of each problem, as illustrated in Figure 107. A similar procedure is utilized with a slightly different

I want to learn how to read better.................................. ⬛ ◻ ▫ ○
I wish I had more "pep"... ⬛ ◻ ▫ ○
In the Junior Inventory, Form S, pupils check each statement as a big problem (by marking the big box), a middle-sized problem (by marking the middle-sized box), a little problem (by marking the little box), or no problem (by marking the circle).

Fig. 107. Sample Items from SRA Junior Inventory. (Reproduced by permission of Science Research Associates.)

set of problem areas in the SRA Youth Inventory (69), for grades 7 to 12. Responses to both of these inventories yield a score in each area that may be evaluated in terms of norms provided for this purpose, but such a quantification of responses is of dubious value.

Mention may also be made of the Bell Adjustment Inventory (13), which has continued in active use since its initial appearance in 1934. The Student Form, designed for the rapid screening of high school and college students for counseling purposes, yields adjustment scores in four areas: home, health, social, and emotional. A less widely used Adult Form added a fifth score in occupational adjustment. Items for the Bell Inventories were selected largely from existing inventories and were grouped into the five categories in terms of their apparent content. Final item selection within each category was based on internal consistency, responses to each item being evaluated against total score on the preliminary scale for the appropriate area.

As a final example of inventories relying primarily upon content validation we may consider the California Test of Personality (78). Available in five levels, this inventory undertakes to span the age range from kindergarten to college students and unselected adults. In the type of scores obtained and the proposed interpretations of such scores, the California Test of Personality resembles empirically developed personality tests. In its construction, however, content validation appears to have predominated. Separate scores are found in 12 areas, identified by such labels as sense of personal worth, withdrawing tendencies, social skills, and school relations. From these part scores, a total adjustment score and two subtotals covering personal and social adjustment are also computed. National norms are provided for evaluating these 15 scores.

It should be added that with all these inventories some efforts have been made toward empirical validation of scores in each problem area. Few personality tests in use today rest their claims entirely on content validity. All tests cited in this section, however, have relied principally on content validity in the formulation, selection, and grouping of items.

EMPIRICAL CRITERION KEYING

Early Inventories. Empirical criterion keying refers to the development of a scoring key in terms of some external criterion. Such a procedure involves the selection of items to be retained and the assignment of scoring weights to each response. In the construction of the previously cited Woodworth Personal Data Sheet, some of the statistical checks applied in the final selection of items pointed the way for criterion keying. Thus no item was retained in this inventory if 25 per cent or more of a normal sample answered it in the unfavorable direction. The rationale underlying this procedure was that a behavior characteristic that occurs with such frequency in an essentially normal sample cannot be indicative of abnormality. The method of contrasted groups was likewise employed in the selection of items. Only symptoms reported at least twice as often in a previously diagnosed psychoneurotic group than in a normal group were retained.

Another early example of criterion keying is provided by the Allport A-S Reaction Study (2, 4, 70). Described as a measure of ascendance-submission (A-S), this inventory seeks to assess the individual's tendency to dominate his associates or be dominated by them in face-to-face contacts of everyday life. Each item begins with a brief description of a situation that might commonly be encountered at a meeting, in school, on a bus, in a repair shop, or in other familiar settings. Two or four alternative ways of meeting the situation are listed, the subject being instructed to indicate which alternative most nearly represents his usual reaction. The responses vary in the degree of ascendance or submission they represent and are weighted accordingly in the scoring.

The scoring weights for the A-S Reaction Study were empirically established on the basis of the criterion ratings obtained by those subjects in the standardization sample who chose each response. Each subject's criterion rating represented a mean of five ratings for social dominance, including a self-rating and four ratings by associates. Following publication of the test, considerable evidence for the validity of total scores has been accumulated, chiefly by the method of contrasted groups. In addition to enjoying wide popularity in its own right, the A-S Reaction Study has influenced the development of many other inventories. This test is one of the most durable of the early personality inventories. It might also be noted that dominance has proved to be one of the most frequently identified and clearly established traits in subsequent factorial analyses of personality.

An examination of questionnaires designed to measure different aspects of personality and bearing dissimilar trait labels reveals many common items. It was this observation that led to the development of the Bernreuter Personality Inventory (16). The 125 Yes-No-? items constituting this inventory were based on questions chosen from four previously existing inventories.[1] Four scoring keys were developed for use with the Bernreuter inventory, each response being assigned a separate weight on each of the four keys. The resulting four scores were described as: B1N—neuroticism, B2S—self-sufficiency, B3I—introversion, and B4D—dominance. The correlations between these scores and the four separate tests from which the Bernreuter was derived ranged from .67 to .94. It thus appeared that a single, short inventory could provide approximately the same information that had previously required four different inventories. This time-saving feature of the Bernreuter probably accounted for much of its popularity.

An analysis of the intercorrelations among the four Bernreuter scores clearly indicates, however, that these scores do not measure four independent aspects of personality. The neuroticism and introversion scores, for example, correlate .95 with each other. Part of this correlation is undoubtedly attributable to the overlap of specific factors and of chance errors, resulting from the use of common items in obtaining the two scores. To a large extent, however, such intercorrelations reflect the overlap that exists among categories commonly used in describing personality. Most of the traditional self-report inventories utilized a priori trait differentiations that were not always borne out by empirical findings.

An early factor analysis of the four Bernreuter scores, conducted by Flanagan (38), demonstrated that two independent measures could be derived from the inventory. These were designated F1C (Confidence) and F2S (Sociability). Scoring keys for these two traits were subsequently added to the test, making a total of six available keys. There is, of course, no justification for using all six keys, since such a practice only further compounds the overlap. The two Flanagan keys should be regarded as substitutes for

[1] Thurstone Personality Schedule (modeled after the earlier Woodworth P.D. Sheet), Laird's Introversion-Extroversion Test, Allport A-S Reaction Study, and Bernreuter's Self-Sufficiency Scale.

the original four. Other factor analyses, using either score or item intercorrelations, have in general confirmed Flanagan's results (cf., e.g., 11). Most studies have found two relatively independent traits which seem to correspond to those identified by Flanagan, although these traits have been described in different terms. Because they correspond more closely to familiar categories, however, the four original keys have been applied more frequently than the two uncorrelated keys. Moreover, the use of correlated factors (oblique axes) is now commonly accepted in factorial research, especially in the area of personality.

The Minnesota Multiphasic Personality Inventory. The outstanding example of criterion keying in personality test construction is to be found in the Minnesota Multiphasic Personality Inventory, commonly known as the MMPI (29, 31, 50, 51, 83). Partly because of its clinical origins and partly because of certain technical innovations, the application of this inventory has attained unprecedented proportions. Since its appearance in 1940 and the publication of its first official manual in 1943, the MMPI has also stimulated a flood of research. In a survey published in 1956, Welsh and Dahlstrom (83) brought together 66 of the most important articles about the MMPI appearing between 1940 and 1954 and included a bibliography of 689 titles. In 1959, *The Fifth Mental Measurements Yearbook* listed 779 references, and the 1960 *Handbook* by Dahlstrom and Welsh (29) contains over 1200.

The MMPI was originally developed "to assay those traits that are commonly characteristic of disabling psychological abnormality" (50). The inventory consists of 550 affirmative statements, which the subject is asked to classify into three categories: *True, False,* and *Cannot say.* In the individual form of the test, the statements are printed on separate cards, which the subject sorts into three stacks. Later, a group form was prepared, in which the statements are printed in a test booklet and the responses are recorded by the subject on an answer sheet. Both forms were designed for adults from about 16 years of age upward, although they have also been employed successfully with somewhat younger adolescents (52). Use of the individual form is generally recommended, especially when testing disturbed patients or persons of low educational or intellecutal level. The MMPI items range widely in content, covering such areas as: health, psychosomatic symptoms, neurological disorders, and motor disturbances; sexual, religious, political, and social attitudes; educational, occupational, family, and marital questions; and many well-known neurotic or psychotic behavior manifestations, such as obsessive and compulsive states, delusions, hallucinations, ideas of reference, phobias, sadistic and masochistic trends, and the like. A few illustrative items are shown below:

I do not tire quickly.

Most people will use somewhat unfair means to gain profit or an advantage rather than to lose it.

I am worried about sex matters.

When I get bored I like to stir up some excitement.

I believe I am being plotted against.

When first published, the MMPI provided scores on nine "clinical scales." Each of these scales consists of items that differentiated between a specified clinical group and a normal control group of approximately 700 persons. The latter were all visitors at the University of Minnesota hospitals, and represented a fairly adequate cross section of the Minnesota population of both sexes between the ages of 16 and 55. The scales were thus developed empirically by criterion keying of items, the criterion being traditional psychiatric diagnosis. By this method, the following scales were prepared:

1. Hs: Hypochondriasis
2. D: Depression
3. Hy: Hysteria
4. Pd: Psychopathic deviate
5. Mf: Masculinity-femininity
6. Pa: Paranoia
7. Pt: Psychasthenia
8. Sc: Schizophrenia
9. Ma: Hypomania

Items for the masculinity-femininity scale were selected in terms of frequency of responses by men and women. High scores on this scale indicate a predominance of interests typical of the opposite sex. Such scores have been found to characterize homosexuals, especially among males, although in individual cases high scores may have other interpretations.

A special feature of the MMPI is its utilization of four so-called validity scales. These scales are not concerned with validity in the technical sense. In effect, they represent checks on carelessness, misunderstanding, malingering, and the operation of special response sets and test-taking attitudes. The validating scores include:

Question Score (?): the total number of items put into the *Cannot say* category.

Lie Score (L): based upon a group of items that make the subject appear in a favorable light, but are unlikely to be truthfully answered in the favorable direction. (E.g., I do not like everyone I know.)

Validity Score (F): determined from a set of items very infrequently answered in the scored direction by the standardization group. Although representing undesirable behavior, these items do not cohere in any pattern of abnormality. Hence it is unlikely that any one subject actually shows all or most of these symptoms. A high F score may indicate scoring errors, carelessness in responding, gross eccentricity, or deliberate malingering.

Correction Score (K): utilizing still another combination of specially chosen items, this score provides a measure of test-taking attitude, related to both L and F, but believed to be more subtle. A high K score may indicate defensiveness or an attempt to "fake good." A low K score may represent excessive frankness and self-criticism or a deliberate attempt to "fake bad."

The first three scores (?, L, F) are ordinarily used for an over-all evaluation of the test record. If any of these scores exceeds a certain maximum value, the record is considered invalid. The K score, on the other hand, was designed to function as a "suppressor variable." It is employed to compute a correction factor which is added to the scores on some of the clinical scales in order to obtain adjusted totals. It should be noted that the utilization of the various validity scales is not completely standardized, but is left partly to the judgment of the clinician. Moreover, the validity scales are constantly undergoing redefinition and revision, in the light of new research.

Since the publication of the MMPI in its initial form, about 200 new scales have been developed, most of them by independent investigators who had not participated in the construction of the original test (29). A Social Introversion (Si) scale has been added to the original nine clinical scales and is now routinely included in the MMPI profiles, with the code number "0." In studies of high school and college students, the Si scale was found to be significantly related to number of extracurricular activities in which the student participated (83). Other scoring scales are applied as the occasion demands. The available scales vary widely in the nature and breadth of the criteria against which items were evaluated. Several scales were developed within normal populations to assess personality traits unrelated to pathology. Some scales have subsequently been applied to the test records of the original MMPI normal standardization sample, thus providing normative data comparable to those of the initial clinical scales (49). Examples of these new scales include Ego Strength (ES), Dependency (Dy),

Dominance (Do), Prejudice (Pr), and Social Status (St). Other scales have been developed for highly specific purposes and are more limited in their applicability.

In its regular administration, the MMPI now yields 14 scores, including the 9 original clinical scales, the Si scale, and the 4 validating scales. Norms on the original control sample of approximately 700 persons are reported in the form of "T scores," or standard scores with a mean of 50 and an *SD* of 10. These standard scores are used in plotting profiles, as illustrated in Figures 108 and 109. Any score of 70 or higher—falling 2 *SD*'s or more above the mean—is generally taken as the cutoff point for the identification of pathological deviations. It should be noted, however, that the clinical significance of the same score may differ from one scale to another. A score of 75 on the Hypochondriasis and on the Schizophrenia scales, for example, may not indicate the same severity of abnormality.

The explanation of low points on the MMPI profile is less clear. Clinicians believe that the occurrence of scores substantially below 50 may have diagnostic significance, but no systematic interpretations have been worked out as yet. It seems likely, however, that marked deviations below 50 also signify maladjustment, rather than indicating superior adjustment. Test-taking attitudes may likewise contribute to the production of low scores. An illustration of possible personality difficulties that may be associated with low MMPI scores is provided by a study of college men with low Pa scores (9). In comparison with a control group whose scores fell within the normal range, the low Pa scorers showed more academic difficulty, a greater proportion of underachievers, and a higher incidence of difficulty with parents. The investigator suggested interpretations of these findings in terms of "repressed or denied hostility."

There is considerable evidence to suggest that, in general, the greater the number and magnitude of deviant scores on the MMPI, the more likely it is that the individual is severely disturbed. For screening purposes, however, shorter and simpler instruments are available. It is clear that the principal applications of the MMPI are to be found in differential diagnosis. In using the inventory for this purpose, the procedure is much more complex than the labels originally assigned to the scales might suggest. The test manual and related publications now caution against literal interpretation of the clinical scales. For example, we cannot assume that a high score on the Schizophrenia scale indicates the presence of schizophrenia. Other psychotic groups show high elevation on this scale, and schizophrenics often score high on other scales. Moreover, such a score may occur in a normal person. It is partly to prevent possible misinterpretations of scores on single scales that the code numbers 0 to 9 have been substituted for the scale names in later publications on the MMPI.

The original clinical scales of the MMPI were based on a traditional psychiatric classification which, though popular, rests upon a dubious theoretical foundation. The artificiality of the categories employed in such traditional schemas has been a matter of concern in abnormal psychology for a long time. The fact that such categories prove unsatisfactory in actual practice is now generally conceded. Another difficulty is that a high score on any one scale may have different implications depending upon the accompanying scores on other scales. In other words, it is the score pattern or profile rather than individual scale scores that should be examined. To facilitate the interpretation of such score patterns, a system of numerical profile coding has been developed. In such codes, the sequence and arrangement of scale numbers show at a glance which are the high and low points in the individual's profile. For instance, the code 49-2 shows high scores in scales 4 (Pd) and 9 (Ma) in decreasing order of size, and a low score in scale 2 (D).

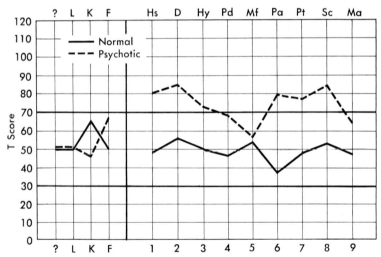

Fig. 108. MMPI Profiles of a Normal Adult and a Psychotic. (Adapted from Weider, 82, pp. 554 and 563, and reproduced by permission of The Ronald Press.)

An Atlas for the Clinical Use of the MMPI (51) provides coded profiles and short case histories of 968 patients, arranged according to similarity of profile pattern. This material is offered as an aid in understanding the diagnostic significance of each profile. A similar codebook utilizing data from over four thousand college students examined in a college counseling center has been prepared for use by counselors (31). Current validation of the

MMPI is proceeding by the accumulation of empirical data about persons who show each profile pattern or code. By such a process, the construct validity of each MMPI code is gradually built up. The MMPI *Handbook* compiled by Dahlstrom and Welsh (29) contains the most comprehensive survey of available interpretive data on major profile patterns.

Examples of the kind of interpretations that are thus evolving include the "neurotic triad," which consists of scales 1, 2, and 3. Codes with high points in these three scales have been found to characterize neurotics. More specifically, "conversion V" codes, beginning with 13 or 31, occur commonly in "immature persons who dodge issues rather than meeting them squarely" (52, p. 23). In this profile, the maximum elevation is still in the first three scales, but scale 3 is higher than 2, thus producing a V-shaped appearance in the first part of the profile. Psychosomatic and other physical symptoms are typical of these profiles. Many psychotic profiles show high points in scales 6, 7, 8, and 9, as well as in the scales of the neurotic triad (cf. Fig. 108). Such a pattern has been designated as the "psychotic tetrad" (29, p. 96).

A series of studies on juvenile delinquents (52), involving both concurrent and predictive validation procedures, showed 49- codes to be characteristic of delinquency. The typical elevation in code 4 is illustrated in the average profile of a group of delinquent girls reproduced in Figure 109. Follow-up studies of unselected ninth grade pupils showed that those with 49- profiles were somewhat more likely to become delinquent. Delinquents with these profiles also tended to respond less favorably to rehabilitation. In terms of test responses, such a profile indicates rebelliousness, conflict with family and society, non-conformity, wide and changeable interests, and overactivity. Certain scales, such as 2 (D) and 0 (Si) seem to function as inhibitors in delinquency codes, high scores in these scales reducing the probability of delinquent behavior. A survey of an adult prison sample likewise yielded a predominance of profiles with 4 high and 0 low (65).

Although the misleading psychiatric labels are dropped, it should be noted that MMPI items are still grouped into scales on the basis of such obsolescent categories. Factorial analyses based on intercorrelations of items and of scales indicate that items would be differently grouped on the basis of their empirically established interrelations (27; 62; 83, pp. 255-281). However, an extensive body of normative data and clinical experience pertaining to the old scales has accumulated over the years. In order not to lose this store of information, later efforts have been directed toward the re-interpretation of the old scales in terms of empirically derived profile codes.

A closely related limitation of the MMPI stems from inadequate relia-

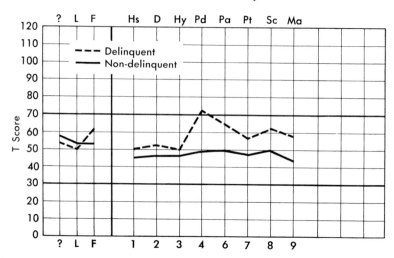

Fig. 109. Mean MMPI Profiles of a Group of Delinquent Girls ($N = 99$) and a Group of Non-Delinquent Girls ($N = 85$). From Hathaway and Monachesi, 52, p. 32; reproduced by permission of the University of Minnesota Press.)

bilities of some of the scales. The effectiveness of any profile analysis is weakened by chance errors in the scores on which it is based. If individual scale scores are unreliable and highly intercorrelated, many of the inter-score differences that determine the profile code may have resulted from chance. Retest reliabilities on normal and abnormal adult samples reported in the manual range from the .50's to the low .90's. The intervals between retests varied from a few days to over a year. Retest coefficients found in a group of college students, however, were generally lower, although only a one-week interval had elapsed between testings (41). The mean of these reliabilities was only .61. Six of the nine coefficients fell below .70, and two fell below .40. Moreover, split-half reliabilities computed for the same college sample showed an even wider variation from scale to scale, ranging from —.05 for scale 6 (Pa) to .81 for scale 7 (Pt).

Still another limitation of the MMPI pertains to the size and representativeness of the normative sample. The standard scores from which all profile codes are derived are expressed in terms of the performance of the control group of approximately 700 Minneapolis adults tested in the original standardization. Such a normative sample appears quite inadequate when compared, for example, with the nationwide standardization samples employed with many of the ability tests discussed in Parts 2 and 3. That the norms may vary appreciably in different normal populations is illustrated by the finding that the means obtained by college students are consistently above 50 on some of the scales (26; 41; 83, pp. 574-578). In one study of

600 college students, 39 per cent received scores above 70 in one or more scales (41). The most satisfactory solution is probably to be found in the gathering of specific norms, at least with reference to the incidence of different profile codes.

Even more than ability tests, personality tests can be expected to show large subcultural as well as cultural differences. As would be anticipated, studies conducted in other countries reveal significant elevation on certain scales when profiles are based on the original Minnesota norms (e.g., 75, 76). Any explanation of such cultural and subcultural differences requires specific knowledge of cultural conditions and other circumstances prevailing within each group. Cultural differentials may operate at many different levels (cf. 8, pp. 567-569, 596-598). Group differences in MMPI scores could, for example, reflect nothing more than differences in interpretation of individual items or of instructions. High elevation in some groups could result from strong traditions of self-depreciation and modesty. Cultural differences in the type of behavior considered socially desirable may likewise influence scores. In still other groups, high scores may indicate the prevalence of genuine emotional problems arising from child-rearing practices, conflicts of social roles, minority group frustrations, and the like.

Other Inventories Derived from the MMPI. Besides stimulating a proliferation of its own scoring scales, the MMPI has served as a basis for the development of certain other inventories. Among these is the Taylor Manifest Anxiety Scale (77). Although not standardized or published, this scale has rapidly gained prominence both in research and in clinical practice. It was originally constructed for use in experiments to test certain hypotheses regarding the effects of drive on learning (74). For this purpose, five clinical psychologists were asked to choose those MMPI statements that they regarded as overt admissions of anxiety. The resulting scale consists of 50 items thus selected, mixed with 175 buffer items drawn largely from the three validity scales (L, F, K).

The item selection procedure followed by Taylor will be recognized as an example of content validation. The clinical psychologists who chose the anxiety items were functioning in the same way as educators who may be asked to evaluate items for an achievement test in social studies. Internal consistency indices were also utilized in the final selection of items. Some evidence of concurrent validity of total scores was later obtained by comparing the performance of neurotic and psychotic patients with that of normal groups. In the course of the subsequent experiments in which this test was administered, data pertaining to its construct validity were likewise accumulated. This test, in fact, has often been cited as an example of construct

validation, probably because of the theoretical setting within which it originated.

It is interesting to note that the administration of the 50 anxiety items in
the context of the Manifest Anxiety Scale apparently leads to somewhat
different responses than are obtained with the same items in the MMPI format. In one study, the correlation between scores on the same set of items
presented in these two settings was only .68. This finding highlights the fact
that an individual's perception of a personality test item may be influenced
by the other items among which it is embedded. Despite its popularity, the
Manifest Anxiety Scale should be regarded as a research instrument only,
until more data on its reliability, validity, and norms become available. The
original scale is suitable for college and unselected adult groups, but a form
for children has subsequently been prepared (18).

An effort to adapt the MMPI for use with normal high school students
and college freshmen led to the development of the Minnesota Counseling
Inventory (14). Many of the 355 true-false items of this inventory are taken
from the MMPI, and several of its scales have a close resemblance to
MMPI scales. With norms based on over 20,000 high school students tested
in ten states, this test provides scores in seven areas, designated as: Family
Relationships, Social Relationships, Emotional Stability, Conformity, Adjustment to Reality, Mood, and Leadership. Although labeled in terms of the
favorable end of the scale, "Conformity," for example, bears a strong resemblance to the MMPI Pd scale, "Adjustment to Reality" to the Sc scale.
There are also two verification scores, similar to MMPI validity scales. Total
scores on the different scales were validated by comparing random samples
of students with groups nominated by teachers as outstanding examples of
the trait in question. Split-half and retest reliabilities are satisfactory, but
some of the scale intercorrelations are about as high as their reliability coefficients. The seven scores are thus not as distinct as their titles imply. Literal interpretation of some of the scales, moreover, would be misleading.
The inventory should be used only by counselors who are sufficiently familiar
with its construction to evaluate scores properly.

As a final example, mention may be made of the California Psychological
Inventory (44), which has been described as "the sane man's MMPI."
Drawing about half of its items from the MMPI, this inventory provides 15
scales derived largely by criterion keying, together with three verification
scales. Items were selected in terms of such criteria as course grades, participation in extracurricular activities, prominence as a leader, and ratings for
various traits. Examples of the scales include dominance, sociability, sense of
well-being, self-control, tolerance, achievement via conformance, achievement

via independence, and flexibility. Standard score norms on over six thousand cases of each sex are provided. Data are reported on retest but not on split-half reliability. High intercorrelations of scales indicate considerable overlap and redundancy. Cross-validation of scale scores against appropriate criteria have yielded rather low correlations. Major emphasis is placed on the interpretation of composite profiles, but the procedures suggested for this purpose are still quite subjective. In its present form, this inventory should be used only by persons well trained in counseling or clinical psychology.

FACTOR ANALYSIS IN TEST DEVELOPMENT

In the effort to arrive at a more systematic classification of personality traits, a number of psychologists have turned to factor analysis. A series of studies by Guilford and his co-workers represents one of the pioneer ventures in this direction (cf. 46, 48). Rather than correlating total scores on existing inventories, these investigators computed the intercorrelations among individual items from many personality inventories. As a by-product of this research, three personality inventories were developed: Inventory of Factors STDCR, Guilford-Martin Inventory of Factors GAMIN, and Guilford-Martin Personnel Inventory. After combining two highly correlated factors to avoid duplication and redefining other factors, a single 10-factor inventory was prepared, known as the Guilford-Zimmerman Temperament Survey (47). This inventory yields separate scores for the following traits, each score based on 30 different items:

G. *General Activity:* Hurrying, liking for speed, liveliness, vitality, production, efficiency vs. slow and deliberate, easily fatigued, inefficient.

R. *Restraint:* Serious-minded, deliberate, persistent vs. carefree, impulsive, excitement-loving.

A. *Ascendance:* Self-defense, leadership, speaking in public, bluffing vs. submissiveness, hesitation, avoiding conspicuousness.

S. *Sociability:* Having many friends, seeking social contacts and limelight vs. few friends and shyness.

E. *Emotional Stability:* Evenness of moods, optimistic, composure vs. fluctuation of moods, pessimism, daydreaming, excitability, feelings of guilt, worry, loneliness, and ill health.

O. *Objectivity:* Thick-skinned vs. hypersensitive, self-centered, suspicious, having ideas of reference, getting into trouble.

F. *Friendliness:* Toleration of hostile action, acceptance of domination, respect for others vs. belligerence, hostility, resentment, desire to dominate, and contempt for others.

T. *Thoughtfulness:* Reflective, observing of self and others, mental poise vs. interest in overt activity and mental disconcertedness.

P. *Personal Relations:* Tolerance of people, faith in social institutions vs. fault-finding, critical of institutions, suspicious, self-pitying.

M. *Masculinity:* Interest in masculine activities, not easily disgusted, hard-boiled, inhibits emotional expression, little interest in clothes and style vs. interest in feminine activities and vocations, easily disgusted, fearful, romantic, emotionally expressive.

The items in the Guilford-Zimmerman Temperament Survey are expressed in the form of affirmative statements, rather than questions. Most concern the examinee directly. A few represent generalizations about other persons. Three examples are given below:

You start work on a new project with a great deal of enthusiasm .... YES   ?   NO

You are often in low spirits .... YES   ?   NO

Most people use politeness to cover up what is really "cut-throat" competition .... YES   ?   NO

The affirmative item form was chosen in the effort to reduce the resistance that a series of direct questions is likely to arouse. In addition, three verification keys are provided to detect falsification and carelessness of response.

Percentile and standard score norms were derived chiefly from college samples. Attention is called to the desirability of interpreting not only single-trait scores but also total profiles. For example, a high score in Emotional Stability is favorable if coupled with a high General Activity score, but may be unfavorable if it occurs in combination with a low General Activity score. In the latter case, the individual may be sluggish, phlegmatic, or lazy. Split-half reliabilities of separate factor scores range from .75 to .85. Higher reliabilities would of course be desirable for the differential interpretation of individual profiles. Similarly, although an effort was made to obtain independent, uncorrelated trait categories, some of the intercorrelations among the 10 traits are still appreciable. Originally presented only on the basis of its factorial validity, the inventory has subsequently been employed in scattered studies of empirical validity, with varied results.

A re-analysis of Guilford's original factorial data led Thurstone (80) to the conclusion that seven major factors would suffice to account for the obtained intercorrelations. In order to measure these seven factors, Thurstone gathered items from a large number of available inventories. Only items pertaining to the behavior of relatively normal persons were included. Items dealing with abnormal or psychiatric classifications and those designed to detect maladjustment were eliminated. After tentative keys had been developed for each of the seven traits, a final set of 20 items for each trait was selected by the method of internal consistency. The resulting inventory, known as the Thurstone Temperament Schedule (79), yields scores in the following traits: Active, Vigorous, Impulsive, Dominant, Stable, Sociable, and Reflective.

Percentile norms are reported for high school and college populations. Reliabilities of separate trait scores are generally low. Only one trait, Dominant, yielded reliabilities in the .80's. All others are below .80, some being in the .40's. The reported intercorrelations of trait scores are low or negligible, with one or two exceptions. Most of the trait categories thus appear to be sufficiently independent for profile interpretation. But the reliabilities fall short of the desirable level for this purpose. A number of concurrent validity studies, chiefly on employee groups, indicate some validity for individual scales against various job-performance and rating criteria.

A somewhat different application of factorial methods to the construction of personality inventories is to be found in the work of Cattell (19, 20). In the effort to arrive at a comprehensive description of personality, Cattell began by assembling all personality trait names occurring both in the dictionary (as compiled by Allport and Odbert, 5) or in the psychiatric and psychological literature. This list was first reduced to 171 trait names by combining obvious synonyms. The 171-trait list was then employed in obtaining associates' ratings of a heterogeneous group of 100 adults. Intercorrelations and factor analyses of these ratings were followed by further ratings of 208 men on a shortened list. Factorial analyses of the latter ratings led to the identification of what Cattell described as "the primary source traits of personality," a designation that seems to imply more universality and stability of results than appear justified by the antecedent research.

Factors identified through the correlation of ratings may reflect in part the influence of social stereotypes and other constant errors of judgment, rather than the subjects' trait organization. Cattell maintains that his identification of primary personality traits is corroborated by the findings of other studies by himself and other investigators, using not only ratings but also such techniques as questionnaires and objective tests. Some of the alleged similarities in trait descriptions, however, appear forced and not too con-

vincing. It should be recalled that an element of subjectivity is likely to enter
into the identification of factors, since the process depends upon an examination of those measures or items having the highest loadings on each factor
(cf. Ch. 13). Hence the cross-identification of factors from different investigations using different measures is difficult. Despite the extensive research conducted by Cattell and his associates over a period of nearly twenty
years, the traits proposed by Cattell must be regarded as tentative.

On the basis of their factorial research, Cattell and his co-workers have
constructed a number of personality inventories, of which the most comprehensive is the Sixteen Personality Factor Questionnaire (24). Designed for
ages 16 and over, this inventory yields 16 scores in such traits as aloof vs.
warm, emotional vs. calm, submissive vs. dominant, glum vs. enthusiastic,
etc. In addition, a "motivational distortion" or verification key is provided
for one of the forms (C). Owing to the shortness of the scales, reliabilities of
factor scores for any single form are generally low. Even when two forms
are combined, several split-half coefficients fall below .80. Available information on normative samples and other aspects of test construction is inadequate. Empirical validation data include average profiles for various occupational groups and psychiatric syndromes.

A similar inventory suitable for ages 12 to 18 has also been developed
(25), and another for ages 8 to 12 (67). In addition, separate inventories
have been published within more limited areas, including anxiety (21), introversion-extroversion (22), and neuroticism (23). These areas correspond
to certain second-order factors identified among correlated first-order factors.
All of these inventories are experimental instruments requiring further development, standardization, and validation.

Factor analysis provides a technique for grouping personality inventory
items into relatively homogeneous and independent clusters. Such a grouping
should facilitate the investigation of validity against empirical criteria. It
should also permit a more effective combination of scores for the prediction
of specific criteria. Homogeneity and factorial purity are desirable goals in
test construction. But they are not substitutes for empirical validity.

FORCED CHOICE AND THE SOCIAL
DESIRABILITY VARIABLE

The forced-choice technique was simultaneously developed by several
psychologists working in industry or in the armed services during the decade
of the 1940's (cf. 10, 55, 71, 73, 81). Essentially, it requires the subject to
choose between two descriptive terms or phrases that appear equally accept-

able but differ in validity. The paired phrases may both be desirable or both undesirable. A tetrad form of item may also be employed, in which two desirable and two undesirable phrases are included; sometimes a fifth alternative is added, giving a pentad item form. In such cases, the subject must indicate which phrase is most characteristic and which least characteristic of himself. Another variant incorporates three phrases, equated for desirability, from which the subject must choose the most and the least applicable.

The construction of a forced-choice inventory requires two principal types of information regarding each descriptive phrase, viz., its social desirability or "preference index" and its empirical validity or "discriminative index." The latter may be determined on the basis of any specific criterion the inventory is designed to predict, such as academic achievement or success on a particular kind of job. Social desirability can be found by having the items rated for this variable by a representative group, or by ascertaining the frequency with which the item is endorsed in self-descriptions. In a series of studies on many different groups, Edwards (33) has shown that frequency of choice and judged social desirability correlate between .80 and .90. In other words, the *average* self-description of a population agrees closely with its average description of a desirable personality.

Such a relationship cannot be attributed primarily to the deliberate faking of personality test responses, since equally high correlations were found when subjects filled out questionnaires anonymously. To some extent, the correlation reflects a façade effect, or a response set to put up a good front, of which the subject himself may not be fully aware. A more pervasive lack of insight about one's own characteristics and actual self-deception may likewise be involved. It is also likely, of course, that the social stereotype of desirable characteristics in any one culture is affected by the prevalent behavior patterns of its members and vice versa.

In order to investigate further the relation of the social desirability variable (SD) to personality test responses, Edwards (33) developed a special social desirability scale. Beginning with 150 heterogeneous MMPI items taken largely from the three validating keys, Edwards selected 79 items that yielded complete agreement among judges with regard to social desirability ratings. Through item analyses against total scores in this preliminary scale, he shortened the list to 39 items. This SD scale correlated .81 with the K scale of the MMPI, partly because of common items between the two scales. Individual scores on this scale can be correlated with scores on any personality test as a check on the degree to which the social desirability variable has been ruled out of test responses. Whatever the cause of the relation, in so far as social desirability is correlated with test scores the effectiveness of the test in discriminating individual differences in other traits is reduced. To be sure, the individual's SD score may be useful in its own right for diagnostic or predictive purposes. But the score should be recognized as such, rather than being misinterpreted as a measure of some other variable.

One way of reducing the contribution of the social desirability variable in personality test scores is through the use of the forced-choice technique. If the paired alternatives are truly equated in social desirability for the population in question, the opportunity for dissembling and faking is minimized. This is one of the principal appeals of the forced-choice item form, especially in industrial and military situations. At the same time, it cannot be assumed that the perceived desirability of items remains unchanged for all purposes. The relative desirability of the same items for salesmen or for physicians, for example, may differ from their desirability when judged in terms of general cultural norms. Thus a forced-choice test whose items were equated in general social desirability could still be faked when taken by job applicants, candidates for admission to professional schools, and other specifically oriented groups. It is possible, of course, to devise more subtle items which can be equated in frequency of choice within specific groups.

The forced-choice technique may also serve to reduce ambiguity and related difficulties in the interpretation of items. For example, in the traditional "Yes-No" type of item, many subjects experience difficulty in choosing a response alternative because their characteristic behavior appears to fall between the clear-cut "Yes" and "No" answers. Nor is the inclusion of a "?" category a very satisfactory solution, since such a response may indicate failure to understand the question, uncertainty, inapplicability of the item, or any intermediate degree of the behavior under consideration. The use of terms designating amount, degree, or frequency is also open to ambiguity of interpretation. It has been demonstrated, for example, that subjects differ widely in the meanings which they attach to such terms as "often," "frequently," "usually," "rarely," and the like (72). By requiring a relative rather than an absolute judgment, the forced-choice technique reduces these sources of ambiguity. In this item form, the individual is called upon to state only which of two descriptions is more nearly applicable to himself.

The forced-choice technique was utilized in the development of the Jurgensen Classification Inventoy (55, 56). Designed especially for industrial application, this inventory provides no general norms or scoring key. Test users are expected to develop scoring keys by empirical tryout against local criteria. The manual describes the steps that should normally be followed in such criterion keying of test items, and furnishes many helpful suggestions and aids to facilitate the work.

Essentially this process involves the determination of a discriminative index for each response and the assignment of scoring weights on this basis. These weights can be positive, negative, or zero, depending upon whether the given response occurs significantly more often in upper, lower, or neither criterion group. For example, if successful salesmen choose a certain response significantly more often than unsuccessful salesmen, that response would receive a positive weight in the key. In so far as the personality qualifications for different jobs vary widely, the practice of criterion keying against specific job criteria would seem desirable. Many test users, unfortunately, may lack the time or facilities for carrying out the necessary research.

The Jurgensen Classification Inventory was the first commercially available inventory to employ the forced-choice technique. Its items pertain to the kinds of persons the subject regards as most and least irritating, the ways in which he would most prefer and least prefer to be considered by others, personal likes and dislikes, preferred activities or modes of behavior, and the types of persons the subject dislikes. Sample items from this inventory are reproduced below, together with abridged instructions:

Mark the one which you think is MOST irritating and the one which you think is LEAST irritating.

    People who are

        Bluffers..M   L

        Complainers.......................................M   L

        Interrupters ....M   L

Decide which reputation you would MOST prefer to have, and which you would LEAST prefer to have.

    Considered

        Calm..M   L

        Alert ....M   L

        Friendly ....M   L

Mark the item you prefer, using XX if your preference is strong, and X if it is weak.

    Have interesting work with moderate pay ———

    Have uninteresting work with high pay ———

Another example of forced-choice technique is provided by the Personal Inventory (PI), developed by Shipley and his associates during World War II (71). This instrument was employed as a psychiatric screening device by the Navy. Each item consisted of a pair of statements, the subject being required to check the alternative that better described him. The items were paired so as to be approximately equated in social acceptance but sharply contrasted in frequency of choice by emotionally maladjusted and normal subjects. Psychiatric diagnosis provided the criterion for the latter purpose.

Two short inventories employing forced-choice items are the Gordon Personal Profile (42) and the Gordon Personal Inventory (43). The items in these inventories were chosen by means of factor analyses to measure eight personality traits. The traits included in the Profile are designated as Ascendancy, Responsibility, Emotional Stability, and Sociability; those included in the Inventory, as Cautiousness, Original Thinking, Personal Relations, and Vigor. In addition, an over-all adjustment score may be computed from the Profile. In both tests, each item contains four statements, corresponding to the four traits being measured. The subject indicates which of the four statements is most like him, and which least like him. A typical item from the Gordon Personal Profile is given below:

Able to make important decisions without help.

Does not mix easily with new people.

Inclined to be tense or high-strung.

Sees a job through despite difficulties.

Retest and internal-consistency reliabilities of the eight factor scores fall mostly in the .80's. Some appreciable intercorrelations among factor scores remain. Empirical validity data are promising but meager for the Profile and as yet unavailable for the more recently published Inventory.

The most ambitious attempt to measure the effect of the social desirability variable in a personality inventory and to control its operation by means of the forced-choice technique is to be found in the Edwards Personal Preference Schedule (32). Since this test also illustrates the use of personality theory in test construction, further discussion of it will be postponed until the next section.

Mention should likewise be made of the application of the forced-choice technique to the construction of *rating scales*. This type of rating scale has been developed for use by supervisors in the merit rating of industrial employees, as well as in the evaluation of military officers (10, 73, 81). Although useful in certain situations, the forced-choice technique has proved less effective when applied to ratings than to self-report inventories. One reason is that these ratings are assigned in very specific contexts. In addition, the experienced supervisors who use such rating scales are better able to "break the key" than is the case with most examinees (59, 81). Owing to his greater job familiarity, the supervisor is more likely to recognize the differential validity or job relevance of alternate items. This opens the way for intentional or unintentional bias to affect the ratings. It is just the operation of such rater bias that the forced-choice technique was designed to minimize. There is empirical evidence, however, that supervisors can, when so directed, alter the ratings on a forced-choice scale in either a favorable or unfavorable direction. Moreover, the more able supervisors tend to be more successful in thus "breaking the key."

To be sure, the forced-choice technique may still reduce—although it does not eliminate—the operation of rater bias. Moreover, it may be possible to formulate more subtle items, whose face validity is approximately equated even for experienced supervisors. The forced-choice technique simply raises the level of sophistication needed to "break the key." It does not eliminate the possibility of so doing.

PERSONALITY THEORY IN TEST DEVELOPMENT

Personality theories have usually originated in clinical settings. The amount of experimental verification to which they have subsequently been subjected varies tremendously from one theoretical system to another. Regardless of the extent of such objective verification, a number of personality tests have been constructed within the framework of one or another personality theory. Clinically formulated hypotheses have been especially prominent in the development of projective techniques, to be considered in Chapter 20. Among the personality theories that have stimulated test development, one of the most prolific has been the manifest need system proposed by H. A. Murray and his associates at the Harvard Psychological Clinic (64). The most comprehensive inventory designed to assess the strength of such needs is the Edwards Personal Preference Schedule (32).

Beginning with 15 needs drawn from Murray's list, Edwards prepared sets of items whose content appeared to fit each of these needs. When these items were administered in traditional "Yes-No" form to a group of college students, frequency of endorsement correlated .87 with the judged social desirability (SD) of the items. As a result, Edwards adopted the forced-choice format, placing in each pair items that were matched in SD. Several independent experiments demonstrated that, when judged in terms of general cultural norms, the SD of items remains remarkably stable in groups differing in sex, age, education, socioeconomic level, or nationality (33). Consistent results were also obtained when the judgments of hospitalized psychiatric patients were compared with those of normal groups.

Edwards, however, did not recheck the SD scale values of his statements when presented in pairs. Later research suggested that the SD values do change under these conditions (28). Not only are there significant differences in SD scale values of paired items, but a correlation of .88 was found between the redetermined scale values of paired items and their frequency of endorsement. It is also relevant to note that studies on faking indicate that scores on the EPPS *can* be deliberately altered to create more favorable impressions, especially for specific purposes (17, 30). The latter possibility, of course, exists in any forced-choice test in which items were equated in terms of general social norms only. On the whole, it appears that the social desirability variable was not as fully controlled in the EPPS as had been anticipated.

Correlations of the 15 EPPS scores with the social desirability scale, however, are lower than those of other inventories. Only two of the EPPS correlations were significant (at the .05 level) and these were low (.32). With such tests as the MMPI and the Guilford-Zimmerman, on the other hand, the SD scale yielded a number of correlations between .50 and .80 (32, 33).

The 15 needs covered by the EPPS, together with abbreviated descriptions of each, are as follows:

Achievement: To do one's best, to accomplish something very difficult or significant.

Deference: To let others make decisions, to conform to what is expected of one.

Order: To have regular times and ways for doing things, to keep things neat and well organized.

Exhibition: To be the center of attention, to say witty things or talk about personal achievements.

Autonomy: To be independent of others in making decisions, to avoid responsibilities and obligations.

Affiliation: To be loyal, to participate in friendly groups, to share or do things with friends.

Intraception: To analyze one's motives and feelings, to observe and understand the feelings of others.

Succorance: To receive help or affection from others, to have others be sympathetic and understanding.

Dominance: To persuade and influence others, to supervise others, to be regarded as a leader.

Abasement: To feel guilty when one has done wrong, to accept blame, to feel timid or inferior.

Nurturance: To help friends or others in trouble, to forgive others, to be generous with others.

Change: To do new and different things, to meet new people, to take up new fads and fashions.

Endurance: To keep at a job until it is finished, to avoid being interrupted while hard at work.

Heterosexuality: To go out with or be in love with one of the opposite sex, to tell or listen to sex jokes.

Aggression: To attack contrary points of view, to become angry, to make fun of others or tell them off.

The inventory consists of 210 different pairs of forced-choice statements, in which items from each of the 15 scales are paired off twice against items from the other 14. In addition, 15 pairs are repeated in identical form to provide an index of respondent consistency. A profile stability score can also be found by correlating the individual's odd and even scores in the 15 variables. Both percentile and T-score norms are provided for college men ($N = 749$) and college women ($N = 760$), based on students in 29 colleges scattered over the country. Additional percentile norms are provided from a general adult sample, including 4031 men and 4932 women. Drawn from urban and rural areas in 48 states, these respondents constituted a consumer-purchase panel used for market surveys (58). The need for specific group norms on personality tests is highlighted by the large and significant mean differences found between this consumer panel and the college sample. The normal percentile chart used in plotting individual scores is illustrated in Figure 110.

Retest reliabilities of the 15 scales range from .74 to .88; split-half, from .60 to .87. Score intercorrelations are satisfactorily low, the highest being .46 and many being close to zero. It might be noted parenthetically that many of the intercorrelations are negative—a necessary result of the forced-choice technique. On such a test, it is impossible for an individual to receive a high score or a low score consistently on all variables. What the profile shows is the relative strength of the different needs.

The validity data reported in the manual are so meager and tangential as to be virtually negligible. Since the publication of the test, however, a number of independent studies have contributed information toward the construct validation of several scales. In one such study (15), subjects were

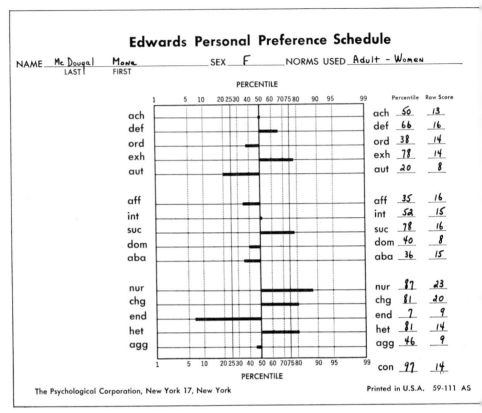

Fig. 110. Profile on the Edwards Personal Preference Schedule. (Reproduced by permission of The Psychological Corporation.)

put through three experimental task situations requiring the explicit demonstration of dependent or independent behavior. Subjects who had scored high on deference and low on autonomy showed more reliance on others for approval and for help. No relationship was found, however, between these scale scores and conformity to the opinions and demands of others. Also relevant to the construct validity of the various scales are a number of significant group differences in mean scores with reference to age, sex, education, socioeconomic level, and other demographic variables (57, 58).

Considerably more information is required for the confident interpretation of EPPS profiles in counseling, selection, and other practical applications. Further work on the control of the social desirability variable, as well as norms on other groups, would also seem desirable. In its present stage, the EPPS is a highly promising research instrument which has contributed several ingenious innovations in test construction.

EVALUATION OF PERSONALITY INVENTORIES

It should now be apparent that the construction and use of personality inventories are beset with special difficulties over and above the common problems encountered in all psychological testing. The question of faking and malingering is far more acute in personality measurement than in aptitude testing. The behavior measured by personality tests is also more changeable than that measured by tests of ability. The latter fact complicates the determination of test reliability, since the stability of the test is likely to become confused with broad, systematic behavioral changes (cf. Ch. 5). Even over relatively short intervals, it cannot be assumed that variations in test response are restricted to the test itself and do not characterize the area of non-test behavior under consideration.

Another problem is presented by the greater specificity of responses in the sphere of personality. For example, an individual might be quite sociable and extroverted at the office, but rather shy and introverted at formal social receptions. Or a student who cheats on examinations might be scrupulously honest in money matters. Such specificity is in turn related to the difficulty of grouping items into clearly defined categories or "personality traits." There is certainly less agreement among the different schemas of classification proposed in the personality than in the aptitude area.

Finally, the search for adequate criterion data for the establishment of validity has generally proved less successful in personality tests. For this reason, personality test constructors have sometimes resorted to such makeshifts as correlations with other tests, internal consistency, or content validity.

To a large extent, the problems cited above are shared by all types of personality tests. But for the present we shall limit our discussion to self-report inventories. The acknowledged deficiencies of current personality inventories may be met in at least two major ways. First, personality inventories may be recognized as intrinsically crude instruments and their application restricted accordingly. Second, various procedures for improving the inventories may be explored. Most psychologists today would probably accept some combination of the two approaches, although a few may align themselves exclusively behind one or the other (cf., e.g., 36, 37, 45, 60, 66).

A specific illustration of the first approach is provided by the use of a personality inventory merely as a springboard for a clinical interview. In such cases, the interviewer might not even score the inventory in the standard manner, but might simply examine the subject's answers with a view to identifying problem areas for further probing during the interview. Other current practices stemming from a recognition of the pitfalls presented by personality inventories pertain to the interpretation of "poor" versus "good" scores, and the use of inventories in counseling versus selection. In most situations a "poor," or unfavorably deviant, score is likely to signify maladjustment, while a "good" score may be ambiguous. It is also evident that the motivation to create a favorable impression is much stronger in the job applicant than in the person seeking help from a counselor or in the subject of a research project (53). Even in the latter situations, however, complete candor cannot be assumed, because of the prevalence of rationalizations, defensive reactions, and other façade effects.

Attempts to improve self-report inventories by direct attack upon the major sources of difficulty have been described throughout this chapter. Among such efforts may be mentioned the application of factor analysis as a means of arriving at more systematic trait categories, the keying of individual items against highly specific criteria, the use of a forced-choice technique, the development of verification and correction scales, and the preparation of "subtle" items whose diagnostic significance is less apparent to the respondent. Such items, for example, may present rationalizations that have been found to be indicative of certain more basic personality traits. It can be readily seen that each of these procedures is directed toward one or more of the special difficulties outlined above.

Personality inventories may also be evaluated at a more basic level, in terms of their theoretical assumptions and underlying rationale. A whole volume could easily be devoted to this discussion. For the present purpose, however, a consideration of two frequently recurring and related questions will suffice. The first concerns the type of information that personality inventories are designed to elicit. The second pertains to the inherent ambiguity of inventory responses.

Because the early personality inventories were designed as a rapid substitute for the psychiatric interview, it is frequently assumed that the response to each question is an index of the presence or absence of the specific symptom or other behavior characteristic described by the question. In the light of the usual procedures for selecting test items and validating the inventories, however, such an assumption appears unwarranted. As in any psychological test, the responses should be operationally interpreted in terms of the criteria against which validity was established (7).

The distinction between these alternative ways of interpreting inventory items has been repeatedly emphasized in the literature (cf., e.g., 19, 35, 60, 61). Various terms have been suggested to differentiate the two types of interpretation. Among them are "factual versus psychological," "veridical versus diagnostic," and "literal versus symptomatic." The already familiar distinction between content validity and the various types of empirical validity may serve in this connection. In effect, the factual-veridical-literal interpretation is based upon the inspectionally determined content validity of the questions, while the psychological-diagnostic-symptomatic interpretation stems from the empirically established relationships of the inventory responses to various appropriate criteria. As Meehl put it, the personality inventory response "constitutes an intrinsically interesting and significant bit of verbal behavior, the non-test correlates of which must be discovered by empirical means" (60, p. 297).

Elsewhere, in characterizing the approach followed in the construction of the MMPI, Meehl wrote,

. . . the verbal type of personality inventory is *not* most fruitfully seen as a "self-rating" or self-description whose value requires the assumption of accuracy on the part of the testee in his observations of self. Rather is the response to a test item taken as an intrinsically interesting segment of verbal behavior, knowledge regarding which may be of more value than any knowledge of the "factual" material about which the item superficially purports to inquire. Thus if a hypochondriac says that he has "many headaches" the fact of interest is that he *says* this (61, p. 9).

In the same vein, Cattell cites the following illustration:

The questionnaire asks, "Would you enjoy being a sailor in a submarine?" If the subject replies "Yes," one does not assume that he would in fact be happy as a sailor in a submarine. One observes, perhaps, that good librarians as opposed to bad librarians more frequently answer "No" to this question, and one uses it empirically as an index of librarianship interests or temperament (19, p. 344).

A self-report inventory is indubitably a series of standardized verbal stimuli. When proper test-construction procedures have been followed, the responses elicited by these stimuli are scored in terms of their empirically established behavior correlates. They are thus treated like any other psychological test responses. That questionnaire responses may correspond to the subject's *perception* of reality (66) does not alter this situation. It merely provides one hypothesis to account for the empirically established validity of certain items.

In line with the empirical validation of personality test responses as such is the research on *response styles* (12, 40, 54). Originally investigated in connection with the development of verification and correction keys, response styles are coming to be regarded as possible diagnostic indicators in their own right, and their validity is being explored from this point of view. Among such response styles are defensiveness, susceptibility to façade effects, and tendency to choose items in terms of their social desirability. Another example is acquiescence, or the inclination to answer affirmatively regardless of the content of the statement. Still another is the tendency to choose atypical responses.

Personality inventories have been vigorously attacked on the grounds that their responses are necessarily ambiguous. A classic exposition of this difficulty was given by Allport, who wrote:

The stimulus-situation is assumed to be identical for each subject, and his response is assumed to have constant significance. A test will assume, for example—and with some justification in terms of statistical probability—that a person who conspicuously takes a front seat at church or at an entertainment should as a rule receive a plus score for ascendance. But the fact of the matter is that this person *may* seek a front seat not because he is ascendant but because he is hard of hearing. Or a test will assume again, with statistical (empirical) justification, that a person who confesses to keeping a diary is introverted; yet upon closer inspection (which no test can give) it may turn out that the diary is almost wholly an expense account, kept not because of introversion but because of money-mindedness. It is a fallacy to assume that all people have the same psychological reasons for their similar responses. At the level of personality it cannot be said with certainty that the same symptoms in two people indicate the same trait, nor that different responses necessarily indicate different traits. All mental tests fail to allow sufficiently for an individual interpretation of cause and effect sequences (3, p. 449).

An empirical demonstration of such response ambiguity was provided in a study by Eisenberg (34). Personality inventory items of the "Yes-?-No" type were administered to 219 college students. Following completion of the inventory, the students were asked to write a sentence or two indicating why they had answered each item as they did. A survey of these explanatory statements revealed a wide range of interpretations for each response. Even more disturbing was the discovery that the identical explanation was sometimes given for opposite answers. For example, to the question "Do you like to be alone?" 55 subjects appended explanations indicating that they liked to be alone when they had work to do, "but not socially." Of these, 18 had marked "Yes" in answering the question, 17 had marked "No," and 20 "?."

It is possible, of course, to reduce the frequency of ambiguous or equivocal responses by formulating items more specifically and clearly. One remedy for the situation obviously lies in this direction. The argument has also been advanced, however, that item vagueness should be retained, since it allows more free play to individual interpretation, which might in turn reflect characteristic attitudes, motives, and emotional states (cf., e.g., 35).

Whether vaguely worded questions yield more or less valid responses on personality inventories can be determined only by empirical correlation with appropriate criteria and by other experimental procedures. It is possible that for the measurement of certain personality characteristics, questions permitting a certain degree of subjectivity of interpretation are more effective. But it would be hazardous to generalize regarding all types of ambiguous items and all personality characteristics.

Apart from practical problems of test construction, the prevalence of response ambiguity is itself of theoretical interest. Why is ambiguity a more serious problem in personality testing than in aptitude testing? The answer can be found in the *greater standardization of the individual's reactional biography in the intellectual sphere* (cf. 6). For example, the system of formal education in our culture assures relative uniformity of interpretation for, let us say, vocabulary or arithmetic computation items. But no such fund of common antecedent experience is available for the preparation of personality test items. This difficulty is similar to that encountered in the construction of aptitude tests for infants and young children, who have not yet been exposed to a highly standardized educational curriculum (cf. Ch. 11).

It may be added that the very organization of behavior into traits is affected by the degree of uniformity of the pertinent experiential background (cf. 6). Factor pattern analyses of the emotional and motivational aspects of behavior have generally yielded trait categories that are less consistent and more difficult to interpret than those of aptitudes. This fact has been amply illustrated in this chapter.

Some psychologists have maintained that, in the domain of personality, the individual can be effectively described only in terms of his own peculiar behavior interrelationships, rather than in terms of common traits (cf., e.g., 3). This approach represents an extreme reaction to the relatively unstandardized nature of the emotional and motivational aspects of the individual's reactional biography. It is undoubtedly true that an intensive study of the individual case will yield the richest and most precise picture of the person. But the judicious use of common techniques and normative data should materially aid such an analysis.

REFERENCES

1. Allen, R. M. *Personality assessment procedures: psychometric, projective, and other approaches.* N. Y.: Harper, 1958.

2. Allport, G. W. A test for ascendance-submission. *J. abnorm. soc. Psychol.,* 1928, 23, 118-136.

3. Allport, G. W. *Personality: a psychological interpretation.* N. Y.: Holt, Rinehart and Winston, 1937.

4. Allport, G. W., and Allport, F. H. *A-S Reaction Study.* Boston: Houghton Mifflin, 1928-1939.

5. Allport, G. W., and Odbert, H. S. Trait-names, a psycholexical study. *Psychol. Monogr.,* 1936, 47.

6. Anastasi, Anne. The nature of psychological "traits." *Psychol. Rev.,* 1948, 55, 127-138.

7. Anastasi, Anne. The concept of validity in the interpretation of test scores. *Educ. psychol. Measmt.,* 1950, 10, 67-78.

8. Anastasi, Anne. *Differential psychology.* (3rd ed.) N. Y.: Macmillan, 1958.

9. Anderson, W. The MMPI: low Pa scores. *J. counsel. Psychol.,* 1956, 3, 226-228.

10. Baier, D. E. Reply to Travers' "A critical review of the validity and rationale of the forced-choice technique." *Psychol. Bull.,* 1951, 48, 421-434.

11. Banks, Charlotte, and Keir, Gertrude. A factorial analysis of items in the Bernreuter Personality Inventory. *Brit. J. Psychol., Stat. Sect.,* 1952, 5, 19-30.

12. Barnes, E. H. Response bias and the MMPI. *J. consult. Psychol.,* 1956, 20, 371-374.

13. Bell, H. M. *The Adjustment Inventory.* Palo Alto, Calif.: Consulting Psychologists Press, 1934-1939.

14. Berdie, R. F., and Layton, W. L. *Minnesota Counseling Inventory.* N. Y.: Psychol. Corp., 1953-1957.

15. Bernadin, A. C., and Jessor, R. A construct validation of the Edwards Personal Preference Schedule with respect to dependency. *J. consult. Psychol.,* 1957, 21, 63-67.

16. Bernreuter, R. G. *The Personality Inventory.* Palo Alto, Calif.: Consulting Psychologists Press, 1935-1938.

17. Borislow, B. The Edwards Personal Preference Schedule (EPPS) and fakability. *J. appl. Psychol.,* 1958, 42, 22-27.

18. Castaneda, A., McCandless, B. R., and Palermo, D. S. The children's form of the Manifest Anxiety Scale. *Child Develpm.,* 1956, 27, 317-327.

19. Cattell, R. B. *Description and measurement of personality.* Tarrytown-on-Hudson, N. Y.: World Book Co., 1946.

20. Cattell, R. B. *Personality and motivation structure and measurement.* Tarrytown-on-Hudson, N. Y.: World Book Co., 1957.

21. Cattell, R. B. *The IPAT Anxiety Scale.* Champaign, Ill.: Inst. Pers. Abil. Test., 1957.

22. Cattell, R. B., *et al. Contact Personality Factor Test.* Champaign, Ill.: Inst. Pers. Abil. Test., 1954-1956.

23. Cattell, R. B., *et al. IPAT Neurotic Personality Factor Test.* Champaign, Ill.: Inst. Pers. Abil. Test., 1955.

24. Cattell, R. B., *et al. Sixteen Personality Factor Questionnaire.* (Rev. ed.) Champaign, Ill.: Inst. Pers. Abil. Test., 1956-1957.

25. Cattell, R. B., *et al. IPAT High School Personality Questionnaire.* (Formerly

called The IPAT Junior Personality Quiz.) Champaign, Ill.: Inst. Pers. Abil. Test., 1958.

26. Clark, J. H. The interpretation of the MMPI profiles of college students; mean scores for male and female groups. *J. soc. Psychol.,* 1954, 40, 319-321.

27. Comrey, A. L. Comparison of two analytic rotation procedures. *Psychol. Rep.,* 1959, 5, 201-209. (Contains references to earlier articles in the series of factorial analyses of MMPI scales.)

28. Corah, M. L., *et al.* Social desirability as a variable in the Edwards Personal Preference Schedule. *J. consult. Psychol.,* 1958, 22, 70-72.

29. Dahlstrom, W. G., and Welsh, G. S. *An MMPI handbook: a guide to use in clinical practice and research.* Minneapolis: Univer. Minn. Press, 1960.

30. Dicken, C. F. Simulated patterns on the Edwards Personal Preference Schedule. *J. appl. Psychol.,* 1959, 43, 372-378.

31. Drake, L. E., and Oetting, E. R. *An MMPI codebook for counselors.* Minneapolis: Univer. Minn. Press, 1959.

32. Edwards, A. L. *Edwards Personal Preference Schedule.* N. Y.: Psychol. Corp., 1953-1959.

33. Edwards, A. L. *The social desirability variable in personality assessment and research.* N. Y.: Dryden, 1957.

34. Eisenberg, P. Individual interpretation of psychoneurotic inventory items. *J. gen. Psychol.,* 1941, 25, 19-40.

35. Elias, G. Self-evaluation questionnaires as projective measures of personality. *J. consult. Psychol.,* 1951, 15, 496-500.

36. Ellis, A. The validity of personality questionnaires. *Psychol. Bull.,* 1946, 43, 385-440.

37. Ellis, A. Recent research with personality inventories. *J. consult. Psychol.,* 1953, 17, 45-49.

38. Flanagan, J. C. *Factor analysis in the study of personality.* Stanford Univer., Calif.: Stanford Univer. Press, 1935.

39. Franz, S. I. *Handbook of mental examination methods.* (2nd Ed.) N. Y.: Macmillan, 1919.

40. Fulkerson, S. C. An acquiescence key for the MMPI. *USAF Sch. Aviat. Med. Rep.,* 1958, No. 58-71.

41. Gilliland, A. R., and Colgin, R. Norms, reliability, and forms of the MMPI. *J. consult. Psychol.,* 1951, 15, 435-438.

42. Gordon, L. V. *Gordon Personal Profile.* Tarrytown-on-Hudson, N. Y.: World Book Co., 1953-1954.

43. Gordon, L. V. *Gordon Personal Inventory.* Tarrytown-on-Hudson, N. Y.: World Book Co., 1956.

44. Gough, H. G. *California Psychological Inventory.* Palo Alto, Calif.: Consulting Psychologists Press, 1956-1957.

45. Guilford, J. P. New standards for test evaluation. *Educ. psychol. Measmt.,* 1946, 6, 427-438.

46. Guilford, J. P. *Personality.* N. Y.: McGraw-Hill, 1959.

47. Guilford, J. P., and Zimmerman, W. S. *The Guilford-Zimmerman Temperament Survey.* Beverly Hills, Calif.: Sheridan Supply Co., 1949-1955.

48. Guilford, J. P., and Zimmerman, W. S. Fourteen dimensions of temperament. *Psychol. Monogr.*, 1956, 70, No. 10.

49. Hathaway, S. R., and Briggs, P. F. Some normative data on new MMPI scales. *J. clin. Psychol.*, 1957, 13, 364-368.

50. Hathaway, S. R., and McKinley, J. C. *Minnesota Multiphasic Personality Inventory, Revised Edition*, N. Y.: Psychol. Corp., 1951.

51. Hathaway, S. R., and Meehl, P. E. *An atlas for the clinical use of the MMPI.* Minneapolis: Univer. Minn. Press, 1951.

52. Hathaway, S. R., and Monachesi, E. D. *Analyzing and predicting juvenile delinquency with the MMPI.* Minneapolis: Univer. Minn. Press, 1953.

53. Heron, A. The effects of real-life motivation on questionnaire response. *J. appl. Psychol.*, 1956, 40, 65-68.

54. Jackson, D. N., and Messick, S. Content and style in personality assessment. *Psychol. Bull.*, 1958, 55, 243-252.

55. Jurgensen, C. E. Report on the "classification inventory," a personality test for industrial use. *J. appl. Psychol.*, 1944, 28, 445-460.

56. Jurgensen, C. E. *Jurgensen Classification Inventory.* Minneapolis: Author, 1947-1950.

57. Klett, C. J. Performance of high school students on the Edwards Personal Preference Schedule. *J. consult. Psychol.*, 1957, 21, 68-72.

58. Koponen, A. The influence of demographic factors on responses to the Edwards Personal Preference Schedule. Unpublished doctoral dissertation, Columbia Univer., 1957.

59. McDonnell, M. J. An investigation of the relationship between competence of raters and their ability to discern the forced-choice key. Unpublished master's dissertation, Fordham Univer., 1953.

60. Meehl, P. E. The dynamics of "structured" personality tests. *J. clin. Psychol.*, 1945, 1, 296-303.

61. Meehl, P. E. An investigation of a general normality or control factor in personality testing. *Psychol. Monogr.*, 1945, 59, No. 4.

62. Mees, H. LeR. Preliminary steps in the construction of factor scales for the MMPI. Unpublished Project Rep., Univer. Washington, Seattle, July 1959.

63. Mooney, R. L., and Gordon, L. V. *Mooney Problem Check List: 1950 Revision.* N. Y.: Psychol. Corp., 1950.

64. Murray, H. A., *et al. Explorations in personality.* N. Y.: Oxford Univer. Press, 1938.

65. Panton, J. H. MMPI profile configurations among crime classification groups. *J. clin. Psychol.*, 1958, 14, 305-308.

66. Pinneau, S. R., and Milton, A. The ecological veracity of the self-report. *J. genet. Psychol.*, 1958, 93, 249-276.

67. Porter, R. B., and Cattell, R. B. *IPAT Children's Personality Questionnaire.* Champaign, Ill.: Inst. Pers. Abil. Test., 1960.

68. Remmers, H. H., and Bauernfeind, R. H. *SRA Junior Inventory, Form S.* Chicago: Sci. Res. Assoc., 1957.

69. Remmers, H. H., and Shimberg, B. *SRA Youth Inventory, Form S.* Chicago: Sci. Res. Assoc., 1956-1960.

70. Ruggles, R., and Allport, G. W. Recent applications of the A-S Reaction Study. *J. abnorm. soc. Psychol.*, 1939, 34, 518-528.
71. Shipley, W. C., Gray, F. E., and Newbert, N. The personal inventory. *J. clin. Psychol.*, 1946, 2, 318-322.
72. Simpson, R. H. The specific meanings of certain terms indicating different degrees of frequency. *Quart. J. Speech*, 1944, 30, 328-330.
73. Sisson, D. E. Forced-choice—the new Army rating. *Personnel Psychol.*, 1948, 1, 365-381.
74. Spence, K. W. A theory of emotionally based drive (D) and its relation to performance in simple learning situations. *Amer. Psychologist*, 1958, 13, 131-141.
75. Sundberg, N. D. The use of the MMPI for cross-cultural personality study: a preliminary report on the German translation. *J. abnorm. soc. Psychol.*, 1956, 58, 281-283.
76. Taft, R. A cross-cultural comparison of the MMPI. *J. consult. Psychol.*, 1957, 21, 161-164.
77. Taylor, Janet A. A personality scale of manifest anxiety. *J. abnorm. soc. Psychol.*, 1953, 48, 285-290.
78. Thorpe, L. P., Clark, W. W., and Tiegs, E. W. *California Test of Personality, 1953 Revision*. Monterey, Calif.: Calif. Test Bur., 1953.
79. Thurstone, L. L. *Thurstone Temperament Schedule*. Chicago: Sci. Res. Assoc. 1949-1953.
80. Thurstone, L. L. The dimensions of temperament. *Psychometrika*, 1951, 16, 11-20.
81. Travers, R. M. W. A critical review of the validity and rationale of the forced-choice technique. *Psychol. Bull.*, 1951, 48, 62-70.
82. Weider, A. (Ed.) *Contributions toward medical psychology*. Vol. II. N. Y.: Ronald, 1953.
83. Welsh, G. S., and Dahlstrom, W. G. (Eds.) *Basic readings on the MMPI in psychology and medicine*. Minneapolis: Univer. Minn. Press, 1956.

CHAPTER 19

Measures of Interests and Attitudes

The strength and direction of the individual's interests, attitudes, motives, values, and related variables represent an important aspect of his personality. These characteristics materially affect his educational and vocational adjustment, his interpersonal relations, the enjoyment he derives from his avocational pursuits, and other major phases of his daily living. Although certain tests are specifically directed toward the measurement of one or another of these variables, the available instruments cannot be rigidly classified according to such discrete categories as interests, attitudes, values, and the like. Overlapping is the rule. Thus a questionnaire designed to assess the relative strength of different values, such as the practical, aesthetic, or intellectual, may have much in common with interest inventories. Similarly, such a questionnaire might be said to gauge the individual's attitudes toward pure science, art for art's sake, practical applications, and the like.

The study of *interests* has probably received its strongest impetus from vocational and educational counseling. To a slightly lesser extent, the development of tests in this area has also been stimulated by vocational selection and classification. From the viewpoint of both the worker and the employer, a consideration of the individual's interests is of practical significance. Achievement is a resultant of aptitude and interest. Although these two variables are positively correlated, a high level in one does not necessarily imply a superior status in the other. An individual may have sufficient aptitude for success in a certain type of activity—educational, vocational, or recreational—without the corresponding interest. Or he may be interested in work for which he lacks the prerequisite aptitudes. A measure of both types of variables thus permits a more effective prediction of performance than would be possible from either alone.

The assessment of *opinions and attitudes* originated largely as a problem in social psychology. Attitudes toward different groups have obvious impli-

528

cations for intergroup relations. Similarly, the gauging and prediction of public opinion regarding a wide variety of issues, institutions, or practices are of deep concern to the social psychologist, as well as to the practical worker in business, politics, and other applied fields. In recent years, the measurement of opinions and attitudes has also made rapid strides in the areas of market research and employee relations.

In this chapter, we shall examine typical standardized tests designed to measure interests, attitudes, and related aspects of personality. As in the preceding chapter, attention will be focused upon the paper-and-pencil, verbal, group inventory. The majority of interest and attitude measures in current use are of this type. It should be noted, however, that in this area—as in the measurement of all personality characteristics—other approaches are being increasingly explored. A consideration of non-inventory techniques will be reserved for Chapters 20 and 21.

INTEREST TESTS

It would seem that the most expedient and direct way of determining an individual's interests in different types of work, educational curricula, or recreational activities would be simply to ask him. But there is a vast array of data, gathered chiefly in the 1920's, which shows that answers to direct questions about interests are often unreliable, superficial, and unrealistic (cf. 27, Ch. 5). This is particularly true of children and young people at the ages when information regarding interests is especially useful for counseling purposes.

The reasons for this situation are not hard to find. In the first place, most persons have insufficient information about different jobs, courses of study, and other activities. They are thus unable to judge whether they would really like all that their choice actually involves. Their interest—or lack of interest—in a job may stem from a very limited notion of what the day-by-day work in that field entails. A second, related factor is the prevalence of stereotypes regarding certain vocations. The life of the average doctor, lawyer, or engineer is quite unlike the versions popularized by movies, television, or the less literate magazines. The problem, therefore, is that individuals are rarely in a position to know their own interests in various fields prior to actual participation in those fields. And by the time they have had the benefit of such personal contact, it may be too late to profit from the experience, since a change may be too wasteful.

For this reason, it was soon realized that more indirect and subtle approaches to the determination of interests would have to be explored. One of the most fruitful of these approaches originated in a graduate seminar on interests conducted at the Carnegie Institute of Technology during the academic year 1919-1920 (cf. 27, Ch. 3). Several standardized interest inventories were subsequently prepared as a result of the work begun by their authors while attending this seminar. But the one whose development has been carried furthest is the Vocational Interest Blank (VIB), constructed by E. K. Strong, Jr. (67, 69). Unlike other early tests, the Vocational Interest Blank has undergone continuing research, revision, and extension.

The interest inventories developed by the Carnegie group introduced two principal procedural innovations. First, the items dealt with the subject's liking or dislike for a wide variety of specific activities, objects, or types of persons that he has commonly encountered in daily living. Second, the responses were empirically keyed for different occupations. These interest inventories were thus among the first tests to employ criterion keying of items. It was found that persons engaged in different occupations were characterized by common interests that differentiated them from persons in other occupations. These differences in interests extended not only to matters pertaining directly to job activities, but also to school work, hobbies, sports, types of plays or books the individual enjoyed, social relations, and many other facets of everyday life. It thus proved feasible to question the individual about his interests in relatively familiar things, and thereby determine how closely his interests resembled those of persons successfully engaged in different vocations.

The current form of the Strong VIB consists of 400 items grouped into eight parts. In the first five parts, the subject records his preference by encircling one of the letters L I D, signifying "Like," "Indifferent," and "Dislike," respectively. Each of these five parts is concerned with one of the following five categories: occupations, school subjects, amusements, miscellaneous activities (such as making a speech, repairing a clock, or expressing judgments publicly regardless of criticism), and peculiarities of people. The remaining three parts of the VIB require the subject to rank given activities in order of preference, compare his interest in pairs of items, and rate his present abilities and other characteristics.

The blank is scored with a different key for each occupation. To date, 47 occupational keys are available for scoring the men's form, and 28 for the women's form. New keys are developed from time to time, as data on other occupational groups are gathered. In the development of these occupational scoring keys, the responses of persons successfully engaged in each occupation were compared with those of "men-in-general" (or "women-in-general"). The general reference group consisted of a representative sample of professional and business men.[1] The choice of reference group was based upon the fact that most of the occupational keys dealt with professions and higher business positions. The use of a reference group representative of the total male population proved less effective in bringing out the differentiating interests of the individual occupations. The interests of professional and business men as a group differ so much from those of skilled laborers that the differences between one high-level occupation and another were obscured when the more general reference group was employed. For the same reason, the few available keys for lower-level occupations are not as discriminative as they might be if the reference group had been closer to the socioeconomic level of the occupations concerned (68, Ch. 21 and 22).

It should be noted, however, that other efforts to develop vocational interest scales for lower-level occupations have failed below the skilled-trades level (17). Workers in semiskilled and unskilled jobs seem to be as interchangeable with regard to interests as they are with regard to abilities. There is also extensive evidence to show that at higher levels of the occupational hierarchy (professional, managerial, etc.) job satisfaction is derived chiefly from intrinsic liking for the work, while at the lower levels there is increasing reliance on such extrinsic factors as pay, security, social contacts, and recognition as a person (17). The measurement of vocational interest patterns thus becomes less relevant as we go down the occupational hierarchy.

In the development of the Strong VIB keys, the relative frequencies of each response among, let us say, engineers and men-in-general determined the weight given to that response in the engineer key. These weights can vary from -4 to $+4$. A positive weight indicates that the response occurs more frequently among engineers than among men-in-general, the greater the difference in frequency the higher the weight. A zero weight means that the response fails to differentiate engineers from men-in-general. And a negative weight is assigned to responses obtained less frequently from engineers than from men-in-general. The computation of scoring weights for the first 10 items on the engineer key is illustrated in Table 24. It will be noted that an L response to the item "author of a technical book" receives a weight of $+3$, while a D response to the same item has a weight of -2. An L response to "auctioneer," on the other hand, is scored -1; and a D response, $+2$.

Parenthetically, it might be objected that in Part I of the Strong test, from which the items in Table 24 were taken, the subject is asked to express his interest in many occupations about which he may have little knowledge. But these responses, like all others in the test, are evaluated in terms of their

---

[1] The women-in-general group included samples of professional and business women, as well as a relatively large representation of housewives (68, p. 714).

empirically established correlates, rather than as a direct index of interest in the occupation specified. This interpretation will be recognized as the "symptomatic" treatment of responses which was discussed in the preceding chapter. What may often be obtained in these occupational preference items is the individual's response to the social stereotype evoked by each occupational name. Whether or not these responses have differential significance for different criterion groups is then empirically determined.

TABLE 24.   **Determination of Scoring Weights for Strong Vocational Interest Blank:**
Sample Items from Engineer Key
(From Strong, 68, p. 75)

First Ten Items on Vocational Interest Blank	Percentage of Men Giving Each Response among:						Differences in Percentage between Engineers and "Men-in-General"			Scoring Weights for Engineer Scale		
	"Men-in-General"			Engineers								
	L	I	D	L	I	D	L	I	D	L	I	D
Actor (not movie)	21	32	47	9	31	60	−12	− 1	+13	−1	0	1
Advertiser	33	38	29	14	37	49	−19	− 1	+20	−2	0	2
Architect	37	40	23	58	32	10	+21	− 8	−13	2	−1	−1
Army officer	22	29	49	31	33	36	+ 9	+ 4	−13	1	0	−1
Artist	24	40	36	28	39	33	+ 4	− 1	− 3	0	0	0
Astronomer	26	44	30	38	44	18	+12	0	−12	1	0	−1
Athletic director	26	41	33	15	51	34	−11	+10	+ 1	−1	1	0
Auctioneer	8	27	65	1	16	83	− 7	−11	+18	−1	−1	2
Author of novel	32	38	30	22	44	34	−10	+ 6	+ 4	−1	1	0
Author of technical book	31	41	28	59	32	9	+28	− 9	−19	3	− 1	−2

The total score on each occupational key is simply the algebraic sum of all item weights. Percentile and standard score norms are reported for each occupational group. To simplify interpretation, Strong also gives letter ratings corresponding to certain portions of the standard score distribution. Thus an "A" rating represents a score at or above −½SD, i.e., a point above which approximately 69 per cent of the occupational group in question scored. Similarly, the lower boundary for a "B" rating is set at −2SD, and scores below −2SD are rated "C." A rating of "C" would thus mean that the individual obtained a lower score on that particular key than about 98 per cent of the corresponding occupational sample. It must be borne in mind that a high score on any VIB key simply indicates close resemblance to the interests of persons engaged in that occupation. The test does not, of course, attempt to measure aptitudes for any vocation.

An individual's Vocational Interest Blank could be scored for a single occupation. For selection purposes, for example, we might want to know how closely the applicant's interests resemble those of successful real estate salesmen. More often, however, the blank is scored with most—if not all—available keys. With the resulting set of scores, it is possible to examine the patterning of the individual's interests. This type of analysis provides a more dependable prediction of the individual's reaction to any given type of work. For counseling purposes, a consideration of the entire interest profile is of prime importance.

Group keys are also available for certain interest clusters. These clusters were identified from the correlations of scores on the various occupational keys and were later corroborated by factor analysis (cf. 68, Ch. 8, 9, 14). For example, one cluster—apparently characterized by a common interest in "uplift" or social betterment—includes YMCA physical director, personnel manager, public administrator, YMCA secretary, social science high school teacher, city school superintendent, and minister. Another group comprises physicist, chemist, mathematician, and engineer. And still another consists of sales manager, real estate salesman, and life insurance salesman. Similar groupings are provided for the women's form. But owing to the smaller number of available keys, the classification of women's occupations is much more tentative than that of men's occupations.

A list of the men's occupations falling within each of the groups identified to date can be found on the Report Blank, reproduced in Figure 111. This blank shows the standard scores corresponding to each letter rating. In addition, the stippled area across from each occupation indicates the range of scores that are likely to result from chance on that occupational key. This range was determined by dice throwing and centers around raw scores of zero. The stippled area covers ± 1 *SD,* or the middle 68 per cent of scores in the chance distribution. Scores falling within the stippled area signify neither clear-cut agreement nor disagreement with the interests of persons in the given occupations. For illustrative purposes, the profile of a group of medical students has been plotted in Figure 111. This profile shows the mean standard score of 47 medical students on each of the occupational keys available at the time of testing.

In general, an examination of the individual's score pattern on separate occupational keys is to be preferred to the use of group scales, since the latter are not equally representative of all their constituent occupations (17). With available electronic scoring equipment, it is now feasible to obtain scores on all keys within a very short time. For certain occupations, the nature of the criterion group employed in developing the key should also be carefully considered. Two studies, for example, have revealed significant group differences in VIB performance among several different types of sales-

Measurement of Personality Traits

Report on Vocational Interest Test for Men
(See other side for explanation)

Name .... Age .... Date .... Agency or school .... Case no. ....

Group	Occupation	Raw Score	Standard Score
I	Artist	32	
	Psychologist (rev.)	29	
	Architect	33	
	Physician (rev.)	46	
	Psychiatrist	—	
	Osteopath	—	
	Dentist	41	
	Veterinarian	—	
II	Physicist	—	
	Chemist	38	
	Mathematician	28	
	Engineer	35	
III	Production Manager	31	
IV	Farmer	37	
	Carpenter	19	
	Printer	33	
	Math. Sci. Teacher	34	
	Policeman	29	
	Forest Service	24	
	Army Officer	—	
	Aviator	—	
V	Y.M.C.A. Phys. Dir.	29	
	Personnel Manager	24	
	Public Administrator	—	
	Vocational Counselor	—	
	Y.M.C.A. Secretary	18	
	Soc. Sci. Teacher	24	
	City School Supt.	21	
	Minister	21	
VI	Musician	34	
VII	C.P.A. Partner	—	
VIII	Senior C.P.A.	26	
	Junior Accountant	22	
	Office Worker	28	
	Purchasing Agent	26	
	Banker	23	
	Mortician	—	
	Pharmacist	—	
IX	Sales Manager	25	
	Real Estate Slsmn.	33	
	Life Insurance Slsmn.	28	
X	Advertising Man	32	
	Lawyer	36	
	Author-Journalist	36	
XI	President	30	
	Occupational Level		
	Masculinity-Femininity		
	Specialization Level		
	Interest Maturity		

Fig. 111. Profile of Medical Students on the Strong Vocational Interest Blank, Showing Mean Standard Scores of 47 Students. Group scales are available for Clusters I, II, V, VIII, IX, and X. (Reproduced by permission of Stanford University Press; data from Strong, 68, p. 421.)

men, in addition to the three broad categories for which separate keys are provided (38, 86). Such findings are in line with the trend away from the concept of a general sales personality.

In addition to the occupational keys, the VIB can also be scored with special keys for interest maturity, masculinity-femininity, occupational level, and specialization level. The first of these scales differentiates between the interests of 15- and 25-year-old men. Beyond 25, little change in interest scores has been found. Changes are most rapid between 15 and 20. For this reason, scores on the occupational scales are likely to be too low in the case of men under 20 (cf. 68, Ch. 12).

The masculinity-femininity scale shows the degree of similarity of the individual's interests to the interests characteristic of men or of women, respectively. The occupational-level scale measures the difference between the interests of laboring men, on the one hand, and those of business and professional men, on the other. Mean occupational-level scores range from 64 for lawyers to —44 for unskilled laborers. This scale has been interpreted by some investigators as an index of level of aspiration, motivation, or status drive (17, pp. 115-118).

The most recent addition to the group of non-occupational scales consists of a scale for measuring specialization level (71). Originally designed for differentiating between the interests of specialists and general practitioners in medicine, this scale proved to have discriminative value in other fields requiring advanced specialized study. It was therefore released for general use among college men, with the tentative explanation that it indicates whether or not the individual would enjoy advanced study of a type involving narrow specialization. Other scales of more restricted application have been constructed for special purposes. Examples include scales for differentiating specialties within the fields of medicine, psychology, and engineering (70, pp. 159-161). In the construction of such specialty scales, the reference group consists of members of the occupation as a whole, rather than the men-in-general sample.

Odd-even reliabilities of the VIB scales average .88. With one exception, all fall above .80. Long-range retests of men originally tested in college have shown good stability. Over intervals of approximately 18 years, the median retest correlation was .69 (70, p. 63). The scales correlated were those corresponding to each individual's actual occupation at the time of the follow-up. Those scales having the highest odd-even reliabilities also exhibited the highest long-range stability. The stability of interest profiles was also checked. For this purpose, each individual's scores on 34 scales, obtained on the initial test, were correlated with his retest scores on the same 34 scales. Over a 22-

year period, the median correlation for all individuals was .74, again indicating remarkable stability (70, pp. 64-65). In line with the increasing interest in response style, some attention has been given to the relative frequency of likes (L) and dislikes (D) marked by an individual on the VIB. Conspicuous differences in this regard have been found among occupational groups, as reflected in the corresponding keys. That such a response tendency is a fairly stable individual characteristic was demonstrated in an analysis of the Physician key responses of 71 physicians tested in 1927 (as college students) and again in 1949 (80). Over this 22-year period, the L scores correlated .54 and the D scores .62, both coefficients being significant well beyond the .01 level.

From the viewpoint of validity, follow-up studies have also indicated considerable correspondence between initial interest scores and eventual choice of occupation. In terms of expectancy ratios (cf. Ch. 7), the chances are 78:22 that a man with an A rating in an occupation will enter that occupation, and the chances are 83:17 that a man with a C rating will not enter the occupation (70, p. 42). These ratios were computed by checking VIB scores of 663 students with the occupations in which they were engaged 18 years later (70, p. 43). Indices of job satisfaction yielded low but significant correlations with interest scores in the individual's own occupational field. These correlations were about as high with initial interest scores (18 years earlier) as with present retest scores (70, p. 114). All in all, the VIB represents one of the most successful approaches to the measurement of nonintellectual variables.

Another widely used interest test is the Kuder Preference Record—Vocational (40). Developed more recently than the VIB, this test followed a different approach in the selection and scoring of items. Its major purpose was to indicate relative interest in a small number of broad areas, rather than in specific occupations. The items were originally formulated and tentatively grouped on the basis of content validity. This was followed by extensive item analyses on high school and adult groups. The object of such item analyses was the development of item groups showing high internal consistency and low correlations with other groups. This aim was reasonably well fulfilled for most of the scales.

The items in the Kuder—Vocational are of the forced-choice triad type. For each of three activities listed, the respondent indicates which he would like most and which he would like least. Two sample triads are illustrated in Figure 112. The test provides 10 interest scales plus a verification scale for detecting carelessness and failure to follow directions. The interest scales include: Outdoor (agricultural, naturalistic), Mechanical, Computational,

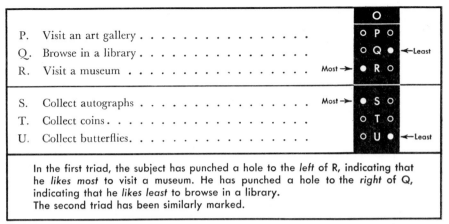

Fig. 112. Sample Items from Kuder Preference Record—Vocational. (Reproduced by permission of Science Research Associates.)

Scientific, Persuasive, Artistic, Literary, Musical, Social Service, and Clerical. Separate sex norms are available for high school, college, and adult groups. Total scores in the 10 interest areas are plotted on a normal percentile chart, as illustrated in Figure 113.

The reliabilities of the Kuder scales, as determined by the Kuder-Richardson technique, cluster around .90. Stability over intervals of about a year or less also appears to be satisfactory. Little information is available regarding stability over longer periods. There is some evidence to suggest that, especially in the case of high school students, shifts in high and low interest areas are relatively frequent when retests are several years apart (34, 49, 55, 60). Studies on the simulation of interest scores have shown that faking is possible to some extent on both the Kuder and the Strong; but visibility is somewhat greater on the Kuder, owing to the more obvious nature of its items (20, 47).

The manual for the Kuder Preference Record provides an extensive list of occupations, grouped according to their major interest area or pair of interest areas. For example, radio operator is classified under Mechanical; landscape architect, under Outdoor-Artistic. This is an a priori listing in terms of logical or content analysis. In addition, a growing list of empirically established occupational profiles has been included in successive revisions of the manual. The data for these average occupational profiles have been contributed largely by test users. Consequently, many of the groups are small and their representativeness or comparability is often questionable. Some attempts have been made to work out a coding system for Kuder profiles (10, 26, 85), similar to that developed for the MMPI. This suggested coding of occupational

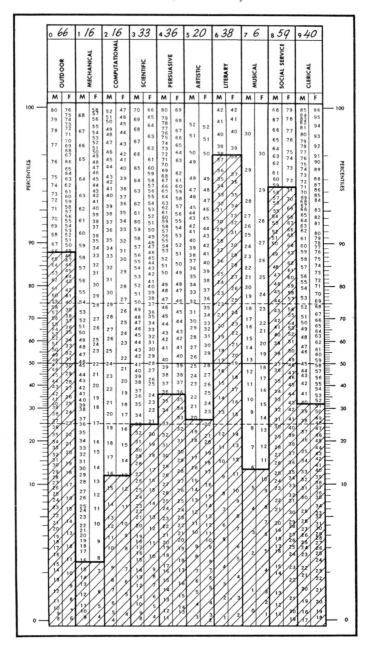

Fig. 113. Profile on Kuder Preference Record—Vocational. (Reproduced by permission of Science Research Associates.)

profiles is based upon empirically established mean scores for each group, rather than upon a priori classifications. Efforts have also been made to develop equations for finding total scores for specific occupations or other criterion groups.

More recently, the Kuder Preference Record—Occupational (42) has been developed through criterion keying procedures similar to those followed in the Strong VIB. Incorporating many items drawn from the earlier, Vocational form, the Kuder—Occupational currently provides 38 occupational scores plus a verification score. Some of the scales are designed for very specifically defined occupational groups, as illustrated by county agricultural agent, counseling psychologist, department store salesman, and radio station manager. Kuder-Richardson reliabilities of individual scales are lower than in the Kuder—Vocational, partly because empirical validity against occupational criteria was given priority over internal consistency in item selection. Median retest reliabilities of .79 and .86 are reported for high school and college samples, respectively. No evidence for long-range stability is given, however. Although the occupational keys were cross-validated on new samples, the available data pertain to concurrent validity only, and not to predictive validity.

It will be noted that recent developments in connection with both the Kuder and Strong inventories have been such as to reduce the initial differences between the approaches of these two instruments to the measurement of interests. On the one hand, occupational-interest clusters, group scales, and profile analysis have broadened the interpretation of VIB scores. On the other hand, occupational scores have been derived for the Kuder—Vocational; and the newly developed Kuder—Occupational has substituted criterion keying against specific occupations for internal consistency of items within broadly defined interest areas.

Still another member of the Kuder family of interest inventories is the Kuder Preference Record—Personal (41). Although developed earlier than the Kuder—Occupational, this inventory has not been widely used and should be considered as an experimental instrument. Again using the triad item form, it provides a verification score and five scores designed to show relative preference for being in groups (Sociable), for familiar and stable situations (Practical), for dealing with ideas (Theoretical), for avoiding conflicts (Agreeable), and for directing others (Dominant). It can be seen that this test cuts across traditional interest areas and some of the personality factors described in the preceding chapter. Correlations with other interest and personality tests, however, raise doubts about the identification of the characteristics measured by the five scales. Certainly the scale labels should not be interpreted literally without considerably more construct validation.

Although the Strong VIB and the Kuder—Vocational are the most widely used instruments for the measurement of interests, many other inventories have been developed. Some are specifically directed toward the appraisal of educational or recreational interests (cf., e.g., 32; 72; 73, Ch. 18). Others have a predominantly vocational slant, like the Strong and Kuder—Occupational. Still others deal with relatively broad interest areas, like the Kuder—Vocational. Well-known examples include the Thurstone Interest Schedule (76), the Guilford-Shneidman-Zimmerman Interest Survey (32), and the Occupational Interest Inventory prepared by Lee and Thorpe (45). In all of these inventories, items were selected and grouped on the basis of their apparent content validity, although internal consistency procedures were followed in the further refinement of scales. All should be regarded as preliminary or experimental instruments.

Corroboration for several of the interest areas covered by the Guilford-Shneidman-Zimmerman Interest Survey was later provided by an extensive factor analysis of interests conducted by Guilford and his associates (30). Based upon the intercorrelations of 95 ten-item interest tests, this study sampled an unusually wide range of interests. The number of subjects was large, including 600 airmen and 720 officer candidates in the Air Force, for whom separate correlation matrices were computed and analyzed. Of the 24 factors identified for airmen and the 23 for officers, 17 were common to both groups. These common factors were described as follows:

A. Mechanical Interest
B. Scientific Interest
C. Adventure vs. Security
D. Social Welfare
E. Aesthetic Appreciation
F. Cultural Conformity
G. Self-Reliance vs. Dependence
H. Aesthetic Expression
I. Clerical Interest
J. Need for Diversion
K. Autistic Thinking
L. Need for Attention
M. Resistance to Restriction
N. Business Interest
O. Outdoor Work Interest
P. Physical Drive
Q. Aggression

Several of these factors suggest the role of culture in structuring interest patterns. A number follow traditional occupational categories characteristic of our society, as illustrated by Mechanical, Scientific, Social Welfare, Clerical, and Business interests. To a lesser extent, this is also true of Aesthetic Appreciation, Aesthetic Expression, and Outdoor Work interests. Certain factors are strongly reminiscent of traits measured by such personality inventories as the Edwards and the MMPI. More will be said about the overlap of interest and "personality" traits in the last section of this chapter.

OPINION AND ATTITUDE SURVEYS

An attitude is often defined as a tendency to react favorably or unfavorably toward a designated class of stimuli, such as a national or racial group, a custom, or an institution. It is evident that, when so defined, attitudes cannot be directly observed, but must be inferred from overt behavior, both verbal and non-verbal (29, Ch. 9; 48). In more objective terms, the concept of attitude may be said to connote response consistency with regard to certain categories of stimuli (11). In actual practice, the term "attitude" has been most frequently associated with social stimuli and with emotionally toned responses.

Opinion is sometimes differentiated from attitude, but the proposed distinctions are neither consistent nor logically defensible. More often the two terms are used interchangeably, and they will be so employed in this discussion. Common usage, however, has popularized the expressions "opinion polling" and "attitude scales" to indicate two distinct methodologies employed in attitude-opinion surveys (48). Although arbitrary, the association of opinions with polls and of attitudes with scales has become conventional.

Opinion polling represents a single-question approach. The answers are usually in the form of "yes" or "no," although an "undecided" category is often included. Sometimes a larger number of response alternatives is provided. In other cases, the subject may be asked to rank items in order of preference. Under special circumstances, the questions may be of the "open-end" type, in which the subject is free to formulate the answer in his own words. Prior to tabulation, the answers to such open-end questions must be coded, or classified on the basis of their essential content. Regardless of the form in which the questions and answers are expressed, the final results are reported in terms of the percentages of persons giving each type of answer.

Attitude scales, on the other hand, yield a score based on the individual's responses to a series of questions pertaining to the issue under investigation. To be sure, opinion polls may also contain more than one question. But the replies to these questions are kept separate rather than being combined. In the construction of an attitude scale, moreover, the different questions are designed to measure a single attitude, or unidimensional variable, and some objective procedures are usually followed in the effort to approximate this goal. The questions used in opinion polls, on the other hand, may be quite unrelated. Attitude scales are also characteristically concerned with intensity of response.

Both polls and attitude scales have been widely used for a variety of purposes. *Public opinion research* is a well-known example (12, 48, 50, 56). Besides the familiar and controversial election forecasts undertaken by commercial pollsters, nationwide polls are carried out regularly on many social, political, economic, and international questions of popular interest. The object of such surveys is similar to that of any other procedures for gauging public opinion, and the resulting information can be put to a number of practical uses. The large-scale nature of these surveys and the rapidity with which answers are required have encouraged the utilization of polling, rather than attitude scale, techniques. But attitude scales have also found a place in public opinion research. An example is provided by "public morale surveys," such as that conducted by Rundquist and Sletto (61) during the depression years of the 1930's. Attitude scales have likewise been employed to explore the attitudes of more narrowly defined publics, such as farmers or persons living in certain areas.

Market research (5) has much in common with public opinion studies. Because of similar practical demands, polling techniques have served as the principal tool in both fields. The consumer public, or potential consumer public, to which market research is directed can usually be more specifically defined than the population to be sampled in public opinion polls. Such a consumer public would of course vary somewhat with the nature of the particular commodity under consideration. The object of market research is to investigate consumer needs and reactions in reference to products, services, or advertisements. The resulting information may be used for such purposes as choosing the most effective advertisement for a specific article, improving a type of service, preparing a new model, or designing a new product to meet consumer specifications.

Another major field of application is to be found in the measurement of *employee attitudes and morale* (6, Chs. 3, 4, 5; 51). Both single-question and scale procedures have been utilized for this purpose. Some surveys are concerned with an over-all estimate of favorable or unfavorable attitude toward the job or the company. More often, the investigation yields a profile of attitudes toward different aspects of the job situation. An example of an instrument designed for the latter purpose is the SRA Employee Inventory (8), which consists of 78 items chosen to sample attitudes in such areas as job demands, working conditions, pay, supervisor-employee interpersonal relations, adequacy of communication, and identification with the company. Subsequent factor analyses of this inventory, however, have failed to support the classification of items into the original categories (2, 3, 84). Either the total score on job attitude or revised keys on the objectively identified factors should be used. In the more carefully conducted employee attitude surveys, it is customary to construct special instruments for use in a given company. It is thus possible to tailor each question to local conditions and to obtain reactions to more specific characteristics of the particular job situation.

Attitude surveys are also employed to check the effectiveness of *education and training*. They may, for example, provide an index for evaluating different instructors or instructional practices. The Survey of Student Opinions administered by the Air Force in its navigation training program illustrates such an application (14). To be sure, if misused by supervisors as a basis for criticism of subordinates or for other unfavorable administrative action, these procedures may seriously undermine morale. But if used wisely and constructively, they can provide information that will be helpful to the individual instructor. Attitude surveys have also been utilized in measuring the changes in student attitudes toward literature, art, different racial or cultural groups, social and economic questions, or other pertinent matters, following a given course of study or other educational program (cf., e.g., 64).

One of the earliest and most extensive applications of attitude surveys is to be found in *research in social psychology, personality theory, and related areas*. Practically every textbook on social psychology contains sections on attitudes and their measurement. Sociologists are likewise concerned with attitudes, although some are skeptical regarding the feasibility of quantification and objective measurement in this area. Among the many problems investigated through attitude surveys may be mentioned group differences in attitudes, the role of attitudes in intergroup relations, background factors associated with the development of attitudes, the interrelations of attitudes (including factor analyses), trends and temporal shifts in attitudes, the experimental alteration of attitudes through interpolated experiences, and parent-child relations. Two instruments that have served as a basis for an unusually large amount of research on a variety of psychological problems are the California F scale designed as a measure of authoritarianism (59, 79) and the Parental Attitude Research Instrument (PARI), constructed by psychologists in the Child Development Section of the National Institute of Mental Health (62).

The measurement of attitudes is a subject of recurrent controversy and debate. Whether verbally expressed opinions can be regarded as indicators of "real" attitudes has frequently been questioned. In part, this problem concerns the relationship between verbal and non-verbal overt behavior. In other words, does the individual suit his actions to his words—or to his attitude scale score? Discrepancies between verbally expressed attitudes and overt behavior have been noted in a number of studies (16, 44). In an investigation on college students, for example, a correlation of only .02 was found between scores on an anonymous but secretly coded scale of attitude toward cheating and actual cheating behavior in scoring examination papers (16). Considerable cheating was found despite the strong attitude against cheating professed by the group as a whole. There is, of course, little room for diversity of socially acceptable opinion about cheating, a fact that may account in part for the lack of correspondence between verbal and non-verbal behavior in this situation.

It has been further pointed out that even observations of overt behavior may not always provide an accurate index of attitude. For example, an individual may both profess strong religious beliefs and attend church regularly, not because of his religious convictions but as a means of gaining social acceptance in his community. Such a possibility raises the further question of the relationship between "public" and "private" attitudes. How do the individual's publicly expressed attitudes compare with the opinions he voices in conversation with intimate friends or with the stranger in the club car whom he never expects to meet again? Public opinion surveys are usually "public" in more than one sense. They represent a verbal expression of attitudes by the public and to the public.

To some extent, anonymous expressions of attitudes may provide a closer approximation to private attitudes; but the two cannot be assumed to be identical. Moreover, the individual's verbally expressed attitudes, even when reported "privately" or anonymously, may sometimes differ from his general, unvocalized attitudinal responses. The latter represent vague feelings or other implicit reactions that have not been overtly verbalized by the individual.

The relationship between "what the person says" and "what he does," as well as the relationship between publicly and privately expressed attitudes, will be recognized as special instances of *validity*. Attitude scales and opinion polls may be validated against a number of criteria, such as membership in contrasted groups, ratings by close acquaintances, and biographical data secured through intensive interviews or case studies. Because of the practical difficulties in obtaining such criterion data, however, investigators have frequently relied upon the familiar makeshifts involving validation by internal consistency or by correlation with another attitude scale. All too often, resort has been made to a superficial kind of content validity based upon the examination and classification of questions according to the topics covered. For opinion polling, validation is rarely attempted at all.

It is admittedly true that the validation of attitude measures presents a difficult problem. In most practical situations, the validity concept can be reduced to a question of how far one can generalize from test results. Many attitude or opinion surveys are conducted for the stated purpose of systematically exploring verbally reported attitudes. In such a case, the criterion should itself be defined in terms of verbally expressed attitudes. In other instances, very different purposes are to be served by the survey. More attention, however, should be given to the explicit formulation of the objectives of each survey, as well as to the precise definition of the criterion. And as a prerequisite to further advances in the development of validation procedures, the very concept of attitude needs additional clarification.

Data on *reliability* are also scanty, especially with reference to polling. Yet in the case of polling techniques, with their reliance upon single questions, reliability is most likely to be suspect.

Attitude surveys also present a number of methodological problems. These problems are not fundamentally different from those encountered in the construction and administration of other types of psychological tests, but they are accentuated in the measurement of attitudes. The major difficulties center about the formulation of questions, the administration of the survey, and the procurement of an adequate sampling of the population (cf. 48).

Proper formulation of questions is especially important in polling techniques, owing to their reliance upon single questions and to the usual lack of time for extensive pretesting and item analysis. It has been repeatedly demonstrated that survey results may be substantially altered by changing the form in which questions and answers are expressed (cf. 12, 48). Many "rules" for good question writing have been listed. Among the pertinent factors to be considered are ambiguity, leading and loaded questions, unfamiliar terms, confusing and complex wording, the use of negatives and double negatives, the number of alternative answers, and the form in which responses are given. The results obtained with any one question may likewise be affected by its context, as determined by preceding questions, opening remarks, or stated sponsorship of the survey. References to stereotypes, such as Fascist or Communist, may alter the subject's response, since he is likely to respond to the emotionally toned stereotype rather than to the specific content of the question.

The conditions under which the survey is conducted may also influence the results. In surveys of employee attitudes, for instance, precautions are generally taken to insure anonymity of replies by having unsigned questionnaires dropped into a ballot box or mailed to an outside consulting organization. For the same reason, interviews are often conducted by persons not connected with the company and unacquainted with individual workers. Whenever feasible, anonymity is a desirable condition in most types of attitude surveys, because it encourages frankness and is more likely to evoke "private" attitudes. Similarly, whether the responses are obtained individually or in groups, in face-to-face oral interviews or in writing, in person or by telephone, represent important procedural questions. Each of these techniques has its characteristic advantages and disadvantages. But it cannot be assumed that all these methods yield interchangeable results.

The role of the interviewer has itself been the subject of extensive research. For certain types of surveys, such as those employing unguided and "depth" interviews or open-end questions, highly trained and experienced interviewers are essential. All interviewers, however, need special qualifications and preparation. Checking procedures are also desirable as a means of controlling the accuracy and honesty of individual interviewers. Of special psychological interest are studies showing that attitude survey results are influenced by interviewer bias as well as by certain recognizable characteristics of the interviewers, such as their socioeconomic level, race, and other group memberships (12, 39, 57).

The problem of *sampling* is of fundamental importance in all attitude surveys. It is especially acute in public opinion polling and market surveys. In order to obtain a satisfactory sample, it is first necessary to define and describe the population to be surveyed. Then a sample must be chosen that will be representative of that population. When the population is large and heterogeneous, as in the case of voters in a national election, it becomes extremely difficult to secure a truly representative cross section. Biased samples, containing a disproportionate number of persons of certain types, are likely to give incorrect estimates of population opinions.

Although a number of sampling procedures have been carefully worked out (cf. 48), poor sampling remains one of the principal weaknesses of public opinion polls and—to a lesser extent—of market surveys. The path of the pollster is beset with sampling pitfalls. For example, persons in lower socioeconomic levels tend to be less accessible and less cooperative for survey purposes. Consequently, they are often under-represented in such polls. Similarly, individuals who fill out and return mailed questionnaires often differ systematically from those who fail to reply. In many cases, the mail respondents tend to be more favorably inclined toward the company or organization that may be sponsoring the survey, and their responses reflect this favorable bias.

All of the problems considered above—including validity, reliability, questionnaire construction, administration, and sampling—are encountered in varying degrees in both opinion polling and attitude measurement. From a technical viewpoint, attitude scales are clearly superior to opinion polls. In their construction and use, attitude scales are more nearly similar to psychological tests. Although by their very nature most polls and many attitude surveys must be custom-made to meet specific needs, at least some attitude scales have been developed for general use. In the following section, we shall examine in more detail the procedures employed in the development and application of attitude scales. Typical examples of available standardized scales will be considered.

ATTITUDE SCALES

Attitude scales are designed to provide a quantitative measure of the individual's relative position along a unidimensional attitude continuum. Special procedures have been devised in an attempt to achieve comparability of scores from scale to scale, equality of distances between scale units, and unidimensionality or homogeneity of items. Thurstone's adaptation of psychophysical methods to the quantification of judgment data represents an important milestone in attitude scale construction (77). By these procedures, Thurstone and his co-workers prepared about thirty scales for measuring attitude toward war, Communism, Negroes, Chinese, capital punishment, the church, patriotism, censorship, and many other institutions, practices, issues, or groups of people.

The construction of the Thurstone-type scales may be illustrated by considering the Scale for Measuring Attitude toward the Church, the development of this scale having been fully reported in published form (78). Essentially the same procedure was followed in preparing all other scales in the series. The first step was to gather a large number of statements regarding the church. These statements were obtained principally by asking several groups of people to write out their opinions about the church. The list was supplemented with statements taken from current literature. A search was made for expressions of opinion ranging from extremely favorable, through neutral, to extremely unfavorable. From the material thus collected, a list of 130 carefully edited, short statements was drawn up.

These statements, each mimeographed on a separate slip, were then given to each of 300 judges for sorting into 11 piles, from A to K. The judges were instructed to put in category A those statements they believed expressed the highest appreciation of the value of the church, in category F those expressing a neutral position, and in category K those expressing the strongest depreciaton of the church. In the intervening piles, statements were to be arranged in accordance with the degree of appreciation or depreciation they expressed. This sorting procedure has been described as the method of "equal-appearing intervals," although the judges were not actually told that the intervals between piles were to appear equal. It should also be noted that the judges were not asked to indicate their own attitudes toward the church, but were requested only to classify the statements.

The percentage of judges who placed each statement in the different categories constituted the basic data for computing the "scale values" of the statements. The method is illustrated in Figure 114. On the baseline of the cumulative frequency graph are the numbers 1 to 11, corresponding to categories A to K, which are treated as equally spaced points on the scale. The vertical axis shows the percentage of judges placing the statement in or below each category. The 50th percentile, or median position, assigned by the judges to the statement can be read directly from the graph. This median position is taken as the *scale value* of the statement. It will be noted that for one of the statements illustrated (No. 39), which is quite favorable to the church, the scale value is 1.8. The other statement (No. 8) has a scale value of 6.7. Once the scale values were computed for all statements, the next step was to select those statements whose scale values were equally spaced along the attitude continuum.

Besides the scale value, or median position, of each statement, the graphs also show the variability or spread of positions assigned to it by the different judges. The index of variability employed for this purpose (Q) is simply the distance between the 25th and 75th percentile points. Reference to Figure 114 shows that the judges agreed closely in the placement of statement 39, but varied widely in classifying statement 8. This difference is reflected in the Q's of 1.3 and 3.6, respectively, which were obtained for the two statements. This measure of variability was taken as an index of the *ambiguity* of statements. Thus ambiguous or double-barreled statements, which are variously interpreted by different judges, would tend to be less consistently classified. Accordingly, statements yielding high Q's were eliminated from the final scale.

The statements were also checked for *irrelevance*. This was accomplished by presenting the 130 statements to subjects with the instructions to mark those statements with which they agreed. The responses were then analyzed statistically to determine their internal consistency. Statements that failed to meet the criterion of internal consistency were excluded as being irrelevant to the variable under consideration.

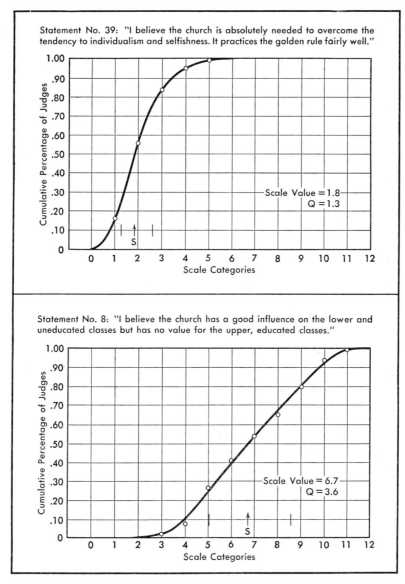

Statement No. 39: "I believe the church is absolutely needed to overcome the tendency to individualism and selfishness. It practices the golden rule fairly well."

Statement No. 8: "I believe the church has a good influence on the lower and uneducated classes but has no value for the upper, educated classes."

Fig. 114. Determination of Scale Values for Thurstone-Type Attitude Scale. (Adapted from Thurstone and Chave, 78, pp. 37, 39; reproduced by permission of University of Chicago Press.)

The final scales thus comprise items that proved to be relatively unambiguous, relevant, and evenly distributed over the range of scale values. The resulting Scale for Measuring Attitude toward the Church consists of 45 items. Most of the other scales in the series have been prepared in two parallel forms, each containing 20 to 22 statements. The sequence of statements is random with respect to scale values. The latter are not, of course, shown on the test blank.

In taking any of the Thurstone-type attitude scales, the subject marks all statements with which he agrees. His score is simply the median scale value of the statements he has endorsed. Parallel-form reliabilities of such scores generally fall between .70 and .90, clustering in the low .80's. Some validation studies have been undertaken, principally by means of contrasted groups or self-ratings. But the available evidence for validity is meager.

The Thurstone technique has been applied to the development of attitude scales for many purposes. Thurstone-type scales have been constructed, for example, to measure the attitude of employees toward their company. A few statements from one of these scales, with their corresponding scale values, are shown below (82):

I think this company treats its employees better than any other company does 10.4

If I had to do it over again I'd still work for this company. 9.5

The workers put as much over on the company as the company puts over on them. 5.1

You've got to have "pull" with certain people around here to get ahead. .   2.1

An honest man fails in this company. 0.8

A difficulty inherent in the development of Thurstone-type scales pertains to the possible effects of the judges' own attitudes upon their classification of the statements. Thurstone recognized this problem, stating that "if the scale is to be regarded as valid, the scale values of the statements should not be affected by the opinions of the people who help to construct it," and adding "until experimental evidence may be forthcoming, we shall make the assumption that the scale values of the statements are independent of the attitude distribution of the readers who sort the statements (78, p. 92). A number of early studies corroborated Thurstone's original assumption, in so far as scale values did not differ appreciably when redetermined on groups known to differ in their own attitudes (4, 23, 35, 54).

Later investigations, however, found that under certain conditions scale values are significantly affected by judges' attitudes (22, 24, 37, 43). Thus large and significant shifts in the scale values of statements about war occurred from 1930 to 1940 (22). Similar differences were obtained with the scale on attitude toward Negroes, when items were rescaled on several Negro and white groups (37). The constancy of scale values reported by the earlier studies appeared to have resulted in part from the failure to include subjects with a sufficiently wide range of attitudes. Moreover, it was a common practice in these studies, as in Thurstone's original work, to discard the records of judges who placed 30 or more statements in a single pile. Such a massing of statements was regarded as evidence of careless sorting. It has subsequently been demonstrated, however, that these disproportionate groupings are more likely to occur among individuals whose own views are extreme (37).

In general, intergroup differences in item placement are reduced when ambiguous items with large inter-judge variability (Q) are eliminated and when only items separated by large scale differences are chosen (24). On the other hand, if judges are presented with ambiguous and relatively neutral items and if the conditions of judgment are not highly controlled—as when judges are allowed to determine how many categories to use—the classification of items is so strongly affected by the judges' own opinions as to permit the use of this procedure itself as a disguised attitude test (43).

Another approach to the construction of attitude scales is that followed by Likert (46). Unlike Thurstone-type scales, the Likert scaling procedure does not require the classification of items by a group of judges. Items are selected solely on the basis of the responses of subjects to whom they are administered in the course of developing the test. Internal consistency is often the only criterion for item selection, although external criteria may be employed when available.

The Likert-type scale, moreover, calls for a graded response to each statement. The response is usually expressed in terms of the following five categories: strongly agree (SA), agree (A), undecided (U), disagree (D), and strongly disagree (SD). The individual statements are either clearly favorable or clearly unfavorable. To score the scale, the alternative responses are credited 5, 4, 3, 2, or 1, respectively, from the favorable to the unfavorable end. For example, "strongly agree" with a favorable statement would receive a score of 5, as would "strongly disagree" with an unfavorable statement. The sum of the item credits represents the individual's total score, which must be interpreted in terms of empirically established norms.

An example of a modified Likert-type scale is the Minnesota Teacher Attitude Inventory (15). Designed to assess pupil-teacher relations, this test was developed by administering over seven hundred items to 100 teachers nominated by their principals as superior in pupil-teacher relations and 100 nominated as inferior. Cross-validation of the resulting 150-item inventory in different groups yielded concurrent validity coefficients of .46 to .60 with a composite criterion derived from principal's estimate, pupils' ratings, and evaluation by a visiting expert. Two sample items from this inventory are shown below.

Most pupils are resourceful when left on their own.

A teacher should never acknowledge his ignorance of a topic in the presence of his pupils.

For each statement, respondents mark SA, A, U, D, or SD. The scores assigned to these responses are based on criterion keying, as in the Strong VIB, rather than on arbitrary 1 to 5 weights. Since its publication, this test has been widely used in research. For practical application in selection and counseling, more information is needed, especially with regard to predictive validity and the interpretation of norms from different groups.

Mention should also be made of the work of Guttman on "scalogram analysis" and of Lazarsfeld on "latent structure analysis" (66). These techniques were developed largely during World War II, in connection with a monumental project on the measurement of soldier opinions. Both are essentially procedures for determining the unidimensionality or homogeneity of items through an analysis of the responses given by a trial group of subjects. The approaches of Guttman and Lazarsfeld provide theoretical models, or conceptual frameworks, for attitude measurement, which represent promising starting points for further research. In their present form, however, these techniques are still limited by a number of unresolved difficulties, both theoretical and practical. A general survey of techniques for the construction of attitude scales can be found in Edwards (21).

OTHER MEASURES OF INTERESTS, ATTITUDES, AND RELATED VARIABLES

There remain a few well-known instruments which have much in common with interest tests, attitude scales, or both, but which do not fall clearly into either category. Some of these tests also include measures of other personality variables, thus overlapping the categories covered in Chapter 18. Moreover, each of these instruments exhibits unique features in its content, use, or construction procedures.

The Allport-Vernon-Lindzey Study of Values (1) was designed to measure the relative prominence of six basic interests, motives, or evaluative attitudes. Originally suggested by Spranger's *Types of Men* (65), the value categories may be described as follows:

Theoretical: Characterized by a dominant interest in the discovery of truth and by an empirical, critical, rational, "intellectual" approach.

Economic: Emphasizing useful and practical values; conforming closely to the prevailing stereotype of the "average American business man."

Aesthetic: Placing the highest value on form and harmony; judging and enjoying each unique experience from the standpoint of its grace, symmetry, or fitness.

Social: Originally defined as love of people, this category has been more narrowly limited in later revisions of the test to cover only altruism and philanthropy.

Political: Primarily interested in personal power, influence, and renown; not necessarily limited to the field of politics.

Religious: Mystical, concerned with the unity of all experience, and seeking to comprehend the cosmos as a whole.

Items for the Study of Values were first formulated on the basis of the theoretical framework provided by Spranger. The criterion for the final item selection was internal consistency within each of the six areas. Intercorrelations of scores on the current form reveal no substantial overlap among any of these areas. The items are arranged in random order in the test booklet, with no clue regarding the categories according to which they will be scored. Each item requires the preferential rating of either two or four alternatives falling in different value categories. Two sample items are reproduced in Figure 115.

By an ingenious arrangement of answer spaces, scoring is simplified and requires no key other than simple instructions printed on a detachable page of the test booklet. Total scores on the six values are plotted in the form of a profile (cf. Fig 116). It should be noted that, owing to the item form employed in this test, final scores reflect only *relative* strength in the six areas. Thus it would be impossible to obtain high or low scores in all areas.

The general norms are based on a college population and are reported separately for men and women. Comparative data are also provided on samples from different types of colleges and on various occupational groups. The split-half reliabilities of the six scores range from .73 to .90. Retests after one or two months yielded reliabilities between .77 and .93 for the six scales.

Validity has been checked partly by the method of contrasted groups. Profiles of various educational and occupational samples exhibit significant differences in the expected directions. For example, medical students ob-

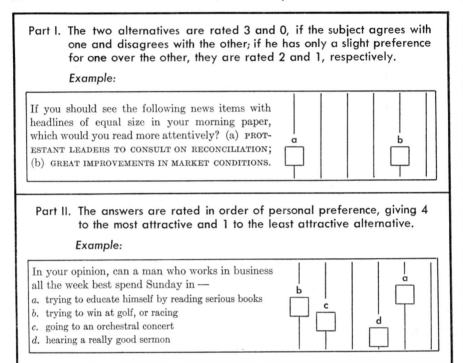

Part I. The two alternatives are rated 3 and 0, if the subject agrees with one and disagrees with the other; if he has only a slight preference for one over the other, they are rated 2 and 1, respectively.

Example:

If you should see the following news items with headlines of equal size in your morning paper, which would you read more attentively? (a) PROTESTANT LEADERS TO CONSULT ON RECONCILIATION; (b) GREAT IMPROVEMENTS IN MARKET CONDITIONS.

a   b

Part II. The answers are rated in order of personal preference, giving 4 to the most attractive and 1 to the least attractive alternative.

Example:

In your opinion, can a man who works in business all the week best spend Sunday in —
a. trying to educate himself by reading serious books
b. trying to win at golf, or racing
c. going to an orchestral concert
d. hearing a really good sermon

a   b   c   d

Fig. 115. Sample Items from Allport-Vernon-Lindzey Study of Values. (Reproduced by permission of Houghton Mifflin Company.)

tained their highest scores in the theoretical area, theological students in the religious area. More extensive validation data have been gathered with the first edition of the Study of Values, which was in use for about twenty years, although some comparable data are also available for the revised form (13, 19, 52, 83). Some relationship has been demonstrated between value profiles and academic achievement, especially when relative achievement in different fields is considered. Data are also available on the correlation of value scores with self-ratings and associates' ratings. Other overt behavioral indices of attitudes with which scores on the Study of Values have been compared include newspaper reading, descriptions of one's "ideal person," club membership, church attendance, and the like. Significant relationships in the expected directions have likewise been reported with a number of other tests, such as Strong VIB and Thurstone attitude scales. Finally, some studies have shown significant changes in score following specific types of experience, such as a period of study under different "styles" of education.

It might be noted that a Pictorial Study of Values (63) has been prepared for subjects with linguistic or reading difficulties. Pictures for this test were

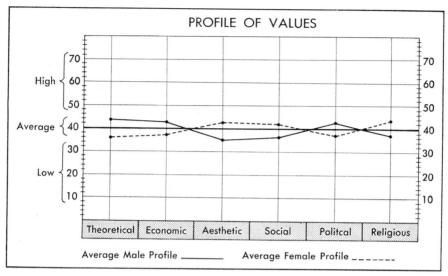

Fig. 116. Sex Differences on the Allport-Vernon-Lindzey Study of Values. (Reproduced by permission of Houghton Mifflin Company.)

assigned to each of the six scales on the basis of their correlations with Allport-Vernon-Lindzey scores in a sample of 100 cases. Although providing a promising idea for test development, in its present form this test is not ready for general use.

A test that combines measures of interests and attitudes with the assessment of certain emotional and social characteristics is the Attitude-Interest Analysis Test developed by Terman and Miles (74, 75). Commonly known as the M–F Test, this instrument represents the first and most extensive attempt to construct a measure of masculinity-femininity by empirical criterion keying. Other MF scales, such as those included in the MMPI, VIB, and Guilford-Zimmerman Temperament Survey, have subsequently appeared; but these scales are based on fewer and more limited types of items than are found in the Terman-Miles test. It cannot be assumed that these different scales are interchangeable. The correlations between their scores are usually low (18).

The development of the Terman-Miles test began with an exhaustive search of the psychological literature for types of test content that yielded the most pronounced sex differences. The preliminary sets of items prepared on this basis were then administered to many hundreds of persons, ranging from elementary school children to college students and many adult groups. The principal criterion for item selection was the relative proportion of men and women giving each response. Items that yielded significant sex differences were retained, while those that failed to discriminate between men and women were discarded. The direction of sex difference in frequency of response determined whether the particular response was scored as masculine or feminine. The final test was prepared in two equivalent forms, each consisting of seven subtests: Word Association, Inkblot Association, Information, Emotional and Ethical Attitudes, Interests, Opinions, and Introvertive Response. It will be noted that, although concerned predominantly with interests and attitudes, the test also includes measures of other personality characteristics, such as introversion-extroversion. Some of the subtests, moreover, utilize adaptations of projective techniques and other testing procedures to be considered in Chapters 20 and 21.

In interpreting MF scores on either the Terman-Miles or other scales designed for the same purpose, two points should be borne in mind. First, MF scores show only the degree to which the individual's responses agree with those most characteristic of men or women in the culture within which the test was developed. For the Terman-Miles test, the culture is that of the United States in the 1930's. Second, it should be noted that such tests were deliberately designed so as to exaggerate sex differences. The behavior of men and women has much in common. The MF tests, however, concentrate only upon the differences. Although these tests can be used to determine the extent to which the individual approximates the norm for his or her sex, they do not provide a basis for establishing the amount of sex difference in psychological traits.

As a final example of a test that cuts across some of the traditional categories we may consider The DF Opinion Survey (31) prepared by Guilford and his associates. Yielding separate scores in 10 "dynamic factors" (DF), this test was designed to measure needs (as in the Edwards Personal Preference Schedule) and broad interest areas (as in the Kuder—Vocational). The 10 factors covered by the test are based largely on Guilford's previously cited factor analyses of interests. Guilford classifies needs, interests, and attitudes as dynamic factors within the general area of motivation (29, p. 205). Examples of the traits for which scores are provided in The DF Opinion Survey include need for attention, liking for thinking, aesthetic appreciation, adventure versus security, and cultural conformity.

THE PLACE OF INTERESTS IN PERSONALITY THEORY

The measurement of interests began as a relatively specific, minor, and tangential development in the study of personality. Early interest inventories were oriented chiefly toward the prediction of the individual's eventual acceptance or rejection of particular job functions. From these modest beginnings, interest tests are gradually coming to play a major role in the formulation of personality theory. The impetus for these developments is coming from several different sources. Factorial analyses of interest items, as illustrated by the work of Guilford (30), have demonstrated the interconnections of interests with other important dimensions of personality. The previously cited DF Opinion Survey, combining interests and needs, highlights the broadening concept of interests and the recognition of their motivational aspects.

A large number of studies have revealed significant associations between measured vocational interests and other aspects of personality. Research on alcoholics, male homosexuals, neurotics, and persons with other psychiatric disabilities has shown a predominance of certain characteristic vocational interest patterns in each group (25, 33, 53). Scores on such inventories as the Strong VIB and the Kuder—Vocational have proved to be related to performance on other personality tests, such as the MMPI and the Study of Values (9, 17, 28, 36). Some investigators have provided personality descriptions of normal persons scoring high or low on particular vocational interest scales. In a survey of 1000 male University of Minnesota freshmen, scores on certain VIB occupational scales were found to be significantly correlated with other measured emotional and attitudinal variables (17, Ch. 4). For example, students scoring high in the social service or business contact clusters of occupational keys obtained higher social adjustment scores than those scoring high in other clusters. On economic conservatism, these same two groups scored in opposite ways, those with high social service interests being more liberal than those with high business contact interests (17, pp. 118-119).

More detailed personality evaluations of individuals receiving high scores on different occupational interest scales are to be found in a study of 100 Air Force officers conducted at the University of California (cf. 17, pp. 128-129). Each subject was given a battery of tests, including the Strong VIB, and also underwent an intensive assessment program through interviews and other observational techniques. On the basis of the available information, subjects were described by eight clinical psychologists in terms of 76 designated personality variables. Correlations of these trait ratings with each of the VIB occupational keys revealed a number of statistically significant relations. For illustrative purposes, the personality descriptions associated with high scores on two keys are summarized below:

High Scorers on Mathematician Key: Self-abasing, concerned with philosophical problems, introspective, lacking in social poise, lacking confidence in own ability, sympathetic, reacts poorly to stress, not persuasive in personal contacts, not an effective leader, not ostentatious, not aggressive or socially ascendant.

High Scorers on Real Estate Salesman Key: Self-indulgent, guileful, cynical, opportunistic, aggressive, persuasive, ostentatious, may arouse hostility in others, not sympathetic, not concerned with philosophical problems, not lacking confidence in own ability, not self-abasing.

From a different angle, it is now widely recognized that the choice of an occupation often reflects the individual's basic emotional needs and that occupational adjustment is a major aspect of general life adjustment (7, 17, 36, 58). There are many different ways of dealing with interpersonal relations and other life problems. No one way is universally better than others. When he chooses a vocation, each individual is to some extent selecting those adjustment techniques, life patterns, and roles most congenial to himself. The measurement of vocational interests—and more specifically the identification of those occupational groups whose interests and attitudes the individual shares most closely—thus becomes a focal point in the understanding of different personalities. Direct studies of the characteristics of persons in different occupations have been contributing to a growing fund of factual material for implementing this approach (cf., e.g., 58).

In line with the above viewpoint, Holland (36) has come full circle in developing an inventory of occupational titles as a measure of personality characteristics. In this test, the respondent merely indicates whether he likes or dislikes each of 300 occupations. Although constructed largely in terms of content validity and internal consistency, the resulting scales yield significant differences between matched samples of psychiatric patients and normal controls. Interest profiles of students in different curricula were also consistent with expectation. The inventory provides 10 "personality" scales, as illustrated by Physical Activity, Intellectuality, Responsibility, Conformity, etc. There are also three response set scales, including Question (number of items left blank), Infrequency (number of rare items marked), and Acquiescence (number of items "liked"). How effective this inventory will ultimately prove to be in either research or practice remains to be seen. But its development illustrates current emphasis on vocational choices as clues to personality.

From still another angle, Tyler (81) regards the study of interests as a way of identifying the choices that the individual makes at various stages. These choices are both a reflection of the kind of person he is and a forecast of what he is likely to become. As each choice is made—choice of friends, recreations, courses, jobs, and the like—the individual's subsequent experiences are thereby channeled into certain paths. Alternative developmental routes are eliminated at each choice point. Translating the predictive validity of the Strong VIB into these terms, Tyler writes:

An A signifies that the person's characteristic pattern of acceptance and rejection of life's varied possibilities is like the choice pattern characteristic of persons in a certain occupation. What we should expect then to be able to predict from such a score is . . . the way he will make his choices at later junctures of his life. This makes sense of the high degree of validity Strong's recent studies have shown for the test (81, p. 78).

The measurement of interests promises to be a lively field of test development and research in the years ahead. Having proved so far to be among the most successful tests outside the aptitude domain, interest inventories are now well on the way to attaining theoretical respectability. At the same time, we can anticipate that the interpretation of interest profiles will show further advances in depth and sophistication.

REFERENCES

1. Allport, G. W., Vernon, P. E., and Lindzey, G. *Study of Values.* (3rd ed.) Boston: Houghton Mifflin, 1960.
2. Ash, P. The SRA Employee Inventory: a statistical analysis. *Personnel Psychol.,* 1954, 7, 337-364.
3. Baehr, Melany E. A factorial study of the SRA Employee Inventory. *Personnel Psychol.,* 1954, 7, 319-336.
4. Beyle, H. C. A scale for the measurement of attitude toward candidates for elective government office. *Amer. polit. Sci. Rev.,* 1932, 26, 527-544.
5. Blankenship, A. B. (Ed.) *How to conduct consumer and opinion research.* N. Y.: Harper, 1946.
6. Blum, M. L. *Industrial psychology and its social foundations.* (2nd ed.) N. Y.: Harper, 1956.
7. Bordin, E. S. A theory of vocational interests as dynamic phenomena. *Educ. psychol. Measmt.,* 1943, 3, 49-65.
8. Burns, R. K., *et al. SRA Employee Inventory.* Chicago: Sci. Res. Assoc., 1951-1958.
9. Bursch, C. W. Certain relationships between the Kuder Preference Record and the Minnesota Multiphasic Personality Inventory. *Calif. J. educ. Res.,* 1952, 3, 224-227.
10. Callis, R., Engram, W. C., and McGowan, J. F. Coding the Kuder Preference Record—Vocational. *J. appl. Psychol.,* 1954, 38, 359-363.
11. Campbell, D. T. The indirect assessment of social attitudes. *Psychol. Bull.,* 1950, 47, 15-38.

12. Cantril, H. *Gauging public opinion.* Princeton, N. J.: Princeton Univer. Press, 1944.

13. Cantril, H., and Allport, G. W. Recent applications of the "study of values." *J. abnorm. soc. Psychol.,* 1933, 28, 259-273.

14. Carter, L. F. (Ed.) *Psychological research on navigator training.* (AAF Aviation Psychology Program, Research Reports. Rep. No. 10.) Washington: Govt. Printing Office, 1947.

15. Cook, W. W., Leeds, C., and Callis, R. *The Minnesota Teacher Attitude Inventory.* N. Y.: Psychol. Corp., 1951.

16. Corey, S. M. Professed attitudes and actual behavior. *J. educ. Psychol.,* 1937, 28, 271-280.

17. Darley, J. G., and Hagenah, Theda. *Vocational interest measurement: theory and practice.* Minneapolis: Univer. Minn. Press, 1955.

18. de Cillis, Olga, and Orbison, W. D. A comparison of the Terman-Miles M–F Test and the Mf scale of the MMPI. *J. appl. Psychol.,* 1950, 34, 338-342.

19. Duffy, Elizabeth. A critical review of investigations employing the Allport-Vernon *Study of Values* and other tests of evaluative attitude. *Psychol. Bull.* 1940, 37, 597-612.

20. Durnall, E. J., Jr. Falsification of interest patterns on the Kuder Preference Record. *J. educ. Psychol.,* 1954, 45, 240-243.

21. Edwards, A. L. *Techniques of attitude scale construction.* N. Y.: Appleton-Century-Crofts, 1957.

22. Farnsworth, P. R. Shifts in the values of opinion items. *J. Psychol.,* 1943, 16, 125-128.

23. Ferguson, L. W. The influence of individual attitudes on construction of an attitude scale. *J. soc. Psychol.,* 1935, 6, 115-117.

24. Fishman, J. A., and Lorge, I. The influence of judges' characteristics on item judgments and on Thurstone scaling via the method of ranks (utilization of judges with varying national, religious, and experiential backgrounds). *J. soc. Psychol.,* 1959, 49, 187-205.

25. Force, R. C. Development of a covert test for the detection of alcoholism by a keying of the Kuder Preference Record. *Quart. J. Stud. Alcohol,* 1958, 19, 72-78.

26. Frandsen, A. N. A note on Wiener's coding of Kuder Preference Record profiles. *Educ. psychol. Measmt.,* 1952, 12, 137-139.

27. Fryer, D. *Measurement of interests.* N. Y.: Holt, Rinehart and Winston, 1931.

28. Garman, G. D., and Uhr, L. An anxiety scale for the Strong Vocational Interest Inventory: development, cross-validation, and subsequent tests of validity. *J. appl. Psychol.,* 1958, 42, 241-246.

29. Guilford, J. P. *Personality.* N. Y.: McGraw-Hill, 1959.

30. Guilford, J. P., et al. A factor analysis study of human interests. *Psychol. Monogr.,* 1954, 68, No. 4.

31. Guilford, J. P., Christensen, P. R., and Bond, N. A., Jr. *The DF Opinion Survey.* Beverly Hills, Calif.: Sheridan Supply Co., 1956.

32. Guilford, J. P., Shneidman, E. S., and Zimmerman, W. S. *The Guilford-Shneidman-Zimmerman Interest Survey.* Beverly Hills, Calif.: Sheridan Supply Co., 1948.

33. Haselkorn, H. The vocational interests of a group of male homosexuals. *J. counsel. Psychol.*, 1956, 3, 8-11.
34. Herzberg, F., and Bouton, A. A further study of the stability of the Kuder Preference Record. *Educ. psychol. Measmt.*, 1954, 14, 326-331.
35. Hinckley, E. D. The influence of individual opinion on construction of an attitude scale. *J. soc. Psychol.*, 1932, 3, 283-296.
36. Holland, J. L. A personality inventory employing occupational titles. *J. appl. Psychol.*, 1958, 42, 336-342.
37. Hovland, C. I., and Sherif, M. Judgmental phenomena and scales of attitude measurement: item displacement in Thurstone scales. *J. abnorm. soc. Psychol.*, 1952, 47, 822-832.
38. Hughes, J. L., and McNamara, W. J. Limitations on the use of Strong sales keys for selection and counseling. *J. appl. Psychol.*, 1958, 42, 93-96.
39. Katz, D. Do interviewers bias poll results? *Publ. Opin. Quart.*, 1942, 6, 248-268.
40. Kuder, G. F. *Kuder Preference Record—Vocational.* Chicago: Sci. Res. Assoc., 1934-1956.
41. Kuder, G. F. *Kuder Preference Record—Personal.* Chicago: Sci. Res. Assoc., 1948-1954.
42. Kuder, G. F. *Kuder Preference Record—Occupational.* Chicago: Sci. Res. Assoc., 1956-1958.
43. La Fave, L., and Sherif, M. *Placement of items on a controversial social issue.* (*Pre-Publication Report*) Norman, Okla.; Authors, Univer. of Oklahoma, August 1959.
44. LaPiere, R. T. Attitudes vs. actions. *Social Forces,* 1934, 13, 230-237.
45. Lee, E. A., and Thorpe, L. P. *Occupational Interest Inventory, 1956 Revision.* Monterey, Calif.: Calif. Test Bur., 1956.
46. Likert, R. A technique for the measurement of attitudes. *Arch. Psychol.,* 1932, No. 140.
47. Longstaff, H. P. Fakability of the Strong Interest Blank and the Kuder Preference Record. *J. appl. Psychol.,* 1948, 32, 360-369.
48. McNemar, Q. Opinion-attitude methodology. *Psychol. Bull.,* 1946, 43, 289-374.
49. Mallinson, G. G., and Crumrine, W. M. An investigation of the stability of interests of high school students. *J. educ. Res.,* 1952, 45, 369-383.
50. Meier, N. C., and Saunders, H. W. (Eds.) *The polls and public opinion.* N. Y.: Holt, Rinehart and Winston, 1949.
51. Moore, B. V. Use of attitude surveys in personnel practice. In L. L. Thurstone (Ed.), *Applications of psychology.* N. Y.: Harper, 1952. Pp. 55-66.
52. Nickels, J. B., and Renzaglia, G. A. Some additional data on the relationship between expressed and measured values. *J. appl. Psychol.,* 1958, 42, 99-104.
53. Patterson, C. H. Interest tests and the emotionally disturbed client. *Educ. psychol. Measmt.,* 1957, 17, 264-280.
54. Pintner, R., and Forlano, G. The influence of attitude upon scaling of attitude items. *J. soc. Psychol.,* 1937, 8, 39-45.

55. Reid, J. W. Stability of measured Kuder interests in young adults. *J. educ. Res.,* 1951, 45, 307-312.

56. Remmers, H. H. *Introduction to opinion and attitude measurement.* N. Y.: Harper, 1955.

57. Robinson, D., and Rohde, Sylvia. Two experiments with an anti-Semitism poll. *J. abnorm. soc. Psychol.,* 1946, 41, 136-144.

58. Roe, Anne. *The psychology of occupations.* N. Y.: Wiley, 1956.

59. Rokeach, M. Political and religious dogmatism; an alternative to the authoritarian personality. *Psychol. Monogr.,* 1956, 70, No. 18.

60. Rosenberg, N. Stability and maturation of Kuder interest patterns of medical, law, and business school alumni. *J. appl. Psychol.,* 1953, 37, 367-369.

61. Rundquist, E. A., and Sletto, R. F. *Personality in the depression.* Minneapolis: Univer. Minn. Press, 1936.

62. Schaefer, E. S., and Bell, R. Q. Development of a parental attitude research instrument. *Child Develpm.,* 1958, 29, 339-361.

63. Shooster, C. *Pictorial Study of Values.* Chicago: Psychometr. Affil., 1957.

64. Smith, E. R., Tyler, R. W., et al. *Appraising and recording student progress.* N. Y.: Harper, 1942.

65. Spranger, E. (transl. by P. J. W. Pigors). *Types of men.* Halle: Niemeyer, 1928.

66. Stouffer, S. A., et al. *Measurement and prediction (Studies in social psychology in World War II, vol. IV).* Princeton, N. J.: Princeton Univer. Press, 1950.

67. Strong, E. K., Jr. *Strong Vocational Interest Blank for Men, Revised.* Stanford Univer., Calif.: Stanford Univer. Press, 1938-1959.

68. Strong, E. K., Jr. *Vocational interests of men and women.* Stanford Univer., Calif.: Stanford Univer. Press, 1943.

69. Strong, E. K., Jr. *Strong Vocational Interest Blank for Women, Revised.* Stanford Univer., Calif.: Stanford Univer. Press, 1946-1959.

70. Strong, E. K., Jr. *Vocational interests 18 years after college.* Minneapolis: Univer. Minn. Press, 1955.

71. Strong, E. K., Jr., and Tucker, A. C. The use of vocational interest scales in planning a medical career. *Psychol. Monogr.,* 1952, 66, No. 9.

72. Super, D. E. *Avocational interest patterns.* Stanford Univer., Calif.: Stanford Univer. Press, 1940.

73. Super, D. E. *Appraising vocational fitness.* N. Y.: Harper, 1949.

74. Terman, L. M., and Miles, Catherine C. *Sex and personality: studies in masculinity and femininity.* N. Y.: McGraw-Hill, 1936.

75. Terman, L. M., and Miles, Catherine C. *Manual of information and directions for use of Attitude-Interest Analysis Test (M–F Test).* N. Y.: McGraw-Hill, 1938.

76. Thurstone, L. L. *Thurstone Interest Schedule.* N. Y.: Psychol. Corp., 1947.

77. Thurstone, L. L. *The measurement of values.* Chicago: Univer. Chicago Press, 1959.

78. Thurstone, L. L., and Chave, E. J. *The measurement of attitude.* Chicago: Univer. Chicago Press, 1929.

79. Titus, H. E., and Hollander, E. P. The California F scale in psychological research: 1950-1955. *Psychol. Bull.,* 1957, 54, 47-64.
80. Tyler, Leona E. Distinctive patterns of likes and dislikes over a twenty-two year period. *J. counsel. Psychol.,* 1959, 6, 234-237.
81. Tyler, Leona E. Toward a workable psychology of individuality. *Amer. Psychologist,* 1959, 14, 75-81.
82. Uhrbrock, R. S. Attitudes of 4430 employees. *J. soc. Psychol.,* 1934, 5, 365-377.
83. Vernon, P. E., and Allport, G. W. A test for personal values. *J. abnorm. soc. Psychol.,* 1931, 26, 231-248.
84. Wherry, R. J. An orthogonal re-rotation of the Baehr and Ash studies of the SRA Employee Inventory. *Personnel Psychol.,* 1954, 7, 365-380.
85. Wiener, D. N. Empirical occupational groupings of Kuder Preference Record profiles. *Educ. psychol. Measmt.,* 1951, 11, 273-279.
86. Witkin, A. A. Differential interest patterns in salesmen. *J. appl. Psychol.,* 1956, 40, 338-340.

CHAPTER 20

Projective Techniques

The chief distinguishing feature of projective techniques is to be found in their assignment of a relatively *unstructured* task, i.e., a task that permits an almost unlimited variety of possible responses. In order to allow free play to the subject's imagination, only brief, general instructions are provided. For the same reason, the test stimuli are usually vague and equivocal. The underlying hypothesis is that the way in which the individual perceives and interprets the test material, or "structures" the situation, will reflect fundamental aspects of his psychological functioning. In other words, it is expected that the test materials will serve as a sort of screen upon which the subject "projects" his characteristic ideas, attitudes, strivings, fears, conflicts, aggressions, and the like.

Typically, projective instruments also represent *disguised* testing procedures, in so far as the subject is rarely aware of the type of psychological interpretation that will be made of his responses. Projective techniques are likewise characterized by a *global* approach to the appraisal of personality. Attention is focused upon a composite picture of the whole personality, rather than upon the measurement of separate traits.

Although the term "projective technique" was first applied to this type of instrument by Frank (43) in an article appearing in 1939, such techniques had been in use for many years prior to that date. Projective methods originated within a clinical setting and have remained predominantly a tool for the clinician. Some have evolved from therapeutic procedures (such as art therapy) employed with psychiatric patients. In their theoretical framework, most projective techniques reflect the influence of psychoanalytic concepts. The emphasis placed upon a global or holistic approach, moreover, will be recognized as a contribution of Gestalt psychology. It should be noted, of course, that the specific techniques need not be evaluated in the light of these particular theoretical slants or historical origins. A procedure may prove to be

564

practically useful or empirically valid for reasons other than those initially cited to justify its introduction.

In line with their typically global approach, projective techniques have been concerned not only with emotional and social characteristics, evidences of maladjustment, interests, attitudes, and motives, but also with certain intellectual aspects of the individual's behavior. Examples of the latter include "general intellectual level," originality, and characteristic methods of attacking problems. Certain adaptations of projective techniques have been specially designed for the measurement of attitudes (33, 103), and thus supplement the instruments described in Chapter 19. Examples of projective attitude tests will be cited in the appropriate sections of this chapter. Still other approaches to attitude measurement will be illustrated in Chapter 21.

The array of projective techniques that have been published or described in the literature is large and steadily growing. Once the underlying principle is grasped, it is relatively easy to design a "new model" that may exhibit varying degrees of resemblance to earlier instruments. Whether the new technique represents a real improvement over existing procedures is much more difficult to demonstrate. Few projective instruments have advanced beyond the stage of preliminary exploration. It might be added that almost any psychological test, for whatever purpose designed, can also serve as a projective instrument. Intelligence tests, for example, have been employed in this fashion by some clinicians (cf. 44).

For the present purpose, only a few outstanding examples of projective techniques can be considered. Similarly, a critical examination of individual instruments would be beyond the scope of the present volume. Instead, a summary evaluation of such instruments as a group will be given in the last section of the chapter. More extensive surveys and fuller discussions of specific techniques are available in a number of published sources, such as Abt and Bellak (1), Anderson and Anderson (10), Bell (19), Brower and Abt (26), Watson (101), and Weider (102). Critiques from different angles can also be found in articles by Cronbach (36, 37) and Eysenck (41), among others. *The Mental Measurements Yearbooks* devote a separate section to projective techniques, where critical reviews of all instruments cited in this chapter can be found.

Projective techniques have been classified with reference to various parameters, such as nature of the stimuli presented, method of administration, manner of interpreting responses, and test-construction procedures. Lindzey (64) has proposed a classification in terms of mode of response. Not only does such a classification focus upon a characteristic that is important in its own right, but it also shows close agreement with a composite classification

based on all major attributes of well-known projective techniques. This classification, which will be followed in the present chapter, groups projective
techniques into five categories:

(1) *associative techniques,* in which the subject must respond to a stimulus by
giving the first word, image, or percept that occurs to him;

(2) *construction procedures,* requiring the subject to create or construct a
product, such as a story;

(3) *completion tasks,* such as completing sentences or stories;

(4) *choice or ordering devices,* calling for the rearrangement of pictures, recording of preferences, and the like;

(5) *expressive methods,* such as drawing, which differ from construction procedures in that the subject's style or method is evaluated as well as the finished product.

ASSOCIATIVE TECHNIQUES

Word Association. A technique that antedated the current flood of projective tests by more than half a century is the word association test (19,
Ch. 2). Originally known as the "free association test," this technique was
first systematically described by Galton in 1879 (47). Wundt subsequently
introduced it into the psychological laboratory, where it was adapted to many
uses. The procedure involves simply the presentation of a series of discon-
nected words, to each of which the subject is told to respond by giving the
first word that comes to his mind. The early experimental psychologists, as
well as the first mental testers, saw in such association tests a tool for the
exploration of thinking processes.

The clinical application of word association methods was stimulated largely
by the psychoanalytic movement, although other psychiatrists, such as Kraepelin, had previously investigated such techniques. Among the psychoana-
lysts, Jung's contribution to the systematic development of the word association test is most conspicuous (58). Jung selected stimulus words to represent
common "emotional complexes." The responses were analyzed with reference
to reaction time and content, the latter being classified according to the general character of the association, such as contrast, supraordinate, modifying
adjective, sound association, and the like. Overt expressions of emotional
tension, such as laughing, flushing, and hand movements, were also noted.

The test was then readministered with the subject being instructed to try to recall the original responses. Changes in response words and other features of the subject's retest behavior provided further diagnostic clues.

More recently, a word association technique was developed at the Menninger Clinic by Rapaport, Gill, and Schafer (81, Ch. 2). In its general orientation, this adaptation reveals its kinship to the earlier Jung test. The 60-word list contains a preponderance of words selected for their psychoanalytic significance, many of them being associated with psychosexual conflicts. According to its authors, the test had a dual aim: to aid in detecting impairment of thought processes and to suggest areas of significant internal conflicts. Results are analyzed with reference to such characteristics as proportion of common or popular responses, reaction times, associative disturbances, and impaired reproduction on retest.

A different approach to the word association test is illustrated by the early work of Kent and Rosanoff (59). Designed principally as a psychiatric screening instrument, the Kent-Rosanoff Free Association Test utilized completely objective scoring and statistical norms. The stimulus words consisted of 100 common, neutral words, chosen because they tend to evoke the same associations from people in general. For example, to the word "table," most people respond "chair"; to "dark," they say "light." A set of frequency tables was prepared—one for each stimulus word—showing the number of times each response was given in a standardization sample of 1000 normal adults.

In scoring the test, the median frequency value of the responses that the subject gave to the 100 stimulus words was employed as an "index of commonality." Any responses not found in the normative tables were designated as "idiosyncratic." Comparisons of psychotics with normals suggested that psychotics give more idiosyncratic responses and obtain a lower index of commonality than the normals. The test fell into disuse, however, with the gradual realization that the frequency of different responses also varies widely with age, socioeconomic and educational level, regional and cultural background, and other factors. The task of developing adequate normative tables would thus be prohibitive, unless the test were to be used within a narrowly delimited population.

A number of investigators have been exploring the possibilities of utilizing *homographs* as stimuli for free association, with promising results. Homographs are words that are spelled identically but have two or more distinctly different meanings. For example, "ring" may refer to an article of jewelry or to the sound of a bell; "friction" may refer to the operation of a machine or to interpersonal relations. By means of criterion keying, experimental versions of homograph tests have been developed for measuring such traits as masculinity-femininity (48), leadership (35, 49), and emotional dependence upon one's social environment (98).

The free association method has also been employed in the appraisal of *interest and attitudes*. A free association interest test was developed by Wyman (104) for analyzing the interests of gifted children. This investigation was part of the well-known study of gifted children conducted under the direction of Terman at Stanford University. In the Wyman test, the responses were scored with reference to "intellectual interest," "social interest," and "activity interest."

Another adaptation of the word association technique for the study of attitudes is illustrated by the work of Murray and Morgan (77). Their procedure was to have the examiner read a list of 48 words—such as "father," "Communism," and "religion"—to each of which the subject was to respond by giving "the most descriptive adjectives" he could think of. The subject was led to believe that the test was designed to measure the range of his vocabulary. Actually, however, the responses were analyzed with respect to the ratio of appreciative to depreciative adjectives.

Mention may likewise be made of the use of the word association technique as a *"lie detector."* This application was also initiated by Jung, and has subsequently been subjected to extensive research—both in the laboratory and in practical situations (cf. 31, Ch. 9; 32, Ch. 11). The rationale offered to justify the employment of word association in the detection of lying or guilt is similar to that which underlies its utilization in uncovering areas of emotional conflict. Content analysis, reaction time, and response disturbances have all been explored as indices of lying or guilt. Frequently, physiological measures of emotional excitement are obtained concurrently with the verbal responses. The word lists chosen for lie detection purposes are usually custom-made to cover distinctive features of the particular crime or other situation under investigation. Whether word association has any practical value as a lie detector is still a moot point. Its effectiveness certainly varies widely with the specific circumstances under which it is used.

The Rorschach Inkblots. The best-known and most widely discussed projective technique is undoubtedly the Rorschach. Developed by the Swiss psychiatrist, Hermann Rorschach, this technique was first described in 1921 (84). Although standardized series of inkblots had previously been utilized by psychologists in studies of imagination and other functions, Rorschach was the first to apply inkblots to the diagnostic investigation of the personality as a whole. In the development of this technique, Rorschach experimented with a large number of inkblots which he administered to different psychiatric groups. By a process of trial and error, those response characteristics that differentiated between the various psychiatric syndromes were gradually incorporated into the scoring system. The scoring procedures were further sharpened by supplementary testing of mental defectives, normals, artists, scholars, and other persons of known characteristics. Rorschach's methodology thus represented an early, informal, and relatively subjective application of criterion keying.

The Rorschach utilizes 10 cards,[1] on each of which is printed a bilaterally symmetrical inkblot similar to that illustrated in Figure 117. Five of the blots are executed in shades of gray and black only; two contain additional touches of bright red; and the remaining three combine several pastel shades. As the subject is shown each inkblot, he is asked to tell what he sees—what

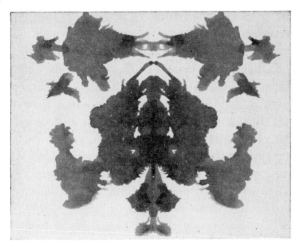

Fig. 117.   An Inkblot of the Type Employed in the Rorschach Technique.

the blot could represent. Besides keeping a verbatim record of the subject's responses to each card, the examiner notes time of responses, position or positions in which cards are held, spontaneous remarks, emotional expressions, and other incidental behavior of the subject during the test session. Following the presentation of all 10 cards, the examiner questions the subject systematically regarding the parts and aspects of each blot to which the associations were given. During this inquiry, the subject also has an opportunity to clarify and elaborate his earlier responses.

The 10 cards are the only part of the Rorschach actually shared by the various techniques bearing that name. Several clinicians have developed

[1] The cards, or plates, are printed by Hans Huber, in Berne, Switzerland. They can be obtained in America from Grune & Stratton or from a number of test distributors, such as C. H. Stoelting and The Psychological Corporation.

their own Rorschach "systems," the major differences among them being in the scoring and interpretation of responses (17, 18, 55, 60, 61, 79, 90). Some of these systems are characterized by exaggerated claims regarding the applicability and effectiveness of the technique, or by naïve metaphorical interpretation of responses, or by procedures so highly subjective as to render communication and replication difficult. Among the most widely used Rorschach techniques in America is that developed by Beck (17), which also adheres most closely to the original procedure followed by Rorschach.

The most common scoring categories employed with the Rorschach include location, determinants, and content. *Location* refers to the part of the blot with which the subject associates each response. Does he use the whole blot, a common detail, an unusual detail, white space, or some combination of these areas? The *determinants* of the response include form, color, shading, and "movement." Although there is of course no movement in the blot itself, the subject's perception of the blot as a representation of a moving object is scored in this category. Further differentiations are made within these categories. For example, human movement, animal movement, and abstract or inanimate movement are separately scored. Similarly, shading may be perceived by the subject as representing depth, texture, hazy forms such as clouds, or achromatic reproductions of colors as in a photograph.

The treatment of *content* varies from one scoring system to another, although certain major categories are regularly employed. Chief among these are human figures, human details (or parts of human figures), animal figures, animal details, and anatomical diagrams. Other broad scoring categories include inanimate objects, plants, maps, clouds, blood, x-rays, sexual objects, and symbols. A *popularity* score is often found on the basis of the relative frequency of different responses among people in general. For each of the 10 cards, certain responses are scored as popular because of their common occurrence.

Further analysis of Rorschach responses is based upon the relative number of responses falling into the various categories, as well as upon certain ratios and interrelations among different categories. Examples of the sort of qualitative interpretations that have commonly been utilized with Rorschach responses include the association of "whole" responses with conceptual thinking, of "color" responses with emotionality, and of "human movement" responses with imagination and fantasy life. In the usual application of the Rorschach, major emphasis is placed on the final "global" description of the individual, in which the clinician integrates the results from different parts of the protocol and takes into account the interrelations of different scores and indices. In actual practice, information derived from outside sources, such as other tests, interviews, and case history records, is also utilized in preparing such global descriptions.

Although the Rorschach is considered to be applicable from the preschool to the adult level, its normative data were derived largely from adult groups. This limitation also characterizes the general fund of clinical experience accumulated through the use of the Rorschach and employed in the qualitative interpretation of protocols. In the effort to extend the empirical framework for Rorschach interpretation to other age groups, Ames and her co-workers at the Gesell Institute of Child Development at Yale collected and published Rorschach norms on children between the ages of 2 and 10 years (2), on adolescents between the ages of 10 and 16 (4), and on older persons from the age of 70 up (3).

Some of the underlying assumptions of traditional Rorschach scoring have been called into question by a growing body of research findings. Comparative studies with standard and achromatic series of Rorschach cards, for example, have demonstrated that color itself has no effect on most of the response characteristics customarily attributed to it (16). There is also evidence that verbal aptitude influences several Rorschach scores commonly interpreted as indicators of personality traits (67, 87). In one study (87), an analysis of the verbal complexity of individual Rorschach responses given by 100 persons revealed that "movement" responses tended to be longer and linguistically more complex than "form" responses. It was also found that verbal complexity of Rorschach responses was highly correlated with the subjects' scores on a verbal aptitude test, as well as with age and educational level.

A major complicating factor in the interpretation of Rorschach scores is the total number of responses—known as response productivity or R (42). Because of large individual differences in R, the practice of considering the absolute number of responses in various categories is obviously misleading. If two individuals or groups differ in R, they are also likely to differ in the same direction in the number of responses falling in specific categories. Thus the differences found in certain categories may be only an artifact resulting from the variation in total number of responses. Nor is the use of percentages a completely satisfactory solution. For example, a protocol containing many responses is likely to include a smaller *proportion* of "whole" responses, since the number of "whole" responses that can reasonably be perceived in the blots is quite limited, while associations to isolated details of the blots may continue indefinitely.

To these intrinsic characteristics of the Rorschach scores may be added the empirical fact that response productivity appears to be closely related to age, intellectual level, and amount of education. Even more disturbing is the finding that R varies significantly from one examiner to another (cf. 15, 50). All of these results suggest that R, which may itself be a major determinant of many of the common Rorschach scores, is influenced by factors quite extraneous to the basic personality variables allegedly measured by the Rorschach. Findings such as these strike at the very foundation upon which the entire elaborate superstructure of Rorschach scoring is supported.

Nor can any encouragement be found in empirical studies of Rorschach validity. Despite a bibliography of over two thousand publications on the Rorschach, the vast majority of interpretive relationships that form the basis of Rorschach scoring have never been empirically validated. The number of published studies that have *failed* to demonstrate a significant relation between Rorschach scores, combinations of scores, or global evaluations and relevant criteria is truly impressive. The Rorschach was found to have little or no predictive or concurrent validity when checked against such criteria as psychiatric diagnosis, response to psychotherapy, various determinations of personality or intellectual traits in normal persons, success or failure in a wide variety of occupations in which personality qualities play an important part, and presence of various conflicts, fears, attitudes, or fantasies independently identified in patients. Those studies that appear to provide positive results have been shown to contain serious methodological defects. Further attention to some of these methodological problems will be given in the concluding section of this chapter. For more detailed evaluation of the Rorschach technique itself, the reader is urged to examine the unusually thorough discussions of this instrument by four independent reviewers in *The Fifth Mental Measurements Yearbook*.

Partly as a result of the predominantly negative findings of validation studies, there has been a shift of emphasis from traditional perceptual or formal scoring to content analysis of Rorschach responses (105, 106). Rorschach himself and most of his followers have relied most heavily on the perceptual bases of the subject's associations to the inkblots, as illustrated by location, color, form, shading, etc. Implicit in such an approach are the assumptions that the subject's responses to the Rorschach cards are indicative of his usual perceptual responses and that personality traits influence perception. In contrast to this approach, content analysis concentrates on *what* the subject perceives in the blots. Such content can then be treated in much the same way as one would treat any material reported by the subject during a clinical interview (cf. 105). Results obtained through this approach appear somewhat more promising than those utilizing perceptual scoring procedures.

In line with the growing tendency to use the Rorschach as an adjunct to the clinical interview, attention is also being given to the role of interpersonal factors in Rorschach responses. There is considerable evidence to show that the social interaction of a particular subject with a particular examiner influences many aspects of the subject's responses and of the examiner's interpretation of such responses (72, 88, 90). In the light of all available data, it would seem best at this stage to regard the Rorschach as an interview aid for the skilled clinician, rather than as a test. This is not to deny the possibility that a valid, objectively scorable inkblot test of personality characteristics may be developed in the future. Experimentation along these lines is in progress (cf., e.g., 57), and some of it may prove fruitful.

CONSTRUCTION PROCEDURES

In contrast to the associative techniques discussed in the preceding section, the type of projective instrument now under consideration requires more complex and somewhat more controlled intellectual activities on the part of the subject. Thus in telling or writing a story that fits a given picture, the individual is bound by certain implicit conventions regarding grammatical expression, logical organization, unity of content, congruence with all elements in the picture, and the like. The instructions, too, frequently focus on quality of production, by introducing the task as a test of imagination or intelligence. Interpretation of responses is typically based on content analysis of a rather qualitative nature. With the gradual realization that content analysis of projective techniques may be more fruitful than formal scoring, there has been an increasing tendency on the part of clinicians to turn to these story construction techniques, which provide more opportunities for content analysis than does the Rorschach.

Thematic Apperception Test. The original and basic test in the present category is the Thematic Apperception Test (TAT) developed by Murray and his staff at the Harvard Psychological Clinic (13; 53; 75; 76; 102, pp. 636-649). Not only has this test been used much more widely than other story construction techniques, but it has also served as a model for the development of later instruments in this class. The TAT materials consist of 19 cards containing vague pictures in black and white and one blank card. The subject is asked to make up a story to fit each picture, telling what led up to the event shown in the picture, describing what is happening at the moment and what the characters are feeling and thinking, and giving the outcome. In the case of the blank card, the subject is instructed to imagine some picture on the card, describe it, and then tell a story about it. The original procedure outlined by Murray (75) requires two one-hour sessions, 10 cards being employed during each session. The cards reserved for the second session were deliberately chosen to be more unusual, dramatic, and bizarre, and the accompanying instructions urge the subject to give free play to his imagination. Four overlapping sets of 20 cards are available—for boys, girls, men over 14, and women over 14. Most clinicians use abridged sets of specially selected cards, seldom giving more than 10 cards to a single respondent. A card from the second set is shown in Figure 118.

Fig. 118. One of the Pictures Used in the Thematic Apperception Test. (Reproduced by permission of Harvard University Press.)

In interpreting TAT stories, the examiner first determines who is the "hero," the character of either sex with whom the subject has presumably identified himself. The content of the stories is then analyzed principally in reference to Murray's list of "needs" and "press." Several of the proposed needs were described in the preceding chapter, in connection with the Edwards Personal Preference Schedule. Examples include achievement, aggression, nurturance, and sex. Press refers to environmental forces that may facilitate or interfere with the satisfaction of needs. Being attacked or criticized by another person, receiving affection, being comforted, and exposure to physical danger as in a shipwreck are illustrations of press. In assessing the importance or strength of a particular need or press for the individual, special attention is given to the intensity, duration, and frequency of its occurrence in different stories, as well as to the "uniqueness" of its association with a given picture. The assumption is made that unusual material, which departs from the common responses to each picture, is more likely to have significance for the individual.

A fair amount of normative information has been published regarding the most frequent response characteristics for each card, including the way each card is perceived, the themes developed, the roles ascribed to the characters, emotional tones expressed, speed of responses, length of stories, and the like (cf. 13; 53; 101, Ch. 16). Although these normative data provide a general framework for interpreting individual responses, most clinicians rely heavily on "subjective norms" built up through their own experience with the test. A number of quantitative scoring schemes and rating scales have been developed that yield good scorer reliability. Since their application is rather time consuming, however, such scoring procedures are seldom used in clinical practice. Although typically given as an individual oral test in the clinical situation, the TAT may also be administered in writing and as a group test. There is some evidence suggesting that under the latter conditions productivity of meaningful material may be facilitated.

The TAT has been used extensively in personality research. Several investigations have been concerned with the assumptions that underlie TAT interpretations, such as self-identification with the hero and personal significance of uncommon responses (63). Although they cannot establish concurrent or predictive validity of the TAT for specific uses, such studies contribute to the construct validation of TAT interpretations. A basic assumption that TAT shares with other projective techniques is that present motivational and emotional condition of the subject affects his responses to an unstructured test situation. A considerable body of experimental data is available to show that such conditions as hunger, sleep deprivation, social frustration, and the experience of failure in a preceding test situation significantly affect TAT responses (cf. 13). While supporting the projective hypothesis, the sensitivity of the TAT to such temporary conditions may complicate the detection of more enduring individual traits.

Some of the research on the effect of personality characteristics on TAT responses has dealt with the concurrent validity of the TAT in differentiating various clinical groups. A number of studies employing rather sophisticated experimental designs have been concerned with the detection of aggressive tendencies. In interpreting the results of such investigations, it has been repeatedly pointed out that the hypothesized relation between aggression in fantasy—as revealed in the TAT—and aggression in overt behavior is not a simple one. Depending upon other concomitant personality characteristics, high aggression in fantasy may be associated with either high or low overt aggression. There is some evidence suggesting that, if strong aggressive tendencies are accompanied by high anxiety or fear of punishment, expressions of aggression will tend to be high in fantasy and low in overt behavior; when anxiety and fear of punishment are low, high fantasy aggression is associated with high overt aggression (78, 80).

Lack of significant correlation between expressions of aggression in TAT stories and in overt behavior in a random sample of cases is thus consistent with expectation, since the relation may be positive in some individuals and negative in others. Obviously, however, such a lack of correlation is also consistent with the hypothesis that the test has no validity at all in detecting aggressive tendencies. What is needed, of course, is more studies using complex experimental designs that permit an analysis of the conditions under which each assumption is applicable. With reference to different needs, it has been suggested by Murray and others that whether the correlation between overt and fantasy expression is positive or negative may depend in part on whether the satisfaction of a particular need is encouraged or inhibited in a given culture. All of these findings again highlight the fact that personality trait scores should not be interpreted without reference to other traits or concomitant circumstances.

It is apparent that the TAT can provide rich material for personality research or for qualitative interpretation by an experienced clinician. But attempts to use it as an objective test in its present form could yield very misleading results. Also relevant is the finding that, like the Rorschach, the TAT has proved susceptible to examiner and situational variables (72, 100). The interpersonal relation of examiner and subject influences TAT responses, as it influences the results of any interviewing technique.

Adaptations of the TAT and Related Tests. A number of adaptations of the TAT have been developed for special purposes. These exhibit varying degrees of resemblance to the original. Where to draw the line between modified versions of the TAT and new tests based on the same general approach as the TAT is arbitrary. Several versions of the TAT have been prepared for use in attitude surveys, especially for studying attitudes toward labor problems and toward various minority groups (cf. 33, p. 16). In one adaptation, for example, ambiguous pictures portraying labor situations were intermingled with the usual TAT cards. Other investigators have designed special sets of cards showing intergroup contacts and other relevant scenes.

Some TAT adaptations have focused on the intensive measurement of a single need or drive, such as sex or aggression (13). Of special interest is the extensive research on the achievement motive conducted by McClelland and his associates (70). To measure the individual's need for achievement, McClelland selected four pictures, two of which were taken from the TAT. The cards portray men working at a machine, a boy at a desk with a book, a father and son picture, and a boy who is apparently daydreaming. Detailed scoring schemas have been developed for scoring the resulting stories with regard to expressions of the achievement drive (13, pp. 179-204; 70).

One revision of the TAT was prepared for use with Negroes, since it was found that Negro respondents were often unable to identify sufficiently with the characters portrayed on the original cards (97). In the revised form, the original pictures were utilized, but Negro figures were substituted for white persons on all cards except a few whose nature made the change unnecessary. Several subsequent studies have shown, however, that neither total number of words nor number of ideas in stories by Negroes differed significantly between the original and Negro forms. Since Negroes living in the American culture are unaccustomed to seeing pictures of Negroes, the use of such pictures tends to focus attention on racial problems. The test may thus be useful in exploring racial attitudes and stereotypes among both Negroes and whites, but its advantages for clinical evaluation of individual Negroes have been questioned. Other variants of the TAT have been developed for use in different cultures. Such variants usually substitute culturally more appropriate situations, besides modifying the appearance and dress of the characters.

Although the TAT is said to be applicable to children as young as 4 years, other forms for young subjects have also been prepared. Among them are the Symonds Picture-Story Test for adolescents, the Children's Apperception Test (CAT), and the Michigan Picture Test. In the Symonds test (93, 94), the TAT pictures were replaced by drawings representing situations of concern to adolescents, most of the cards portraying teen-age boys or girls. The CAT (20, 21) employs pictures of animals rather than people, on the assumption that young children identify more readily with animals than with human beings. The various animals in the pictures are portrayed in typically human situations, in the characteristic anthropomorphic style of a child's picture book. The pictures are designed to evoke fantasies relating to such problems as those of feeding and other oral activity, sibling rivalry, parent-child relations, aggression, toilet-training, and other childhood experiences. Contrary to the authors' assumption, several studies with children from the first grade up have found either no significant difference or—more often—greater productivity with human than with animal pictures (12, 22, 46, 62).

The Michigan Picture Test (11) was developed in the course of an investigation of the emotional reactions of children between the ages of 8 and 14, conducted by the Michigan Department of Mental Health. The test consists of 16 TAT-like pictures, chosen to represent intrafamilial conflicts, feelings of personal inadequacy, sexual difficulties, and other emotional problems. Scores are based on seven psychological needs, four of which were found useful in discriminating between groups of well-adjusted and poorly adjusted children. Scoring is highly objective, interscorer reliability for all needs and all grade levels averaging .98. One of the scores computed is a "tension index," showing the frequency of verbalized expressions of unresolved conflict. The authors report expectancy ratios indicating the probability that a child with a given tension index will fall into the well-adjusted or poorly adjusted category. In comparison with other projective devices, the Michigan test is unusual in the quality of its test-construction procedures and of the accompanying manual. Although promising results are reported from a few studies, it is too early to determine how useful the test will prove in practice.

Mention may also be made of several available story-telling techniques utilizing auditory stimuli. Such tests should prove useful in testing the blind or persons with defective vision, although they are not limited to these purposes. In one such test (14), 10 sets of sound situations are presented on records. A wide variety of sounds are included, such as typewriter, dialogue, foghorn, wind, explosions, and train crash. After listening to each set, the subject makes up a story incorporating as many of the sounds as he can. As in the TAT, the story should tell what happened, what led up to the sounds, and what was the outcome.

The Blacky Pictures. Originally devised as a means of investigating certain psychoanalytic hypotheses, The Blacky Pictures (23) concentrate on the assessment of various areas of psychosexual development. The materials consist of 10 cards with cartoon-like drawings. These drawings concern a dog named Blacky, who could be of either sex, as well as his mother, father, and sibling— who could also be of either sex. The test was designed for adults, but is described as being suitable also for children. The procedure is similar to that of the TAT, in that the subject tells a story about each picture. As each card is presented, however, the examiner adds a preliminary statement that structures the situation a little more than in the usual projective test. Following the completion of each story, the subject is asked a set of standardized questions.

Although an ingenious research tool, this test can have little practical value until more empirical information is obtained as to what it measures.

Make A Picture Story. Still another variation of the storytelling procedure is illustrated by the Make A Picture Story (MAPS), developed by Shneidman (91). Like the TAT, this test is presented to the subject as a measure of his imaginative and creative abilities. In this case, however, the subject first creates his own dramatic situations by choosing figures to go with a given background, and then he develops a story around the scene. The test provides 22 pictorial backgrounds, ranging from such highly structured ones as a living-room or a bathroom to such ambiguous ones as a dream, a stage, or a cave-like opening. One completely blank background is also included. There are 67 cut-out cardboard figures, including 19 male adults, 11 female adults, 2 adults of indeterminate sex, 12 children, 10 minority group figures (such as Negroes, Jews, Orientals), 6 legendary or fictitious characters (such as Santa Claus), 2 animals (dog and snake), and 5 silhouettes and figures with blank faces. Most of the figures are fully clothed, but a few are partly clothed or nude.

Figure 119 shows the assortment of characters furnished with the MAPS

Fig. 119. Materials for Use with MAPS (Make A Picture Story) Technique. (Courtesy The Psychological Corporation.)

test, as well as one of the backgrounds, a forest scene, against which four figures have been arranged on wooden stands. In administering the test, the examiner presents the backgrounds one at a time, asking the subject to select one or more figures, place them against the background, and "tell a story about who the characters are, what they are doing and thinking and how they feel, and how the whole thing turns out." Usually about half of the backgrounds are employed, the particular choice varying somewhat with the nature of the specific case. At the end, the subject may be asked to choose his own background from those that are left.

A formal scoring system has been worked out that takes into account which figures are chosen, how many are used, where they are placed, how they are handled by the subject, and what relationships they are said to bear to each other. Since the chief aim of this test is the investigation of the "psychosocial aspects of fantasy production," the scoring categories relate principally to interpersonal relationships. Scoring elements were selected by criterion keying against a schizophrenic and a normal sample. Available data, however, are insufficient to permit an evaluation of the concurrent validity of the proposed scoring key. It is also possible, of course, to submit the content of the stories to a thematic analysis of the type employed with the TAT.

COMPLETION TASKS

In completion tasks, the subject may be required to complete sentences, stories, arguments, or conversations. All available projective completion tests utilize verbal material, although some combine pictorial and verbal stimuli. The subject's responses, however, are always verbal, but they may be reported orally or in writing. Completion tests lend themselves to both group and individual administration. Since they provide opportunities for content analysis as well as for formal scoring, they are being employed increasingly for a variety of purposes.

Sentence Completion. Unlike the incomplete sentences found in measures of verbal aptitude, those utilized in projective tests permit highly varied completions. Generally, only the opening words are provided, the subject being required to write the ending. A few typical examples are shown below:

I feel . . .
What annoys me . . .
My mind . . .
If I had my way . . .
Women . . .

As in the development of adjustment inventories, the construction of projective sentence completion tests has been characterized by extensive borrowing of items. It is therefore difficult to trace the original authorship of items or sets of items. Several current versions, moreover, have many common items.

As a typical illustration, we may consider the Rotter Incomplete Sentences Blank (86). This test comprises 40 incomplete sentences, or "stems." The directions to the subject read: "Complete these sentences to express *your real feelings.* Try to do every one. Be sure to make a complete sentence." Each completion is rated on a seven-point scale according to the degree of adjustment or maladjustment indicated. Illustrative completions corresponding to each rating are given in the manual. With the aid of these specimen responses, fairly objective scoring is possible. The sum of the individual ratings provides a total adjustment score that can be used for screening purposes. The response content can also be examined clinically for more specific diagnostic clues. Validation studies have yielded some promising results. The manual gives a well-balanced, conservative evaluation of the strengths and weaknesses of the test, thereby providing a welcome contrast to the exaggerated claims made for most projective instruments.

In the Sentence Completions Test developed by Rohde (82, 83), a system of quantitative scoring has been worked out in terms of Murray's needs and press. Since such scoring is rather time consuming, however, qualitative content analysis may be employed instead. Normative data have been gathered on junior high school and normal adult groups. Comparative results are also available from neurotic and psychotic samples. Other variants of the sentence completion method have also been employed in studying intergroup attitudes (cf. 33). In general, the sentence completion technique can be readily adapted for specific purposes. This is one of its advantages, in both a clinical and a research setting.

Story Completion. In story completion tests, the subject is generally given one or more brief descriptions of dramatic incidents or unfinished plots, which he then uses as a nucleus for writing his own story. An oral procedure may be substituted, especially with children. The multiple-choice form has also been employed in such story completion tests.

Still another version is illustrated by the Test of Insight into Human Nature (89), so labeled in order to arouse interest and at the same time disguise the true purpose of the test. Each item in this test describes an incident involving a conflict situation. The subject is asked to write answers to two questions pertaining to each incident: (*a*) "What did he (or she) do and why?" and (*b*) "How did he (or she) feel?" The major areas of conflict sampled by the test include family, opposite sex, social and friendship relations, vocation, religious and moral beliefs, and health. A quantitative scoring scheme is provided, but the empirical data on which it was based are very inadequate. Responses can also be subjected to qualitative content analysis.

Argument Completion. Murray and Morgan (77) prepared an argument completion test as a means of exploring attitudes. The subject is given 10 cards, on each of which is printed a brief description of the beginning of an argument between two young men. In each case, the subject is to continue the argument to its termination, employing a realistic dialogue. The examinee is given the impression that his powers of argumentation are being tested. It is expected, however, that in the process of carrying out the task he will reveal which side of the argument he favors.

Rosenzweig Picture-Frustration Study. Combining pictorial and verbal material, the Rosenzweig Picture-Frustration Study (P-F) was designed in terms of the author's theory of frustration and aggression (85). This test is available in a form for children (4 to 13 years) and a form for adults (14 years and older). Each form comprises a series of cartoon-like drawings, depicting two principal characters. One of these persons is involved in a mildly frustrating situation of common occurrence; the other is saying something that either occasions the frustration or calls attention to the frustrating circumstances. The subject is instructed to write in the blank caption box what the frustrated person would answer. He is urged to give the very first reply that comes to his mind. The frustrating situations are of two types: (*a*) "ego-blocking," in which some obstruction, personal or impersonal, impedes, disappoints, deprives, or otherwise thwarts the individual directly; and (*b*) "superego-blocking," in which the individual is insulted, accused, or otherwise incriminated by another person. An item from the adult form is reproduced in Figure 120.

The Picture-Frustration Study is based on the assumption that the subject identifies with the frustrated character in each picture and projects his own reaction tendencies in the replies given. In scoring the test, each reply is classified with reference to type of reaction and direction of aggression. Type of reaction includes: "obstacle-dominance," in which the frustrating object is emphasized in the response; "ego-defense," in which attention is focused on the protection of the thwarted individual; and "need-persistence," in which the solution of the frustrating problem is paramount. Direction of aggression is scored as: "extrapunitive," or turned out upon the environment; "intropunitive," or turned in upon the subject; and "impunitive," or turned off in an attempt at glossing over or evading the situation. The percentage of responses falling into each of these categories is determined. A group conformity rating (GCR), showing the subject's tendency to give responses that agree with the modal responses of the standardization sample, may also be obtained.

Fig. 120. Illustrative Item from Rosenzweig P-F Study. (Reproduced by permission of Saul Rosenzweig.)

Norms for the P-F Study have been gathered on many special groups, but no systematic national norms are available, nor is sufficient information given regarding the characteristics of normative samples. Separate norms are provided with translations prepared for use in several countries of Europe, Asia, and Africa. Both temporal stability and interitem consistency of the test are low. A revision utilizing item analysis to obtain higher internal consistency would be desirable, as long as performance on separate items is summated to yield total scores. Interscorer agreement is only moderate. Validity studies have yielded some positive and some negative results.

Being more limited in coverage, more highly structured, and relatively objective in its scoring procedures, the P-F Study lends itself better to statistical analysis than most other projective techniques. More systematic efforts have also been made to gather norms and to check its reliability and validity. In its present form, however, its value as an objective instrument has not been established. Its use must therefore be circumscribed by the same cautions applying to other projective techniques.

Like a number of other projective instruments, the P-F Study has been adapted by other investigators for research on attitudes (cf. 33, 103). The general approach of the P-F Study has been followed in specially designed tests for studying attitudes toward minority groups (27) and opinions on the prevention of war (45).

CHOICE OR ORDERING DEVICES

Tests in this category require the subject to choose the items or arrangements that best fit a specified criterion such as meaningfulness or attractiveness. Such tests necessarily present a more highly structured stimulus situation and require simpler responses from the subject than most other projective techniques. As a result, objective, quantitative scoring systems are applicable, but they are likely to be laborious owing to the many possible combinations of responses. Although the two examples cited in this section are quite dissimilar in a number of ways, both may be regarded as falling between projective tests and the "objective" personality tests to be discussed in the next chapter. They are also alike in that both utilize pictorial material.

Szondi Test. In the Szondi Test (40, 95, 96) the subject is shown 48 photographs of psychiatric patients of both sexes, grouped into sets of eight. Each set contains pictures representing the following diagnostic categories: a homosexual, a sadistic murderer, an epileptic, a hysteric, a catatonic schizophrenic, a paranoid schizophrenic, a depressive, and a manic. The subject is instructed to select the two pictures he "likes most" and the two he "dislikes most" in each set. He is not, of course, given any indication of the psychiatric classification of the persons photographed. It is recommended that the test be administered at least six, and preferably ten, times with at least a one-day interval between administrations.

To score the Szondi Test, it is necessary first to find the number of pictures liked and disliked in each of the eight categories. The test is based on the assumption that each person can be described in terms of eight factors or "need-systems," which correspond to the categories of the photographs. It is further assumed that the selection or rejection of photographs indicates the relative tension existing in these need-systems. The final interpretive process is quite complex, taking into account not only the relative number of photographs of each kind chosen, but also the interplay of the need-systems and the temporal changes in the subject's responses.

The Szondi Test is probably one of the least promising of the currently popular projective techniques. Its theoretical rationale—both as originally presented by Szondi and as revamped by Deri—appears particularly weak and farfetched. Attempts at empirical validation of its various assumptions have so far yielded overwhelmingly negative results (25).

Tomkins-Horn Picture Arrangement Test. The development of the PAT (99) was influenced both by the general approach of the TAT and by the authors' observation that personality factors seemed to affect performance on the Picture Arrangement test of the Weschsler-Bellevue (cf. Ch. 12). Each of the 25 items of the PAT consists of three sketches presented in a round-robin arrangement so as to minimize positional set. The subject's task is to indicate the order of the three pictures "which makes the best sense" and to write a sentence for each of the three pictures to tell the story. All items deal with interpersonal relations. Since the test was originally designed for use in the selection and guidance of industrial personnel, more than half of its items portray a work situation.

Administration of the PAT is simple and suitable for testing large groups. Quantitative scoring is completely objective but time consuming. However, the test can be hand scored by a clerk or machine scored. Any subject's scores are based on those responses that are rare (frequency less than 5 per cent) among persons of his age, IQ, and educational level. It is the uncommon responses that a subject gives that are believed to be diagnostic for him. The authors have worked out 655 scoring patterns, representing significant response combinations. Once the quantitative score pattern has been identified for the individual, it is then interpreted by the clinical psychologist who may also refer to the subject's written material at this stage.

The attempt to develop an empirical system of pattern scoring is one of the contributions of this test. Another noteworthy feature is to be found in its unusually good norms. Through the resources of the Gallup Poll organization, the PAT was administered to 1500 persons constituting a representative sample of the United States population. In addition, comparative data were obtained on over seven hundred psychiatric patients in 84 clinics and mental hospitals. A vocabulary test given at the same time made possible the publication of subgroup norms with reference to intelligence as well as age, education, and other demographic variables.

On the negative side, no data are provided on interitem consistency. Temporal stability over a three-week interval proved to be low. And validity data are lacking. On the whole, the PAT has some ingenious features; it provides far better norms than most projective techniques; and it should be useful in research or as an adjunct to the clinical interview. But like many personality tests, it is not ready for general psychometric application.

EXPRESSIVE METHODS

As pointed out earlier in the chapter, expressive methods differ from construction techniques such as the TAT and MAPS in that the former consider the subject's method or style as well as the characteristics of the finished product. Another distinguishing feature of projective techniques in the present category is that they serve as therapeutic as well as diagnostic devices (64). Through the opportunities for self-expression that these techniques afford, it is believed that the individual not only reveals his difficulties but also relieves them. The principal projective techiques in this category include drawing and painting, play activities, and psychodrama.

Drawing and Painting. The use of drawing and painting for diagnostic as well as therapeutic purposes has a long and voluminous history (cf. 5; 6; 7; 8; 19, Ch. 17-19; 52). Few standardized instruments have emerged from this vast area of clinical practice and research. It will be recalled that drawings have also been utilized in non-projective testing, as illustrated by the Goodenough Draw-a-Man Test described in Chapter 10. In the restandardization of that test by Harris, however, projective uses of the drawings as an approach to personality were also explored (52).

Although almost every art medium, technique, and type of subject matter has been investigated in the search for significant diagnostic clues, special attention has centered upon drawings of the *human figure*. A well-known example is provided by the Machover Draw-a-Person Test (71). In this test, the subject is provided with a letter-size sheet of paper and a medium-soft pencil, and is told simply to "draw a person." For young children, the instructions may be altered to "draw somebody" or "draw a boy or a girl." Upon completion of the first drawing, the subject is asked to draw a person of the opposite sex from that of the first figure. While the subject draws, the examiner notes his comments, the sequence in which different parts are drawn, and other procedural details. The drawing may be followed by an inquiry, in which the subject is asked to make up a story about each person drawn, "as if he were a character in a play or novel." A series of questions is employed during the inquiry to elicit specific information about age, schooling, occupation, family, and other facts associated with the characters portrayed.

Scoring of the Draw-a-Person Test is essentially qualitative, involving the preparation of a composite personality description from an analysis of many features of the drawings. Among the factors considered in this connection are the absolute and relative size of the male and female figures, their position on the page, quality of lines, sequence of parts drawn, stance, front or profile view, position of arms, depiction of clothing, and background and grounding effects. Special interpretations are given for the omission of different bodily parts, disproportions, shading, amount and distribution of details, erasures, symmetry, and other stylistic features. There is also detailed discussion of the significance of each major body part, such as head, individual facial features, hair, neck, shoulders, breast, trunk, hips, and extremities.

The interpretive guide for the Draw-a-Person Test abounds in sweeping generalizations, such as "Disproportionately large heads will often be given by individuals suffering from organic brain disease," or "The sex given the proportionately larger head is the sex that is accorded more intellectual and social authority." But no evidence is provided in support of these statements. Reference is made to a file of "thousands of drawings" examined in clinical contexts, and a few selected cases are cited for illustrative purposes. No systematic presentation of data, however, accompanies the published report of the test.

Validation studies by other investigators have yielded conflicting results. Attempts to develop semi-objective scoring procedures which utilize rating scales or checklists have met with little success (cf., e.g., 9). The test may be more successful with children and other relatively naïve subjects than with sophisticated adult groups. Although it appears to differentiate between seriously disturbed persons and normals, its discriminative value within relatively normal groups is questionable. Some of the pertinent studies are inconclusive owing to their failure to cross-validate.

Another drawing test that has aroused considerable interest, as witnessed by the number of relevant research publications, is the House-Tree-Person Projective Technique (H-T-P) devised by Buck (28). In this test, the subject is told to draw as good a picture of a house as he can, the same instructions being repeated in turn with "tree" and "person." Meanwhile, the examiner takes copious notes on time, sequence of parts drawn, spontaneous comments by the subject, and expressions of emotion. The completion of the drawings is followed by an oral inquiry, including a long set of standardized questions. The drawings are analyzed both quantitatively and qualitatively, chiefly on the basis of their formal or stylistic characteristics.

In discussing the rationale underlying the choice of objects to be drawn,

Buck maintains that "house" should arouse associations concerning the subject's home and those living with him; "tree" should evoke associations pertaining to his life role and his ability to derive satisfaction from his environment in general; and "person" should call up associations dealing with interpersonal relations. Some clinicians may find helpful leads in such drawings, when they are considered jointly with other information about the individual case. But the elaborate and lengthy administrative and scoring procedures described by Buck appear unwarranted in the light of the highly inadequate nature of the supporting data.

In addition to drawing, several other art media have been tried in both diagnostic and therapeutic situations. Outstanding among them is *finger painting* (cf. 10, Ch. 14). Finger paints are spread directly with the hand upon a large sheet of glossy paper. They thus combine some of the aspects of painting and modeling. Simplicity of use is an important asset of this technique. Subjects with no previous art training or experience can readily produce many pleasing and satisfying designs. The fact that such paints can be easily washed off with clear water is a further practical advantage. For children, they also provide some of the attraction of playing with mud, smearing, or simply "making a mess." These features of finger paints are considered particularly important by some clinicians.

In the interpretation of finger paintings, as in the projective use of all paintings and drawings, some attempts have been made to attach specific diagnostic significance to the objects portrayed and to the formal characteristics of the products. Systems of more or less uniform symbols, often of a psychoanalytic nature, have been proposed for such purposes. Pending the empirical demonstration of the validity of specific signs, however, such interpretations are of dubious value. In their present stage of development, drawing and painting techniques can probably serve best by providing leads for the clinician to follow up through interviewing or other procedures.

Play Techniques. Play and dramatic objects, such as puppets, dolls, toys, and miniatures, have also been utilized in projective testing (cf. 19, Ch. 22). Originating in play therapy with children, these materials have subsequently been adapted for the diagnostic testing of both adults and children. The objects are usually selected because of their expected associative value. Among the articles most frequently employed for these purposes, for example, are dolls representing adults and children of both sexes and various age levels, furniture, bathroom and kitchen fixtures, and other household furnishings. Play with such articles is expected to reveal the child's attitudes toward his own family, as well as sibling rivalries, fears, aggressions, conflicts, and the like. The examiner notes what items the child chooses, what he does with them, his verbalizations, emotional expressions, and other overt behavior.

With children, these techniques often take the form of free play with the collection of toys that the examiner simply makes available. With adults, the materials are presented with general instructions to carry out some task of a highly unstructured nature. These instructions may, of course, also be employed with children. Frequently the task has certain dramatic features, as in the arrangement of figures on a miniature stage set. Several investigators have used play techniques in studying prejudice and other intergroup attitudes (33, p. 17).

One attempt to standardize projective "toy tests" is represented by the World Test. First developed in England by Lowenfeld (68), this test has been adapted, revised, and restandardized by Buhler and her associates (29, 30), Bolgar and Fischer (24), and others (cf. 19, Ch. 23). The materials consist of a large number of miniature pieces—from 150 to 300 in different forms—including houses, people, animals, bridges, trees, cars, fences, and other common objects that might be found outdoors. The subject is told to construct whatever he would like, using a large table top, the floor, or a sandbox as a base. In the various adaptations of the World Test, the responses have been evaluated in a number of ways. Some interpretive systems rely chiefly on formal properties of procedure and product, such as sequence of pieces chosen, number and variety of objects included, rigidity of organization, and the like. Others place more emphasis on content and symbolism. Accompanying verbalizations and other expressive reactions are also considered.

Psychodrama. In this technique (74; 19, Ch. 24), the subject himself enacts various roles on a stage, while a "director" (examiner-therapist) guides the general procedure. The active participation of an audience is also considered to be an integral aspect of this process. The subject's behavior is observed in a number of appropriately chosen situations. For example, the subject may be instructed that he is on the stage with an imaginary person and that he is to invent a relationship with this character, identifying the person, time, place, and activity. The subsequent action and conversation are left entirely up to the subject. This situation is designed to reveal what a social relationship means to the subject, as well as his manner of communicating with another person. In some situations, additional live actors, known as "auxiliary egos," play specified roles with the subject. Examples of some of the other situations include acting with real or imaginary objects; silent action that utilizes only gestures and gross bodily movements; rapid shifting from one role to another; and reversal of roles, in which the subject and another person trade places in the course of a scene. Into the various situations, the director may introduce a wide range of themes, such as love, death, family, economic problems, status, and security.

From a practical point of view, the application of psychodrama is limited by its demands in time, personnel, and physical facilities, although simplified versions are often employed. Lack of adequate standardization, with regard to administration, recording, and especially interpretation, is a serious drawback. A more fundamental limitation stems from the absence of validating data. It has been asserted that this technique needs no validation, since it utilizes samples of actual behavior. To be sure, all tests do so. But the question of validity remains nevertheless. To what extent does the subject's behavior on the psychodrama stage correlate with—or to what extent does it serve as a dependable indicator of—his behavior in other situations?

CRITICAL EVALUATION

It is evident that projective techniques differ widely among themselves. Some appear more promising than others because of more favorable empirical findings, sounder theoretical orientation, or both. Regarding some techniques, such as the Rorschach, voluminous data have been gathered, albeit their interpretation is often uncertain. About others little is known, either because of their recent origin, or because objective verification is hindered by the intrinsic nature of the instruments or by the attitudes of their exponents.

To evaluate each instrument individually and to attempt to summarize the extensive pertinent literature would require a separate volume. Within this chapter, critical comments have been interjected only in the cases of instruments that presented unique features—whether of a favorable or unfavorable nature. There are certain points, however, that apply to a greater or lesser extent to the bulk of projective techniques. These points can be conveniently considered in summary form.

Rapport and Applicability. Most projective techniques represent an effective means for "breaking the ice" during the initial contacts between subject and examiner. The task is usually intrinsically interesting and often entertaining to the subject. It tends to divert the subject's attention away from himself and thus reduces embarrassment and defensiveness. And it offers little or no threat to his prestige, since any response he gives is "right."

It should be noted parenthetically, however, that some projective techniques may have poor face validity for normal and superior adults—a fact that diminishes their acceptability for industrial selection, military screening or classification, and similar purposes. Wechsler's objections to the adult use of traditional, child-oriented intelligence tests (cf. Ch. 12) apply with even greater cogency to certain projective techniques. It is not difficult to predict the reactions of an Air Force pilot when confronted with four anthropomorphic portraits of dogs labeled "Blacky," "Papa," "Mama," and "Tippy," respectively!

On the other hand, projective techniques may be especially useful with young children, illiterates, and persons with language handicaps or speech defects. Non-verbal media would be readily applicable to all of these groups. And oral responses to pictorial and other non-language stimuli could be secured from the first two. With all these verbally limited groups, projective techniques may help the subject to communicate with the examiner. These techniques may also aid the subject in clarifying for himself some of his own behavior that he had not previously verbalized.

Faking. In general, projective instruments are less susceptible to faking than are self-report inventories. The purpose of projective techniques is usually disguised. Even if an individual has some psychological sophistication and is familiar with the general nature of a particular instrument, such as the Rorschach or TAT, it is still unlikely that he can predict the intricate ways in which his responses will be scored and interpreted. Moreover, the subject soon becomes absorbed in the task and hence is less likely to resort to the customary disguises and restraints of interpersonal communication.

On the other hand, it cannot be assumed that projective tests are completely immune to faking. Several experiments with the Rorschach, TAT, and other projective instruments have shown that significant differences do occur when subjects are instructed to alter their responses so as to create favorable or unfavorable impressions, or when they are given statements suggesting that certain types of responses are more desirable (72). In a particularly well-controlled study, Davids and Pildner (39) administered a battery of self-report and projective tests to two groups of college students, one of which took the tests as genuine job applicants, the other as participants in a research project. Under these conditions, the job applicants obtained significantly better-adjusted scores than the research subjects on the self-report but *not* on the projective tests. Certain types of projective test items, however, were found to be susceptible to faking. Thus sentence completion stems expressed in the first person yielded significantly more favorable responses than those expressed in the third person.

Standardization. It is obvious that most projective techniques are inadequately standardized with respect to both administration and scoring. Yet there is evidence that even subtle differences in the phrasing of verbal instructions and in examiner-subject relationships can appreciably alter performance on these tests (15, 72, 88, 90). Even when employing identical instructions, some examiners may be more encouraging or reassuring, others more threatening, owing to their general manner and appearance. Such differences may affect response productivity, defensiveness, stereotypy, imaginativeness, and other basic performance characteristics. In the light of these findings, problems of administration and testing conditions assume even greater importance than in other psychological tests.

Equally serious is the lack of objectivity in scoring. It will be recalled that even when objective scoring systems have been developed, the final steps in the evaluation and integration of the raw data depend upon the skill and clinical experience of the examiner. Such a situation has several implications. In the first place, it reduces the number of examiners who are properly qualified to employ the technique and thus limits the range of its effective application. It also means that the results obtained by different examiners may not be comparable, a fact that complicates research with the instrument. But perhaps the most disturbing implication is that the interpreting of scores is often as projective for the examiner as the test stimuli are for the subject. In other words, the final interpretation of projective test responses may reveal more about the theoretical orientation, favorite hypotheses, and personality idiosyncrasies of the examiner than it does about the subject's personality dynamics.

Norms. Another conspicuous deficiency common to most projective instruments pertains to normative data. Such data may be completely lacking, grossly inadequate, or based upon vaguely described populations. In the absence of adequate objective norms, the clinician falls back upon his "general clinical experience" to interpret projective test performance. But such a frame of reference is subject to all the distortions of memory that are themselves reflections of theoretical bias, preconceptions, and other idiosyncrasies of the clinician. Moreover, any one clinician's contacts may have been limited largely to persons who are atypical in education, socioeconomic level, sex ratio, age distribution, or other relevant characteristics. In at least one respect, the clinician's experience is almost certain to produce a misleading picture, since he deals predominantly with maladjusted or pathological cases. He thus lacks sufficient firsthand familiarity with the characteristic reactions of normal people. The Rorschach norms gathered by Ames and her associates on children, adolescents, and persons over 70 represent a recent effort to correct some of the more obvious lacks. The representative nationwide sample examined in the standardization of the Tomkins-Horn Picture Arrangement Test is an outstanding exception to the traditional practices followed in projective test development.

Interpretation of projective test performance often involves subgroup norms, of either a subjective or an objective nature. Thus the clinician may have a general subjective picture of what constitutes a "typical" schizophrenic or psychoneurotic performance on a particular test. Or the published data may provide qualitative or quantitative norms that delineate the characteristic performance of different diagnostic groups. In either case, the subgroup norms may lead to faulty interpretations unless the subgroups were equated in other respects. For example, if the schizophrenics and normals on whom the norms were derived differed also in mean educational level, the observed disparities between schizophrenic and normal performance may have resulted from educational inequality rather than from schizophrenia. Similar systematic or constant errors may operate in the comparison of various psychiatric syndromes. For example, schizophrenics as a group tend to be younger than manic-depressives; anxiety neurotics are likely to come from higher educational and socioeconomic levels than hysterics.

Reliability. In view of the relatively unstandardized scoring procedures and the inadequacies of normative data, *scorer reliability* becomes an important consideration in projective testing. For projective techniques, a proper measure of scorer reliability should include not only the more objective preliminary scoring, but also the final integrative and interpretive stages. It is not enough, for example, to demonstrate that examiners who have mastered the same system of Rorschach scoring agree closely in their tallying of such characteristics as whole, unusual detail, or color responses. On a projective test like the Rorschach, these raw quantitative measures cannot be interpreted directly from a table of norms, as in the usual type of psychological test. Interpretive scorer reliability is concerned with the extent to which different examiners attribute the same personality characteristics to the subject on the basis of their interpretations of the identical record.

Few adequate studies have been conducted on the scorer reliability of projective tests. Some investigations have revealed marked divergencies in the interpretations given by reasonably well-qualified test users. A fundamental ambiguity in such results stems from the unknown contribution of the interpreter's skill. Neither high nor low scorer reliability can be directly generalized to other scorers differing appreciably from those utilized in the particular investigation.

Attempts to measure other types of test reliability have fared equally poorly in the field of projective testing. Coefficients of *equivalence* or internal consistency, when computed, have usually been low. In such tests as the Rorschach and TAT, it has been argued that different cards are not comparable and hence should not be used in finding split-half reliabilities. One solution, of course, would be to construct a parallel form that *is* comparable. It should also be noted that in so far as responses to different Rorschach or TAT cards are combined in arriving at a total estimate of any personality characteristic, intercard agreement is assumed. Yet empirical results have rarely supported this assumption. A careful investigation of TAT reliability, for example, yielded internal consistency correlations ranging from —.07 to .34 for 10 of the major themes, such as achievement, aggression, etc. (34).

Retest reliability also presents special problems. With long intervals, genuine personality changes may occur which the test should detect. With short intervals, a retest may show no more than recall of original responses. When the investigators instructed their subjects to write different TAT stories on a retest, in order to determine whether the same themes would recur, most of the scored variables yielded insignificant retest correlations (65). It is also relevant to note that many scores derived from projective techniques are based upon very inadequate response samples. In the case of the Rorschach, for instance, the number of responses within a given individual's protocol that fall into such categories as animal movement, human movement, shading, color, unusual detail, and the like may be so few as to yield extremely unreliable indices. Large chance variations are to be expected under such circumstances. Ratios and percentages computed with such unreliable measures are even more unstable than the individual measures themselves (cf. 36, pp. 411-412).

Validity. For any test, the most fundamental question is that of validity. Most empirical validation studies of projective tests have been concerned with *concurrent validity*. Of these, many have compared the performance of contrasted groups, such as occupational or diagnostic groups. As was pointed out in connection with norms, however, these groups often differ in other respects, such as age or education. Other investigations of concurrent validity have used essentially a matching technique, in which personality descriptions derived from test records are compared with descriptions or data about the same subjects taken from case histories, psychiatric interviews, or long-range behavioral records. A few studies have investigated *predictive validity* against such criteria as success in specialized types of training or response to psychotherapy. There has been an increasing trend to investigate the *construct validity* of projective instruments by testing specific hypotheses that underlie the use and interpretation of each test. This approach is illustrated by studies of the effect of hunger, sleep deprivation, drugs, anxiety, and frustration on test performance. as well as by research on examiner and situational variables.

All too often the advocates of a projective technique have based their claims on *content validity,* which in these cases means essentially that the technique appears to fit some particular personality theory. Such assertions can do no more than provide hypotheses for empirical verification. Mention should also be made of what has been variously described as "clinical validity," "subjective validity," and "faith validity." This is simply a feeling of satisfaction, unaccompanied by any demonstrable or communicable proof, reported by some clinicians who use a given technique. It is outside the realm of science.

The large majority of published validation studies on projective techniques are inconclusive because of procedural deficiencies in either experimental controls, statistical analysis, or both (cf. 36, 37, 41). This is especially true of studies concerned with the Rorschach. Some methodological deficiencies may have the effect of producing spurious evidence of test validity where none exists. An example is the contamination of either criterion or test data. Thus the criterion judges may have had some knowledge of the subjects' test performance. Similarly, the examiner may have obtained cues about the subject's characteristics from conversation with the subject in the course of test administration, or from case history material and other non-test sources. The customary control for the latter type of contamination in validation studies is to utilize "blind analysis," in which the test record is interpreted by a scorer who has had no contact with the subject and who has no information about him other than that contained in the test protocol.

Another common source of spurious validity data is failure to cross-validate (cf. Ch. 7). Because of the large number of potential diagnostic signs or scorable elements that can be derived from most projective tests, it is very easy by chance alone to find a set of such signs that differentiate significantly between criterion groups. The validity of such a scoring key, however, will collapse to zero when applied to new samples.

Inadequacies of experimental design may also have the effect of underestimating the validity of a diagnostic instrument. It is widely recognized, for example, that traditional psychiatric categories, such as schizophrenia, manic-depressive psychosis, and hysteria, represent crude and unrealistic classifications of the personality disorders actually manifested by patients. Hence if such diagnostic categories are used as the sole criterion for checking the validity of a personality test, negative results are inconclusive. Those who stress the importance of configural scoring, response patterns, and trait interrelationships in personality assessment have also objected to attempts to validate isolated scores or diagnostic signs derived from projective techniques. That insignificant correlations may result from failure to allow for complex patterns of relationship among personality variables was illustrated by the previously cited studies of aggression indicators in TAT stories.

Few research projects have been so designed as to avoid all the major pitfalls of projective test validation. The advanced student is urged to examine for himself the reports of such studies as those of Henry and Farley (54), Little and Shneidman (66), and Silverman (92), which set a high standard in experimental design. While differing in type of subject examined and in specific problems they set out to investigate, these studies point to a common conclusion: when experienced clinicians are given an opportunity to examine and interpret in their own way subjects' protocols from such projective tests as the Rorschach, TAT, and MAPS, their evaluations of the subjects' personalities tend to match independent case history evaluations significantly better than chance. In so far as can be ascertained, however, the obtained relations are low. Moreover, the relationship appears to be a function of the particular clinician and subject, a number of individual matches being no better than chance. There is also little agreement among evaluations based on different projective techniques, or among different clinicians using the same technique.

Current Trends. When first introduced, many projective techniques were surrounded by an atmosphere of cultism that tended to insulate them from the main stream of psychological research. The isolationism characterizing the exponents of such techniques retarded both the effective development and evaluation of the techniques and their acceptance by the psychological profession. One of the chief developments of personality testing during the 1950's was the attempt on the part of many psychologists to bring projective techniques into the main body of psychological science through a clarification of underlying theoretical rationale as well as carefully designed experimentation.

In the rapidly accumulating research findings on projective techniques, we can recognize certain trends pointing toward future developments. First, well-designed validation studies utilizing blind analyses and adequate experimental controls have demonstrated that even under optimal conditions such techniques have inadequate validity to justify their use as *psychometric tools* in making individual decisions. The utilization of projective techniques as tests thus appears to be on the decline.

Nevertheless, certain projective techniques may serve a useful function as *interviewing aids* in the hands of skilled clinicians. The realization that this is the proper role of projective techniques represents a second major trend. In this connection, qualitative content analysis is proving more fruitful than formal scoring categories. Furthermore, since the clinician is an intrinsic part of the interviewing situation, research on the effects of interpersonal examiner and subject variables on projective performance is relevant to this approach (51, 72, 100).

Borrowing a concept from information theory, Cronbach and Gleser (38, p. 128) characterize interviewing and projective techniques as "wide-band" procedures. Bandwidth, or breadth of coverage, is achieved at the cost of lowered fidelity or dependability of information. Objective psychometric tests characteristically yield a narrow band of information at a high level of dependability. In contrast, projective and interviewing techniques provide a much wider range of information of lower dependability. Moreover, the kinds of data furnished by any one projective technique may vary from individual to individual (38, p. 129). One person's TAT responses, for example, may tell us a good deal about his aggression and little or nothing about his creativity or achievement drive; another person's record may permit a thorough assessment of the degree of creativity or rigidity of his behavior and of the strength of his achievement drive, while revealing little about his aggression. Such a lack of uniformity in the kinds of information provided in individual cases helps to explain the low validities found when projective test responses are analyzed for any single trait across a group of persons.

It is interesting to note that a similar unevenness characterizes clinicians' interpretations of individual records. Thus in their study of the validity of the TAT, Henry and Farley (54, p. 22) conclude:

> There is no single correct way of employing the TAT interpretation. There was little item agreement between judges, but each judge made enough "correct" decisions to yield a highly significant agreement figure. Judges may arrive at essentially the same interpretive implications of the test report, by quite different routes; or judges may differ individually in their ability to utilize TAT predictions in different areas . . . or for different subjects.

The nature of "clinical judgment" through which projective and interviewing data may be utilized in reaching decisions about individual cases is receiving increasing attention from psychologists (56, 69, 73). In this process, the very constructs or categories in terms of which the data are organized are built up inductively through an examination of the particular combination of data available in the individual case. The special function of the clinician is to make predictions from unique or rare combinations of events about which it is impracticable to prepare any statistical table or equation. By creating new constructs to fit the individual case, the clinician can predict from combinations of events that he has never encountered before in any other case. In making his predictions, he can also take into account the varied significance of similar events for different individuals. Such clinical predictions are helpful, provided they are not accepted as final but are constantly tested against information elicited through subsequent inquiry, test responses, reaction to therapy, or other behavior on the part of the subject. It follows from the nature of interviewing and projective techniques that decisions should not be based on any single datum or score obtained from such sources. These techniques serve best in sequential decisions, by suggesting leads for further exploration or hypotheses about the individual for subsequent verification.

A third trend can be seen in the increasing use of projective techniques as *raw materials* for the development of objective tests. In this capacity, projective techniques provide hypotheses, such as possible relationships between specific aspects of perceptual responses and personality traits, around which structured tests can be devised. Such tests are objectively scorable, reducing to a minimim the role of the examiner as data gatherer or as data interpreter. They are typically narrow-band procedures, seeking to provide dependable information about a small segment of personality. To these tests, projective techniques are contributing not only a variety of fresh hypotheses but also testing procedures that minimize faking and façade effects. These objective personality tests are among the newer techniques for personality assessment to be surveyed in the next chapter.

REFERENCES

1. Abt, L. E., and Bellak, L. *Projective psychology.* N. Y.: Knopf, 1950.
2. Ames, Louise B., *et al. Child Rorschach responses: developmental trends from two to ten years.* N. Y.: Hoeber, 1952.
3. Ames, Louise B., *et al. Rorschach responses in old age.* N. Y.: Hoeber, 1954.
4. Ames, Louise B., *et al. Adolescent Rorschach responses: developmental trends from ten to sixteen years.* N. Y.: Hoeber, 1959.
5. Anastasi, Anne, and Foley, J. P., Jr. A survey of the literature on artistic behavior in the abnormal: III. Spontaneous productions. *Psychol. Monogr.,* 1940, 52, No. 6.
6. Anastasi, Anne, and Foley, J. P., Jr. A survey of the literature on artistic behavior in the abnormal: I. Historical and theoretical background. *J. gen. Psychol.,* 1941, 25, 111-142.
7. Anastasi, Anne, and Foley, J. P., Jr. A survey of the literature on artistic behavior in the abnormal: II. Approaches and interrelationships. *Ann. N. Y. Acad. Sci.,* 1941, 42, 1-112.
8. Anastasi, Anne, and Foley, J. P., Jr. A survey of the literature on artistic behavior in the abnormal: IV. Experimental investigations. *J. gen. Psychol.,* 1941, 25, 187-237.
9. Anastasi, Anne, and Foley, J. P., Jr. Psychiatric selection of flying personnel: V. The Human-Figure Drawing Test as an objective psychiatric screening

aid for student pilots. *USAF School of Aviation Medicine, Project No. 21-37-002, Rep. No. 5,* Oct. 1952.

10. Anderson, H. H., and Anderson, Gladys L. *An introduction to projective techniques.* Englewood Cliffs, N. J.: Prentice-Hall, 1951.

11. Andrew, Gwen, *et al. The Michigan Picture Test.* Chicago: Sci. Res. Assoc., 1953.

12. Armstrong, Mary A. S. Children's responses to animal and human figures in thematic pictures. *J. consult. Psychol.,* 1954, 18, 67-70.

13. Atkinson, J. W. (Ed.) *Motives in fantasy, action, and society.* Princeton, N. J.: Van Nostrand, 1958.

14. *Auditory Apperception Test.* Los Angeles: Western Psychol. Serv., 1953.

15. Baughman, E. E. Rorschach scores as a function of examiner difference. *J. proj. Tech.,* 1951, 15, 243-249.

16. Baughman, E. E. The role of the stimulus in Rorschach responses. *Psychol. Bull.,* 1958, 55, 121-147.

17. Beck, S. J. *Rorschach's test.* N. Y.: Grune & Stratton, 1945, 1949, 1952. 3 vols.

18. Beck, S. J. Rorschach test. In A. Weider (Ed.), *Contributions toward medical psychology.* N. Y.: Ronald, 1953. Vol. II, pp. 599-610.

19. Bell, J. E. *Projective techniques.* N. Y.: Longmans, Green, 1948.

20. Bellak, L. *The Thematic Apperception Test and the Children's Apperception Test in clinical use.* N. Y.: Grune & Stratton, 1954.

21. Bellak, L., and Bellak, Sonya S. *Children's Apperception Test.* N. Y.: C.P.S. Co., 1949-1955.

22. Biersdorf, Kathryn R., and Marcuse, F. L. Responses of children to human and to animal pictures. *J. proj. Tech.,* 1953, 17, 455-459.

23. Blum, G. S. *The Blacky Pictures: a technique for the exploration of personality dynamics.* N. Y.: Psychol. Corp., 1950.

24. Bolgar, Hedda, and Fischer, Liselotte K. Personality projection in the World Test. *Amer. J. Orthopsychiat.,* 1947, 17, 117-128.

25. Borstelmann, L. J., and Klopfer, W. G. The Szondi Test: a review and critical evaluation. *Psychol. Bull.,* 1953, 50, 112-132.

26. Brower, D., and Abt, L. E. (Eds.) *Progress in clinical psychology.* Vol. I, Sect. 1. N. Y.: Grune & Stratton, 1952.

27. Brown, J. F. A modification of the Rosenzweig Picture-Frustration Test to study hostile interracial attitudes. *J. Psychol.,* 1947, 24, 247-272.

28. Buck, J. N., and Jolles, I. *H-T-P: House-Tree-Person Projective Technique.* Los Angeles: Western Psychol. Serv., 1946-1956.

29. Buhler, Charlotte. *The Toy World Test.* Los Angeles, Calif.: Author, 1949-1955.

30. Buhler, Charlotte, Lumry, Gayle K., and Carroll, Helen S. World-test standardization studies. *J. Child Psychiat.,* 1951, 2, 2-81.

31. Burtt, H. E. *Legal psychology.* Englewood Cliffs, N. J.: Prentice-Hall, 1931.

32. Burtt, H. E. *Applied psychology.* (2nd ed.) Englewood Cliffs, N. J.: Prentice-Hall, 1957.

33. Campbell, D. T. The indirect assessment of social attitudes. *Psychol. Bull.,* 1950, 47, 15-38.

34. Child, I. L., Frank, Kitty F., and Storm, T. Self-ratings and TAT: their relation to each other and to childhood background. *J. Pers.,* 1956, 25, 96-114.

35. Cobb, Katherine. Measuring leadership in college women by free association. *J. abnorm. soc. Psychol.,* 1952, 47, 126-128.

36. Cronbach, L. J. Statistical methods applied to Rorschach scores: a review. *Psychol. Bull.,* 1949, 46, 393-429.

37. Cronbach, L. J. Assessment of individual differences. *Ann. Rev. Psychol.,* 1956, 7, 173-196.

38. Cronbach, L. J., and Gleser, Goldine C. *Psychological tests and personnel decisions.* Urbana, Ill.: Univer. Ill. Press, 1957.

39. Davids, A., and Pildner, H., Jr. Comparison of direct and projective methods of personality assessment under different conditions of motivation. *Psychol. Monogr.,* 1958, 72, No. 11.

40. Deri, Susan K. *Introduction to the Szondi Test: theory and practice.* N. Y.: Grune & Stratton, 1949.

41. Eysenck, H. J. Personality tests: 1950-1955. In T. H. Fleming (Ed.), *Recent progress in psychology.* London: J. & A. Churchill, 1959. Pp. 118-159.

42. Fiske, D. W., and Baughman, E. E. Relationships between Rorschach scoring categories and the total number of responses. *J. abnorm. soc. Psychol.,* 1953, 48, 25-32.

43. Frank, L. K. Projective methods for the study of personality. *J. Psychol.,* 1939, 8, 389-413.

44. Fromm, Erika, Hartman, Lenore D., and Marschak, Marian. Children's intelligence tests as a measure of dynamic personality functioning. *Amer. J. Orthopsychiat.,* 1957, 27, 134-144.

45. Fromme, A. On the use of certain qualitative methods of attitude research. *J. soc. Psychol.,* 1941, 13, 425-459.

46. Furuya, K. Responses of school-children to human and animal pictures. *J. Proj. Tech.,* 1957, 21, 248-252.

47. Galton, F. Psychometric experiments. *Brain,* 1879, 2, 149-162.

48. Goodenough, Florence L. The use of free association in the objective measurement of personality. In Q. McNemar and Maud A. Merrill (Eds.), *Studies in personality.* N. Y.: McGraw-Hill, 1942. Pp. 87-103.

49. Goodenough, Florence L. Semantic choice and personality structure. *Science,* 1946, 104, 451-456.

50. Guilford, J. P., and Lacey, J. I. (Eds.) *Printed classification tests.* (AAF Aviation Psychology Program, Research Reports. Rep. No. 5.) Washington: Govt. Printing Office, 1947.

51. Hammond, K. R. Representative vs. systematic design in clinical psychology. *Psychol. Bull.,* 1954, 51, 150-159.

52. Harris, D. B., and Goodenough, Florence L. *Children's drawings as measures of intellectual maturity: a revision and extension of the Goodenough Draw-a-Man test.* Tarrytown, N. Y.: Harcourt, Brace and World, (in press).

53. Henry, W. E. *The analysis of fantasy: the thematic apperception technique in the study of personality.* N. Y.: Wiley, 1956.

54. Henry, W. E., and Farley, Jane. The validity of the Thematic Apperception

Test in the study of adolescent personality. *Psychol. Monogr.*, 1959, 73, No. 17.

55. Hertz, Marguerite R. Rorschach: twenty years after. *Psychol. Bull.*, 1942, 39, 529-572.

56. Holt, R. R. Clinical *and* statistical prediction: a reformulation and some new data. *J. abnorm. soc. Psychol.*, 1958, 56, 1-12.

57. Holtzman, W. H. Objective scoring of projective tests. In B. M. Bass and I. A. Berg (Eds.), *Objective approaches to personality assessment.* Princeton, N. J.: Van Nostrand, 1959. Pp. 119-145.

58. Jung, C. G. The association method. *Amer. J. Psychol.*, 1910, 21, 219-269.

59. Kent, Grace H., and Rosanoff, A. J. A study of association in insanity. *Amer. J. Insanity*, 1910, 67, 37-96; 317-390.

60. Klopfer, B., *et al. Developments in the Rorschach technique.* Vol. I and II. Tarrytown-on-Hudson, N. Y.: World Book Co., 1954, 1956.

61. Klopfer, B., and Kelley, D. M. *The Rorschach technique.* Tarrytown-on-Hudson, N. Y.: World Book Co., 1942.

62. Light, B. H. Comparative study of a series of TAT and CAT cards. *J. clin. Psychol.*, 1954, 10, 179-181.

63. Lindzey, G. Thematic Apperception Test: interpretive assumptions and related empirical evidence. *Psychol. Bull.*, 1952, 49, 1-25.

64. Lindzey, G. On the classification of projective techniques. *Psychol. Bull.*, 1959, 56, 158-168.

65. Lindzey, G., and Herman, P. S. Thematic Apperception Test: a note on reliability and situational validity. *J. proj. Tech.*, 1955, 19, 36-42.

66. Little, K. B., and Shneidman, E. S. Congruencies among interpretations of psychological test and anamnestic data. *Psychol. Monogr.*, 1959, 73, No. 6.

67. Lotsof, E. J. Intelligence, verbal fluency, and the Rorschach test. *J. consult. Psychol.*, 1953, 17, 21-24.

68. Lowenfeld, Margaret. The world pictures of children. *Brit. J. med. Psychol.*, 1939, 18, 65-101.

69. McArthur, C. Analyzing the clinical process. *J. counsel. Psychol.*, 1954, 1, 203-207.

70. McClelland, D. C., *et al. The achievement motive.* N. Y.: Appleton-Century-Crofts, 1953.

71. Machover, Karen. *Personality projection in the drawing of the human figure: A method of personality investigation.* Springfield, Ill.: Thomas, 1949.

72. Masling, J. The influence of situational and interpersonal variables in projective testing. *Psychol. Bull.*, 1960, 57, 65-85.

73. Meehl, P. E. *Clinical versus statistical prediction: a theoretical analysis and a review of the evidence.* Minneapolis: Univer. Minn. Press, 1954.

74. Moreno, J. L. *Psychodrama.* N. Y.: Beacon House, 1946.

75. Murray, H. A. *Thematic Apperception Test.* Cambridge, Mass.: Harvard Univer. Press, 1943.

76. Murray, H. A., *et al. Explorations in personality.* N. Y.: Oxford Univer. Press, 1938.

77. Murray, H. A., and Morgan, Christiana D. A clinical study of sentiments: I and II. *Genet. Psychol. Monogr.*, 1945, 32, 3-311.
78. Mussen, P. H., and Naylor, H. K. The relationships between overt and fantasy aggression. *J. abnorm. soc. Psychol.*, 1954, 49, 235-240.
79. Piotrowski, Z. A. *Perceptanalysis: a fundamentally reworked, expanded, and systematized Rorschach method.* N. Y.: Macmillan, 1957.
80. Pittluck, Patricia. The relation between aggressive fantasy and overt behavior. Unpublished doctoral dissertation. Yale Univer., 1950.
81. Rapaport, D., Gill, M., and Schafer, R. *Diagnostic psychological testing.* Vol. II. Chicago: Year Book Publ., 1946.
82. Rohde, Amanda R. *Sentence Completions Test.* (Rev. ed.) Los Angeles: Western Psychol. Serv., 1953-1957.
83. Rohde, Amanda R. *The sentence completion method.* N. Y.: Ronald, 1957.
84. Rorschach, H. (Transl. by P. Lemkau and B. Kronenburg.) *Psychodiagnostics: a diagnostic test based on perception.* Berne: Huber, 1942. (1st German ed., 1921; U. S. distributor, Grune & Stratton.)
85. Rosenzweig, S. *Rosenzweig Picture-Frustration Study.* St. Louis, Mo.: Author, 1947-1949.
86. Rotter, J. B., and Rafferty, Janet E. *The Rotter Incomplete Sentences Blank.* N. Y.: Psychol. Corp., 1950.
87. Sachman, H. An investigation of certain aspects of the validity of the formal Rorschach scoring system in relation to age, education, and vocabulary score. Unpublished doctoral dissertation, Fordham Univer., 1952.
88. Sarason, S. B. *The clinical interaction, with special reference to the Rorschach.* N. Y.: Harper, 1954.
89. Sargent, Helen D. *The Insight Test: a verbal projective test for personality.* N. Y.: Grune & Stratton, 1953.
90. Schafer, R. *Psychoanalytic interpretation in Rorschach testing.* N. Y.: Grune & Stratton, 1954.
91. Shneidman, E. S. *Make A Picture Story.* N. Y.: Psychol. Corp., 1947-1952.
92. Silverman, L. H. A Q-sort of the validity of evaluations made from projective techniques. *Psychol. Monogr.*, 1959, 73, No. 7.
93. Symonds, P. M. *Symonds Picture-Story Test.* N. Y.: Teach. Coll., Columbia Univer., Bur. Publ., 1948.
94. Symonds, P. M. *Adolescent fantasy: an investigation of the picture-story method of personality study.* N. Y.: Teach. Coll., Columbia Univer., Bur. Publ., 1949.
95. Szondi, L. *Szondi Test.* Berne: Huber, 1947-1952. (U. S. distributor: Grune & Stratton.)
96. Szondi, L. *Experimental diagnostics of drives.* N. Y.: Grune & Stratton, 1952.
97. Thompson, C. E. *Thematic Apperception Test: Thompson Modification.* Cambridge, Mass.: Harvard Univer. Press, 1949.
98. Thurstone, L. L. Word associations with homonyms. *Psychometr. Lab., Univer. Chicago,* No. 79, July 1952.
99. Tomkins, S. S., Horn, D., and Miner, J. B. *The Tomkins-Horn Picture Arrangement Test.* N. Y.: Springer, 1944-1957.

100. Veroff, J., Atkinson, J. W., Feld, Sheila C., and Gwin, G. The use of thematic apperception to assess motivation in a nationwide interview study. *Psychol. Monogr.,* 1960, 74, No. 12.

101. Watson, R. I. *The clinical method in psychology.* N. Y.: Harper, 1951.

102. Weider, A. (Ed.) *Contributions toward medical psychology.* Vol. II. N. Y.: Ronald, 1953.

103. Weschler, I. R., and Bernberg, R. Indirect methods of attitude measurement. *Int. J. Opin. Attitude Res.,* 1950, 4, 209-228.

104. Wyman, Jennie B. Tests of intellectual, social, and activity interests. In L. M. Terman, *et al., Genetic studies of genius.* Vol. I. *Mental and physical traits of a thousand gifted children.* Stanford Univer., Calif.: Stanford Univer. Press, 1925. Ch. 16.

105. Zubin, J. Failures of the Rorschach technique. *J. proj. Tech.,* 1954, 18, 303-315.

106. Zubin, J., Eron, L. D., and Sultan, Florence. Current status of the Rorschach test. Symposium, 1955: 1. A psychometric evaluation of the Rorschach experiment. *Amer. J. Orthopsychiat.,* 1956, 26, 773-782.

CHAPTER 21

Other Techniques for
Personality Assessment

The paper-and-pencil inventories and the projective techniques surveyed in the preceding chapters undoubtedly represent the best-known and most widely used types of instruments for the appraisal of personality. Nevertheless, there still remains a rich supply of other devices that are being explored for this purpose. Out of this diversity of approaches may come techniques that will eventually revitalize the measurement of personality and stimulate progress in new directions.

The techniques to be considered in this chapter are extremely heterogeneous in nature. Moreover, they do not fall into clear-cut or generally recognized categories, although several attempts have been made to work out schemas of classification and appropriate terminology (cf. 18, 19, 72, 79). For the purposes of the present discussion, these techniques have been grouped into the following four types, each to be treated in a separate section: situational tests; tests utilizing perceptual, cognitive, or evaluative tasks; tests based on sociometry; and tests designed to assess self concepts and personal constructs. Only a few examples of each type will be described for illustrative purposes.

A few of the instruments to be considered may be regarded as special adaptations of either self-report inventories or projective techniques. As in most classifications, borderline specimens can be found that could be placed in more than one category. In a later section of the chapter, we shall consider some further procedures for the appraisal of personality. These are not properly speaking psychological tests and hence will receive only brief mention.

SITUATIONAL TESTS

Although the term "situational test" was popularized during and following World War II, tests fitting this description had been developed prior to that time. Essentially, a situational test is one that places the subject in a situation closely resembling or simulating a "real-life" criterion situation. Such tests thus show certain basic similarities to the "worksample" technique employed in constructing trade tests (cf. Ch. 17). In the present tests, however, the criterion behavior that is sampled is more varied and complex. Moreover, interest is focused, not upon aptitude or achievement, but upon emotional, social, attitudinal, and other personality variables.

Tests of the Character Education Inquiry. Among the earliest situational tests—although they were not so labeled at the time—were those constructed by Hartshorne, May, and their associates (43, 44, 45) for the Character Education Inquiry (CEI). These tests were designed principally as research instruments for use in an extensive project on the nature and development of character in children. Nevertheless, the techniques can be adapted to other testing purposes, and a number have been so utilized.

In general, the CEI techniques made use of familiar, natural situations within the school child's daily routine. The tests were administered in the form of regular classroom examinations, as part of the pupil's homework, in the course of athletic contests, or as party games. Moreover, the children were not aware that they were being tested, except in so far as ordinary school examinations might be involved in the procedure. At the same time, all of the Hartshorne-May tests represented carefully standardized instruments which yielded objective, quantitative scores.

The CEI tests were designed to measure such behavior characteristics as honesty, persistence, inhibition, and service (cooperation and charity). The largest number of tests in the CEI series were concerned with *cheating*. One group of tests developed for this purpose utilized a duplicating technique. In this technique, common tests such as vocabulary, sentence completion, or arithmetic reasoning were administered in the classroom. The test papers were then collected and a duplicate of each child's responses was made. At a subsequent session, the original, unmarked test papers were returned, and each child scored his own paper from a key. Comparison with the duplicate record revealed any changes the individual had made in scoring his paper.

The same types of test content were employed with the double testing technique. In this case, two equivalent forms of the test were administered, one under unsupervised conditions that provided an opportunity to copy from a key, and the other under supervised conditions that eliminated the possibility of cheating. The maximum drop in score that could be expected without cheating was established empirically by administering the two forms of each test under supervised conditions to a comparable group of subjects. A variant of the same basic technique was employed in athletic contests in which the individual reported his maximum achievement on tests of strength of grip, lung capacity, chinning, and broad jump, following supervised "practice trials."

A third technique for the detection of cheating was based upon improbable achievement. In this case, a task was given under such conditions that achievement above a certain empirically established level indicated cheating. Among the tasks utilized for this purpose were weight discrimination, the solution of various mechanical puzzles, and paper-and-pencil tests of motor coordination. An example of the last-named type of test is provided by the Circles Puzzle. In this test, the subject was instructed to make a mark in each of 10 small, irregularly arranged circles, while keeping his eyes shut. Control tests under conditions that precluded peeking indicated that a score of more than 13 correctly placed marks in a total of three trials was highly improbable. By peeking, however, the child might obtain a higher score.

Honesty was also measured by means of a few tests designed to detect *stealing* and *lying* behavior. Tests of stealing can be illustrated by the Magic Square—an arithmetical puzzle requiring coins for its solution. The object of the puzzle was to arrange coins in such a way that the sums of all rows, columns, and diagonals were the same. Upon completion of the task, subjects were instructed to return the boxes containing the puzzles and coins. Through code numbers on the puzzles, it was possible for the examiner to identify any subjects who failed to return all the coins.

An example of a lying test from the Hartshorne-May series is provided by a written questionnaire consisting of items of the sort subsequently utilized in the L-scale of the MMPI (cf. Ch. 18). Each form of this test included 36 questions to be answered "yes" or "no" by the subject. Typical questions are shown below (43, pp. 98-99):

Did you ever act greedily by taking more than your share of anything?

Are you always on time at school or for other appointments?

Do you always smile when things go wrong?

Did you ever say anything about your teacher that you would be unwilling to say to her face?

On the basis of empirical investigations, it was decided that a subject who answered 24 or more of these questions in the socially approved direction was probably lying.

To measure *persistence,* the subjects were given different tasks appealing to a variety of interests and were permitted to work as long as they wished. Persistence scores were based upon the time the subject spent on the problem before voluntarily stopping. The tasks included a variety of mechanical and paper-and-pencil puzzles, as well as a story completion test. In administering the story completion test, the examiner read three stories involving danger or adventure. Each was stopped at a point of suspense. The subjects were then given sheets on which the ending of the story was printed in a form that made reading difficult. Moreover, as the end of the story was approached, the difficulty of deciphering the words was further increased by the spacing of the letters and by the indiscriminate mixture of capitals and small letters. The three successive levels of difficulty are illustrated below (44, p. 294):

CHARLESLIFTEDLUCILLETOHISBACK"PUTYOURARMSTIGHT AROUNDMYNECKANDHOLDON

NoWhoWTogETBaCkONthETREStle.HoWTOBRingTHaTTerrIfIEDBURDeN OFAChILDuPtOSafeTY

fiN ALly tAp-tAPC AME ARHYTH Month eBriD GeruNNing fee Tfee Tcom INGtow ArdT Hem

The subjects were instructed to draw lines separating the words as they read. The examiner could thus determine how far each individual had proceeded before giving up, as well as the time devoted to the task. It might be noted parenthetically that, regardless of how this test is scored, the resulting measure is likely to depend upon a number of aptitude variables, quite apart from the subject's persistence in the given task.

Tests of *inhibition* required the subjects to resist the tendency to respond to more attractive stimuli than were provided by the task at hand. For example, an arithmetic test was administered to the same subjects under normal and distracting conditions. For the latter purpose, the problems were presented on a sheet covered with cartoon-like sketches, verbal comments, and other miscellaneous doodles. The larger the difference between the two scores, the less successful the subject had been in resisting the "pull" of the distracting material.

Most of the CEI tests proved to have good discriminative power, yielding a wide range of individual differences in scores. Reliability also appeared to be fairly satisfactory. Although it was not feasible to obtain estimates of reliability for all tests, most had retest or alternate-form reliabilities in the .70's and .80's. Validity was more difficult to establish. Correlations with ratings by teachers and classmates were generally low, but such ratings were themselves quite unreliable and of doubtful validity. In evaluating what today would be called the construct validity of their instruments, Hartshorne and May found intercorrelations of the many different tests within each category. These correlations proved to be low, indicating considerable specificity in the behavior surveyed by the tests. Although tests utilizing similar techniques correlated highly with each other, when all honesty tests were considered, their average intercorrelation was only .227. Moreover, several of the individual correlations between honesty tests were practically zero. Similar results were obtained when tests within the persistence, inhibition, and service areas were intercorrelated.

It should be noted that the variables investigated in the Character Education Inquiry represent categories derived primarily from the ethical and social evaluation of behavior. In so far as can be determined from available data, however, these categories do not correspond to "traits" in the sense in which this concept is used in the factorial analysis of behavioral organization. For example, the relative strength of different interests, values, or motives for a given individual may determine his persistence or his tendency to cheat in specific situations. The child who is motivated to excel in school work is not necessarily concerned about his achievement in athletic contests or social games. And the child who lies to win approbation may not be at all inclined to pilfer coins. When first published, the findings of the CEI research aroused a storm of controversy. From the standpoint of test construction, however, this project not only contributed many ingenious techniques but also demonstrated that standardized procedures and objective, quantitative scoring could be used successfully with real-life situations.

Situational Stress Tests. Like the tests developed in the CEI program, situational stress tests are realistic and disguised. The principal difference in the case of stress tests is to be found in the introduction of features designed to arouse anxiety or to produce other emotional disturbances. Among the stimuli that have been employed to induce emotional stress may be mentioned: electric shock; expectation of shock or pain that does not materialize; falling and disruption of body balance; startle-producing stimuli, such as loud noise, sudden explosion, water spray, or air blast; threat of apparent physical danger; distractions; criticism and razzing; time pressure in the performance of an assigned task; failure or threat of failure; and a variety of interpersonal conflicts involving examiners, observers, co-workers, or helpers. A number of these conditions derive their stressful nature from the fact that the subject is highly motivated to succeed in the task at hand or to make a favorable impression upon his observers.

The subject's reactions to stress may be determined through the use of physiological measures of emotion, objective records of performance, or qualitative observations and rating procedures. In many cases, a combination of these measures may yield the most satisfactory information. Whenever feasible, it is also desirable to make observations during a control, or pre-stress period, as well as during a post-stress period (47). The control observations provide a measure of normal performance for each individual, in terms of which his behavior under stress may be evaluated. The post-stress period permits an appraisal of the individual's recovery from stress. A post-stress interview is likewise helpful in obtaining supplementary information regarding the subject's emotional involvement, his interpretation of the situation, and other questions bearing on the intensity of stress actually experienced by each individual.

One type of situational stress test is illustrated by the Observational Stress Test developed during World War II as part of a test battery for the selection of Air Force pilots (41, pp. 660-663; 61, pp. 811-814). This test was designed to measure the subject's ability to resist confusion and distraction in performing a complex coordination task similar to that of piloting a plane. The apparatus provided seven controls—a pedal, a stick, and five levers—which were to be reset continually by the subject in response to signal lights and a buzzer. Electric clocks recorded the speed with which correct settings were made throughout the test period. In addition to the confusing nature of the complex and constantly changing task, executed under time pressure, the examiner introduced criticism and threat of failure through such standardized comments as the following:

Set the controls . . . You must work more quickly . . . Your scores are not nearly good enough yet. Remember we are rating you the same way a primary instructor would rate you on your flying . . . You will have to do things exactly right or you are through . . . Are you letting a simple test like this confuse you? . . .

Among the most ambitious projects concerned with the development and use of situational stress tests was that undertaken by the Office of Strategic Services (OSS) during World War II (63, 66). The object of this testing program was the evaluation of candidates for assignment to military intelligence. The principal assessment program consisted of a three-day session of intensive testing and observation. During this period, the candidates lived together in small groups, under almost continuous scrutiny by members of the assessment staff. Besides specially constructed situational tests, the program included aptitude tests, projective techniques, intensive interviewing, and general observations under casual and informal conditions. Several of the situational tests were modeled after techniques developed in the German and British armies.

An example of an OSS situational stress test is provided by the Construction Test, in which a five-foot cube had to be assembled from wooden poles, blocks, and pegs. The subject was informed that, since it was impossible for one man to complete the task within the ten minutes allotted to it, he would be given two helpers. Actually, the helpers were psychologists who played prearranged roles. One followed a policy of inertia and passive resistance; the other obstructed the work by making impractical suggestions, asking irrelevant and often embarrassing questions, and needling the candidate with ridicule and criticism. So well did the helpers succeed in frustrating the candidates that the construction was never completed in the history of the assessment program. The subject's emotional and interpersonal reactions in this situation were observed and evaluated qualitatively.

Available validity data on situational stress tests are meager (41, 52, 60, 66). A major difficulty arises from the lack of suitable criterion data. In the OSS project, for example, the diversity of individual assignments reduced the possibility of evaluating field performance under comparable conditions for different members of the group. Unreliability of criterion ratings also tends to reduce validity estimates. With these qualifications, it must be noted that, when determined, predictive validity of situational stress tests has proved to be low. Although a few techniques may be promising for special purposes, the contribution of these tests rarely justifies the time, equipment, and highly trained personnel that their administration requires.

"Leaderless Group" and Related Techniques. A relatively common type of situational test utilizes a "leaderless group" as a device for appraising such characteristics as cooperation, teamwork, resourcefulness, initiative, and leadership. In such tests, a task is assigned that requires the cooperative efforts of a group of examinees, none of whom is designated as leader or given specific responsibilities. Examples from the OSS program include the Brook Situation, involving the transfer of personnel and equipment across a brook with maximum speed and safety; and the Wall Situation, in which men and materials had to be conveyed over a double wall separated by an imaginary canyon.

A promising variant of this technique is the Leaderless Group Discussion

(LGD). Requiring a minimum of equipment and time, this technique has been used widely in the selection of such groups as military officers, civil service supervisors and administrators, industrial executives and management trainees, sales trainees, teachers, and social workers (cf. 8). It has also been employed in research on leadership (10, 20), on the effects of counseling (68), and on the selection of clinical psychology trainees (53). Essentially, the group is assigned a topic for discussion during a specified period. Examiners observe and rate each person's performance, but do not participate in the discussion. Although often used under informal and unstandardized conditions, the LGD has been subjected to considerable research (8). Bass (10) has worked out objective indices of each individual's leadership in terms of his effectiveness in changing group opinion.

Validity studies suggest that LGD techniques are among the most effective applications of situational tests. Many significant and sizeable correlations have been found between ratings from LGD performance and follow-up or concurrent ratings obtained in military, industrial, and social settings (cf. 8; 40, p. 262). Some of these correlations are as high as .60. It is also interesting to note that leadership ratings based on a one-hour LGD correlated over .60 with leadership assessment from three days of situational testing in the OSS program (66). A similar correlation between LGD and an entire battery of situational tests was found by Vernon (88) in a British study.

Information relevant to the construct validity of the LGD is provided by correlations with certain personality tests, such as the Ascendance and Sociability scores of the Guilford-Zimmerman Temperament Survey, both of which yield significant positive correlations with LGD ratings. Factor analyses of performance in leaderless group situations have revealed three major factors: (*a*) "individual prominence"—efforts to stand out from others and individually achieve various personal goals; (*b*) "group goal facilitation"— efforts to assist the group in achieving goals toward which the group is oriented; and (*c*) "group sociability"—efforts to establish and maintain cordial and socially satisfying relations with other group members.

Neither LGD nor other, more elaborate situational tests, however, have proved valid as devices for assessing broad personality traits (52, 53, 60, 66). All such tests appear to be most effective when they approximate actual "worksamples" of the criterion behavior they are designed to predict. The LGD tests in particular have some validity in predicting performance in jobs requiring a certain amount of verbal communication, verbal problem-solving, and acceptance by peers. Another factor that seems to increase the predictive validity of situational tests is job familiarity on the part of the raters (46, 88). Such a finding again suggests that situational tests work best when the subject's performance is interpreted as a worksample rather than in terms of underlying personality variables. Flanagan (3, 32) has developed a number of situational techniques that are closely modeled after actual job activities and are scored in terms of a checklist of desirable and undesirable actions. A typical problem used in evaluating naval officers requires the examinee to discuss with a junior officer an unsatisfactory performance report he is about to submit (3, p. 2). The circumstances leading up to the unsatisfactory report are described and the examinee is then observed in his handling of the interview.

PERCEPTUAL, COGNITIVE, AND EVALUATIVE TASKS

A major trend in personality testing today is the development of a wide variety of simple and comparatively objective tests, most of which are of the paper-and-pencil type. In common with the previously discussed situational tests, these techniques can be characterized as relatively structured and disguised. Rather than attempting to utilize complex, lifelike, or realistic situations, however, these tests present the subject with an artificial task bearing little or no resemblance to the criterion to be predicted. The tests under consideration represent efforts to identify behavior that may serve as a valid predictor of a criterion, without being a direct sample of criterion behavior. For this reason, these techniques have sometimes been described as "indirect" tests.

These tests have also been characterized by some writers as "objective tests." Such a designation, however, does not adequately differentiate them from other types of personality tests, since all psychological tests are objective when properly constructed, administered, and evaluated. In earlier chapters we have seen, for example, how personality inventories and projective techniques can be used as objective tests, although frequently they are not so employed. When applied to personality tests, moreover, the term "objective" has been given widely varied meanings by different writers (cf. 89). Campbell (19) uses the term in a very special sense to indicate that the subject perceives the task as having an objectively correct solution. This definition would differentiate most tests in this section from both self-report and projective tests. Cattell (21, 24) applies the term to all except self-appraisal techniques. Still other writers base their criterion of objectivity in personality assessment on interscorer consistency and the elimination of examiner variables.

Although there is as yet no satisfactory or generally accepted label for the type of tests to be considered in this section, we can readily identify their common differentiating features. First, the subject is *task-oriented,* rather than being report-oriented as in personality questionnaires. He is given an objective task to perform, rather than being asked to describe his habitual behavior. Second, the purpose of these tests is *disguised,* the subject not realizing which aspects of his performance are to be scored. Third, the tasks set for the subject are *structured.* In this feature lies their principal difference from the tasks utilized in projective techniques. To be sure, structuring is a matter of degree. As a group, however, the tests now under consideration are more highly structured than are typical projective devices.

A fourth and related feature pertains to the *apparent existence of a "right solution"* for each task or problem—at least from the subject's viewpoint. Thus many of the tests are presented in the guise of aptitude measures, in which the subject endeavors to give "correct" answers. True, the instruments are not actually treated as aptitude tests, nor are they scored on the basis of right and wrong responses. But the subject's approach to the test is nevertheless quite unlike that encouraged by projective tests, in which "anything goes." Finally, the rationale underlying the construction of such tests is often based upon the concept of *personality style,* or broad stylistic traits of behavior, which may be manifested in a wide variety of dissimilar activities or "media." In this respect, the approach is similar to that of projective techniques.

Major research projects that include the development of a number of personality tests in the present category have been conducted under the direction of Thurstone (84, 87), MacKinnon (59), Cattell (21, 24), Eysenck (31), and others. In addition to these comprehensive and continuing projects, other investigators have been engaged in developing single tests of the same nature for specific purposes. It might be added that several tests discussed in earlier chapters could also be included in the present category. This is true, for example, of the various sorting and perceptual tests described in Chapter 12, the Porteus Mazes cited in Chapter 10, and some of the more highly standardized projective techniques covered in Chapter 20.

Perceptual Functions. One of the principal sources of the simple, objective personality tests under consideration is to be found in the area of perceptual functions. A rapidly growing body of experimental literature has demonstrated significant relationships between the individual's attitudinal, motivational, or emotional characteristics and his performance on perceptual or cognitive tasks (cf., e.g., 14, 17, 49, 91). It should also be recognized that a number of projective techniques—notably the Rorschach—are essentially perceptual tests.

Of the factors identified in factorial analyses of perception, two that have proved particularly fruitful in personality research are speed of closure and flexibility of closure (67, 82). The first involves the rapid recognition of a familiar word, object, or other figure in a relatively unorganized or mutilated visual field. Typical items from a test found to be highly saturated with this factor (Street Gestalt Completion) are reproduced in Figure 121. Flexibility

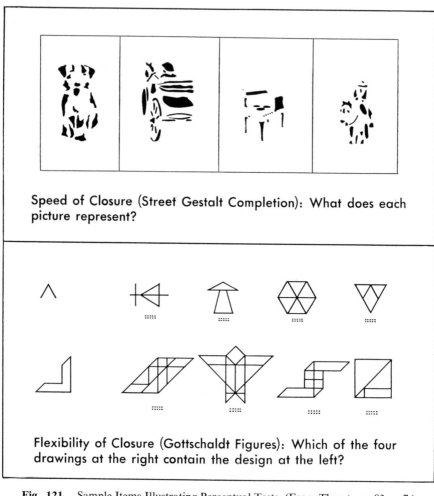

Speed of Closure (Street Gestalt Completion): What does each picture represent?

Flexibility of Closure (Gottschaldt Figures): Which of the four drawings at the right contain the design at the left?

Fig. 121.   Sample Items Illustrating Perceptual Tests. (From Thurstone, 83, p. 7.)

of closure requires the identification of a figure amid distracting and confusing details. Two items from a test with a high loading in this factor (Gottschaldt Figures) are also shown in Figure 121. Several studies have reported suggestive data indicating possible relationships between each of these factors and personality traits (59, 67, 82). In one investigation (67), for example, persons who excelled in speed of closure tended to rate themselves as sociable, quick in reactions, artistic, self-confident, systematic, neat and precise, and disliking logical and theoretical problems. In contrast, those scoring high in flexibility of closure had high self-ratings on such traits as socially retiring, independent of the opinions of others, analytical, interested in theoretical and scientific problems, and disliking rigid systematization and routine.

In other tests, the subject is presented with conflicting perceptual cues. For example, in the Stroop Color Word Test (82), the subject first reads printed color names from a card as quickly as possible; on a second card, he names the colors of rows of dots as fast as he can. The third card contains color names printed in colors that do not correspond to the names. For example, the word "blue" might be printed in red. The subject is required to name each color as rapidly as possible while ignoring the words. Finally, he is told to read each word while ignoring the colors. Increase in time required from trial 1 to 4 (reading words) and from trial 2 to 3 (naming colors) shows the extent of blocking caused by the conflicting cues.

Several tests have been designed to provide objective indices of color or form dominance. It will be recalled that this is one of the response determinants emphasized in traditional Rorschach scoring. Although there is evidence of a slight tendency for individuals to favor either form or color in their perceptions, intercorrelations of different form-color tests are low (51). One such test, developed by Thurstone (86, 87), presents a motion-picture film in which small colored figures move in a straight line across a clock face. If the individual follows constant color in spite of flickering shapes, he will report movement in one direction; if he follows constant shape in spite of flickering colors, he will report movement in the opposite direction.

Conflicting perceptual cues also underlie the tests devised by Witkin and his associates (91) in a 10-year study of perceptual space orientation. Through various tests utilizing a rod and frame that could be independently moved, a tilting chair, and a tilting room, these investigators were able to show that individuals differ widely in their "field dependence," or the extent to which their perception of the upright is influenced by the surrounding visual field. Considerable evidence was amassed to indicate that this perceptual trait is a relatively stable, consistent characteristic, having a certain amount of generality. Thus both odd-even and retest reliabilities were high, and most of the intercorrelations among the different spatial orientation tests were significant. Of even more interest are the significant correlations between the orientation tests and the Embedded-Figure Test (similar to the

Gottschaldt Figures illustrated in Figure 121), which may be regarded as measuring field dependence in a purely visual, paper-and-pencil situation. The authors also report some suggestive relationships between field dependence scores and personality characteristics, but these relationships need to be checked under more carefully controlled conditions.

Controlled Verbal Association. Another type of personality test is based upon partially controlled verbal associations. Such tests are similar to the free word association tests described in the preceding chapter, the principal difference being found in the more restrictive nature of the tasks assigned in the present tests. Several tests of this type were devised for use in the previously cited Thurstone project (84, 85). One example is the Verbal Emphasis Test, designed to measure differences in the speed with which the subject can make cognitive and affective discriminations in the meanings of words. Sixty word pairs are projected serially on a screen, the subject being instructed to indicate, by pressing the appropriate key, which of the two words is the stronger. One half of the pairs require "cognitive" discriminations, as in "colossal—large." The other half call for affective discriminations between either positively or negatively toned words. The former is illustrated by "interested—enthusiastic," the latter by "miserable—unhappy." It is thus possible to compare median reaction time for cognitive and affective discriminations, as well as for positively and negatively toned word-pairs within the latter category.

A second illustration is provided by a Synonyms-Antonyms Test. There are two parts to this test, in each of which adjectives are exposed on a screen, one at a time. In the first part, the subject is asked to give an opposite, or antonym, for each word. In the second part, administered on another day, he gives a synonym. The adjectives in each list are of three types: affectively positive, stating complimentary facts about people; affectively negative, describing uncomplimentary human qualities; and affectively neutral, referring to such physical properties as shiny, damp, or legible. Three scores can be found, corresponding to three hypotheses regarding personality indicators. Thus the subject's speed of response can be compared on: (a) synonyms and antonyms, (b) affectively toned and neutral stimuli, and (c) complimentary and uncomplimentary adjectives.

An ingenious technique is employed in a Recognition Test. The subject is provided with a stack of cards, on each of which is printed a word with one letter missing. The subject is instructed to read each word aloud as soon as he recognizes it. Scattered randomly in the list are 50 homonyms, which can be pronounced as either verbs or non-verbs (usually nouns). An example is "object," which can be accented on either syllable. The hypothesis underlying this test is that persons giving predominantly verb-responses are more active than those who give a majority of noun-responses.

Aesthetic Preferences. Still another approach utilizes aesthetic preferences as indices of personality factors. As a part of the previously mentioned MacKinnon project, Barron (6) and Barron and Welsh (7) asked subjects to indicate whether they liked or disliked each of a set of drawings and small colored reproductions of paintings. The results showed certain correspondences between the type of drawing and the type of painting preferred by individual subjects. With regard to personality, subjects showing a preference for simple-symmetrical drawings and realistic-traditional paintings described themselves significantly more often as contented, gentle, conservative, unaffected, patient, and peaceable. Those who liked complex-asymmetrical figures and "modern" paintings, on the other hand, chose such self-descriptions as gloomy, loud, unstable, bitter, cool, dissatisfied, pessimistic, emotional, irritable, and pleasure-seeking. Such findings are, of course, tentative until confirmed by cross-validation. But the nature of the particular adjectives chosen significantly more often by each group suggests that there may be more than a chance association between the subject's self-perception and his aesthetic preferences.

In the effort to demonstrate the unimportance of specific test content in personality measurement, Berg (12) prepared a Perceptual Reaction Test consisting of 60 abstract designs. To each design, the subject responds by checking "Like Much," "Like Slightly," "Dislike Slightly," or "Dislike Much." Despite the simplicity and abstract nature of its content, the test apparently evokes response sets that are correlated with other behavior manifestations. Through an analysis of deviant responses on this test, for example, it proved possible to construct scales for differentiating several common psychiatric disorders.

Another attempt to utilize aesthetic responses in the development of personality tests is to be found in the IPAT Music Preference Test of Personality (25, 26, 28). This test consists of 100 short piano selections reproduced on two sides of a phonograph record. For each musical excerpt, the subject records "Like," "Indifferent," or "Dislike." On the basis of factor analysis, the 100 items were classified into 11 groups, each yielding a separate factor score. Only 7 of these factor scores are interpreted, however, owing to the very low odd-even reliability of the remaining four.

Evidence for the validity of the IPAT Music Preference Test of Personality, as well as for the psychological interpretations of the music preference factors, was derived in part from correlations with Cattell's Sixteen Personality Factor Questionnaire (cf. Ch. 18). Additional evidence was based upon certain relations discovered with psychiatric syndromes. In an attempt to express the essential common characteristics of the items classified under each factor, musicians were asked to analyze the selections within the various categories. The type of results obtained may be illustrated with Factor 1. According to the musicians' descriptions, a high score on this factor indicates *liking* for music which builds "upsurging feeling and increasing emotion, through an increase in aesthetic pace, breadth, and harmonic color," and a *dislike* for music invoking a "sombre, relaxed mood through resolved harmonics, fairly constant aesthetic pace, and controlled expression." For the same factor, statistical analysis of the data suggested that a high score is associated with emotional adjustment, freedom from acute neurotic symptoms and from bodily signs of emotionality, peace of mind, trustfulness, and freedom from jealousy. A low score, on the other hand, appeared to be related to "jitteriness," overwroughtness, exhaustion, bodily symptoms of emotionality, resentment, and suspiciousness. This factor further distinguished between normals and psychotics at the .01 level of significance, the difference being largest in the case of chronic alcoholics.

Humor. Reactions to humor have likewise been explored as possible indicators of personality variables. The IPAT Humor Test of Personality (23, 27, 58), available in three forms, provides jokes and cartoons to be evaluated by the subject. Each form of the test contains approximately 100 items. In Form A, the subject chooses the joke he considers funnier in each pair. In Forms B and C, he checks "Good" or "Poor" for each joke or cartoon. A sample item from Form A is reproduced below:

(*a*) Epitaph to a waiter:
   By and by
   God caught his eye.

(*b*) One prehistoric man to another:
   "Now that we've learned to communicate with each other—shut up!"

Although Form A yields more reliable scores, the arrangement followed in Forms B and C provides additional information on the subject's general readiness to rate an item as funny. The items were again grouped into clusters on the basis of intercorrelations and factor analysis, a separate score being found in each factor.

Evaluation of Proverbs. Some personality tests elicit subjects' reactions to proverbs or aphorisms. For example, in the "Famous Sayings" test developed by Bass (9), the subject responds to each of 130 statements by indicating whether he agrees, disagrees, or is uncertain. Scales identified as Hostility, Fear of Failure, and Conventional Mores were derived through factor analysis. A Social Acquiescence score is also found on the basis of the subject's general acceptance or rejection of items. Apart from the factorial analyses and a few significant correlations with certain personality inventory scores, validity data for this test were based largely on significant differences between various occupational, regional, educational, and clinical groups.

Interests and Attitudes. Finally, mention may be made of the use of relatively objective, task-oriented tests in the appraisal of interests and attitudes. Some of the earliest attempts to measure interests centered around the use of tests of information, learning, and distraction (cf. 34). It is certainly reasonable to expect that an individual will more readily learn and retain information related to his interests, and that material appealing to his interests will prove to be more distracting to him than material in which he is not interested. These early tests, however, did not prove as successful as interest inventories such as the VIB (cf. Ch. 19), and hence were soon abandoned. More recently, efforts to construct "indirect" tests of interest have been renewed (cf. 18, 22, 79, 90).

A number of information tests have been developed for research on attitudes. The knowledge an individual has acquired is apt to reflect his selective perception and retention of facts, as well as his biased sources of information. We are likely to notice and to remember those facts that are in line with our expectations or hypotheses, and to overlook and forget others. Moreover, when no information is available on a given question, the direction of guessing may be determined by the subject's attitude; this tendency has been utilized in the *error-choice technique* (42), in which the respondent is forced to choose between two equally incorrect alternatives reflecting opposed biases. The items in error-choice tests are such that the correct answers are not generally familiar to the majority of respondents. Hence the errors are not readily apparent. Attitude bias on the part of the subject is revealed by systematic errors in one direction, as opposed to random errors.

Among the many other techniques utilized for the measurement of attitudes may be mentioned perception and memory tests, in which distortions and errors reflect bias; the evaluation of arguments, syllogistic conclusions, inferences, and the like; prediction of the outcomes of described events; estimation of group opinions, the estimated opinions being presumably colored by the subject's own views; judging character from the photographs of persons identified as members of different minority groups, occupations, etc.; expressing approval or disapproval of pictured or described incidents involving intergroup relations; and rating jokes, some of which pertain to minority-group members.

Still other procedures are illustrated by an investigation of the development of racial attitudes among children from the kindergarten through the eighth grade (48). In one test constructed for this study, a set of 12 photographs of pleasant-looking Negro and white boys was shown to the child, with the instructions to "pick out the one you like best, next best, next best, and so on until all are ranked." The score was based upon discrepancies in the ranks assigned to the Negro and white boys. The same 12 photographs were employed in another test in which the subject was asked to select photographs according to instructions such as the following: "Show me all those you want to sit next to on a street car"; "Show me all those that you would go swimming with"; and "Show me all those that you'd like to have for a cousin."

The last-mentioned test represents a pictorial and somewhat disguised adaptation of an earlier technique utilized in the Bogardus Social Distance Scale (15). In the Bogardus test, which is more closely related to an attitude inventory, the subject is given a list of national, racial, socioeconomic, religious, and other special groups, with the instructions to mark each of seven given types of relationships to which he would be willing to admit members of the group. These relationships range from "close kinship by marriage" to "exclusion from one's country." The relationships checked by the subject are then used as a basis for determining the "social distance" of each group from the individual.

Many other techniques could be added to the list. Considerable ingenuity has been exercised in devising novel and subtle ways of assessing interests and attitudes, as well as other personality traits. A number of the proposed techniques, moreover, reflect a healthy tendency toward integration of concepts or procedures derived from test construction, experimental psychology, and clinical practice. It should be reiterated, however, that few if any of the procedures described in this section have advanced beyond the stage of exploratory research.

SOCIOMETRY

Sociometry is essentially a procedure for recording interpersonal attractions among the members of a group. The technique has been highly developed and elaborated by Moreno (62), who applied it to a wide variety of groups and problems. Ordinarily it is used with a group of persons who have been together long enough to be acquainted with one another, as in a class, factory, institution, club, or military unit. Each individual is asked to choose one or more group members with whom he would like to study, work, eat lunch, play, or carry out any other designated function. Subjects may be asked to nominate as many group members as they wish, or a specified number (such as first, second, and third choice), or only one person for each function.

Sociometric data may be analyzed in various ways. A favorite procedure is to prepare a *sociogram* (cf. 50, 62), as illustrated in Figure 122. This

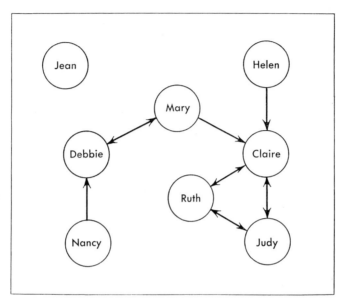

Fig. 122. A Sociogram. Eight girls in a school club are asked to choose a partner with whom they would like to work on a specific project; each is allowed two choices.

diagram shows the expressed preferences of a hypothetical group of eight girls, when each was allowed two choices. In sociometric lingo, Claire is a "star," having been chosen by four of the eight girls. Jean is an "isolate" who has neither made nor received any choices. Although Helen and Nancy both chose a preferred partner, they too received no choices. Some writers would classify them as isolates along with Jean; others reserve the term "unchosen" for this category (55). The sociogram also serves to reveal the presence of cliques of various sizes. In Figure 122, Claire, Ruth, and Judy form a closely knit triangle through their mutual choices. Debbie and Mary constitute a mutual pair, but Mary is also an intermediary between this pair and the previously mentioned triangle. With larger groups, the sociogram may show still other features of group structure.

Sociograms have been put to many uses both in research and in the practical management of groups. The sociogram of a group may serve as a basis for assigning individuals to subgroups where they will function congenially. Or it may suggest ways for improving the cohesiveness and effectiveness of the total group. Thus a particular group may have many isolates; it may be torn apart by strong cliques; or it may exhibit other features that interfere with its unified functioning. Sociograms may be obtained on different occasions to determine the effects of intervening factors upon group structure. They may also be utilized in studying attitudes toward minority group members within a group.

From the standpoint of individual differences, sociometric data can help in identifying isolates as well as leaders. In addition, several indices can be computed for a more precise assessment of each individual (55, 62). Such indices may show, for example, the number of times an individual has been nominated by his associates—either for a specific function or for all functions combined. If more than one choice is permitted, the number of first choices received can be similarly recorded. When number of choices is unlimited, an index of social "expansiveness" may be found from the number of other persons the individual chooses.

Sociometric nominations have generally proved to be one of the most dependable of rating techniques. When checked against a variety of practical criteria dependent upon interpersonal relations, such ratings have been found to have good predictive validity (55). These findings are understandable when we consider some of the features of sociometry. First, the number of raters is large, including all group members. Second, an individual's peers are often in a particularly favorable position to observe his typical behavior. They may thus be better judges of certain interpersonal traits than teachers, supervisors, and other outside observers. Third, and probably most important, is the fact that the opinions of group members—right or wrong—influence their actions and hence partly determine the nature of the individual's subsequent interactions with the group. Other comparable groups may be expected to react toward the individual in a similar fashion. Sociometric ratings may thus be said to have content validity in the same sense as worksamples.

An ingenious adaptation of sociometric techniques is provided by the Syracuse Scales of Social Relations, prepared by Gardner and Thompson (35, 36). While retaining the advantages of peer nominations, these scales permit better standardization of procedure and scoring. Designed principally for use in the classroom, the Syracuse scales are available at three levels: elementary (grades 5-6), junior high school (grades 7-9), and senior high school (grades 10-12). To provide a uniform and broad frame of reference, the individual is first instructed to select five names "from all persons he has ever known" to represent key points on his scale. Every member of the class is then assigned a position in this scale with regard to two questions. These questions were selected from the Murray system of needs (cf. Chs. 18 and 20) as being especially important at each of the three levels covered by the scales. Accordingly, the subject is asked to evaluate his classmates as:

- a possible source of aid when troubled by a personal problem (succorance: included at all three levels)

- someone to help him do something well so people will praise him (achievement-recognition: elementary)

- someone to look up to as an ideal (deference: junior high)

- a person whose company he would enjoy at a party or recreation (playmirth: senior high)

Scores are based on the scale positions assigned to an individual by all his classmates. Several measures can be computed to describe both group and individual characteristics. For the individual, the midscore of *ratings received* indicates how his classmates regard him, while the midscore of *ratings given* shows how well his classmates as a group satisfy the particular need for him. An advantage of these scores is that they are comparable for all needs, individuals, and groups (35). For further individual evaluation, percentile norms from a large standardization sample are also provided for each grade. In view of the care exercised in their development and the favorable nature of available research findings, these scales appear very promising for a variety of purposes.

SELF CONCEPTS AND PERSONAL CONSTRUCTS

A number of current approaches to personality assessment have concentrated on the way the individual views himself and others. Such techniques reflect the influence of phenomenological psychology, which focuses on how events are *perceived* by the individual (54, 76). The individual's self description thus becomes of primary importance in its own right, rather than being regarded as a second-best substitute for other behavioral observations. Interest also centers on the extent of self acceptance shown by the individual. Another common feature of all procedures to be considered in this section is their applicability to idiosyncratic, intensive investigation of the individual case. For this reason, they are of special interest to the clinical psychologist. Many of them, in fact, have originated within a clinical setting.

Self Conceptualization. One device explicitly directed toward eliciting a self concept is the Adjective Check List, prepared by Gough (37, 38, 39). In this test, the subject is presented with a list of 300 common adjectives, arranged alphabetically from "absent-minded" to "zany," and is instructed to check all those he considers to be descriptive of himself. This checklist has been used extensively in the previously mentioned personality assessment program directed by MacKinnon at the University of California. In one investigation, for example, the Adjective Check List was administered to graduate students participating in the assessment program, and item analyses were conducted with reference to a number of ratings by instructors and by assessment staff members. The subject's responses were analyzed on the assumption that "any systematic tendencies observed in the analysis would reveal important aspects of self-perception, whether or not the descriptions could be accepted as objectively true" (37, p. 1). This quotation typifies the rationale underlying the construction of self-concept tests.

Responses on the Adjective Check List or on similar descriptive inventories have also been compared with performance on several of the perceptual, cognitive, and evaluative tests described in the preceding section. Illustrative findings from the California project and from investigations conducted elsewhere were cited in that section. Any empirically established correspondences between self descriptions and performance on one of these indirect personality tests would contribute toward the construct validation of both instruments.

It might be argued that such self-concept tests as the Adjective Check List do not differ essentially from the self-report inventories discussed in Chapter 18. True, but it would be more accurate to say that self-report inventories are actually measures of self concept. That many psychologists regard personality inventories in this light has already been noted in Chapters 18 and 19.

The interpretation of personality inventory responses in terms of self conceptualization forms the basis of a provocative hypothesis formulated by Loevinger (56, 57). Bringing together many disparate findings from her own research and that of others, Loevinger proposes a personality trait which she defines as the capacity to conceptualize oneself, or to "assume distance" from oneself and one's impulses. According to Loevinger, it is the manifestations of this trait in personality inventories that have been described in such terms as façade, test-taking defensiveness, response set, social desirability, acquiescence, and personal style. In common with a number of other psychologists, Loevinger regards such test-taking attitudes, not as instrumental errors to be ruled out, but as the major source of valid variance in personality inventories.

On the basis of data from many sources, Loevinger suggests that ability to form a self concept increases with age, intelligence, education, and socio-economic level. At the lowest point, illustrated by the infant, the individual is incapable of self conceptualization. As the ability develops, he gradually forms a stereotyped, conventional, and socially acceptable concept of himself. This stage Loevinger considers to be typical of adolescence. With increasing maturity, the individual progresses beyond such a stereotyped concept to a differentiated and realistic self concept. At this point, he is fully aware of his idiosyncracies and accepts himself for what he is. Loevinger maintains that the level of self conceptualization attained by the individual is a basic determiner of his impulse control, social attitudes, and other important aspects of personality.

According to Loevinger, many (if not most) persons fail to reach the final stage of differentiated self concept. In so far as personality inventory responses are evaluated in terms of normative data, individuals whose self concepts are at the stereotyped conventional stage receive higher or "better adjusted" scores. In the course of psychotherapy, some persons may advance beyond this stage to the individualized self concept and hence may show a decline in scores on adjustment inventories (57). Such a hypothesis could account for the apparent failures of personality inventories when used in a clinical setting. The finding by some investigators (e.g., 71) that, when evaluated in terms of personality inventory norms, college seniors appear to have poorer emotional adjustment than college freshmen may have a similar explanation. Essentially, Loevinger argues that the capacity for self conceptualization is an important personality trait and that the relation of this trait to personality inventory scores is not linear but curvilinear.

Several testing techniques have been based on comparisons between the individual's self concept and his concepts of "average," "ideal," or other similar categories (13, 69, 70). Or, the individual's "private" self concept may be compared with his "social" self concept, i.e., his most accurate estimate of himself as he believes other people see him (16). Many variations of these procedures could readily be formulated to test specific hypotheses. Such techniques lend themselves especially well to the detection of conflicts, through discrepancies in the various concepts. Several have yielded promising results, although they are still in an experimental stage.

Q **Sort.** One of the special techniques suitable for investigating self concepts is the *Q* sort developed by Stephenson (78). In this technique, the subject is given a set of cards containing statements or trait names which he must sort into piles ranging from "most characteristic" to "least characteristic" of himself. The items may come from a standard list, but more often are designed to fit the individual case. To insure uniform distribution of ratings, a "forced-normal" distribution is used, the subject being instructed to place a specified number of cards in each pile. Such a distribution can be prepared for any size of item sample by reference to a normal curve table. It should be noted that, like the forced-choice technique discussed in Chapter 18, the Q sort yields "ipsative" rather than "normative" data. In other words, the individual tells us which he considers his strong and which his weak traits, but not how strong he believes himself to be in comparison with another person or some outside norm.

Q sorts have been employed to study a variety of psychological problems. When applied to an investigation of individual personality, the subject is often asked to re-sort the same set of items within different frames of reference. For example, he may sort the items as they apply to himself and to other persons, such as his father, his mother, or his wife. Similarly, he may sort the items as they apply to himself in different settings, such as job, home, or social situations. Q sorts can likewise be obtained for the individual as he believes he actually is, as he believes others see him, and as he would like to be. To observe change, Q sorts may be obtained successively at different stages during psychotherapy. The degree of similarity or difference among various Q sorts has often been found by computing correlations among them. When a large number of Q sorts has been obtained, the intercorrelations have sometimes been factor-analyzed to identify common elements or group factors through certain sortings.

Q technique represents a systematization of self-rating procedures. It can also be employed as a basis for rating others. For example, a clinician or interviewer may record his evaluation of an individual by means of a Q sort. Although some of the statistical procedures that have been employed in analyzing Q-sort data are questionable (29), the Q sort provides a useful rating technique for both psychological research and practice.

The Semantic Differential. This technique was originally developed by Osgood and his associates (64) as a tool for research on the psychology of meaning. It was only later that its possibilities for personality assessment were recognized. The Semantic Differential represents a standardized and quantified procedure for measuring the connotations of any given concept for the individual. Each concept is rated on a 7-point graphic scale as being more closely related to one or the other of a pair of opposites, such as good-bad or fast-slow. Every concept to be investigated is paired in turn with each scale, as illustrated below:

CHILD   valuable _____:_____:_____:_____:_____:_____:_____ worthless

HATRED   tense   _____:_____:_____:_____:_____:_____ relaxed

SEX   strong   _____:_____:_____:_____:_____:_____ weak

CHILD   large   _____:_____:_____:_____:_____:_____ small

Some of the scales can be applied literally to a particular concept, as in the rating of Child on the large-small scale. Many of the ratings are obviously influenced by common metaphorical usage, as when a person is described as "cold." When a scale appears totally inapplicable to a concept, the subject would presumably check the middle position.

Although of relatively recent origin, the Semantic Differential has already been employed in considerable research, which has contributed to its construct validation. Tests carried out at four age levels from the first grade to college showed that, with increasing age, subjects tend to agree more closely with each other in the connotations of common objects (cf. 64, p. 289). Intercorrelations and factorial analyses of different scales have revealed three major factors: *Evaluative,* with high loadings in such scales as good-bad, valuable-worthless, and clean-dirty; *Potency,* found in such scales as strong-weak, large-small, and heavy-light; and *Activity,* identified in such scales as active-passive, fast-slow, and sharp-dull. The evaluative factor is the most conspicuous, accounting for the largest percentage of total variance.

Responses on the Semantic Differential can be analyzed in several ways. The over-all similarity of any two concepts for an individual or a group can be determined in terms of their positions on all scales. The connotations of all concepts rated by an individual can be investigated by computing the "score" of each concept in the three principal factors described above. An approximation of these factor scores can be found by averaging the ratings of each concept on those scales having the highest loadings on each factor. Thus on a scale extending from $+3$ to -3, a given individual's concept of "My Brother" might rate -2 in the evaluative factor, 0.1 in potency, and 2.7 in activity.

The loadings of the three factors in each concept can be more easily visualized by means of three-dimensional models, as illustrated in Figure 123. These models are taken from an intensive study of a well-known case of multiple personality, in which the patient shifted back and forth between sharply contrasted "selves" (80, 81). The one self, designated as "Eve White," was meek, self-critical, frustrated, and unhappy. The other, "Eve Black," was irresponsible, self-centered, fun-loving, and mischievous. "Jane,"

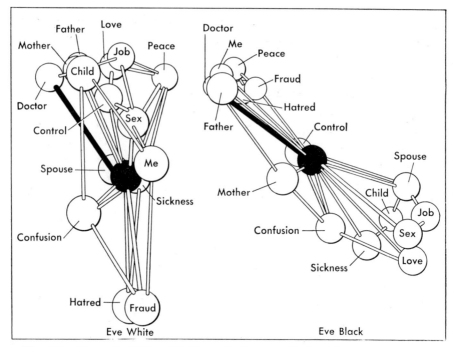

Fig. 123. Semantic Differential: Semantic Patterns Obtained in a Case of Multiple Personality. (From Osgood and Luria, 65, pp. 584, 585.)

a third, more highly integrated and better-adjusted personality, emerged in the course of therapy and eventually seemed to be replacing the other two. A blind analysis of the Semantic Differential patterns of Eve White and Eve Black led to personality descriptions that agreed remarkably well with the case reports of the therapists (64, 65).

Figure 123 shows the Semantic Differential patterns of Eve White and Eve Black as they appeared early in therapy. In these diagrams, "good" is at the top, "active" at the left, and "weak" toward the reader. The dark circle is at the zero point for all three dimensions. The dark line connecting this circle to "Doctor" (who retained approximately the same position in all diagrams) serves to orient the patterns in "semantic space." A number of contrasts are apparent between the two patterns. Eve White places "Me" much lower in the evaluative dimension than does Eve Black. The latter also shows less differentiation of concepts along the evaluative dimension. Eve Black's distorted values are further indicated by her placing Hate and Fraud along with Peace, Father, Doctor, and herself toward the good end of the scale, while Child, Spouse, Job, Sex, and Love are classified with Confusion and Sickness toward the bad end. In Eve White's pattern, the separation of Love and Sex and the neutral position of Spouse reflect some of her adjustment difficulties in marriage. Changes occurring in the course of therapy were also accompanied by shifts in the position of concepts in subsequent Semantic Differential patterns.

Role Construct Repertory Test. A technique devised specifically as an aid in clinical practice is the Role Construct Repertory Test (Rep Test) developed by Kelly (54). This test has common features with a number of other personality tests, notably the Semantic Differential and the various sorting tests used to study concept formation (Ch. 12). In the Rep Test, however, the objects to be sorted are persons who are important in the subject's life. And unlike the Semantic Differential, the Rep Test requires the subject himself to designate the scales, dimensions, or constructs in terms of which he characterizes these persons.

The development of the Rep Test is intimately related to Kelly's personality theory. A basic proposition in this theory is that the concepts or constructs an individual uses to perceive objects or events influence his behavior. In the course of psychotherapy, it is frequently necessary to build new constructs and to discard some old constructs before progress can be made.

The Rep Test is designed to help the clinician identify some of the client's important constructs about people. Although the test can be administered in many ways, including both group and individual versions, one of its simpler variants will serve to illustrate its essential characteristics. In this variant, the subject is first given a Role Title List and asked to name a person in his experience who fits each role title. A few examples are:

A teacher you liked

Your father

Your wife or present girl friend

A person with whom you have been closely associated recently who appears to dislike you

The examiner next selects three of the persons named and asks, "In what *important way* are two of them alike but different from the third?" This procedure is repeated with many other sets of three names, in which some of the names recur in different combinations. The Rep Test yields a wealth of qualitative data. A simplified factor-analytic procedure has also been developed for quantitative identification of constructs that are important for each individual.

FURTHER PROCEDURES FOR THE APPRAISAL OF PERSONALITY

The tests considered in this and the preceding three chapters give ample evidence of the variety of approaches that have been followed in the assessment of personality variables. Earlier chapters provided a picture of the diversity of procedures commonly grouped under projective techniques and under self-report inventories. In this chapter, we have examined several relatively new types of tests, including situational tests; task-oriented structured tests utilizing perceptual, cognitive, and evaluative functions; procedures based on sociometry; and a number of attempts to systematize the exploration of self concepts and personal constructs.

Nor does this survey by any means exhaust the methods that have been utilized for the appraisal of personality. Research on possible *physical and physiological* indicators of personality characteristics has been going on for many decades, although so far the results have been largely negative (cf. 4, Ch. 5; 21, Chs. 7 and 15; 22; 40, Ch. 14). Among the physiological measures investigated in this connection are muscle tension, basal metabolic rate, blood pressure, pulse rate, and galvanic skin reaction. Considerable research has been directed toward investigating possible relationships between intellectual or personality variables and critical flicker frequency (CFF), or the rate at which a flickering light is first seen to fuse. It is believed that CFF may serve as an index of the efficiency of functioning of the nervous system. Electroencephalography, or the measurement of the electrical activity of the brain, has likewise been used in the study of personality deviations. Interest in the possible relation of body build to personality factors has been periodically revived by theories of constitutional types, of which the most recent is that of Sheldon (cf. 4, Ch. 6; 74; 75).

A sizable body of literature dealing with *expressive movements* has likewise accumulated (2; 5, Chs. 15-16; 11, Chs. 13-15 and 21; 40, Ch. 11; 77; 92). Expressive movements have been defined as "those aspects of movement which are distinctive enough to differentiate one individual from another" (2, p. vii). Such reactions include not only gross bodily movements like walking, gesturing, and performing various motor tasks, but also handwriting and speech. Handwriting has received special attention, because it represents a relatively permanent product of motor responses, which is easy to obtain and can be re-examined at leisure (5, Ch. 15; 11, Ch. 14; 77). Available data on the relationships between characteristics of handwriting or other expressive movements and personality variables, however, are negative or inconclusive.

Many types of *personal documents,* such as letters, diaries, autobiographies, and art products, have likewise been subjected to intensive investigation for possible clues to attitudes, emotional traits, and other aspects of personality (cf. 1; 73, pp. 323-330). One attempt to quantify the evaluation of verbal self-reports is to be found in the discomfort-relief quotient (DRQ) proposed by Dollard and Mowrer (30). This index is a ratio of the number of words indicating discomfort (unhappiness, tension, suffering) to the number of words indicating relief (satisfaction, comfort, enjoyment). It may also be found by using sentences or thought units in place of words.

Direct observations of behavior represent another source of information about personality. Trained observers have made detailed records of the behavior of children in nursery schools, pupils in school, boys in camp, employees on the job, and individuals in a number of other natural situations of daily life. Except for their lack of control over stimulus conditions, such procedures do not differ much from some of the previously discussed situational tests. When practicable, observations may be rendered more complete and accurate through the use of sound recorders, motion pictures, and other automatic recording devices. To obtain a representative picture of the individual's behavior in a given situation, *time sampling* may be employed. This involves a randomized distribution of observation periods. Depending upon the nature and purpose of the observations, such periods may vary in duration from less than a minute to several hours; and they may be concentrated in one day or spaced over several months.

Observations may cover all behavior occurring during the specified period, or they may be limited to a certain type of behavior, such as crying or aggressive behavior in nursery school children. The *critical incident technique,* in which instances of behavior considered to be especially favorable or unfavorable for a given purpose are recorded, is a special example of such selective observation. Thus during a two-month period the supervisor of a research unit may be asked to keep a record of all instances of specific actions characteristic of productive and of unproductive research workers on his staff. This technique, which has been widely applied by Flanagan, forms the basis of a standardized Performance Record (33) designed for use by teachers in charting the personal and social development of elementary school children.

Mention should also be made of the time-honored source of information provided by interviewing techniques (40, Ch. 7). Interviews may vary

from the highly structured (representing little more than an orally administered questionnaire), through patterned or guided interviews covering certain predetermined areas, to non-directive and depth interviews in which the
interviewer merely sets the stage and encourages the subject to talk as freely
as possible. Interviews provide chiefly two kinds of information. First, they
afford an opportunity for direct observation of a rather limited sample of
behavior manifested during the interview situation itself. For example, the
individual's speech, language usage, poise, and manner in meeting a stranger can be noted. A much more important function of interviewing, however, is to elicit life history data. What the individual has done in the past is a
good indicator of what he may do in the future, especially when interpreted
in the light of concomitant circumstances and of the subject's comments regarding his actions.

When properly employed, *rating scales* (40, Ch. 7) can likewise yield
valuable and dependable information not readily available through testing.
Ratings by teachers, job supervisors, officers, counselors, and other trained
observers represent a well-established evaluation procedure. Some of the advantages of peer ratings and peer nominations have already been mentioned
in connection with sociometric techniques. Under the name of "buddy ratings" such peer ratings have been widely and successfully employed in the
armed services. A type of rating procedure that is especially applicable in
obtaining children's ratings of each other is the "Guess Who" technique, first
used by Hartshorne and May in the Character Education Inquiry. In this
technique, the children are given a number of brief "word-pictures" and are
instructed to write under each the name of every classmate who might fit the
description. Examples include (44, p. 88):

This is a jolly good fellow—friends with every one, no matter who they are.

This one is always picking on others and annoying them.

Some of these techniques, including direct observations, interviews, and
ratings, are not tests and should not be evaluated as such. Others represent
areas of inquiry out of which tests or other indicators of personality characteristics may eventually emerge. It should also be noted that many of the
approaches cited in this section are concerned not only with personality
traits in the restricted sense, but with all behavior characteristics.

From the bewildering diversity of techniques or potential techniques that
have been considered, one impression should be clear: The field of personality testing is still in a formative stage. Few if any available instruments have

as yet proved their value empirically to the same extent as have aptitude or achievement tests. Consequently, the tester in this field must proceed warily —at his own risk. Personality testing today offers a real challenge, both to the creative ingenuity of the test constructor and to the scientific vigilance of the test user. Even more than in other branches of psychological testing, the fullest utilization of personality tests requires the ability to recognize promise, without accepting unsupported claims—to be receptive toward what is new, without being credulous toward what is unverified.

REFERENCES

1. Allport, G. W. The use of personal documents in psychological science. *Soc. Sci. Res. Coun. Bull.,* 1942, No. 49.
2. Allport, G. W., and Vernon, P. E. *Studies in expressive movement.* N. Y.: Macmillan, 1933.
3. American Institute for Research. Situational tests for evaluating supervisory skill. *AIR Res. Notes,* 1957, No. 14.
4. Anastasi, Anne. *Differential psychology.* (3rd ed.) N. Y.: Macmillan, 1958.
5. Anderson, H. H., and Anderson, Gladys L. (Eds.) *An introduction to projective techniques.* Englewood Cliffs, N. J.: Prentice-Hall, 1951.
6. Barron, F. Personality style and perceptual choice. *J. Pers.,* 1952, 20, 385-401.
7. Barron, F., and Welsh, G. S. Artistic perception as a possible factor in personality style: its measurement by a figure preference test. *J. Psychol.,* 1952, 33, 199-203.
8. Bass, B. M. The leaderless group discussion. *Psychol. Bull.,* 1954, 51, 465-92.
9. Bass, B. M. *Famous Sayings.* Missoula, Montana: Psychol. Test Specialists, 1957-1958.
10. Bass, B. M. An approach to the objective assessment of successful leadership. In B. M. Bass and I. A. Berg (Eds.), *Objective approaches to personality assessment.* Princeton, N. J.: Van Nostrand, 1959. Ch. VIII.
11. Bell, J. E. *Projective techniques.* N. Y.: Longmans, Green, 1948.
12. Berg, I. A. The unimportance of test item content. In B. M. Bass and I. A. Berg (Eds.), *Objective approaches to personality assessment.* Princeton, N. J.: Van Nostrand, 1959. Ch. V.
13. Bills, R. E., Vance, E. L., and McLean, O. S. An index of adjustment and values. *J. consult. Psychol.,* 1951, 15, 257-261.
14. Blake, R. R., and Ramsey, G. V. (Eds.) *Perception: an approach to personality.* N. Y.: Ronald, 1951.
15. Bogardus, E. L. A social distance scale. *Sociol. soc. Res.,* 1933, 17, 265-271.
16. Brownfain, J. J. Stability of the self-concept as a dimension of personality. *J. abnorm. soc. Psychol.,* 1952, 47, 597-606.
17. Bruner, J. S., and Krech, D. (Eds.) *Perception and personality: a symposium.* Durham, N. C.: Duke Univer. Press, 1950.
18. Campbell, D. T. The indirect assessment of social attitudes. *Psychol. Bull.,* 1950, 47, 15-38.

19. Campbell, D. T. A typology of tests, projective and otherwise. *J. consult. Psychol.*, 1957, 21, 207-210.

20. Carter, L. F. Evaluating the performance of individuals as members of small groups. *Personnel Psychol.*, 1954, 7, 477-484.

21. Cattell, R. B. *Personality and motivation structure and measurement.* Tarrytown-on-Hudson, N. Y.: World Book Co., 1957.

22. Cattell, R. B., *et al.* The objective measurement of dynamic traits. *Educ. psychol. Measmt.*, 1950, 10, 224-248.

23. Cattell, R. B., *et al. IPAT Humor Test of Personality.* Champaign, Ill.: Inst. Pers. Abil. Test., 1953.

24. Cattell, R. B., *et al. Handbook for the objective-analytic personality test batteries.* Champaign, Ill.: Inst. Pers. Abil. Test., 1956.

25. Cattell, R. B., and Anderson, Jean C. *IPAT Music Preference Test of Personality.* Champaign, Ill.: Inst. Pers. Abil. Test., 1953.

26. Cattell, R. B., and Anderson, Jean C. The measurement of personality and behavior disorders by the IPAT music preference test. *J. appl. Psychol.*, 1953, 37, 446-454.

27. Cattell, R. B., and Luborsky, L. B. Personality factors in response to humor. *J. abnorm. soc. Psychol.*, 1947, 42, 402-421.

28. Cattell, R. B., and Saunders, D. R. Musical preferences and personality diagnosis: I. A factorization of one hundred and twenty themes. *J. soc. Psychol.*, 1954, 39, 3-24.

29. Cronbach, L. J., and Gleser, Goldine C. Review of Stephenson, W. The study of behavior: Q-technique and its methodology. *Psychometrika*, 1954, 19, 327-330. (See also reply by Stephenson, 331-333.)

30. Dollard, J., and Mowrer, O. H. A method of measuring tension in written documents. *J. abnorm. soc. Psychol.*, 1947, 42, 3-32.

31. Eysenck, H. J. *The structure of human personality.* London: Methuen, 1953.

32. Flanagan, J. C. Some considerations in the development of situation tests. *Personnel Psychol.*, 1954, 7, 461-464.

33. Flanagan, J. C. *Performance Record for the Personal and Social Development Program.* Chicago: Sci. Res. Assoc., 1956.

34. Fryer, D. *The measurement of interests.* N. Y.: Holt, Rinehart and Winston, 1931.

35. Gardner, E. F., and Thompson, G. G. *Social relations and morale in small groups.* N. Y.: Appleton-Century-Crofts, 1956.

36. Gardner, E. F., and Thompson, G. G. *Syracuse Scales of Social Relations.* Tarrytown-on-Hudson, N. Y.: World Book Co., 1959.

37. Gough, H. G. *Personality characteristics of successful graduate students: a progress note.* Berkeley, Calif.: Inst. Pers. Assess. Res., Univer. Calif., July, 1951.

38. Gough, H. G. *The Adjective Check List.* Berkeley, Calif.: Univer. Calif. Press, 1952.

39. Gough, H. G. *Predicting success in graduate training: a progress report.* Berkeley, Calif.: Inst. Pers. Assess. Res., Univer. Calif., July, 1952.

40. Guilford, J. P. *Personality.* N. Y.: McGraw-Hill, 1959.

41. Guilford, J. P., and Lacey, J. I. (Eds.) *Printed classification tests.* (AAF

Aviation Psychology Program, Research Reports. Rep. No. 5.) Washington: Govt. Printing Office, 1947.

42. Hammond, K. R. Measuring attitudes by error choice; an indirect method. *J. abnorm. soc. Psychol.,* 1948, 43, 38-48.

43. Hartshorne, H., and May, M. A. *Studies in deceit.* N. Y.: Macmillan, 1928.

44. Hartshorne, H., May, M. A., and Maller, J. B. *Studies in service and self-control.* N. Y.: Macmillan, 1929.

45. Hartshorne, H., May, M. A., and Shuttleworth, F. K. *Studies in the organization of character.* N. Y.: Macmillan, 1930.

46. Holmen, M. G., *et al.* An assessment program for OCS applicants. *HumRRO tech. Rep.* 26, 1956.

47. Holtzman, W. H., and Bitterman, M. E. Psychiatric screening of flying personnel: VI. Anxiety and reactions to stress. *USAF School of Aviation Medicine, Project No. 21-37-002,* Rep. No. 6, Dec., 1952.

48. Horowitz, E. L. Development of attitude toward the Negro. *Arch. Psychol.,* 1936, No. 194.

49. Jenkin, N. Affective processes in perception. *Psychol. Bull.,* 1957, 54, 100-127.

50. Jennings, Helen H. *Sociometry in group relations: a work guide for teachers.* Washington: Amer. Coun. Educ., 1948.

51. Keehn, J. D. A factorial study of tests of color-form attitudes. *J. Pers.,* 1955, 23, 295-307.

52. Kelly, E. L. The place of situation tests in evaluating clinical psychologists. *Personnel Psychol.,* 1954, 7, 484-492.

53. Kelly, E. L., and Fiske, D. W. *The prediction of performance in clinical spychology.* Ann Arbor, Mich.: Univer. Mich. Press, 1951.

54. Kelly, G. A. *The psychology of personal constructs.* Vol. 1. *A theory of personality.* N. Y.: Norton, 1955.

55. Lindzey, G., and Borgatta, E. F. Sociometric measurement. In G. Lindzey (Ed.), *Handbook of social psychology.* Cambridge, Mass.: Addison-Wesley, 1954. Vol. 1, Ch. 11.

56. Loevinger, Jane. A theory of test response. *Proc. 1958 invit. Conf. test. Probl., Educ. Test. Serv.,* 1959, 36-47.

57. Loevinger, Jane, and Ossorio, A. G. Evaluation of therapy by self-report: a paradox. *Amer. Psychologist,* 1958, 13, 366.

58. Luborsky, L. B., and Cattell, R. B. The validation of personality factors in humor. *J. Pers.,* 1947, 15, 283-291.

59. MacKinnon, D. W. Tests for the measurement of personal effectiveness. *Proc. 1951 invit. Conf. test. Probl., Educ. Test. Serv.,* 1952, 73-81.

60. MacKinnon, D. W. An assessment study of Air Force officers: Part V. Summary and applications. *WADC tech. Rep.* 58-91 (V), Wright Air Develpm. Center, 1958.

61. Melton, A. W. (Ed.) *Apparatus tests.* (AAF Aviation Psychology Program, Research Reports. Rep. No. 4.) Washington: Govt. Printing Office, 1947.

62. Moreno, J. L. *Who shall survive? Foundations of sociometry, group psychotherapy, and sociodrama.* (2nd ed.) Beacon, N. Y.: Beacon House, 1953. (*Sociometry Monogr.,* No. 29.)

63. Murray, H. A., and MacKinnon, D. W. Assessment of OSS personnel. *J. consult. Psychol.*, 1946, 10, 76-80.

64. Osgood, C. E., *et al. The measurement of meaning.* Urbana, Ill.: Univer. Ill. Press, 1957.

65. Osgood, C. E., and Luria, Zella. A blind analysis of a case of multiple personality using the semantic differential. *J. abnorm. soc. Psychol.*, 1954, 49, 579-591.

66. OSS Assessment Staff. *Assessment of men: selection of personnel for the Office of Strategic Services.* N. Y.: Holt, Rinehart and Winston, 1948.

67. Pemberton, Carol L. The closure factors related to temperament. *J. Pers.*, 1952, 21, 159-175.

68. Pepinsky, H. B., Siegel, L., and Vanatta, A. The criterion in counseling: a group participation scale. *J. abnorm. soc. Psychol.*, 1952, 47, 415-419.

69. Rogers, C. R. Measuring personality adjustment in children nine to thirteen years of age. *Teach. Coll., Columbia Univer., Contrib. Educ.*, 1931.

70. Rogers, C. R., and Dymond, Rosalind F. (Eds.) *Psychotherapy and personality change.* Chicago: Univer. Chicago Press, 1954.

71. Sanford, N. (Ed.) Personality development during the college years. *J. soc. Issues*, 1956, 12, 3-70.

72. Scheier, I. H. What is an "objective" test? *Psychol. Rep.*, 1958, 4, 147-157.

73. Selltiz, Claire, *et al. Research methods in social relations.* (Rev. ed.) N. Y.: Holt, Rinehart and Winston, 1959.

74. Sheldon, W. H. *Varieties of delinquent youth.* N. Y.: Harper, 1949.

75. Sheldon, W. H., and Stevens, S. S. *The varieties of temperament.* N. Y.: Harper, 1942.

76. Snygg, D., and Combs, A. W. *Individual behavior: a perceptual approach to behavior.* (Rev. ed.) N. Y.: Harper, 1959.

77. Sonneman, U. *Handwriting analysis as a psychodiagnostic tool.* N. Y.: Grune & Stratton, 1950.

78. Stephenson, W. *The study of behavior: Q-technique and its methodology.* Chicago: Univer. Chicago Press, 1953.

79. Straus, M. A. Direct, indirect, and disguised measurement in rural sociology. *Wash. Agric. Exp. Stations, State Coll. Wash., Tech. Bull.*, 26, 1957.

80. Thigpen, C. H., and Cleckley, H. A case of multiple personality. *J. abnorm. soc. Psychol.*, 1954, 49, 135-151.

81. Thigpen, C. H., and Cleckley, H. *The three faces of Eve.* N. Y.: McGraw-Hill, 1957.

82. Thurstone, L. L. A factorial study of perception. *Psychometr. Monogr.*, No. 4, 1944.

83. Thurstone, L. L. Some primary abilities in visual thinking. *Psychometr. Lab., Univer. Chicago*, No. 59, August, 1950.

84. Thurstone, L. L. Experimental tests of temperament. In *Essays in psychology dedicated to David Katz.* Uppsala, Sweden: Almquist & Wiksells, 1951. Pp. 248-262.

85. Thurstone, L. L. Objective tests of temperament: tests of verbal associations. *Psychometr. Lab., Univer. Chicago*, No. 72, July, 1951.

86. Thurstone, L. L. Progress report on a color-form test. *Psychometr. Lab., Univer. Chicago,* No. 80, July, 1952.
87. Thurstone, L. L. The development of objective measures of temperament. *Psychometr. Lab., Univer. N. Carolina,* No. 1, April, 1953.
88. Vernon, P. E. The validation of civil service selection board procedures. *Occup. Psychol.,* 1950, 24, 75-95.
89. Watson, R. I. Historical review of objective personality testing: the search for objectivity. In B. M. Bass and I. A. Berg (Eds.), *Objective approaches to personality assessment.* Princeton, N. J.: Van Nostrand, 1959. Ch. I.
90. Weschler, I. R., and Bernberg, R. E. Indirect methods of attitude measurement. *Int. J. Opin. Attit. Res.,* 1950, 4, 209-228.
91. Witkin, H. A., *et al. Personality through perception: an experimental and clinical study.* N. Y.: Harper, 1954.
92. Wolff, W. *The expression of personality.* N. Y.: Harper, 1943.

Test Publishers

Below are the names and addresses of some of the larger American publishers and distributors of psychological tests. Catalogues of current tests can be obtained from these publishers on request. For names and addresses of other test publishers, see the Publisher's Directory in the latest *Mental Measurements Yearbook*.

California Test Bureau, Del Monte Research Park, Monterey, California.
Consulting Psychologists Press, 270 Town and Country Village, Palo Alto, California.
Educational Test Bureau, 720 Washington Avenue, S.E., Minneapolis 14, Minnesota.
Educational Testing Service, Cooperative Test Division, 20 Nassau Street, Princeton, New Jersey.
Harcourt, Brace and World, Inc., Tarrytown, New York.
Houghton Mifflin Company, 2 Park Street, Boston 7, Massachusetts.
Institute for Personality and Ability Testing, 1602 Coronado Drive, Champaign, Illinois.
Psychological Corporation, 304 East 45th Street, New York 17, New York.
Psychological Test Specialists, Box 1441, Missoula, Montana.
Psychometric Affiliates, Box 1625, Chicago 90, Illinois.
Public School Publishing Company, 345 Calhoun Street, Cincinnati 19, Ohio.
Science Research Associates, Inc., 259 East Erie Street, Chicago, Illinois.
Sheridan Supply Company, P. O. Box 837, Beverly Hills, California.
C. H. Stoelting Company, 424 North Homan Avenue, Chicago 24, Illinois.
Western Psychological Services, Box 775, Beverly Hills, California.

Author Index

In order not to crowd the text with names of investigators, relatively few authors' names have been directly cited in the discussion, the majority of references being reported by number only. All these references, however, have been included in the Author Index. When looking up such a reference, the reader should find the author's name in the bibliography at the end of the particular chapter, note the number of the reference, and then locate that number on the given page of the text. References to bibliographies have been set in italics in the Author Index.

Subject Index